PENGUIN  CLASSICS

A JOURNEY TO THE WESTERN ISLANDS OF SCOTLAND
AND
THE JOURNAL OF A TOUR TO THE HEBRIDES

SAMUEL JOHNSON (1709–84) was born in Lichfield and educated at Lichfield Grammar School and Pembroke College, Oxford. A notable moral essayist, critic, poet and lexicographer, Johnson's powerful personality and his long career made him the dominating literary figure of the century. He met Boswell in 1763 and the latter became his devoted follower; ten years later, at the respective ages of sixty-three and thirty-two, they began their tour of Scotland. Johnson's account of his journey is a superb illustration of his wisdom, his prejudices and the range of his interests.

JAMES BOSWELL (1740–95) was born in Edinburgh and studied law at Edinburgh University and at Utrecht. At the insistence of his domineering father he practised as an advocate, but he was greatly interested in politics and writing. He travelled in Europe during 1765–6 and made the acquaintance of Voltaire and Rousseau, and developed an interest in Corsican affairs. His *Account of Corsica* (1768) and a less successful sequel (1769) brought him the fame he so desired. Boswell is best remembered for his masterly biography of Johnson and as Peter Levi states in the introduction, 'we probably owe the *Life of Johnson* as well as this slighter sketch to that surprising expedition of theirs so late in the season, between August and November, 1773.'

PETER LEVI, classical scholar, archaeologist and poet, was born in 1931. He translated *The Psalms* and Pausanias' *Guide to Greece* for Penguin Classics, as well as a collection of Yevtushenko (with R. Milner-Gulland) for the Penguin Modern Poets. He also edited *The Penguin Book of English Christian Verse*. He wrote more than sixty books, including *The Light Garden of the Angel King*, an account of his travels in Afghanistan; *A Bottle in the Shade*; *The Penguin History of Greek Literature*; and biographies of Alfred Lord Tennyson, John Milton and Edward Lear. Peter Levi was Professor of Poetry at the University of Oxford from 1984 to 1989. He died on 1 February 2000.

Samuel Johnson

A JOURNEY TO
THE WESTERN ISLANDS
OF SCOTLAND

❧

James Boswell

THE JOURNAL OF
A TOUR TO THE HEBRIDES

❧

Edited, with an Introduction and Notes,
by Peter Levi

Penguin Books

PENGUIN BOOKS

Published by the Penguin Group
Penguin Books Ltd, 80 Strand, London WC2R 0RL, England
Penguin Putnam Inc., 375 Hudson Street, New York, New York 10014, USA
Penguin Books Australia Ltd, 250 Camberwell Road, Camberwell, Victoria 3124, Australia
Penguin Books Canada Ltd, 10 Alcorn Avenue, Toronto, Ontario, Canada M4V 3B2
Penguin Books India (P) Ltd, 11 Community Centre, Panchsheel Park, New Delhi – 110 017, India
Penguin Books (NZ) Ltd, Cnr Rosedale and Airborne Roads, Albany, Auckland, New Zealand
Penguin Books (South Africa) (Pty) Ltd, 24 Sturdee Avenue, Rosebank 2196, South Africa

Penguin Books Ltd, Registered Offices: 80 Strand, London WC2R 0RL, England

www.penguin.com

Johnson's *Journey to the Western Islands of Scotland*
first published in 1775
Boswell's *Journal of a Tour to the Hebrides with Samuel Johnson LL.D.*
first published in 1786
Published in Penguin Classics 1984

18

Introduction and notes copyright © Peter Levi, 1984
All rights reserved

Printed in England by Clays Ltd, St Ives plc
Filmset in 9/11pt Monophoto Photina
Map drawn by Reg Piggot

FOR
DEIRDRE

CONTENTS

ACKNOWLEDGEMENTS

The text printed here is from Johnson's first edition and Boswell's third, but without Boswell's appendices, which are of little interest except to compliment his Scottish friends. I have used the commentaries available: Chapman's edition of the two books together, the Yale Johnson and L. F. Powell's revision of Birkbeck Hill's Oxford *Boswell*, and as this last in particular is the repository of the research of generations, I am constantly indebted to it. I found John Wain's *Life of Johnson* profoundly interesting and really helpful. I got a few thoughts from W. J. Bate's *Samuel Johnson* also. I had recourse to guide-books of every kind and to various Ordnance Survey maps. Moray Maclaren's guide was the best, but Tom Weir also has plenty to contribute. Of more general works, W. B. Blaikie's *Origins of the Forty-Five* (Edinburgh, 1916), Ewen Maclauchlan on Ossianic poetry in the *Celtic Magazine* for 1880 and 1881, and H. G. Graham's *Social Life of Scotland in the Eighteenth Century* threw light on some problems. But the pleasantest part of my own brief research was reading old travel books, and travelling myself in Western Scotland. I am grateful for help to St Catherine's, my Oxford college, to the library of Christ Church, to the Bodleian library, to the National Gallery of Scotland, the British Museum Department of Prints and Drawings, and the West Highland Museum at Fort William. Above all I am grateful to my wife for constant encouragement and help of every kind.

INTRODUCTION

The first thought that is likely to occur to a new reader of these two works is of Scotland, how empty and how beautiful it must have been in the eighteenth century, and how strange. The journey may be diverting but the vanished or withered world must have been magical. It is true that the most attractive and solitary parts of Scotland still await every explorer as they awaited old Samuel Johnson and young James Boswell. It is even true that the modern traveller may often exclaim sadly, 'How could they have missed Appin and Lismore?' or 'What about this or that standing stone?' or 'What a pity to miss Rhum and Invergarry, with the story of Iain the family bard who washed seven human heads in the water-spring. 'But the picture of Scotland that Johnson in particular uncovers is a very different matter. Easy tourists like ourselves may feel reproved by it. All the same, Johnson enjoyed his Scottish journey and Boswell exulted in it. The year was 1773; they were sixty-three and thirty-two years old. They had known each other for ten years, and this expedition was an old project. It matured almost too late, because the war of 1745 was the beginning of the end of ancient Scotland, and the processes of change in the Highlands were already gathering speed.

It was in 1773 that the first emigration ship from Fort William sailed away with 425 highlanders. In the following years, privateers and slave-ships or quasi-slave-ships worked the Hebrides. Seven were recorded in 1774 alone. The destruction of Scottish forests was already in spate, not only for ships' timbers but for charcoal and to feed the furnaces of the big water-powered iron-works operated by southerners. Bonawe still stands as an example of the latter. The clan system was in decay. Edinburgh Calvinism had reached St Kilda. The whisky industry was still mostly illegal and its rough product mostly uncontrolled. Scotland was held down by a string of forts. 'We came too late,' wrote Dr Johnson, 'to see what we expected.'

All the same, Scotland in 1773 was still a relatively wild place; it was romantic, and they both rejoiced in it. Boswell wept over the memorials of 1745; he was or had been a secret Catholic. Dr Johnson had vehement Jacobite sympathies, although in his own account of the journey he suppressed them; King George himself appears to have read it in manuscript. Comparison of Boswell's and Johnson's treatment of Flora Macdonald is revealing. But in private company, and under provocation, Johnson announced in 1775 that 'George the First knew nothing, and desired to know nothing; did nothing, and desired to do nothing; the only good thing that is told of him, is that he wished to restore the crown to its hereditary successor.' In 1777 Johnson caused some upset at Ashbourne, in Derbyshire, by maintaining in the house of a Whig Justice of the Peace that 'if England were fairly polled, the present King would be sent away tonight, and his adherents hanged tomorrow'.

Apart from his omnivorous curiosity about literature and learned institutions, what Johnson specially wanted in Scotland was to understand wild or primitive or savage life. At the moment when he conceived his Scottish book, he had just got for the first time into utterly wild and grand countryside. He felt some of the emotions in the Highlands that Darwin in the *Beagle* felt when he saw his first savage, though Johnson came to love the Scots and to respect them. 'Our business,' says Boswell, 'was with life and manners.' It may be true that the whole work of great writers exists in germ in a few short pages; certainly some parts of Johnson's Scottish book convey a sense of Rasselas come true. He was proud to be adventurous. 'I have now the pleasure,' he wrote from Skye, 'of going where nobody goes, and seeing what nobody sees.'

Samuel Johnson was not wholeheartedly an antiquary; Boswell, being as maggotty-witted as Aubrey, and a most patriotic Scot, was closer to that type of traveller. Johnson was an explorer of a kind, but a moral explorer: he was not quite a scientist, nor simply an aesthete in pursuit of the picturesque. Agricultural improvement was to him a natural interest. British travel writing was already well established by 1773, and the great county histories were already appearing. Johnson had read Sacheverell on the Isle of Man, and the Elizabethan Sir John Davies on the state of Ireland, which suggested questions about Scotland. Not only Dovedale and the Peak, celebrated by Hobbes and Cotton, but the Lake District was already famous through Thomas Gray's *Journal in the Lakes* (1769), and Scotland itself had already revealed the sublime, the picturesque and the romantic in a high degree in the watercolours of Paul Sandby. Gray had been in Scotland in 1765, and Johnson, who probably read his account in the later seventies, thought well of Gray as a travel writer. Already in 1759 Lord Breadalbane wrote, 'It has been the fashion this year to travel into the Highlands,' and by 1773 he found the number of English visitors at his house burdensome, 'sixteen often at table for several days together'.

It is worth pausing to notice that Paul Sandby, the founding father of English topographic painting and the first artist to capture the genius of place with the freshness and immediacy of watercolour sketching and the strong discipline of eighteenth-century drawing technique, had his training in the Military Drawing Department at the Tower of London, and served in Scotland in the survey for a new road to Fort George under Colonel Watson in the years following 1745. In a drawing by him in the British Museum of high-landers under guard it is clear enough his sympathies are with them. He was one of the earliest members appointed to the new Royal Academy in 1768, and Dr Johnson, the friend of Reynolds, must certainly have known him and at some time seen his work. His brother Thomas had made drawings for Cumberland in 1746; Paul Sandby, in addition to many sketches of Scottish life and landscape, drew for the official survey of Scottish castles.

Johnson reveals in Boswell's records that he was a sharp observer of the real shape of things, but in his own writing, although he precisely describes, yet he seldom visually evokes what he sees: a phrase or two flares like a fire in the dark, but that is all. His ideal is to make a series of sternly objective verbal models of reality: they are meant to be unambiguous. His prose, and his understanding of Scotland, are none the worse for that; indeed, never has a true poet suppressed his poetry to better effect than Dr Johnson; that is the most important clue to his career. As he says, he dreamed of being a poet and woke to find himself a lexicographer. But we are very lucky that while Johnson was observing Scotland, Boswell was observing Johnson; the two books admirably complement each other. Boswell's journal takes a rather original form. Johnson was writing in an accepted, almost a classic form, and about territory where he was not the first to venture.

Thomas Pennant's *Tour in Scotland 1769* had appeared in 1771; for thoroughness, Johnson could not hope to rival it.* 'Pennant speaks of bears,' he said; and again, 'Pennant seems to have seen a great deal which we did not see: when we travel again let us look better about us.' There had been British travel books ever since Addison, though Pennant set a new standard that Johnson recognized. Smollett's rather pedantic and heavily derivative travels abroad had appeared in 1766, and Sterne's dizzy counterblast, the *Sentimental Journey*, in 1768. Some stray withering remarks about north-east England in Smollett's *Humphrey Clinker* (1771) hardly improved his record. Addison's victory was one of style, but he already listed the interest of foreign places as being the works of nature, the variety of governments, curiosities and antiquities. That seems a sensible and classic formula, if by government it comprehends the kind of thing Johnson seeks out in human societies, and the essential note that such an inquiry is always an inquiry into change.

* Pennant's *Tour in Scotland 1769* appeared in 1771, his *Supplement to the Tour* in 1772, and his *Tour in Scotland and Voyage to the Hebrides 1772* in two parts, in 1774 and 1776.

Sterne is pleasanter to read than Smollett, but one has enough of him sooner; he was the author of many unreadable pages, the worst of which are his *Rabelaisian Fragment*. But his classification of travellers is amusing and concerns us here: idle travellers; inquisitive travellers; lying travellers; proud travellers; vain travellers; splenetic travellers; the travellers of necessity; the delinquent and felonious traveller; the unfortunate and innocent traveller; the simple traveller; the sentimental traveller. Dr Johnson was chiefly an inquisitive and Boswell chiefly a sentimental traveller, but some of each had rubbed off onto the other.

Apart from Martin Martin, whom we shall discuss later, and apart from renaissance authorities whose knowledge was largely second-hand, the earliest British traveller to write well about Scotland was Richard Pococke, later an Irish bishop, and a fascinating wanderer in Greece, the Levant, Egypt and Switzerland. He was in Scotland in 1746. Unfortunately, he died of apoplexy during a visitation of his Irish diocese, and his papers languished unprinted until the late nineteenth century.

Johnson's ideal traveller was Thomas Pennant, for the simple reason that Pennant noticed and recorded more than any other published account. Like Johnson, Pennant was not quite an antiquary nor simply an aesthete; his writings are very full and still most useful, particularly on Wales. He was born in 1726, a year after William Stukely (born 1687), whom one may fairly call an archaeological traveller, had walked and mapped Hadrian's Wall from end to end. Stukely, incidentally, was what Sterne would call a traveller of necessity, since as a doctor of medicine he believed that only constant walking tours could cure his gout. But Pennant was a naturalist, a friend of Buffon and a correspondent of Linnaeus. His first tour was in Cornwall as an undergraduate, in search of minerals and fossils. Oxford gave him an honorary degree in 1771: Johnson's came in 1775. Pennant's first Scottish tour had been in 1769; in 1772 he made a second, which included the Lakes and the Hebrides. There is no doubt that it was he, rather than Johnson, who first revealed Scotland to the English, and Wales as well. His only failure as a traveller was in Ireland, where he kept too few notes 'owing to the extreme conviviality of the country'.

When Johnson said of Pennant, 'he's the best traveller I ever read; he observes more things than anyone else does', he apparently had at the back of his mind an idea which is reasonable but quite naive. When the learned old man first found himself among Scottish mountains, he remarked that they would have surprised him greatly, had he not already seen the Peak, which was near enough to Lichfield for him to have known it well. He was pleased to see what mountains looked like, to see the reality behind the word. One may recollect that as late as 1788 Gilbert White of Selborne, who had not seen the Peak, could refer to 'the vast range of mountains called the Sussex Downs'. It seems that Johnson thought the purpose of travelling was largely in order to understand what was meant by the words used for the phenomena of nature. On the island of Coll he gazed at sand dunes and brooded about deserts. In his criticism of pastoral poetry, he had once made a similar point, quite earnestly, about the renaissance poet Sannazaro. That was in an essay in 1750, and it comes close to the motive for his longing to travel:

> Another obstacle to the general reception of this kind of poetry is the ignorance of maritime pleasures, in which the greater part of mankind must always live. To all the inland inhabitants of every region, the sea is only known as an immense diffusion of waters, over which men pass from one country to another, and in which life is frequently lost. They have, therefore, no opportunity of tracing, in their own thoughts, the descriptions of winding shores and calm bays, nor can they look on the poem in which they are mentioned, with other sensations than on a sea chart, or on the metrical geography of Dionysius.

Johnson was then five years from producing his dictionary; no doubt he writes too much as a lexicographer. But his journey in Scotland was certainly intended as research into things that needed to be better understood and more clearly defined. He did wish 'to be generally acquainted with the works of nature', among which one should remember that Buffon includes mankind.

It is a relief that Johnson never saw the Druid Temple Lord Glenorchy had built at Taymouth Castle in the 1750s. But what he expected to find even in the Western Islands was a wilder and earlier state of things than he ever in fact encountered there. His notions of their life were formed in childhood from Martin Martin's *Description of the Western Islands of Scotland* (1703), which saw many later editions and a copy of which it is said he carried on his journey. Martin Martin was a doctor who took a Leyden degree, and a factor to the Macleods. He was a Skye man, full of natural curiosity and local loyalty. He 'had the advantage of seeing Foreign Places, and the honour of Conversing with some of the Royal Society, who raised his natural Curiosity to survey the Isles of Scotland'. Martin's *Western Islands* is a kind of gazetteer; Johnson came to think it ill-written and plainly wished to outdo it, but the seeds of many of his thoughts and some of his sentences are scattered in its pages. A modern reader will find much of its information of the greatest interest, and its prose style attractive. It has a smell of the seventeenth century, even a ghostly odour of Thomas Browne (Martin may well have been born before 1660). His best writing is to be found in his *A Late Voyage to St Kilda, Etc.* (1698). He died in 1719. He appears to have been patronized by Sir Robert Sibbald of the Royal College of Physicians, who was appointed in 1682 Geographer of Scotland to Charles II.

The happiness and health of the islanders, the question of second sight, natural economy, antiquities, orchards and trees, whisky, language, dress, architecture, religion and education, and particularly 'Manuscripts in the Irish Character and Language', are subjects of Martin's that Johnson investigated. There is no doubt, alas, that the sun had set on Martin's world by 1773; that fact, and Martin's far wider coverage of the islands seemed to taunt Samuel Johnson. It was he and not Boswell who 'thought we should see many more'. 'We thought of sailing about easily from island to island.' But the seas were roughening, the season as well as the year was late. The distances were small, but so were the boats. Even at Staffa, 'so lately raised to renown by Mr Banks' (through the pages of Pennant), it was too dangerous to land. I had the same experience there far earlier in the season fifteen years ago.

We know that Boswell got his basic route for Johnson's journey from the Reverend Kenneth Macaulay, the Presbyterian minister under the Duke of Argyll's patronage who visited St Kilda and half wrote, but largely had written for him, an account of that remote island (1764, reprinted 1974). In general, Macaulay's book is an unsuccessful attempt to outdo Martin. He makes an interesting apology for his publication in his excellent, almost certainly ghost-written concluding pages. He discusses the possibility and nature of happiness on an island like St Kilda and the protection of natural religion by distance and ignorance. 'At any rate I think the St Kildians may be ranked among the greatest curiosities of the moral world.' These pages must have stirred some interest in the author of *Rasselas* and the *Rambler* essays; they may even owe something to his influence. But Johnson's behaviour, and even his observations in Scotland, are far looser and more human than poor Macaulay's, and Boswell's infinitely so.

Johnson at sixty-three was just at the high point of a laborious and distinguished career, and at last he was ready to relax. He had finished his dictionary at the age of forty-six, and in 1761, at fifty-two, he was granted an annual pension of three hundred pounds, comparatively a substantial sum. Four years later he finished his *Shakespeare*. It is not only the authority, but the vast scale of these enterprises that impresses. The summer that the pension was awarded he spent travelling, for the first time in his life, with Reynolds in Devonshire and the south-west. We know also that he nursed an ambition to see all the English cathedrals before he died: an ambition that few if any readers of these words will probably have fulfilled, even under today's easier though less pleasant conditions. When he set out for Scotland he began a high-spirited late season of his life. It had been put off from year to year, and maybe the old Corsican General Paoli's tour with Boswell in 1771 turned the scales and brought it about. If Paoli could do it, it was practicable. In December of 1772 Boswell 'was much disappointed that you did not come to Scotland last autumn'. Yet once the Scottish journey was over, Johnson travelled in 1774 in Wales, in 1775 in France, in 1776 with Boswell to the Peak District, then once again in 1777 they met there, and in 1778 Johnson attended a Militia camp in Lincolnshire as the guest of Captain Langton. Johnson and Boswell even had their eye on the Baltic and the North. Can they have meant Russia as well as Sweden? Johnson went on travelling until he was sixty-nine.

For Boswell the Scottish journey, or at any rate his publication of it, was an even more important milestone. He was famous from his youth for a book about Corsica. He was the heir to a grand, if not great estate, and a member of the Scottish Bar, where somewhat curiously he had sometimes to plead before his father, a judge, often it seems unsuccessfully. It is not possible even to sketch in a few lines the ramifications of his character. He shares with his fellow-countryman Lord Byron a fullness of self-expression and a variety that defy easy analysis. It is evident that Johnson loved him like a son; perhaps James Boswell took over this role from Garrick. Their occasional quarrels are as embarrassing as intimate family quarrels. When Johnson quarrelled with Boswell's real father, which sounds as though it was both a fearsome spectacle and very funny indeed, Boswell is almost silent on the subject.

We must think away the *Life of Johnson* which was still unwritten. All that Boswell had when Johnson died at the end of 1784 were notes, and his own journals, and some letters. The best part of these papers so far as their Johnson material was concerned was Boswell's journal of the Scottish tour. In publishing it, with the help and encouragement of that great Shakespearian scholar Edmond Malone, he was staking his claim to be the full biographer of Johnson; or more than that even: he was beginning to fill out the brilliant picture of a character fully imagined, fully created on paper – a new achievement in English prose, and one that has perhaps never been bettered.

It is interesting to see the degree to which both Johnson in much of his writing, and Boswell in the *Journal* and then the *Life of Johnson*, were leaning over into the territory of the novel, just beginning to be colonized in their lifetime. Many of Boswell's observations, and some of Johnson's tricks of treatment, would today be called novelistic. This point about Johnson was well made by John Wain in his recent sympathetic and fascinating *Life* of the great man. It is even truer, in a different way, about Boswell, who says of a projected account of his own early days in London: 'The account will be as like a no el as what is strictly true can be.' It is as if different elements of the novel were floating about off-stage, as if they had half materialized, or as if they had only to come together. Was it the passionate and sober devotion to truth of Johnson's generation or his circle that prevented the novel from being born earlier? Or some ghost of classical propriety? Why did Johnson neglect Fielding while he revelled in Shakespeare? At any rate, Boswell's *Journal* in particular poses some interesting problems about the interrelations of literature and reality. The two writers will often pleasingly confuse one another's account of the same day, spent together.

We are lucky to know quite a lot about how these two very different works were composed. We know that Boswell was an experienced and a very full diarist, and that Johnson read Boswell's Scottish journals in their original form during their journey, although after he had conceived of a book of his own. We have had for some time since their rediscovery at Malahide the original manuscript, almost complete, of Boswell's journals, and some of Malone's intelligent and modest work on them has also come to light. We can trace revisions through the three early editions. Boswell's self-censorship and self-editing add significantly to what we know about him. Johnson also kept a journal, now lost, which he used in London in composing his book. It almost certainly resembled the French journal of 1775 which Boswell thought jejune (and by his standards it was), but which luckily he prints in the *Life of Johnson*. That reads like a series of chapter and paragraph headings; the structure is iron, and the book that could emerge from it is already determined. Opinions as well as facts were already fully formed. The journal of Johnson's Welsh journey in 1774, which has recently come to light and was printed in Powell's revision of Birkbeck Hill's *Boswell*, is much fuller, almost a book already. Johnson also had access in London to his own much fresher and more novelistic letters from Scotland to Mrs Thrale. In an ideal world the Malahide manuscript, Boswell's published book, Johnson's book and his letters should all be open on one's desk at once, because of their constant interplay.

Some of the self-editing that Boswell did after the old man's death is simply literary. Using his recollection of Johnson's speaking style, he makes many sentences more dramatic and more immediate by adding a 'Sir' or slightly sharpening the syntax. It is impossible to know whether his recollection was general or at least in most instances particular. I have found sometimes that memory, jolted by a note of conversation made many years ago and then forgotten, can be fuller and sharper than the note ever was, and particularly so in the case of an old and loved friend. It seems that for Boswell the process of rewriting increased rather than decreased the quality of dramatic immediacy and freshness which is so exciting in his portrait of Johnson.

On occasion entire incidents are suppressed. Not unnaturally he suppresses most of his personal fear of infestation by lice; also, alas, he cut out what he thought boring, but historians are pleased to know, about how credit operated, and the difficulty of obtaining money on even a large island. A bill had to be changed with an emigrant ship, because there was 'hardly any specie in Sky'. 'I got one and twenty shillings in Portree, which is a wonderful store.' Even more annoyingly he cuts out an accurate account of what was eaten and drunk. The hostess and her daughters ate oat-bread, but 'Mr Johnson and I had excellent cakes of flour'. He suppresses a moment when he went too far in teasing Johnson and got badly snubbed, this not because of the snub but because of the gravity of his insult to Johnson.

More significantly, he suppresses his wife's objection to the entire expedition. 'Madam,' replied Johnson, 'we do not go there as to a paradise. We go to see something different from what we are accustomed to see.' He suppresses what he feels about his own extravagance of behaviour at a moment when he went out alone to pray, flinging his arms around an ancient cross that stood on Inchkenneth. Johnson had written to Mrs Thrale about that incident: 'Boswell, who is very pious, went into it [a chapel] at night to perform his devotions, but came back in haste, for fear of spectres.' Boswell suppresses another prayer, one that was fortunately answered, on the way to Iona, where 'I put up a petition to God to make the waves more still'. And on Iona itself, which was, as it was meant to be, the climax of their expedition, Boswell suppresses how deeply and in what a romantic way he was moved.

He was lawyer to the Macleans in an important case, which not surprisingly in the end they lost, to recover their lands from the Dukes of Argyll, who had calmly conquered them in a private war in the 1690s. What he suppresses on Iona, where the grandeur of his friend Maclean is by no means underestimated but rather dramatized, is that he went alone to the Swearing Stone and swore some kind of clan loyalty to Maclean and his family. And yet a few days later, when he proudly paraded Johnson at Inveraray, where the Argylls made much of their famous visitor, the same Boswell was surprised and hurt to be snubbed by the Duchess. One may well feel, as Boswell's self-censorship suggests that he himself felt, that his true world was polite, political, compromising London, of which Edinburgh was a provincial image, and that a certain unreality infected the deeper stirrings of his soul. One cannot resist recording another endearing absurdity of Boswell on Iona. He records his prayer, then the fact that he read aloud a sermon on prayer by Dr Ogden. 'I had a serious joy in hearing my voice, while it was filled with Ogden's admirable eloquence, resounding in the ancient cathedral.'

Boswell likes to laugh at Johnson, but he is careful not to overdo the laughter. There was an evening when Johnson in high spirits imitated a kangaroo, an animal at that time newly discovered. Boswell suppressed that pleasing scene. Was it tact about Johnson's personal awkwardness, his neurotic spasms, or was it that Johnson had seen this passage and disliked it, or was it just the difficulty of conveying this uninhibited scene? If Boswell feared he might attract mockery in London, he was right. In 1786, almost as soon as *Journal of a Tour to the Hebrides with Samuel Johnson* appeared, Rowlandson produced a very amusing series of satiric sketches, 'after designs by Samuel Collings', called *The Picturesque Beauties of Boswell*. One of the funniest is an imaginary picture of the quarrel between Johnson and Lord Auchinleck, which Boswell forbore to describe in detail.

Questions of religion and politics open an entry into a far more important matter, so far as these books are concerned. However finely Johnson sounded his trumpet-note on Iona, and however widely his sentences there were admired, it remains true that he was unwilling to be impressed or pre-occupied by mere antiquities, castles or graves or stone circles. He had an element in common, outside politics and religion, with the Argylls. Almost within living memory that family, as heads of the aggressive and successful Campbell clan, had washed with blood and scorched with gunpowder the innocent hillsides of Glencoe, the most idyllic and wild piece of pastoral land-scape in Scotland. But there is no doubt that the Argylls in 1773 represented progress and modernity and success in the modern world. They were progres-sive paternalists as well as ruthless lords.

The clan age of Scotland, to which we have little access as historians, though as anthropologists we may understand and admire clan society, was full of calamities, rapes, feuds and revenges, the piling up of heads and the burning alive of families to the sound of bagpipes. Johnson treated these deplorable stories with healthy irony and hostility. He was keenly interested in the education and the economic progress of the Scottish islanders in a better future. He tempted Boswell to suggest he should found a great college on Little Colonsay, 'the master to be a clergyman of the Church of England'. The conclusion of all Johnson's observations was that 'whatever enlarges hope, will exalt courage; after having seen the deaf taught arithmetick, who would be afraid to cultivate the Hebrides?'

However much he respected feudal authority or warmed to old manners, he did not regret the lost age, only the chance to observe it. 'That animating rabble has now ceased,' he said of the retinue of the chieftains. At Inveraray Robert Mylne was building a model town for the Duke of Argyll which still stands, and which represents the purest ideals of eighteenth-century architectural planning. It is as logical and functional as its French equivalent Les Salines, but it is not as beautiful. It is tempting to suggest that a closer analogy to the architectural style of Inveraray is at Berwick on Tweed, the King's Arms Hotel and Vanbrugh's toy fort as counterparts to the inn where Johnson stayed and the Duke of Argyll's new house and park, a pretty Gothick toy if ever there was one.

Johnson had no sympathy with Highland lairds who increased rents and depopulated their lands; he clearly hated them. Nor did he seek or envisage any radical solution to Scottish evils. His sympathies were with liberality and paternalism, and with modern enterprise. He understood the usefulness of the new military roads and the siting of Tobermory (Johnson's Tobor Morar) where he landed on Mull. Boswell reports twelve or fourteen ships in the bay. Martin and earlier writers had already noticed the place, and it was probably well known to generations of local fishermen, but its foundation as a town was due to the British Fisheries Society, an offshoot of the Highland Society of London founded in 1786, acting under the guidance of the Duke of Argyll, the most active developer and improver in Scotland.

The Duke's being a Whig or a Tory has little significance, certainly much less than Johnson gave to such questions. Johnson's Toryism, if it was not provincial local patriotism, a traditional loyalty of religion extended to politics, was a refusal of the ugly modern forces that increased their strength throughout his lifetime: corruption, exploitation and powerful cruelty that he felt would once have been inadmissible. He was committedly on the side of American Indians, Negro slaves, the British poor, and every other underdog he knew. It is important to realize that these attitudes could go together with the most progressive analysis of human society. There is a crucial sense in which Johnson belongs outside an English context, to the European Enlightenment.

That is not how he is usually seen. But Johnson believed utterly in the republic of letters, the community of learning, with the whole of man and nature for its object, and all human enterprise and improvement depending on it. His roots were in the renaissance; hence his attachment to such writers as Buchanan. As for the practicality of his interests, there is a record that he worked for some time alone in London on a new process for the improvement of British china and porcelain. His examples of how to waste time and money conclude with 'one makes collections of shells, and another searches the world for tulips and carnations'. In his treatment of the poet

Shenstone as a landscape gardener he finds it hard to subdue his scorn to a gentle rumble: 'Perhaps a sullen and surly speculator may think such performances rather the sport than the business of human reason.' What Johnson had in common with the Enlightenment was intellectual hope and courage, and the wish to be a benefactor of mankind. He declared in so many words that the happiness of twenty thousand is twenty thousand times as important as one man's happiness.

It was not only in England that deep thought was being given in those years to the nature of human society, to society as a long development. One of the officers with whom Johnson chatted at Fort Augustus had fought the American Indians; he had taken part in the Ohio expedition. Indians and Scots were much the same to him. Johnson had written about Europeans from an Indian point of view in the *Idler* of November 1759, in unforgettable phrases. From his boyhood, he had read the Jesuit records of native peoples, and they had fired his mind. Enlightened intellectuals from Voltaire to Diderot in France, and by the mid-century even in Spain and Mexico, where their stimulus was the Aztecs and Incas, had seen the importance of such problems; they had begun to realize that human nature must be understood through human development. Scotland was an instance close to home.

Johnson's view of human conditions was always harsh. It was well supplied by his experience of life, but in the last analysis I think it was based on Juvenal, an author he quoted at length by heart and an influence almost greater on his prose than on his verse, and rooted in a stern Roman morality. His observation of evil in the Argyll policy of abolishing the old class of semi-independent 'tacksmen', and substituting tenants and those who could be manipulated, might have been derived from several chains of reasoning. The uprising of 1745 lay close to the root of the policy. Johnson probably derived his objection from a dislike of the raised rents and exploitation that went with it, though at the same time he was disturbed by a vaster alteration, the withering away of a world. But he ends like this, like a Roman philosopher: 'Without intelligence man is not social, he is only gregarious; and little intelligence will there be, where all are constrained to daily labour, and every mind must wait upon the hand.' Johnson's own mind is like a courageous lantern in the darkness: the policies of the Argylls may seem to offer a vaster effulgence, but they have their dark element. When British ships in 1746 went round a remote bit of Argyll coast, pillaging and burning the houses of Jacobites, murdering any they caught and destroying all food, the then Duke of Argyll objected only that the houses were his property and their shells should have been left standing.

Boswell preserves the huffs and woofs and the 'warts-and-all' aspect of

Johnson: some signs of his age, for instance, and some notes on his spirits at different times and his casual conversation. This is valuable mostly as a fore-runner of the *Life*, which appeared in 1791 and crowned the prose achieve-ments of the eighteenth century. We are told it was Reynolds's confirmation 'of my being able to preserve his conversation in an authentick and lively manner' in the *Journal of a Tour* that gave Boswell the confidence for his great work. Boswell does present a lively and obviously authentic Johnson, and often suggests a motive or a context, though he can add nothing to Johnson's reasoning, but only diffuse it or distract from it.

There are some puzzles about the journey which will occur to modern readers where Boswell throws little light, and some places with a beguiling later history that he could not have foreseen. We can understand the penetra-tion of the Highlands by way of Inverness and the Great Glen. That was the classic route from Berwick on Tweed; it was determined by physical geography. Fort George is still standing; that is the old depot of the Seaforth Highlanders. When it was built it cost £160,000 and it could hold 2,500 men, slightly more than Prince Charles Edward reviewed at Aberchalder in 1745, before burning down the predecessor of Fort George. At Fort Augustus things are more complicated. A large part of one wall of the old fort survives, and makes it clear that the Lovat Arms occupies the ground where most of that fort stood. It dated from 1716 and held only 300 men. The highlanders knocked it down in 1746, and the later and grander fort down by the lake, substantial traces of which are to be seen in the layout and the walls of the Benedictine school, is the one where Johnson was enter-tained. It never heard an angry cannon-shot; it was sold off for £5,000 in 1867 to Lord Lovat, who employed Hansom and the younger Pugin to transform it. About the same time Fort William was sold off to make a railway station.

Why did Boswell strike north for Skye from Fort Augustus, by a tough route to an inconvenient port? Mallaig and the Mallaig route were created later by the railway, just as Oban was. The people were Catholic, the population sparse and beyond Campbell control, and the country was some-what unknown. But Bernera on the coast opposite Skye had been a garrison for years, and a place on the map at least as early as *The English Pilot* of 1715. The road that led there was a military track. It was hazardous and hard to follow, and may have surprised Boswell as much as it alarmed Johnson. Today its earlier stretches are harder to trace than the last rough twelve miles, because the road has been constantly improved. Even so, most modern travellers who trace it will be astonished that Boswell chose it. The reason must be that it was mapped, and that the Reverend Mr Macaulay knew nothing about any Mallaig route. Boswell offers the barest of route-plans to illustrate his book; without a guide it would be useless.

The Wordsworths in 1808 travelled the Highlands on wheels; but in 1773 one had to ride a small pony. To imagine the state of the military roads and droving tracks that Johnson used, one should simply go and test them now for oneself. I recommend the path from Kilmore south of Oban by Loch Nant to Kilchrenan, some eleven miles, not all easy going. If that is not possible, one might consider the Order issued by Colonel Montgomery at Fort William in May of 1792 against the ploughing up of military roads, the turning of ploughs and drawing of harrows on them, the laying of seaweed or manure or the piling up of unwanted stones on them. The droving tracks were not the green lanes one might expect, or the grassy ways you will sometimes see in Scotland. The route that island cattle took to southern markets was a rough one, even apart from the swimming of Loch Awe between the twin inns at Taychreggan and Port Sonachan (the North Port and South Port of the Ordnance Survey), both of the inns being, I think, later than Johnson's time. The cattle seem to have moved about ten or twelve miles a day: from Loch Nell near Oban to Taychreggan is not much more, and the cattle track from Port Sonachan to Inveraray may be less. In two months at that rate cattle could reach London.

But to use the same routes at greater speed on small ponies when one is over sixty would certainly be, as Johnson found it, extremely fatiguing. There have been some modern attempts to retrace the 1773 journey, none of them so far as I can tell under anything like the original conditions, and none of them quite complete. The most interesting of these pilgrimages were those of the Reverend James Bailey in 1787, George Birkbeck Hill in 1890, and Moray Maclaren in 1948. Today the route would be more easily walked than ridden. A recent attempt to recreate and film the droving of cattle along part of it for television ended as fatuously as one might expect, with the cattle straying at night and refusing to enter the cold water of the lochs. Yet there is no doubt about Johnson's and Boswell's route, and no doubt of the scale on which Scottish cattle were driven in the eighteenth century to southern markets. The central Scottish market was at Falkirk. How early? As early as the 1680s the government had boats on the lochs to prevent the movement of stolen cattle, and Kintyre cattle were reaching Stirling before 1600. One of the pleasantest witnesses to those long roads is John Clare, in the suppressed 'July' of his 'Shepherd's Calendar', recently published.

> Scotch droves of beasts a little breed
> In swelterd weary mood proceed

A patient race from Scottish hills
To fatten by our pasture rills
Lean wi the wants of mountain soil
But short and stout for travels toyl
Wi cockd up horns and curling crown
And dewlap bosom hanging down ...
And shepherds as they trample by
Leaves oer their hooks a wondering eye
To witness men so oddly clad
In petticoats of banded plaid
Wi blankets oer their shoulders slung
To camp at night the fields among
When they for rest on commons stop
And blue cap like a stocking top
Cockt oer their faces summer brown
Wi scarlet tazzles on the crown ...

If I have seemed to linger too long over this picture of the cattle and the survival or revival of the kilt in 1823, when John Clare's poem was written, that is because in order fully to taste what Johnson and Boswell have to offer one must understand a very slow time-scale, a vanished way of life, the hardness of travelling, the comparative peace and silence of Scotland, the brave intrusion of any musical instrument, and such things as the slow plodding of cattle from end to end of the United Kingdom. In Johnson's years the normal way to get to London from Scotland was by the waggon from Newcastle. This had six wheels and eight horses, and it took eighteen days, travelling twenty-five miles every day. From Glasgow one had to ride or to sail, which might take a month. Johnson was lucky to find a coach; they do not appear to have been regular on such a long journey, though a coach did run between Edinburgh and Glasgow twice a week, taking twelve hours each way. Meanwhile, between 1763 and 1775, twenty thousand highlanders and islanders emigrated, four thousand in one year leaving from Skye alone, and the price of Highland cattle doubled or trebled in three years.

'You and I, Sir,' said Boswell to Johnson in 1776, 'have, I think, seen together the extremes of what can be seen in Britain: the wild rough island of Mull, and Blenheim Park.' Well, there were and are wilder islands than Mull, and if Blenheim and Stowe once offered the extreme of cultivated landscape, one still imagines Samuel Johnson as preferring London. One of his advantages over Boswell is that he had no pretensions. 'Is not every garden a botanick garden?' the old gentleman inquired. But Boswell's advantage is that although he censors his own extravagant behaviour, and Johnson's as well where necessary, he permits Johnson more extravagance, however slightly more, than Johnson permits himself. He unbuttons Johnson. He wakes him from his perfect prose as Pygmalion wakened the statue. He makes it possible, indeed he makes it inevitable for us to enter into his love affair with the old man.

Johnson is more attractive than Boswell chiefly because of the way Boswell writes about him. We can hardly believe in the gay, gentle, elegant Boswell that Johnson sketches: he is just another of those polite paintings of eighteenth-century faces, so wreathed in compliment and convention that the faces seem part of the frames. Boswell's self-knowledge contains a little self-disgust, and the slightly rank taste of his writings which makes him so readable is also what blocks us from whole-hearted acceptance of him. He is slightly embarrassed, slightly embarrassing; his special gift is self-conscious-ness. But Johnson with his prejudices and passions is, as Juvenal says of the satirist, an old dog mouthing and mumbling an old bone, instead of just swallowing his dinner and trotting on as Boswell would. They are both deeply melancholy men; their comradeship in high spirits is not unreal to either of them, but it is Johnson's melancholy, his passions and his needs which go deeper. His was a life with no solutions and probably no illusions about any-thing but love.

Still, some of his prejudices are strange, or strange to us. He genuinely believed that civilized manners are the product of kings and their courts, from which they soak down to permeate human societies. Where does that view come from? Some philosopher of the eighteenth century, or an interpretation of Shakespeare, or a sense of degree and propriety from conservative Derbyshire and Staffordshire, provincial Lichfield? Johnson's view that old Scottish manners depended on the numerous courts of chieftains is as strange to me as his friend Gibbon's explanation that disbelief in ancient Roman religion must have spread through servants overhearing the jokes of their masters as they waited at table.

The most deadly attack on Johnson I have ever read is by William Cobbett, the chip on whose shoulder is authentic English oak of solid antiquity and great weight. This side of idolatry, Cobbett is my hero. He speaks of 'Old dread-death and dread-devil Johnson, that teacher of moping and melancholy. If the writings of this time-saving, mean, dastardly old pensioner had got a firm hold of the people at large, the people would have been bereft of their souls. These writings, aided by the charm of their pompous sound, were fast making their ways, till light, reason and the French revolution confined them to the shelves of repentant, married old rakes and those of old stock-jobbers with young wives standing in need of something to keep down their unruly ebullitions.' It seems to be a rule of light and reason and revolution that every new wave seeks to drown the one before it.

Cobbett's objection is to Johnson's melancholy moralism and religious rigour. I doubt whether it could be sustained today that Johnson's Church and God did more harm than the European or the British movement which shook them off, and it is not true that the intellectual seduction which lurks in Johnson's own writings consists of a pompous sound. 'Zadok the priest and Nathan the prophet' is a pompous sound; Johnson does not ever sound like that. I am inclined to believe that Cobbett's Johnson is as imaginary as his French revolution. Cobbett is quarrelling with himself, perhaps, or his younger self. And Johnson on Scotland is far more informative and useful than Cobbett's brief Scottish pages. Yet it remains true that he who dines with Johnson should use a long spoon.

The quarrel with Lord Auchinleck becomes more interesting than ever in the light of Cobbett's invective. Boswell's father 'was as sanguine a Whig and Presbyterian, as Dr Johnson was a Tory and Church of England man', and the explosion of the two volcanoes seems to have begun in premonitory rumblings during the early days of the visit. On Wednesday it rained, and Johnson was irritated to be asked how he liked the Highlands. 'Who *can* like the Highlands? – I like the inhabitants very well.' On Thursday Johnson and Boswell discussed the nature of melancholy. On Friday Johnson told a local minister, 'Sir, you know no more of our Church than a Hottentot.' The final explosion, if Boswell has the order of days right, was over Cromwell and Charles I. We know that Lord Auchinleck praised Cromwell to Johnson 'for teaching Kings they had a joint in their necks'. This crumb of information comes to us through Walter Scott. The two old men quarrelled badly. Yet Johnson was not always consumed with hatred of Cromwell; at Inverness he gave the devil his due: 'He introduced by useful violence the arts of peace.' I think that the reason Johnson found Auchinleck so provoking and vice versa has to do with Johnson's scarcely suppressed rage about the state of Scotland.

His prose is majestic. He has a tighter and a looser style, and uses both with easy transition. He can never give the perfect illusion of artlessness that Addison can give, and one can see that he often spoke much as he wrote. The expression of ideas was harder work for Johnson than for Addison, but the result has great advantages. Part of his attraction is intellectual: one is interested to know what he thinks, to trace his coherence, to savour his common sense. To make common sense sound unpredictable is one of his weapons. In 1773, Johnson was a practised essayist, a formidable scholar and a mature inquirer. A lifetime of vast reading had crumbled into the humus of his mind. The windows at Banff, the nuts by the roadside at Loch Ness, the stone arrowheads found in the Hebrides and 'the mischiefs of emigration' are all grist for the same kind of encyclopaedic prose because they are all understood in a context that can range the world and history. The intelligence of his memory is what is so striking. His eye is hawk-like to pick out what is relevant, and even in light of passing analogies he can fix what he sees with an unexpected and precise comparison. His narrative power, for example in the death of Hugh Macdonald, and his analytic power, for example in the long discussion of tacksmen and tenantry, are as remarkable in the *Journey to the Western Islands* as anywhere in his works.

For years after his return to London, Johnson thought continually about Scotland and Scottish affairs. He worked on proofs of Lord Hailes's *Annals of Scotland*, did what he could to get a young Macaulay into Oxford, forwarded books in Gaelic to the Bodleian library. He was deeply grieved by the death of Maclean of Coll in 1774; a year or so later he entertained young Coll's brother, the new laird, for some weeks in London. He did turn aside from northern interests to travel in Wales and France, but only because the Thrales invited him; that meant going in luxury, and he more or less loved Mrs Thrale. It is more important to us that Johnson's Scottish journey had cemented his friendship with Boswell: we probably owe the *Life of Johnson* as well as this slighter sketch to that surprising expedition of theirs so late in the season, between August and November, 1773.

Map of Johnson's and Boswell's Route

The Tour through SCOTLAND and the HEBRIDES in 1773

A JOURNEY TO
THE WESTERN ISLANDS
OF SCOTLAND

by

Samuel Johnson

I had desired to visit the Hebrides, or Western Islands of Scotland, so long, that I scarcely remember how the wish was originally excited; and was in the Autumn of the year 1773 induced to undertake the journey, by finding in Mr Boswell a companion, whose acuteness would help my inquiry, and whose gaiety of conversation and civility of manners are sufficient to counteract the inconveniencies of travel, in countries less hospitable than we have passed.

On the eighteenth of August we left Edinburgh, a city too well known to admit description, and directed our course northward, along the eastern coast of Scotland, accompanied the first day by another gentleman,[1] who could stay with us only long enough to shew us how much we lost at separation.

As we crossed the Frith of Forth, our curiosity was attracted by Inch Keith, a small island, which neither of my companions had ever visited, though, lying within their view, it had all their lives solicited their notice. Here, by climbing with some difficulty over shattered crags, we made the first experiment of unfrequented coasts. Inch Keith is nothing more than a rock covered with a thin layer of earth, not wholly bare of grass, and very fertile of thistles. A small herd of cows grazes annually upon it in the summer. It seems never to have afforded to man or beast a permanent habitation.

We found only the ruins of a small fort, not so injured by time but that it might be easily restored to its former state. It seems never to have been intended as a place of strength, nor was built to endure a siege, but merely to afford cover to a few soldiers, who perhaps had the charge of a battery, or were stationed to give signals of approaching danger. There is therefore no provision of water within the walls, though the spring is so near, that it might have been easily enclosed. One of the stones had this inscription: MARIA REG. 1564. It has probably been neglected from the time that the whole island had the same king.

We left this little island with our thoughts employed awhile on the different appearance that it would have made, if it had been placed at the same distance from London, with the same facility of approach; with what emulation of price a few rocky acres would have been purchased, and with what expensive industry they would have been cultivated and adorned.

When we landed, we found our chaise ready, and passed through King-horn, Kirkaldy, and Cowpar,[2] places not unlike the small or straggling market-towns in those parts of England where commerce and manufactures have not yet produced opulence.

Though we were yet in the most populous part of Scotland, and at so small a distance from the capital, we met few passengers.

The roads are neither rough nor dirty; and it affords a southern stranger a new kind of pleasure to travel so commodiously without the interruption of toll-gates. Where the bottom is rocky, as it seems commonly to be in Scotland, a smooth way is made indeed with great labour, but it never wants repairs; and in those parts where adventitious materials are necessary, the ground once consolidated is rarely broken; for the inland commerce is not great, nor are heavy commodities often transported otherwise than by water. The carriages in common use are small carts, drawn each by one little horse; and a man seems to derive some degree of dignity and importance from the reputation of possessing a two-horse cart.

ST ANDREWS

At an hour somewhat late we came to St Andrews, a city once archiepiscopal; where that university still subsists in which philosophy was formerly taught by Buchanan,[3] whose name has as fair a claim to immortality as can be conferred by modern latinity, and perhaps a fairer than the instability of vernacular languages admits.

We found, that by the interposition of some invisible friend,[4] lodgings had been provided for us at the house of one of the professors,[5] whose easy civility quickly made us forget that we were strangers; and in the whole time of our stay we were gratified by every mode of kindness, and entertained with all the elegance of lettered hospitality.

In the morning we rose to perambulate a city, which only history shews to have once flourished, and surveyed the ruins of ancient magnificence, of which even the ruins cannot long be visible, unless some care be taken to preserve them; and where is the pleasure of preserving such mournful memorials?[6] They have been till very lately so much neglected, that every man carried away the stones who fancied that he wanted them.

The cathedral, of which the foundations may be still traced, and a small part of the wall is standing, appears to have been a spacious and majestick building, not unsuitable to the primacy of the kingdom. Of the architecture, the poor remains can hardly exhibit, even to an artist, a sufficient specimen. It was demolished, as is well known, in the tumult and violence of Knox's reformation.

Not far from the cathedral, on the margin of the water, stands a fragment of the castle, in which the archbishop anciently resided. It was never very large, and was built with more attention to security than pleasure. Cardinal Beatoun is said to have had workmen employed in improving its fortifications at the time when he was murdered by the ruffians of reformation,[7] in the manner of which Knox has given what he himself calls a merry narrative.

The change of religion in Scotland, eager and vehement as it was, raised an epidemical enthusiasm, compounded of sullen scrupulousness and warlike ferocity, which, in a people whom idleness resigned to their own thoughts, and who, conversing only with each other, suffered no dilution of their zeal from the gradual influx of new opinions, was long transmitted in its full strength from the old to the young, but by trade and intercourse with England, is now visibly abating, and giving way too fast to their laxity of practice and indifference of opinion, in which men, not sufficiently instructed to find the middle point, too easily shelter themselves from rigour and constraint.

The city of St Andrews, when it had lost its archiepiscopal preeminence, gradually decayed: one of its streets is now lost; and in those that remain, there is the silence and solitude of inactive indigence and gloomy depopulation.

The university, within a few years, consisted of three colleges, but is now reduced to two; the college of St Leonard being lately dissolved by the sale of its buildings and the appropriation of its revenues to the professors of the two others.[8] The chapel of the alienated college is yet standing, a fabrick not inelegant of external structure; but I was always, by some civil excuse, hindred from entering it. A recent[9] attempt, as I was since told, has been made to convert it into a kind of green-house, by planting its area with shrubs. This new method of gardening is unsuccessful; the plants do not hitherto prosper. To what use it will next be put I have no pleasure in conjecturing. It is something that its present state is at least not ostentatiously displayed. Where there is yet shame, there may in time be virtue.

The dissolution of St Leonard's college was doubtless necessary; but of that necessity there is reason to complain. It is surely not without just reproach, that a nation, of which the commerce is hourly extending, and the wealth encreasing, denies any participation of its prosperity to its literary societies; and while its merchants or its nobles are raising palaces, suffers its universities to moulder into dust.

Of the two colleges yet standing, one is by the institution of its founder appropriated to Divinity.[10] It is said to be capable of containing fifty students;

but more than one must occupy a chamber. The library, which is of late erection, is not very spacious, but elegant and luminous.

The doctor,[11] by whom it was shewn, hoped to irritate or subdue my English vanity by telling me, that we had no such repository of books in England.

Saint Andrews seems to be a place eminently adapted to study and education, being situated in a populous, yet a cheap country, and exposing the minds and manners of young men neither to the levity and dissoluteness of a capital city, nor to the gross luxury of a town of commerce, places naturally unpropitious to learning; in one the desire of knowledge easily gives way to the love of pleasure, and in the other, is in danger of yielding to the love of money.

The students however are represented as at this time not exceeding a hundred. Perhaps it may be some obstruction to their increase that there is no episcopal chapel in the place. I saw no reason for imputing their paucity to the present professors; nor can the expence of an academical education be very reasonably objected. A student of the highest class may keep his annual session, or as the English call it, his term, which lasts seven months, for about fifteen pounds, and one of lower rank for less than ten; in which board, lodging, and instruction are all included.

The chief magistrate resident in the university, answering to our vice-chancellor, and to the *rector magnificus* on the continent, had commonly the title of Lord Rector; but being addressed only as 'Mr Rector' in an inauguratory speech by the present chancellor,[12] he has fallen from his former dignity of style. Lordship was very liberally annexed by our ancestors to any station or character of dignity: They said, the 'Lord General', and 'Lord Ambassador'; so we still say 'my Lord' to the judge upon the circuit, and yet retain in our Liturgy 'the Lords of the Council'.

In walking among the ruins of religious buildings, we came to two vaults over which had formerly stood the house of the sub-prior. One of the vaults was inhabited by an old woman, who claimed the right of abode there, as the widow of a man whose ancestors had possessed the same gloomy mansion for no less than four generations. The right, however it began, was considered as established by legal prescription, and the old woman lives undisturbed. She thinks however that she has a claim to something more than sufferance; for as her husband's name was Bruce, she is allied to royalty, and told Mr Boswell that when there were persons of quality in the place, she was distinguished by some notice; that indeed she is now neglected, but she spins a thread, has the company of her cat, and is troublesome to nobody.

Having now seen whatever this ancient city offered to our curiosity, we left it with good wishes, having reason to be highly pleased with the attention that was paid us. But whoever surveys the world must see many things that give him pain. The kindness of the professors did not contribute to abate the uneasy remembrance of an university declining, a college alienated, and a church profaned and hastening to the ground.

St Andrews indeed has formerly suffered more atrocious ravages and more extensive destruction, but recent evils affect with greater force. We were reconciled to the sight of archiepiscopal ruins. The distance of a calamity from the present time seems to preclude the mind from contact of sympathy. Events long past are barely known; they are not considered. We read with as little emotion the violence of Knox and his followers, as the irruptions of Alaric and the Goths. Had the university been destroyed two centuries ago, we should not have regretted it; but to see it pining in decay and struggling for life, fills the mind with mournful images and ineffectual wishes.

ABERBROTHIC

As we knew sorrow and wishes to be vain, it was now our business to mind our way. The roads of Scotland afford little diversion to the traveller, who seldom sees himself either encountered or overtaken, and who has nothing to contemplate but grounds that have no visible boundaries, or are separated by walls of loose stone. From the bank of the Tweed to St Andrews I had never seen a single tree, which I did not believe to have grown up far within the present century. Now and then about a gentleman's house stands a small plantation, which in Scotch is called a *policy*, but of these there are few, and those few all very young. The variety of sun and shade is here utterly unknown. There is no tree for either shelter or timber. The oak and the thorn is equally a stranger, and the whole country is extended in uniform nakedness, except that in the road between Kirkaldy and Cowpar, I passed for a few yards between two hedges. A tree might be a show in Scotland as a horse in Venice. At St Andrews Mr Boswell found only one, and recommended it to my notice; I told him that it was rough and low, or looked as if I thought so.[13] This, said he, is nothing to another a few miles off. I was still less delighted to hear that another tree was not to be seen nearer. Nay, said a gentleman that stood by, I know but of this and that tree in the county.

The Lowlands of Scotland had once undoubtedly an equal portion of woods with other countries. Forests are every where gradually diminished, as architecture and cultivation prevail by the increase of people and the introduction of arts. But I believe few regions have been denuded like this, where many centuries must have passed in waste without the least thought of future supply. Davies observes in his account of Ireland,[14] that no Irishman had ever planted an orchard. For that negligence some excuse might be drawn from an unsettled state of life, and the instability of property; but in Scotland possession has long been secure, and inheritance regular, yet it may be doubted whether before the Union any lowlander between Edinburgh and England had ever set a tree.

Of this improvidence no other account can be given than that it probably began in times of tumult, and continued because it had begun. Established custom is not easily broken, till some great event shakes the whole system of things, and life seems to recommence upon new principles. That before the union the Scots had little trade and little money, is no valid apology; for plantation is the least expensive of all methods of improvement. To drop a seed into the ground can cost nothing, and the trouble is not great of protecting the young plant, till it is out of danger; though it must be allowed to have some difficulty in places like these, where they have neither wood for palisades, nor thorns for hedges.

Our way was over the Firth of Tay, where, though the water was not wide, we paid four shillings for ferrying the chaise. In Scotland the necessaries of life are easily procured, but superfluities and elegancies are of the same price at least as in England, and therefore may be considered as much dearer.

We stopped a while at Dundee, where I remember nothing remarkable, and mounting our chaise again, came about the close of the day to Aberbrothick.[15]

The monastery of Aberbrothick is of great renown in the history of Scotland. Its ruins afford ample testimony of its ancient magnificence:[16] its extent might, I suppose, easily be found by following the walls among the grass and weeds, and its height is known by some parts yet standing. The arch of one of the gates is entire, and of another only so far dilapidated as to diversify the appearance. A square apartment of great loftiness is yet standing; its use I could not conjecture, as its elevation was very disproportionate to its area. Two corner towers, particularly attracted our attention. Mr Boswell, whose inquisitiveness is seconded by great activity, scrambled in at a high window, but found the stairs within broken, and could not reach the top. Of the other tower we were told that the inhabitants sometimes climbed it, but we did not immediately discern the entrance, and as the night was gathering upon us, thought proper to desist. Men skilled in architecture might do what we did not attempt: They might probably form an exact ground-plot of this venerable edifice. They may from some parts yet standing conjecture its general form, and perhaps by comparing it with other buildings of the same kind and the same age, attain an idea very near to truth. I should scarcely have regretted my journey, had it afforded nothing more than the sight of Aberbrothick.

MONTROSE

Leaving these fragments of magnificence, we travelled on to Montrose, which we surveyed in the morning, and found it well built, airy, and clean. The townhouse is a handsome fabrick with a portico. We then went to view the English chapel,[17] and found a small church, clean to a degree unknown in any other part of Scotland, with commodious galleries, and what was yet less expected, with an organ.

At our inn we did not find a reception such as we thought proportionate to the commercial opulence of the place; but Mr Boswell desired me to observe that the innkeeper was an Englishman, and I then defended him as well as I could.

When I had proceeded thus far, I had opportunities of observing what I had never heard, that there are many beggars in Scotland. In Edinburgh the proportion is, I think, not less than in London, and in the smaller places it is far greater than in English towns of the same extent. It must, however, be allowed that they are not importunate, nor clamorous. They solicit silently, or very modestly, and therefore though their behaviour may strike with more force the heart of a stranger, they are certainly in danger of missing the attention of their countrymen. Novelty has always some power, an unaccustomed mode of begging excites an unaccustomed degree of pity. But the force of novelty is by its own nature soon at an end; the efficacy of outcry and perseverance is permanent and certain.

The road from Montrose exhibited a continuation of the same appearances. The country is still naked, the hedges are of stone, and the fields so generally plowed that it is hard to imagine where grass is found for the horses that till them. The harvest, which was almost ripe, appeared very plentiful.

Early in the afternoon Mr Boswell observed that we were at no great distance from the house of Lord Monboddo.[18] The magnetism of his conversation easily drew us out of our way, and the entertainment which we received would have been a sufficient recompence for a much greater deviation.

The roads beyond Edinburgh, as they are less frequented, must be expected to grow gradually rougher; but they were hitherto by no means incommodious. We travelled on with the gentle pace of a Scotch driver, who having no rivals in expedition, neither gives himself nor his horses unnecessary trouble. We did not affect the impatience we did not feel, but were satisfied with the company of each other as well riding in the chaise, as sitting at an inn. The night and the day are equally solitary and equally safe; for where there are so few travellers, why should there be robbers?

ABERDEEN

We came somewhat late to Aberdeen, and found the inn so full, that we had some difficulty in obtaining admission, till Mr Boswell made himself known: His name overpowered all objection, and we found a very good house and civil treatment.

I received the next day a very kind letter from Sir Alexander Gordon, whom I had formerly known in London, and after a cessation of all intercourse for near twenty years found here professor of physic in the King's College. Such unexpected renewals of acquaintance may be numbered among the most pleasing incidents of life.

The knowledge of one professor soon procured me the notice of the rest, and I did not want any token of regard, being conducted wherever there was any thing which I desired to see, and entertained at once with the novelty of the place, and the kindness of communication.

To write of the cities of our own island with the solemnity of geographical description, as if we had been cast upon a newly discovered coast, has the appearance of very frivolous ostentation; yet as Scotland is little known to the greater part of those who may read these observations, it is not super-fluous to relate, that under the name of Aberdeen are comprised two towns standing about a mile distant from each other, but governed, I think, by the same magistrates.[19]

Old Aberdeen is the ancient episcopal city, in which are still to be seen the remains of the cathedral. It has the appearance of a town in decay, being built in times when commerce was yet unstudied, with very little attention to the commodities of the harbour.

New Aberdeen has all the bustle of prosperous trade, and all the shew of increasing opulence. It is built by the waterside. The houses are large and lofty, and the streets spacious and clean. They build almost wholly with the granite used in the new pavement of the streets of London, which is well known not to want hardness, yet they shape it easily. It is beautiful and must be very lasting.

What particular parts of commerce are chiefly exercised by the merchants of Aberdeen, I have not inquired. The manufacture which forces itself upon a stranger's eye is that of knit-stockings, on which the women of the lower class are visibly employed.

In each of these towns there is a college, or in stricter language, an university; for in both there are professors of the same parts of learning, and the colleges hold their sessions and confer degrees separately, with total independence of one on the other.

In old Aberdeen stands the King's College, of which the first president was Hector Boece, or Boethius,[20] who may be justly reverenced as one of the revivers of elegant learning. When he studied at Paris, he was acquainted with Erasmus, who afterwards gave him a public testimony of his esteem, by inscribing to him a catalogue of his works. The stile of Boethius, though, perhaps, not always rigorously pure, is formed with great diligence upon ancient models, and wholly uninfected with monastic barbarity. His history is written with elegance and vigour, but his fabulousness and credulity are justly blamed. His fabulousness, if he was the author of the fictions, is a fault for which no apology can be made; but his credulity may be excused in an age, when all men were credulous. Learning was then rising on the world; but ages so long accustomed to darkness, were too much dazzled with its light to see any thing distinctly. The first race of scholars, in the fifteenth century, and some time after, were, for the most part, learning to speak, rather than to think, and were therefore more studious of elegance than of truth. The contemporaries of Boethius thought it sufficient to know what the ancients had delivered. The examination of tenets and of facts was reserved for another generation.

Boethius, as president of the university, enjoyed a revenue of forty Scottish marks, about two pounds four shillings and sixpence of sterling money. In the present age of trade and taxes, it is difficult even for the imagination so to raise the value of money, or so to diminish the demands of life, as to suppose four and forty shillings a year an honourable stipend; yet it was probably equal, not only to the needs, but to the rank of Boethius. The wealth of England was undoubtedly to that of Scotland more than five to one, and it is known that Henry the Eighth, among whose faults avarice was never reckoned, granted to Roger Ascham, as a reward of his learning, a pension of ten pounds a year.

The other, called the Marischal College, is in the new town. The hall is large and well lighted. One of its ornaments is the picture of Arthur Johnston, who was principal of the college, and who holds among the Latin poets of Scotland the next place to the elegant Buchanan.[21]

In the library I was shewn some curiosities; a Hebrew manuscript of exquisite penmanship, and a Latin translation of Aristotle's Politicks by Leonardus Aretinus, written in the Roman character with nicety and beauty, which, as the art of printing has made them no longer necessary, are not now to be found. This was one of the latest performances of the transcribers, for Aretinus died[22] but about twenty years before typography was invented. This version has been printed, and may be found in libraries, but is little read; for the same books have been since translated both by Victorius and

43

Lambinus,[23] who lived in an age more cultivated, but perhaps owed in part to Aretinus that they were able to excel him. Much is due to those who first broke the way to knowledge, and left only to their successors the task of smoothing it.

In both these colleges the methods of instruction are nearly the same; the lectures differing only by the accidental difference of diligence, or ability in the professors. The students wear scarlet gowns and the professors black, which is, I believe, the academical dress in all the Scottish universities, except that of Edinburgh, where the scholars are not distinguished by any particular habit. In the King's College there is kept a public table, but the scholars of the Marischal College are boarded in the town. The expence of living is here, according to the information that I could obtain, somewhat more than at St Andrews.

The course of education is extended to four years, at the end of which those who take a degree, who are not many, become masters of arts, and whoever is a master may, if he pleases, immediately become a doctor. The title of doctor, however, was for a considerable time bestowed only on physicians. The advocates are examined and approved by their own body; the ministers were not ambitious of titles, or were afraid of being censured for ambition; and the doctorate in every faculty was commonly given or sold into other countries. The ministers are now reconciled to distinction, and as it must always happen that some will excel others, have thought graduation a proper testimony of uncommon abilities or acquisitions.

The indiscriminate collation of degrees has justly taken away that respect which they originally claimed as stamps, by which the literary value of men so distinguished was authoritatively denoted. That academical honours, or any others should be conferred with exact proportion to merit, is more than human judgment or human integrity have given reason to expect. Perhaps degrees in universities cannot be better adjusted by any general rule than by the length of time passed in the public profession of learning. An English or Irish doctorate cannot be obtained by a very young man, and it is reasonable to suppose, what is likewise by experience commonly found true, that he who is by age qualified to be a doctor, has in so much time gained learning sufficient not to disgrace the title, or wit sufficient not to desire it.

The Scotch universities hold but one term or session in the year. That of St Andrews continues seven months,[24] that of Aberdeen only five, from the first of November to the first of April.

In Aberdeen there is an English chapel, in which the congregation was numerous and splendid. The form of public worship used by the Church of England is in Scotland legally practised in licensed chapels served by clergymen of English or Irish ordination, and by tacit connivance quietly permitted in separate congregations supplied with ministers by the successors of the bishops who were deprived at the Revolution.[25]

We came to Aberdeen on Saturday August 21. On Monday we were invited into the town-hall, where I had the freedom of the city given me by the Lord Provost. The honour conferred had all the decorations that politeness could add, and what I am afraid I should not have had to say of any city south of the Tweed, I found no petty officer bowing for a fee.

The parchment containing the record of admission is, with the seal appending, fastened to a riband and worn for one day by the new citizen in his hat.

By a lady[26] who saw us at the chapel, the Earl of Errol was informed of our arrival, and we had the honour of an invitation to his seat, called Slanes Castle,[27] as I am told, improperly, from the castle of that name, which once stood at a place not far distant.

The road beyond Aberdeen grew more stony, and continued equally naked of all vegetable decoration. We travelled over a tract of ground near the sea, which not long ago, suffered a very uncommon, and unexpected calamity. The sand of the shore was raised by a tempest in such quantities, and carried to such a distance, that an estate was overwhelmed and lost. Such and so hopeless was the barrenness superinduced, that the owner, when he was required ruined to pay the usual tax, desired rather to resign the ground.

SLANES CASTLE. THE BULLER OF BUCHAN

We came in the afternoon to Slanes Castle, built upon the margin of the sea, so that the walls of one of the towers seem only a continuation of a perpendicular rock, the foot of which is beaten by the waves. To walk round the house seemed impracticable. From the windows the eye wanders over the sea that separates Scotland from Norway, and when the winds beat with violence must enjoy all the terrifick grandeur of the tempestuous ocean. I would not for my amusement wish for a storm; but as storms, whether wished or not, will sometimes happen, I may say, without violation of humanity, that I should willingly look out upon them from Slanes Castle.[28]

When we were about to take our leave, our departure was prohibited by the countess till we should have seen two places upon the coast, which she rightly considered as worthy of curiosity, Dun Buy and the Buller of Buchan, to which Mr Boyd[29] very kindly conducted us.

Dun Buy, which in Erse is said to signify the Yellow Rock, is a double protuberance of stone, open to the main sea on one side, and parted from the land by a very narrow channel on the other. It has its name and its colour from the dung of innumerable sea-fowls, which in the Spring chuse this place as convenient for incubation, and have their eggs and their young taken in great abundance. One of the birds that frequent this rock has, as we were told, its body not larger than a duck's, and yet lays eggs as large as those of a goose. This bird is by the inhabitants named a Coot. That which is called Coot in England, is here a Cooter.[30]

Upon these rocks there was nothing that could long detain attention, and we soon turned our eyes to the Buller, or Bouilloir of Buchan,[31] which no man can see with indifference, who has either sense of danger or delight in rarity. It is a rock perpendicularly tubulated, united on one side with a high shore, and on the other rising steep to a great height, above the main sea. The top is open, from which may be seen a dark gulf of water which flows into the cavity, through a breach made in the lower part of the inclosing rock. It has the appearance of a vast well bordered with a wall. The edge of the Buller is not wide, and to those that walk round, appears very narrow. He that ventures to look downward sees, that if his foot should slip, he must fall from his dreadful elevation upon stones on one side, or into the water on the other. We however went round, and were glad when the circuit was completed.

When we came down to the sea, we saw some boats, and rowers, and resolved to explore the Buller at the bottom. We entered the arch, which the water had made, and found ourselves in a place, which, though we could not think ourselves in danger, we could scarcely survey without some recoil of the mind. The bason in which we floated was nearly circular, perhaps thirty yards in diameter. We were inclosed by a natural wall, rising steep on every side to a height which produced the idea of insurmountable confinement. The interception of all lateral light caused a dismal gloom. Round us was a perpendicular rock, above us the distant sky, and below an unknown profundity of water. If I had any malice against a walking spirit, instead of laying him in the Red Sea, I would condemn him to reside in the Buller of Buchan.

But terrour without danger is only one of the sports of fancy, a voluntary agitation of the mind that is permitted no longer than it pleases. We were soon at leisure to examine the place with minute inspection, and found many cavities which, as the watermen told us, went backward to a depth[32] which they had never explored. Their extent we had not time to try; they are said to serve different purposes. Ladies come hither sometimes in the summer with collations, and smugglers make them store-houses for clandestine merchandise. It is hardly to be doubted but the pirates of ancient times often used them as magazines of arms, or repositories of plunder.

To the little vessels used by the northern rowers,[33] the Buller may have served as a shelter from storms, and perhaps as a retreat from enemies; the entrance might have been stopped, or guarded with little difficulty, and though the vessels that were stationed within would have been battered with stones showered on them from above, yet the crews would have lain safe in the caverns.

Next morning we continued our journey, pleased with our reception at Slanes Castle, of which we had now leisure to recount the grandeur and the elegance; for our way afforded us few topics of conversation. The ground was neither uncultivated nor unfruitful; but it was still all arable. Of flocks or herds there was no appearance. I had now travelled two hundred miles in Scotland and seen only one tree not younger than myself.

BAMFF

We dined this day at the house of Mr Frazer of Streichton, who shewed us in his grounds some stones yet standing of a druidical circle, and what I began to think more worthy of notice, some forest trees of full growth.[34]

At night we came to Bamff, where I remember nothing that particularly claimed my attention. The ancient towns of Scotland have generally an appearance unusual to Englishmen. The houses, whether great or small, are for the most part built of stones. Their ends are now and then next the streets, and the entrance into them is very often by a flight of steps, which reaches up to the second story, the floor which is level with the ground being entered only by stairs descending within the house.

The art of joining squares of glass with lead is little used in Scotland, and in some places is totally forgotten. The frames of their windows are all of wood. They are more frugal of their glass than the English, and will often, in houses not otherwise mean, compose a square of two pieces, not joining like cracked glass, but with one edge laid perhaps half an inch over the other. Their windows do not move upon hinges, but are pushed up and drawn down in grooves, yet they are seldom accommodated with weights and pullies. He that would have his window open must hold it with his hand, unless what may be sometimes found among good contrivers, there be a nail which he may stick into a hole, to keep it from falling.

What cannot be done without some uncommon trouble or particular expedient, will not often be done at all. The incommodiousness of the Scotch windows keeps them very closely shut. The necessity of ventilating human habitations has not yet been found by our northern neighbours; and even in houses well built and elegantly furnished, a stranger may be sometimes forgiven, if he allows himself to wish for fresher air.

These diminutive observations seem to take away something from the dignity of writing, and therefore are never communicated but with hesitation, and a little fear of abasement and contempt. But it must be remembered, that life consists not of a series of illustrious actions, or elegant enjoyments; the greater part of our time passes in compliance with necessities, in the performance of daily duties, in the removal of small inconveniencies, in the procurement of petty pleasures; and we are well or ill at ease, as the main stream of life glides on smoothly, or is ruffled by small obstacles and frequent interruption. The true state of every nation is the state of common life. The manners of a people are not to be found in the schools of learning, or the palaces of greatness, where the national character is obscured or obliterated by travel or instruction, by philosophy or vanity; nor is public happiness to be estimated by the assemblies of the gay, or the banquets of the rich. The great mass of nations is neither rich nor gay: they whose aggregate constitutes the people, are found in the streets, and the villages, in the shops and farms; and from them collectively considered, must the measure of general prosperity be taken. As they approach to delicacy a nation is refined, as their conveniencies are multiplied, a nation, at least a commercial nation, must be denominated wealthy.

ELGIN

Finding nothing to detain us at Bamff, we set out in the morning, and having breakfasted at Cullen, about noon came to Elgin, where in the inn, that we supposed the best, a dinner was set before us, which we could not eat. This was the first time, and except one, the last, that I found any reason to complain of a Scotish table; and such disappointments, I suppose, must be expected in every country, where there is no great frequency of travellers.

The ruins of the cathedral of Elgin afforded us another proof of the waste of reformation. There is enough yet remaining to shew, that it was once magnificent. Its whole plot is easily traced. On the north side of the choir, the chapter-house, which is roofed with an arch of stone, remains entire; and on the south side, another mass of building, which we could not enter, is preserved by the care of the family of Gordon; but the body of the church is a mass of fragments.

A paper was here put into our hands, which deduced from sufficient authorities the history of this venerable ruin. The church of Elgin had, in the intestine tumults of the barbarous ages, been laid waste by the irruption of a highland chief, whom the bishop had offended;[35] but it was gradually restored to the state, of which the traces may be now discerned, and was at last not destroyed by the tumultuous violence of Knox, but more shamefully suffered to dilapidate by deliberate robbery and frigid indifference. There is still extant, in the books of the council, an order, of which I cannot remember the date,[36] but which was doubtless issued after the Reformation, directing that the lead, which covers the two cathedrals of Elgin and Aberdeen, shall be taken away, and converted into money for the support of the army. A Scotch army was in those times very cheaply kept; yet the lead of two churches must have born so small a proportion to any military expence, that it is hard not to believe the reason alleged to be merely popular, and the money intended for some private purse. The order however was obeyed; the two churches were stripped, and the lead was shipped to be sold in Holland. I hope every reader will rejoice that this cargo of sacrilege was lost at sea.

Let us not however make too much haste to despise our neighbours.[37] Our own cathedrals are mouldering by unregarded dilapidation. It seems to be part of the despicable philosophy of the time to despise monuments of sacred magnificence, and we are in danger of doing that deliberately, which the Scots did not do but in the unsettled state of an imperfect constitution.

Those who had once uncovered the cathedrals never wished to cover them again; and being thus made useless, they were first neglected, and perhaps, as the stone was wanted, afterwards demolished.

Elgin seems a place of little trade, and thinly inhabited. The episcopal cities of Scotland, I believe, generally fell with their churches, though some of them have since recovered by a situation convenient for commerce. Thus Glasgow, though it has no longer an archbishop, has risen beyond its original state by the opulence of its traders; and Aberdeen, though its ancient stock has decayed, flourishes by a new shoot in another place.

In the chief street of Elgin, the houses jut over the lowest story, like the old buildings of timber in London, but with greater prominence; so that there is sometimes a walk for a considerable length under a cloister, or portico, which is now indeed frequently broken, because the new houses have another form, but seems to have been uniformly continued in the old city.

FORES. CALDER. FORT GEORGE

We went forwards the same day to Fores, the town to which Macbeth was travelling, when he met the weird sisters in his way. This to an Englishman is classic ground. Our imaginations were heated, and our thoughts recalled to their old amusements.

We had now a prelude to the Highlands. We began to leave fertility and culture behind us, and saw for a great length of road nothing but heath; yet at Fochabars, a seat belonging to the Duke of Gordon, there is an orchard, which in Scotland I had never seen before, with some timber trees, and a plantation of oaks.

At Fores we found good accommodation, but nothing worthy of particular remark, and next morning entered upon the road, on which Macbeth heard the fatal prediction; but we travelled on not interrupted by promises of kingdoms, and came to Nairn, a royal burgh, which, if once it flourished, is now in a state of miserable decay; but I know not whether its chief annual magistrate has not still the title of Lord Provost.

At Nairn we may fix the verge of the Highlands; for here I first saw peat fires, and first heard the Erse language. We had no motive to stay longer than to breakfast, and went forward to the house of Mr Macaulay, the minister who published an account of St Kilda,[38] and by his direction visited Calder Castle, from which Macbeth drew his second title. It has been formerly a place of strength. The draw-bridge is still to be seen, but the moat is now dry. The tower is very ancient: its walls are of great thickness, arched on the top with stone, and surrounded with battlements. The rest of the house is later, though far from modern.

We were favoured by a gentleman,[39] who lives in the castle, with a letter to one of the officers at Fort George,[40] which being the most regular fortification in the island, well deserves the notice of a traveller, who has never travelled before. We went thither next day, found a very kind reception, were led round the works by a gentleman, who explained the use of every part, and entertained by Sir Eyre Coote, the governour, with such elegance of conversation as left us no attention to the delicacies of his table.

Of Fort George I shall not attempt to give any account. I cannot delineate it scientifically, and a loose and popular description is of use only when the imagination is to be amused. There was every where an appearance of the utmost neatness and regularity. But my suffrage is of little value, because this and Fort Augustus[41] are the only garrisons that I ever saw.

We did not regret the time spent at the fort, though in consequence of our delay we came somewhat late to Inverness, the town which may properly be called the capital of the Highlands. Hither the inhabitants of the inland parts come to be supplied with what they cannot make for themselves: hither the young nymphs of the mountains and valleys are sent for education, and as far as my observation has reached, are not sent in vain.

INVERNESS

Inverness was the last place which had a regular communication by high roads with the southern counties. All the ways beyond it have, I believe, been made by the soldiers in this century. At Inverness therefore Cromwell, when he subdued Scotland, stationed a garrison, as at the boundary of the Highlands. The soldiers seem to have incorporated afterwards with the inhabitants, and to have peopled the place with an English race; for the language of this town has been long considered as peculiarly elegant.[42]

Here is a castle, called the castle of Macbeth, the walls of which are yet standing. It was no very capacious edifice, but stands upon a rock so high and steep, that I think it was once not accessible, but by the help of ladders, or a bridge. Over against it, on another hill, was a fort built by Cromwell, now totally demolished; for no faction of Scotland loved the name of Cromwell, or had any desire to continue his memory.

Yet what the Romans did to other nations, was in a great degree done by Cromwell to the Scots; he civilized them by conquest, and introduced by useful violence the arts of peace. I was told at Aberdeen that the people learned from Cromwell's soldiers to make shoes and to plant kail.[43]

How they lived without kail, it is not easy to guess: they cultivate hardly any other plant for common tables, and when they had not kail they probably had nothing. The numbers that go barefoot are still sufficient to shew that shoes may be spared: they are not yet considered as necessaries of life; for tall boys, not otherwise meanly dressed, run without them in the streets and in the islands; the sons of gentlemen pass several of their first years with naked feet.

I know not whether it be not peculiar to the Scots to have attained the liberal, without the manual arts, to have excelled in ornamental knowledge, and to have wanted not only the elegancies, but the conveniencies of common life. Literature soon after its revival found its way to Scotland, and from the middle of the sixteenth century, almost to the middle of the seventeenth, the politer studies were very diligently pursued. The Latin poetry of *Deliciæ Poëtarum Scotorum* would have done honour to any nation; at least till the publication of May's *Supplement* the English had very little to oppose.[44]

Yet men thus ingenious and inquisitive were content to live in total ignorance of the trades by which human wants are supplied, and to supply them by the grossest means. Till the Union made them acquainted with English manners, the culture of their lands was unskilful, and their domestick life unformed; their tables were coarse as the feasts of Eskimeaux, and their houses filthy as the cottages of Hottentots.

Since they have known that their condition was capable of improvement, their progress in useful knowledge has been rapid and uniform. What remains to be done they will quickly do, and then wonder, like me, why that which was so necessary and so easy was so long delayed. But they must be for ever content to owe to the English that elegance and culture, which, if they had been vigilant and active, perhaps the English might have owed to them.

Here the appearance of life began to alter. I had seen a few women with plaids at Aberdeen; but at Inverness the Highland manners are common. There is I think a kirk,[45] in which only the Erse language is used. There is likewise an English chapel, but meanly built, where on Sunday we saw a very decent congregation.

We were now to bid farewel to the luxury of travelling, and to enter a country upon which perhaps no wheel has ever rolled. We could indeed have used our post-chaise one day longer, along the military road to Fort Augustus,[46] but we could have hired no horses beyond Inverness, and we were not so sparing of ourselves, as to lead them, merely that we might have one day longer the indulgence of a carriage.

At Inverness therefore we procured three horses for ourselves and a servant,[47] and one more for our baggage, which was no very heavy load. We found in the course of our journey the convenience of having disencumbered ourselves, by laying aside whatever we could spare; for it is not to be imagined without experience, how in climbing crags, and treading bogs, and winding through narrow and obstructed passages, a little bulk will hinder, and a little weight will burthen; or how often a man that has pleased himself at home with his own resolution, will, in the hour of darkness and fatigue, be content to leave behind him every thing but himself.

LOUGH NESS

We took two Highlanders to run beside us, partly to shew us the way, and partly to take back from the sea-side the horses, of which they were the owners. One of them was a man of great liveliness and activity, of whom his companion said, that he would tire any horse in Inverness. Both of them were civil and ready-handed. Civility seems part of the national character of Highlanders. Every chieftain is a monarch, and politeness, the natural product of royal government, is diffused from the laird through the whole clan. But they are not commonly dexterous: their narrowness of life confines them to a few operations, and they are accustomed to endure little wants more than to remove them.

We mounted our steeds on the thirtieth[48] of August, and directed our guides to conduct us to Fort Augustus. It is built at the head of Lough Ness, of which Inverness stands at the outlet. The way between them has been cut by the soldiers, and the greater part of it runs along a rock, levelled with great labour and exactness, near the water-side.

Most of the day's journey was very pleasant. The day, though bright, was not hot; and the appearance of the country, if I had not seen the Peak, would have been wholly new. We went upon a surface so hard and level, that we had little care to hold the bridle, and were therefore at full leisure for contemplation. On the left were high and steep rocks shaded with birch, the hardy native of the North, and covered with fern or heath. On the right the limpid waters of Lough Ness were beating their bank, and waving their surface by a gentle agitation. Beyond them were rocks sometimes covered with verdure, and sometimes towering in horrid nakedness. Now and then we espied a little corn-field, which served to impress more strongly the general barrenness.

Lough Ness is about twenty-four miles long, and from one mile to two miles broad. It is remarkable that Boethius, in his description of Scotland, gives it twelve miles of breadth. When historians or geographers exhibit false accounts of places far distant, they may be forgiven, because they can tell but what they are told; and that their accounts exceed the truth may be justly supposed, because most men exaggerate to others, if not to themselves: but Boethius lived at no great distance; if he never saw the lake, he must have been very incurious, and if he had seen it, his veracity yielded to very slight temptations.

Lough Ness, though not twelve miles broad, is a very remarkable diffusion of water without islands. It fills a large hollow between two ridges of high rocks, being supplied partly by the torrents which fall into it on either side, and partly, as is supposed, by springs at the bottom. Its water is remarkably clear and pleasant, and is imagined by the natives to be medicinal. We were told, that it is in some places a hundred and forty fathom deep,[49] a profundity scarcely credible, and which probably those that relate it have never sounded. Its fish are salmon, trout, and pike.

It was said at Fort Augustus, that Lough Ness is open in the hardest winters, though a lake not far from it is covered with ice. In discussing these exceptions from the course of nature, the first question is, whether the fact be justly stated.[50] That which is strange is delightful, and a pleasing error is not willingly detected. Accuracy of narration is not very common, and there are few so rigidly philosophical, as not to represent as perpetual, what is only frequent, or as constant, what is really casual. If it be true that Lough Ness never freezes, it is either sheltered by its high banks from the cold blasts, and exposed only to those winds which have more power to agitate than congeal; or it is kept in perpetual motion by the rush of streams from the rocks that inclose it. Its profundity though it should be such as is represented can have little part in this exemption; for though deep wells are not frozen, because their water is secluded from the external air, yet where a wide surface is exposed to the full influence of a freezing atmosphere, I know not why the depth should keep it open. Natural philosophy is now one of the favourite studies of the Scottish nation, and Lough Ness well deserves to be diligently examined.

The road on which we travelled, and which was itself a source of entertainment, is made along the rock, in the direction of the lough, sometimes by breaking off protuberances, and sometimes by cutting the great mass of stone to a considerable depth. The fragments are piled in a loose wall on either side, with apertures left at very short spaces, to give a passage to the wintry currents. Part of it is bordered with low trees, from which our guides gathered nuts, and would have had the appearance of an English lane, except that an English lane is almost always dirty. It has been made with great labour, but has this advantage, that it cannot, without equal labour, be broken up.

Within our sight there were goats feeding or playing. The mountains have red deer, but they came not within view; and if what is said of their vigilance and subtlety be true, they have some claim to that palm of wisdom, which the eastern philosopher, whom Alexander interrogated, gave to those beasts which live furthest from men.[51]

Near the way, by the water-side, we espied a cottage. This was the first Highland hut that I had seen; and as our business was with life and manners, we were willing to visit it. To enter a habitation without leave, seems to be not considered here as rudeness or intrusion. The old laws of hospitality still give this licence to a stranger.

A hut is constructed with loose stones, ranged for the most part with some tendency to circularity. It must be placed where the wind cannot act upon it with violence, because it has no cement; and where the water will run easily away, because it has no floor but the naked ground. The wall, which is commonly about six feet high, declines from the perpendicular a little inward. Such rafters as can be procured are then raised for a roof, and covered with heath, which makes a strong and warm thatch, kept from flying off by ropes of twisted heath, of which the ends, reaching from the center of the thatch to the top of the wall, are held firm by the weight of a large stone. No light is admitted but at the entrance, and through a hole in the thatch, which gives vent to the smoke. This hole is not directly over the fire, lest the rain should extinguish it; and the smoke therefore naturally fills the place before it escapes. Such is the general structure of the houses in which one of the nations of this opulent and powerful island has been hitherto content to live. Huts however are not more uniform than palaces; and this which we were inspecting was very far from one of the meanest, for it was divided into several apartments; and its inhabitants possessed such property as a pastoral poet might exalt into riches.

When we entered, we found an old woman boiling goats-flesh in a kettle. She spoke little English, but we had interpreters at hand; and she was willing enough to display her whole system of economy. She has five children, of which none are yet gone from her. The eldest, a boy of thirteen, and her husband, who is eighty years old, were at work in the wood. Her two next sons were gone to Inverness to buy meal, by which oatmeal is always meant. Meal she considered as expensive food, and told us, that in Spring, when the goats gave milk, the children could live without it. She is mistress of sixty goats, and I saw many kids in an enclosure at the end of her house. She had also some poultry. By the lake we saw a potatoe-garden, and a small spot of ground on which stood four shucks,[52] containing each twelve sheaves of barley. She has all this from the labour of their own hands, and for what is necessary to be bought, her kids and her chickens are sent to market.

With the true pastoral hospitality, she asked us to sit down and drink whisky. She is religious, and though the kirk is four miles off, probably eight English miles, she goes thither every Sunday. We gave her a shilling, and she begged snuff; for snuff is the luxury of a Highland cottage.

Soon afterwards we came to the 'General's Hut', so called because it was the temporary abode of Wade,[53] while he superintended the works upon the road. It is now a house of entertainment for passengers, and we found it not ill stocked with provisions.

FALL OF FIERS

Towards evening we crossed, by a bridge, the river which makes the celebrated fall of Fiers. The country at the bridge strikes the imagination with all the gloom and grandeur of Siberian solitude. The way makes a flexure, and the mountains, covered with trees, rise at once on the left hand and in the front. We desired our guides to shew us the fall, and dismounting, clambered over very rugged crags, till I began to wish that our curiosity might have been gratified with less trouble and danger. We came at last to a place where we could overlook the river, and saw a channel torn, as it seems, through black piles of stone, by which the stream is obstructed and broken, till it comes to a very steep descent, of such dreadful depth, that we were naturally inclined to turn aside our eyes.

But we visited the place at an unseasonable time, and found it divested of its dignity and terror. Nature never gives every thing at once. A long continuance of dry weather, which made the rest of the way easy and delightful, deprived us of the pleasure expected from the fall of Fiers. The river having now no water but what the springs supply, showed us only a swift current, clear and shallow, fretting over the asperities of the rocky bottom, and we were left to exercise our thoughts, by endeavouring to conceive the effect of a thousand streams poured from the mountains into one channel, struggling for expansion in a narrow passage, exasperated by rocks rising in their way, and at last discharging all their violence of waters by a sudden fall through the horrid chasm.

The way now grew less easy, descending by an uneven declivity, but without either dirt or danger. We did not arrive at Fort Augustus till it was late. Mr Boswell, who, between his father's merit and his own, is sure of reception wherever he comes, sent a servant before to beg admission and entertainment for that night. Mr Trapaud, the governor, treated us with that courtesy which is so closely connected with the military character. He came out to meet us beyond the gates, and apologized that, at so late an hour, the rules of a garrison suffered him to give us entrance only at the postern.

FORT AUGUSTUS

In the morning we viewed the fort, which is much less than that of St George, and is said to be commanded by the neighbouring hills. It was not long ago taken by the highlanders.[54] But its situation seems well chosen for pleasure, if not for strength; it stands at the head of the lake, and, by a sloop of sixty tuns, is supplied from Inverness with great convenience.

We were now to cross the Highlands towards the western coast, and to content ourselves with such accommodations, as a way so little frequented could afford. The journey was not formidable, for it was but of two days, very unequally divided, because the only house, where we could be entertained, was not further off than a third of the way. We soon came to a high hill, which we mounted by a military road, cut in traverses, so that as we went upon a higher stage, we saw the baggage following us below in a contrary direction. To make this way, the rock has been hewn to a level with labour that might have broken the perseverance of a Roman legion.

The country is totally denuded of its wood, but the stumps both of oaks and firs, which are still found, shew that it has been once a forest of large timber. I do not remember that we saw any animals, but we were told that, in the mountains, there are stags, roebucks, goats and rabbits.

We did not perceive that this tract was possessed by human beings, except that once we saw a corn-field, in which a lady was walking with some gentlemen. Their house was certainly at no great distance, but so situated that we could not descry it.

Passing on through the dreariness of solitude, we found a party of soldiers from the fort, working on the road, under the superintendence of a serjeant. We told them how kindly we had been treated at the garrison, and as we were enjoying the benefit of their labours, begged leave to shew our gratitude by a small present.

ANOCH

Early in the afternoon we came to Anoch, a village in Glenmollison of three huts, one of which is distinguished by a chimney. Here we were to dine and lodge, and were conducted through the first room, that had the chimney, into another lighted by a small glass window. The landlord[55] attended us with great civility, and told us what he could give us to eat and drink. I found some books on a shelf, among which were a volume or more of Prideaux's *Connection*.[56]

This I mentioned as something unexpected, and perceived that I did not please him: I praised the propriety of his language, and was answered that I need not wonder, for he had learned it by grammar.

By subsequent opportunities of observation, I found that my host's diction had nothing peculiar. Those highlanders that can speak English, commonly speak it well, with few of the words, and little of the tone by which a Scotchman is distinguished. Their language seems to have been learned in the army or the navy, or by some communication with those who could give them good examples of accent and pronunciation. By their Lowland neighbours they would not willingly be taught; for they have long considered them as a mean and degenerate race. These prejudices are wearing fast away; but so much of them still remains, that when I asked a very learned minister in the islands, which they considered as their most savage clans: 'Those,' said he, 'that live next the Lowlands.'

As we came hither early in the day, we had time sufficient to survey the place. The house was built like other huts of loose stones, but the part in which we dined and slept was lined with turf and wattled with twigs, which kept the earth from falling. Near it was a garden of turnips and a field of potatoes. It stands in a glen, or valley, pleasantly watered by a winding river.

But this country, however it may delight the gazer or amuse the naturalist, is of no great advantage to its owners. Our landlord told us of a gentleman, who possesses lands, eighteen Scotch miles in length, and three in breadth; a space containing at least a hundred square English miles. He has raised his rents, to the danger of depopulating his farms, and he fells his timber, and by exerting every art of augmentation, has obtained an yearly revenue of four hundred pounds, which for a hundred square miles is three halfpence an acre.

Some time after dinner we were surprised by the entrance of a young woman, not inelegant either in mien or dress, who asked us whether we would have tea. We found that she was the daughter of our host, and desired her to make it. Her conversation, like her appearance, was gentle and pleasing. We knew that the girls of the Highlands are all gentlewomen, and treated her with great respect, which she received as customary and due, and was neither elated by it, nor confused, but repaid my civilities without embarassment, and told me how much I honoured her country by coming to survey it.

She had been at Inverness to gain the common female qualifications, and had, like her father, the English pronunciation. I presented her with a book, which I happened to have about me,[57] and should not be pleased to think that she forgets me.

In the evening the soldiers, whom we had passed on the road, came to spend at our inn the little money that we had given them. They had the true military impatience of coin in their pockets, and had marched at least six miles to find the first place where liquor could be bought. Having never been before in a place so wild and unfrequented, I was glad of their arrival, because I knew that we had made them friends, and to gain still more of their good will, we went to them, where they were carousing in the barn, and added something to our former gift. All that we gave was not much, but it detained them in the barn, either merry or quarrelling, the whole night, and in the morning they went back to their work, with great indignation at the bad qualities of whisky.

We had gained so much the favour of our host, that, when we left his house in the morning, he walked by us a great way, and entertained us with conversation both on his own condition, and that of the country. His life seemed to be merely pastoral, except that he differed from some of the ancient Nomades in having a settled dwelling. His wealth consists of one hundred sheep, as many goats, twelve milk-cows, and twenty-eight beeves ready for the drover.

From him we first heard[58] of the general dissatisfaction, which is now driving the highlanders into the other hemisphere; and when I asked him whether they would stay at home, if they were well treated, he answered with indignation, that no man willingly left his native country. Of the farm, which he himself occupied, the rent had, in twenty-five years, been advanced from five to twenty pounds, which he found himself so little able to pay, that he would be glad to try his fortune in some other place. Yet he owned the reasonableness of raising the Highland rents in a certain degree, and declared himself willing to pay ten pounds for the ground which he had formerly had for five.

Our host having amused us for a time, resigned us to our guides. The journey of this day was long, not that the distance was great, but that the way was difficult. We were now in the bosom of the Highlands, with full leisure to contemplate the appearance and properties of mountainous regions, such as have been, in many countries, the last shelters of national distress, and are every where the scenes of adventures, stratagems, surprises and escapes.

Mountainous countries are not passed but with difficulty, not merely from the labour of climbing; for to climb is not always necessary: but because that which is not mountain is commonly bog, through which the way must be picked with caution. Where there are hills, there is much rain, and the torrents pouring down into the intermediate spaces, seldom find so ready an outlet, as not to stagnate, till they have broken the texture of the ground.

Of the hills, which our journey offered to the view on either side, we did not take the height, nor did we see any that astonished us with their loftiness. Towards the summit of one, there was a white spot, which I should have called a naked rock, but the guides, who had better eyes, and were acquainted with the phenomena of the country, declared it to be snow. It had already lasted to the end of August, and was likely to maintain its contest with the sun, till it should be reinforced by winter.

The height of mountains philosophically considered is properly computed from the surface of the next sea; but as it affects the eye or imagination of the passenger, as it makes either a spectacle or an obstruction, it must be reckoned from the place where the rise begins to make a considerable angle with the plain. In extensive continents the land may, by gradual elevation, attain great height, without any other appearance than that of a plane gently inclined, and if a hill placed upon such raised ground be described, as having its altitude equal to the whole space above the sea, the representation will be fallacious.

These mountains may be properly enough measured from the inland base; for it is not much above the sea. As we advanced at evening towards the western coast, I did not observe the declivity to be greater than is necessary for the discharge of the inland waters.

We passed many rivers and rivulets, which commonly ran with a clear shallow stream over a hard pebbly bottom. These channels, which seem so much wider than the water that they convey would naturally require, are formed by the violence of wintry floods, produced by the accumulation of innumerable streams that fall in rainy weather from the hills, and bursting away with resistless impetuosity, make themselves a passage proportionate to their mass.

Such capricious and temporary waters cannot be expected to produce many fish. The rapidity of the wintry deluge sweeps them away, and the scantiness of the summer stream would hardly sustain them above the ground. This is the reason why in fording the northern rivers, no fishes are seen, as in England, wandering in the water.

Of the hills many may be called with Homer's Ida 'abundant in springs', but few can deserve the epithet which he bestows upon Pelion by 'waving their leaves'. They exhibit very little variety; being almost wholly covered with dark heath, and even that seems to be checked in its growth. What is not heath is nakedness, a little diversified by now and then a stream rushing down the steep. An eye accustomed to flowery pastures and waving harvests is astonished and repelled by this wide extent of hopeless sterility. The appearance is that of matter incapable of form or usefulness, dismissed by nature from her care and disinherited of her favours, left in its original elemental state, or quickened only with one sullen power of useless vegetation.

It will very readily occur, that this uniformity of barrenness can afford very little amusement to the traveller; that it is easy to sit at home and conceive rocks and heath, and waterfalls; and that these journeys are useless labours, which neither impregnate the imagination, nor enlarge the understanding. It is true that of far the greater part of things, we must content ourselves with such knowledge as description may exhibit, or analogy supply; but it is true likewise, that these ideas are always incomplete, and that at least, till we have compared them with realities, we do not know them to be just. As we see more, we become possessed of more certainties, and consequently gain more principles of reasoning, and found a wider basis of analogy.

Regions mountainous and wild, thinly inhabited, and little cultivated, make a great part of the earth, and he that has never seen them, must live unacquainted with much of the face of nature, and with one of the great scenes of human existence.

As the day advanced towards noon, we entered a narrow valley not very flowery, but sufficiently verdant. Our guides told us, that the horses could not travel all day without rest or meat, and intreated us to stop here, because no grass would be found in any other place. The request was reasonable and the argument cogent. We therefore willingly dismounted and diverted ourselves as the place gave us opportunity.

I sat down on a bank,[59] such as a writer of Romance might have delighted to feign. I had indeed no trees to whisper over my head, but a clear rivulet streamed at my feet. The day was calm, the air soft, and all was rudeness, silence, and solitude. Before me, and on either side, were high hills, which by hindering the eye from ranging, forced the mind to find entertainment for itself. Whether I spent the hour well I know not; for here I first conceived the thought of this narration.

We were in this place at ease and by choice, and had no evils to suffer or to fear; yet the imaginations excited by the view of an unknown and untravelled wilderness are not such as arise in the artificial solitude of parks and gardens, a flattering notion of self-sufficiency, a placid indulgence of voluntary delusions, a secure expansion of the fancy, or a cool concentration of the mental powers. The phantoms which haunt a desert are want, and misery, and danger; the evils of dereliction rush upon the thoughts; man is made unwillingly acquainted with his own weakness, and meditation shews him only how little he can sustain, and how little he can perform. There were no traces of inhabitants, except perhaps a rude pile of clods called a summer hut, in which a herdsman had rested in the favourable seasons. Whoever had been in the place where I then sat, unprovided with provisions and ignorant of the country, might, at least before the roads were made, have wandered among the rocks, till he had perished with hardship, before he could have found either food or shelter. Yet what are these hillocks to the ridges of Taurus, or these spots of wildness to the deserts of America?

It was not long before we were invited to mount, and continued our journey along the side of a lough, kept full by many streams, which with more or less rapidity and noise, crossed the road from the hills on the other hand. These currents, in their diminished state, after several dry months, afford, to one who has always lived in level countries, an unusual and delightful spectacle; but in the rainy season, such as every winter may be expected to bring, must precipitate an impetuous and tremendous flood. I suppose the way by which we went, is at that time impassable.

GLENSHEALS

The lough at last ended in a river broad and shallow like the rest, but that it may be passed when it is deeper, there is a bridge over it. Beyond it is a valley called Glensheals, inhabited by the clan of Macrae. Here we found a village called Auknasheals, consisting of many huts, perhaps twenty, built all of dry-stone, that is, stones piled up without mortar.

We had, by the direction of the officers at Fort Augustus, taken bread for ourselves and tobacco for those highlanders who might show us any kindness. We were now at a place where we could obtain milk, but must have wanted bread if we had not brought it. The people of this valley did not appear to know any English, and our guides now became doubly necessary as interpreters. A woman, whose hut was distinguished by greater spaciousness and better architecture, brought out some pails of milk. The villagers gathered about us in considerable numbers, I believe without any evil intention, but with a very savage wildness of aspect and manner. When our meal was over, Mr Boswell sliced the bread, and divided it amongst them, as he supposed them never to have tasted a wheaten loaf before. He then gave them little pieces of twisted tobacco, and among the children we distributed a small handful of halfpence, which they received with great eagerness. Yet I have been since told, that the people of that valley are not indigent; and when we mentioned them afterwards as needy and pitiable, a Highland lady let us know, that we might spare our commiseration; for the dame whose milk we drank had probably more than a dozen milk-cows. She seemed unwilling to take any price, but being pressed to make a demand, at last named a shilling. Honesty is not greater where elegance is less. One of the by-standers, as we were told afterwards, advised her to ask more, but she said a shilling was enough. We gave her half a crown, and I hope got some credit by our behaviour; for the company said, if our interpreters did not flatter us, that they had not seen such a day since the old Laird of Macleod passed through their country.

The Macraes, as we heard afterwards in the Hebrides, were originally an indigent and subordinate clan, and having no farms nor stock, were in great numbers servants to the Maclellans, who, in the war of Charles the First, took arms at the call of the heroic Montrose, and were, in one of his battles, almost all destroyed. The women that were left at home, being thus deprived of their husbands, like the Scythian ladies of old, married their servants,[60] and the Macraes became a considerable race.

THE HIGHLANDS

As we continued our journey, we were at leisure to extend our speculations, and to investigate the reason of those peculiarities by which such rugged regions as these before us are generally distinguished.

Mountainous countries commonly contain the original, at least the oldest race of inhabitants, for they are not easily conquered, because they must be entered by narrow ways, exposed to every power of mischief from those that occupy the heights; and every new ridge is a new fortress, where the defendants have again the same advantages. If the assailants either force the strait, or storm the summit, they gain only so much ground; their enemies are fled to take possession of the next rock, and the pursuers stand at gaze, knowing neither where the ways of escape wind among the steeps, nor where the bog has firmness to sustain them: besides that, mountaineers have an agility in climbing and descending distinct from strength or courage, and attainable only by use.

If the war be not soon concluded, the invaders are dislodged by hunger; for in those anxious and toilsome marches, provisions cannot easily be carried, and are never to be found. The wealth of mountains is cattle, which, while the men stand in the passes, the women drive away. Such lands at last cannot repay the expence of conquest, and therefore perhaps have not been so often invaded by the mere ambition of dominion; as by resentment of robberies and insults, or the desire of enjoying in security the more fruitful provinces.

As mountains are long before they are conquered, they are likewise long before they are civilized. Men are softened by intercourse mutually profitable, and instructed by comparing their own notions with those of others. Thus Cæsar found the maritime parts of Britain made less barbarous by their commerce with the Gauls. Into a barren and rough tract no stranger is brought either by the hope of gain or of pleasure. The inhabitants having neither commodities for sale, nor money for purchase, seldom visit more polished places, or if they do visit them, seldom return.

It sometimes happens that by conquest, intermixture, or gradual refinement, the cultivated parts of a country change their language. The mountaineers then become a distinct nation, cut off by dissimilitude of speech from conversation with their neighbours. Thus in Biscay, the original Cantabrian, and in Dalecarlia, the old Swedish still subsists. Thus Wales and the Highlands speak the tongue of the first inhabitants of Britain, while the other parts have received first the Saxon, and in some degree afterwards the French, and then formed a third language between them.

That the primitive manners are continued where the primitive language is spoken, no nation will desire me to suppose, for the manners of mountaineers are commonly savage, but they are rather produced by their situation than derived from their ancestors.

Such seems to be the disposition of man, that whatever makes a distinction produces rivalry. England, before other causes of enmity were found, was disturbed for some centuries by the contests of the northern and southern counties; so that at Oxford, the peace of study could for a long time be preserved only by chusing annually one of the proctors from each side of the Trent. A tract intersected by many ridges of mountains, naturally divides its inhabitants into petty nations, which are made by a thousand causes enemies to each other. Each will exalt its own chiefs, each will boast the valour of its men, or the beauty of its women, and every claim of superiority irritates competition; injuries will sometimes be done, and be more injuriously defended; retaliation will sometimes be attempted, and the debt exacted with too much interest.

In the Highlands it was a law, that if a robber was sheltered from justice, any man of the same clan might be taken in his place. This was a kind of irregular justice, which, though necessary in savage times, could hardly fail to end in a feud, and a feud once kindled among an idle people with no variety of pursuits to divert their thoughts, burnt on for ages either sullenly glowing in secret mischief, or openly blazing into publick violence. Of the effects of this violent judicature, there are not wanting memorials. The cave is now to be seen to which one of the Campbells, who had injured the Macdonalds, retired with a body of his own clan. The Macdonalds required the offender, and being refused, made a fire at the mouth of the cave, by which he and his adherents were suffocated together.

Mountaineers are warlike, because by their feuds and competitions they consider themselves as surrounded with enemies, and are always prepared to repel incursions, or to make them. Like the Greeks in their unpolished state, described by Thucydides, the highlanders, till lately, went always armed, and carried their weapons to visits, and to church.

Mountaineers are thievish, because they are poor, and having neither manufactures nor commerce, can grow richer only by robbery. They regularly plunder their neighbours, for their neighbours are commonly their enemies; and having lost that reverence for property, by which the order of civil life is preserved, soon consider all as enemies, whom they do not reckon as friends, and think themselves licensed to invade whatever they are not obliged to protect.

By a strict administration of the laws, since the laws have been introduced into the Highlands, this disposition to thievery is very much represt. Thirty years ago no herd had ever been conducted through the mountains, without paying tribute in the night, to some of the clans; but cattle are now driven, and passengers travel without danger, fear, or molestation.

Among a warlike people, the quality of highest esteem is personal courage, and with the ostentatious display of courage are closely connected promptitude of offence and quickness of resentment. The highlanders, before they were disarmed, were so addicted to quarrels, that the boys used to follow any publick procession or ceremony, however festive, or however solemn, in expectation of the battle, which was sure to happen before the company dispersed.

Mountainous regions are sometimes so remote from the seat of government, and so difficult of access, that they are very little under the influence of the sovereign, or within the reach of national justice. Law is nothing without power; and the sentence of a distant court could not be easily executed, nor perhaps very safely promulgated, among men ignorantly proud and habitually violent, unconnected with the general system, and accustomed to reverence only their own lords. It has therefore been necessary to erect many particular jurisdictions, and commit the punishment of crimes, and the decision of right to the proprietors of the country who could enforce their own decrees. It immediately appears that such judges will be often ignorant, and often partial; but in the immaturity of political establishments no better expedient could be found. As government advances towards perfection, provincial judicature is perhaps in every empire gradually abolished.

Those who had thus the dispensation of law, were by consequence themselves lawless. Their vassals had no shelter from outrages and oppressions; but were condemned to endure, without resistance, the caprices of wantonness, and the rage of cruelty.

In the Highlands, some great lords had an hereditary jurisdiction over counties; and some chieftains over their own lands; till the final conquest of the Highlands afforded an opportunity of crushing all the local courts, and of extending the general benefits of equal law to the low and the high, in the deepest recesses of obscurest corners.

While the chiefs had this resemblance of royalty, they had little inclination to appeal, on any question, to superior judicatures. A claim of lands between two powerful lairds was decided like a contest for dominion between sovereign powers. They drew their forces into the field, and right attended on the strongest. This was, in ruder times, the common practice, which the kings of Scotland could seldom control.

Even so lately as in the last years of King William, a battle was fought at Mull Roy, on a plain a few miles to the south of Inverness, between the clans of Mackintosh and Macdonald of Keppoch. Col. Macdonald, the head of a small clan, refused to pay the dues demanded from him by Mackintosh, as his superior lord. They disdained the interposition of judges and laws, and calling each his followers to maintain the dignity of the clan, fought a formal battle, in which several considerable men fell on the side of Mackintosh, without a complete victory to either. This is said to have been the last open war made between the clans by their own authority.

The Highland lords made treaties, and formed alliances, of which some traces may still be found, and some consequences still remain as lasting evidences of petty regality. The terms of one of these confederacies were, that each should support the other in the right, or in the wrong, except against the king.

The inhabitants of mountains form distinct races, and are careful to preserve their genealogies. Men in a small district necessarily mingle blood by intermarriages, and combine at last into one family, with a common interest in the honour and disgrace of every individual. Then begins that union of affections, and co-operation of endeavours, that constitute a clan. They who consider themselves as ennobled by their family, will think highly of their progenitors, and they who through successive generations live always together in the same place, will preserve local stories and hereditary prejudices. Thus every highlander can talk of his ancestors, and recount the outrages which they suffered from the wicked inhabitants of the next valley.

Such are the effects of habitation among mountains, and such were the qualities of the highlanders, while their rocks secluded them from the rest of mankind, and kept them an unaltered and discriminated race. They are now losing their distinction, and hastening to mingle with the general community.

GLENELG

We left Auknasheals and the Macraes in the afternoon, and in the evening came to Ratiken, a high hill on which a road is cut, but so steep and narrow, that it is very difficult.[61] There is now a design of making another way round the bottom. Upon one of the precipices, my horse, weary with the steepness of the rise, staggered a little, and I called in haste to the highlander to hold him. This was the only moment of my journey, in which I thought myself endangered.

Having surmounted the hill at last, we were told that at Glenelg, on the sea-side, we should come to a house of lime and slate and glass. This image of magnificence raised our expectation. At last we came to our inn weary and peevish, and began to inquire for meat and beds.

Of the provisions the negative catalogue was very copious. Here was no meat, no milk, no bread, no eggs, no wine. We did not express much satisfaction. Here however we were to stay. Whisky we might have, and I believe at last they caught a fowl and killed it. We had some bread, and with that we prepared ourselves to be contented, when we had a very eminent proof of Highland hospitality. Along some miles of the way, in the evening, a gentleman's servant had kept us company on foot with very little notice on our part. He left us near Glenelg, and we thought on him no more till he came to us again, in about two hours, with a present from his master of rum and sugar. The man had mentioned his company, and the gentleman, whose name, I think, is Gordon,[62] well knowing the penury of the place, had this attention to two men, whose names perhaps he had not heard, by whom his kindness was not likely to be ever repaid, and who could be recommended to him only by their necessities.

We were now to examine our lodging. Out of one of the beds, on which we were to repose, started up, at our entrance, a man black as a Cyclops from the forge. Other circumstances of no elegant recital concurred to disgust us. We had been frighted by a lady at Edinburgh,[63] with discouraging representations of Highland lodgings. Sleep, however, was necessary. Our highlanders had at last found some hay, with which the inn could not supply them. I directed them to bring a bundle into the room, and slept upon it in my riding coat. Mr Boswell being more delicate, laid himself sheets with hay over and under him, and lay in linen like a gentleman.

SKY. ARMIDEL

In the morning, September the second,[64] we found ourselves on the edge of the sea. Having procured a boat, we dismissed our highlanders, whom I would recommend to the service of any future travellers, and were ferried over to the Isle of Sky. We landed at Armidel, where we were met on the sands by Sir Alexander Macdonald,[65] who was at that time there with his lady, preparing to leave the island and reside at Edinburgh.

Armidel is a neat house, built where the Macdonalds had once a seat, which was burnt in the commotions that followed the Revolution. The walled orchard, which belonged to the former house, still remains. It is well shaded by tall ash trees, of a species, as Mr Janes[66] the fossilist informed me, uncommonly valuable. This plantation is very properly mentioned by Dr Campbell, in his new account of the state of Britain, and deserves attention;[67] because it proves that the present nakedness of the Hebrides is not wholly the fault of Nature.

As we sat at Sir Alexander's table, we were entertained, according to the ancient usage of the North, with the melody of the bagpipe. Every thing in those countries has its history. As the bagpiper was playing, an elderly gentleman informed us, that in some remote time, the Macdonalds of Glengary having been injured, or offended by the inhabitants of Culloden, and resolving to have justice or vengeance, came to Culloden on a Sunday, where finding their enemies at worship, they shut them up in the church, which they set on fire; and this, said he, is the tune that the piper played while they were burning.

Narrations like this, however uncertain, deserve the notice of a traveller, because they are the only records of a nation that has no historians, and afford the most genuine representation of the life and character of the ancient highlanders.

Under the denomination of highlander are comprehended in Scotland all that now speak the Erse language, or retain the primitive manners, whether they live among the mountains or in the islands; and in that sense I use the name, when there is not some apparent reason for making a distinction.

In Sky I first observed the use of brogues, a kind of artless shoes, stitched with thongs so loosely, that though they defend the foot from stones, they do not exclude water. Brogues were formerly made of raw hides, with the hair inwards, and such are perhaps still used in rude and remote parts; but they are said not to last above two days. Where life is somewhat improved, they are now made of leather tanned with oak bark, as in other places, or with the bark of birch, or roots of tormentil, a substance recommended in defect of bark, about forty years ago, to the Irish tanners, by one to whom the parliament of that kingdom voted a reward. The leather of Sky is not completely penetrated by vegetable matter, and therefore cannot be very durable.

My inquiries about brogues, gave me an early specimen of Highland information. One day I was told, that to make brogues was a domestick art, which every man practised for himself, and that a pair of brogues was the work of an hour. I supposed that the husband made brogues as the wife made an apron, till next day it was told me, that a brogue-maker was a trade, and that a pair would cost half a crown. It will easily occur that these representations may both be true, and that, in some places, men may buy them, and in others, make them for themselves; but I had both the accounts in the same house within two days.

Many of my subsequent inquiries upon more interesting topicks ended in the like uncertainty. He that travels in the Highlands may easily saturate his soul with intelligence, if he will acquiesce in the first account. The highlander gives to every question an answer so prompt and peremptory, that skepticism itself is dared into silence, and the mind sinks before the bold reporter in unresisting credulity; but, if a second question be ventured, it breaks the enchantment; for it is immediately discovered, that what was told so confidently was told at hazard, and that such fearlessness of assertion was either the sport of negligence, or the refuge of ignorance.

If individuals are thus at variance with themselves, it can be no wonder that the accounts of different men are contradictory. The traditions of an ignorant and savage people have been for ages negligently heard, and unskilfully related. Distant events must have been mingled together, and the actions of one man given to another. These, however, are deficiencies in story, for which no man is now to be censured. It were enough, if what there is yet opportunity of examining were accurately inspected, and justly represented; but such is the laxity of Highland conversation, that the inquirer is kept in continual suspense, and by a kind of intellectual retrogradation, knows less as he hears more.

In the islands the plaid is rarely worn. The law by which the highlanders have been obliged to change the form of their dress,[68] has, in all the places that we have visited, been universally obeyed. I have seen only one gentleman completely clothed in the ancient habit, and by him it was worn only occasionally and wantonly. The common people do not think themselves under any legal necessity of having coats; for they say that the law against plaids was made by Lord Hardwicke, and was in force only for his life:[69] but the same poverty that made it then difficult for them to change their clothing, hinders them now from changing it again.

The fillibeg, or lower garment, is still very common, and the bonnet almost universal; but their attire is such as produces, in a sufficient degree, the effect intended by the law, of abolishing the dissimilitude of appearance between the highlanders and the other inhabitants of Britain; and, if dress be supposed to have much influence, facilitates their coalition with their fellow-subjects.

What we have long used we naturally like, and therefore the highlanders were unwilling to lay aside their plaid, which yet to an unprejudiced spectator must appear an incommodious and cumbersome dress; for hanging loose upon the body, it must flutter in a quick motion, or require one of the hands to keep it close. The Romans always laid aside the gown when they had any thing to do. It was a dress so unsuitable to war, that the same word which signified a gown signified peace. The chief use of a plaid seems to be this, that they could commodiously wrap themselves in it, when they were obliged to sleep without a better cover.

In our passage from Scotland to Sky, we were wet for the first time with a shower. This was the beginning of the Highland winter, after which we were told that a succession of three dry days was not to be expected for many months. The winter of the Hebrides consists of little more than rain and wind. As they are surrounded by an ocean never frozen, the blasts that come to them over the water are too much softened to have the power of congelation. The salt loughs, or inlets of the sea, which shoot very far into the island, never have any ice upon them, and the pools of fresh water will never bear the walker. The snow that sometimes falls, is soon dissolved by the air, or the rain.

This is not the description of a cruel climate, yet the dark months are here a time of great distress; because the summer can do little more than feed itself, and winter comes with its cold and its scarcity upon families very slenderly provided.

CORIATACHAN IN SKY

The third or fourth day after our arrival at Armidel, brought us an invitation to the isle of Raasay, which lies east of Sky. It is incredible how soon the account of any event is propagated in these narrow countries by the love of talk, which much leisure produces, and the relief given to the mind in the penury of insular conversation by a new topick. The arrival of strangers at a place so rarely visited, excites rumour, and quickens curiosity. I know not whether we touched at any corner, where Fame had not already prepared us a reception.

To gain a commodious passage to Raasay, it was necessary to pass over a large part of Sky. We were furnished therefore with horses and a guide. In the islands there are no roads, nor any marks by which a stranger may find his way. The horseman has always at his side a native of the place, who, by pursuing game, or tending cattle, or being often employed in messages or conduct, has learned where the ridge of the hill has breadth sufficient to allow a horse and his rider a passage, and where the moss or bog is hard enough to bear them. The bogs are avoided as toilsome at least, if not unsafe, and therefore the journey is made generally from precipice to precipice; from which if the eye ventures to look down, it sees below a gloomy cavity, whence the rush of water is sometimes heard.

But there seems to be in all this more alarm than danger. The highlander walks carefully before, and the horse, accustomed to the ground, follows him with little deviation. Sometimes the hill is too steep for the horseman to keep his seat, and sometimes the moss is too tremulous to bear the double weight of horse and man. The rider then dismounts, and all shift as they can.

Journies made in this manner are rather tedious than long. A very few miles require several hours. From Armidel we came at night to Coriatachan, a house very pleasantly situated between two brooks, with one of the highest hills of the island behind it. It is the residence of Mr Mackinnon, by whom we were treated with very liberal hospitality, among a more numerous and elegant company than it could have been supposed easy to collect.

The hill behind the house we did not climb. The weather was rough, and the height and steepness discouraged us. We were told that there is a cairne upon it. A cairne is a heap of stones thrown upon the grave of one eminent for dignity of birth, or splendour of atchievements. It is said that by digging, an urn is always found under these cairnes: they must therefore have been thus piled by a people whose custom was to burn the dead. To pile stones is, I believe, a northern custom, and to burn the body was the Roman practice; nor do I know when it was that these two acts of sepulture were united.

The weather was next day too violent for the continuation of our journey; but we had no reason to complain of the interruption. We saw in every place, what we chiefly desired to know, the manners of the people. We had company, and, if we had chosen retirement, we might have had books.

I never was in any house of the islands, where I did not find books in more languages than one, if I staid long enough to want them, except one from which the family was removed. Literature is not neglected by the higher rank of the Hebridians.

It need not, I suppose, be mentioned, that in countries so little frequented as the islands, there are no houses where travellers are entertained for money. He that wanders about these wilds, either procures recommendations to those whose habitations lie near his way, or, when night and weariness come upon him, takes the chance of general hospitality. If he finds only a cottage, he can expect little more than shelter; for the cottagers have little more for themselves: but if his good fortune brings him to the residence of a gentleman, he will be glad of a storm to prolong his stay. There is, however, one inn by the sea-side at Sconfor, in Sky, where the post-office is kept.

At the tables where a stranger is received, neither plenty nor delicacy is wanting. A tract of land so thinly inhabited, must have much wild-fowl; and I scarcely remember to have seen a dinner without them. The moorgame is every where to be had.[70] That the sea abounds with fish, needs not be told, for it supplies a great part of Europe. The Isle of Sky has stags and roebucks, but no hares. They sell very numerous droves of oxen yearly to England, and therefore cannot be supposed to want beef at home. Sheep and goats are in great numbers, and they have the common domestick fowls.

But as here is nothing to be bought, every family must kill its own meat, and roast part of it somewhat sooner than Apicius would prescribe.[71] Every kind of flesh is undoubtedly excelled by the variety and emulation of English markets; but that which is not best may be yet very far[72] from bad, and he that shall complain of his fare in the Hebrides, has improved his delicacy more than his manhood.

Their fowls are not like those plumped for sale by the poulterers of London, but they are as good as other places commonly afford, except that the geese, by feeding in the sea, have universally a fishy rankness.

These geese seem to be of a middle race, between the wild and domestick kinds. They are so tame as to own a home, and so wild as sometimes to fly quite away.

Their native bread is made of oats, or barley. Of oatmeal they spread very thin cakes, coarse and hard, to which unaccustomed palates are not easily reconciled. The barley cakes are thicker and softer; I began to eat them without unwillingness; the blackness of their colour raises some dislike, but the taste is not disagreeable. In most houses there is wheat flower, with which we were sure to be treated, if we staid long enough to have it kneaded and baked. As neither yeast nor leaven are used among them, their bread of every kind is unfermented. They make only cakes, and never mould a loaf.

A man of the Hebrides, for of the women's diet I can give no account, as soon as he appears in the morning, swallows a glass of whisky; yet they are not a drunken race, at least I never was present at much intemperance; but no man is so abstemious as to refuse the morning dram, which they call a *skalk*.[73]

The word *whisky* signifies water, and is applied by way of eminence to 'strong water', or distilled liquor. The spirit drunk in the North is drawn from barley. I never tasted it, except once for experiment at the inn in Inverary, when I thought it preferable to any English malt brandy. It was strong, but not pungent, and was free from the empyreumatick taste or smell.[74] What was the process I had no opportunity of inquiring, nor do I wish to improve the art of making poison pleasant.

Not long after the dram, may be expected the breakfast, a meal in which the Scots, whether of the Lowlands or mountains, must be confessed to excel us. The tea and coffee are accompanied not only with butter, but with honey, conserves, and marmalades. If an epicure could remove by a wish, in quest of sensual gratifications, wherever he had supped he would breakfast in Scotland.

In the islands however, they do what I found it not very easy to endure. They pollute the tea-table by plates piled with large slices of cheshire cheese, which mingles its less grateful odours with the fragrance of the tea.

Where many questions are to be asked, some will be omitted. I forgot to inquire how they were supplied with so much exotic luxury. Perhaps the French may bring them wine for wool, and the Dutch give them tea and coffee at the fishing season, in exchange for fresh provision. Their trade is unconstrained; they pay no customs, for there is no officer to demand them; whatever therefore is made dear only by impost, is obtained here at an easy rate.

A dinner in the Western Islands differs very little from a dinner in England, except that in the place of tarts, there are always set different preparations of milk. This part of their diet will admit some improvement. Though they have milk, and eggs, and sugar, few of them know how to compound them in a custard. Their gardens afford them no great variety, but they have always some vegetables on the table. Potatoes at least are never wanting, which, though they have not known them long, are now one of the principal parts of their food. They are not of the mealy, but the viscous kind.

Their more elaborate cookery, or made dishes, an Englishman at the first taste is not likely to approve, but the culinary compositions of every country are often such as become grateful to other nations only by degrees; though I have read a French author, who, in the elation of his heart, says, that French cookery pleases all foreigners, but foreign cookery never satisfies a Frenchman.

Their suppers are, like their dinners, various and plentiful. The table is always covered with elegant linen. Their plates for common use are often of that kind of manufacture which is called cream coloured, or queen's ware. They use silver on all occasions where it is common in England, nor did I ever find the spoon of horn, but in one house.[75]

The knives are not often either very bright, or very sharp. They are indeed instruments of which the highlanders have not been long acquainted with the general use. They were not regularly laid on the table, before the prohibition of arms, and the change of dress. Thirty years ago the highlander wore his knife as a companion to his dirk or dagger, and when the company sat down to meat, the men who had knives, cut the flesh into small pieces for the women, who with their fingers conveyed it to their mouths.

There was perhaps never any change of national manners so quick, so great, and so general, as that which has operated in the Highlands, by the last conquest, and the subsequent laws. We came thither too late to see what we expected, a people of peculiar appearance, and a system of antiquated life. The clans retain little now of their original character, their ferocity of temper is softened, their military ardour is extinguished, their dignity of independence is depressed, their contempt of government subdued, and their reverence for their chiefs abated. Of what they had before the late conquest of their country, there remain only their language and their poverty. Their language is attacked on every side. Schools are erected, in which English only is taught, and there were lately some who thought it reasonable to refuse them a version of the holy scriptures, that they might have no monument of their mother-tongue.

That their poverty is gradually abated, cannot be mentioned among the unpleasing consequences of subjection. They are now acquainted with money, and the possibility of gain will by degrees make them industrious. Such is the effect of the late regulations, that a longer journey than to the Highlands must be taken by him whose curiosity pants for savage virtues and barbarous grandeur.

RAASAY

At the first intermission of the stormy weather we were informed, that the boat, which was to convey us to Raasay, attended us on the coast.[76] We had from this time our intelligence facilitated, and our conversation enlarged, by the company of Mr Macqueen, minister of a parish in Sky,[77] whose knowledge and politeness give him a title equally to kindness and respect, and who, from this time, never forsook us till we were preparing to leave Sky, and the adjacent places.

The boat was under the direction of Mr Malcolm Macleod, a gentleman of Raasay. The water was calm, and the rowers were vigorous; so that our passage was quick and pleasant. When we came near the island, we saw the laird's house, a neat modern fabrick, and found Mr Macleod, the proprietor of the island, with many gentlemen, expecting us on the beach. We had, as at all other places, some difficulty in landing. The craggs were irregularly broken, and a false step would have been very mischievous.

It seemed that the rocks might, with no great labour, have been hewn almost into a regular flight of steps; and as there are no other landing places, I considered this rugged ascent as the consequence of a form of life inured to hardships, and therefore not studious of nice accommodations. But I know not whether, for many ages, it was not considered as a part of military policy, to keep the country not easily accessible. The rocks are natural fortifications, and an enemy climbing with difficulty, was easily destroyed by those who stood high above him.

Our reception exceeded our expectations. We found nothing but civility, elegance, and plenty. After the usual refreshments, and the usual conversation, the evening came upon us. The carpet was then rolled off the floor; the musician was called, and the whole company was invited to dance, nor did ever fairies trip with greater alacrity. The general air of festivity, which predominated in this place, so far remote from all those regions which the mind has been used to contemplate as the mansions of pleasure, struck the imagination with a delightful surprise, analogous to that which is felt at an unexpected emersion from darkness into light.

When it was time to sup, the dance ceased, and six and thirty persons sat down to two tables in the same room. After supper the ladies sung Erse songs, to which I listened as an English audience to an Italian opera, delighted with the sound of words which I did not understand.

I inquired the subjects of the songs, and was told of one, that it was a love song, and of another, that it was a farewell composed by one of the islanders that was going, in this epidemical fury of emigration, to seek his fortune in America. What sentiments would rise, on such an occasion, in the heart of one who had not been taught to lament by precedent, I should gladly have known; but the lady, by whom I sat, thought herself not equal to the work of translating.

Mr Macleod is the proprietor of the islands of Raasay, Rona, and Fladda, and possesses an extensive district in Sky. The estate has not, during four hundred years, gained or lost a single acre. He acknowledges Macleod of Dunvegan[78] as his chief, though his ancestors have formerly disputed the pre-eminence.

One of the old Highland alliances has continued for two hundred years, and is still subsisting between Macleod of Raasay and Macdonald of Sky, in consequence of which, the survivor always inherits the arms of the deceased; a natural memorial of military friendship. At the death of the late Sir James Macdonald, his sword was delivered to the present Laird of Raasay.

The family of Raasay consists of the laird, the lady, three sons and ten daughters. For the sons there is a tutor in the house, and the lady is said to be very skilful and diligent in the education of her girls. More gentleness of manners, or a more pleasing appearance of domestick society, is not found in the most polished countries.

Raasay is the only inhabited island in Mr Macleod's possession. Rona and Fladda afford only pasture for cattle, of which one hundred and sixty winter in Rona, under the superintendence of a solitary herdsman.

The length of Raasay is, by computation, fifteen miles, and the breadth two. These countries have never been measured, and the computation by miles is negligent and arbitrary. We observed in travelling, that the nominal and real distance of places had very little relation to each other.[79] Raasay probably contains near a hundred square miles. It affords not much ground, notwithstanding its extent, either for tillage, or pasture; for it is rough, rocky, and barren. The cattle often perish by falling from the precipices. It is like the other islands, I think, generally naked of shade, but it is naked by neglect; for the laird has an orchard, and very large forest trees grow about his house. Like other hilly countries it has many rivulets. One of the brooks turns a corn-mill, and at least one produces trouts.

In the streams or fresh lakes of the islands, I have never heard of any other fish than trouts and eels. The trouts, which I have seen, are not large; the colour of their flesh is tinged as in England. Of their eels I can give no account, having never tasted them; for I believe they are not considered as wholesome food.

It is not very easy to fix the principles upon which mankind have agreed to eat some animals, and reject others; and as the principle is not evident, it is not uniform. That which is selected as delicate in one country, is by its neighbours abhorred as loathsome. The Neapolitans lately refused to eat potatoes in a famine. An Englishman is not easily persuaded to dine on snails with an Italian, on frogs with a Frenchman, or on horse-flesh with a Tartar. The vulgar inhabitants of Sky, I know not whether of the other islands, have not only eels, but pork and bacon in abhorrence, and accordingly I never saw a hog in the Hebrides, except one at Dunvegan.

Raasay has wild fowl in abundance, but neither deer, hares, nor rabbits. Why it has them not, might be asked, but that of such questions there is no end. Why does any nation want what it might have? Why are not spices transplanted to America? Why does tea continue to be brought from China?[80] Life improves but by slow degrees, and much in every place is yet to do. Attempts have been made to raise roebucks in Raasay, but without effect. The young ones it is extremely difficult to rear, and the old can very seldom be taken alive.

Hares and rabbits might be more easily obtained. That they have few or none of either in Sky, they impute to the ravage of the foxes, and have therefore set, for some years past, a price upon their heads, which, as the number was diminished, has been gradually raised, from three shillings and sixpence to a guinea, a sum so great in this part of the world, that, in a short time, Sky may be as free from foxes, as England from wolves. The fund for these rewards is a tax of sixpence in the pound, imposed by the farmers on themselves, and said to be paid with great willingness.

The beasts of prey in the islands are foxes, otters, and weasels. The foxes are bigger than those of England; but the otters exceed ours in a far greater proportion. I saw one at Armidel, of a size much beyond that which I supposed them ever to attain; and Mr Maclean, the heir of Col, a man of middle stature, informed me that he once shot an otter, of which the tail reached the ground, when he held up the head to a level with his own.[81] I expected the otter to have a foot particularly formed for the art of swimming; but upon examination, I did not find it differing much from that of a spaniel. As he preys in the sea, he does little visible mischief, and is killed only for his fur. White otters are sometimes seen.

In Raasay they might have hares and rabbits, for they have no foxes. Some depredations, such as were never made before, have caused a suspicion that a fox has been lately landed in the island by spite or wantonness. This imaginary stranger has never yet been seen, and therefore, perhaps, the mischief was done by some other animal. It is not likely that a creature so ungentle, whose head could have been sold in Sky for a guinea, should be kept alive only to gratify the malice of sending him to prey upon a neighbour: and the passage from Sky is wider than a fox would venture to swim, unless he were chased by dogs into the sea, and perhaps than his strength would enable him to cross. How beasts of prey came into any islands is not easy to guess. In cold countries they take advantage of hard winters, and travel over the ice: but this is a very scanty solution; for they are found where they have no discoverable means of coming.

The corn of this island is but little. I saw the harvest of a small field. The women reaped the corn, and the men bound up the sheaves. The strokes of the sickle were timed by the modulation of the harvest song, in which all their voices were united. They accompany in the Highlands every action, which can be done in equal time, with an appropriated strain, which has, they say, not much meaning; but its effects are regularity and cheerfulness. The ancient proceleusmatick[82] song, by which the rowers of gallies were animated, may be supposed to have been of this kind. There is now an oar-song used by the Hebridians.

The ground of Raasay seems fitter for cattle than for corn, and of black cattle I suppose the number is very great. The laird himself keeps a herd of four hundred, one hundred of which are annually sold. Of an extensive domain, which he holds in his own hands, he considers the sale of cattle as repaying him the rent, and supports the plenty of a very liberal table with the remaining product.

Raasay is supposed to have been very long inhabited. On one side of it they show caves, into which the rude nations of the first ages retreated from the weather. These dreary vaults might have had other uses. There is still a cavity near the house called the oar-cave, in which the seamen, after one of these piratical expeditions, which in rougher times were very frequent, used, as tradition tells, to hide their oars. This hollow was near the sea, that nothing so necessary might be far to be fetched; and it was secret, that enemies, if they landed, could find nothing. Yet it is not very evident of what use it was to hide their oars from those, who, if they were masters of the coast, could take away their boats.

A proof much stronger of the distance at which the first possessors of this island lived from the present time, is afforded by the stone heads of arrows which are very frequently picked up. The people call them Elf-bolts, and believe that the fairies shoot them at the cattle. They nearly resemble those which Mr Banks[83] has lately brought from the savage countries in the Pacifick Ocean, and must have been made by a nation to which the use of metals was unknown.

The number of this little community has never been counted by its ruler, nor have I obtained any positive account, consistent with the result of political computation. Not many years ago, the late laird led out one hundred men upon a military expedition.[84] The sixth part of a people is supposed capable of bearing arms: Raasay had therefore six hundred inhabitants. But because it is not likely, that every man able to serve in the field would follow the summons, or that the chief would leave his lands totally defenceless, or take away all the hands qualified for labour, let it be supposed, that half as many might be permitted to stay at home. The whole number will then be nine hundred, or nine to a square mile; a degree of populousness greater than those tracts of desolation can often show. They are content with their country, and faithful to their chiefs, and yet uninfected with the fever of migration.

Near the house, at Raasay, is a chapel unroofed and ruinous, which has long been used only as a place of burial. About the churches, in the islands, are small squares inclosed with stone, which belong to particular families, as repositories for the dead. At Raasay there is one, I think, for the proprietor, and one for some collateral house.

It is told by Martin,[85] that at the death of the lady of the island, it has been here the custom to erect a cross. This we found not to be true. The stones that stand about the chapel at a small distance, some of which perhaps have crosses cut upon them, are believed to have been not funeral monuments, but the ancient boundaries of the sanctuary or consecrated ground.

Martin was a man not illiterate: he was an inhabitant of Sky, and therefore was within reach of intelligence, and with no great difficulty might have visited the places which he undertakes to describe; yet with all his opportunities, he has often suffered himself to be deceived. He lived in the last century, when the chiefs of the clans had lost little of their original influence. The mountains were yet unpenetrated, no inlet was opened to foreign novelties, and the feudal institutions operated upon life with their full force. He might therefore have displayed a series of subordination and a form of government, which, in more luminous and improved regions, have been long forgotten, and have delighted his readers with many uncouth customs that are now disused, and wild opinions that prevail no longer. But he probably had not knowledge of the world sufficient to qualify him for judging what would deserve or gain the attention of mankind. The mode of life which was familiar to himself, he did not suppose unknown to others, nor imagined that he could give pleasure by telling that of which it was, in his little country, impossible to be ignorant.

What he has neglected cannot now be performed. In nations, where there is hardly the use of letters, what is once out of sight is lost for ever. They think but little, and of their few thoughts, none are wasted on the past, in which they are neither interested by fear nor hope. Their only registers are stated observances and practical representations.[86] For this reason an age of ignorance is an age of ceremony. Pageants, and processions, and commemorations, gradually shrink away, as better methods come into use of recording events, and preserving rights.

It is not only in Raasay that the chapel is unroofed and useless; through the few islands which we visited, we neither saw nor heard of any house of prayer, except in Sky, that was not in ruins. The malignant influence of Calvinism has blasted ceremony and decency together; and if the remembrance of papal superstition is obliterated, the monuments of papal piety are likewise effaced.

It has been, for many years, popular to talk of the lazy devotion of the Romish clergy; over the sleepy laziness of men that erected churches, we may indulge our superiority with a new triumph, by comparing it with the fervid activity of those who suffer them to fall.

Of the destruction of churches, the decay of religion must in time be the consequence; for while the publick acts of the ministry are now performed in houses, a very small number can be present; and as the greater part of the islanders make no use of books, all must necessarily live in total ignorance who want the opportunity of vocal instruction.

From these remains of ancient sanctity, which are every where to be found, it has been conjectured, that, for the last two centuries, the inhabitants of the islands have decreased in number. This argument, which supposes that the churches have been suffered to fall, only because they were no longer necessary, would have some force, if the houses of worship still remaining were sufficient for the people. But since they have now no churches at all, these venerable fragments do not prove the people of former times to have been more numerous, but to have been more devout. If the inhabitants were doubled with their present principles, it appears not that any provision for publick worship would be made. Where the religion of a country enforces consecrated buildings, the number of those buildings may be supposed to afford some indication, however uncertain, of the populousness of the place; but where by a change of manners a nation is contented to live without them, their decay implies no diminution of inhabitants.

Some of these dilapidations are said to be found in islands now uninhabited; but I doubt whether we can thence infer that they were ever peopled. The religion of the middle age, is well known to have placed too much hope in lonely austerities. Voluntary solitude was the great act[87] of propitiation, by which crimes were effaced, and conscience was appeased; it is therefore not unlikely, that oratories were often built in places where retirement was sure to have no disturbance.

Raasay has little that can detain a traveller, except the laird and his family; but their power wants no auxiliaries. Such a feat of hospitality, amidst the winds and waters, fills the imagination with a delightful contrariety of images. Without is the rough ocean and the rocky land, the beating billows and the howling storm: within is plenty and elegance, beauty and gaiety, the song and the dance. In Raasay, if I could have found an Ulysses, I had fancied a Phæacia.[88]

DUNVEGAN

At Raasay, by good fortune, Macleod, so the chief of the clan is called, was paying a visit, and by him we were invited to his seat at Dunvegan. Raasay has a stout boat, built in Norway, in which, with six oars, he conveyed us back to Sky. We landed at Port Re, so called, because James the Fifth of Scotland, who had curiosity to visit the islands, came into it. The port is made by an inlet of the sea, deep and narrow, where a ship lay waiting to dispeople Sky, by carrying the natives away to America.

In coasting Sky, we passed by the cavern in which it was the custom, as Martin relates, to catch birds in the night, by making a fire at the entrance. This practice is disused; for the birds, as is known often to happen, have changed their haunts.

Here we dined at a publick house, I believe the only inn of the island,[89] and having mounted our horses, travelled in the manner already described, till we came to Kingsborough, a place distinguished by that name, because the King lodged here when he landed at Port Re. We were entertained with the usual hospitality by Mr Macdonald and his lady, Flora Macdonald, a name that will be mentioned in history, and if courage and fidelity be virtues, mentioned with honour.[90] She is a woman of middle stature, soft features, gentle manners, and elegant presence.

In the morning we sent our horses round a promontory to meet us, and spared ourselves part of the day's fatigue, by crossing an arm of the sea.[91] We had at last some difficulty in coming to Dunvegan; for our way led over an extensive moor, where every step was to be taken with caution, and we were often obliged to alight, because the ground could not be trusted. In travelling this watery flat, I perceived that it had a visible declivity, and might without much expence or difficulty be drained. But difficulty and expence are relative terms, which have different meanings in different places.

To Dunvegan we came, very willing to be at rest, and found our fatigue amply recompensed by our reception. Lady Macleod, who had lived many years in England, was newly come hither with her son[92] and four daughters, who knew all the arts of southern elegance, and all the modes of English economy. Here therefore we settled, and did not spoil the present hour with thoughts of departure.

Dunvegan is a rocky prominence, that juts out into a bay, on the west side of Sky. The house, which is the principal seat of Macleod, is partly old and partly modern; it is built upon the rock, and looks upon the water. It forms two sides of a small square: on the third side is the skeleton of a castle of unknown antiquity, supposed to have been a Norwegian fortress, when the Danes were masters of the islands. It is so nearly entire, that it might have easily been made habitable, were there not an ominous tradition in the family, that the owner shall not long outlive the reparation. The grandfather of the present laird, in defiance of prediction, began the work, but desisted in a little time, and applied his money to worse uses.

As the inhabitants of the Hebrides lived, for many ages, in continual expectation of hostilities, the chief of every clan resided in a fortress. This house was accessible only from the water, till the last possessor opened an entrance by stairs upon the land.

They had formerly reason to be afraid, not only of declared wars and authorized invaders, or of roving pirates, which, in the northern seas, must have been very common; but of inroads and insults from rival clans, who, in the plenitude of feudal independence, asked no leave of their Sovereign to make war on one another. Sky has been ravaged by a feud between the two mighty powers of Macdonald and Macleod. Macdonald having married a Macleod, upon some discontent dismissed her, perhaps because she had brought him no children. Before the reign of James the Fifth, a Highland laird made a trial of his wife for a certain time, and if she did not please him, he was then at liberty to send her away. This however must always have offended, and Macleod resenting the injury, whatever were its circumstances, declared, that the wedding had been solemnized without a bonfire, but that the separation should be better illuminated; and raising a little army, set fire to the territories of Macdonald, who returned the visit, and prevailed.

Another story may show the disorderly state of insular neighbourhood. The inhabitants of the Isle of Egg, meeting a boat manned by Macleods, tied the crew hand and foot, and set them a-drift. Macleod landed upon Egg, and demanded the offenders; but the inhabitants refusing to surrender them, retreated to a cavern, into which they thought their enemies unlikely to follow them. Macleod choked them with smoke, and left them lying dead by families as they stood.[93]

Here the violence of the weather confined us for some time, not at all to our discontent or inconvenience. We would indeed very willingly have visited the islands, which might be seen from the house scattered in the sea, and I was particularly desirous to have viewed Isay; but the storms did not permit us to launch a boat, and we were condemned to listen in idleness to the wind, except when we were better engaged by listening to the ladies.

We had here more wind than waves, and suffered the severity of a tempest, without enjoying its magnificence. The sea being broken by the multitude of islands, does not roar with so much noise, nor beat the storm with such foamy violence, as I have remarked on the coast of Sussex. Though, while I was in the Hebrides, the wind was extremely turbulent, I never saw very high billows.

The country about Dunvegan is rough and barren. There are no trees, except in the orchard, which is a low sheltered spot surrounded with a wall.

When this house was intended to sustain a siege, a well was made in the court, by boring the rock downwards, till water was found, which though so near to the sea, I have not heard mentioned as brackish, though it has some hardness, or other qualities, which make it less fit for use; and the family is now better supplied from a stream, which runs by the rock, from two pleasing water-falls.

Here we saw some traces of former manners, and heard some standing traditions. In the house is kept an ox's horn, hollowed so as to hold perhaps two quarts, which the heir of Macleod was expected to swallow at one draught, as a test of his manhood, before he was permitted to bear arms, or could claim a seat among the men.[94] It is held that the return of the laird to Dunvegan, after any considerable absence, produces a plentiful capture of herrings; and that, if any woman crosses the water to the opposite islands, the herrings will desert the coast. Boethius tells the same of some other place. This tradition is not uniform. Some hold that no woman may pass, and others that none may pass but a Macleod.

Among other guests, which the hospitality of Dunvegan brought to the table, a visit was paid by the laird and lady of a small island south of Sky, of which the proper name is Muack, which signifies swine. It is commonly called Muck, which the proprietor not liking, has endeavoured, without effect, to change to Monk. It is usual to call gentlemen in Scotland by the name of their possessions, as Raasay, Bernera, Loch Buy, a practice necessary in countries inhabited by clans, where all that live in the same territory have one name, and must be therefore discriminated by some addition. This gentleman, whose name, I think, is Maclean, should be regularly called Muck; but the appellation, which he thinks too coarse for his island, he would like still less for himself, and he is therefore addressed by the title of, Isle of Muck.[95]

This little island, however it be named, is of considerable value. It is two English miles long, and three quarters of a mile broad, and consequently contains only nine hundred and sixty English acres. It is chiefly arable. Half of this little dominion the laird retains in his own hand, and on the other half, live one hundred and sixty persons, who pay their rent by exported corn. What rent they pay, we were not told, and could not decently inquire. The proportion of the people to the land is such, as the most fertile countries do not commonly maintain.

The laird having all his people under his immediate view, seems to be very attentive to their happiness. The devastation of the small-pox, when it visits places where it comes seldom, is well known. He has disarmed it of its terrour at Muack, by inoculating eighty of his people. The expence was two shillings and sixpence a head. Many trades they cannot have among them, but upon occasion, he fetches a smith from the Isle of Egg, and has a tailor from the main land, six times a year. This island well deserved to be seen, but the laird's absence left us no opportunity.

Every inhabited island has its appendant and subordinate islets. Muck, however small, has yet others smaller about it, one of which has only ground sufficient to afford pasture for three wethers.

At Dunvegan I had tasted lotus, and was in danger of forgetting that I was ever to depart, till Mr Boswell sagely reproached me with my sluggishness and softness. I had no very forcible defence to make; and we agreed to pursue our journey. Macleod accompanied us to Ulinish, where we were entertained by the sheriff of the Island.[96]

ULINISH

Mr Macqueen travelled with us, and directed our attention to all that was worthy of observation. With him we went to see an ancient building, called a dun or borough. It was a circular inclosure, about forty-two feet in diameter, walled round with loose stones, perhaps to the height of nine feet. The walls are very thick, diminishing a little towards the top, and though in these countries, stone is not brought far, must have been raised with much labour. Within the great circle were several smaller rounds of wall, which formed distinct apartments. Its date, and its use are unknown. Some suppose it the original seat of the chiefs of the Macleods. Mr Macqueen thought it a Danish fort.

The entrance is covered with flat stones, and is narrow, because it was necessary that the stones which lie over it, should reach from one wall to the other; yet, strait as the passage is, they seem heavier than could have been placed where they now lie, by the naked strength of as many men as might stand about them. They were probably raised by putting long pieces of wood under them, to which the action of a long line of lifters might be applied. Savages, in all countries, have patience proportionate to their unskilfulness, and are content to attain their end by very tedious methods.

If it was ever roofed, it might once have been a dwelling, but as there is no provision for water, it could not have been a fortress. In Sky, as in every other place, there is an ambition of exalting whatever has survived memory, to some important use, and referring it to very remote ages. I am inclined to suspect, that in lawless times, when the inhabitants of every mountain stole the cattle of their neighbour, these inclosures were used to secure the herds and flocks in the night. When they were driven within the wall, they might be easily watched, and defended as long as could be needful; for the robbers durst not wait till the injured clan should find them in the morning.

The interior inclosures, if the whole building were once a house, were the chambers of the chief inhabitants. If it was a place of security for cattle, they were probably the shelters of the keepers.

From the dun we were conducted to another place of security, a cave carried a great way under ground, which had been discovered by digging after a fox. These caves, of which many have been found, and many probably remain concealed, are formed, I believe, commonly by taking advantage of a hollow, where banks or rocks rise on either side. If no such place can be found, the ground must be cut away. The walls are made by piling stones against the earth, on either side. It is then roofed by larger stones laid across the cavern, which therefore cannot be wide. Over the roof, turfs were placed, and the grass was suffered to grow; and the mouth was concealed by bushes, or some other cover.

These caves were represented to us as the cabins of the first rude inhabitants, of which, however, I am by no means persuaded. This was so low, that no man could stand upright in it. By their construction they are all so narrow, that two can never pass along them together, and being subterraneous, they must be always damp. They are not the work of an age much ruder than the present; for they are formed with as much art as the construction of a common hut requires. I imagine them to have been places only of occasional use, in which the islander, upon a sudden alarm, hid his utensils, or his cloaths, and perhaps sometimes his wife and children.

This cave we entered, but could not proceed the whole length, and went away without knowing how far it was carried. For this omission we shall be blamed, as we perhaps have blamed other travellers; but the day was rainy, and the ground was damp. We had with us neither spades nor pickaxes, and if love of ease surmounted our desire of knowledge, the offence has not the invidiousness of singularity.

Edifices, either standing or ruined, are the chief records of an illiterate nation. In some part of this journey, at no great distance from our way, stood a shattered fortress, of which the learned minister, to whose communication we are much indebted, gave us an account.

Those, said he, are the walls of a place of refuge, built in the time of James the Sixth, by Hugh Macdonald, who was next heir to the dignity and fortune of his chief. Hugh, being so near his wish, was impatient of delay; and had art and influence sufficient to engage several gentlemen in a plot against the laird's life. Something must be stipulated on both sides; for they would not dip their hands in blood merely for Hugh's advancement. The compact was formerly written, signed by the conspirators, and placed in the hands of one Macleod.

It happened that Macleod had sold some cattle to a drover, who, not having ready money, gave him a bond for payment. The debt was discharged, and the bond re-demanded; which Macleod, who could not read, intending to put into his hands, gave him the conspiracy. The drover, when he had read the paper, delivered it privately to Macdonald; who, being thus informed of his danger, called his friends together, and provided for his safety. He made a publick feast, and inviting Hugh Macdonald and his confederates, placed each of them at the table between two men of known fidelity. The compact of conspiracy was then shewn, and every man confronted with his own name. Macdonald acted with great moderation. He upbraided Hugh, both with disloyalty and ingratitude; but told the rest, that he considered them as men deluded and misinformed. Hugh was sworn to fidelity, and dismissed with his companions; but he was not generous enough to be reclaimed by lenity; and finding no longer any countenance among the gentlemen, endeavoured to execute the same design by meaner hands. In this practice he was detected, taken to Macdonald's castle, and imprisoned in the dungeon. When he was hungry, they let down a plentiful meal of salted meat; and when, after his repast, he called for drink, conveyed to him a covered cup, which, when he lifted the lid, he found empty. From that time they visited him no more, but left him to perish in solitude and darkness.

We were then told of a cavern by the sea-side, remarkable for the powerful reverberation of sounds. After dinner we took a boat, to explore this curious cavity. The boatmen, who seemed to be of a rank above that of common drudges, inquired who the strangers were, and being told we came one from Scotland, and the other from England, asked if the Englishman could recount a long genealogy. What answer was given them, the conversation being in Erse, I was not much inclined to examine.

They expected no good event of the voyage; for one of them declared that he heard the cry of an English ghost. This omen I was not told till after our return, and therefore cannot claim the dignity of despising it.

The sea was smooth. We never left the shore, and came without any disaster to the cavern, which we found rugged and misshapen, about one hundred and eighty feet long, thirty wide in the broadest part, and in the loftiest, as we guessed, about thirty high. It was now dry, but at high water the sea rises in it near six feet. Here I saw what I had never seen before, limpets and mussels in their natural state. But, as a new testimony to the veracity of common fame, here was no echo to be heard.

We then walked through a natural arch in the rock, which might have pleased us by its novelty, had the stones, which incumbered our feet, given us leisure to consider it. We were shown the gummy seed of the kelp, that fastens itself to a stone, from which it grows into a strong stalk.

In our return, we found a little boy upon the point of a rock, catching with his angle, a supper for the family. We rowed up to him, and borrowed his rod, with which Mr Boswell caught a cuddy.

The cuddy is a fish of which I know not the philosophical name.[97] It is not much bigger than a gudgeon, but is of great use in these islands, as it affords the lower people both food, and oil for their lamps. Cuddies are so abundant, at some times of the year, that they are caught like whitebait in the Thames, only by dipping a basket and drawing it back.

If it were always practicable to fish, these islands could never be in much danger from famine; but unhappily in the winter, when other provision fails, the seas are commonly too rough for nets, or boats.

TALISKER IN SKY

From Ulinish, our next stage was to Talisker, the house of Colonel Macleod, an officer in the Dutch service, who, in this time of universal peace, has for several years been permitted to be absent from his regiment. Having been bred to physick, he is consequently a scholar, and his lady, by accompanying him in his different places of residence, is become skilful in several languages.

Talisker is the place beyond all that I have seen, from which the gay and the jovial seem utterly excluded; and where the hermit might expect to grow old in meditation, without possibility of disturbance or interruption. It is situated very near the sea, but upon a coast where no vessel lands but when it is driven by a tempest on the rocks. Towards the land are lofty hills streaming with water-falls. The garden is sheltered by firs or pines, which grow there so prosperously, that some, which the present inhabitant planted, are very high and thick.

At this place we very happily met Mr Donald Maclean, a young gentleman, the eldest son of the Laird of Col,[98] heir to a very great extent of land, and so desirous of improving his inheritance, that he spent a considerable time among the farmers of Hertfordshire, and Hampshire, to learn their practice. He worked with his own hands at the principal operations of agriculture, that he might not deceive himself by a false opinion of skill, which, if he should find it deficient at home, he had no means of completing. If the world has agreed to praise the travels and manual labours of the Czar of Muscovy,[99] let Col have his share of the like applause, in the proportion of his dominions to the empire of Russia.

This young gentleman was sporting in the mountains of Sky, and when he was weary with following his game, repaired for lodging to Talisker. At night he missed one of his dogs, and when he went to seek him in the morning, found two eagles feeding on his carcass.

Col, for he must be named by his possessions, hearing that our intention was to visit Iona,[100] offered to conduct us to his chief, Sir Allan Maclean, who lived in the isle of Inch Kenneth,[101] and would readily find us a convenient passage. From this time was formed an acquaintance, which being begun by kindness, was accidentally continued by constraint; we derived much pleasure from it, and I hope have given him no reason to repent it.

The weather was now almost one continued storm, and we were to snatch some happy intermission to be conveyed to Mull, the third island of the Hebrides, lying about a degree south of Sky, whence we might easily find our way to Inch Kenneth, where Sir Allan Maclean resided, and afterward to Iona.

For this purpose, the most commodious station that we could take was Armidel, which Sir Alexander Macdonald had now left to a gentleman, who lived there as his factor or steward.

In our way to Armidel was Coriatachan, where we had already been, and to which therefore we were very willing to return. We staid however so long at Talisker, that a great part of our journey was performed in the gloom of the evening. In travelling even thus almost without light thro' naked solitude, when there is a guide whose conduct may be trusted, a mind not naturally too much disposed to fear may preserve some degree of cheerfulness; but what must be the solitude of him who should be wandering, among the craggs and hollows, benighted, ignorant, and alone?

The fictions of the Gothick romances were not so remote from credibility as they are now thought. In the full prevalence of the feudal institution, when violence desolated the world, and every baron lived in a fortress, forests and castles were regularly succeeded by each other, and the adventurer might very suddenly pass from the gloom of woods, or the ruggedness of moors, to seats of plenty, gaiety, and magnificence. Whatever is imaged in the wildest tale, if giants, dragons, and enchantment be excepted, would be felt by him, who, wandering in the mountains without a guide, or upon the sea without a pilot, should be carried amidst his terror and uncertainty, to the hospitality and elegance of Raasay or Dunvegan.

To Coriatachan at last we came, and found ourselves welcomed as before. Here we staid two days, and made such inquiries as curiosity suggested. The house was filled with company, among whom Mr Macpherson[102] and his sister distinguished themselves by their politeness and accomplishments. By him we were invited to Ostig, a house not far from Armidel, where we might easily hear of a boat, when the weather would suffer us to leave the Island.

OSTIG IN SKY

At Ostig, of which Mr Macpherson is minister, we were entertained for some days, then removed to Armidel, where we finished our observations on the island of Sky.

As this island lies in the fifty-seventh degree, the air cannot be supposed to have much warmth. The long continuance of the sun above the horizon, does indeed sometimes produce great heat in northern latitudes; but this can only happen in sheltered places, where the atmosphere is to a certain degree stagnant, and the same mass of air continues to receive for many hours the rays of the sun, and the vapours of the earth. Sky lies open on the west and north to a vast extent of ocean, and is cooled in the summer by perpetual ventilation, but by the same blasts is kept warm in winter. Their weather is not pleasing. Half the year is deluged with rain. From the autumnal to the vernal equinox, a dry day is hardly known, except when the showers are suspended by a tempest. Under such skies can be expected no great exuberance of vegetation. Their winter overtakes their summer, and their harvest lies upon the ground drenched with rain. The autumn struggles hard to produce some of our early fruits. I gathered gooseberries in September; but they were small, and the husk was thick.

Their winter is seldom such as puts a full stop to the growth of plants, or reduces the cattle to live wholly on the surplusage of the summer. In the year seventy-one they had a severe season, remembered by the name of the Black Spring, from which the island has not yet recovered. The snow lay long upon the ground, a calamity hardly known before. Part of their cattle died for want, part were unseasonably sold to buy sustenance for the owners; and, what I have not read or heard of before, the kine that survived were so emaciated and dispirited, that they did not require the male at the usual time. Many of the roebucks perished.

The soil, as in other countries, has its diversities. In some parts there is only a thin layer of earth spread upon a rock, which bears nothing but short brown heath, and perhaps is not generally capable of any better product. There are many bogs or mosses of greater or less extent, where the soil cannot be supposed to want depth, though it is too wet for the plow. But we did not observe in these any aquatick plants. The vallies and the mountains are alike darkened with heath. Some grass, however, grows here and there, and some happier spots of earth are capable of tillage.

Their agriculture is laborious, and perhaps rather feeble than unskilful. Their chief manure is sea-weed, which, when they lay it to rot upon the field, gives them a better crop than those of the Highlands. They heap sea shells upon the dunghill, which in time moulder into a fertilizing substance. When they find a vein of earth where they cannot use it, they dig it up, and add it to the mould of a more commodious place.

Their corn grounds often lie in such intricacies among the craggs, that there is no room for the action of a team and plow. The soil is then turned up by manual labour, with an instrument called a crooked spade, of a form and weight which to me appeared very incommodious, and would perhaps be soon improved in a country where workmen could be easily found and easily paid. It has a narrow blade of iron fixed to a long and heavy piece of wood, which must have, about a foot and a half above the iron, a knee or flexure with the angle downwards. When the farmer encounters a stone which is the great impediment of his operations, he drives the blade under it, and bringing the knee or angle to the ground, has in the long handle a very forcible lever.

According to the different mode of tillage, farms are distinguished into 'long land' and 'short land'. Long land is that which affords room for a plow, and short land is turned up by the spade.

The grain which they commit to the furrows thus tediously formed, is either oats or barley. They do not sow barley without very copious manure, and then they expect from it ten for one, an increase equal to that of better countries; but the culture is so operose that they content themselves commonly with oats; and who can relate without compassion, that after all their diligence they are to expect only a triple increase? It is in vain to hope for plenty, when a third part of the harvest must be reserved for seed.

When their grain is arrived at the state which they must consider as ripeness, they do not cut, but pull the barley: to the oats they apply the sickle. Wheel carriages they have none, but make a frame of timber, which is drawn by one horse with the two points behind pressing on the ground. On this they sometimes drag home their sheaves, but often convey them home in a kind of open panier, or frame of sticks upon the horse's back.

Of that which is obtained with so much difficulty, nothing surely ought to be wasted; yet their method of clearing their oats from the husk is by parching them in the straw. Thus with the genuine improvidence of savages, they destroy that fodder for want of which their cattle may perish. From this practice they have two petty conveniencies. They dry the grain so that it is easily reduced to meal, and they escape the theft of the thresher. The taste contracted from the fire by the oats, as by every other scorched substance, use must long ago have made grateful. The oats that are not parched must be dried in a kiln.

The barns of Sky I never saw. That which Macleod of Raasay had erected near his house was so contrived, because the harvest is seldom brought home dry as by perpetual perflation to prevent the mow from heating.

Of their gardens I can judge only from their tables. I did not observe that the common greens were wanting, and suppose, that by choosing an advantageous exposition, they can raise all the more hardy esculent plants. Of vegetable fragrance or beauty they are not yet studious. Few vows are made to Flora in the Hebrides.

They gather a little hay, but the grass is mown late; and is so often almost dry and again very wet, before it is housed, that it becomes a collection of withered stalks without taste or fragrance; it must be eaten by cattle that have nothing else, but by most English farmers would be thrown away.

In the islands I have not heard that any subterraneous treasures have been discovered, though where there are mountains, there are commonly minerals. One of the rocks in Col has a black vein, imagined to consist of the ore of lead; but it was never yet opened or essayed. In Sky a black mass was accidentally picked up, and brought into the house of the owner of the land, who found himself strongly inclined to think it a coal, but unhappily it did not burn in the chimney. Common ores would be here of no great value; for what requires to be separated by fire, must, if it were found, be carried away in its mineral state, here being no fewel for the smelting-house or forge. Perhaps by diligent search in this world of stone, some valuable species of marble might be discovered. But neither philosophical curiosity, nor commercial industry, have yet fixed their abode here, where the importunity of immediate want supplied but for the day, and craving on the morrow, has left little room for excursive knowledge or the pleasing fancies of distant profit.

They have lately found a manufacture considerably lucrative. Their rocks abound with kelp, a sea-plant, of which the ashes are melted into glass. They burn kelp in great quantities, and then send it away in ships, which come regularly to purchase them. This new source of riches has raised the rents of many maritime farms; but the tenants pay, like all other tenants, the additional rent with great unwillingness; because they consider the profits of the kelp as the mere product of personal labour, to which the landlord contributes nothing. However, as any man may be said to give, what he gives the power of gaining, he has certainly as much right to profit from the price of kelp as of any thing else found or raised upon his ground.

This new trade has excited a long and eager litigation between Macdonald and Macleod, for a ledge of rocks, which, till the value of kelp was known, neither of them desired the reputation of possessing.

The cattle of Sky are not so small as is commonly believed.[103] Since they have sent their beeves in great numbers to southern marts, they have probably taken more care of their breed. At stated times the annual growth of cattle is driven to a fair, by a general drover, and with the money, which he returns to the farmer, the rents are paid.

The price regularly expected, is from two to three pounds a head: there was once one sold for five pounds. They go from the islands very lean, and are not offered to the butcher, till they have been long fatted in English pastures.

Of their black cattle, some are without horns, called by the Scots 'humble' cows, as we call a bee an 'humble' bee, that wants a sting. Whether this difference be specifick, or accidental, though we inquired with great diligence, we could not be informed. We are not very sure that the bull is ever without horns, though we have been told, that such bulls there are. What is produced by putting a horned and unhorned male and female together, no man has ever tried, that thought the result worthy of observation.

Their horses are, like their cows, of a moderate size. I had no difficulty to mount myself commodiously by the favour of the gentlemen. I heard of very little cows in Barra, and very little horses in Rum, where perhaps no care is taken to prevent that diminution of size, which must always happen, where the greater and the less copulate promiscuously, and the young animal is restrained from growth by penury of sustenance.

The goat is the general inhabitant of the earth, complying with every difference of climate, and of soil. The goats of the Hebrides are like others; nor did I hear any thing of their sheep, to be particularly remarked.

In the penury of these malignant regions, nothing is left that can be converted to food. The goats and the sheep are milked like the cows. A single meal of a goat is a quart, and of a sheep a pint. Such at least was the account, which I could extract from those of whom I am not sure that they ever had inquired.

The milk of goats is much thinner than that of cows, and that of sheep is much thicker. Sheeps milk is never eaten before it is boiled: as it is thick, it must be very liberal of curd, and the people of St Kilda form it into small cheeses.

The stags of the mountains are less than those of our parks, or forests, perhaps not bigger than our fallow deer. Their flesh has no rankness, nor is inferiour in flavour to our common venison. The roebuck I neither saw nor tasted. These are not countries for a regular chase. The deer are not driven with horns and hounds. A sportsman, with his gun in his hand, watches the animal, and when he has wounded him, traces him by the blood.

They have a race of brinded greyhounds, larger and stronger than those with which we course hares, and those are the only dogs used by them for the chase.

Man is by the use of fire-arms made so much an overmatch for other animals, that in all countries, where they are in use, the wild part of the creation sensibly diminishes. There will probably not be long, either stags or roebucks in the islands. All the beasts of chase would have been lost long ago in countries well inhabited, had they not been preserved by laws for the pleasure of the rich.

There are in Sky neither rats nor mice, but the weasel is so frequent, that he is heard in houses rattling behind chests or beds, as rats in England. They probably owe to his predominance that they have no other vermin; for since the great rat took possession of this part of the world, scarce a ship can touch at any port, but some of his race are left behind. They have within these few years began to infest the isle of Col, where being left by some trading vessel, they have increased for want of weasels to oppose them.[104]

The inhabitants of Sky, and of the other islands, which I have seen, are commonly of the middle stature, with fewer among them very tall or very short, than are seen in England, or perhaps, as their numbers are small, the chances of any deviation from the common measure are necessarily few. The tallest men that I saw are among those of higher rank. In regions of barrenness and scarcity, the human race is hindered in its growth by the same causes as other animals.

The ladies have as much beauty here as in other places, but bloom and softness are not to be expected among the lower classes, whose faces are exposed to the rudeness of the climate, and whose features are sometimes contracted by want, and sometimes hardened by the blasts. Supreme beauty is seldom found in cottages or work-shops, even where no real hardships are suffered. To expand the human face to its full perfection, it seems necessary that the mind should co-operate by placidness of content, or consciousness of superiority.

Their strength is proportionate to their size, but they are accustomed to run upon rough ground, and therefore can with great agility skip over the bog, or clamber the mountain. For a campaign in the wastes of America, soldiers better qualified could not have been found. Having little work to do, they are not willing, nor perhaps able to endure a long continuance of manual labour, and therefore considered as habitually idle.

Having never been supplied with these accommodations, which life extensively diversified with trades affords, they supply their wants by very insufficient shifts, and endure many inconveniences, which a little attention would easily relieve. I have seen a horse carrying home the harvest on a crate. Under his tail was a stick for a crupper, held at the two ends by twists of straw. Hemp will grow in their islands, and therefore ropes may be had. If they wanted hemp, they might make better cordage of rushes, or perhaps of nettles, than of straw.

Their method of life neither secures them perpetual health, nor exposes them to any particular diseases. There are physicians in the islands, who, I believe, all practise chirurgery, and all compound their own medicines.

It is generally supposed, that life is longer in places where there are few opportunities of luxury; but I found no instance here of extraordinary longevity. A cottager grows old over his oaten cakes, like a citizen at a turtle feast. He is indeed seldom incommoded by corpulence. Poverty preserves him from sinking under the burden of himself, but he escapes no other injury of time. Instances of long life are often related, which those who hear them are more willing to credit than examine. To be told that any man has attained a hundred years, gives hope and comfort to him who stands trembling on the brink of his own climacterick.

Length of life is distributed impartially to very different modes of life in very different climates; and the mountains have no greater examples of age and health than the low lands, where I was introduced to two ladies of high quality; one of whom, in her ninety-fourth year, presided at her table with the full exercise of all her powers; and the other has attained her eighty-fourth, without any diminution of her vivacity, and with little reason to accuse time of depredations on her beauty.[105]

93

In the islands, as in most other places, the inhabitants are of different rank, and one does not encroach here upon another. Where there is no commerce nor manufacture, he that is born poor can scarcely become rich; and if none are able to buy estates, he that is born to land cannot annihilate his family by selling it. This was once the state of these countries. Perhaps there is no example, till within a century and half, of any family whose estate was alienated otherwise than by violence or forfeiture. Since money has been brought amongst them, they have found, like others, the art of spending more than they receive; and I saw with grief the chief of a very ancient clan, whose island was condemned by law to be sold for the satisfaction of his creditors.[106]

The name of highest dignity is laird, of which there are in the extensive Isle of Sky only three, Macdonald, Macleod, and Mackinnon. The laird is the original owner of the land, whose natural power must be very great, where no man lives but by agriculture; and where the produce of the land is not conveyed through the labyrinths of traffick, but passes directly from the hand that gathers it to the mouth that eats it. The laird has all those in his power that live upon his farms. Kings can, for the most part, only exalt or degrade. The laird at pleasure can feed or starve, can give bread, or withold it. This inherent power was yet strengthened by the kindness of consanguinity, and the reverence of patriarchal authority. The laird was the father of the clan, and his tenants commonly bore his name. And to these principles of original command was added, for many ages, an exclusive right of legal jurisdiction.

This multifarious, and extensive obligation operated with force scarcely credible. Every duty, moral or political, was absorbed in affection and adherence to the chief. Not many years have passed since the clans knew no law but the laird's will. He told them to whom they should be friends or enemies, what King they should obey, and what religion they should profess.

When the Scots first rose in arms against the succession of the house of Hanover, Lovat, the Chief of the Frasers, was in exile for a rape. The Frasers were very numerous, and very zealous against the government. A pardon was sent to Lovat. He came to the English camp, and the clan immediately deserted to him.

Next in dignity to the laird is the tacksman; a large taker or leaseholder of land, of which he keeps part, as a domain, in his own hand, and lets part to under tenants. The tacksman is necessarily a man capable of securing to the laird the whole rent, and is commonly a collateral relation. These 'tacks', or subordinate possessions, were long considered as hereditary, and the occupant was distinguished by the name of the place at which he resided. He held a middle station, by which the highest and the lowest orders were connected. He paid rent and reverence to the laird, and received them from the tenants. This tenure still subsists, with its original operation, but not with the primitive stability. Since the islanders, no longer content to live, have learned the desire of growing rich, an ancient dependent is in danger of giving way to a higher bidder, at the expence of domestick dignity and hereditary power. The stranger, whose money buys him preference, considers himself as paying for all that he has, and is indifferent about the laird's honour or safety. The commodiousness of money is indeed great; but there are some advantages which money cannot buy, and which therefore no wise man will by the love of money be tempted to forego.

I have found in the higher parts of Scotland, men not defective in judgment or general experience, who consider the tacksmen as a useless burden of the ground, as a drone who lives upon the product of an estate, without the right of property, or the merit of labour, and who impoverishes at once the landlord and the tenant. The land, say they, is let to the tacksman at six-pence an acre, and by him to the tenant at ten-pence. Let the owner be the immediate landlord to all the tenants; if he sets the ground at eight-pence, he will increase his revenue by a fourth part, and the tenant's burthen will be diminished by a fifth.

Those who pursue this train of reasoning, seem not sufficiently to inquire whither it will lead them, nor to know that it will equally shew the propriety of suppressing all wholesale trade, of shutting up the shops of every man who sells what he does not make, and of extruding all whose agency and profit intervene between the manufacturer and the consumer. They may, by stretching their understandings a little wider, comprehend, that all those who by undertaking large quantities of manufacture, and affording employment to many labourers, make themselves considered as benefactors to the publick, have only been robbing their workmen with one hand, and their customers with the other. If Crowley[107] had sold only what he could make, and all his smiths had wrought their own iron with their own hammers, he would have lived on less, and they would have sold their work for more. The salaries of superintendents and clerks would have been partly saved, and partly shared, and nails been sometimes cheaper by a farthing in a hundred. But then if the smith could not have found an immediate purchaser, he must have deserted his anvil; if there had by accident at any time been more sellers than buyers, the workmen must have reduced their profit to nothing, by underselling one another; and as no great stock could have been in any hand, no sudden demand of large quantities could have been answered, and the builder must have stood still till the nailer could supply him.

According to these schemes, universal plenty is to begin and end in universal misery. Hope and emulation will be utterly extinguished; and as all must obey the call of immediate necessity, nothing that requires extensive views, or provides for distant consequences, will ever be performed.

To the southern inhabitants of Scotland, the state of the mountains and the islands is equally unknown with that of Borneo or Sumatra. Of both they have only heard a little, and guess the rest. They are strangers to the language and the manners, to the advantages and wants of the people, whose life they would model, and whose evils they would remedy.

Nothing is less difficult than to procure one convenience by the forfeiture of another. A soldier may expedite his march by throwing away his arms. To banish the tacksman is easy, to make a country plentiful by diminishing the people, is an expeditious mode of husbandry; but that abundance, which there is nobody to enjoy, contributes little to human happiness.

As the mind must govern the hands, so in every society the man of intelligence must direct the man of labour. If the tacksmen be taken away, the Hebrides must in their present state be given up to grossness and ignorance; the tenant, for want of instruction, will be unskilful, and for want of admonition will be negligent. The laird in these wide estates, which often consist of islands remote from one another, cannot extend his personal influence to all his tenants; and the steward having no dignity annexed to his character, can have little authority among men taught to pay reverence only to birth, and who regard the tacksman as their hereditary superior; nor can the steward have equal zeal for the prosperity of an estate profitable only to the laird, with the tacksman, who has the laird's income involved in his own.

The only gentlemen in the Islands are the lairds, the tacksmen, and the ministers, who frequently improve their livings by becoming farmers. If the tacksmen be banished, who will be left to impart knowledge, or impress civility? The laird must always be at a distance from the greater part of his lands; and if he resides at all upon them, must drag his days in solitude, having no longer either a friend or a companion; he will therefore depart to some more comfortable residence, and leave the tenants to the wisdom and mercy of a factor.

Of tenants there are different orders, as they have greater or less flock. Land is sometimes leased to a small fellowship, who live in a cluster of huts, called a Tenants Town, and are bound jointly and separately for the payment of their rent. These, I believe, employ in the care of their cattle, and the labour of tillage, a kind of tenants yet lower; who having a hut, with grass for a certain number of cows and sheep, pay their rent by a stipulated quantity of labour.

The condition of domestick servants, or the price of occasional labour, I do not know with certainty. I was told that the maids have sheep, and are allowed to spin for their own clothing; perhaps they have no pecuniary wages, or none but in very wealthy families. The state of life, which has hitherto been purely pastoral, begins now to be a little variegated with commerce; but novelties enter by degrees, and till one mode has fully prevailed over the other, no settled notion can be formed.

Such is the system of insular subordination, which, having little variety, cannot afford much delight in the view, nor long detain the mind in contemplation. The inhabitants were for a long time perhaps not unhappy; but their content was a muddy mixture of pride and ignorance, an indifference for pleasures which they did not know, a blind veneration for their chiefs, and a strong conviction of their own importance.

Their pride has been crushed by the heavy hand of a vindictive conqueror, whose severities have been followed by laws, which, though they cannot be called cruel, have produced much discontent, because they operate upon the surface of life, and make every eye bear witness to subjection. To be compelled to a new dress has always been found painful.

Their chiefs being now deprived of their jurisdiction, have already lost much of their influence; and as they gradually degenerate from patriarchal rulers to rapacious landlords, they will divest themselves of the little that remains.

That dignity which they derived from an opinion of their military importance, the law, which disarmed them, has abated. An old gentleman, delighting himself with the recollection of better days, related, that forty years ago, a chieftain walked out attended by ten or twelve followers, with their arms rattling. That animating rabble has now ceased. The chief has lost his formidable retinue; and the highlander walks his heath unarmed and defenceless, with the peaceable submission of a French peasant or English cottager.

Their ignorance grows every day less, but their knowledge is yet of little other use than to shew them their wants. They are now in the period of education, and feel the uneasiness of discipline, without yet perceiving the benefit of instruction.

The last law, by which the highlanders are deprived of their arms, has operated with efficacy beyond expectation. Of former statutes made with the same design, the execution had been feeble, and the effect inconsiderable.

Concealment was undoubtedly practised, and perhaps often with connivance. There was tenderness, or partiality, on one side, and obstinacy on the other. But the law, which followed the victory of Culloden, found the whole nation dejected and intimidated; informations were given without danger, and without fear, and the arms were collected with such rigour, that every house was despoiled of its defence.

To disarm part of the Highlands, could give no reasonable occasion of complaint. Every government must be allowed the power of taking away the weapon that is lifted against it. But the loyal clans murmured, with some appearance of justice, that after having defended the King, they were forbidden for the future to defend themselves; and that the sword should be forfeited, which had been legally employed. Their case is undoubtedly hard, but in political regulations, good cannot be complete, it can only be predominant.

Whether by disarming a people thus broken into several tribes, and thus remote from the seat of power, more good than evil has been produced, may deserve inquiry. The supreme power in every community has the right of debarring every individual, and every subordinate society from self-defence, only because the supreme power is able to defend them; and therefore where the governor cannot act, he must trust the subject to act for himself. These islands might be wasted with fire and sword before their sovereign would know their distress. A gang of robbers, such as has been lately found confederating themselves in the Highlands, might lay a wide region under contribution. The crew of a petty privateer might land on the largest and most wealthy of the islands, and riot without control in cruelty and waste. It was observed by one of the chiefs of Sky, that fifty armed men might, without resistance, ravage the country. Laws that place the subjects in such a state, contravene the first principles of the compact of authority: they exact obedience and yield no protection.

It affords a generous and manly pleasure to conceive a little nation gathering its fruits and tending its herds with fearless confidence, though it lies open on every side to invasion, where, in contempt of walls and trenches, every man sleeps securely with his sword beside him; where all on the first approach of hostility come together at the call to battle, as at a summons to a festal show; and committing their cattle to the care of those whom age or nature has disabled, engage the enemy with that competition for hazard and for glory, which operate in men that fight under the eye of those, whose dislike or kindness they have always considered as the greatest evil or the greatest good.

This was, in the beginning of the present century, the state of the Highlands. Every man was a soldier, who partook of national confidence, and interested himself in national honour. To lose this spirit, is to lose what no small advantage will compensate.

It may likewise deserve to be inquired, whether a great nation ought to be totally commercial? Whether amidst the uncertainty of human affairs, too much attention to one mode of happiness may not endanger others? Whether the pride of riches must not sometimes have recourse to the protection of courage? And whether, if it be necessary to preserve in some part of the empire the military spirit, it can submit more commodiously in any place, than in remote and unprofitable provinces, where it can commonly do little harm, and whence it may be called forth at any sudden exigence?

It must however be confessed, that a man, who places honour only in successful violence, is a very troublesome and pernicious animal in time of peace; and that the martial character cannot prevail in a whole people, but by the diminution of all other virtues. He that is accustomed to resolve all right into conquest, will have very little tenderness or equity. All the friendship in such a life can be only a confederacy of invasion, or alliance of defence. The strong must flourish by force, and the weak subsist by stratagem.

Till the highlanders lost their ferocity, with their arms, they suffered from each other all that malignity could dictate, or precipitance could act. Every provocation was revenged with blood, and no man that ventured into a numerous company, by whatever occasion brought together, was sure of returning without a wound. If they are now exposed to foreign hostilities, they may talk of the danger, but can seldom feel it. If they are no longer martial, they are no longer quarrelsome. Misery is caused for the most part, not by a heavy crush of disaster, but by the corrosion of less visible evils, which canker enjoyment, and undermine security. The visit of an invader is necessarily rare, but domestick animosities allow no cessation.

The abolition of the local jurisdictions, which had for so many ages been exercised by the chiefs, has likewise its evil and its good. The feudal constitution naturally diffused itself into long ramifications of subordinate authority. To this general temper of the government was added the peculiar form of the country, broken by mountains into many subdivisions scarcely accessible but to the natives, and guarded by passes, or perplexed with intricacies, through which national justice could not find its way.

The power of deciding controversies, and of punishing offences, as some such power there must always be, was intrusted to the lairds of the country, to those whom the people considered as their natural judges. It cannot be supposed that a rugged proprietor of the rocks, unprincipled and unenlightened, was a nice resolver of entangled claims, or very exact in proportioning punishment to offences. But the more he indulged his own will, the more he held his vassals in dependance. Prudence and innocence, without the favour of the chief, conferred no security; and crimes involved no danger, when the judge was resolute to acquit.

When the chiefs were men of knowledge and virtue, the convenience of a domestick judicature was great. No long journies were necessary, nor artificial delays could be practised; the character, the alliances, and interests of the litigants were known to the court, and all false pretences were easily detected. The sentence, when it was past, could not be evaded; the power of the laird superseded formalities, and justice could not be defeated by interest or stratagem.

I doubt not but that since the regular judges have made their circuits through the whole country, right has been every where more wisely, and more equally distributed; the complaint is, that litigation is grown troublesome, and that the magistrates are too few, and therefore often too remote for general convenience.

Many of the smaller islands have no legal officer within them. I once asked, if a crime should be committed, by what authority the offender could be seized? and was told, that the laird would exert his right; a right which he must now usurp, but which surely necessity must vindicate, and which is therefore yet exercised in lower degrees, by some of the proprietors, when legal processes cannot be obtained.

In all greater questions, however, there is now happily an end to all fear or hope from malice or from favour. The roads are secure in those places through which, forty years ago, no traveller could pass without a convoy. All trials of right by the sword are forgotten, and the mean are in as little danger from the powerful as in other places. No scheme of policy has, in any country, yet brought the rich and poor on equal terms into courts of judicature. Perhaps experience, improving on experience, may in time effect it.

Those who have long enjoyed dignity and power, ought not to lose it without some equivalent. There was paid to the chiefs by the publick, in exchange for their privileges, perhaps a sum greater than most of them had ever possessed, which excited a thirst for riches, of which it shewed them the use. When the power of birth and station ceases, no hope remains but from the prevalence of money. Power and wealth supply the place of each other. Power confers the ability of gratifying our desire without the consent of others. Wealth enables us to obtain the consent of others to our gratification. Power, simply considered, whatever it confers on one, must take from another. Wealth enables its owner to give to others, by taking only from himself. Power pleases the violent and proud: wealth delights the placid and the timorous. Youth therefore flies at power, and age grovels after riches.

The chiefs, divested of their prerogatives, necessarily turned their thoughts to the improvement of their revenues, and expect more rent, as they have less homage. The tenant, who is far from perceiving that his condition is made better in the same proportion, as that of his landlord is made worse, does not immediately see why his industry is to be taxed more heavily than before. He refuses to pay the demand, and is ejected; the ground is then let to a stranger, who perhaps brings a larger stock, but who, taking the land at its full price, treats with the laird upon equal terms, and considers him not as a chief, but as a trafficker in land. Thus the estate perhaps is improved, but the clan is broken.

It seems to be the general opinion, that the rents have been raised with too much eagerness. Some regard must be paid to prejudice. Those who have hitherto paid but little, will not suddenly be persuaded to pay much, though they can afford it. As ground is gradually improved, and the value of money decreases, the rent may be raised without any diminution of the farmer's profits: yet it is necessary in these countries, where the ejection of a tenant is a greater evil, than in more populous places, to consider not merely what the land will produce, but with what ability the inhabitant can cultivate it. A certain flock can allow but a certain payment; for if the land be doubled, and the flock remains the same, the tenant becomes no richer. The proprietors of the Highlands might perhaps often increase their income, by subdividing the farms, and allotting to every occupier only so many acres as he can profitably employ, but that they want people.

There seems now, whatever be the cause, to be through a great part of the Highlands a general discontent. That adherence, which was lately professed by every man to the chief of his name, has now little prevalence; and he that cannot live as he desires at home, listens to the tale of fortunate islands, and happy regions, where every man may have land of his own, and eat the product of his labour without a superior.

Those who have obtained grants of American lands, have, as is well known, invited settlers from all quarters of the globe; and among other places, where oppression might produce a wish for new habitations, their emissaries would not fail to try their persuasions in the isles of Scotland, where at the time when the clans were newly disunited from their chiefs, and exasperated by unprecedented exactions, it is no wonder that they prevailed.

Whether the mischiefs of emigration were immediately perceived, may be justly questioned. They who went first, were probably such as could best be spared; but the accounts sent by the earliest adventurers, whether true or false, inclined many to follow them; and whole neighbourhoods formed parties for removal; so that departure from their native country is no longer exile. He that goes thus accompanied, carries with him all that makes life pleasant. He sits down in a better climate, surrounded by his kindred and his friends: they carry with them their language, their opinions, their popular songs, and hereditary merriment: they change nothing but the place of their abode; and of that change they perceive the benefit.

This is the real effect of emigration, if those that go away together settle on the same spot, and preserve their ancient union. But some relate that these adventurous visitants of unknown regions, after a voyage passed in dreams of plenty and felicity, are dispersed at last upon a sylvan wilderness, where their first years must be spent in toil, to clear the ground which is afterwards to be tilled, and that the whole effect of their undertaking is only more fatigue and equal scarcity.

Both accounts may be suspected. Those who are gone will endeavour by every art to draw others after them; for as their numbers are greater, they will provide better for themselves. When Nova Scotia was first peopled, I remember a letter, published under the character of a New Planter, who related how much the climate put him in mind of Italy.[108] Such intelligence the Hebridians probably receive from their transmarine correspondents. But with equal temptations on interest, and perhaps with no greater niceness of veracity, the owners of the islands spread stories of American hardships to keep their people content at home.

Some method to stop this epidemick desire of wandering, which spreads its contagion from valley to valley, deserves to be sought with great diligence. In more fruitful countries, the removal of one only makes room for the succession of another: but in the Hebrides, the loss of an inhabitant leaves a lasting vacuity; for nobody born in any other parts of the world will choose this country for their residence; and an island once depopulated will remain a desert, as long as the present facility of travel gives every one, who is discontented and unsettled, the choice of his abode.

Let it be inquired, whether the first intention of those who are fluttering on the wing, and collecting a flock that they may take their flight, be to attain good, or to avoid evil. If they are dissatisfied with that part of the globe, which their birth has allotted them, and resolve not to live without the pleasures of happier climates; if they long for bright suns, and calm skies, and flowery fields, and fragrant gardens, I know not by what eloquence they can be persuaded, or by what offers they can be hired to stay.

But if they are driven from their native country by positive evils, and disgusted by ill-treatment, real or imaginary, it were fit to remove their grievances, and quiet their resentment; since, if they have been hitherto undutiful subjects, they will not much mend their principles by American conversation.

To allure them into the army, it was thought proper to indulge them in the continuance of their national dress. If this concession could have any effect, it might easily be made.[109] That dissimilitude of appearance, which was supposed to keep them distinct from the rest of the nation, might disincline them from coalescing with the Pensylvanians, or people of Connecticut. If the restitution of their arms will reconcile them to their country, let them have again those weapons, which will not be more mischievous at home than in the Colonies. That they may not fly from the increase of rent, I know not whether the general good does not require that the landlords be, for a time, restrained in their demands, and kept quiet by pensions proportionate to their loss.

To hinder insurrection, by driving away the people, and to govern peaceably, by having no subjects, is an expedient that argues no great profundity of politicks. To soften the obdurate, to convince the mistaken, to mollify the resentful, are worthy of a statesman; but it affords a legislator little self-applause to consider, that where there was formerly an insurrection, there is now a wilderness.

It has been a question often agitated without solution, why those northern regions are now so thinly peopled, which formerly overwhelmed with their armies the Roman empire. The question supposes what I believe is not true, that they had once more inhabitants than they could maintain, and overflowed only because they were full.

This is to estimate the manners of all countries and ages by our own. Migration, while the state of life was unsettled, and there was little communication of intelligence between distant places, was among the wilder nations of Europe, capricious and casual. An adventurous projector heard of a fertile coast unoccupied, and led out a colony; a chief of renown for bravery, called the young men together, and led them out to try what fortune would present. When Cæsar was in Gaul, he found the Helvetians preparing to go they knew not whither, and put a stop to their motions.[110] They settled again in their own country, where they were so far from wanting room, that they had accumulated three years provision for their march.

The religion of the north was military; if they could not find enemies, it was their duty to make them: they travelled in quest of danger, and willingly took the chance of Empire or Death. If their troops were numerous, the countries from which they were collected are of vast extent, and without much exuberance of people great armies may be raised where every man is a soldier. But their true numbers were never known. Those who were conquered by them are their historians, and shame may have excited them to say, that they were overwhelmed with multitudes. To count is a modern practice, the ancient method was to guess; and when numbers are guessed they are always magnified.

Thus England has for several years been filled with the achievements of seventy thousand highlanders employed in America.[111] I have heard from an English officer, not much inclined to favour them, that their behaviour deserved a very high degree of military praise; but their number has been much exaggerated. One of the ministers told me, that seventy thousand men could not have been found in all the Highlands, and that more than twelve thousand never took the field. Those that went to the American war, went to destruction. Of the old Highland regiment, consisting of twelve hundred, only seventy-six survived to see their country again.

The Gothick swarms have at least been multiplied with equal liberality. That they bore no great proportion to the inhabitants, in whose countries they settled, is plain from the paucity of northern words now found in the provincial languages.[112] Their country was not deserted for want of room, because it was covered with forests of vast extent; and the first effect of plenitude of inhabitants is the destruction of wood. As the Europeans spread over America, the lands are gradually laid naked.

I would not be understood to say, that necessity had never any part in their expeditions. A nation, whose agriculture is scanty or unskilful, may be driven out by famine. A nation of hunters may have exhausted their game. I only affirm that the northern regions were not, when their irruptions subdued the Romans, overpeopled with regard to their real extent of territory, and power of fertility. In a country fully inhabited, however afterward laid waste, evident marks will remain of its former populousness. But of Scandinavia and Germany, nothing is known but that as we trace their state upwards into antiquity, their woods were greater, and their cultivated ground was less.

That causes very different from want of room may produce a general disposition to seek another country is apparent from the present conduct of the highlanders, who are in some places ready to threaten a total secession. The numbers which have already gone, though like other numbers they may be magnified, are very great, and such as if they had gone together and agreed upon any certain settlement, might have founded an independent government in the depths of the western continent. Nor are they only the lowest and most indigent; many men of considerable wealth have taken with them their train of labourers and dependants; and if they continue the feudal scheme of polity, may establish new clans in the other hemisphere.

That the immediate motives of their desertion must be imputed to their landlords, may be reasonably concluded, because some lairds of more prudence and less rapacity have kept their vassals undiminished. From Raasa only one man had been seduced, and at Col there was no wish to go away.

The traveller who comes hither from more opulent countries, to speculate upon the remains of pastoral life, will not much wonder that a common highlander has no strong adherence to his native soil; for of animal enjoyments, or of physical good, he leaves nothing that he may not find again wheresoever he may be thrown.

The habitations of men in the Hebrides may be distinguished into huts and houses. By a house, I mean a building with one story over another; by a hut, a dwelling with only one floor. The laird, who formerly lived in a castle, now lives in a house; sometimes sufficiently neat, but seldom very spacious or splendid. The tacksmen and the ministers have commonly houses. Wherever there is a house, the stranger finds a welcome, and to the other evils of exterminating tacksmen may be added the unavoidable cessation of hospitality, or the devolution of too heavy a burden on the ministers.

Of the houses little can be said. They are small, and by the necessity of accumulating stores, where there are so few opportunities of purchase, the rooms are very heterogeneously filled. With want of cleanliness it were ingratitude to reproach them. The servants having been bred upon the naked earth, think every floor clean, and the quick succession of guests, perhaps not always over-elegant, does not allow much time for adjusting their apartments.

Huts are of many gradations; from murky dens, to commodious dwellings.

The wall of a common hut is always built without mortar, by a skilful adaptation of loose stones. Sometimes perhaps a double wall of stones is raised, and the intermediate space filled with earth. The air is thus completely excluded. Some walls are, I think, formed of turfs, held together by a wattle, or texture of twigs. Of the meanest huts, the first room is lighted by the entrance, and the second by the smoke-hole. The fire is usually made in the middle. But there are huts, or dwellings, of only one story, inhabited by gentlemen, which have walls cemented with mortar, glass windows, and boarded floors. Of these all have chimneys, and some chimneys have grates.

The house and the furniture are not always nicely suited. We were driven once, by missing a passage, to the hut of a gentleman, where, after a very liberal supper, when I was conducted to my chamber, I found an elegant bed of Indian cotton, spread with fine sheets. The accommodation was flattering; I undressed myself, and felt my feet in the mire. The bed stood upon the bare earth, which a long course of rain had softened to a puddle.

In pastoral countries the condition of the lowest rank of people is sufficiently wretched. Among manufacturers, men that have no property may have art and industry, which make them necessary, and therefore valuable. But where flocks and corn are the only wealth, there are always more hands than work, and of that work there is little in which skill and dexterity can be much distinguished. He therefore who is born poor never can be rich. The son merely occupies the place of the father, and life knows nothing of progression or advancement.

The petty tenants, and labouring peasants, live in miserable cabins, which afford them little more than shelter from the storms. The Boor of Norway is said to make all his own utensils. In the Hebrides, whatever might be their ingenuity, the want of wood leaves them no materials. They are probably content with such accommodations as stones of different forms and sizes can afford them.

Their food is not better than their lodging. They seldom taste the flesh of land animals; for here are no markets. What each man eats is from his own flock. The great effect of money is to break property into small parts. In towns, he that has a shilling may have a piece of meat; but where there is no commerce, no man can eat mutton but by killing a sheep.

Fish in fair weather they need not want; but, I believe, man never lives long on fish, but by constraint; he will rather feed upon roots and berries.

The only fewel of the islands is peat. Their wood is all consumed, and coal they have not yet found. Peat is dug out of the marshes, from the depth of one foot to that of six. That is accounted the best which is nearest the surface. It appears to be a mass of black earth held together by vegetable fibres. I know not whether the earth be bituminous, or whether the fibres be not the only combustible part; which, by heating the interposed earth red hot, make a burning mass. The heat is not very strong nor lasting. The ashes are yellowish, and in a large quantity. When they dig peat, they cut it into square pieces, and pile it up to dry beside the house. In some places it has an offensive smell. It is like wood charked[113] for the smith. The common method of making peat fires, is by heaping it on the hearth; but it burns well in grates, and in the best houses is so used.

The common opinion is, that peat grows again where it has been cut; which, as it seems to be chiefly a vegetable substance, is not unlikely to be true, whether known or not to those who relate it.

There are water mills in Sky and Raasa; but where they are too far distant, the house-wives grind their oats with a quern, or hand-mill, which consists of two stones, about a foot and a half in diameter; the lower is a little convex, to which the concavity of the upper must be fitted. In the middle of the upper stone is a round hole, and on one side is a long handle. The grinder sheds the corn gradually into the hole with one hand, and works the handle round with the other. The corn slides down the convexity of the lower stone, and by the motion of the upper is ground in its passage. These stones are found in Lochabar.

The islands afford few pleasures, except to the hardy sportsman, who can tread the moor and climb the mountain. The distance of one family from another, in a country where travelling has so much difficulty, makes frequent intercourse impracticable. Visits last several days, and are commonly paid by water; yet I never saw a boat furnished with benches, or made commodious by any addition to the first fabrick. Conveniencies are not missed where they never were enjoyed.

The solace which the bagpipe can give, they have long enjoyed; but among other changes, which the last Revolution introduced, the use of the bagpipe begins to be forgotten. Some of the chief families still entertain a piper, whose office was anciently hereditary. Macrimmon was piper to Macleod, and Rankin to Maclean of Col.

The tunes of the bagpipe are traditional. There has been in Sky, beyond all time of memory, a college of pipers, under the direction of Macrimmon, which is not quite extinct.[114] There was another in Mull, superintended by Rankin, which expired about sixteen years ago. To these colleges, while the pipe retained its honour, the students of musick repaired for education. I have had my dinner exhilarated by the bagpipe, at Armidale, at Dunvegan, and in Col.

The general conversation of the islanders has nothing particular. I did not meet with the inquisitiveness of which I have read, and suspect the judgment to have been rashly made. A stranger of curiosity comes into a place where a stranger is seldom seen: he importunes the people with questions, of which they cannot guess the motive, and gazes with surprise on things which they, having had them always before their eyes, do not suspect of any thing wonderful. He appears to them like some being of another world, and then thinks it peculiar that they take their turn to inquire whence he comes, and whither he is going.

The islands were long unfurnished with instruction for youth, and none but the sons of gentlemen would have any literature. There are now parochial schools, to which the lord of every manor pays a certain stipend.

Here the children are taught to read; but by the rule of their institution, they teach only English, so that the natives read a language which they may never use or understand. If a parish, which often happens, contains several islands, the school being but in one, cannot assist the rest. This is the state of Col, which, however, is more enlightened than some other places; for the deficiency is supplied by a young gentleman, who, for his own improvement, travels every year on foot over the Highlands to the session at Aberdeen; and at his return, during the vacation, teaches to read and write in his native island.[115]

In Sky there are two grammar schools, where boarders are taken to be regularly educated. The price of board is from three pounds, to four pounds ten shillings a year, and that of instruction is half a crown a quarter. But the scholars are birds of passage, who live at school only in the summer; for in winter provisions cannot be made for any considerable number in one place. This periodical dispersion impresses strongly the scarcity of these countries.

Having heard of no boarding-school for ladies nearer than Inverness, I suppose their education is generally domestick. The elder daughters of the higher families are sent into the world, and may contribute by their acquisitions to the improvement of the rest.

Women must here study to be either pleasing or useful. Their deficiencies are seldom supplied by very liberal fortunes. A hundred pounds is a portion beyond the hope of any but the laird's daughter. They do not indeed often give money with their daughters; the question is, how many cows a young lady will bring her husband. A rich maiden has from ten to forty; but two cows are a decent fortune for one who pretends to no distinction.

The religion of the islands is that of the Kirk of Scotland. The gentlemen with whom I conversed are all inclined to the English liturgy; but they are obliged to maintain the established minister, and the country is too poor to afford payment to another, who must live wholly on the contribution of his audience.[116]

They therefore all attend the worship of the Kirk, as often as a visit from their minister, or the practicability of travelling gives them opportunity; nor have they any reason to complain of insufficient pastors; for I saw not one in the islands, whom I had reason to think either deficient in learning, or irregular in life; but found several with whom I could not converse without wishing, as my respect increased, that they had not been Presbyterians.

The ancient rigour of Puritanism is now very much relaxed, though all are not yet equally enlightened. I sometimes met with prejudices sufficiently malignant, but they were prejudices of ignorance. The ministers in the islands had attained such knowledge as may justly be admired in men, who have no motive to study, but generous curiosity, or, what is still better, desire of usefulness; with such politeness as so narrow a circle of converse could not have supplied, but to minds naturally disposed to elegance.

Reason and truth will prevail at last. The most learned of the Scottish doctors would now gladly admit a form of prayer,[117] if the people would endure it. The zeal or rage of congregations has its different degrees. In some parishes the Lord's Prayer is suffered: in others it is still rejected as a form; and he that should make it part of his supplication would be suspected of heretical pravity.

The principle upon which extemporary prayer was originally introduced, is no longer admitted. The minister formerly, in the effusion of his prayer, expected immediate, and perhaps perceptible inspiration, and therefore thought it his duty not to think before what he should say. It is now universally confessed, that men pray as they speak on other occasions, according to the general measure of their abilities and attainments. Whatever each may think of a form prescribed by another, he cannot but believe that he can himself compose by study and meditation a better prayer than will rise in his mind at a sudden call; and if he has any hope of supernatural help, why may he not as well receive it when he writes as when he speaks.

In the variety of mental powers, some must perform extemporary prayer with much imperfection; and in the eagerness and rashness of contradictory opinions, if publick liturgy be left to the private judgment of every minister, the congregation may often be offended or misled.

There is in Scotland, as among ourselves, a restless suspicion of popish machinations, and a clamour of numerous converts to the Romish religion. The report is, I believe, in both parts of the island equally false. The Romish religion is professed only in Egg and Canna, two small islands, into which the Reformation never made its way.[118] If any missionaries are busy in the Highlands, their zeal entitles them to respect, even from those who cannot think favourably of their doctrine.

The political tenets of the islanders I was not curious to investigate, and they were not eager to obtrude. Their conversation is decent and inoffensive. They disdain to drink for their principles, and there is no disaffection at their tables. I never heard a health offered by a highlander that might not have circulated with propriety within the precincts of the King's palace.

Legal government has yet something of novelty to which they cannot perfectly conform. The ancient spirit, that appealed only to the sword, is yet among them. The tenant of Scalpa, an island belonging to Macdonald, took no care to bring his rent; when the landlord talked of exacting payment, he declared his resolution to keep his ground, and drive all intruders from the island, and continued to feed his cattle as on his own land, till it became necessary for the Sheriff to dislodge him by violence.

The various kinds of superstition which prevailed here, as in all other regions of ignorance, are by the diligence of the ministers almost extirpated.

Of Browny, mentioned by Martin, nothing has been heard for many years. Browny was a sturdy fairy; who, if he was fed, and kindly treated, would, as they said, do a great deal of work. They now pay him no wages, and are content to labour for themselves.

In Troda, within these three-and-thirty years, milk was put every Saturday for *Greogach*, or the 'Old Man with the Long Beard'.[119] Whether *Greogach* was courted as kind, or dreaded as terrible, whether they meant, by giving him the milk, to obtain good, or avert evil, I was not informed. The minister is now living by whom the practice was abolished.

They have still among them a great number of charms for the cure of different diseases; they are all invocations, perhaps transmitted to them from the times of popery, which increasing knowledge will bring into disuse.

They have opinions, which cannot be ranked with superstition, because they regard only natural effects. They expect better crops of grain, by sowing their seed in the moon's increase. The moon has great influence in vulgar philosophy. In my memory it was a precept annually given in one of the English Almanacks, 'to kill hogs when the moon was increasing, and the bacon would prove the better in boiling'.

We should have had little claim to the praise of curiosity, if we had not endeavoured with particular attention to examine the question of the second sight.[120] Of an opinion received for centuries by a whole nation, and supposed to be confirmed through its whole descent, by a series of successive facts, it is desirable that the truth should be established, or the fallacy detected.

The second sight is an impression made either by the mind upon the eye, or by the eye upon the mind, by which things distant or future are perceived, and seen as if they were present. A man on a journey far from home falls from his horse, another, who is perhaps at work about the house, sees him bleeding on the ground, commonly with a landscape of the place where the accident befalls him. Another seer, driving home his cattle, or wandering in idleness, or musing in the sunshine, is suddenly surprised by the appearance of a bridal ceremony, or funeral procession, and counts the mourners or attendants, of whom, if he knows them, he relates the names, if he knows them not, he can describe the dresses. Things distant are seen at the instant when they happen. Of things future I know not that there is any rule for determining the time between the sight and the event.

This receptive faculty, for power it cannot be called, is neither voluntary nor constant. The appearances have no dependence upon choice: they cannot be summoned, detained, or recalled. The impression is sudden, and the effect often painful.

By the term second sight, seems to be meant a mode of seeing, superadded to that which Nature generally bestows. In the Erse it is called *taisch*;[121] which signifies likewise a spectre, or a vision. I know not, nor is it likely that the highlanders ever examined, whether by *taisch*, used for second sight, they mean the power of seeing, or the thing seen.

I do not find it to be true, as it is reported, that to the second sight nothing is presented but phantoms of evil. Good seems to have the same proportion in those visionary scenes, as it obtains in real life: almost all remarkable events have evil for their basis; and are either miseries incurred, or miseries escaped. Our sense is so much stronger of what we suffer, than of what we enjoy, that the ideas of pain predominate in almost every mind. What is recollection but a revival of vexations, or history but a record of wars, treasons, and calamities? Death, which is considered as the greatest evil, happens to all. The greatest good, be it what it will, is the lot but of a part.

That they should often see death is to be expected; because death is an event frequent and important. But they see likewise more pleasing incidents. A gentleman told me, that when he had once gone far from his own island, one of his labouring servants predicted his return, and described the livery of his attendant, which he had never worn at home; and which had been, without any previous design, occasionally given him.

Our desire of information was keen, and our inquiry frequent. Mr Boswell's frankness and gaiety made every body communicative; and we heard many tales of these airy shows, with more or less evidence and distinctness.

It is the common talk of the Lowland Scots, that the notion of the second sight is wearing away with other superstitions; and that its reality is no longer supposed, but by the grossest people. How far its prevalence ever extended, or what ground it has lost, I know not. The islanders of all degrees, whether of rank or understanding, universally admit it, except the ministers, who universally deny it, and are suspected to deny it, in consequence of a system, against conviction. One of them honestly told me, that he came to Sky with a resolution not to believe it.[122]

Strong reasons for incredulity will readily occur. This faculty of seeing things out of sight is local, and commonly useless. It is a breach of the common order of things, without any visible reason or perceptible benefit. It is ascribed only to a people very little enlightened; and among them, for the most part, to the mean and the ignorant.

To the confidence of these objections it may be replied, that by presuming to determine what is fit, and what is beneficial, they presuppose more knowledge of the universal system than man has attained; and therefore depend upon principles too complicated and extensive for our comprehension; and that there can be no security in the consequence, when the premises are not understood; that the second sight is only wonderful because it is rare, for, considered in itself, it involves no more difficulty than dreams, or perhaps than the regular exercise of the cogitative faculty; that a general opinion of communicative impulses, or visionary representations, has prevailed in all ages and all nations; that particular instances have been given, with such evidence, as neither Bacon nor Boyle[123] has been able to resist; that sudden impressions, which the event has verified, have been felt by more than own or publish them; that the second sight of the Hebrides implies only the local frequency of a power, which is nowhere totally unknown; and that where we are unable to decide by antecedent reason, we must be content to yield to the force of testimony.

By pretension to second sight, no profit was ever sought or gained. It is an involuntary affection, in which neither hope nor fear are known to have any part. Those who profess to feel it, do not boast of it as a privilege, nor are considered by others as advantageously distinguished. They have no temptation to feign; and their hearers have no motive to encourage the imposture.

To talk with any of these seers is not easy. There is one living in Sky, with whom we would have gladly conversed; but he was very gross and ignorant, and knew no English. The proportion in these countries of the poor to the rich is such, that if we suppose the quality to be accidental, it can very rarely happen to a man of education; and yet on such men it has sometimes fallen. There is now a second-sighted gentleman in the Highlands, who complains of the terrors to which he is exposed.

The foresight of the seers is not always prescience: they are impressed with images, of which the event only shews them the meaning. They tell what they have seen to others, who are at that time not more knowing than themselves, but may become at last very adequate witnesses, by comparing the narrative with its verification.

To collect sufficient testimonies for the satisfaction of the publick, or of ourselves, would have required more time than we could bestow. There is, against it, the seeming analogy of things confusedly seen, and little understood; and for it, the indistinct cry of national persuasion, which may be perhaps resolved at last into prejudice and tradition. I never could advance my curiosity to conviction; but came away at last only willing to believe.

As there subsists no longer in the islands much of that peculiar and discriminative form of life, of which the idea had delighted our imagination, we were willing to listen to such accounts of past times as would be given us. But we soon found what memorials were to be expected from an illiterate people, whose whole time is a series of distress; where every morning is labouring with expedients for the evening; and where all mental pains or pleasure arose from the dread of winter, the expectation of spring, the caprices of their chiefs, and the motions of the neighbouring clans; where there was neither shame from ignorance, nor pride in knowledge; neither curiosity to inquire, nor vanity to communicate.

The chiefs indeed were exempt from urgent penury, and daily difficulties; and in their houses were preserved what accounts remained of past ages. But the chiefs were sometimes ignorant and careless, and sometimes kept busy by turbulence and contention; and one generation of ignorance effaces the whole series of unwritten history. Books are faithful repositories, which may be a while neglected or forgotten; but when they are opened again, will again impart their instruction: memory, once interrupted, is not to be recalled. Written learning is a fixed luminary, which, after the cloud that had hidden it has past away, is again bright in its proper station. Tradition is but a meteor, which, if once it falls, cannot be rekindled.

It seems to be universally supposed, that much of the local history was preserved by the bards, of whom one is said to have been retained by every great family. After these bards were some of my first inquiries; and I received such answers as, for a while, made me please myself with my increase of knowledge; for I had not then learned how to estimate the narration of a highlander.

They said that a great family had a bard and a *senachi*, who were the poet and historian of the house;[124] and an old gentleman told me that he remembered one of each. Here was a dawn of intelligence. Of men that had lived within memory, some certain knowledge might be attained. Though the office had ceased, its effects might continue; the poems might be found, though there was no poet.

Another conversation indeed informed me, that the same man was both bard and *senachi*. This variation discouraged me; but as the practice might be different in different times, or at the same time in different families, there was yet no reason for supposing that I must necessarily sit down in total ignorance.

Soon after I was told by a gentleman,[125] who is generally acknowledged the greatest master of Hebridian antiquities, that there had indeed once been both bards and *senachies*; and that *senachi* signified 'the man of talk', or of conversation; but that neither bard nor *senachi* had existed for some centuries. I have no reason to suppose it exactly known at what time the custom ceased, nor did it probably cease in all houses at once. But whenever the practice of recitation was disused, the works, whether poetical or historical, perished with the authors; for in those times nothing had been written in the Earse language.

Whether the 'man of talk' was a historian, whose office was to tell truth, or a story-teller, like those which were in the last century, and perhaps are now among the Irish, whose trade was only to amuse, it now would be vain to inquire.[126]

Most of the domestick offices were, I believe, hereditary; and probably the laureat of a clan was always the son of the last laureat. The history of the race could not otherwise be communicated, or retained; but what genius could be expected in a poet by inheritance?

The nation was wholly illiterate. Neither bards nor *senachies* could write or read;[127] but if they were ignorant, there was no danger of detection; they were believed by those whose vanity they flattered.

The recital of genealogies, which has been considered as very efficacious to the preservation of a true series of ancestry, was anciently made, when the heir of the family came to manly age. This practice has never subsisted within time of memory, nor was much credit due to such rehearsers, who might obtrude fictitious pedigrees, either to please their masters, or to hide the deficiency of their own memories.

Where the chiefs of the Highlands have found the histories of their descent is difficult to tell; for no Earse genealogy was ever written. In general this only is evident, that the principal house of a clan must be very ancient, and that those must have lived long in a place, of whom it is not known when they came thither.

Thus hopeless are all attempts to find any traces of Highland learning. Nor are their primitive customs and ancient manner of life otherwise than very faintly and uncertainly remembered by the present race.

The peculiarities which strike the native of a commercial country, proceeded in a great measure from the want of money. To the servants and dependents that were not domesticks, and if an estimate be made from the capacity of any of their old houses which I have seen, their domesticks could have been but few, were appropriated certain portions of land for their support. Macdonald has a piece of ground yet, called the bards or *senachies* field. When a beef was killed for the house, particular parts were claimed as fees by the several officers, or workmen. What was the right of each I have not learned. The head belonged to the smith, and the udder of a cow to the piper: the weaver had likewise his particular part; and so many pieces followed these prescriptive claims, that the laird's was at last but little.[128]

The payment of rent in kind has been so long disused in England, that it is totally forgotten. It was practised very lately in the Hebrides, and probably still continues, not only in St Kilda, where money is not yet known, but in others of the smaller and remoter islands. It were perhaps to be desired, that no change in this particular should have been made. When the laird could only eat the produce of his lands, he was under the necessity of residing upon them; and when the tenant could not convert his stock into more portable riches, he could never be tempted away from his farm, from the only place where he could be wealthy. Money confounds subordination, by overpowering the distinctions of rank and birth, and weakens authority by supplying power of resistance, or expedients for escape. The feudal system is formed for a nation employed in agriculture, and has never long kept its hold where gold and silver have become common.

Their arms were anciently the *glaymore*,[129] or great two-handed sword, and afterwards the two-edged sword and target, or buckler, which was sustained on the left arm. In the midst of the target, which was made of wood, covered with leather, and studded with nails, a slender lance, about two feet long, was sometimes fixed; it was heavy and cumberous, and accordingly has for some time past been gradually laid aside. Very few targets were at Culloden. The dirk, or broad dagger, I am afraid, was of more use in private quarrels than in battles. The Lochaber-ax is only a slight alteration of the old English bill.

After all that has been said of the force and terrour of the Highland sword, I could not find that the art of defence was any part of common education. The gentlemen were perhaps sometimes skilful gladiators, but the common men had no other powers than those of violence and courage. Yet it is well known, that the onset of the highlanders was very formidable. As an army cannot consist of philosophers, a panick is easily excited by any unwonted mode of annoyance. New dangers are naturally magnified; and men accustomed only to exchange bullets at a distance, and rather to hear their enemies than see them, are discouraged and amazed when they find themselves encountered hand to hand, and catch the gleam of steel flashing in their faces.

The Highland weapons gave opportunity for many exertions of personal courage, and sometimes for single combats in the field; like those which occur so frequently in fabulous wars. At Falkirk, a gentleman now living, was, I suppose after the retreat of the King's troops, engaged at a distance from the rest with an Irish dragoon. They were both skilful swordsmen, and the contest was not easily decided: the dragoon at last had the advantage, and the highlander called for quarter; but quarter was refused him, and the fight continued till he was reduced to defend himself upon his knee. At that instant one of the Macleods came to his rescue; who, as it is said, offered quarter to the dragoon, but he thought himself obliged to reject what he had before refused, and, as battle gives little time to deliberate, was immediately killed.[130]

Funerals were formerly solemnized by calling multitudes together, and entertaining them at great expence. This emulation of useless cost has been for some time discouraged, and at last in the Isle of Sky is almost suppressed.

Of the Earse language, as I understand nothing, I cannot say more than I have been told. It is the rude speech of a barbarous people, who had few thoughts to express, and were content, as they conceived grossly, to be grossly understood. After what has been lately talked of Highland bards, and Highland genius, many will startle when they are told, that the Earse never was a written language;[131] that there is not in the world an Earse manuscript a hundred years old; and that the sounds of the highlanders were never expressed by letters, till some little books of piety were translated, and a metrical version of the Psalms was made by the Synod of Argyle.[132] Whoever therefore now writes in this language, spells according to his own perception of the sound, and his own idea of the power of the letters. The Welsh and the Irish are cultivated tongues. The Welsh, two hundred years ago, insulted their English neighbours for the instability of their Orthography;[133] while the Earse merely floated in the breath of the people, and could therefore receive little improvement.

When a language begins to teem with books, it is tending to refinement; as those who undertake to teach others must have undergone some labour in improving themselves, they set a proportionate value on their own thoughts, and wish to enforce them by efficacious expressions; speech becomes embodied and permanent; different modes and phrases are compared, and the best obtains an establishment. By degrees one age improves upon another. Exactness is first obtained, and afterwards elegance. But diction, merely vocal, is always in its childhood. As no man leaves his eloquence behind him, the new generations have all to learn. There may possibly be books without a polished language, but there can be no polished language without books.

That the bards could not read more than the rest of their countrymen, it is reasonable to suppose; because, if they had read, they could probably have written; and how high their compositions may reasonably be rated, an inquirer may best judge by considering what stores of imagery, what principles of ratiocination, what comprehension of knowledge, and what delicacy of elocution he has known any man attain who cannot read. The state of the bards was yet more hopeless. He that cannot read, may now converse with those that can; but the bard was a barbarian among barbarians, who, knowing nothing himself, lived with others that knew no more.

There has lately been in the islands one of these illiterate poets, who hearing the Bible read at church, is said to have turned the sacred history into verse.[134] I heard part of a dialogue, composed by him, translated by a young lady in Mull, and thought it had more meaning than I expected from a man totally uneducated; but he had some opportunities of knowledge; he lived among a learned people. After all that has been done for the instruction of the highlanders, the antipathy between their language and literature still continues; and no man that has learned only Earse is, at this time, able to read.

The Earse, has many dialects, and the words used in some islands are not always known in others. In literate nations, though the pronunciation, and sometimes the words of common speech may differ, as now in England, compared with the south of Scotland, yet there is a written diction, which pervades all dialects, and is understood in every province. But where, the whole language is colloquial, he that has only one part, never gets the rest, as he cannot get it but by change of residence.

In an unwritten speech, nothing that is not very short is transmitted from one generation to another. Few have opportunities of hearing a long composition often enough to learn it, or have inclination to repeat it so often as is necessary to retain it; and what is once forgotten is lost for ever. I believe there cannot be recovered, in the whole Earse language, five hundred lines of which there is any evidence to prove them a hundred years old. Yet I hear that the father of Ossian boasts of two chests more of ancient poetry, which he suppresses, because they are too good for the English.[135]

He that goes into the Highlands with a mind naturally acquiescent, and a credulity eager for wonders, may come back with an opinion very different from mine; for the inhabitants knowing the ignorance of all strangers in their language and antiquities, perhaps are not very scrupulous adherents to truth; yet I do not say that they deliberately speak studied falsehood, or have a settled purpose to deceive. They have inquired and considered little, and do not always feel their own ignorance. They are not much accustomed to be interrogated by others; and seem never to have thought upon interrogating themselves; so that if they do not know what they tell to be true, they likewise do not distinctly perceive it to be false.

Mr Boswell was very diligent in his inquiries; and the result of his investigations was, that the answer to the second question was commonly such as nullified the answer to the first.

We were a while told, that they had an old translation of the Scriptures; and told it till it would appear obstinacy to inquire again. Yet by continued accumulation of questions we found, that the translation meant, if any meaning there were, was nothing else than the Irish Bible.[136]

We heard of manuscripts that were, or that had been in the hands of somebody's father, or grandfather; but at last we had no reason to believe they were other than Irish. Martin mentions Irish, but never any Earse manuscripts, to be found in the islands in his time.

I suppose my opinion of the poems of Ossian is already discovered. I believe they never existed in any other form than that which we have seen. The editor, or author, never could shew the original; nor can it be shewn by any other; to revenge reasonable incredulity, by refusing evidence, is a degree of insolence, with which the world is not yet acquainted; and stubborn audacity is the last refuge of guilt. It would be easy to shew it if he had it; but whence could it be had? It is too long to be remembered, and the language formerly had nothing written. He has doubtless inserted names that circulate in popular stories, and may have translated some wandering ballads, if any can be found; and the names, and some of the images being recollected, make an inaccurate auditor imagine, by the help of Caledonian bigotry, that he has formerly heard the whole.

I asked a very learned minister in Sky,[137] who had used all arts to make me believe the genuineness of the book, whether at last he believed it himself? But he would not answer. He wished me to be deceived, for the honour of his country; but would not directly and formally deceive me. Yet has this man's testimony been publickly produced, as of one that held *Fingal* to be the work of Ossian.

It is said, that some men of integrity profess to have heard parts of it, but they all heard them when they were boys; and it was never said that any of them could recite six lines. They remember names, and perhaps some proverbial sentiments; and, having no distinct ideas, coin a resemblance without an original. The persuasion of the Scots, however, is far from universal; and in a question so capable of proof, why should doubt be suffered to continue? The editor has been heard to say, that part of the poem was received by him, in the Saxon character. He has then found, by some peculiar fortune, an unwritten language, written in a character which the natives probably never beheld.

I have yet supposed no imposture but in the publisher,[138] yet I am far from certainty, that some translations have not been lately made, that may now be obtruded as parts of the original work. Credulity on one part is a strong temptation to deceit on the other, especially to deceit of which no personal injury is the consequence, and which flatters the author with his own ingenuity. The Scots have something to plead for their easy reception of an improbable fiction: they are seduced by their fondness for their supposed ancestors. A Scotchman must be a very sturdy moralist, who does not love Scotland better than truth: he will always love it better than inquiry; and if falsehood flatters his vanity, will not be very diligent to detect it. Neither ought the English to be much influenced by Scotch authority; for the past and present state of the whole Earse nation, the lowlanders are as least as ignorant as ourselves. To be ignorant is painful; but it is dangerous to quiet our uneasiness by the delusive opiate of hasty persuasion.

But this is the age in which those who could not read, have been supposed to write; in which the giants of antiquated romance have been exhibited as realities. If we know little of the ancient highlanders, let us not fill the vacuity with Ossian. If we have not searched the Magellanick regions, let us however forbear to people them with 'patagons'.[139]

Having waited some days at Armidel, we were flattered at last with a wind that promised to convey us to Mull. We went on board a boat that was taking in kelp, and left the Isle of Sky behind us. We were doomed to experience, like others, the danger of trusting to the wind, which blew against us, in a short time, with such violence, that we, being no seasoned sailors, were willing to call it a tempest. I was sea-sick and lay down. Mr Boswell kept the deck. The master knew not well whither to go; and our difficulties might perhaps have filled a very pathetick page, had not Mr Maclean of Col, who, with every other qualification which insular life requires, in a very active and skilful manner, piloted us safe into his own harbour.[140]

COL

In the morning we found ourselves under the Isle of Col, where we landed; and passed the first day and night with Captain Maclean,[141] a gentleman who has lived some time in the East Indies; but having dethroned no Nabob, is not too rich to settle in his own country.

Next day the wind was fair, and we might have had an easy passage to Mull; but having, contrarily to our own intention, landed upon a new island, we would not leave it wholly unexamined. We therefore suffered the vessel to depart without us, and trusted the skies for another wind.

Mr Maclean of Col, having a very numerous family, has, for some time past, resided at Aberdeen, that he may superintend their education, and leaves the young gentleman, our friend,[142] to govern his dominions, with the full power of a Highland chief. By the absence of the laird's family, our entertainment was made more difficult, because the house was in a great degree disfurnished; but young Col's kindness and activity supplied all defects, and procured us more than sufficient accommodation.

Here I first mounted a little Highland steed; and if there had been many spectators, should have been somewhat ashamed of my figure in the march.[143] The horses of the islands, as of other barren countries, are very low: they are indeed musculous and strong, beyond what their size gives reason for expecting; but a bulky man upon one of their backs makes a very disproportionate appearance.

From the habitation of Captain Maclean we went to Grissipol, but called by the way on Mr Hector Maclean, the minister of Col, whom we found in a hut, that is, a house of only one floor, but with windows and chimney; and not inelegantly furnished. Mr Maclean has the reputation of great learning: he is seventy-seven years old, but not infirm, with a look of venerable dignity, excelling what I remember in any other man.

His conversation was not unsuitable to his appearance. I lost some of his goodwill, by treating a heretical writer with more regard than, in his opinion, a heretick could deserve.[144] I honoured his orthodoxy, and did not much censure his asperity. A man who has settled his opinions, does not love to have the tranquillity of his conviction disturbed; and at seventy-seven it is time to be in earnest.

Mention was made of the Earse translation of the New Testament, which has been lately published, and of which the learned Mr Macqueen of Sky spoke with commendation; but Mr Maclean said he did not use it, because he could make the text more intelligible to his auditors by an extemporary version. From this I inferred, that the language of the translation was not the language of the Isle of Col.

He has no publick edifice for the exercise of his ministry; and can officiate to no greater number, than a room can contain; and the room of a hut is not very large. This is all the opportunity of worship that is now granted to the inhabitants of the island, some of whom must travel thither perhaps ten miles. Two chapels were erected by their ancestors, of which I saw the skeletons, which now stand faithful witnesses of the triumph of Reformation.

The want of churches is not the only impediment to piety: there is likewise a want of ministers. A parish often contains more islands than one; and each island can have the minister only in its own turn. At Raasa they had, I think, a right to service only every third Sunday. All the provision made by the present ecclesiastical constitution, for the inhabitants of about a hundred square miles, is a prayer and sermon in a little room, once in three weeks: and even this parsimonious distribution is at the mercy of the weather; and in those islands where the minister does not reside, it is impossible to tell how many weeks or months may pass without any publick exercise of religion.

GRISSIPOL in COL

After a short conversation with Mr Maclean, we went on to Grissipol, a house and farm tenanted by Mr Macsweyn, where I saw more of the ancient life of a highlander, than I had yet found. Mrs Macsweyn could speak no English, and had never seen any other places than the islands of Sky, Mull, and Col, but she was hospitable and good-humoured, and spread her table with sufficient liberality. We found tea here, as in every other place, but our spoons were of horn.

The house of Grissipol stands by a brook very clear and quick; which is, I suppose, one of the most copious streams in the island. This place was the scene of an action, much celebrated in the traditional history of Col, but which probably no two relaters will tell alike.

Some time, in the obscure ages, Macneil of Barra married the Lady Maclean, who had the Isle of Col for her jointure. Whether Macneil detained Col, when the widow was dead, or whether she lived so long as to make her heirs impatient, is perhaps not now known. The younger son, called John Gerves, or John the Giant, a man of great strength, who was then in Ireland, either for safety, or for education, dreamed of recovering his inheritance; and getting some adventurers together, which, in those unsettled times, was not hard to do, invaded Col. He was driven away, but was not discouraged, and collecting new followers, in three years came again with fifty men. In his way he stopped at Artorinish in Morvern, where his uncle was prisoner to Macleod, and was then with his enemies in a tent. Maclean took with him only one servant, whom he ordered to stay at the outside; and where he should see the tent pressed outwards, to strike with his dirk; it being the intention of Maclean, as any man provoked him, to lay hands upon him, and push him back. He entered the tent alone, with his 'Lochabar-axe' in his hand,[145] and struck such terror into the whole assembly, that they dismissed his uncle.

When he landed at Col, he saw the sentinel, who kept watch towards the sea, running off to Grissipol, to give Macneil, who was there with a hundred and twenty men, an account of the invasion. He told Macgill, one of his followers, that if he intercepted that dangerous intelligence, by catching the courier, he would give him certain lands in Mull. Upon this promise, Macgill pursued the messenger, and either killed, or stopped him; and his posterity, till very lately, held the lands in Mull.

The alarm being thus prevented, he came unexpectedly upon Macneil. Chiefs were in those days never wholly unprovided for an enemy. A fight ensued, in which one of their followers is said to have given an extraordinary proof of activity, by bounding backwards over the brook of Grissipol. Macneil being killed, and many of his clan destroyed, Maclean took possession of the Island, which the Macneils attempted to conquer by another invasion, but were defeated and repulsed.

Maclean, in his turn, invaded the estate of the Macneils, took the castle of Brecacig,[146] and conquered the Isle of Barra, which he held for seven years, and then restored it to the heirs.

CASTLE OF COL

From Grissipol, Mr Maclean conducted us to his father's seat; a neat new house, erected near the old castle, I think, by the last proprietor. Here we were allowed to take our station, and lived very commodiously, while we waited for moderate weather and a fair wind, which we did not so soon obtain, but we had time to get some information of the present state of Col, partly by inquiry, and partly by occasional excursions.

Col is computed to be thirteen miles in length, and three in breadth.[147] Both the ends are the property of the Duke of Argyle, but the middle belongs to Maclean, who is called Col, as the only laird.

Col is not properly rocky; it is rather one continued rock, of a surface much diversified with protuberances, and covered with a thin layer of earth, which is often broken, and discovers the stone. Such a soil is not for plants that strike deep roots; and perhaps in the whole island nothing has ever yet grown to the height of a table. The uncultivated parts are clothed with heath, among which industry has interspersed spots of grass and corn; but no attempt has yet been made to raise a tree. Young Col, who has a very laudable desire of improving his patrimony, purposes some time to plant an orchard; which, if it be sheltered by a wall, may perhaps succeed. He has introduced the culture of turnips, of which he has a field, where the whole work was performed by his own hand. His intention is to provide food for his cattle in the winter. This innovation was considered by Mrs Macsweyn as the idle project of a young head, heated with English fancies; but he has now found that turnips will really grow, and that hungry sheep and cows will really eat them.

By such acquisitions as these, the Hebrides may in time rise above their annual distress. Wherever heath will grow, there is reason to think something better may draw nourishment; and by trying the production of other places, plants will be found suitable to every soil.

Col has many lochs, some of which have trouts and eels, and others have never yet been stocked; another proof of the negligence of the islanders, who might take fish in the inland waters, when they cannot go to sea.[148]

Their quadrupeds are horses, cows, sheep, and goats. They have neither deer, hares, nor rabbits. They have no vermin, except rats, which have been lately brought thither by sea, as to other places; and are free from serpents, frogs, and toads.

The harvest in Col, and in Lewis, is ripe sooner than in Sky; and the winter in Col is never cold, but very tempestuous. I know not that I ever heard the wind so loud in any other place; and Mr Boswell observed, that its noise was all its own, for there were no trees to increase it.[149]

Noise is not the worst effect of the tempests; for they have thrown the sand from the shore over a considerable part of the land; and it is said still to encroach and destroy more and more pasture; but I am not of opinion, that by any surveys or landmarks, its limits have been ever fixed, or its progression ascertained. If one man has confidence enough to say, that it advances, nobody can bring any proof to support him in denying it. The reason why it is not spread to a greater extent, seems to be, that the wind and rain come almost together, and that it is made close and heavy by the wet before the storms can put it in motion. So thick is the bed, and so small the particles, that if a traveller should be caught by a sudden gust in dry weather, he would find it very difficult to escape with life.

For natural curiosities, I was shown only two great masses of stone, which lie loose upon the ground; one on top of a hill, and the other at a small distance from the bottom.[150] They certainly were never put into their present places by human strength or skill; and though an earthquake might have broken off the lower stone, and rolled it into the valley, no account can be given of the other, which lies on the hill, unless, which I forgot to examine, there be still near it some higher rock, from which it might be torn. All nations have a tradition, that their earliest ancestors were giants, and these stones are said to have been thrown up and down by a giant and his mistress.[151] There are so many more important things, of which human knowledge can give no account, that it may be forgiven us, if we speculate no longer on two stones in Col.

This island is very populous. About nine-and-twenty years ago, the fencible[152] men of Col were reckoned one hundred and forty, which is the sixth of eight hundred and forty; and probably some contrived to be left out of the list. The minister told us, that a few years ago the inhabitants were eight hundred, between the ages of seven and of seventy. Round numbers are seldom exact. But in this case the authority is good, and the errour likely to be little. If to the eight hundred be added what the laws of computation require, they will be increased to at least a thousand; and if the dimensions of the country have been accurately related, every mile maintains more than twenty-five.

This proportion of habitation is greater than the appearance of the country seems to admit; for wherever the eye wanders, it sees much waste and little cultivation. I am more inclined to extend the land, of which no measure has ever been taken, than to diminish the people, who have been really numbered. Let it be supposed, that a computed mile contains a mile and a half, as was commonly found true in the mensuration of the English roads, and we shall then allot nearly twelve to a mile, which agrees much better with ocular observation.

Here, as in Sky and other islands, are the laird, the tacksmen, and the under tenants. Mr Maclean, the laird, has very extensive possessions, being proprietor, not only of far the greater part of Col, but of the extensive island of Rum, and a very considerable territory in Mull.

Rum is one of the larger islands,[153] almost square, and therefore of great capacity in proportion to its sides. By the usual method of estimating computed extent, it may contain more than a hundred and twenty square miles. It originally belonged to Clanronald, and was purchased by Col; who, in some dispute about the bargain, made Clanronald prisoner, and kept him nine months in confinement. Its owner represents it as mountainous, rugged, and barren. In the hills there are red deer. The horses are very small, but of a breed eminent for beauty. Col, not long ago, bought one of them from a tenant; who told him, that as he was of a shape uncommonly elegant, he could not sell him but at a high price; and that whoever had him should pay a guinea and a half. There are said to be in Barra a race of horses yet smaller, of which the highest is not above thirty-six inches.

The rent of Rum is not great. Mr Maclean declared, that he should be very rich, if he could set his land at two-pence halfpenny an acre. The inhabitants are fifty-eight families,[154] who continued papists for some time after the laird became a Protestant. Their adherence to their old religion was strengthened by the countenance of the laird's sister, a zealous Romanist, till one Sunday, as they were going to mass under the conduct of their patroness, Maclean met them on the way, gave one of them a blow on the head with a 'yellow stick', I suppose a cane, for which the Earse had no name, and drove them to the kirk, from which they have never since departed. Since the use of this method of conversion, the inhabitants of Egg and Canna, who continue papists, call the Protestantism of Rum, the religion of the Yellow Stick.

The only popish islands are Egg and Canna. Egg is the principal island of a parish, in which, though he has no congregation, the Protestant minister resides. I have heard of nothing curious in it, but the cave in which a former generation of the islanders were smothered by Macleod.

If we had travelled with more leisure, it had not been fit to have neglected the popish islands.[155] Popery is favourable to ceremony; and among ignorant nations, ceremony is the only preservative of tradition. Since protestantism was extended to the savage parts of Scotland, it has perhaps been one of the chief labours of the ministers to abolish stated observances, because they continued the remembrance of the former religion. We therefore who came to hear old traditions, and see antiquated manners, should probably have found them amongst the papists.[156]

Canna, the other popish island, belongs to Clanronald. It is said not to comprise more than twelve miles of land, and yet maintains as many inhabitants as Rum.

We were at Col under the protection of the young laird, without any of the distresses, which Mr Pennant, in a fit of simple credulity, seems to think almost worthy of an elegy by Ossian. Wherever we roved, we were pleased to see the reverence with which his subjects regarded him. He did not endeavour to dazzle them by any magnificence of dress: his only distinction was a feather in his bonnet; but as soon as he appeared, they forsook their work and clustered about him: he took them by the hand, and they seemed mutually delighted. He has the proper disposition of a chieftain, and seems desirous to continue the customs of his house. The bagpiper played regularly, when dinner was served, whose person and dress made a good appearance; and he brought no disgrace upon the family of Rankin, which has long supplied the Lairds of Col with hereditary musick.

The tacksmen of Col seem to live with less dignity and convenience than those of Sky; where they had good houses, and tables not only plentiful, but delicate. In Col only two houses pay the window tax; for only two have six windows, which, I suppose, are the laird's and Mr Macsweyn's.

The rents have, till within seven years, been paid in kind, but the tenants finding that cattle and corn varied in their price, desired for the future to give their landlord money; which, not having yet arrived at the philosophy of commerce, they consider as being every year of the same value.

We were told of a particular mode of undertenure. The tacksman admits some of his inferiour neighbours to the cultivation of his grounds, on condition that performing all the work, and giving a third part of the seed, they shall keep a certain number of cows, sheep, and goats, and reap a third part of the harvest. Thus by less than the tillage of two acres they pay the rent of one.

There are tenants below the rank of tacksmen, that have got smaller tenants under them; for in every place, where money is not the general equivalent, there must be some whose labour is immediately paid by daily food.

A country that has no money, is by no means convenient for beggars, both because such countries are commonly poor, and because charity requires some trouble and some thought. A penny is easily given upon the first impulse of compassion, or impatience of importunity; but few will deliberately search their cupboards or their granaries to find out something to give. A penny is likewise easily spent; but victuals, if they are unprepared, require houseroom, and fire, and utensils, which the beggar knows not where to find.

Yet beggars there sometimes are, who wander from island to island. We had, in our passage to Mull, the company of a woman and her child, who had exhausted the charity of Col. The arrival of a beggar on an island is accounted a sinistrous event. Every body considers that he shall have the less for what he gives away. Their alms, I believe, is generally oatmeal.

Near to Col is another island called Tireye, eminent for its fertility. Though it has but half the extent of Rum, it is so well peopled, that there have appeared, not long ago, nine hundred and fourteen at a funeral. The plenty of this island enticed beggars to it, who seemed so burdensome to the inhabitants, that a formal compact was drawn up, by which they obliged themselves to grant no more relief to casual wanderers, because they had among them an indigent woman of high birth, whom they considered as entitled to all that they could spare. I have read the stipulation, which was indited with juridical formality, but was never made valid by regular subscription.

If the inhabitants of Col have nothing to give, it is not that they are oppressed by their landlord: their leases seem to be very profitable. One farmer,[157] who pays only seven pounds a year, has maintained seven daughters and three sons, of whom the eldest is educated at Aberdeen for the ministry; and now, at every vacation, opens a school in Col.[158]

Life is here, in some respects, improved beyond the condition of some other islands. In Sky what is wanted can only be bought, as the arrival of some wandering pedlar may afford an opportunity; but in Col there is a standing shop, and in Mull there are two. A shop in the islands, as in other places of little frequentation, is a repository of every thing requisite for common use. Mr Boswell's journal was filled, and he bought some paper in Col. To a man that ranges the streets of London, where he is tempted to contrive wants for the pleasure of supplying them, a shop affords no image worthy of attention; but in an island, it turns the balance of existence between good and evil. To live in perpetual want of little things, is a state not indeed of torture, but of constant vexation. I have in Sky had some difficulty to find ink for a letter; and if a woman breaks her needle, the work is at a stop.

As it is, the islanders are obliged to content themselves with succedaneous[159] means for many common purposes. I have seen the chief man of a very wide district riding with a halter for a bridle, and governing his hobby with a wooden curb.

The people of Col, however, do not want dexterity to supply some of their necessities. Several arts which make trades, and demand apprenticeships in great cities, are here the practices of daily economy. In every house candles are made, both moulded and dipped. Their wicks are small shreds of linen cloth. They all know how to extract from the cuddy, oil for their lamps. They all tan skins, and make brogues.

As we travelled through Sky, we saw many cottages, but they very frequently stood single on the naked ground. In Col, where the hills opened a place convenient for habitation, we found a petty village, of which every hut had a little garden adjoining; thus they made an appearance of social commerce and mutual offices, and of some attention to convenience and future supply. There is not in the Western Islands any collection of buildings that can make pretensions to be called a town, except in the Isle of Lewis, which I have not seen.

If Lewis is distinguished by a town, Col has also something peculiar. The young laird has attempted what no islander perhaps ever thought on. He has begun a road capable of a wheel-carriage. He has carried it about a mile, and will continue it by annual elongation from his house to the harbour.

Of taxes here is no reason for complaining; they are paid by a very easy composition. The malt-tax for Col is twenty shillings.[160] Whisky is very plentiful: there are several stills in the island, and more is made than the inhabitants consume.

The great business of insular policy is how to keep the people in their own country. As the world has been let in upon them, they have heard of happier climates, and less arbitrary government; and if they are disgusted, have emissaries among them ready to offer them land and houses, as a reward for deserting their chief and clan. Many have departed both from the main of Scotland, and from the islands; and all that go may be considered as subjects lost to the British crown; for a nation scattered in the boundless regions of America resembles rays diverging from a focus. All the rays remain, but the heat is gone. Their power consisted in their concentration: when they are dispersed, they have no effect.

It may be thought that they are happier by the change; but they are not happy as a nation, for they are a nation no longer. As they contribute not to the prosperity of any community, they must want that security, that dignity, that happiness, whatever it be, which a prosperous community throws back upon individuals.

The inhabitants of Col have not yet learned to be weary of their heath and rocks, but attend their agriculture and their dairies, without listening to American seducements.

There are some however who think that this emigration has raised terrour disproportionate to its real evil; and that it is only a new mode of doing what was always done. The Highlands, they say, never maintained their natural inhabitants; but the people, when they found themselves too numerous, instead of extending cultivation, provided for themselves by a more compendious method, and sought better fortune in other countries. They did not indeed go away in collective bodies, but withdrew invisibly, a few at a time; but the whole number of fugitives was not less, and the difference between other times and this, is only the same as between evaporation and effusion.

This is plausible, but I am afraid it is not true. Those who went before, if they were not sensibly missed, as the argument supposes, must have gone either in less number, or in a manner less detrimental, than at present; because formerly there was no complaint. Those who then left the country were generally the idle dependants on overburdened families, or men who had no property; and therefore carried away only themselves. In the present eagerness of emigration, families, and almost communities, go away together. Those who were considered as prosperous and wealthy sell their stock and carry away the money. Once none went away but the useless and poor; in some parts there is now reason to fear, that none will stay but those who are too poor to remove themselves, and too useless to be removed at the cost of others.

Of antiquity there is not more knowledge in Col than in other places; but every where something may be gleaned.

How ladies were proportioned, when there was no money, it would be difficult for an Englishman to guess. In 1649, Maclean of Dronart[161] in Mull married his sister Fingala to Maclean of Coll, with a hundred and eighty kine; and stipulated, that if she became a widow, her jointure should be three hundred and sixty. I suppose some proportionate tract of land was appropriated to their pasturage.

The disposition to pompous and expensive funerals, which has at one time or other prevailed in most parts of the civilized world, is not yet suppressed in the islands, though some of the ancient solemnities are worn away, and singers are no longer hired to attend the procession. Nineteen years ago, at the burial of the Laird of Col, were killed thirty cows, and about fifty sheep. The number of the cows is positively told, and we must suppose other victuals in like proportion.

Mr Maclean informed us of an odd game, of which he did not tell the original, but which may perhaps be used in other places, where the reason of it is not yet forgot. At New Year's eve, in the hall or castle of the laird, where, at festal seasons, there may be supposed a very numerous company, one man dresses himself in a cow's hide, upon which other men beat with sticks.[162] He runs with all this noise round the house, which all the company quits in a counterfeited fright: the door is then shut. At New Year's eve there is no great pleasure to be had out of doors in the Hebrides. They are sure soon to recover from their terror enough to solicit for re-admission; which, for the honour of poetry, is not to be obtained but by repeating a verse, with which those that are knowing and provident take care to be furnished.

Very near the house of Maclean stands the castle of Col, which was the mansion of the laird, till the house was built. It is built upon a rock, as Mr Boswell remarked, that it might not be mined. It is very strong, and having been not long uninhabited, is yet in repair. On the wall was, not long ago, a stone with an inscription, importing, that 'if any man of the clan of Maclonich shall appear before this castle, though he come at midnight, with a man's head in his hand, he shall there find safety and protection against all but the King'.

This is an old Highland treaty made upon a very memorable occasion. Maclean, the son of John Gerves, who recovered Col, and conquered Barra, had obtained, it is said, from James the Second, a grant of the lands of Lochiel, forfeited, I suppose, by some offence against the state.

Forfeited estates were not in those days quietly resigned; Maclean, therefore, went with an armed force to seize his new possessions, and, I know not for what reason, took his wife with him. The Camerons rose in defence of their chief, and a battle was fought at the head of Loch Ness, near the place where Fort Augustus now stands, in which Lochiel obtained the victory, and Maclean, with his followers, was defeated and destroyed.

The lady fell into the hands of the conquerors, and being found pregnant was placed in the custody of Maclonich, one of a tribe or family branched from Cameron, with orders, if she brought a boy, to destroy him, if a girl, to spare her.

Maclonich's wife, who was with child likewise, had a girl about the same time at which Lady Maclean brought a boy, and Maclonich with more generosity to his captive, than fidelity to his trust, contrived that the children should be changed.

Maclean being thus preserved from death, in time recovered his original patrimony; and in gratitude to his friend, made his castle a place of refuge to any of the clan that should think himself in danger; and, as a proof of reciprocal confidence, Maclean took upon himself and his posterity the care of educating the heir of Maclonich.

This story, like all other traditions of the Highlands, is variously related, but though some circumstances are uncertain, the principal fact is true. Maclean undoubtedly owed his preservation to Maclonich; for the treaty between the two families has been strictly observed: it did not sink into disuse and oblivion, but continued in its full force while the chieftains retained their power. I have read a demand of protection, made not more than thirty-seven years ago, for one of the Maclonichs, named Ewen Cameron, who had been accessary to the death of Macmartin, and had been banished by Lochiel, his lord, for a certain term; at the expiration of which he returned married from France, but the Macmartins, not satisfied with the punishment, when he attempted to settle, still threatened him with vengeance. He therefore asked, and obtained shelter in the Isle of Col.

The power of protection subsists no longer, but what the law permits is yet continued, and Maclean of Col now educates the heir of Maclonich.

There still remains in the islands, though it is passing fast away, the custom of fosterage.[163] A laird, a man of wealth and eminence, sends his child, either male or female, to a tacksman, or tenant, to be fostered. It is not always his own tenant, but some distant friend that obtains this honour; for an honour such as trust is very reasonably thought. The terms of fosterage seem to vary in different islands. In Mull the father sends with his child a certain number of cows, to which the same number is added by the fosterer.

The father appropriates a proportionable extent of ground, without rent, for their pasturage. If every cow brings a calf, half belongs to the fosterer, and half to the child; but if there be only one calf between two cows, it is the child's, and when the child returns to the parents, it is accompanied by all the cows given, both by the father and by the fosterer, with half of the increase of the stock by propagation. These beasts are considered as a portion, and called *macalive*[164] cattle, of which the father has the produce, but is supposed not to have the full property, but to owe the same number to the child, as a portion to the daughter, or a stock for the son.

Children continue with the fosterer perhaps six years, and cannot, where this is the practice, be considered as burdensome. The fosterer, if he gives four cows, receives likewise four, and has, while the child continues with him, grass for eight without rent, with half the calves, and all the milk, for which he pays only four cows when he dismisses his *dalt*,[165] for that is the name for a foster child.

Fosterage is, I believe, sometimes performed upon more liberal terms. Our friend, the young Laird of Col, was fostered by Macsweyn of Grissipol. Macsweyn then lived a tenant to Sir James Macdonald in the Isle of Sky; and therefore Col, whether he sent him cattle or not, could grant him no land. The *dalt*, however, at his return, brought back a considerable number of *macalive* cattle, and of the friendship so formed there have been good effects. When Macdonald raised his rents, Macsweyn was, like other tenants, discontented, and, resigning his farm, removed from Sky to Col, and was established at Grissipol.

These observations we made by favour of the contrary wind that drove us to Col, an island not often visited; for there is not much to amuse curiosity, or to attract avarice.

The ground has been hitherto, I believe, used chiefly for pasturage. In a district, such as the eye can command, there is a general herdsman, who knows all the cattle of the neighbourhood, and whose station is upon a hill, from which he surveys the lower grounds; and if one man's cattle invade another's grass, drives them back to their own borders. But other means of profit begin to be found; kelp is gathered and burnt, and sloops are loaded with the concreted ashes. Cultivation is likely to be improved by the skill and encouragement of the present heir, and the inhabitants of those obscure vallies will partake of the general progress of life.

The rents of the parts which belong to the Duke of Argyle, have been raised from fifty-five to one hundred and five pounds, whether from the land or the sea I cannot tell. The bounties of the sea have lately been so great, that a farm in Southuist has risen in ten years from a rent of thirty pounds to one hundred and eighty.

He who lives in Col, and finds himself condemned to solitary meals, and incommunicable reflection, will find the usefulness of that middle order of tacksmen, which some who applaud their own wisdom are wishing to destroy. Without intelligence man is not social, he is only gregarious; and little intelligence will there be, where all are constrained to daily labour, and every mind must wait upon the hand.

After having listened for some days to the tempest, and wandered about the island till our curiosity was satisfied, we began to think about our departure. To leave Col in October was not very easy. We however found a sloop which lay on the coast to carry kelp; and for a price which we thought levied upon our necessities, the master agreed to carry us to Mull, whence we might readily pass back to Scotland.

MULL

As we were to catch the first favourable breath, we spent the night not very elegantly, nor pleasantly in the vessel, and were landed next day at Tobor Morar,[166] a port in Mull, which appears to an unexperienced eye formed for the security of ships; for its mouth is closed by a small island, which admits them through narrow channels into a bason sufficiently capacious. They are indeed safe from the sea, but there is a hollow between the mountains, through which the wind issues from the land with very mischievous violence.

There was no danger while we were there, and we found several other vessels at anchor; so that the port had a very commercial appearance.

The young Laird of Col, who had determined not to let us lose his company, while there was any difficulty remaining, came over with us. His influence soon appeared; for he procured us horses, and conducted us to the house of Doctor Maclean, where we found very kind entertainment, and very pleasing conversation. Miss Maclean, who was born, and had been bred at Glasgow, having removed with her father to Mull, added to other qualifications, a great knowledge of the Earse language, which she had not learned in her childhood, but gained by study, and was the only interpreter of Earse poetry that I could ever find.

The Isle of Mull is perhaps in extent the third of the Hebrides. It is not broken by waters, nor shot into promontories, but is a solid and compact mass, of breadth nearly equal to its length. Of the dimensions of the larger islands, there is no knowledge approaching to exactness. I am willing to estimate it as containing about three hundred square miles.

Mull had suffered like Sky by the black winter of seventy-one, in which, contrary to all experience, a continued frost detained the snow eight weeks upon the ground. Against a calamity never known, no provision had been made, and the people could only pine in helpless misery. One tenant was mentioned, whose cattle perished to the value of three hundred pounds; a loss which probably more than the life of man is necessary to repair. In countries like these, the descriptions of famine become intelligible. Where by vigorous and artful cultivation of a soil naturally fertile, there is commonly a superfluous growth both of grain and grass; where the fields are crowded with cattle; and where every hand is able to attract wealth from a distance, by making something that promotes ease, or gratifies vanity, a dear year produces only a comparative want, which is rather seen than felt, and which terminates commonly in no worse effect, than that of condemning the lower orders of the community to sacrifice a little luxury to convenience, or at most a little convenience to necessity.

But where the climate is unkind, and the ground penurious, so that the most fruitful years will produce only enough to maintain themselves; where life unimproved, and unadorned, fades into something little more than naked existence, and every one is busy for himself, without any arts by which the pleasure of others may be increased; if to the daily burden of distress any additional weight be added, nothing remains but to despair and die. In Mull the disappointment of a harvest, or a murrain among the cattle, cuts off the regular provision; and they who have no manufactures can purchase no part of the superfluities of other countries. The consequence of a bad season is here not scarcity, but emptiness; and they whose plenty was barely a supply of natural and present need, when that slender stock fails, must perish with hunger.

All travel has its advantages. If the passenger visits better countries, he may learn to improve his own, and if fortune carries him to worse, he may learn to enjoy it.

Mr Boswell's curiosity strongly impelled him to survey Iona, or Icolmkil, which was to the early ages the great school of theology, and is supposed to have been the place of sepulture for the ancient kings. I, though less eager, did not oppose him.

That we might perform this expedition, it was necessary to traverse a great part of Mull. We passed a day at Dr Maclean's, and could have been well contented to stay longer. But Col provided us horses, and we pursued our journey. This was a day of inconvenience, for the country is very rough, and my horse was but little. We travelled many hours through a tract, black and barren, in which, however, there were the reliques of humanity; for we found a ruined chapel in our way.

It is natural, in traversing this gloom of desolation, to inquire, whether something may not be done to give nature a more cheerful face, and whether those hills and moors that afford heath cannot with a little care and labour bear something better? The first thought that occurs is to cover them with trees, for that in many of these naked regions trees will grow, is evident, because stumps and roots are yet remaining; and the speculatist hastily proceeds to censure that negligence and laziness that has omitted for so long a time so easy an improvement.

To drop seeds into the ground, and attend their growth, requires little labour and no skill. He who remembers that all the woods, by which the wants of man have been supplied from the Deluge till now, were self-sown, will not easily be persuaded to think all the art and preparation necessary, which the Georgick writers[167] prescribe to planters. Trees certainly have covered the earth with very little culture. They wave their tops among the rocks of Norway, and might thrive as well in the Highlands and Hebrides.

But there is a frightful interval between the seed and timber. He that calculates the growth of trees, has the unwelcome remembrance of the shortness of life driven hard upon him. He knows that he is doing what will never benefit himself; and when he rejoices to see the stem rise, is disposed to repine that another shall cut it down.

Plantation is naturally the employment of a mind unburdened with care, and vacant to futurity, saturated with present good, and at leisure to derive gratification from the prospect of posterity. He that pines with hunger, is in little care how others shall be fed. The poor man is seldom studious to make his grandson rich. It may be soon discovered, why in a place, which hardly supplies the cravings of necessity, there has been little attention to the delights of fancy, and why distant convenience is unregarded, where the thoughts are turned with incessant solicitude upon every possibility of immediate advantage.

Neither is it quite so easy to raise large woods, as may be conceived. Trees intended to produce timber must be sown where they are to grow; and ground sown with trees must be kept useless for a long time, inclosed at an expence from which many will be discouraged by the remoteness of the profit, and watched with that attention, which, in places where it is most needed, will neither be given nor bought. That it cannot be plowed is evident; and if cattle be suffered to graze upon it, they will devour the plants as fast as they rise. Even in coarser countries, where herds and flocks are not fed, not only the deer and the wild goats will browse upon them, but the hare and rabbit will nibble them. It is therefore reasonable to believe, what I do not remember any naturalist to have remarked, that there was a time when the world was very thinly inhabited by beasts, as well as men, and that the woods had leisure to rise high before animals had bred numbers sufficient to intercept them.

Sir James Macdonald, in part of the wastes of his territory, set or sowed trees, to the number, as I have been told, of several millions, expecting, doubtless, that they would grow up into future navies and cities; but for want of inclosure, and of that care which is always necessary, and will hardly ever be taken, all his cost and labour have been lost, and the ground is likely to continue an useless heath.

Having not any experience of a journey in Mull, we had no doubt of reaching the sea by day-light, and therefore had not left Dr Maclean's very early. We travelled diligently enough, but found the country, for road there was none, very difficult to pass. We were always struggling with some obstruction or other, and our vexation was not balanced by any gratification of the eye or mind. We were now long enough acquainted with hills and heath to have lost the emotion that they once raised, whether pleasing or painful, and had our mind employed only on our own fatigue. We were however sure, under Col's protection, of escaping all real evils. There was no house in Mull to which he could not introduce us. He had intended to lodge us, for that night, with a gentleman that lived upon the coast, but discovered on the way, that he then lay in bed without hope of life.

We resolved not to embarrass a family, in a time of so much sorrow, if any other expedient could be found; and as the island of Ulva was over against us, it was determined that we should pass the strait and have recourse to the laird, who, like the other gentlemen of the islands, was known to Col. We expected to find a ferry-boat, but when at last we came to the water, the boat was gone.

We were now again at a stop. It was the sixteenth of October, a time when it is not convenient to sleep in the Hebrides without a cover, and there was no house within our reach, but that which we had already declined.

ULVA

While we stood deliberating, we were happily espied from an Irish ship, that lay at anchor in the strait. The master saw that we wanted a passage, and with great civility sent us his boat, which quickly conveyed us to Ulva, where we were very liberally entertained by Mr Macquarry.[168]

To Ulva we came in the dark, and left it before noon the next day. A very exact description therefore will not be expected. We were told, that it is an island of no great extent, rough and barren, inhabited by the Macquarrys; a clan not powerful nor numerous, but of antiquity, which most other families are content to reverence. The name is supposed to be a depravation of some other; for the Earse language does not afford it any etymology. Macquarry is proprietor both of Ulva and some adjacent Islands, among which is Staffa, so lately raised to renown by Mr Banks.[169]

When the islanders were reproached with their ignorance, or insensibility of the wonders of Staffa, they had not much to reply. They had indeed considered it little, because they had always seen it; and none but philosophers, nor they always, are struck with wonder, otherwise than by novelty. How would it surprise an unenlightened ploughman, to hear a company of sober men, inquiring by what power the hand tosses a stone, or why the stone, when it is tossed, falls to the ground!

Of the ancestors of Macquarry, who thus lies hid in his unfrequented island, I have found memorials in all places where they could be expected.

Inquiring after the reliques of former manners, I found that in Ulva, and, I think, no where else, is continued the payment of the *mercheta mulierum*; a fine in old times due to the laird at the marriage of a virgin.[170] The original of this claim, as of our tenure of Borough English, is variously delivered. It is pleasant to find ancient customs in old families. This payment, like others, was, for want of money, made anciently in the produce of the land. Macquarry was used to demand a sheep, for which he now takes a crown, by that inattention to the uncertain proportion between the value and the denomination of money, which has brought much disorder into Europe. A sheep has always the same power of supplying human wants, but a crown will bring at one time more, at another less.

Ulva was not neglected by the piety of ancient times: it has still to show what was once a church.

INCH KENNETH

In the morning we went again into the boat, and were landed on Inch Kenneth, an island about a mile long, and perhaps half a mile broad, remarkable for pleasantness and fertility.[171] It is verdant and grassy, and fit both for pasture and tillage; but it has no trees. Its only inhabitants were Sir Allan Maclean, and two young ladies, his daughters, with their servants.

Romance does not often exhibit a scene that strikes the imagination more than this little desert in these depths of western obscurity, occupied not by a gross herdsman, or amphibious fisherman, but by a gentleman and two ladies, of high birth, polished manners, and elegant conversation, who, in a habitation raised not very far above the ground, but furnished with unexpected neatness and convenience, practised all the kindness of hospitality, and refinement of courtesy.

Sir Allan is the chieftain of the great clan of Maclean, which is said to claim the second place among the Highland families, yielding only to Macdonald.[172] Though by the misconduct of his ancestors, most of the extensive territory, which would have descended to him, has been alienated, he still retains much of the dignity and authority of his birth. When soldiers were lately wanting for the American war, application was made to Sir Allan, and he nominated a hundred men for the service, who obeyed the summons, and bore arms under his command.

He had then, for some time, resided with the young ladies in Inch Kenneth, where he lives not only with plenty, but with elegance, having conveyed to his cottage a collection of books, and what else is necessary to make his hours pleasant.

When we landed, we were met by Sir Allan and the ladies, accompanied by Miss Macquarry, who had passed some time with them, and now returned to Ulva with her father.

We all walked together to the mansion, where we found one cottage for Sir Allan, and I think two more for the domesticks and the offices. We entered, and wanted little that palaces afford. Our room was neatly floored, and well lighted; and our dinner, which was dressed in one of the other huts, was plentiful and delicate.

In the afternoon Sir Allan reminded us, that the day was Sunday, which he never suffered to pass without some religious distinction, and invited us to partake in his acts of domestick worship; which I hope neither Mr Boswell nor myself will be suspected of a disposition to refuse. The elder of the ladies read the English service.[173]

Inch Kenneth was once a seminary of ecclesiasticks, subordinate, I suppose, to Icolmkill.[174] Sir Allan had a mind to trace the foundation of the college, but neither I nor Mr Boswell, who 'bends' a keener 'eye on vacancy', were able to perceive them.

Our attention, however, was sufficiently engaged by a venerable chapel, which stands yet entire, except that the roof is gone. It is about sixty feet in length, and thirty in breadth. On one side of the altar is a bas relief of the blessed Virgin, and by it lies a little bell; which, though cracked, and without a clapper, has remained there for ages, guarded only by the venerableness of the place. The ground round the chapel is covered with grave-stones of chiefs and ladies; and still continues to be a place of sepulture.

Inch Kenneth is a proper prelude to Icolmkill. It was not without some mournful emotion that we contemplated the ruins of religious structures, and the monuments of the dead.

On the next day we took a more distinct view of the place, and went with the boat to see the oysters in the bed, out of which the boat-men forced up as many as were wanted. Even Inch Kenneth has a subordinate island, named Sandiland, I suppose, in contempt, where we landed, and found a rock, with a surface of perhaps four acres, of which one is naked stone, another spread with sand and shells, some of which I picked up for their glossy beauty, and two covered with a little earth and grass, on which Sir Allan has a few sheep. I doubt not but when there was a college at Inch Kenneth, there was a hermitage upon Sandiland.

Having wandered over those extensive plains, we committed ourselves again to the winds and waters; and after a voyage of about ten minutes, in which we met with nothing very observable, were again safe upon dry ground.

We told Sir Allan our desire of visiting Icolmkill, and entreated him to give us his protection, and his company. He thought proper to hesitate a little, but the ladies hinted, that as they knew he would not finally refuse, he would do better if he preserved the grace of ready compliance. He took their advice, and promised to carry us on the morrow in his boat.

We passed the remaining part of the day in such amusements as were in our power. Sir Allan related the American campaign, and at evening one of the ladies played on her harpsichord, while Col and Mr Boswell danced a Scottish reel with the other.

We could have been easily persuaded to a longer stay upon Inch Kenneth, but life will not be all passed in delight. The session at Edinburgh was approaching, from which Mr Boswell could not be absent.[175]

In the morning our boat was ready: it was high and strong. Sir Allan victualled it for the day, and provided able rowers. We now parted from the young Laird of Col, who had treated us with so much kindness, and concluded his favours by consigning us to Sir Allan. Here we had the last embrace of this amiable man, who, while these pages were preparing to attest his virtues, perished in the passage between Ulva and Inch Kenneth.[176]

Sir Allan, to whom the whole region was well known, told us of a very remarkable cave, to which he would show us the way. We had been disappointed already by one cave, and were not much elevated by the expectation of another.

It was yet better to see it, and we stopped at some rocks on the coast of Mull. The mouth is fortified by vast fragments of stone, over which we made our way, neither very nimbly, nor very securely. The place, however, well repaid our trouble. The bottom, as far as the flood rushes in, was encumbered with large pebbles, but as we advanced was spread over with smooth sand. The breadth is about forty-five feet: the roof rises in an arch, almost regular, to a height which we could not measure; but I think it about thirty feet.

This part of our curiosity was nearly frustrated; for though we went to see a cave, and knew that caves are dark, we forgot to carry tapers, and did not discover our omission till we were wakened by our wants. Sir Allan then sent one of the boat-men into the country, who soon returned with one little candle. We were thus enabled to go forward, but could not venture far. Having passed inward from the sea to a great depth, we found on the right hand a narrow passage, perhaps not more than six feet wide, obstructed by great stones, over which we climbed and came into a second cave, in breadth twenty-five feet. The air in this apartment was very warm, but not oppressive, nor loaded with vapours. Our light showed no tokens of a feculent or corrupted atmosphere. Here was a square stone, called, as we are told, Fingal's Table.

If we had been provided with torches, we should have proceeded in our search, though we had already gone as far as any former adventurer, except some who are reported never to have returned; and, measuring our way back, we found it more than a hundred and sixty yards, the eleventh part of a mile.

Our measures were not critically exact, having been made with a walking pole, such as it is convenient to carry in these rocky countries, of which I guessed the length by standing against it. In this there could be no great errour, nor do I much doubt but the highlander, whom we employed, reported the number right. More nicety however is better, and no man should travel unprovided with instruments for taking heights and distances.

There is yet another cause of errour not always easily surmounted, though more dangerous to the veracity of itinerary narratives, than imperfect mensuration. An observer deeply impressed by any remarkable spectacle, does not suppose, that the traces will soon vanish from his mind, and having commonly no great convenience for writing, defers the description to a time of more leisure, and better accommodation.

He who has not made the experiment, or who is not accustomed to require rigorous accuracy from himself, will scarcely believe how much a few hours take from certainty of knowledge, and distinctness of imagery; how the succession of objects will be broken, how separate parts will be confused, and how many particular features and discriminations will be compressed and conglobated into one gross and general idea.

To this dilatory notation must be imputed the false relations of travellers, where there is no imaginable motive to deceive. They trusted to memory, what cannot be trusted safely but to the eye, and told by guess what a few hours before they had known with certainty. Thus it was that Wheeler and Spon described with irreconcilable contrariety things which they surveyed together, and which both undoubtedly designed to show as they saw them.[177]

When we had satisfied our curiosity in the cave, so far as our penury of light permitted us, we clambered again to our boat, and proceeded along the coast of Mull to a headland, called Atun, remarkable for the columnar form of the rocks, which rise in a series of pilasters with a degree of regularity, which Sir Allan thinks not less worthy of curiosity than the shore of Staffa.

Not long after we came to another range of black rocks, which had the appearance of broken pilasters, set one behind another to a great depth. This place was chosen by Sir Allan for our dinner. We were easily accommodated with seats, for the stones were of all heights, and refreshed ourselves and our boatmen, who could have no other rest till we were at Icolmkill.

The evening was now approaching, and we were yet at a considerable distance from the end of our expedition. We could therefore stop no more to make remarks in the way, but set forward with some degree of eagerness. The day soon failed us, and the moon presented a very solemn and pleasing scene. The sky was clear, so that the eye commanded a wide circle: the sea was neither still nor turbulent: the wind neither silent nor loud. We were never far from one coast or another, on which, if the weather had become violent, we could have found shelter, and therefore contemplated at ease the region through which we glided in the tranquillity of the night, and saw now a rock and now an island grow gradually conspicuous and gradually obscure. I committed the fault which I have just been censuring, in neglecting, as we passed, to note the series of this placid navigation.

We were very near an island, called Nun's Island, perhaps from an ancient convent. Here is said to have been dug the stone that was used in the buildings of Icolmkill. Whether it is now inhabited we could not stay to inquire.

At last we came to Icolmkill, but found no convenience for landing. Our boat could not be forced very near the dry ground, and our highlanders carried us over the water.

We were now treading[178] that illustrious island, which was once the luminary of the Caledonian regions, whence savage clans and roving barbarians derived the benefits of knowledge, and the blessings of religion. To abstract the mind from all local emotion would be impossible, if it were endeavoured, and would be foolish, if it were possible. Whatever withdraws us from the power of our senses; whatever makes the past, the distant, or the future predominate over the present, advances us in the dignity of thinking beings. Far from me and from my friends, be such frigid philosophy as may conduct us indifferent and unmoved over any ground which has been dignified by wisdom, bravery, or virtue. That man is little to be envied, whose patriotism would not gain force upon the plain of Marathon, or whose piety would not grow warmer among the ruins of Iona.

We came too late to visit monuments: some care was necessary for ourselves. Whatever was in the island, Sir Allan could command, for the inhabitants were Macleans; but having little they could not give us much. He went to the headman of the island, whom Fame (but Fame delights in amplifying) represents as worth no less than fifty pounds. He was perhaps proud enough of his guests, but ill prepared for our entertainment; however, he soon produced more provision than men not luxurious require. Our lodging was next to be provided. We found a barn well stocked with hay, and made our beds as soft as we could.

In the morning we rose and surveyed the place. The churches of the two convents are both standing, though unroofed. They were built of unhewn stone, but solid, and not inelegant. I brought away rude measures of the buildings, such as I cannot much trust myself, inaccurately taken, and obscurely noted. Mr Pennant's delineations, which are doubtless exact, have made my unskilful descriptions less necessary.

The episcopal church consists of two parts, separated by the belfry, and built at different times. The original church had, like others, the altar at one end, and tower at the other; but as it grew too small, another building of equal dimension was added, and the tower then was necessarily in the middle.

That these edifices are of different ages seems evident. The arch of the first church is Roman, being part of a circle; that of the additional building is pointed, and therefore Gothick, or Saracenical; the tower is firm, and wants only to be floored and covered.

Of the chambers or cells belonging to the monks, there are some walls remaining, but nothing approaching to a complete apartment.

The bottom of the church is so incumbered with mud and rubbish, that we could make no discoveries of curious inscriptions, and what there are have been already published. The place is said to be known where the black stones lie concealed,[179] on which the old Highland chiefs, when they made contracts and alliances, used to take the oath, which was considered as more sacred than any other obligation, and which could not be violated without the blackest infamy. In those days of violence and rapine, it was of great importance to impress upon savage minds the sanctity of an oath, by some particular and extraordinary circumstances. They would not have recourse to the black stones, upon small or common occasions, and when they had established their faith by this tremendous sanction, inconstancy and treachery were no longer feared.

The chapel of the nunnery is now used by the inhabitants as a kind of general cow-house, and the bottom is consequently too miry for examination. Some of the stones which covered the later abbesses have inscriptions, which might yet be read, if the chapel were cleaned. The roof of this, as of all the other buildings, is totally destroyed, not only because timber quickly decays when it is neglected, but because in an island utterly destitute of wood, it was wanted for use, and was consequently the first plunder of needy rapacity.

The chancel of the nuns' chapel is covered with an arch of stone, to which time has done no injury; and a small apartment communicating with the choir, on the north side, like the chapter-house in cathedrals, roofed with stone in the same manner, is likewise entire.

In one of the churches was a marble altar, which the superstition of the inhabitants has destroyed. Their opinion was, that a fragment of this stone was a defence against shipwrecks, fire, and miscarriages. In one corner of the church the bason for holy water is yet unbroken.

The cemetery of the nunnery was, till very lately, regarded with such reverence that only women were buried in it. These reliques of veneration always produce some mournful pleasure. I could have forgiven a great injury more easily than the violation of this imaginary sanctity.

South of the chapel stand the walls of a large room, which was probably the hall, or refectory of the nunnery. This apartment is capable of repair. Of the rest of the convent there are only fragments.

Besides the two principal churches, there are, I think, five chapels yet standing, and three more remembered. There are also crosses, of which two bear the names of St John and St Matthew.

A large space of ground about these consecrated edifices is covered with grave-stones, few of which have any inscription. He that surveys it, attended by an insular antiquary, may be told where the Kings of many nations are buried, and if he loves to sooth his imagination with the thoughts that naturally rise in places where the great and the powerful lie mingled with the dust, let him listen in submissive silence; for if he asks any questions, his delight is at an end.

Iona has long enjoyed, without any very credible attestation, the honour of being reputed the cemetery of the Scottish Kings. It is not unlikely, that, when the opinion of local sanctity was prevalent, the chieftains of the isles, and perhaps some of the Norwegian or Irish princes were reposited in this venerable enclosure. But by whom the subterraneous vaults are peopled is now utterly unknown. The graves are very numerous, and some of them undoubtedly contain the remains of men, who did not expect to be so soon forgotten.[180]

Not far from this awful ground, may be traced the garden of the monastery: the fishponds are yet discernible, and the aqueduct, which supplied them, is still in use.

There remains a broken building, which is called the Bishop's house, I know not by what authority. It was once the residence of some man above the common rank, for it has two stories, and a chimney. We were shewn a chimney at the other end, which was only a nich, without perforation, but so much does antiquarian credulity, or patriotick vanity prevail, that it was not much more safe to trust the eye of our instructor than the memory.

There is in the island one house more, and only one, that has a chimney: we entered it, and found it neither wanting repair nor inhabitants; but to the farmers, who now possess it, the chimney is of no great value; for their fire was made on the floor, in the middle of the room, and notwithstanding the dignity of their mansion, they rejoiced, like their neighbours, in the comforts of smoke.

It is observed, that ecclesiastical colleges are always in the most pleasant and fruitful places. While the world allowed the monks their choice, it is surely no dishonour that they chose well. The island is remarkably fruitful. The village near the churches is said to contain seventy families, which, at five in a family, is more than a hundred inhabitants to a mile. There are perhaps other villages; yet both corn and cattle are annually exported.

But the fruitfulness of Iona is now its whole prosperity. The inhabitants are remarkably gross, and remarkably neglected: I know not if they are visited by any minister. The island, which was once the metropolis of learning and piety, has now no school for education, nor temple for worship, only two inhabitants that can speak English, and not one that can write or read.

The people are of the clan of Maclean; and though Sir Allan had not been in the place for many years, he was received with all the reverence due to their chieftain. One of them being sharply reprehended by him, for not sending him some rum, declared after his departure, in Mr Boswell's presence, that he had no design of disappointing him, 'for,' said he, 'I would cut my bones for him; and if he had sent his dog for it, he should have had it.'

When we were to depart, our boat was left by the ebb at a great distance from the water, but no sooner did we wish it afloat, than the islanders gathered round it, and by the union of many hands, pushed it down the beach; every man who could contribute his help seemed to think himself happy in the opportunity of being, for a moment, useful to his chief.

We now left those illustrious ruins, by which Mr Boswell was much affected, nor would I willingly be thought to have looked upon them without some emotion. Perhaps, in the revolutions of the world, Iona may be sometime again the instructress of the western regions.

It was no long voyage to Mull, where, under Sir Allan's protection, we landed in the evening, and were entertained for the night by Mr Macleod,[181] a minister that lives upon the coast, whose elegance of conversation, and strength of judgment, would make him conspicuous in places of greater celebrity. Next day we dined with Dr Maclean, another physician, and then travelled on to the house of a very powerful laird, Maclean of Lochbuy; for in this country every man's name is Maclean.

Where races are thus numerous, and thus combined, none but the chief of a clan is addressed by his name. The Laird of Dunvegan is called Macleod, but other gentlemen of the same family are denominated by the places where they reside, as Raasa, or Talisker. The distinction of the meaner people is made by their Christian names. In consequence of this practice, the late Laird of Macfarlane, an eminent genealogist, considered himself as disrespectfully treated, if the common addition was applied to him. Mr Macfarlane, said he, may with equal propriety be said to many; but I, and I only, am Macfarlane.

Our afternoon journey was through a country of such gloomy desolation, that Mr Boswell thought no part of the Highlands equally terrifick, yet we came without any difficulty, at evening, to Lochbuy, where we found a true Highland laird, rough and haughty, and tenacious of his dignity; who, hearing my name, inquired whether I was of the Johnstons of Glencoe, or of Ardnamurchan.

Lochbuy has, like the other insular chieftains, quitted the castle that sheltered his ancestors, and lives near it, in a mansion not very spacious or splendid.[182] I have seen no houses in the islands much to be envied for convenience or magnificence, yet they bear testimony to the progress of arts and civility, as they shew that rapine and surprise are no longer dreaded, and are much more commodious than the ancient fortresses.

The castles of the Hebrides, many of which are standing, and many ruined, were always built upon points of land, on the margin of the few. For the choice of this situation there must have been some general reason, which the change of manners has left in obscurity. They were of no use in the days of piracy, as defences of the coast; for it was equally accessible in other places. Had they been sea-marks or light-houses, they would have been of more use to the invader than the natives, who could want no such directions on their own waters: for a watch-tower, a cottage on a hill would have been better, as it would have commanded a wider view.

If they be considered merely as places of retreat, the situation seems not well chosen; for the laird of an island is safest from foreign enemies in the center: on the coast he might be more suddenly surprised than in the inland parts; and the invaders, if their enterprise miscarried, might more easily retreat. Some convenience, however, whatever it was, their position on the shore afforded; for uniformity of practice seldom continues long without good reason.

A castle in the islands is only a single tower of three or four stories, of which the walls are sometimes eight or nine feet thick, with narrow windows, and close winding stairs of stone. The top rises in a cone, or pyramid of stone, encompassed by battlements. The intermediate floors are sometimes frames of timber, as in common houses, and sometimes arches of stone, or alternately stone and timber; so that there was very little danger from fire. In the center of every floor, from top to bottom, is the chief room, of no great extent, round which there are narrow cavities, or recesses, formed by small vacuities, or by a double wall. I know not whether there be ever more than one fire-place. They had not capacity to contain many people, or much provision; but their enemies could seldom stay to blockade them; for if they failed in the first attack, their next care was to escape.

The walls were always too strong to be shaken by such desultory hostilities; the windows were too narrow to be entered, and the battlements too high to be scaled. The only danger was at the gates, over which the wall was built with a square cavity, not unlike a chimney, continued to the top. Through this hollow the defendants let fall stones upon those who attempted to break the gate, and poured down water, perhaps scalding water, if the attack was made with fire. The castle of Lochbuy was secured by double doors, of which the outer was an iron grate.

In every castle is a well and a dungeon. The use of the well is evident. The dungeon is a deep subterraneous cavity, walled on the sides, and arched on the top, into which the descent is through a narrow door, by a ladder or a rope, so that it seems impossible to escape, when the rope or ladder is drawn up. The dungeon was, I suppose, in war, a prison for such captives as were treated with severity, and, in peace, for such delinquents as had committed crimes within the laird's jurisdiction; for the mansions of many lairds were, till the late privation of their privileges, the halls of justice to their own tenants.

As these fortifications were the productions of mere necessity, they are built only for safety, with little regard to convenience, and with none to elegance or pleasure. It was sufficient for a laird of the Hebrides, if he had a strong house, in which he could hide his wife and children from the next clan. That they are not large nor splendid is no wonder. It is not easy to find how they were raised, such as they are, by men who had no money, in countries where the labourers and artificers could scarcely be fed. The buildings in different parts of the islands shew their degrees of wealth and power. I believe that for all the castles which I have seen beyond the Tweed, the ruins yet remaining of some one of these which the English built in Wales, would supply materials.[183]

These castles afford another evidence that the fictions of romantick chivalry had for their basis the real manners of the feudal times, when every lord of a seignory lived in his hold lawless and unaccountable, with all the licentiousness and insolence of uncontested superiority and unprincipled power. The traveller, whoever he might be, coming to the fortified habitation of a chieftain, would, probably, have been interrogated from the battlements, admitted with caution at the gate, introduced to a petty monarch, fierce with habitual hostility, and vigilant with ignorant suspicion; who, according to his general temper, or accidental humour, would have seated a stranger as his guest at the table, or as a spy confined him in the dungeon.

Lochbuy means the Yellow Lake, which is the name given to an inlet of the sea, upon which the castle of Mr Maclean stands. The reason for the appellation we did not learn.[184]

We were now to leave the Hebrides, where we had spent some weeks with sufficient amusement, and where we had amplified our thoughts with new scenes of nature, and new modes of life. More time would have given us a more distinct view, but it was necessary that Mr Boswell should return before the courts of justice were opened; and it was not proper to live too long upon hospitality, however liberally imparted.

Of these islands it must be confessed, that they have not many allurements, but to the mere lover of naked nature. The inhabitants are thin, provisions are scarce, and desolation and penury give little pleasure.

The people collectively considered are not few, though their numbers are small in proportion to the space which they occupy. Mull is said to contain six thousand, and Sky fifteen thousand. Of the computation respecting Mull, I can give no account; but when I doubted the truth of the numbers attributed to Sky, one of the ministers exhibited such facts as conquered my incredulity.

Of the proportion, which the product of any region bears to the people, an estimate is commonly made according to the pecuniary price of the necessaries of life; a principle of judgment which is never certain, because it supposes what is far from truth, that the value of money is always the same, and so measures an unknown quantity by an uncertain standard. It is competent enough when the markets of the same country, at different times, and those times not too distant, are to be compared; but of very little use for the purpose of making one nation acquainted with the state of another. Provisions, though plentiful, are sold in places of great pecuniary opulence for nominal prices, to which, however scarce, where gold and silver are yet scarcer, they can never be raised.

In the Western Islands there is so little internal commerce, that hardly any thing has a known or settled rate. The price of things brought in, or carried out, is to be considered as that of a foreign market; and even this there is some difficulty in discovering, because their denominations of quantity are different from ours; and when there is ignorance on both sides, no appeal can be made to a common measure.

This, however, is not the only impediment. The Scots, with a vigilance of jealousy which never goes to sleep, always suspect that an Englishman despises them for their poverty, and to convince him that they are not less rich than their neighbours, are sure to tell him a price higher than the true. When Lesley,[185] two hundred years ago, related so punctiliously, that a hundred hen eggs, new laid, were sold in the islands for a peny, he supposed that no inference could possibly follow, but that eggs were in great abundance. Posterity has since grown wiser; and having learned, that nominal and real value may differ, they now tell no such stories, lest the foreigner should happen to collect, not that eggs are many, but that pence are few.

Money and wealth have by the use of commercial language been so long confounded, that they are commonly supposed to be the same; and this prejudice has spread so widely in Scotland, that I know not whether I found a man or woman, whom I interrogated concerning payments of money, that could surmount the illiberal desire of deceiving me, by representing every thing as dearer than it is.

From Lochbuy we rode a very few miles to the side of Mull, which faces Scotland, where, having taken leave of our kind protector, Sir Allan, we embarked in a boat, in which the seat provided for our accommodation was a heap of rough brushwood; and on the twenty-second of October reposed at a tolerable inn on the main land.

On the next day we began our journey southwards.[186] The weather was tempestuous. For half the day the ground was rough, and our horses were still small. Had they required much restraint, we might have been reduced to difficulties; for I think we had amongst us but one bridle. We fed the poor animals liberally, and they performed their journey well. In the latter part of the day, we came to a firm and smooth road, made by the soldiers, on which we travelled with great security, busied with contemplating the scenè about us. The night came on while we had yet a great part of the way to go, though not so dark, but that we could discern the cataracts which poured down the hills, on one side, and fell into one general channel that ran with great violence on the other. The wind was loud, the rain was heavy, and the whistling of the blast, the fall of the shower, the rush of the cataracts, and the roar of the torrent, made a nobler chorus of the rough musick of nature than it had ever been my chance to hear before. The streams, which ran cross the way from the hills to the main current, were so frequent, that after a while I began to count them; and, in ten miles, reckoned fifty-five, probably missing some, and having let some pass before they forced themselves upon my notice. At last we came to Inverary, where we found an inn, not only commodious, but magnificent.

The difficulties of peregrination were now at an end. Mr Boswell had the honour of being known to the Duke of Argyle, by whom we were very kindly entertained at his splendid seat, and supplied with conveniences for surveying his spacious park and rising forests.[187]

After two days stay at Inverary we proceeded southward over Glencroe, a black and dreary region, now made easily passable by a military road, which rises from either end of the glen by an acclivity not dangerously steep, but sufficiently laborious. In the middle, at the top of the hill, is a seat with this inscription, REST, AND BE THANKFUL. Stones were placed to mark the distances, which the inhabitants have taken away, resolved, they said, 'to have no new miles'.

In this rainy season the hills streamed with waterfalls, which, crossing the way, formed currents on the other side, that ran in contrary directions as they fell to the north and south of the summit. Being, by the favour of the duke, well mounted, I went up and down the hill with great convenience.

From Glencroe we passed through a pleasant country to the banks of Loch Lomond, and were received at the house of Sir James Colquhoun, who is owner of almost all the thirty islands of the loch, which we went in a boat next morning to survey. The heaviness of the rain shortened our voyage, but we landed on one island planted with yew, and stocked with deer, and on another containing perhaps not more than half an acre, remarkable for the ruins of an old castle, on which the osprey builds her annual nest. Had Loch Lomond been in a happier climate, it would have been the boast of wealth and vanity to own one of the little spots which it incloses, and to have employed upon it all the arts of embellishment. But as it is, the islets, which court the gazer at a distance, disgust him at his approach, when he finds, instead of soft lawns and shady thickets, nothing more than uncultivated ruggedness.

Where the loch discharges itself into a river, called the Leven, we passed a night with Mr Smollet, a relation of Doctor Smollet, to whose memory he has raised an obelisk on the bank near the house in which he was born. The civility and respect which we found at every place, it is ungrateful to omit, and tedious to repeat. Here we were met by a post-chaise, that conveyed us to Glasgow.

To describe a city so much frequented as Glasgow, is unnecessary. The prosperity of its commerce appears by the greatness of many private houses, and a general appearance of wealth. It is the only episcopal city whose cathedral was left standing in the rage of Reformation.[188] It is now divided into many separate places of worship, which, taken all together, compose a great pile, that had been some centuries in building, but was never finished; for the change of religion intercepted its progress, before the cross isle was added, which seems essential to a Gothick cathedral.

The college has not had a sufficient share of the increasing magnificence of the place. The session was begun; for it commences on the tenth of October, and continues to the tenth of June, but the students appeared not numerous, being, I suppose, not yet returned from their several homes. The division of the academical year into one session, and one recess, seems to me better accommodated to the present state of life, than that variegation of time by terms and vacations derived from distant centuries, in which it was probably convenient, and still continued in the English universities. So many solid months as the Scotch scheme of education joins together, allow and encourage a plan for each part of the year; but with us, he that has settled himself to study in the college is soon tempted into the country, and he that has adjusted his life in the country, is summoned back to his college.

Yet when I have allowed to the universities of Scotland a more rational distribution of time, I have given them, so far as my inquiries have informed me, all that they can claim. The students, for the most part, go thither boys, and depart before they are men; they carry with them little fundamental knowledge, and therefore the superstructure cannot be lofty. The grammar schools are not generally well supplied; for the character of a school-master being there less honourable than in England, is seldom accepted by men who are capable to adorn it, and where the school has been deficient, the college can effect little.

Men bred in the universities of Scotland cannot be expected to be often decorated with the splendours of ornamental erudition, but they obtain a mediocrity of knowledge, between learning and ignorance, not inadequate to the purposes of common life, which is, I believe, very widely diffused among them, and which countenanced in general by a national combination so invidious, that their friends cannot defend it, and actuated in particulars by a spirit of enterprise, so vigorous, that their enemies are constrained to praise it, enables them to find, or to make their way to employment, riches, and distinction.

From Glasgow we directed our course to Auchinleck, an estate devolved, through a long series of ancestors, to Mr Boswell's father, the present possessor. In our way we found several places remarkable enough in themselves, but already described by those who viewed them at more leisure, or with much more skill; and stopped two days at Mr Campbell's, a gentleman married to Mrs Boswell's sister.[189]

Auchinleck, which signifies a 'stony field', seems not now to have any particular claim to its denomination. It is a district generally level, and sufficiently fertile, but like all the western side of Scotland, incommoded by very frequent rain. It was, with the rest of the country, generally naked, till the present possessor finding, by the growth of some stately trees near his old castle, that the ground was favourable enough to timber, adorned it very diligently with annual plantations.

Lord Auchinleck, who is one of the Judges of Scotland, and therefore not wholly at leisure for domestick business or pleasure, has yet found time to make improvements in his patrimony. He has built a house of hewn stone, very stately, and durable, and has advanced the value of his lands with great tenderness to his tenants.

I was, however, less delighted with the elegance of the modern mansion, than with the sullen dignity of the old castle. I clambered with Mr Boswell among the ruins, which afford striking images of ancient life. It is, like other castles, built upon a point of rock, and was, I believe, anciently surrounded with a moat. There is another rock near it, to which the drawbridge, when it was let down, is said to have reached. Here, in the ages of tumult and rapine, the laird was surprised and killed by the neighbouring chief, who perhaps might have extinguished the family, had he not in a few days been seized and hanged, together with his sons, by Douglas, who came with his forces to the relief of Auchinleck.

At no great distance from the house runs a pleasing brook, by a red rock, out of which has been hewn a very agreeable and commodious summer-house, at less expence, as Lord Auchinleck told me, than would have been required to build a room of the same dimensions. The rock seems to have no more dampness than any other wall. Such opportunities of variety it is judicious not to neglect.

We now returned to Edinburgh, where I passed some days with men of learning, whose names want no advancement from my commemoration, or with women of elegance, which perhaps disclaims a pedant's praise.

The conversation of the Scots grows every day less unpleasing to the English; their peculiarities wear fast away; their dialect is likely to become in half a century provincial and rustick, even to themselves. The great, the learned, the ambitious, and the vain, all cultivate the English phrase, and the English pronunciation, and in splendid companies Scotch is not much heard, except now and then from an old lady.[190]

There is one subject of philosophical curiosity to be found in Edinburgh, which no other city has to shew; a college of the deaf and dumb, who are taught to speak, to read, to write, and to practice arithmetick, by a gentleman, whose name is Braidwood. The number which attends him is, I think, about twelve, which he brings together into a little school, and instructs according to their several degrees of proficiency.

I do not mean to mention the instruction of the deaf as new. Having been first practised upon the son of a constable of Spain, it was afterwards cultivated with much emulation in England, by Wallis and Holder,[191] and was lately professed by Mr Baker,[192] who once flattered me with hopes of seeing his method published. How far any former teachers have succeeded, it is not easy to know; the improvement of Mr Braidwood's pupils is wonderful. They not only speak, write, and understand what is written, but if he that speaks looks towards them, and modifies his organs by distinct and full utterance, they know so well what is spoken, that it is an expression scarcely figurative to say, they hear with the eye. That any have attained to the power mentioned by Burnet,[193] of feeling sounds, by laying a hand on the speaker's mouth, I know not; but I have seen so much, that I can believe more; a single word, or a short sentence, I think, may possibly be so distinguished.

It will readily be supposed by those that consider this subject, that Mr Braidwood's scholars spell accurately. Orthography is vitiated among such as learn first to speak, and then to write, by imperfect notions of the relation between letters and vocal utterance; but to those students every character is of equal importance; for letters are to them not symbols of names, but of things; when they write they do not represent a sound, but delineate a form.

This school I visited, and found some of the scholars waiting for their master, whom they are said to receive at his entrance with smiling countenances and sparkling eyes, delighted with the hope of new ideas. One of the young ladies had her slate before her, on which I wrote a question consisting of three figures, to be multiplied by two figures. She looked upon it, and quivering her fingers in a manner which I thought very pretty, but of which I know not whether it was art or play, multiplied the sum regularly in two lines, observing the decimal place; but did not add the two lines together, probably disdaining so easy an operation. I pointed at the place where the sum total should stand, and she noted it with such expedition as seemed to shew that she had it only to write.

It was pleasing to see one of the most desperate of human calamities capable of so much help: whatever enlarges hope, will exalt courage; after having seen the deaf taught arithetick, who would be afraid to cultivate the Hebrides?

Such are the things which this journey has given me an opportunity of seeing, and such are the reflections which that sight has raised. Having passed my time almost wholly in cities, I may have been surprised by modes of life and appearances of nature, that are familiar to men of wider survey and more varied conversation. Novelty and ignorance must always be reciprocal, and I cannot but be conscious that my thoughts on national manners, are the thoughts of one who has seen but little.

THE JOURNAL OF
A TOUR TO THE HEBRIDES
WITH SAMUEL JOHNSON, LL.D.

by

James Boswell

DEDICATION

MY DEAR SIR,

In every narrative, whether historical or biographical, authenticity is of the utmost consequence. Of this I have ever been so firmly persuaded, that I inscribed a former work to that person who was the best judge of its truth.[1] I need not tell you I mean General Paoli; who, after his great, though unsuccessful, efforts to preserve the liberties of his country, has found an honourable asylum in Britain, where he has now lived many years the object of Royal regard and private respect; and whom I cannot name without expressing my very grateful sense of the uniform kindness which he has been pleased to shew me.[2]

The friends of Doctor Johnson can best judge, from internal evidence, whether the numerous conversations which form the most valuable part of the ensuing pages, are correctly related. To them, therefore I wish to appeal, for the accuracy of the portrait here exhibited to the world.

As one of those who were intimately acquainted with him, you have a title to this address.[3] You have obligingly taken the trouble to peruse the original manuscript of this tour, and can vouch for the strict fidelity of the present publication. Your literary alliance with our much lamented friend, in consequence of having undertaken to render one of his labours more complete, by your edition of Shakespeare, a work which I am confident will not disappoint the expectations of the publick, gives you another claim. But I have a still more powerful inducement to prefix your name to this volume, as it gives me an opportunity of letting the world know that I enjoy the honour and happiness of your friendship; and of thus publickly testifying the sincere regard with which I am,

> My dear Sir,
> Your very faithful
> And obedient servant,

LONDON,
20 September 1785.

JAMES BOSWELL.

ADVERTISEMENT

TO THE THIRD EDITION

Animated by the very favourable reception which two large impressions of this work have had, it has been my study to make it as perfect as I could in this edition, by correcting some inaccuracies which I discovered myself, and some which the kindness of friends or the scrutiny of adversaries pointed out. A few notes are added, of which the principal object is, to refute misrepresentation and calumny.

To the animadversions in the periodical journals of criticism, and in the numerous publications to which my book has given rise, I have made no answer. Every work must stand or fall by its own merit. I cannot, however, omit this opportunity of returning thanks to a gentleman who published defence of my journal, and has added to the favour by communicating his name to me in a very obliging letter.[4]

It would be an idle waste of time to take any particular notice of the futile remarks, to many of which, a petty national resentment, unworthy of my countrymen, has probably given rise; remarks, which have been industriously circulated in the publick prints by shallow or envious cavillers, who have endeavoured to persuade the world that Dr Johnson's character has been *lessened* by recording such various instances of his lively wit and acute judgment, on every topick that was presented to his mind. In the opinion of every person of taste and knowledge that I have conversed with, it has been greatly *heightened*; and I will venture to predict, that this specimen of the colloquial talents and extemporaneous effusions of my illustrious fellow-traveller will become still more valuable, when, by the lapse of time, he shall have become an *ancient*;[5] when all those who can now bear testimony to the transcendent powers of his mind, shall have passed away; and no other memorial of this great and good man shall remain, but the following Journal, the other anecdotes and letters preserved by his friends, and those incomparable works, which have for many years been in the highest estimation, and will be read and admired as long as the English language shall be spoken or understood.

LONDON, 15 August 1786.   J.B.

He was of an admirable pregnancy of wit, and that pregnancy much improved by continual study from his childhood; by which he had gotten such a promptness in expressing his mind, that his extemporal speeches were little inferior to his premeditated writings. Many, no doubt, had read as much and perhaps more than he; but scarce ever any concocted his reading into judgement as he did.

BAKER'S CHRONICLE[6]

Dr Johnson had for many years given me hopes that we should go together, and visit the Hebrides. Martin's *Account* of those islands had impressed us with a notion that we might there contemplate a system of life almost totally different from what we had been accustomed to see; and, to find simplicity and wildness, and all the circumstances of remote time or place, so near to our native great island, was an object within the reach of reasonable curiosity. Dr Johnson has said in his *Journey*, 'that he scarcely remembered how the wish to visit the Hebrides was excited'; but he told me, in summer, 1763, that his father put Martin's *Account* into his hands when he was very young, and that he was much pleased with it. We reckoned there would be some inconveniencies and hardships, and perhaps a little danger; but these we were persuaded were magnified in the imagination of every body. When I was at Ferney,[7] in 1764, I mentioned our design to Voltaire. He looked at me, as if I had talked of going to the North Pole, and said, 'You do not insist on my accompanying you?' 'No, sir.' 'Then I am very willing you should go.' I was not afraid that our curious expedition would be prevented by such apprehensions; but I doubted that it would not be possible to prevail on Dr Johnson to relinquish, for some time, the felicity of a London life, which, to a man who can enjoy it with full intellectual relish, is apt to make existence in any narrower sphere seem insipid or irksome. I doubted that he would not be willing to come down from his elevated state of philosophical dignity; from a superiority of wisdom among the wise, and of learning among the learned; and from flashing his wit upon minds bright enough to reflect it.

He had disappointed my expectations so long, that I began to despair; but in spring, 1773, he talked of coming to Scotland that year with so much firmness, that I hoped he was at last in earnest. I knew that, if he were once launched from the metropolis, he would go forward very well; and I got our common friends there to assist in setting him afloat. To Mrs Thrale in particular, whose enchantment over him seldom failed, I was much obliged. It was, 'I'll give thee a wind.' 'Thou art kind.'[8] To attract him, we had invitations from the chiefs Macdonald and Macleod; and, for additional aid, I wrote to Lord Elibank, Dr William Robertson, and Dr Beattie.[9]

To Dr Robertson, so far as my letter concerned the present subject, I wrote as follows:

Our friend, Mr Samuel Johnson, is in great health and spirits; and, I do think, has a serious resolution to visit Scotland this year. The more attraction, however, the better; and therefore, though I know he will be happy to meet you there, it will forward the scheme, if, in your answer to this, you express yourself concerning it with that power of which you are so happily possessed, and which may be so directed as to operate strongly upon him.

His answer to that part of my letter was quite as I could have wished. It was written with the address and persuasion of the historian of America.

When I saw you last, you gave us some hopes that you might prevail with Mr Johnson to make that excursion to Scotland, with the expectation of which we have long flattered ourselves. If he could order matters so, as to pass some time in Edinburgh, about the close of the summer session, and then visit some of the Highland scenes, I am confident he would be pleased with the grand features of nature in many parts of this country: he will meet with many persons here who respect him, and some whom I am persuaded he will think not unworthy of his esteem. I wish he would make the experiment. He sometimes cracks his jokes upon us; but he will find that we can distinguish between the stabs of malevolence, and 'the rebukes of the righteous, which are like excellent oil,* and break not the head'. Offer my best compliments to him, and assure him that I shall be happy to have the satisfaction of seeing him under my roof.

To Dr Beattie I wrote,

The chief intention of this letter is to inform you, that I now seriously believe Mr Samuel Johnson will visit Scotland this year: but I wish that every power of attraction may be employed to secure our having so valuable an acquisition, and therefore I hope you will without delay write to me what I know you think, that I may read it to the mighty sage, with proper emphasis, before I leave London, which I must soon. He talks of you with the same warmth that he did last year. We are to see as much of Scotland as we can, in the months of August and September. We shall not be long of being at Marischal College.† He is particularly desirous of seeing some of the Western Islands.

* Our friend Edmund Burke, who by this time had received some pretty severe strokes from Dr Johnson, on account of the unhappy difference in their politicks, upon my repeating this passage to him, exclaimed, 'Oil of vitriol!'

† This, I find, is a Scotticism. I should have said, 'It will not be long before we shall be at Marischal College.'

Dr Beattie did better: *ipse venit*. He was, however, so polite as to wave his privilege of *nil mihi rescribas*,[10] and wrote from Edinburgh, as follows:

Your very kind and agreeable favour of the 20th of April overtook me here yester-day, after having gone to Aberdeen, which place I left about a week ago. I am to set out this day for London, and hope to have the honour of paying my respects to Mr Johnson and you, about a week or ten days hence. I shall then do what I can, to enforce the topick you mentioned; but at present I cannot enter upon it, as I am in a very great hurry; for I intend to begin my journey within an hour or two.

He was as good as his word, and threw some pleasing motives into the northern scale. But, indeed, Mr Johnson loved all that he heard from one whom he tells us, in his *Lives of the Poets*, Gray[11] found 'a poet, a philosopher, and a good man'.

My Lord Elibank did not answer my letter to his lordship for some time. The reason will appear, when we come to the Isle of Sky. I shall then insert my letter, with letters from his lordship, both to myself and Mr Johnson. I beg it may be understood, that I insert my own letters, as I relate my own sayings, rather as keys to what is valuable belonging to others, than for their own sake.

Luckily Mr Justice (now Sir Robert) Chambers, who was about to sail for the East Indies, was going to take leave of his relations at Newcastle, and he conducted Dr Johnson to that town. Mr Scott, of University College, Oxford, (now Dr Scott, of the Commons[12]) accompanied him from thence to Edinburgh. With such propitious convoys did he proceed to my native city. But, lest metaphor should make it be supposed he actually went by sea, I choose to mention that he travelled in post-chaises, of which the rapid motion was one of his most favourite amusements.

Dr Samuel Johnson's character, religious, moral, political, and literary, nay his figure and manner, are, I believe, more generally known than those of almost any man; yet it may not be superfluous here to attempt a sketch of him. Let my readers then remember that he was a sincere and zealous Christian, of high Church of England and monarchical principles, which he would not tamely suffer to be questioned; steady and inflexible in maintaining the obligations of piety and virtue, both from a regard to the order of society, and from a veneration for the Great Source of all order; correct, nay stern in his taste; hard to please, and easily offended, impetuous and irritable in his temper, but of a most humane and benevolent heart; having a mind stored with a vast and various collection of learning and knowledge, which he communicated with peculiar perspicuity and force, in rich and choice expression. He united a most logical head with a most fertile imagination, which gave him an extraordinary advantage in arguing; for he could reason close or wide, as he saw best for the moment. He could, when he chose it, be the greatest sophist that ever wielded a weapon in the schools of declamation; but he indulged this only in conversation; for he owned he sometimes talked for victory; he was too conscientious to make errour permanent and pernicious, by deliberately writing it. He was conscious of his superiority. He loved praise when it was brought to him; but was too proud to seek for it. He was somewhat susceptible of flattery. His mind was so full of imagery, that he might have been perpetually a poet. It has been often remarked, that in his poetical pieces, which it is to be regretted are so few, because so excellent, his style is easier than in his prose. There is deception in this: it is not easier, but better suited to the dignity of verse; as one may dance with grace, whose motions, in ordinary walking – in the common step – are awkward. He had a constitutional melancholy, the clouds of which darkened the brightness of his fancy, and gave a gloomy cast to his whole course of thinking: yet, though grave and awful in his deportment, when he thought it necessary or proper, he frequently indulged himself in pleasantry and sportive sallies. He was prone to superstition, but not to credulity. Though his imagination might incline him to a belief of the marvellous, and the mysterious, his vigorous reason examined the evidence with jealousy. He had a loud voice, and a slow deliberate utterance, which no doubt gave some additional weight to the sterling metal of his conversation. Lord Pembroke said once to me at Wilton, with a happy pleasantry, and some truth, that 'Dr Johnson's sayings would not appear so extra-ordinary, were it not for his *bow-wow way*': but I admit the truth of this only on some occasions. The *Messiah*, played upon the Canterbury organ, is more sublime than when played upon an inferior instrument: but very slight musick will seem grand, when conveyed to the ear through that majestick medium. *While therefore Doctor Johnson's sayings are read, let his manner be taken along with them.* Let it however be observed, that the sayings themselves are generally great; that, though he might be an ordinary composer at times, he was for the most part a Handel. His person was large, robust, I may say approaching to the gigantick, and grown unwieldy from corpulency. His countenance was naturally of the craft of an ancient statue, but somewhat disfigured by the scars of that evil, which, it was formerly imagined, the royal touch could cure. He was now in his sixty-fourth year, and was become a little dull of hearing. His sight had always been some-what weak; yet, so much does mind govern, and even supply the deficiency of organs, that his perceptions were uncommonly quick and accurate. His head, and sometimes also his body, shook with a kind of motion like the effect of a palsy: he appeared to be frequently disturbed by cramps, or convulsive contractions,* of the nature of that distemper called St Vitus's dance. He wore a full suit of plain brown clothes, with twisted-hair buttons of the same colour, a large bushy greyish wig, a plain shirt, black worsted stockings, and silver buckles. Upon this tour, when journeying, he wore boots, and a very wide brown cloth great coat, with pockets which might have almost held the two volumes of his folio dictionary; and he carried in his hand a large English oak stick. Let me not be censured for mentioning such minute particulars. Every thing relative to so great a man is worth observing. I remember Dr Adam Smith, in his rhetorical lectures at Glasgow, told us he was glad to know that Milton wore latchets in his shoes, instead of buckles. When I mention the oak stick, it is but letting Hercules have his club; and, by-and-by, my readers will find this stick will bud, and produce a good joke.

This imperfect sketch of 'the combination and the form' of that Wonderful Man, whom I venerated and loved while in this world, and after whom I gaze with humble hope, now that it has pleased Almighty God to call him to a better world, will serve to introduce to the fancy of my readers the capital object of the following journal, in the course of which I trust they will attain to a considerable degree of acquaintance with him.

His prejudice against Scotland was announced almost as soon as he began to appear in the world of letters. In his *London*, a poem, are the following nervous lines:

> For who would leave, unbrib'd, Hibernia's land?
> Or change the rocks of Scotland for the Strand?
> There none are swept by sudden fate away;
> But all, whom hunger spares, with age decay.

The truth is, like the ancient Greeks and Romans, he allowed himself to look upon all nations but his own as barbarians: not only Hibernia, and Scotland, but Spain, Italy, and France, are attacked in the same poem. If he was particularly prejudiced against the Scots, it was because they were more in his way; because he thought their success in England rather exceeded the due proportion of their real merit; and because he could not but see

---

* Such they appeared to me; but since the first edition, Sir Joshua Reynolds has observed to me, 'that Dr Johnson's extraordinary gestures were only habits, in which he indulged himself at certain times. When in company, where he was not free, or when engaged earnestly in conversation, he never gave way to such habits, which proves that they were not involuntary', I still however think, that these gestures were involuntary; for surely had not that been the case, he would have restrained them in the publick streets.

in them that nationality which I believe no liberal-minded Scotsman will deny. He was indeed, if I may be allowed the phrase, at bottom much of a John Bull; much of a blunt 'true born Englishman'. There was a stratum of common clay under the rock of marble. He was voraciously fond of good eating; and he had a great deal of that quality called humour, which gives an oiliness and a gloss to every other quality.

I am, I flatter myself, completely a citizen of the world. In my travels through Holland, Germany, Switzerland, Italy, Corsica, France, I never felt myself from home; and I sincerely love 'every kindred and tongue and people and nation'. I subscribe to what my late truly learned and philosophical friend Mr Crosbie said, that the English are better animals than the Scots; they are nearer the sun; their blood is richer, and more mellow: but when I humour any of them in an outrageous contempt of Scotland, I fairly own I treat them as children. And thus I have, at some moments, found myself obliged to treat even Dr Johnson.

To Scotland however he ventured; and he returned from it in great humour, with his prejudices much lessened, and with very grateful feelings of the hospitality with which he was treated; as is evident from that admirable work, his *Journey to the Western Islands of Scotland*, which, to my utter astonishment, has been misapprehended, even to rancour, by many of my countrymen.

To have the company of Chambers and Scott, he delayed his journey so long, that the court of session, which rises on the eleventh of August, was broke up before he got to Edinburgh.

On Saturday the fourteenth of August, 1773, late in the evening, I received a note from him, that he was arrived at Boyd's inn, at the head of the Canongate.[13] I went to him directly. He embraced me cordially; and I exulted in the thought, that I now had him actually in Caledonia. Mr Scott's amiable manners, and attachment to our Socrates, at once united me to him. He told me that, before I came in, the Doctor had unluckily had a bad specimen of Scottish cleanliness. He then drank no fermented liquor. He asked to have his lemonade made sweeter; upon which the waiter, with his greasy fingers, lifted a lump of sugar, and put it into it. The Doctor, in indignation, threw it out of the window. Scott said, he was afraid he would have knocked the waiter down. Mr Johnson told me, that such another trick was played him at the house of a lady in Paris. He was to do me the honour to lodge under my roof. I regretted sincerely that I had not also a room for Mr Scott. Mr Johnson and I walked arm-in-arm up the High Street, to my house in James's court:[14] it was a dusky night: I could not prevent his being assailed by the evening effluvia of Edinburgh. I heard a late baronet, of some distinction in the political world in the beginning of the present reign, observe, that 'walking the streets of Edinburgh at night was pretty perilous, and a good deal odoriferous'. The peril is much abated, by the care which the magistrates have taken to enforce the city laws against throwing foul water from the windows; but, from the structure of the houses in the old town, which consist of many stories, in each of which a different family lives, and there being no covered sewers, the odour still continues. A zealous Scotsman would have wished Mr Johnson to be without one of his five senses upon this occasion. As we marched slowly along, he grumbled in my ear, 'I smell you in the dark!' But he acknowledged that the breadth of the street, and the loftiness of the buildings on each side, made a noble appearance.

My wife had tea ready for him, which it is well known he delighted to drink at all hours, particularly when sitting up late, and of which his able defence against Mr Jonas Hanway should have obtained him a magnificent reward from the East India Company. He shewed much complacency upon finding that the mistress of the house was so attentive to his singular habit; and as no man could be more polite when he chose to be so, his address to her was most courteous and engaging; and his conversation soon charmed her into a forgetfulness of his external appearance.

I did not begin to keep a regular full journal till some days after we had set out from Edinburgh; but I have luckily preserved a good many fragments of his *Memorabilia* from his very first evening in Scotland.

We had, a little before this, had a trial for murder, in which the judges had allowed the lapse of twenty years since its commission as a plea in bar, in conformity with the doctrine of prescription in the civil law, which Scotland and several other countries in Europe have adopted. He at first disapproved of this; but then he thought there was something in it, if there had been for twenty years a neglect to prosecute a crime which was *known*. He would not allow that a murder, by not being *discovered* for twenty years, should escape punishment. We talked of the ancient trial by duel. He did not think it so absurd as is generally supposed; 'For,' said he, 'it was only allowed when the question was *in equilibrio*, as when one affirmed and another denied; and they had a notion that Providence would interfere in favour of him who was in the right. But as it was found that in a duel, he who was in the right had not a better chance than he who was in the wrong, therefore society instituted the present mode of trial, and gave the advantage to him who is in the right.'

We sat till near two in the morning, having chatted a good while after my wife left us. She had insisted, that to shew all respect to the Sage, she would give up her own bed-chamber to him, and take a worse. This

I cannot but gratefully mention, as one of a thousand obligations which I owe her, since the great obligation of her being pleased to accept of me as her husband.

Sunday, 15th August

Mr Scott came to breakfast, at which I introduced to Dr Johnson, and him, my friend Sir William Forbes, now of Pitsligo;[15] a man of whom too much good cannot be said; who, with distinguished abilities and application in his profession of a banker, is at once a good companion, and a good Christian; which I think is saying enough. Yet it is but justice to record, that once, when he was in a dangerous illness, he was watched with the anxious apprehension of a general calamity; day and night his house was beset with affectionate inquiries; and, upon his recovery, *Te deum* was the universal chorus from the hearts of his countrymen.

Mr Johnson was pleased with my daughter Veronica,* then a child of about four months old. She had the appearance of listening to him. His motions seemed to her to be intended for her amusement; and when he stopped, she fluttered, and made a little infantine noise, and a kind of signal for him to begin again. She would be held close to him; which was a proof, from simple nature, that his figure was not horrid. Her fondness for him endeared her still more to me, and I declared she should have five hundred pounds of additional fortune.

We talked of the practice of the law. William Forbes said, he thought an honest lawyer should never undertake a cause which he was satisfied was not a just one. 'Sir,' said Mr Johnson, 'a lawyer has no business with the justice or injustice of the cause which he undertakes, unless his client asks his opinion, and then he is bound to give it honestly. The justice or

---

* The saint's name of *Veronica* was introduced into our family through my great grandmother Veronica, Countess of Kincardine, a Dutch lady of the noble house of Sommelsdyck, of which there is a full account in Bayle's *Dictionary*. The family had once a princely right in Surinam. The governour of that settlement was appointed by the States General, the town of Amsterdam, and Sommelsdyck. The States General have acquired Sommelsdyck's right; but the family has still great dignity and opulence, and by intermarriages is connected with many other noble families. When I was at the Hague, I was received with all the affection of kindred. The present Sommelsdyck has an important charge in the Republick, and is as worthy a man as lives. He has honoured me with his correspondence for these twenty years. My great grandfather, the husband of Countess Veronica, was Alexander, Earl of Kincardine, that eminent Royalist whose character is given by Burnet in his *History of his own Times*. From him the blood of Bruce flows in my veins. Of such ancestry who would not be proud? And, as *Nihil est, nisi hoc sciat alter*, is peculiarly true of genealogy, who would not be glad to seize a fair opportunity to let it be known?[16]

injustice of the cause is to be decided by the judge. Consider, sir; what is the purpose of courts of justice? It is, that every man may have his cause fairly tried, by men appointed to try causes. A lawyer is not to tell what he knows to be a lie: he is not to produce what he knows to be a false deed; but he is not to usurp the province of the jury and of the judge, and determine what shall be the effect of evidence – what shall be the result of legal argument. As it rarely happens that a man is fit to plead his own cause, lawyers are a class of the community, who, by study and experience, have acquired the art and power of arranging evidence, and of applying to the points of issue what the law has settled. A lawyer is to do for his client all that his client might fairly do for himself, if he could. If, by a superiority of attention, of knowledge, of skill, and a better method of communication, he has the advantage of his adversary, it is an advantage to which he is entitled. There must always be some advantage, on one side or other; and it is better that advantage should be had by talents, than by chance. If lawyers were to undertake no causes till they were sure they were just, a man might be precluded altogether from a trial of his claim, though, were it judicially examined, it might be found a very just claim.' This was sound practical doctrine, and rationally repressed a too refined scrupulosity of conscience.

Emigration was at this time a common topick of discourse. Dr Johnson regretted it as hurtful to human happiness: 'For,' said he, 'it spreads mankind which weakens the defence of a nation, and lessens the comfort of living. Men, thinly scattered, make a shift, but a bad shift, without many things. A smith is ten miles off: they'll do without a nail or a staple. A taylor is far from them: they'll botch their own clothes. It is being concentrated which produces high convenience.'

Sir William Forbes, Mr Scott, and I, accompanied Mr Johnson to the chapel, founded by Lord Chief Baron Smith, for the Service of the Church of England.[17] The Reverend Mr Carre, the senior clergyman, preached from these words, 'Because the Lord reigneth, let the earth be glad.' I was sorry to think Mr Johnson did not attend to the sermon, Mr Carre's low voice not being strong enough to reach his hearing. A selection of Mr Carre's sermons has, since his death, been published by Sir William Forbes, and the world has acknowledged their uncommon merit. I am well assured Lord Mansfield has pronounced them to be excellent.

Here I obtained a promise from Lord Chief Baron Orde, that he would dine at my house next day. I presented Mr Johnson to his Lordship, who politely said to him, 'I have not the honour of knowing you; but I hope for it, and to see you at my house. I am to wait on you tomorrow.' This respectable English judge will be long remembered in Scotland, where he built an elegant house, and lived in it magnificently.[18] His own ample fortune, with the addition of his salary, enabled him to be splendidly hospitable. It may be fortunate for an individual amongst ourselves to be Lord Chief Baron; and a most worthy man now has the office; but, in my opinion, it is better for Scotland in general, that some of our publick employments should be filled by gentlemen of distinction from the south side of the Tweed, as we have the benefit of promotion in England. Such an interchange would make a beneficial mixture of manners, and render our union more complete. Lord Chief Baron Orde was on good terms with us all, in a narrow country filled with jarring interests and keen parties; and, though I well knew his opinion to be the same with my own, he kept himself aloof at a very critical period indeed, when the Douglas cause shook the sacred security of birthright in Scotland to its foundation; a cause, which had it happened before the Union, when there was no appeal to a British House of Lords, would have left the great fortress of honours and of property in ruins.[19]

When we got home, Dr Johnson desired to see my books. He took down Ogden's *Sermons on Prayer*, on which I set a very high value, having been much edified by them, and he retired with them to his room. He did not stay long, but soon joined us in the drawing room. I presented to him Mr Robert Arbuthnot, a relation of the celebrated Dr Arbuthnot,[20] and a man of literature and taste. To him we were obliged for a previous recommendation, which secured us a very agreeable reception at St Andrews, and which Dr Johnson, in his *Journey*, ascribes to 'some invisible friend'.

Of Dr Beattie, Mr Johnson said, 'Sir, he has written like a man conscious of the truth, and feeling his own strength. Treating your adversary with respect, is giving him an advantage to which he is not entitled. The greatest part of men cannot judge of reasoning, and are impressed by character; so that, if you allow your adversary a respectable character, they will think, that though you differ from him, you may be in the wrong. Sir, treating your adversary with respect, is striking soft in a battle.[21] And as to Hume – a man who has so much conceit as to tell all mankind that they have been bubbled for ages, and he is the wise man who sees better than they – a man who has so little scrupulosity as to venture to oppose those principles which have been thought necessary to human happiness – is he to be surprised if another man comes and laughs at him? If he is the great man he thinks himself, all this cannot hurt him: it is like throwing peas against a rock.' He added 'something much too rough',[22] both as to Mr Hume's head and heart, which I suppress. Violence is, in my opinion, not suitable to the Christian cause. Besides, I always lived on good terms with Mr Hume, though I have frankly told him, I was not clear that it was right in me to keep company with him. 'But', said I, 'how much better are you than your books!' He was cheerful, obliging, and instructive; he was charitable to the poor; and many an agreeable hour have I passed with him: I have preserved some entertaining and interesting memoirs of him, particularly when he knew himself to be dying, which I may some time or other communicate to the world. I shall not, however, extol him so very highly as Dr Adam Smith does, who says, in a letter to Mr Strahan the printer (not a confidential letter to his friend, but a letter which is published* with all formality): 'Upon the whole, I have always considered him, both in his life time and since his death, as approaching as nearly to the idea of a perfectly wise and virtuous man as perhaps the nature of human frailty will permit.' Let Dr Smith consider: Was not Mr Hume blest with good health, good spirits, good friends, a competent and increasing fortune? And had he not also a perpetual feast of fame? But, as a learned friend has observed to me, 'What trials did he undergo, to prove the perfection of his virtue? Did he ever experience any great instance of adversity?' When I read this sentence, delivered by my old Professor of Moral Philosophy, I could not help exclaiming with the Psalmist, 'Surely I have now more understanding than my teachers!'

While we were talking, there came a note to me from Dr William Robertson.

Dear Sir,

I have been expecting every day to hear from you, of Dr Johnson's arrival. Pray, what do you know about his motions? I long to take him by the hand. I write this from the college, where I have only this scrap of paper. Ever yours,

Sunday.   W.R.

It pleased me to find Dr Robertson thus eager to meet Dr Johnson. I was glad I could answer, that he was come: and I begged Dr Robertson might be with us as soon as he could.

---

*This letter, though shattered by the sharp shot of Dr Horne of Oxford's wit, in the character of 'One of the People called Christians', is still prefixed to Mr Hume's excellent *History of England*, like a poor invalid on the piquet guard, or like a list of quack medicines sold by the same bookseller, by whom a work of whatever nature is published; for it has no connection with his *History*, let it have what it may with what are called his Philosophical Works. A worthy friend of mine in London was lately consulted by a lady of quality, of most distinguished merit, what was the best History of England for her son to read. My friend recommended Hume's. But, upon recollecting that its usher was a superlative panegyrick on one, who endeavoured to sap the credit of our holy religion, he revoked his recommendation. I am really sorry for this ostentatious alliance; because I admire *The Theory of Moral Sentiments*, and value the greatest part of *An Inquiry into the Nature and Causes of the Wealth of Nations*. Why should such a writer be so forgetful of human comfort, as to give any countenance to that dreary infidelity which would 'make us poor indeed!'

Sir William Forbes, Mr Scott, Mr Arbuthnot, and another gentleman dined with us.[23] 'Come, Dr Johnson,' said I, 'it is commonly thought that our veal in Scotland is not good. But here is some which I believe you will like.' There was no catching him: JOHNSON. 'Why, sir, what is commonly thought, I should take to be true. *Your* veal may be good; but that will only be an exception to the general opinion; not a proof against it.'

Dr Robertson, according to the custom of Edinburgh at that time, dined in the interval between the forenoon and afternoon service, which was then later than now; so we had not the pleasure of his company till dinner was over, when he came and drank wine with us. And then began some animated dialogue, of which here follows a pretty full note.

We talked of Mr Burke. Dr Johnson said, he had great variety of knowledge, store of imagery, copiousness of language. ROBERTSON. 'He has wit too.' JOHNSON. 'No, sir; he never succeeds there. 'Tis low; 'tis conceit. I used to say, Burke never once made a good joke.* What I most envy Burke for, is,

---

*This was one of the points upon which Dr Johnson was strangely heterodox. For, surely, Mr Burke, with his other remarkable qualities, is also distinguished for his wit, and for wit of all kinds too; not merely that power of language which Pope chooses to denominate wit,

> True wit is Nature to advantage drest;
> What oft was thought, but ne'er so well exprest.

but surprising allusions, brilliant sallies of vivacity, and pleasant conceits. His speeches in Parliament are strewed with them. Take, for instance, the variety which he has given in his wide range, yet exact detail, when exhibiting his Reform Bill. And his conversation abounds in wit. Let me put down a specimen. I told him, I had seen, at a blue stocking assembly, a number of ladies sitting round a worthy and tall friend of ours, listening to his literature. 'Ay,' said he, 'like maids round a May-pole.' I told him, I had found a perfect definition of human nature, as distinguished from the animal. An ancient philosopher said, man was a 'two-legged animal without feathers', upon which his rival sage had a cock plucked bare, and set him down in the school before all the disciples, as a 'Philosophick Man'. Dr Franklin said, man was 'a tool-making animal', which is very well; for no animal but man makes a thing, by means of which he can make another thing. But this applies to very few of the species. My definition of man is, 'a Cooking Animal'. The beasts have memory, judgment, and all the faculties and passions of our mind, in a certain degree; but no beast is a cook. The trick of the monkey using the cat's paw to roast a chestnut, is only a piece of shrewd malice in that *turpissima bestia*, which humbles us so sadly by its similarity to us. Man alone can dress a good dish; and every man whatever is more or less a cook, in seasoning what he himself eats. 'Your definition is good,' said Mr Burke, 'and I now see the full force of the common proverb, "There is *reason* in roasting of eggs".' When Mr Wilkes, in his days of tumultuous opposition, was borne upon the shoulders of the mob, Mr Burke (as Mr Wilkes told me himself, with classical admiration,) applied to him what Horace says of Pindar,

> ... numeris*que fertur*
> LEGE solutis.

Sir Joshua Reynolds, who agrees with me entirely as to Mr Burke's fertility of wit, said, that this was 'dignifying a pun'. He also observed, that he has often heard Burke say, in the course his being constantly the same. He is never what we call humdrum; never unwilling to begin to talk, nor in haste to leave off.' BOSWELL. 'Yet he can listen.' JOHNSON. 'No; I cannot say he is good at that. So desirous is he to talk, that, if one is speaking at this end of the table, he'll speak to somebody at the other end. Burke, sir, is such a man, that if you met him for the first time in the street where you were stopped by a drove of oxen, and you and he stepped aside to take shelter but for five minutes, he'd talk to you in such a manner, that, when you parted, you would say, this is an extraordinary man. Now, you may be long enough with me, without finding any thing extraordinary.' He said, he believed Burke was intended for the law; but either had not money enough to follow it, or had not diligence enough. He said, he could not understand how a man could apply to one thing, and not to another. Robertson said, one man had more judgment, another more imagination. JOHNSON. 'No, sir; it is only, one man has more mind than another. He may direct it differently; he may, by accident, see the success of one kind of study, and take a desire to excel in it. I am persuaded that, had Sir Isaac Newton applied to poetry, he would have made a very fine epick poem. I could as easily apply to law as to tragick poetry.' BOSWELL.

---

of an evening, ten good things, each of which would have served a noted wit (whom he named) to live upon for a twelvemonth.

I find,[24] since the former edition, that some persons have objected to the instances which I have given of Mr Burke's wit, as not doing justice to my very ingenious friend; the specimens produced having, it is alleged, more of conceit than real wit, and being merely sportive sallies of the moment, not justifying the encomium which they think with me, he undoubtedly merits. I was well aware, how hazardous it was to exhibit particular instances of wit, which is of so airy and spiritual a nature as often to elude the hand that attempts to grasp it. The excellence and efficacy of a *bon mot* depend frequently so much on the occasion on which it is spoken, on the particular manner of the speaker, on the person of whom it is applied, the previous introduction, and a thousand minute particulars which cannot be easily enumerated, that it is always dangerous to detach a witty saying from the group to which it belongs, and to see it before the eye of the spectator, divested of those concomitant circumstances, which gave it animation, mellowness, and relief. I ventured, however, at all hazards to put down the first instances that occurred to me, as proofs of Mr Burke's lively and brilliant fancy; but am very sensible that his numerous friends could have suggested many of a superior quality. Indeed, the being in company with him, for a single day, is sufficient to shew that what I have asserted is well founded; and it was only necessary to have appeaied to all who know him intimately, for a complete refutation of the heterodox opinion entertained by Dr Johnson on this subject. *He* allowed Mr Burke, as the reader will find hereafter, to be a man of consummate and unrivalled abilities in every light except that now under consideration; and the variety of his allusions, and splendour of his imagery, have made such an impression on *all the rest* of the world, that superficial observers are apt to overlook his other merits, and to suppose that *wit* is his chief and most prominent excellence; when in fact it is only one of the many talents that he possesses, which are so various and extraordinary, that it is very difficult to ascertain precisely the rank and value of each.

'Yet, sir, you did apply to tragick poetry, not to law.' JOHNSON. 'Because, sir, I had not money to study law. Sir, the man who has vigour, may walk to the east, just as well as to the west, if he happens to turn his head that way.' BOSWELL. 'But, sir, 'tis like walking up and down a hill; one man will naturally do the one better than the other. A hare will run up a hill best, from her fore-legs being short; a dog down.' JOHNSON. 'Nay, sir; that is from mechanical powers. If you make mind mechanical, you may argue in that manner. One mind is a vice, and holds fast; there's a good memory. Another is a file; and he is a disputant, a controversialist. Another is a razor; and he is sarcastical.' We talked of Whitefield. He said, he was at the same college with him,²⁵ and knew him 'before he began to be better than other people' (smiling); that he believed he sincerely meant well, but had a mixture of politicks and ostentation: whereas Wesley thought of religion only.* Robertson said, Whitefield had strong natural eloquence, which, if cultivated, would have done great things. JOHNSON. 'Why, sir, I take it, he was at the height of what his abilities could do, and was sensible of it. He had the ordinary advantages of education; but he chose to pursue that oratory which is for the mob.' BOSWELL. 'He had great effect on the passions.' JOHNSON. 'Why, sir, I don't think so. He could not represent a succession of pathetick images. He vociferated, and made an impression. *There*, again, was a mind like a hammer.' Dr Johnson now said, a certain eminent political friend of ours²⁶ was wrong, in his maxim of sticking to a certain set of *men* on all occasions. 'I can see that a man may do right to stick to a *party*,' said he; 'that is to say, he is a *Whig*, or he is a *Tory*, and he thinks one of those parties upon the whole the best, and that to make it prevail, it must be generally supported, though, in particulars, it may be wrong. He takes its faggot of principles, in which there are fewer rotten sticks than in the other, though some rotten sticks to be sure; and they cannot well be separated. But, to bind one's self to one man, or one set of men (who may be right to-day and wrong to-morrow), without any general preference of system, I must disapprove.'†

*That cannot be said now, after the flagrant part which Mr John Wesley took against our American brethren, when, in his own name, he threw amongst his enthusiastic flock, the very individual combustibles of Dr Johnson's *Taxation no Tyranny*; and after the intolerant spirit which he manifested against our fellow Christians of the Roman Catholick Communion, for which that able champion, Father O'Leary, has given him so hearty a drubbing. But I should think myself very unworthy, if I did not at the same time acknowledge Mr John Wesley's merit, as a veteran 'Soldier of Jesus Christ', who has, I do believe, 'turned many from darkness into light, and from the power of Satan to the living God'.

† If due attention were paid to this observation, there would be more virtue, even in politicks. What Dr Johnson justly condemned, has, I am sorry to say, greatly increased in the present reign. At the distance of four years from this conversation, 21st February 1777, My Lord Archbishop of York, in his 'Sermon before the Society for the Propagation of the Gospel in Foreign Parts', thus indignantly describes the then state of parties:

He told us of Cooke,[27] who translated Hesiod, and lived twenty years on a translation of Plautus, for which he was always taking subscriptions; and that he presented Foote to a club, in the following singular manner: 'This is the nephew of the gentleman who was lately hung in chains for murdering his brother.'[28]

In the evening I introduced to Mr Johnson* two good friends of mine, Mr William Nairne, advocate, and Mr Hamilton of Sundrum, my neighbour in the country, both of whom supped with us. I have preserved nothing of what passed, except that Dr Johnson displayed another of his heterodox opinions – a contempt of tragick acting. He said, 'the action of all players in tragedy is bad. It should be a man's study to repress those signs of emotion and passion, as they are called.' He was of a directly contrary opinion to that of Fielding, in his *Tom Jones*; who makes Partridge say, of Garrick, 'why, I could act as well as he himself. I am sure, if I had seen a ghost, I should have looked in the very same manner, and done just as he did.' For, when I asked him, 'Would not you, sir, start as Mr Garrick does, if you saw a ghost?' He answered, 'I hope not. If I did, I should frighten the ghost.'

Monday, 16th August

Dr William Robertson came to breakfast. We talked of Ogden on Prayer. Dr Johnson said, 'The same arguments which are used against God's hearing

---

'Parties once had a *principle* belonging to them, absurd perhaps, and indefensible, but still carrying a notion of *duty*, by which honest minds might easily be caught.

'But they are now *combinations of individuals*, who, instead of being the sons and servants of the community, make a league for advancing their *private interests*. It is their business to hold high the notion of *political honour*. I believe and trust, it is not injurious to say, that such a bond is no better than that by which the lowest and wickedest combinations are held together; and that it denotes the last stage of political depravity.'

To find a thought, which just shewed itself to us from the mind of *Johnson*, thus appearing again at such a distance of time, and without any communication between them, enlarged to full growth in the mind of *Markham*, is a curious object of philosophical contemplation. That two such great and luminous minds should have been so dark in one corner – that *they* should have held it to be 'wicked rebellion in the British subjects established in America, to resist the abject condition of holding all their property at the mercy of British subjects remaining at home, while their allegiance to our common Lord the King was to be preserved inviolate' – is a striking proof to me, either that 'He who fitteth in Heaven', scorns the loftiness of human pride, or that the evil spirit, whose personal existence I strongly believe, and even in this age am confirmed in that belief by a Fell, nay, by a Hurd, has more power than some choose to allow.

* It may be observed, that I sometimes call my great friend, *Mr* Johnson, sometimes *Dr* Johnson; though he had at this time a doctor's degree from Trinity College, Dublin. The University of Oxford afterwards conferred it upon him by a diploma, in very honourable terms. It was some time before I could bring myself to call him Doctor; but, as he has been long known by that title, I shall give it to him in the rest of this *Journal*.

prayer, will serve against his rewarding good, and punishing evil. He has resolved, he has declared, in the former case as in the latter.' He had last night looked into Lord Hailes's *Remarks on the History of Scotland*. Dr Robertson and I said, it was a pity Lord Hailes did not write greater things. His lordship had not then published his *Annals of Scotland*. JOHNSON. 'I remember I was once on a visit at the house of a lady for whom I had a high respect. There was a good deal of company in the room. When they were gone, I said to this lady, "What foolish talking have we had!" "Yes," said she, "but while they talked, you said nothing." I was struck with reproof. How much better is the man who does nothing. Besides, I love anecdotes. I fancy mankind may come, in time, to write all aphoristically, except in narrative; grow weary of preparation, and connection, and illustration, and all those arts by which a big book is made. If a man is to wait till he weaves anecdotes into a system, we may be long in getting them, and get but a few, in comparison of what we might get.'

Dr Robertson said, the notions of Eupham Macallan, a fanatick woman, of whom Lord Hailes gives a sketch, were still prevalent among some of the Presbyterians; and therefore it was right in Lord Hailes, a man of known piety, to undeceive them.[29]

We walked out, that Dr Johnson might see some of the things which we have to shew at Edinburgh. We went to the Parliament House, where the Parliament of Scotland sat, and where the Ordinary Lords of Session hold their courts; and to the New Session House adjoining to it, where our Court of Fifteen (the fourteen Ordinaries, with the Lord President at their head) sit as a court of Review. We went to the Advocates' Library, of which Dr Johnson took a cursory view, and then to what is called the *Laigh* (or Under) Parliament House, where the records of Scotland, which has an universal security by register, are deposited, till the great Register Office be finished. I was pleased to behold Dr Samuel Johnson rolling about in this old magazine of antiquities. There was, by this time, a pretty numerous circle of us attending upon him. Somebody talked of happy moments for composition; and how a man can write at one time, and not at another. 'Nay,' said Dr Johnson, 'a man may write at any time, if he will set himself *doggedly** to it.'

I here began to indulge old Scottish sentiments, and to express a warm regret, that, by our union with England, we were no more – our independent kingdom was lost. JOHNSON. 'Sir, never talk of your independency, who could

---

*This word is commonly used to signify *sullenly, gloomily*; and in that sense alone it appears in Dr Johnson's *Dictionary*. I suppose he meant by it, 'with an *obstinate resolution*, similar to that of a sullen man'.

let your Queen remain twenty years in captivity, and then be put to death, without even a pretence of justice, without your ever attempting to rescue her; and such a Queen too! as every man of any gallantry of spirit would have sacrificed his life for.' Worthy MR JAMES KERR, Keeper of the Records. 'Half our nation was bribed by English money.' JOHNSON. 'Sir, that is no defence: that makes you worse.' Good MR BROWN, Keeper of the Advocates Library. 'We had better say nothing about it.' BOSWELL. 'You would have been glad, however, to have had us last war, sir, to fight your battles!' JOHNSON. 'We should have had you for the same price, though there had been no Union, as we might have had Swiss, or other troops. No, no, I shall agree to a separation. You have only to *go home.*' Just as he had said this, I to divert the subject, shewed him the signed assurances of the three successive Kings of the Hanover family, to maintain the Presbyterian establishment in Scotland. 'We'll give you that,' said he, 'into the bargain.'

We next went to the great church of St Giles, which has lost its original magnificence in the inside, by being divided into four places of Presbyterian worship.[30] 'Come,' said Dr Johnson jocularly to Principal Robertson,* 'let me see what was once a church!' We entered that division which was formerly called the New Church, and of late the High Church, so well known by the eloquence of Dr Hugh Blair. It is now very elegantly fitted up; but it was then shamefully dirty. Dr Johnson said nothing at the time; but when we came to the great door of the Royal Infirmary, where, upon a board, was this inscription, CLEAN YOUR FEET! he turned about slyly, and said, 'There is no occasion for putting this at the doors of your churches!'

We then conducted him down the Post-house stairs, Parliament Close, and made him look up from the Cow-gate to the highest building in Edinburgh (from which he had just descended), being thirteen floors or stories from the ground upon the back elevation; the front wall being built upon the edge of the hill, and the back wall rising from the bottom of the hill several stories before it comes to a level with the front wall. We proceeded to the College, with the Principal at our head. Dr Adam Fergusson, whose *Essay on the History of Civil Society* gives him a respectable place in the ranks of literature, was with us. As the College buildings are indeed very mean, the Principal said to Dr Johnson, that he must give them the same epithet that a Jesuit did when shewing a poor college abroad: *Hæ miseriæ nostræ.*[31] Dr Johnson was, however, much pleased with the library, and with the

---

*I have hitherto called him Dr William Robertson, to distinguish him from Dr James Robertson, who is soon to make his appearance. But 'Principal', from his being the head of our college, is his usual designation, and is shorter; so I shall use it hereafter.

conversation of Dr James Robertson, Professor of Oriental Languages, the Librarian. We talked of Kennicot's edition of the Hebrew Bible,[32] and hoped it would be quite faithful. JOHNSON. 'Sir, I know not any crime so great that a man could contrive to commit, as poisoning the sources of eternal truth.'

I pointed out to him where there formerly stood an old wall enclosing part of the college, which I remember bulged out in a threatening manner, and of which there was a common tradition similar to that concerning Bacon's study at Oxford, that it would fall upon some very learned man.[33] It had some time before this been taken down, that the street might be widened, and a more convenient wall built. Dr Johnson, glad of an opportunity to have a pleasant hit at Scottish learning, said, 'they have been afraid it never would fall'.

We shewed him the Royal Infirmary, for which, and for every other exertion of generous publick spirit in his power, that noble-minded citizen of Edinburgh, George Drummond, will be ever held in honourable remembrance. And we were too proud not to carry him to the Abbey of Holyrood House, that beautiful piece of architecture, but, alas! that deserted mansion of royalty, which Hamilton of Bangour, in one of his elegant poems, calls

A virtuous palace, where no monarch dwells.

I was much entertained while Principal Robertson fluently harangued to Dr Johnson, upon the spot, concerning scenes of his celebrated *History of Scotland*. We surveyed that part of the palace appropriated to the Duke of Hamilton, as Keeper, in which our beautiful Queen Mary lived, and in which David Rizzio was murdered; and also the State Rooms. Dr Johnson was a great reciter of all sorts of things serious or comical. I over-heard him repeating here, in a kind of muttering tone, a line of the old ballad, 'Johnny Armstrong's Last Good-Night':

'And ran him through the fair body!'*

We returned to my house, where there met him, at dinner, the Duchess of Douglas, Sir Adolphus Oughton, Lord Chief Baron, Sir William Forbes, Principal Robertson, Mr Cullen, advocate. Before dinner, he told us of a curious conversation between the famous George Faulkner and him.[34]

_____

* The stanza from which he took this line is,
   But then rose up all Edinburgh,
   They rose up by thousands three;
   A cowardly Scot came John behind,
   And ran him through the fair body!

George said that England had drained Ireland of fifty thousand pounds in specie, annually, for fifty years. 'How so, sir!' said Dr Johnson, 'you must have a very great trade?' 'No trade.' 'Very rich mines?' 'No mines.' 'From whence, then, does all this money come?' 'Come! why out of the blood and bowels of the poor people of Ireland!'

He seemed to me to have an unaccountable prejudice against Swift; for I once took a liberty to ask him, if Swift had personally offended him, and he told me, he had not. He said to-day, 'Swift is clear, but he is shallow. In coarse humour, he is inferior to Arbuthnot; in delicate humour, he is inferior to Addison: so he is inferior to his contemporaries; without putting him against the whole world. I doubt if the *Tale of a Tub* was his: it has so much more thinking, more knowledge, more power, more colour, than any of the works which are indisputably his. If it was his, I shall only say, he was *impar sibi*.'[35]

We gave him as good a dinner as we could. Our Scotch muir-fowl, or growse, were then abundant, and quite in season; and, so far as wisdom and wit can be aided by administering agreeable sensations to the palate, my wife took care that our great guest should not be deficient.

Sir Adolphus Oughton, then our Deputy Commander in Chief, who was not only an excellent officer, but one of the most universal scholars I ever knew, had learned the Erse language, and expressed his belief in the authenticity of Ossian's poetry. Dr Johnson took the opposite side of that perplexed question; and I was afraid the dispute would have run high between them. But Sir Adolphus, who had a very sweet temper, changed the discourse, grew playful, laughed at Lord Monboddo's notion[36] of men having tails, and called him a Judge, *a posteriori*, which amused Dr Johnson; and thus hostilities were prevented.

At supper we had Dr Cullen, his son the advocate, Dr Adam Fergusson, and Mr Crosbie, advocate.[37] Witchcraft was introduced. Mr Crosbie said, he thought it the greatest blasphemy to suppose evil spirits counteracting the Deity, and raising storms, for instance, to destroy his creatures. JOHNSON. 'Why, sir, if moral evil be consistent with the government of the Deity, why may not physical evil be also consistent with it? It is not more strange that there should be evil spirits, than evil embodied spirits. And as to storms, we know there are such things; and it is no worse that evil spirits raise them, than that they rise.' CROSBIE. 'But it is not credible, that witches should have effected what they are said in stories to have done.' JOHNSON. 'Sir, I am not defending their credibility. I am only saying, that your arguments are not good, and will not overturn the belief of witchcraft.' (Dr Fergusson said to me, aside, 'He is right.') 'And then, sir, you have all mankind, rude and civilized, agreeing in the belief of the agency of preternatural powers. You must take evidence: you must consider, that wise and great men have condemned witches to die.'[38] CROSBIE. 'But an Act of Parliament put an end to witchcraft.' JOHNSON. 'No, sir; witchcraft had ceased; and therefore an Act of Parliament was passed to prevent persecution for what was not witchcraft. Why it ceased, we cannot tell, as we cannot tell the reason of many other things.' Dr Cullen, to keep up the gratification of mysterious disquisition, with the grave address for which he is remarkable in his companionable as in his professional hours, talked, in a very entertaining manner, of people walking and conversing in their sleep. I am very sorry I have no note of this. We talked of the *Ouran-Outang*, and of Lord Monboddo's thinking that he might be taught to speak. Dr Johnson treated this with ridicule. Mr Crosbie said, that Lord Monboddo believed the existence of every thing possible; in short, that all which is in *posse* might be found in *esse*. JOHNSON. 'But, sir, it is as possible that the *Ouran-Outang* does not speak, as that he speaks. However, I shall not contest the point. I should have thought it not possible to find a Monboddo; yet *he* exists.' I again mentioned the stage. JOHNSON. 'The appearance of a player, with whom I have drun ̇ tea, counteracts the imagination that he is the character he represents. Nay, you know, nobody imagines that he is the character he represents. They say, "See *Garrick!* how he looks to-night! See how he'll clutch the dagger!" That is the buz of the theatre.'

Tuesday, 17th August

Sir William Forbes came to breakfast, and brought with him Dr Blacklock,[39] whom he introduced to Dr Johnson, who received him with a most humane complacency. 'Dear Blacklock, I am glad to see you!' Blacklock seemed to be much surprised, when Dr Johnson said, 'it was easier to him to write poetry than to compose his *Dictionary*. His mind was less on the stretch in doing the one than the other. Besides; composing a dictionary requires books and a desk: you can make a poem walking in the fields, or lying in bed.' Dr Blacklock spoke of scepticism in morals and religion, with apparant uneasiness, as if he wished for more certainty. Dr Johnson, who had thought it all over, and whose vigorous understanding was fortified by much experience, thus encouraged the blind bard to apply to higher speculations what we willingly submit to in common life: in short, he gave him more familiarly the able and fair reasoning of Butler's *Analogy*: 'Why, sir, the greatest concern we have in this world, the choice of our profession, must be determined without demonstrative reasoning. Human life is not yet so well known, as that we can have it. And take the case of a man who is ill. I call two physicians: they differ in opinion. I am not to lie down, and die between them: I must do something.' The conversation then turned on atheism; on that horrible book, *Système de la Nature*;[40] and on the supposition of an eternal necessity, without design, without a governing mind. JOHNSON. 'If it were so, why has it ceased? Why don't we see men thus produced around us now? Why, at least, does it not keep pace, in some measure, with the progress of time? If it stops because there is now no need of it, then it is plain there is, and ever has been, an all-powerful intelligence. But stay!' said he, with one of his satyrick laughs. 'Ha! ha! ha! I shall suppose Scotchmen made necessarily, and Englishmen by choice.'

At dinner this day, we had Sir Alexander Dick, whose amiable character, and ingenious and cultivated mind, are so generally known (he was then on the verge of seventy, and is now (1785) eighty-one, with his faculties entire, his heart warm, and his temper gay); Sir David Dalrymple; Lord Hailes; Mr Maclaurin, advocate; Dr Gregory, who now worthily fills his father's medical chair; and my uncle, Dr Boswell. This was one of Dr Johnson's best days. He was quite in his element. All was literature and taste, without any interruption. Lord Hailes, who is one of the best philologists in Great Britain, who has written papers in the *World*, and a variety of other works in prose and in verse, both Latin and English, pleased him highly. He told him, he had discovered the *Life of Cheynel*, in the *Student*, to be his. JOHNSON. 'No one else knows it.' Dr Johnson had, before this, dictated to me a law-paper, upon a question purely in the law of Scotland, concerning 'vicious intro-mission', that is to say, intermeddling with the effects of a deceased person, without a regular title; which formerly was understood to subject the inter-meddler to payment of all the defunct's debts. The principle has of late been relaxed. Dr Johnson's argument was, for a renewal of its strictness. The paper was printed, with additions by me, and given into the Court of Session. Lord Hailes knew Dr Johnson's part not to be mine, and pointed out exactly where it began, and where it ended. Dr Johnson said, 'It is much, now, that his lordship can distinguish so.'

In Dr Johnson's *Vanity of Human Wishes*, there is the following passage:

> The teeming mother, anxious for her race,
> Begs, for each birth, the fortune of a face:
> Yet *Vane* could tell, what ills from beauty spring;
> And *Sedley* curs'd the charms which pleas'd a king.[41]

Lord Hailes told him, he was mistaken in the instances he had given of unfortunate fair ones; for neither Vane nor Sedley had a title to that descrip-tion. His Lordship has since been so obliging as to send me a note of this, for the communication of which I am sure my readers will thank me.

The lines in the tenth Satire of Juvenal, according to my alteration, should have run thus:

> Yet *Shore** could tell—;
> And *Valiere*† curs'd—.

The first was a penitent by compulsion, the second by sentiment; though the truth is, Mademoiselle de la Valiere threw herself (but still from sentiment) in the King's way.

'Our friend chose Vane, who was far from being well-looked; and Sedley, who was so ugly, that Charles II said, his brother had her by way of penance.'

Mr Maclaurin's[42] learning and talents enabled him to do his part very well in Dr Johnson's company. He produced two epitaphs upon his father, the celebrated mathematician. One was in English, of which Dr Johnson did not change one word. In the other, which was in Latin, he made several alterations. In place of the very words of Virgil, *Ubi luctus et pavor et plurima mortis imago*, he wrote *Ubi luctus regnant et pavor*.[43] He introduced the word *prorsus* into the line *Mortalibus prorsus non absit solatium* and after *Hujus enim scripta evolve*, he added, *Mentemque tantarum rerum capacem corpori caduco superstitem crede*;[44] which is quite applicable to Dr Johnson himself.‡

Mr Murray, advocate, who married a niece of Lord Mansfield's and is now one of the Judges of Scotland, by the title of Lord Henderland, sat with us a part of the evening; but did not venture to say any thing, that I remember, though he is certainly possessed of talents which would have enabled him to have shewn himself to advantage, if too great anxiety had not prevented him.

---

* Mistress of Edward IV.

† Mistress of Louis XIV.

‡ Mr Maclaurin's epitaph, as engraved on a marble tombstone, in the Gray-Friars church-yard, Edinburgh:

> *Infra situs est*
> COLIN MACLAURIN
> *Mathes. olim in Acad. Edin. Prof.*
> *Electus ipso Newtono suadente.*
> *H. L. P. F.*
> *Non ut nomini paterno consulat,*
> *Nam tali auxilio nil eget;*
> *Sed ut in hoc infelici campo,*
> *Ubi luctus regnant et pavor,*
> *Mortalibus prorsus non absit solatium:*
> *Hujus enim scripta evolve,*
> *Mentemque tantarum rerum capacem*
> *Corpori caduco superstitem crede.*

At supper we had Dr Alexander Webster,[45] who, though not learned, had such a knowledge of mankind, such a fund of information and entertainment, so clear a head and such accommodating manners, that Dr Johnson found him a very agreeable companion.

When Dr Johnson and I were left by ourselves, I read to him my notes of the opinions of our Judges upon the questions of Literary Property. He did not like them; and said, 'they make me think of your Judges not with that respect which I should wish to do'. To the argument of one of them, that there can be no property in blasphemy or nonsense, he answered, 'then your rotten sheep are mine! By that rule, when a man's house falls into decay, he must lose it.' I mentioned an argument of mine, that literary performances are not taxed. As Churchill says,

> No statesman yet has thought it worth his pains
> To tax our labours, or excite our brains;

and therefore they are not property. 'Yet,' said he, 'we hang a man for stealing a horse, and horses are not taxed.' Mr Pitt has since put an end to that argument.

Wednesday, 18th August

On this day we set out from Edinburgh. We should gladly have had Mr Scott to go with us; but he was obliged to return to England. I have given a sketch of Dr Johnson: my readers may wish to know a little of his fellow traveller. Think then, of a gentleman of ancient blood, the pride of which was his predominant passion. He was then in his thirty-third year, and had been about four years happily married. His inclination was to be a soldier; but his father, a respectable judge, had pressed him into the profession of the law. He had travelled a good deal, and seen many varieties of human life. He had thought more than any body supposed, and had a pretty good stock of general learning and knowledge. He had all Dr Johnson's principles, with some degree of relaxation. He had rather too little, than too much prudence, and, his imagination being lively, he often said things of which the effect was very different from the intention. He resembled sometimes

The best good man, with the worst natur'd muse.[46]

He cannot deny himself the vanity of finishing with the encomium of Dr Johnson, whose friendly partiality to the companion of his Tour represents him as one, 'whose acuteness would help my inquiry, and whose gaiety of conversation, and civility of manners, are sufficient to counteract the inconveniences of travel, in countries less hospitable than we have passed'.

Dr Johnson thought it unnecessary to put himself to the additional expense of bringing with him Francis Barber, his faithful black servant; so we were attended only by my man, Joseph Ritter, a Bohemian; a fine stately fellow above six feet high, who had been over a great part of Europe, and spoke many languages. He was the best servant I ever saw. Let not my readers disdain his introduction! For Dr Johnson gave him this character: 'Sir, he is a civil man, and a wise man.'

From an erroneous apprehension of violence, Dr Johnson had provided a pair of pistols, some gun-powder, and a quantity of bullets: but upon being assured we should run no risk of meeting any robbers, he left his arms and ammunition in an open drawer, of which he gave my wife the charge. He also left in that drawer one volume of a pretty full and curious *Diary of his Life*, of which I have a few fragments; but the book has been destroyed. I wish female curiosity had been strong enough to have had it all transcribed, which might easily have been done; and I should think the theft, being *pro bono publico*, might have been forgiven. But I may be wrong. My wife told me she never once looked into it. She did not seem quite easy when we left her: but away we went!

Mr Nairne, advocate,[47] was to go with us as far as St Andrews. It gives me pleasure that, by mentioning his name, I connect his title to the just and handsome compliment paid him by Dr Johnson, in his book: 'A gentleman who could stay with us only long enough to make us know how much we lost by his leaving us.' When we came to Leith, I talked with perhaps too boasting an air, how pretty the Frith of Forth looked; as indeed, after the prospect from Constantinople, of which I have been told, and that from Naples, which I have seen, I believe the view of that Frith and its environs, from the Castle Hill of Edinburgh, is the finest prospect in Europe. 'Ay,' said Dr Johnson, 'that is the state of the world. Water is the same every where.

*Una est injusti cœrula forma maris.**

I told him the port here was the mouth of the river or water of Leith. 'Not *Lethe*,' said Mr Nairne. 'Why, sir,' said Dr Johnson, 'when a Scotchman

---

* *Non illic urbes, non tu mirabere silvas:*
 Una est injusti cœrula forma maris.
 Ovid, *Amor*. II. xi.
 Nor groves nor towns the ruthless ocean shows;
 Unvaried still its azure surface flows.

sets out from this port for England, he forgets his native country.' NAIRNE. 'I hope, sir, you will forget England here.' JOHNSON. 'Then 'twill be still more *Lethe*.' He observed of the pier or quay, 'you have no occasion for so large a one: your trade does not require it: but you are like a shopkeeper who takes a shop, not only for what he has to put into it, but that it may be believed he has a great deal to put into it'. It is very true, that there is now, comparatively, little trade upon the eastern coast of Scotland. The riches of Glasgow shew how much there is in the west; and perhaps we shall find trade travel westward on a great scale, as well as a small.

We talked of a man's drowning himself. JOHNSON. 'I should never think it time to make away with myself.' I put the case of Eustace Budgell, who was accused of forging a will, and sunk himself in the Thames, before the trial of its authenticity came on. 'Suppose, sir,' said I, 'that a man is absolutely sure, that, if he lives a few days longer, he shall be detected in a fraud, the consequence of which will be utter disgrace and expulsion from society.' JOHNSON. 'Then, sir, let him go abroad to a distant country; let him go to some place where he is *not* known. Don't let him go to the devil where he *is* known!'

He then said, 'I see a number of people bare-footed here: I suppose you all went so before the Union. Boswell, your ancestors went so, when they had as much land as your family has now. Yet *Auchinleck* is the *Field of Stones*: there would be bad going bare-footed here. The *lairds*, however, did it.' I bought some *speldings*, fish (generally whitings) salted and dried in a particular manner, being dipped in the sea and dried in the sun, and eaten by the Scots by way of a relish. He had never seen them, though they are sold in London. I insisted on *scottifying** his palate; but he was very reluctant. With difficulty I prevailed with him to let a bit of one of them lie in his mouth. He did not like it.

In crossing the Frith, Dr Johnson determined that we should land upon Inch Keith. On approaching it, we first observed a high rocky shore. We coasted about, and put into a little bay on the north-west. We clambered up a very steep ascent, on which was very good grass, but rather a profusion of thistles. There were sixteen head of black cattle grazing upon the island. Lord Hailes observed to me, that Brantome[48] calls it *L'isle des Chevaux*, and that it was probably 'a *safer* stable' than many others in his time. The fort, with an inscription on it, MARIA RE 1564, is strongly built.[49] Dr Johnson examined it with much attention. He stalked like a giant among the luxuriant

---

* My friend, General Campbell, Governour of Madras, tells me, that they make *speldings* in the East Indies, particularly at Bombay, where they call them *Bambaloes*.

thistles and nettles. There are three wells in the island; but we could not find one in the fort. There must probably have been one, though now filled up, as a garrison could not subsist without it. But I have dwelt too long on this little spot. Dr Johnson afterwards bade me try to write a description of our discovering Inch Keith, in the usual style of travellers, describing fully every particular; stating the grounds on which we concluded that it must have once been inhabited, and introducing many sage reflections; and we should see how a thing might be covered in words, so as to induce people to come and survey it. All that was told might be true, and yet in reality there might be nothing to see. He said, 'I'd have this island. I'd build a house, make a good landing-place, have a garden, and vines, and all sorts of trees. A rich man, of a hospitable turn, here, would have many visitors from Edinburgh.' When we had got into our boat again, he called to me, 'Come, now, pay a classical compliment to the island on quitting it.' I happened luckily, in allusion to the beautiful Queen Mary, whose name is upon the fort, to think of what Virgil makes Æneas say, on having left the country of his charming Dido:

*Invitus, regina, tuo de littore cessi.**

'Very well hit off!' said he.

We dined at Kinghorn,[50] and then got into a post-chaise. Mr Nairne and his servant, and Joseph, rode by us. We stopped at Cupar, and drank tea. We talked of Parliament; and I said, I supposed very few of the members knew much of what was going on, as indeed very few gentlemen know much of their own private affairs. JOHNSON. 'Why, sir, if a man is not of a sluggish mind, he may be his own steward. If he will look into his affairs, he will soon learn. So it is as to publick affairs. There must always be a certain number of men of business in Parliament.' BOSWELL. 'But consider, sir; what is the House of Commons? Is not a great part of it chosen by peers? Do you think, sir, they ought to have such an influence?' JOHNSON. 'Yes, sir. Influence must ever be in proportion to property; and it is right it should.' BOSWELL. 'But is there not reason to fear that the common people may be oppressed?' JOHNSON. 'No, sir. Our great fear is from want of power in government. Such a storm of vulgar force has broke in.' BOSWELL. 'It has only roared.' JOHNSON. 'Sir, it has roared, till the Judges in Westminster Hall have been afraid to pronounce sentence in opposition to the popular cry. You are frightened by what is no longer dangerous, like Presbyterians

* Unhappy queen!
  Unwilling I forsook your friendly state.
                                    DRYDEN

by popery.' He then repeated a passage, I think, in Butler's *Remains*, which ends, 'and would cry, Fire! Fire! in Noah's flood'.*

We had a dreary drive, in a dusky night, to St Andrews, where we arrived late.[51] We found a good supper at Glass's inn, and Dr Johnson revived agreeably. He said, 'the collection called *The Muses' Welcome to King James*[52] (first of England, and sixth of Scotland), on his return to his native kingdom, shewed that there was then abundance of learning in Scotland; and that the conceits in that collection, with which people find fault, were mere mode'. He added, 'we could not now entertain a sovereign so; that Buchanan[53] had spread the spirit of learning amongst us, but we had lost it during the civil wars'. He did not allow the Latin poetry of Pitcairne so much merit as has been usually attributed to it; though he owned that one of his pieces, which he mentioned, but which I am sorry is not specified in my notes, was 'very well'. It is not improbable that it was the poem which Prior has so elegantly translated.[54]

After supper, we made a procession to Saint Leonard's College, the landlord walking before us with a candle, and the waiter with a lantern. That college had some time before been dissolved; and Dr Watson, a professor here (the historian of Phillip II), had purchased the ground, and what buildings remained. When we entered his court, it seemed quite academical; and we found in his house very comfortable and genteel accommodation.†

Thursday, 19th August

We rose much refreshed.[55] I had with me a map of Scotland,[56] a Bible, which was given me by Lord Mountstuart when we were together in Italy, and Ogden's *Sermons on Prayer*. Mr Nairne introduced us to Dr Watson, whom

*The passage quoted by Dr Johnson is in the *Character of the Assembly-man*, Butler's *Remains*, p. 232, edit. 1754. 'He preaches, indeed, both in season and out of season; for he rails at Popery, when the land is almost lost in Presbytery; and would cry Fire! Fire! in Noah's flood.'

There is reason to believe that this piece was not written by Butler, but by Sir John Birkenhead; for Wood, in his *Athenæ Oxonienses*, Vol. II. p. 460, enumerates it among that gentleman's works, and gives the following account of it:

'The *Assembly-man* (or *The Character of an Assembly-man*) written 1647, Lond. 1662–3, in three sheets in qu. The copy of it was taken from the author by those who said they could not rob, because all was theirs; so excised what they liked not; and so mangled and reformed it, that it was no character of an Assembly, but of themselves. At length, after it had slept several years, the author published it, to avoid false copies. It is also reprinted in a book entit. *Wit and Loyalty Revived*, in a collection of some smart satyrs in verse and prose on the late times. Lond. 1682, qu. said to be written by Abr. Cowley, Sir John Birkenhead, and Hudibras, alias Sam. Butler.' For this information I am indebted to Mr Reed, of Staple Inn.

† My *Journal*, from this day inclusive, was read by Dr Johnson.

we found a well-informed man, of very amiable manners. Dr Johnson, after they were acquainted, said, 'I take great delight in him.' His daughter, a very pleasing young lady, made breakfast. Dr Watson observed, that Glasgow University had fewer home-students, since trade increased, as learning was rather incompatible with it. JOHNSON. 'Why, sir, as trade is now carried on by subordinate hands, men in trade have as much leisure as others; and now learning itself is a trade. A man goes to a bookseller, and gets what he can. We have done with patronage. In the infancy of learning, we find some great man praised for it. This diffused it among others. When it becomes general, an author leaves the great, and applies to the multitude.' BOSWELL. 'It is a shame that authors are not now better patronized.' JOHNSON. 'No, sir. If learning cannot support a man, if he must sit with his hands across till somebody feeds him, it is as to him a bad thing, and it is better as it is. With patronage, what flattery! What falsehood! While a man is *in equilibrio*, he throws truth among the multitude, and lets them take it as they please: in patronage, he must say what pleases his patron, and it is an equal chance whether that be truth or falsehood.' WATSON. 'But is not the case now, that, instead of flattering one person, we flatter the age?' JOHNSON. 'No, sir. The world always lets a man tell what he thinks, his own way. I wonder however, that so many people have written, who might have let it alone. That people should endeavour to excel in conversation, I do not wonder; because in conversation praise is instantly reverberated.'

We talked of change of manners. Dr Johnson observed, that our drinking less than our ancestors was owing to the change from ale to wine. 'I remember,' said he, 'when all the *decent* people in Lichfield got drunk every night, and were not the worse thought of. Ale was cheap, so you pressed strongly. When a man must bring a bottle of wine, he is not in such haste. Smoking has gone out. To be sure, it is a shocking thing, blowing smoke out of our mouths into other people's mouths, eyes, and noses, and having the same thing done to us. Yet I cannot account, why a thing which requires so little exertion, and yet preserves the mind from total vacuity, should have gone out. Every man has something by which he calms himself: beating with his feet, or so.* I remember when people in England changed a shirt only once a week: a Pandour,⁵⁷ when he gets a shirt, greases it to make it last. Formerly, good tradesmen had no fire but in the kitchen; never in the parlour, except on Sunday. My father, who was a magistrate of Lichfield, lived thus. They never began to have a fire in the parlour, but on leaving off business, or some great revolution of their life.' Dr Watson said, the hall was as a kitchen, in old

* Dr Johnson used to practice this himself very much.

squires' houses. JOHNSON. 'No, sir. The hall was for great occasions, and never was used for domestick reflection.' We talked of the Union, and what money it had brought into Scotland. Dr Watson observed, that a little money formerly went as far as a great deal now. JOHNSON. 'In speculation, it seems that a smaller quantity of money, equal in value to a larger quantity, if equally divided, should produce the same effect. But it is not so in reality. Many more conveniences and elegancies are enjoyed where money is plentiful, than where it is scarce. Perhaps a great familiarity with it, which arises from plenty, makes us more easily part with it.'

After what Dr Johnson had said of St Andrews, which he had long wished to see, as our oldest university, and the seat of our Primate in the days of episcopacy, I can say little. Since the publication of Dr Johnson's book, I find that he has been censured for not seeing here the ancient chapel of St Rule, a curious piece of sacred architecture. But this was neither his fault nor mine. We were both of us abundantly desirous of surveying such sort of antiquities: but neither of us knew of this. I am afraid the censure must fall on those who did not tell us of it. In every place, where there is any thing worthy of observation, there should be a short printed directory for strangers, such as we find in all the towns of Italy, and in some of the towns in England. I was told that there is a manuscript account of St Andrews, by Martin,[58] secretary to Archbishop Sharp; and that one Douglas has published a small account of it.[59] I inquired at a bookseller's, but could not get it. Dr Johnson's veneration for the Hierarchy is well known. There is no wonder then, that he was affected with a strong indignation, while he beheld the ruins of religious magnificence. I happened to ask where John Knox was buried. Dr Johnson burst out, 'I hope in the high-way. I have been looking at his reformations.'

It was a very fine day. Dr Johnson seemed quite wrapt up in the contemplation of the scenes which were now presented to him. He kept his hat off while he was upon any part of the ground where the cathedral had stood. He said well, that 'Knox had set on a mob, without knowing where it would end; and that differing from a man in doctrine was no reason why you should pull his house about his ears'. As we walked in the cloisters, there was a solemn echo, while he talked loudly of a proper retirement from the world. Mr Nairne said, he had an inclination to retire. I called Dr Johnson's attention to this, that I might hear his opinion if it was right. JOHNSON. 'Yes, when he has done his duty to society. In general, as every man is obliged not only to "love God, but his neighbour as himself", he must bear his part in active life; yet there are exceptions. Those who are exceedingly scrupulous (which I do not approve, for I am no friend to scruples), and find their scrupulosity invincible, so that they are quite in the dark, and know not what they shall do, or those who can not resist temptations, and find they make themselves worse by being in the world, without making it better, may retire. I never read of a hermit, but in imagination I kiss his feet; never of a monastery, but I could fall on my knees, and kiss the pavement. But I think putting young people there, who know nothing of life, nothing of retirement, is dangerous and wicked. It is a saying as old as Hesiod,

$$\text{ἔργα νεῶν, βούλαι τε μεσῶν, εὐχαί τε γερόντων.}^*$$

That is a very noble line: not that young men should not pray, or old men not give counsel, but that every season of life has its proper duties. I have thought of retiring, and have talked of it to a friend; but I find my vocation is rather to active life.' I said, *some* young monks might be allowed, to shew that it is not age alone that can retire to pious solitude; but he thought this would only shew that they could not resist temptation.

He wanted to mount the steeples, but it could not be done. There are no good inscriptions here. Bad Roman characters he naturally mistook for half Gothick, half Roman. One of the steeples, which he was told was in danger, he wished not to be taken down; 'for,' said he, 'it may fall on some of the posterity of John Knox; and no great matter!' Dinner was mentioned. JOHNSON. 'Ay, ay; amidst all these sorrowful scenes, I have no objection to dinner.'

We went and looked at the castle, where Cardinal Beaton was murdered, and then visited Principal Murison at his college, where is a good library-room;[60] but the principal was abundantly vain of it, for he seriously said to Dr Johnson, 'you have not such a one in England'.

The professors entertained us with a very good dinner. Present: Murison, Shaw, Cooke, Hill, Haddo, Watson, Flint, Brown. I observed, that I wondered to see him eat so well, after viewing so many sorrowful scenes of ruined religious magnificence. 'Why,' said he, 'I am not sorry, after seeing these gentlemen; for they are not sorry.' Murison said, all sorrow was bad, as it was murmuring against the dispensations of Providence. JOHNSON. 'Sir, sorrow is inherent in humanity. As you cannot judge two and two to be either five, or three, but certainly four, so, when comparing a worse present state with a better which is past, you cannot but feel sorrow. It is not cured by reason, but by the incursion of present objects, which wear out the past. You need not murmur, though you are sorry.' MURISON. 'But St Paul says, "I have learnt, in whatever state I am, therewith to be content." ' JOHNSON. 'Sir, that relates to riches and poverty; for we see St Paul, when he had a thorn in the flesh, prayed earnestly to have it removed; and then he could not be content.'

* Let youth in deeds, in counsel man engage;
  Prayer is the proper duty of old age.

Murison, thus refuted, tried to be smart, and drank to Dr Johnson, 'Long may you lecture!' Dr Johnson afterwards, speaking of his not drinking wine, said, 'The Doctor spoke of *lecturing*' (looking to him). 'I give all these lectures on water.'

He defended requiring subscription in those admitted to universities, thus: 'As all who come into the country must obey the King, so all who come into an university must be of the Church.'

And here I must do Dr Johnson the justice to contradict a very absurd and ill-natured story, as to what passed at St Andrews. It has been circulated, that, after grace was said in English, in the usual manner, he with the greatest marks of contempt, as if he had held it to be no grace in an university, would not sit down till he had said grace aloud in Latin. This would have been an insult indeed to the gentlemen who were entertaining us. But the truth was precisely thus. In the course of conversation at dinner, Dr Johnson, in very good humour, said, 'I should have expected to have heard a Latin grace, among so many learned men: we had always a Latin grace at Oxford. I believe I can repeat it.' Which he did, as giving the learned men in one place a specimen of what was done by the learned men in another place.

We went and saw the church, in which is Archbishop Sharp's monument.[61] I was struck with the same kind of feelings with which the churches of Italy impressed me. I was much pleased, to see Dr Johnson actually in St Andrews, of which we had talked so long. Professor Haddo was with us this afternoon, along with Dr Watson. We looked at St Salvador's College. The rooms for students seemed very commodious, and Dr Johnson said, the chapel was the neatest place of worship he had seen. The key of the library could not be found; for it seems Professor Hill, who was out of town, had taken it with him. Dr Johnson told a joke he had heard of a monastery abroad, where the key of the library could never be found.

It was somewhat dispiriting, to see this ancient archiepiscopal city now sadly deserted. We saw in one of its streets a remarkable proof of liberal toleration; a nonjuring clergyman, strutting about in his canonicals, with a jolly countenance and a round belly, like a well-fed monk.[62]

We observed two occupations united in the same person, who had hung out two sign-posts. Upon one was, JAMES HOOD, WHITE IRON SMITH (i.e. tin-plate worker). Upon another, THE ART OF FENCING TAUGHT, BY JAMES HOOD. Upon this last were painted some trees, and two men fencing, one of whom had hit the other in the eye, to shew his great dexterity; so that the art was well taught. JOHNSON. 'Were I studying here, I should go and take a lesson. I remember Hope, in his book on this art, says, "the Scotch are very good fencers".'

191

We returned to the inn, where we had been entertained at dinner, and drank tea in company with some of the professors, of whose civilities I beg leave to add my humble and very grateful acknowledgement to the honourable testimony of Dr Johnson, in his *Journey*.

We talked of composition, which was a favourite topick of Dr Watson's, who first distinguished himself by lectures on rhetorick. JOHNSON. 'I advised Chambers, and would advise every young man beginning to compose, to do it as fast as he can, to get a habit of having his mind to start promptly; it is so much more difficult to improve in speed than in accuracy.' WATSON. 'I own I am for much attention to accuracy in composing, lest one should get bad habits of doing it in a slovenly manner.' JOHNSON. 'Why, sir, you are confounding *doing* inaccurately with the *necessity* of doing inaccurately. A man knows when his composition is inaccurate, and when he thinks fit he'll correct it. But, if a man is accustomed to compose slowly, and with difficulty, upon all occasions, there is danger that he may not compose at all, as we do not like to do that which is not done easily; and, at any rate, more time is consumed in a small matter than ought to be.' WATSON. 'Dr Hugh Blair has taken a week to compose a sermon.' JOHNSON. 'Then, sir, that is for want of the habit of composing quickly, which I am insisting one should acquire.' WATSON. 'Blair was not composing all the week, but only such hours as he found himself disposed for composition.' JOHNSON. 'Nay, sir, unless you tell me the time he took, you tell me nothing. If I say I took a week to walk a mile, and have had the gout five days, and been ill otherwise another day, I have taken but one day. I myself have composed about forty sermons.[63] I have begun a sermon after dinner, and sent it off by the post that night. I wrote forty-eight of the printed octavo pages of the *Life of Savage* at a sitting; but then I sat up all night. I have also written six sheets in a day of translation from the French.' BOSWELL. 'We have all observed how one man dresses himself slowly, and another fast.' JOHNSON. 'Yes, sir; it is wonderful how much time some people will consume in dressing; taking up a thing and looking at it, and laying it down, and taking it up again. Every one should get the habit of doing it quickly. I would say to a young divine, "Here is your text; let me see how soon you can make a sermon." Then I'd say, "Let me see how much better you can make it." Thus I should see both his powers and his judgement.'

We all went to Dr Watson's to supper. Miss Sharp, great grandchild of Archbishop Sharp, was there; as was Mr Craig, the ingenious architect of the new town of Edinburgh, and nephew of Thomson, to whom Dr Johnson has since done so much justice, in his *Lives of the Poets*.

We talked of memory, and its various modes. JOHNSON. 'Memory will play strange tricks. One sometimes loses a single word. I once lost *fugaces* in the Ode *Posthume, Posthume.*[64] I mentioned to him, that a worthy gentleman of my acquaintance actually forgot his own name. JOHNSON. 'Sir, that was a morbid oblivion.'

Friday, 20th August

Dr Shaw, the professor of divinity, breakfasted with us. I took out my Ogden *On Prayer*, and read some of it to the company. Dr Johnson praised him. 'Abernethy,'[65] said he, 'allows only of a physical effect of prayer upon the mind, which may be produced many ways, as well as by prayer; for instance, by meditation. Ogden goes farther. In truth, we have the consent of all nations for the efficacy of prayer, whether offered up by individuals, or by assemblies; and Revelation has told us, it will be effectual.' I said, 'Leechman seemed to incline to Abernethy's doctrine.'[66] Dr Watson observed, that Leechman meant to shew, that, even admitting no effect to be produced by prayer, respecting the Deity, it was useful to our own minds. He had given only a part of his system: Dr Johnson thought he should have given the whole.

Dr Johnson enforced the strict observance of Sunday. 'It should be different,' he observed, 'from another day. People may walk, but not throw stones at birds. There may be relaxation, but there should be no levity.'

We went and saw Colonel Nairne's garden and grotto. Here was a fine old plane tree. Unluckily the colonel said, there was but this and another large tree in the county. This assertion was an excellent cue for Dr Johnson, who laughed enormously, calling to me to hear it. He had expatiated to me on the nakedness of that part of Scotland which he had seen. His *Journey* has been violently abused, for what he has said upon this subject. But let it be considered, that, when Dr Johnson talks of trees, he means trees of good size, such as he was accustomed to see in England; and of these there are certainly very few upon the *eastern coast* of Scotland. Besides, he said, that he meant to give only a map of the road; and let any traveller observe how many trees, which deserve the name, he can see from the road from Berwick to Aberdeen. Had Dr Johnson said, 'there are *no* trees' upon this line, he would have said what is colloquially true; because, by no trees, in common speech, we mean few. When he is particular in counting, he may be attacked. I know not how Colonel Nairne came to say there were but *two* large trees in the county of Fife. I did not perceive that he smiled. There are certainly not a great many; but I could have shewn him more than two at Balmuto,[67] from whence my ancestors came, and which now belongs to a branch of my family.

The grotto was ingeniously constructed. In the front of it were petrified stocks of fir, plane, and some other tree. Dr Johnson said, 'Scotland has no right to boast of this grotto; it is owing to personal merit. I never denied personal merit to many of you.' Professor Shaw said to me, as we walked, 'This is a wonderful man: he is master of every subject he handles.' Dr Watson allowed him a very strong understanding, but wondered at his total inattention to established manners, as he came from London.

I have not preserved, in my *Journal*, any of the conversation which passed between Dr Johnson and Professor Shaw; but I recollect Dr Johnson said to me afterwards, 'I took much to Shaw.'

We left St Andrews about noon, and some miles from it observing, at Leuchars, a church with an old tower, we stopped to look at it. The *manse*, as the parsonage-house is called in Scotland, was close by. I waited on the minister, mentioned our names, and begged he would tell us what he knew about it. He was a very civil old man; but could only inform us, that it was supposed to have stood eight hundred years. He told us, there was a colony of Danes in his parish; that they had landed at a remote period of time, and still remained a distinct people. Dr Johnson shrewdly inquired whether they had brought women with them. We were not satisfied as to this colony.

We saw, this day, Dundee and Aberbrothick, the last of which Dr Johnson has celebrated in his *Journey*. Upon the road we talked of the Roman Catholick faith. He mentioned (I think) Tillotson's argument against transubstantiation; 'That we are as sure we see bread and wine only, as that we read in the Bible the text on which that false doctrine is founded. We have only the evidence of our senses for both. If,' he added, 'God had never spoken figuratively, we might hold that he speaks literally, when he says, "This is my body".' BOSWELL. 'But what do you say, sir, to the ancient and continued tradition of the Church upon this point?' JOHNSON. 'Tradition, sir, has no place, where the Scriptures are plain; and tradition cannot persuade a man into a belief of transubstantiation. Able men, indeed, have *said* they believed it.'

This is an awful subject. I did not then press Dr Johnson upon it; nor shall I now enter upon a disquisition concerning the import of those words uttered by our Saviour,* which had such an effect upon many disciples, that they 'went back, and walked no more with him'. The Catechism and solemn office for Communion, in the Church of England, maintain a mysterious belief in more than a mere commemoration of the death of Christ, by partaking of the elements of bread and wine.

* 'Then Jesus said unto them, verily, verily, I say unto you, except ye eat the flesh of the son of man, and drink his blood, ye have no life in you.' See St John's Gospel, chap. vi. 53, and following verses.

Dr Johnson put me in mind, that, at St Andrews, I had defended my profession very well, when the question had again been started, whether a lawyer might honestly engage with the first side that offers him a fee. 'Sir,' said I, 'it was with your arguments against Sir William Forbes: but it was much that I could wield the arms of Goliath.'

He said, our judges had not gone deep in the question concerning literary property. I mentioned Lord Monboddo's opinion, that if a man could get a work by heart, he might print it, as by such an act the mind is exercised. JOHNSON. 'No, sir; a man's repeating it no more makes it his property, than a man may sell a cow which he drives home.' I said, printing an abridgement of a work was allowed, which was only cutting the horns and tail off the cow. JOHNSON. 'No, sir; 'tis making the cow have a calf.'

About eleven at night we arrived at Montrose. We found but a sorry inn, where I myself saw another waiter put a lump of sugar with his fingers into Dr Johnson's lemonade, for which he called him 'Rascal!' It put me in great glee that our landlord was an Englishman. I rallied the Doctor upon this, and he grew quiet. Both Sir John Hawkins's and Dr Burney's *History of Musick* had then been advertised. I asked if this was not unlucky: would not they hurt one another? JOHNSON. 'No, sir. They will do good to one another. Some will buy the one, some the other, and compare them; and so a talk is made about a thing, and the books are sold.'

He was angry at me for proposing to carry lemons with us to Sky, that he might be sure to have his lemonade. 'Sir,' said he, 'I do not wish to be thought that feeble man who cannot do without any thing. Sir, it is very bad manners to carry provisions to any man's house, as if he could not entertain you. To an inferior, it is oppressive; to a superior, it is insolent.'

Having taken the liberty, this evening, to remark to Dr Johnson, that he very often sat quite silent for a long time, even when in company with only a single friend, which I myself had sometimes sadly experienced, he smiled and said, 'It is true, sir. Tom Tyers' (for so he familiarly called our ingenious friend, who, since his death, has paid a biographical tribute to his memory) 'Tom Tyers[68] described me the best. He once said to me, "Sir, you are like a ghost: you never speak till you are spoken to." '*

Saturday, 21st August

Neither the Rev. Mr Nisbet, the established minister, nor the Rev. Mr Spooner, the episcopal minister, were in town. Before breakfast, we went and saw the

* This description of Dr Johnson, appears to have been borrowed from *Tom Jones*, Book XI. chap. ii. 'The other, who like a ghost, only wanted to be spoke to, readily answered,' &c.

town-hall, where is a good dancing-room, and other rooms for tea-drinking. The appearance of the town from it is very well; but many of the houses are built with their ends to the street, which looks awkward. When we came down from it, I met Mr Gleg, a merchant here. He went with us to see the English chapel. It is situated on a pretty dry spot, and there is a fine walk to it. It is really an elegant building, both within and without. The organ is adorned with green and gold. Dr Johnson gave a shilling extraordinary to the clerk, saying, 'He belongs to an honest church.' I put him in mind, that episcopals were but *dissenters* here; they were only *tolerated*. 'Sir,' said he, 'we are here, as Christians in Turkey.' He afterwards went into an apothecary's shop, and ordered some medicine for himself, and wrote the prescription in technical characters.[69] The boy took him for a physician.

I doubted much which road to take, whether to go by the coast, or by Lawrence Kirk and Monboddo. I knew Lord Monboddo and Dr Johnson did not love each other: yet I was unwilling not to visit his lordship; and was also curious to see them together.* I mentioned my doubts to Dr Johnson, who said, he would go two miles out of his way to see Lord Monboddo. I therefore sent Joseph forward, with the following note.

My dear Lord,   *Montrose, 21 August.*

Thus far I am come with Mr Samuel Johnson. We must be at Aberdeen to-night. I know you do not admire him so much as I do; but I cannot be in this country without making you a bow at your old place, as I do not know if I may again have an opportunity of seeing Monboddo. Besides, Mr Johnson says, he would go two miles out of his way to see Lord Monboddo. I have sent forward my servant, that we may know if your lordship be at home. I am ever, my dear lord,

                            Most sincerely yours,
                            JAMES BOSWELL.

As we travelled onwards from Montrose, we had the Grampion hills in our view, and some good land around us, but void of trees and hedges. Dr Johnson has said ludicrously, in his *Journey*, that the *hedges* were of *stone*; for, instead of the verdant *thorn* to refresh the eye, we found the bare *wall* or *dike* intersecting the prospect.[70] He observed, that it was wonderful to see a country so divested, so denuded of trees.

We stopped at Lawrence Kirk, where our great grammarian, Ruddiman, was once schoolmaster. We respectfully remembered that excellent man and eminent scholar, by whose labours a knowledge of the Latin language will

---

* There were several points of similarity between them: learning, clearness of head, precision of speech, and a love of research on many subjects which people in general do not investigate. Foote paid Lord Monboddo the compliment of saying, that he was 'an Elzevir edition of Johnson'.

It has been shrewdly observed that Foote must have meant a diminutive, or *pocket* edition.

be preserved in Scotland, if it shall be preserved at all. Lord Gardenston, one of our judges, collected money to raise a monument to him at this place, which I hope will be well executed. I know my father gave five guineas towards it.[71] Lord Gardenston is the proprietor of Lawrence Kirk, and has encouraged the building of a manufacturing village, of which he is exceedingly fond, and has written a pamphlet upon it, as if he had founded Thebes, in which, however there are many useful precepts strongly expressed. The village seemed to be irregularly built, some of the houses being of clay, some of brick, and some of brick and stone. Dr Johnson observed, they thatched well here.

I was a little acquainted with Mr Forbes, the minister of the parish. I sent to inform him that a gentleman desired to see him. He returned for answer, 'that he would not come to a stranger'. I then gave my name, and he came. I remonstrated to him for not coming to a stranger; and, by presenting him to Dr Johnson, proved to him what a stranger might sometimes be. His Bible inculcates 'be not forgetful to entertain strangers', and mentions the same motive. He defended himself by saying, he had once come to a stranger who sent for him; and he found him 'a little worth person!'

Dr Johnson insisted on stopping at the inn, as I told him that Lord Gardenston had furnished it with a collection of books, that travellers might have entertainment for the mind, as well as the body. He praised the design, but wished there had been more books, and those better chosen.

About a mile from Monboddo, where you turn off the road, Joseph was waiting to tell us my lord expected us to dinner. We drove over a wild moor. It rained, and the scene was somewhat dreary. Dr Johnson repeated, with solemn emphasis, Macbeth's speech on meeting the witches. As we travelled on, he told me, 'Sir, you got into our club by doing what a man can do.* Several of the members wished to keep you out. Burke told me, he doubted if you were fit for it: but, now you are in, none of them are sorry. Burke says, that you have so much good humour naturally, it is scarce a virtue.' BOSWELL. 'They were afraid of you, sir, as it was you who proposed me.' JOHNSON. 'Sir, they knew, that if they refused you, they'd probably never have got in another. I'd have kept them all out. Beauclerk was very earnest for you.' BOSWELL. 'Beauclerk has a keenness of mind which is very uncommon.' JOHNSON. 'Yes, sir; and every thing comes from him so easily. It appears to me that I labour, when I say a good thing.' BOSWELL. 'You are loud, sir; but it is not an effort of mind.'

---

*This, I find, is considered as obscure. I suppose Dr Johnson meant, that I assiduously and earnestly recommended myself to some of the members, as in a canvass for an election into Parliament.

Monboddo is a wretched place, wild and naked, with a poor old house; though, if I recollect right, there are two turrets which mark an old baron's residence. Lord Monboddo received us at his gate most courteously; pointed to the Douglas arms upon his house, and told us that his great-grandmother was of that family. 'In such houses,' said he, 'our ancestors lived, who were better men than we.' 'No, no, my lord,' said Dr Johnson. 'We are as strong as they, and a great deal wiser.' This was an assault upon one of Lord Monboddo's capital dogmas, and I was afraid there would have been a violent altercation in the very close, before we got into the house. But his lordship is distinguished not only for 'ancient metaphysicks', but for ancient *politesse, la vieille cour,* and he made no reply.

His lordship was drest in a rustick suit, and wore a little round hat; he told us, we now saw him as Farmer Burnett, and we should have his family dinner, a farmer's dinner. He said, 'I should not have forgiven Mr Boswell, had he not brought you here, Dr Johnson.' He produced a very long stalk of corn, as a specimen of his crop, and said, 'You see here the *lætas segetes.*'[72] He added, that Virgil seemed to be as enthusiastick a farmer as he, and was certainly a practical one. JOHNSON. 'It does not always follow, my lord, that a man who has written a good poem on an art, has practised it. Philip Miller told me, that in Philips's "Cyder", a poem, all the precepts were just, and indeed better than in books written for the purpose of instructing; yet Philips had never made cyder.'

I started the subject of emigration. JOHNSON. 'To a man of mere animal life, you can urge no argument against going to America, but that it will be some time before he will get the earth to produce. But a man of any intellectual enjoyment will not easily go and immerse himself and his posterity for ages in barbarism.'

He and my lord spoke highly of Homer. JOHNSON. 'He had all the learning of his age. The shield of Achilles shews a nation in war, a nation in peace; harvest sport, nay stealing.'* MONBODDO. 'Ay, and what we' (looking to me) 'would call a parliament-house scene; a cause pleaded.' JOHNSON. 'That is part of the life of a nation in peace. And there are in Homer such characters of heroes, and combinations of qualities of heroes, that the united

---

* My note of this is much too short. *Brevis esse laboro, obscurus fio.* Yet as I have resolved that *the very* Journal *which Dr Johnson read,* shall be presented to the publick, I will not expand the text in any considerable degree, though I may occasionally supply a word to complete the sense, as I fill up the blanks of abbreviation in the writing; neither of which can be said to change the genuine *Journal.* One of the best criticks of our age conjectures that the imperfect passage above has probably been as follows: 'In his book we have an accurate display of a nation in war, and a nation in peace; the peasant is delineated as truly as the general; nay, even harvest-sport, and the modes of ancient theft are described.'

powers of mankind ever since have not produced any but what are to be found there.' MONBODDO. 'Yet no character is described.' JOHNSON. 'No; they all develope themselves. Agamemnon is always a gentleman-like character; he has always βασιλικόν τι.[73] That the ancients held so, is plain from this; that Euripides, in his *Hecuba*, makes him the person to interpose.'* MONBODDO. 'The history of manners is the most valuable. I never set a high value on any other history.' JOHNSON. 'Nor I; and therefore I esteem biography, as giving us what comes near to ourselves, what we can turn to use.' BOSWELL. 'But in the course of general history, we find manners. In wars, we see the dispositions of people, their degrees of humanity, and other particulars.' JOHNSON. 'Yes; but then you must take all the facts to get this; and it is but a little you get.' MONBODDO. 'And it is that little which makes history valuable.' Bravo! thought I; they agree like two brothers. MONBODDO. 'I am sorry, Dr Johnson, you were not longer at Edinburgh, to receive the homage of our men of learning.' JOHNSON. 'My lord, I received great respect and great kindness.' BOSWELL. 'He goes back to Edinburgh after our tour.' We talked of the decrease of learning in Scotland, and the *Muses' Welcome*. JOHNSON. 'Learning is much decreased in England, in my remembrance.' MONBODDO. 'You, sir, have lived to see its decrease in England, I its extinction in Scotland.' However, I brought him to confess that the High School of Edinburgh did well. JOHNSON. 'Learning has decreased in England, because learning will not do so much for a man as formerly. There are other ways of getting preferment. Few bishops are now made for their learning. To be a bishop, a man must be learned in a learned age, factious in a factious age; but always of eminence. Warburton[74] is an exception; though his learning alone did not raise him. He was first an antagonist to Pope, and helped Theobald to publish his *Shakspeare*; but, seeing Pope the rising man, when Crousaz attacked his *Essay on Man*, for some faults which it has, and some which it has not, Warburton defended it in the *Review* of that time. This brought him acquainted with Pope, and he gained his friendship. Pope introduced him to Allen, Allen married him to his niece: so, by Allen's interest and his own,[75] he was made a bishop. But then his learning was the *sine qua non*: he knew how to make the most of it; but I do not find by any dishonest means.' MONBODDO. 'He is a great man.' JOHNSON. 'Yes; he has great knowledge,

* Dr Johnson modestly said, he had not read Homer so much as he wished he had done. But this conversation shews how well he was acquainted with the Mœonian bard; and he has shewn it still more in his criticism upon Pope's *Homer*, in his *Life* of that poet. My excellent friend, Mr Langton, told me, he was once present at a dispute between Dr Johnson and Mr Burke, on the comparative merits of Homer and Virgil, which was carried on with extraordinary abilities on both sides. Dr Johnson maintained the superiority of Homer.

great power of mind. Hardly any man brings greater variety of learning to bear upon his point.' MONBODDO. 'He is one of the greatest lights of your church.' JOHNSON. 'Why, we are not so sure of his being very friendly to us. He blazes, if you will, but that is not always the steadiest light. Lowth is another bishop who has risen by his learning.'[76]

Dr Johnson examined young Arthur, Lord Monboddo's son, in Latin. He answered very well; upon which he said, with complacency, 'Get you gone! When King James comes back,* you shall be in the "Muses' Welcome"!' My lord and Dr Johnson disputed a little, whether the savage or the London shopkeeper had the best existence; his lordship, as usual, preferring the savage. My lord was extremely hospitable, and I saw both Dr Johnson and him liking each other better every hour.

Dr Johnson having retired for a short time, his lordship spoke of his conversation as I could have wished. Dr Johnson had said, 'I have done greater feats with my knife than this;' though he had eaten a very hearty dinner. My lord, who affects or believes he follows an abstemious system, seemed struck with Dr Johnson's manner of living. I had a particular satisfaction in being under the roof of Monboddo, my lord being my father's old friend, and having been always very good to me. We were cordial together. He asked Dr Johnson and me to stay all night. When I said we *must* be at Aberdeen, he replied, 'Well, I am like the Romans: I shall say to you, "Happy to come – happy to depart!"' He thanked Dr Johnson for his visit. JOHNSON. 'I little thought, when I had the honour to meet your lordship in London, that I should see you at Monboddo.' After dinner, as the ladies were going away, Dr Johnson would stand up. He insisted that politeness was of great consequence in society. 'It is,' said he, 'fictitious benevolence. It supplies the place of it amongst those who see each other only in publick, or but little. Depend upon it, the want of it never fails to produce something disagreeable to one or other. I have always applied to good breeding, what Addison in his *Cato* says of honour:

> Honour's a sacred tie; the law of Kings;
> The noble mind's distinguishing perfection,
> That aids and strengthens Virtue where it meets her,
> And imitates her actions where she is not.

When he took up his large oak stick, he said, 'My lord, that's *Homerick*;' thus pleasantly alluding to his lordship's favourite writer.

Gory, my lord's black servant, was sent as our guide, to conduct us to the

* I find, some doubt has been entertained concerning Dr Johnson's meaning here. It is to be supposed that he meant, 'when a king shall again be entertained in Scotland'.

high road. The circumstance of each of them having a black servant was another point of similarity between Johnson and Monboddo.[77] I observed how curious it was to see an African in the north of Scotland, with little or no difference of manners from those of the natives. Dr Johnson laughed to see Gory and Joseph riding together most cordially. 'Those two fellows,' said he, 'one from Africa, the other from Bohemia, seem quite at home.' He was much pleased with Lord Monboddo to-day. He said, he would have pardoned him for a few paradoxes, when he found he had so much that was good: but that, from his appearance in London, he thought him all paradox; which would not do. He observed, that his lordship had talked no paradoxes to-day. 'And as to the savage and the London shopkeeper,' said he, 'I don't know but I might have taken the side of the savage equally, had any body else taken the side of the shopkeeper.' He had said to my lord, in opposition to the value of the savage's courage, that it was owing to his limited power of thinking, and repeated Pope's verses, in which 'Macedonia's madman' is introduced, and the conclusion is,

Yet ne'er looks forward farther than his nose.

I objected to the last phrase, as being low. JOHNSON. 'Sir, it is intended to be low: it is satire. The expression is debased, to debase the character.'

When Gory was about to part from us, Dr Johnson called to him, 'Mr Gory, give me leave to ask you a question! Are you baptized?' Gory told him he was, and confirmed by the Bishop of Durham. He then gave him a shilling.

We had tedious driving this afternoon, and were somewhat drowsy. Last night I was afraid Dr Johnson was beginning to faint in his resolution; for he said, 'If we must ride much, we shall not go; and there's an end on't.' To-day, when he talked of Sky with spirit, I said, 'Why, sir, you seemed to me to despond yesterday. You are a delicate Londoner; you are a maccaroni; you can't ride.' JOHNSON. 'Sir, I shall ride better than you. I was only afraid I should not find a horse able to carry me.' I hoped then there would be no fear of getting through our wild tour.

We came to Aberdeen at half an hour past eleven. The New Inn, we were told, was full. This was comfortless. The waiter, however, asked if one of our names was Boswell, and brought me a letter left at the inn: it was from Mr Thrale, enclosing one to Dr Johnson. Finding who I was, we were told they would contrive to lodge us by putting us for a night into a room with two beds. The waiter said to me in the broad strong Aberdeenshire dialect, 'I thought I knew you, by your likeness to your father.' My father puts up at the New Inn, when on his circuit. Little was said to-night. I was to sleep in a little press-bed in Dr Johnson's room. I had it wheeled out into the dining-room, and there I lay very well.

Sunday, 22d August

I sent a message to Professor Thomas Gordon, who came and breakfasted with us. He had secured seats for us at the English chapel. We found a respectable congregation, and an admirable organ, well played by Mr Tait.

We walked down to the shore. Dr Johnson laughed to hear that Cromwell's soldiers taught the Aberdeen people to make shoes and stockings, and to plant cabbages. He asked, if weaving the plaids was ever a domestick art in the Highlands, like spinning or knitting. They could not inform him here. But he conjectured probably, that where people lived so remote from each other, it was likely to be a domestick art; as we see it was among the ancients, from Penelope. I was sensible to-day, to an extraordinary degree, of Dr Johnson's excellent English pronunciation. I cannot account for its striking me more now than any other day: but it was as if new to me; and I listened to every sentence which he spoke, as to a musical composition. Professor Gordon gave him an account of the plan of education in his college. Dr Johnson said, it was similar to that at Oxford. Waller the poet's great grandson was studying here. Dr Johnson wondered that a man should send his son so far off, when there were so many good schools in England. He said, 'At a great school there is all the splendour and illumination of many minds; the radiance of all is concentrated in each, or at least reflected upon each. But we must own that neither a dull boy, nor an idle boy, will do so well at a great school as at a private one. For at a great school there are always boys enough to do well easily, who are sufficient to keep up the credit of the school; and after whipping being tried to no purpose, the dull or idle boys are left at the end of a class, having the appearance of going through the course, but learning nothing at all. Such boys may do good at a private school, where constant attention is paid to them, and they are watched. So that the question of publick or private education is not properly a general one; but whether one or the other is best for *my son*.'

We were told the present Mr Waller[78] was a plain country gentleman; and his son would be such another. I observed, a family could not expect a poet but in a hundred generations. 'Nay,' said Dr Johnson, 'not one family in a hundred can expect a poet in a hundred generations.' He then repeated Dryden's celebrated lines,[79]

Three poets in three distant ages born, &c.

and a part of a Latin translation of it done at Oxford:* he did not then say by whom.

He received a card from Sir Alexander Gordon, who had been his acquaintance twenty years ago in London, and who, 'if forgiven for not answering a line from him', would come in the afternoon. Dr Johnson rejoiced to hear of him, and begged he would come and dine with us. I was much pleased to see the kindness with which Dr Johnson received his old friend Sir Alexander; a gentleman of good family, Lismore, but who had not the estate. The King's College here made him Professor of Medicine, which affords him a decent subsistence. He told us that the value of the stockings exported from Aberdeen was, in peace, a hundred thousand pounds; and amounted, in time of war, to one hundred and seventy thousand pounds. Dr Johnson asked, what made the difference? Here we had a proof of the comparative sagacity of the two professors. Sir Alexander answered, 'Because there is more occasion for them in war.' Professor Thomas Gordon answered, 'Because the Germans, who are our great rivals in the manufacture of stockings, are otherwise employed in time of war.' JOHNSON. 'Sir, you have given a very good solution.'

At dinner, Dr Johnson ate several plate-fulls of Scotch broth, with barley and peas in it, and seemed very fond of the dish. I said, 'You never ate it before.' JOHNSON. 'No, sir; but I don't care how soon I eat it again.' My cousin, Miss Dallas, formerly of Inverness, was married to Mr Riddoch, one of the ministers of the English chapel here. He was ill, and confined to his room; but she sent us a kind invitation to tea, which we all accepted. She was the same lively, sensible, cheerful woman, as ever. Dr Johnson here threw out some jokes against Scotland. He said, 'You go first to Aberdeen; then to *Enbru* (the Scottish pronunciation of Edinburgh); then to Newcastle, to be polished by the colliers; then to York; then to London.' And he laid hold of a little girl, Stuart Dallas, niece to Mrs Riddoch, and, representing himself as a giant, said, he would take her with him! telling her, in a hollow voice, that he lived in a cave, and had a bed in the rock, and she should have a bed cut opposite to it!

He thus treated the point, as to prescription of murder in Scotland. 'A jury

* *London, 2d May,* 1778. Dr Johnson acknowledged that he was himself the authour of the translation above alluded to, and dictated it to me as follows:

> *Quos laudet vates Graius Romanus et Anglus*
>   *Tres tria temporibus secla dedere suis.*
> *Sublime ingenium Graius; Romanus habebat*
>   *Carmen grande sonans; Anglus utrumque tulit.*
> *Nil majus Natura capit: clarare priores*
>   *Quæ potuere duos tertius unus habet.*

in England would make allowance for deficiencies of evidence, on account of lapse of time: but a general rule that a crime should not be punished, or tried for the purpose of punishment, after twenty years, is bad. It is cant to talk of the King's advocate delaying a prosecution from malice. How unlikely is it the King's advocate should have malice against persons who commit murder, or should even know them at all. If the son of the murdered man should kill the murderer who got off merely by prescription, I would help him to make his escape; though, were I upon his jury, I would not acquit him. I would not advise him to commit such an act. On the contrary, I would bid him submit to the determination of society, because a man is bound to submit to the inconveniences of it, as he enjoys the good: but the young man, though politically wrong, would not be morally wrong. He would have to say, "Here I am amongst barbarians, who not only refuse to do justice, but encourage the greatest of all crimes. I am therefore in a state of nature: for, so far as there is now law, it is a state of nature: and consequently, upon the eternal and immutable law of justice, which requires that he who sheds man's blood should have his blood shed, I will stab the murderer of my father." '

We went to our inn, and sat quietly. Dr Johnson borrowed, at Mr Riddoch's, a volume of Massilon's *Discourses on the Psalms*:[80] but I found he read little in it. Ogden too he sometimes took up, and glanced at; but threw it down again. I then entered upon religious conversation. Never did I see him in a better frame: calm, gentle, wise, holy. I said, 'Would not the same objection hold against the Trinity as against transubstantiation?' 'Yes,' said he, 'if you take three and one in the same sense. If you do, to be sure you cannot believe it: but the three persons in the Godhead are Three in one sense, and One in another. We cannot tell how; and that is the mystery!'

I spoke of the satisfaction of Christ. He said his notion was, that it did not atone for the sins of the world; but, by satisfying divine justice, by shewing that no less than the Son of God suffered for sin, it shewed to men and innumerable created beings, the heinousness of it, and therefore rendered it unnecessary for divine vengeance to be exercised against sinners, as it otherwise must have been; that in this way it might operate even in favour of those who had never heard of it: as to those who did hear of it, the effect it should produce would be repentance and piety, by impressing upon the mind a just notion of sin: that original sin was the propensity to evil, which no doubt was occasioned by the fall. He presented this solemn subject in a new light to me,*

* My worthy, intelligent, and candid friend, Dr Kippis, informs me, that several divines have thus explained the mediation of our Saviour. What Dr Johnson now delivered, was but a temporary opinion; for he afterwards was fully convinced of the propitiatory sacrifice, as I shall shew at large in my future work, *The Life of Samuel Johnson, LL.D.*

and rendered much more rational and clear the doctrine of what our Saviour has done for us, as it removed the notion of imputed righteousness in co-operating; whereas by this view, Christ has done all already that he had to do, or is ever to do, for mankind, by making his great satisfaction; the consequences of which will affect each individual according to the particular conduct of each. I would illustrate this by saying, that Christ's satisfaction resembles a sun placed to shew light to men, so that it depends upon themselves whether they will walk the right way or not, which they could not have done without that sun, 'the sun of righteousness'. There is, however, more in it than merely giving light – 'a light to lighten the Gentiles': for we are told, there is 'healing under his wings'. Dr Johnson said to me, 'Richard Baxter commends a treatise by Grotius, *De Satisfactione Christi*.[81] I have never read it: but I intend to read it; and you may read it.' I remarked, upon the principle now laid down, we might explain the difficult and seemingly hard text, 'They that believe shall be saved; and they that believe not shall be damned.' They that believe shall have such an impression made upon their minds, as will make them act so that they may be accepted by God.

We talked of one of our friends taking ill,[82] for a length of time, a hasty expression of Dr Johnson's to him, on his attempting to prosecute a subject that had a reference to religion, beyond the bounds within which the Doctor thought such topicks should be confined in a mixed company. JOHNSON. 'What is to become of society, if a friendship of twenty years is to be broken off for such a cause?' As Bacon says,

> Who then to frail mortality shall trust,
> But limns the water, or but writes in dust.[83]

I said, he should write expressly in support of Christianity; for that, although a reverence for it shines through his works in several places, that is not enough. 'You know,' said I, 'what Grotius has done, and what Addison has done. You should do also.' He replied, 'I hope I shall.'

Monday, 23d August

Principal Campbell, Sir Alexander Gordon, Professor Gordon, and Professor Ross, visited us in the morning, as did Dr Gerard, who had come six miles from the country on purpose. We went and saw the Marischal College,* and at one o'clock we waited on the magistrates in the town hall, as they had invited us in order to present Dr Johnson with the freedom of the town, which Provost Jopp did with a very good grace. Dr Johnson was much pleased

---

* Dr Beattie was so kindly entertained in England, that he had not yet returned home.

with this mark of attention, and received it very politely. There was a pretty numerous company assembled. It was striking to hear all of them drinking 'Dr Johnson! Dr Johnson!' in the town-hall of Aberdeen, and then to see him with his burgess-ticket, or diploma,* in his hat, which he wore as he walked along the street, according to the usual custom. It gave me great satisfaction to observe the regard, and indeed fondness too, which every body here had for my father.

While Sir Alexander Gordon conducted Dr Johnson to old Aberdeen, Professor Gordon and I called on Mr Riddoch, whom I found to be a grave worthy clergyman. He observed, that, whatever might be said of Dr Johnson while he was alive, he would, after he was dead, be looked upon by the world with regard and astonishment, on account of his *Dictionary*.

Professor Gordon and I walked over to the Old College, which Dr Johnson had seen by this time. I stepped into the chapel, and looked at the tomb of the founder, Archbishop Elphinston, of whom I shall have occasion to write in my History of James IV of Scotland, the patron of my family.

We dined at Sir Alexander Gordon's. The Provost, Professor Ross, Professor Dunbar, Professor Thomas Gordon, were there. After dinner came in Dr Gerard, Professor Leslie, Professor Macleod. We had little or no conversation in the morning; now we were but barren. The professors seemed afraid to speak.

Dr Gerard told us that an eminent printer was very intimate with Warburton. JOHNSON. 'Why, sir, he has printed some of his works, and perhaps bought the property of some of them. The intimacy is such as one of the professors here may have with one of the carpenters who is repairing the college.' 'But,' said Gerard, 'I saw a letter from him to this printer, in which he says, that the one half of the clergy of the Church of Scotland are fanaticks, and the other half infidels.' JOHNSON. 'Warburton has accustomed himself to write letters just as he speaks, without thinking any more of what he throws out. When I read Warburton first, and observed his force, and his contempt of mankind, I thought he had driven the world before him; but I soon found that was not the case; for Warburton, by extending his abuse, rendered it ineffectual.'

* Dr Johnson's burgess-ticket was in these words:

Aberdoniæ, vigesimo tertio die mensis Augusti, anno Domini millesimo septingentesimo septuagesimo tertio, in presentia honorabilium virorum, Jacobi Jopp, armigeri, præpositi, Adami Duff, Gulielmi Young, Georgii Marr, et Gulielmi Forbes, Balivorum, Gulielmi Rainie Decani guildæ, et Joannis Nicoll Thesaurarii dicti burgi.

Quo die vir generosus et doctrina clarus, Samuel Johnson, LL. D. receptus et admissus fuit in municipes et fratres guildæ præfati burgi de Aberdeen. In deditissimi amoris et affectus ac eximiæ observantiæ tesseram, quibus dicti Magistratus eum amplectuntur. Extractum per me,

ALEX. CARNEGIE.

He told me, when we were by ourselves, that he thought it very wrong in the printer, to shew Warburton's letter, as it was raising a body of enemies against him. He thought it foolish in Warburton to write so to the printer; and added, 'Sir, the worst way of being intimate, is by scribbling.' He called Warburton's *Doctrine of Grace* a poor performance, and so he said was Wesley's *Answer*. 'Warburton,' he observed, 'had laid himself very open. In particular, he was weak enough to say, that, in some disorders of the imagination, people had spoken with tongues, had spoken languages which they never knew before; a thing as absurd as to say, that, in some disorders of the imagination, people had been known to fly.'

I talked of the difference of genius, to try if I could engage Gerard in a disquisition with Dr Johnson; but I did not succeed. I mentioned, as a curious fact, that Locke had written verses. JOHNSON. 'I know of none, sir, but a kind of exercise prefixed to Dr Sydenham's *Works*, in which he has some conceits about the dropsy, in which water and burning are united; and how Dr Sydenham removed fire by drawing off water, contrary to the usual practice, which is to extinguish fire by bringing water upon it. I am not sure that there is a word of all this; but it is such kind of talk.'*

---

*All this, as Dr Johnson suspected at the time, was the immediate invention of his own lively imagination; for there is not one word of it in Mr Locke's complimentary performance. My readers will, I have no doubt, like to be satisfied, by comparing them; and, at any rate, it may entertain them to read verses composed by our great metaphysician, when a Bachelor in Physick.

AUCTORI, IN TRACTATUM EJUS DE FEBRIBUS.

Febriles æstus, victumque ardoribus orbem
  Flevit, non tantis par Medicina malis.
  Et post mille artes, medicæ tentamina curae,
  Ardet adhuc Febris; nec velit arte regi.
Præda sumus flammis; solum hoc speramus ab igne,
  Ut restet paucus, quem capit urna, cinis.
Dum quærit medicus febris caussamque, modumque,
  Flammarum et tenebras, et sine luce faces;
Quas tractat patitur flammas, et febre calescens,
  Corruit ipse suis victima rapta focis.
Qui tardos potuit morbos, artusque trementes,
  Sistere, febrili se videt igne rapi.
Sic faber exesos fulsit tibicine muros;
  Dum trahit antiquas lenta ruina domos.
Sed si flamma vorax miseras incenderit ædes,
  Unica flagrantes tunc sepelire salus.
Fit fuga, tectonicas nemo tunc invocat artes;
  Cum perit artificis non minus usta domus.
Se tandem Sydenham febrisque Scholæque furori

We spoke of *Fingal*. Dr Johnson said calmly, 'If the poems were really translated, they were certainly first written down. Let Mr Macpherson deposite the manuscript in one of the colleges at Aberdeen, where there are people who can judge; and, if the professors certify the authenticity, then there will be an end of the controversy. If he does not take this obvious and easy method, he gives the best reason to doubt; considering too, how much is against it *a priori*.'

We sauntered after dinner in Sir Alexander's garden, and saw his little grotto, which is hung with pieces of poetry written in a fair hand. It was

---

Opponens, morbi quærit, et artis opem.
Non temere incusat tectæ putedinis ignes;
  Nec fictus, febres qui fovet, humor erit,
Non bilem ille movet, nulla hic pituita; Salutis
  Quæ spes, si fallax ardeat intus aqua?
Nec doctas magno rixas ostentat hiatu,
  Quis ipsis major febribus ardor inest.
Innocuas placide corpus jubet urere flammas,
  Et justo rapidos temperat igne focos.
Quid febrim exstinguat, varius quid postulat usus,
  Solari ægrotos, qua potes arte, docet.
Hactenus ipsa suum timuit Natura calorem,
  Dum sæpe incerto, quo calet, igne perit:
Dum reparat tacitos male provida sanguinis ignes,
  Prælusit busto, fit calor iste rogus.
Jam secura suas foveant præcordia flammas,
  Quem Natura negat, dat Medicina modum.
Nec solum faciles compescit sanguinis æstus,
  Dum dubia est inter spemque metumque salus;
Sed fatale malum domuit, quodque astra malignum
  Credimus, iratam vel genuisse Stygem.
Extorsit Lachesi cultros, Pestique venenum
  Abstulit, et tantos non sinit esse metus.
Quis tandem arte nova domitam mitescere Pestem
  Credat, et antiquas ponere posse minas?
Post tot mille neces, cumulataque funera busto,
  Victa jacet, parvo vulnere, dira Lues.
Ætheriæ quanquam spargunt contagia flammæ,
  Quicquid inest istis ignibus, ignis erit.
Delapsæ cœlo flammæ licet acrius urant,
  Has gelida exstingui non nisi morte putas?
Tu meliora paras victrix Medicina; tuusque,
  Pestis quæ superat cuncta, triumphus eris.
Vive liber, victis febrilibus ignibus; unus
  Te simul et mundum qui manet, ignis erit.

J. Lock, *A. M.* Ex. Aede Christi, Oxon.

agreeable to observe the contentment and kindness of this quiet, benevolent man. Professor Macleod was brother to Macleod of Talisker, and brother-in-law to the Laird of Col. He gave me a letter to young Col. I was weary of this day, and began to think wishfully of being again in motion. I was uneasy to think myself too fastidious, whilst I fancied Dr Johnson quite satisfied. But he owned to me that he was fatigued and teased by Sir Alexander's doing too much to entertain him. I said, it was all kindness. JOHNSON. 'True, sir: but sensation is sensation.' BOSWELL. 'It is so: we feel pain equally from the surgeon's probe, as from the sword of the foe.'

We visited two booksellers' shops, and could not find Arthur Johnston's *Poems*.[84] We went and sat near an hour at Mr Riddoch's. He could not tell distinctly how much education at the college here costs, which disgusted Dr Johnson. I had pledged myself that we should go to the inn, and not stay supper. They pressed us, but he was resolute. I saw Mr Riddoch did not please him. He said to me, afterwards, 'Sir, he has no vigour in his talk.' But my friend should have considered that he himself was not in good humour; so that it was not easy to talk to his satisfaction. We sat contentedly at our inn. He then became merry, and observed how little we had either heard or said at Aberdeen: that the Aberdonians had not started a single *mawkin* (the Scottish word for hare) for us to pursue.

Tuesday, 24th August

We set out about eight in the morning, and breakfasted at Ellon. The land-lady said to me, 'Is not this the great Doctor that is going about through the country?' I said, 'Yes.' 'Ay,' said she, 'we heard of him, I made an errand into the room on purpose to see him. There's something great in his appearance: it is a pleasure to have such a man in one's house; a man who does so much good. If I had thought of it, I would have shewn him a child of mine, who has had a lump on his throat for some time.' 'But,' said I, 'he is not a doctor of physick.' 'Is he an oculist?' said the landlord. 'No,' said I, 'he is only a very learned man.' LANDLORD. 'They say he is the greatest man in England, except Lord Mansfield.' Dr Johnson was highly entertained with this, and I do think he was pleased too. He said, 'I like the exception: to have called me the greatest man in England, would have been an unmeaning compliment: but the exception marked that the praise was in earnest; and, in *Scotland*, the exception must be *Lord Mansfield*, or – *Sir John Pringle*.'[85]

He told me a good story of Dr Goldsmith. Graham,[86] who wrote *Telemachus, a Masque*, was sitting one night with him and Dr Johnson, and was half drunk. He rattled away to Dr Johnson: 'You are a clever fellow, to be sure;

but you cannot write an essay like Addison, or verses like the *Rape of the Lock*.' At last he said,* '*Doctor, I should be happy to see you at Eaton.*' 'I shall be glad to wait on you,' answered Goldsmith. 'No,' said Graham, ' 'tis not you I mean, Dr *Minor*; 'tis Dr *Major*, there.' Goldsmith was excessively hurt by this. He afterwards spoke of it himself. 'Graham,' said he, 'is a fellow to make one commit suicide.'

We had received a polite invitation to Slains castle. We arrived there just at three o'clock, as the bell for dinner was ringing. Though, from its being just on the north-east Ocean, no trees will grow here, Lord Errol has done all that can be done. He has cultivated his fields so as to bear rich crops of every kind, and he has made an excellent kitchen-garden, with a hot-house. I had never seen any of the family: but there had been a card of invitation written by the honourable Charles Boyd, the earl's brother. We were conducted into the house, and at the dining-room door were met by that gentleman, whom both of us at first took to be Lord Errol; but he soon corrected our mistake. My lord was gone to dine in the neighbourhood, at an entertainment given by Mr Irvine of Drum. Lady Errol received us politely, and was very attentive to us during the time of dinner. There was nobody at table but her ladyship, Mr Boyd, and some of the children, their governour and governess. Mr Boyd put Dr Johnson in mind of having dined with him at Cumming the Quaker's, along with Mr Hall and Miss Williams: this was a bond of connection between them. For me, Mr Boyd's acquaintance with my father was enough. After dinner, Lady Errol favoured us with a sight of her young family, whom she made stand up in a row. There were six daughters and two sons. It was a very pleasing sight.

Dr Johnson proposed our setting out. Mr Boyd said, he hoped we would stay all night; his brother would be at home in the evening, and would be very sorry if he missed us. Mr Boyd was called out of the room. I was very desirous to stay in so comfortable a house, and I wished to see Lord Errol. Dr Johnson, however, was right in resolving to go, if we were not asked again, as it is best to err on the safe side in such cases, and to be sure that one is quite welcome. To my great joy, when Mr Boyd returned, he told Dr Johnson that it was Lady Errol who had called him out, and said that she would never let Dr Johnson into the house again, if he went away that night; and that she had ordered the coach, to carry us to view a great curiosity

---

* I am sure I have related this story exactly as Dr Johnson told it to me; but a friend who has often heard him tell it, informs me that he usually introduced a circumstance which ought not to be omitted. 'At last, sir, Graham, having now got to about the pitch of looking at one man, and talking to another, said *Doctor* &c. 'What effect,' Dr Johnson used to add, 'this had on Goldsmith, who was as irascible as a hornet, may be easily conceived.'

on the coast, after which we should see the house. We cheerfully agreed.

Mr Boyd was engaged, in 1745–6, on the same side with many unfortunate mistaken noblemen and gentlemen. He escaped, and lay concealed for a year in the island of Arran, the ancient territory of the Boyds. He then went to France, and was about twenty years on the continent. He married a French lady, and now lived very comfortably at Aberdeen, and was much at Slains castle. He entertained us with great civility. He had a pompousness or formal plenitude in his conversation which I did not dislike. Dr Johnson said, there was too much elaboration in his talk. It gave me pleasure to see him, a steady branch of the family, setting forth all its advantages with much zeal. He told us that Lady Errol was one of the most pious and sensible women in the island; had a good head, and as good a heart. He said, she did not use force or fear in educating her children. JOHNSON. 'Sir, she is wrong; I would rather have the rod to be the general terror to all, to make them learn, than tell a child, if you do thus or thus, you will be more esteemed than your brothers or sisters. The rod produces an effect which terminates itself. A child is afraid of being whipped, and gets his task, and there's an end on't; whereas, by exciting emulation, and comparisons of superiority, you lay the foundation of lasting mischief; you make brothers and sisters hate each other.'

During Mr Boyd's stay in Arran, he had found a chest of medical books, left by a surgeon there, and had read them till he acquired some skill in physick, in consequence of which he is often consulted by the poor. There were several here waiting for him as patients. We walked round the house till stopped by a cut made by the influx of the sea. The house is built quite upon the shore; the windows look upon the main ocean, and the King of Denmark is Lord Errol's nearest neighbour on the north-east.

We got immediately into the coach, and drove to Dunbui, a rock near the shore, quite covered with sea-fowls; then to a circular bason of large extent, surrounded with tremendous rocks. On the quarter next the sea, there is a high arch in the rock, which the force of the tempest has driven out. This place is called Buchan's Buller, or the Buller of Buchan, and the country people call it the Pot. Mr Boyd said it was so called from the French *Bouloir*. It may be more simply traced from *Boiler* in our own language. We walked round this monstrous cauldron. In some places, the rock is very narrow; and on each side there is a sea deep enough for a man of war to ride in; so that it is somewhat horrid to move along. However, there is earth and grass upon the rock, and a kind of road marked out by the print of feet; so that one makes it out pretty safely: yet it alarmed me to see Dr Johnson striding irregularly along. He insisted on taking a boat, and sailing into the Pot. We did so. He was stout, and wonderfully alert. The Buchan-men all shewing their teeth, and speaking with that strange sharp accent which distinguishes them, was to me a matter of curiosity. He was not sensible of the difference of pronunciation in the south and north of Scotland, which I wondered at.

As the entry into the Buller is so narrow that oars cannot be used as you go in, the method taken is to row very hard when you come near it, and give the boat such a rapidity of motion that it glides in. Dr Johnson observed what an effect this scene would have had, were we entering into an unknown place. There are caves of considerable depth; I think, one on each side. The boatmen had never entered either of them far enough to know the size. Mr Boyd told us that it is customary for the company at Peterhead well, to make parties, and come and dine in one of the caves here.

He told us, that, as Slains is at a considerable distance from Aberdeen, Lord Errol, who has a very large family, resolved to have a surgeon of his own. With this view he educated one of his tenant's sons, who is now settled in a very neat house and farm just by, which we saw from the road. By the salary which the earl allows him, and the practice which he has had, he is in very easy circumstances. He had kept an exact account of all that had been laid out on his education, and he came to his lordship one day, and told him that he had arrived at a much higher situation than ever he expected; that he was now able to repay what his lordship had advanced, and begged he would accept of it. The earl was pleased with the generous gratitude and genteel offer of the man; but refused it. Mr Boyd also told us, Cumming the Quaker first began to distinguish himself, by writing against Dr Leechman on prayer,[87] to prove it unnecessary, as God knows best what should be, and will order it without our asking – the old hackneyed objection.

When we returned to the house we found coffee and tea in the drawing-room. Lady Errol was not there, being, as I supposed, engaged with her young family. There is a bow-window fronting the sea. Dr Johnson repeated the ode, *Jam satis terris*,[88] while Mr Boyd was with his patients. He spoke well in favour of entails, to preserve lines of men whom mankind are accustomed to reverence. His opinion was that so much land should be entailed as that families should never fall into contempt, and as much left free as to give them all the advantages of property in case of any emergency. 'If,' said he, 'the nobility are suffered to sink into indigence, they of course become corrupt; they are ready to do whatever the king chooses; therefore it is fit they should be kept from becoming poor, unless it is fixed that when they fall below a certain standard of wealth they shall lose their peerages. We know the House of Peers have made noble stands, when the House of Commons durst not. The two last years of Parliament they dare not contradict the populace.'

This room is ornamented with a number of fine prints, and with a whole length picture of Lord Errol, by Sir Joshua Reynolds. This led Dr Johnson and me to talk of our amiable and elegant friend, whose panegyrick he concluded by saying, 'Sir Joshua Reynolds, sir, is the most invulnerable man I know; the man with whom if you should quarrel, you would find the most difficulty how to abuse.'

Dr Johnson observed, the situation here was the noblest he had ever seen, better than Mount Edgecumbe, reckoned the first in England; because, at Mount Edgecumbe, the sea is bounded by land on the other side, and, though there is there the grandeur of a fleet, there is also the impression of there being a dock-yard, the circumstances of which are not agreeable. At Slains is an excellent old house. The noble owner has built of brick, along the square in the inside, a gallery, both on the first and second story, the house being no higher; so that he has always a dry walk, and the rooms, to which formerly there was no approach but through each other, have now all separate entries from the gallery, which is hung with Hogarth's works, and other prints. We went and sat a while in the library.[89] There is a valuable numerous collection. It was chiefly made by Mr Falconer, husband to the late Countess of Errol in her own right. This earl has added a good many modern books.

About nine the earl came home. Captain Gordon of Park was with him. His lordship put Dr Johnson in mind of their having dined together in London, along with Mr Beauclerk. I was exceedingly pleased with Lord Errol. His dignified person and agreeable countenance, with the most unaffected affability, gave me high satisfaction. From perhaps a weakness, or, as I rather hope, more fancy and warmth of feeling than is quite reasonable, my mind is ever impressed with admiration for persons of high birth, and I could, with the most perfect honesty, expatiate on Lord Errol's good qualities; but he stands in no need of my praise. His agreeable manners and softness of address prevented that constraint which the idea of his being Lord High Constable of Scotland might otherwise have occasioned. He talked very easily and sensibly with his learned guest. I observed that Dr Johnson, though he shewed that respect to his lordship, which, from principle, he always does to high rank, yet, when they came to argument, maintained that manliness which becomes the force and vigour of his understanding. To shew external deference to our superiors, is proper: to seem to yield to them in opinion, is meanness.* The earl said grace, both before and after supper, with much

---

* Lord Chesterfield, in his letters to his son, complains of one who argued in an indiscriminate manner with men of all ranks. Probably the noble lord had felt with some uneasiness what it was to encounter stronger abilities than his own. If a peer will engage at foils with his inferior in station, he must expect that his inferior in station will avail himself of every advantage; otherwise it

decency. He told us a story of a man who was executed at Perth, some years ago, for murdering a woman who was with child by him, and a former child he had by her. His hand was cut off: he was then pulled up; but the rope broke, and he was forced to lie an hour on the ground, till another rope was brought from Perth, the execution being in a wood at some distance, at the place where the murders were committed. 'There,' said my lord, 'I see the hand of Providence.' I was really happy here. I saw in this nobleman the best dispositions and best principles; and I saw him, in my mind's eye, to be the representative of the ancient Boyds of Kilmarnock. I was afraid he might have urged drinking, as, I believe, he used formerly to do, but he drank port and water out of a large glass himself, and let us do as we pleased. He went with us to our rooms at night; said, he took the visit very kindly; and told me, my father and he were very old acquaintances; that I now knew the way to Slains, and he hoped to see me there again.

I had a most elegant room; but there was a fire in it which blazed; and the sea, to which my windows looked, roared; and the pillows were made of the feathers of some sea-fowl, which had to me a disgreeable smell: so that, by all these causes, I was kept awake a good while. I saw, in imagination, Lord Errol's father, Lord Kilmarnock (who was beheaded on Tower Hill in 1746), and I was somewhat dreary. But the thought did not last long, and I fell asleep.

Wednesday, 25th August

We got up between seven and eight, and found Mr Boyd in the dining-room, with tea and coffee before him, to give us breakfast. We were in an admirable humour. Lady Errol had given each of us a copy of an ode by Beattie, on the birth of her son, Lord Hay. Mr Boyd asked Dr Johnson, how he liked it. Dr Johnson, who did not admire it, got off very well, by taking it out, and reading the second and third stanzes of it with much melody. This, without his saying

---

is not a fair trial of strength and skill. The same will hold in a contest of reason, or of wit. A certain king entered the lists of genius with Voltaire. The consequence was, that, though the king had great and brilliant talents, Voltaire had such a superiority that his majesty could not bear it; and the poet was dismissed, or escaped, from that court. In the reign of James I of England, Crichton, Lord Sanquhar, a peer of Scotland, from a vain ambition to excel a fencing-master in his own art, played at rapier and dagger with him. The fencing-master, whose fame and bread were at stake, put out one of his lordship's eyes. Exasperated at this, Lord Sanquhar hired ruffians, and had the fencing-master assassinated; for which his lordship was capitally tried, condemned, and hanged. Not being a peer of England, he was tried by the name of Robert Crichton, Esq.; but he was admitted to be a baron of three hundred years standing. See the *State Trials*; and the *History of England* by Hume, who applauds the impartial justice executed upon a man of high rank.

a word, pleased Mr Boyd. He observed, however, to Dr Johnson, that the expression as to the family of Errol,

A thousand years have seen it shine

compared with what went before, was an anticlimax, and that it would have been better

Ages have seen, &c.

Dr Johnson said, 'So great a number as a thousand is better. *Dolus latet in universalibus.*[90] Ages might be only two ages.' He talked of the advantage of keeping up the connections of relationship, which produce much kindness. 'Every man,' said he, 'who comes into the world, has need of friends. If he has to get them for himself, half his life is spent, before his merit is known. Relations are a man's ready friends who support him. When a man is in real distress, he flies into the arms of his relations. An old lawyer, who had much experience in making wills, told me, that after people had deliberated long, and thought of many for their executors, they settled at last by fixing on their relations. This shews the universality of the principle.'

I regretted the decay of respect for men of family, and that a Nabob[91] now would carry an election from them. JOHNSON. 'Why, sir, the Nabob will carry it by means of his wealth, in a country where money is highly valued, as it must be where nothing can be had without money; but, if it comes to personal preference, the man of family will always carry it. There is generally a *scoundrelism* about a low man.' Mr Boyd said, that was a good *ism*.

I said, I believed mankind were happier in the ancient feudal state of subordination, than they are in the modern state of independency. JOHNSON. 'To be sure, the *chief* was: but we must think of the number of individuals. That *they* were less happy, seems plain; for that state from which all escape as soon as they can, and to which none return after they have left it, must be less happy; and this is the case with the state of dependance on a chief or great man.'

I mentioned the happiness of the French in their subordination, by the reciprocal benevolence and attachment between the great and those in lower rank. Mr Boyd gave us an instance of their gentlemanly spirit. An old *Chevalier de Malthe*, of ancient *noblesse*, but in low circumstances, was in a coffee-house at Paris, where was Julien, the great manufacturer at the Gobelins, of the fine tapestry, so much distinguished both for the figures and the colours. The chevalier's carriage was very old. Says Julien, with a plebeian insolence, 'I think, sir, you had better have your carriage new painted.' The chevalier looked at him with indignant contempt, and answered, 'Well, sir, you may take it home and *dye* it!' All the coffee-house rejoiced at Julien's confusion.

We set out about nine. Dr Johnson was curious to see one of those structures which northern antiquarians call a Druid's temple.[92] I had a recollection of one at Strichen; which I had seen fifteen years ago; so we went four miles out of our road, after passing Old Deer, and went thither. Mr Fraser, the proprietor, was at home, and shewed it to us. But I had augmented it in my mind; for all that remains is two stones set up on end, with a long one laid upon them, as was usual and one stone at a little distance from them.[93] That stone was the capital one of the circle which surrounded what now remains. Mr Fraser was very hospitable.* There was a fair at Strichen; and he had several of his neighbours from it at dinner. One of them, Dr Fraser, who had been in the army, remembered to have seen Dr Johnson at a lecture on experimental philosophy, at Lichfield. The doctor recollected being at the lecture; and he was surprised to find here somebody who knew him.

Mr Fraser sent a servant to conduct us by a short passage into the highroad. I observed to Dr Johnson, that I had a most disagreeable notion of the life of country gentlemen; that I left Mr Fraser just now, as one leaves a prisoner in a jail. Dr Johnson said, that I was right in thinking them unhappy; for that they had not enough to keep their minds in motion.

I started a thought this afternoon which amused us a great part of the way. 'If,' said I, 'our club should come and set up in St Andrews, as a college, to teach all that each of us can, in the several departments of learning and taste, we should rebuild the city: we should draw a wonderful concourse of students.' Dr Johnson entered fully into the spirit of this project. We immediately fell to distributing the offices. I was to teach civil and Scotch law; Burke, politicks and eloquence; Garrick, the art of publick speaking; Langton was to be our Grecian, Colman our Latin professor; Nugent to teach physick;

---

* He is the worthy son of a worthy father, the late Lord Strichen, one of our judges, to whose kind notice I was much obliged. Lord Strichen was a man not only honest, but highly generous; for after his succession to the family estate, he paid a large sum of debts contracted by his predecessor, which he was not under any obligation to pay. Let me here, for the credit of Ayrshire, my own county, record a noble instance of liberal honesty in William Hutchison, drover, in Lanehead, Kyle, who formerly obtained a full discharge from his creditors upon a composition of his debts; but upon being restored to good circumstances, invited his creditors last winter to a dinner, without telling the reason, and paid them their full sums, principal and interest. They presented him with a piece of plate, with an inscription to commemorate this extraordinary instance of true worth; which should make some people in Scotland blush, while, though mean themselves, they strut about under the protection of great alliance conscious of the wretchedness of numbers who have lost by them, to whom they never think of making reparation, but indulge themselves and their families in most unsuitable expence.

Lord Charlemont, modern history; Beauclerk, natural philosophy; Vesey, Irish antiquities, or Celtick learning;* Jones, Oriental learning; Goldsmith, poetry and ancient history; Chamier, commercial politicks; Reynolds, painting, and the arts which have beauty for their object; Chambers, the law of England. Dr Johnson at first said, 'I'll trust theology to nobody but myself.' But, upon due consideration, that Percy is a clergyman, it was agreed that Percy should teach practical divinity and British antiquities; Dr Johnson himself, logick, metaphysicks and scholastick divinity. In this manner did we amuse ourselves, each suggesting, and each varying or adding, till the whole was adjusted. Dr Johnson said, we only wanted a mathematician since Dyer died, who was a very good one; but as to every thing else, we should have a very capital university.†

We got at night to Banff. I sent Joseph on to Duff house: but Earl Fife was not at home, which I regretted much, as we should have had a very elegant reception from his lordship. We found here but an indifferent inn.‡ Dr Johnson wrote a long letter to Mrs Thrale. I wondered to see him write so much so easily. He verified his own doctrine that 'a man may always write when he will set himself *doggedly* to it'.

---

* Since the first edition, it has been suggested by one of the clubs, who knew Mr Vesey better than Dr Johnson and I, that we did not assign him a proper place; for he was quite unskilled in Irish antiquities and Celtick learning, but might with propriety have been made professor of architecture, which he understood well, and has left a very good specimen of his knowledge and taste in that art, by an elegant house built on a plan of his own formation, at Lucan, a few miles from Dublin.

† Our club, originally at the Turk's Head, Gerrard Street, then at Prince's, Sackville Street, now at Baxter's Dover Street, which at Mr Garrick's funeral acquired a *name* for the first time, and was called The Literary Club, was instituted in 1764, and now consists of thirty-five members. It has, since 1773, been greatly augmented; and though Dr Johnson with justice observed, that, by losing Goldsmith, Garrick, Nugent, Chamier, Beauclerk, we had lost what would make an eminent club, yet when I mention, as an accession, Mr Fox, Dr George Fordyce, Sir Charles Bunbury, Lord Offory, Mr Gibbon, Dr Adam Smith, Mr R. B. Sheridan, the Bishops of Kilaloe and St Asaph, Dean Marlay, Mr Steevens, Mr Dunning, Sir Joseph Banks, Dr Scott of the Commons, Earl Spencer, Mr Windham of Norfolk, Lord Elliot, Mr Malone, Dr Joseph Warton, the Rev. Thomas Warton, Lord Lucan, Mr Burke junior, Lord Palmerston, Dr Burney, Sir William Hamilton, and Dr Warren, it will be acknowledged that we might establish a second university of high reputation.

‡ Here, unluckily, the windows had no pullies; and Dr Johnson, who was constantly eager for fresh air, had much struggling to get one of them kept open. Thus he had a notion impressed upon him, that this wretched defect was general in Scotland; in consequence of which he has erroneously enlarged upon it in his *Journey*. I regretted that he did not allow me to read over his book before it was printed. I should have changed very little; but I should have suggested an alteration in a few places where he has laid himself open to be attacked. I hope I should have prevailed with him to omit or soften his assertion, that 'a Scotsman must be a sturdy moralist, who does not prefer Scotland to truth', for I really think it is not founded; and it is harshly said.

Thursday, 26th August

We got a fresh chaise here, a very good one, and very good horses. We breakfasted at Cullen. They set down dried haddocks broiled, along with our tea. I ate one; but Dr Johnson was disgusted by the sight of them, so they were removed. Cullen has a comfortable appearance, though but a very small town, and the houses mostly poor buildings.

I called on Mr Robertson, who has the charge of Lord Findlater's affairs, and was formerly Lord Monboddo's clerk, was three times in France with him, and translated Condamine's *Account of the Savage Girl*,[94] to which his lordship wrote a preface, containing several remarks of his own. Robertson said, he did not believe so much as his lordship did; that it was plain to him, the girl confounded what she imagined with what she remembered: that, besides, she perceived Condamine and Lord Monboddo forming theories, and she adapted her story to them.

Dr Johnson said, 'It is a pity to see Lord Monboddo publish such notions as he has done; a man of sense, and of so much elegant learning. There would be little in a fool doing it; we should only laugh; but when a wise man does it, we are sorry. Other people have strange notions; but they conceal them. If they have tails, they hide them; but Monboddo is as jealous of his tail as a squirrel.' I shall here put down some more remarks of Dr Johnson's on Lord Monboddo, which were not made exactly at this time, but come in well from connection. He said, he did not approve of a judge's calling himself *Farmer* Burnett,* and going about with a little round hat. He laughed heartily at his lordship's saying he was an *enthusiastical* farmer; 'for,' said he, 'what can he do in farming by his *enthusiasm?*' Here, however, I think Dr Johnson mistaken. He who wishes to be successful, or happy, ought to be enthusiastical, that is to say, very keen in all the occupations or diversions of life. An ordinary gentleman-farmer will be satisfied with looking at his fields once or twice a day: an enthusiastical farmer will be constantly employed on them; will have his mind earnestly engaged; will talk perpetually of them. But Dr Johnson has much of the *nil admirari* in smaller concerns. That survey of life which gave birth to his *Vanity of Human Wishes* early sobered his mind. Besides, so great a mind as his cannot be moved by inferior objects: an elephant does not run and skip like lesser animals.

---

* It is the custom in Scotland for the judges of the Court of Session to have the title of *Lords*, from their estates; thus Mr Burnett is Lord *Monboddo*, as Mr Home was Lord *Kames*. There is something a little aukward in this; for they are denominated in deeds by their *names*, with the addition of 'one of the Senators of the College of Justice'; and subscribe their Christian and sur-name, as *James Burnett, Henry Home*, even in judicial acts.

Mr Robertson sent a servant with us, to shew us through Lord Findlater's wood, by which our way was shortened, and we saw some part of his domain, which is indeed admirably laid out. Dr Johnson did not choose to walk through it. He always said, that he was not come to Scotland to see fine places, of which there were enough in England; but wild objects – mountains, waterfalls, peculiar manners; in short, things which he had not seen before. I have a notion that he at no time has had much taste for rural beauties. I have myself very little.

Dr Johnson said, there was nothing more contemptible than a country gentleman living beyond his income, and every year growing poorer and poorer. He spoke strongly of the influence which a man has by being rich. 'A man,' said he, 'who keeps his money, has in reality more use from it, than he can have by spending it.' I observed that this looked very like a paradox; but he explained it thus: 'If it were certain that a man would keep his money locked up for ever, to be sure he would have no influence; but, as so many want money, and he has the power of giving it, and they know not but by gaining his favour they may obtain it, the rich man will always have the greatest influence. He again who lavishes his money, is laughed at as foolish, and in a great degree with justice, considering how much is spent from vanity. Even those who partake of a man's hospitality, have but a transient kindness for him. If he has not the command of money, people know he cannot help them, if he would; whereas the rich man always can, if he will, and for the chance of that, will have much weight.' BOSWELL. 'But philosophers and satirists have all treated a miser as contemptible.' JOHNSON. 'He is so philosophically; but not in the practice of life.' BOSWELL. 'Let me see now – I do not know the instances of misers in England, so as to examine into their influence.' JOHNSON. 'We have had few misers in England.' BOSWELL. 'There was Lowther.'[95] JOHNSON. 'Why, sir, Lowther, by keeping his money, had the command of the county, which the family has now lost, by spending it.* I take it, he lent a great deal; and that is the way to have influence, and yet preserve one's wealth. A man may lend his money upon very good security, and yet have his debtor much under his power.' BOSWELL. 'No doubt, sir. He can always distress him for the money; as no man borrows, who is able to pay on demand quite conveniently.'

We dined at Elgin, and saw the noble ruins of the cathedral. Though it rained much, Dr Johnson examined them with a most patient attention. He

*I do not know what was at this time the state of the parliamentary interest of the ancient family of Lowther; a family before the Conquest: but all the nation knows it to be very extensive at present. A due mixture of severity and kindness, œconomy and munificence, characterizes its present Representative.

could not here feel any abhorrence at the Scottish reformers, for he had been told by Lord Hailes, that it was destroyed before the Reformation, by the Lord of Badenoch,* who had a quarrel with the bishop. The bishop's house, and those of the other clergy, which are still pretty entire, do not seem to have been proportioned to the magnificence of the cathedral, which has been of great extent, and had very fine carved work. The ground within the walls of the cathedral is employed as a burying-place. The family of Gordon have their vault here; but it has nothing grand.

We passed Gordon Castle† this forenoon, which has a princely appearance. Fochabers, the neighbouring village, is a poor place, many of the houses being ruinous; but it is remarkable, they have in general orchards well stored with apple-trees. Elgin has what in England are called piazzas, that run in many places on each side of the street. It must have been a much better place formerly. Probably it had piazzas all along the town, as I have seen at Bologna. I approved much of such structures in a town, on account of their conveniency in wet weather. Dr Johnson disapproved of them, 'because,' said he, 'it makes the under story of a house very dark, which greatly over-balances the conveniency, when it is considered how small a part of the year it rains; how few are usually in the street at such times; that many who are might as well be at home; and the little that people suffer, supposing them to be as much wet as they commonly are in walking a street'.

We fared but ill at our inn here; and Dr Johnson said, this was the first time he had seen a dinner in Scotland that he could not eat.

In the afternoon, we drove over the very heath where Macbeth met the witches, according to tradition. Dr Johnson again solemnly repeated

> ' "How far is't called to Fores? What are these,
> So wither'd, and so wild in their attire?
> That look not like the inhabitants o' the earth,
> And yet are on't?" '

* NOTE, by Lord *Hailes*: 'The cathedral of Elgin was burnt by the Lord of Badenoch, because the Bishop of Moray had pronounced an award not to his liking. The indemnification that the see obtained, was, that the Lord of Badenoch stood for three days bare footed at the great gate of the cathedral. The story is in the Chartulary of Elgin.'

† I am not sure whether the duke was at home. But, not having the honour of being much known to his grace, I could not have presumed to enter his castle, though to introduce even so celebrated a stranger. We were at any rate in a hurry to get forward to the wildness which we came to see. Perhaps, if this noble family had still preserved that sequestered magnificence which they maintained when Catholicks, corresponding with the Grand Duke of Tuscany, we might have been induced to have procured proper letters of introduction, and devoted some time to the contemplation of venerable superstitious state.[96]

He repeated a good deal more of *Macbeth*. His recitation was grand and affecting, and, as Sir Joshua Reynolds has observed to me, had no more tone than it should have: it was the better for it. He then parodied the 'All-hail' of the witches to Macbeth, addressing himself to me. I had purchased some land called Dalblair; and, as in Scotland it is customary to distinguish landed men by the name of their estates, I had thus two titles, *Dalblair* and Young *Auchinleck*. So my friend, in imitation of

All hail Macbeth! hail to thee, Thane of Cawdor!

condescended to amuse himself with uttering

All hail Dalblair! hail to thee, Laird of Auchinleck!

We got to Fores at night, and found an admirable inn, in which Dr Johnson was pleased to meet with a landlord who styled himself 'Wine-Cooper, from London'.

Friday, 27th August

It was dark when we came to Fores last night; so we did not see what is called King Duncan's monument.[97] I shall now mark some gleanings of Dr Johnson's conversation. I spoke of *Leonidas*,[98] and said there were some good passages in it. JOHNSON. 'Why, you must *seek* for them.' He said, Paul Whitehead's *Manners* was a poor performance. Speaking of Derrick, he told me he had a kindness for him, and had often said, that if his letters had been written by one of a more established name, they would have been thought very pretty letters.

This morning I introduced the subject of the origin of evil. JOHNSON. 'Moral evil is occasioned by free will, which implies choice between good and evil. With all the evil that there is, there is no man but would rather be a free agent, than a mere machine without the evil; and what is best for each individual, must be best for the whole. If a man would rather be the machine, I cannot argue with him. He is a different being from me.' BOSWELL. 'A man, as a machine, may have agreeable sensations; for instance, he may have pleasure in musick.' JOHNSON, 'No, sir, he can not have pleasure in musick; at least no power of producing musick; for he who can produce musick may let it alone: he who can play upon a fiddle may break it: such a man is not a machine.' This reasoning satisfied me. It is certain, there cannot be a free agent, unless there is the power of being evil as well as good. We must take the inherent possibilities of things into consideration, in our reasonings or conjectures concerning the works of God.

We came to Nairn to breakfast. Though a county town and royal burgh, it is a miserable place. Over the room where we sat, a girl was spinning wool with a great wheel, and singing an Erse song: 'I'll warrant you,' said Dr Johnson, 'one of the songs of Ossian.' He then repeated these lines:[99]

> ' "Verse sweetens toil, however rude the sound.
> All at her work the village maiden sings;
> Nor, while she turns the giddy wheel around
> Revolves the sad vicissitude of things." '

I thought I had heard these lines before. JOHNSON. 'I fancy not, sir; for they are in a detached poem, the name of which I do not remember, written by one Giffard, a parson.'

I expected Mr Kenneth M'Aulay, the minister of Calder, who published the history of St Kilda, a book which Dr Johnson liked, would have met us here, as I had written to him from Aberdeen. But I received a letter from him, telling me that he could not leave home, as he was to administer the sacrament the following Sunday, and earnestly requesting to see us at his manse. 'We'll go,' said Dr Johnson; which we accordingly did. Mrs M'Aulay received us, and told us her husband was in the church distributing tokens.* We arrived between twelve and one o'clock, and it was near three before he came to us.

Dr Johnson thanked him for his book,[101] and said 'it was a very pretty piece of topography'. M'Aulay did not seem much to mind the compliment. From his conversation, Dr Johnson was persuaded that he had not written the book which goes under his name. I myself always suspected so; and I have been told it was written by the learned Dr John M'Pherson of Sky, from the materials collected by M'Aulay.[102] Dr Johnson said privately to me, 'There is a combination in it of which M'Aulay is not capable.' However, he was exceedingly hospitable; and, as he obligingly promised us a route for our tour through the Western Isles, we agreed to stay with him all night.

After dinner, we walked to the old castle of Calder (pronounced Cawder), the Thane of Cawdor's seat. I was sorry that my friend, this 'prosperous gentleman', was not there.[103] The old tower must be of great antiquity. There is a draw-bridge, – what has been a moat – and an ancient court. There is a hawthorn-tree, which rises like a wooden pillar through the rooms of the

---

* In Scotland, there is a great deal of preparation before administering the sacrament. The minister of the parish examines the people as to their fitness, and to those of whom he approves gives little pieces of tin, stamped with the name of the parish, as *tokens*, which they must produce before receiving it. This is a species of priestly power, and sometimes may be abused. I remember a lawsuit brought by a person against his parish minister, for refusing him admission to that sacred ordinance.[100]

castle; for, by a strange conceit, the walls have been built round it. The thickness of the walls, the small slaunting windows, and a great iron door at the entrance on the second story as you ascend the stairs, all indicate the rude times in which this castle was erected. There were here some large venerable trees.[104]

I was afraid of a quarrel between Dr Johnson and Mr M'Aulay, who talked slightingly of the lower English clergy. The Doctor gave him a frowning look, and said, 'This is a day of novelties: I have seen old trees in Scotland, and I have heard the English clergy treated with disrespect.'

I dreaded that a whole evening at Caldermanse would be heavy; however, Mr Grant, an intelligent and well-bred minister in the neighbourhood, was there, and assisted us by his conversation. Dr Johnson, talking of hereditary occupations in the Highlands, said, 'There is no harm in such a custom as this; but it is wrong to enforce it, and oblige a man to be a taylor or a smith, because his father has been one.' This custom, however, is not peculiar to our Highlands; it is well known that in India a similar practice prevails.

Mr M'Aulay began a rhapsody against creeds and confessions. Dr Johnson shewed, that 'what he called "imposition", was only a voluntary declaration of agreement in certain articles of faith, which a church has a right to require, just as any other society can insist on certain rules being observed by its members. Nobody is compelled to be of the church, as nobody is compelled to enter into a society.' This was a very clear and just view of the subject: but, M'Aulay could not be driven out of his track. Dr Johnson said, 'Sir, you are a *bigot to laxness*.'[105]

Mr M'Aulay and I laid the map of Scotland before us; and he pointed out a rout for us from Inverness, by Fort Augustus, to Glenelg, Sky, Mull, Icolmkill, Lorn, and Inveraray, which I wrote down.[106] As my father was to begin the northern circuit about the 18th of September, it was necessary for us to make our tour with great expedition, so as to get to Auchinleck before he set out, or to protract it, so as not to be there till his return, which would be about the 10th of October. By M'Aulay's calculation, we were not to land in Lorn till the 20th of September. I thought that the interruptions by bad days, or by occasional excursions, might make it ten days later; and I thought too, that we might perhaps go to Benbecula, and visit Clanranald,[107] which would take a week of itself.

Dr Johnson went up with Mr Grant to the library, which consisted of a tolerable collection; but the Doctor thought it rather a lady's library, with some Latin books in it by chance, than the library of a clergyman. It had only two of the Latin fathers, and one of the Greek fathers in Latin. I doubted whether Dr Johnson would be present at a Presbyterian prayer. I told Mr

M'Aulay so, and said that the Doctor might sit in the library while we were at family worship. Mr M'Aulay said, he would omit it, rather than give Dr Johnson offence: but I would by no means agree that an excess of politeness, even to so great a man, should prevent what I esteem as one of the best pious regulations. I know nothing more beneficial, more comfortable, more agreeable, than that the little societies of each family should regularly assemble, and unite in praise and prayer to our heavenly Father, from whom we daily receive so much good, and may hope for more in a higher state of existence. I mentioned to Dr Johnson the over-delicate scrupulosity of our host. He said, he had no objection to hear the prayer. This was a pleasing surprise to me; for he refused to go and hear Principal Robertson preach. 'I will hear him,' said he, 'if he will get up into a tree and preach; but I will not give a sanction, by my presence, to a Presbyterian assembly.'

Mr Grant having prayed, Dr Johnson said, his prayer was a very good one; but objected to his not having introduced the Lord's Prayer. He told us, that an Italian of some note in London said once to him, 'We have in our service a prayer called the *Pater Noster*, which is a very fine composition. I wonder who is the author of it.' A singular instance of ignorance in a man of some literature and general inquiry![108]

Saturday, 28th August

Dr Johnson had brought a Sallust with him in his pocket from Edinburgh. He gave it last night to Mr M'Aulay's son, a smart young lad about eleven years old. Dr Johnson had given an account of the education at Oxford, in all its gradations. The advantage of being servitor to a youth of little fortune struck Mrs M'Aulay much. I observed it aloud. Dr Johnson very handsomely and kindly said, that, if they would send their boy to him, when he was ready for the university, he would get him made a servitor, and perhaps would do more for him. He could not promise to do more; but would undertake for the servitorship.*

I should have mentioned that Mr White, a Welchman, who has been many years factor (i.e. steward) on the estate of Calder, drank tea with us last night, and upon getting a note from Mr M'Aulay, asked us to his house. We had not time to accept of his invitation. He gave us a letter of introduction to Mr Ferne, master of stores at Fort George. He shewed it to me. It recommended 'two celebrated gentlemen; no less than Dr Johnson, *author of his*

---

* Dr Johnson did not neglect what he had undertaken. By his interest with the Rev. Dr Adams, master of Pembroke College, Oxford, where he was educated for some time, he obtained a servitorship for young M'Aulay. But it seems he had other views; and I believe went abroad.[109]

Dictionary, and Mr Boswell, known at Edinburgh by the name of Paoli'. He said, he hoped I had no objection to what he had written; if I had, he would alter it. I thought it was a pity to check his effusions, and acquiesced; taking care, however, to seal the letter, that it might not appear that I had read it.

A conversation took place, about saying grace at breakfast (as we do in Scotland) as well as at dinner and supper; in which Dr Johnson said, 'It is enough if we have stated seasons of prayer; no matter when. A man may as well pray when he mounts his horse, or a woman when she milks her cow, (which Mr Grant told us is done in the Highlands), as at meals; and custom is to be followed.'*

We proceeded to Fort George. When we came into the square, I sent a soldier with the letter to Mr Ferne. He came to us immediately, and along with him came Major Brewse of the Engineers, pronounced *Bruce*. He said he believed it was originally the same Norman name with Bruce. That he had dined at a house in London, where were three Bruces, one of the Irish line, one of the Scottish line, and himself of the English line. He said he was shewn it in the Herald's office spelt fourteen different ways. I told him the different spellings of my name. Dr Johnson observed, that there had been great disputes about the spelling of Shakspear's name; at last it was thought it would be settled by looking at the original copy of his will; but, upon examining it, he was found to have written it himself no less than three different ways.

Mr Ferne and Major Brewse first carried us to wait on Sir Eyre Coote,[110] whose regiment, the 37th, was lying here, and who then commanded the fort. He asked us to dine with him, which we agreed to do.

Before dinner we examined the fort. The Major explained the fortification to us, and Mr Ferne gave us an account of the stores. Dr Johnson talked of the proportions of charcoal and salt-petre in making gunpowder, of granulating it, and of giving it a gloss. He made a very good figure upon these topicks. He said to me afterwards, that he had talked *ostentatiously*. We reposed ourselves a little in Mr Ferne's house. He had every thing in neat order as in England; and a tolerable collection of books. I looked into Pennant's *Tour in Scotland*. He says little of this fort; but that 'the barracks, &c. form several streets'. This is aggrandizing. Mr Ferne observed, if he had said they form a square, with a row of buildings before it, he would have given a juster description. Dr Johnson remarked, 'how seldom descriptions correspond with realities; and

* He could not bear to have it thought that, in any instance whatever, the Scots are more pious than the English. I think grace as proper at breakfast as at any other meal. It is the pleasantest meal we have. Dr Johnson has allowed the peculiar merit of breakfast in Scotland.

the reason is, that people do not write them till some time after, and then their imagination has added circumstances'.

We talked of Sir Adolphus Oughton.[111] The Major said, he knew a great deal for a military man. JOHNSON. 'Sir, you will find few men, of any profession, who know more. Sir Adolphus is a very extraordinary man; a man of boundless curiosity and unwearied diligence.'

I know not how the Major contrived to introduce the contest between Warburton and Lowth. JOHNSON. 'Warburton kept his temper all along, while Lowth was in a passion. Lowth published some of Warburton's letters. Warburton drew *him* on to write some very abusive letters, and then asked his leave to publish them; which he knew Lowth could not refuse, after what *he* had done. So that Warburton contrived that he should publish, apparently with Lowth's consent, what could not but shew Lowth in a disadvantageous light.'*

At three the drum beat for dinner. I, for a little while, fancied myself a military man, and it pleased me. We went to Sir Eyre Coote's, at the governour's house, and found him a most gentleman-like man. His lady is a very agreeable woman, with an uncommonly mild and sweet tone of voice. There was a pretty large company: Mr Ferne, Major Brewse, and several officers. Sir Eyre had come from the East Indies by land, through the Desarts of Arabia. He told us, the Arabs could live five days without victuals, and subsist for three weeks on nothing else but the blood of their camels, who could lose so much of it as would suffice for that time, without being exhausted. He highly praised the virtue of the Arabs; their fidelity, if they undertook to conduct any person; and said, they would sacrifice their lives rather than let him be robbed. Dr Johnson, who is always for maintaining the superiority of civilized over uncivilized men, said, 'Why, sir, I can see no superiour virtue in this. A serjeant and twelve men, who are my guard, will die, rather than that I shall be robbed.' Colonel Pennington, of the 37th regiment, took up the argument with a good deal of spirit and ingenuity. PENNINGTON. 'But the soldiers are compelled to this, by fear of punishment.' JOHNSON. 'Well, sir, the Arabs are compelled by the fear of infamy.' PENNINGTON. 'The soldiers have the same fear of infamy, and the fear of punishment besides; so have less virtue; because they act less voluntarily.' Lady Coote observed very well, that it ought to be known if there was not, among the Arabs, some punishment for not being faithful on such occasions.

We talked of the stage. I observed, that we had not now such a company

* Here Dr Johnson gave us part of a conversation held between a Great Personage and him, in the library at the Queen's Palace, in the course of which this contest was considered. I have been at great pains to get that conversation as perfectly preserved as possible. It may perhaps at some future time be given to the publick.

of actors as in the last age; Wilks, Booth, &c. &c. JOHNSON. 'You think so, because there is one who excels all the rest so much: you compare them with Garrick, and see the deficiency. Garrick's great distinction is his universality. He can represent all modes of life, but that of an easy fine-bred gentleman.' PENNINGTON. 'He should give over playing young parts.' JOHNSON. 'He does not take them now; but he does not leave off those which he has been used to play, because he does them better than any one else can do them. If you had generations of actors, if they swarmed like bees, the young ones might drive off the old. Mrs Cibber, I think, got more reputation than she deserved, as she had a great sameness; though her expression was undoubtedly very fine. Mrs Clive was the best player I ever saw. Mrs Pritchard was a very good one; but she had something affected in her manner: I imagine she had some player of the former age in her eye, which occasioned it.'

Colonel Pennington said, Garrick sometimes failed in emphasis; as for instance, in *Hamlet*,

> I will speak *daggers* to her; but use *none*.

instead of

> I will *speak* daggers to her; but *use* none.

We had a dinner of two complete courses, variety of wines, and the regimental band of musick playing in the square, before the window, after it. I enjoyed this day much. We were quite easy and cheerful. Dr Johnson said, 'I shall always remember this fort with gratitude.' I could not help being struck with some admiration, at finding upon this barren sandy point, such buildings, such a dinner, such company: it was like enchantment. Dr Johnson, on the other hand, said to me more rationally, that it did not strike *him* as any thing extraordinary; because he knew, here was a large sum of money expended in building a fort; here was a regiment. If there had been less than what we found, it would have surprized him. *He* looked coolly and deliberately through all the gradations: my warm imagination jumped from the barren sands to the splendid dinner and brilliant company, to borrow the expression of an absurd poet,

> Without ands or ifs,
> I leapt from off the sands upon the cliffs.

The whole scene gave me a strong impression of the power and excellence of human art.

We left the fort between six and seven o'clock: Sir Eyre Coote, Colonel Pennington, and several more, accompanied us down stairs, and saw us into our chaise. There could not be greater attention paid to any visitors. Sir Eyre

spoke of the hardships which Dr Johnson had before him. BOSWELL.
'Considering what he has said of us, we must make him feel something rough
in Scotland.' Sir Eyre said to him, 'You must change your name, sir.'
BOSWELL. 'Ay, to Dr M'Gregor.'[112]

We got safely to Inverness, and put up at Mackenzie's inn. Mr Keith, the
collector of Excise here, my old acquaintance at Ayr, who had seen us at the
fort, visited us in the evening, and engaged us to dine with him next day,
promising to breakfast with us, and take us to the English chapel; so that
we were at once commodiously arranged.

Not finding a letter here that I expected, I felt a momentary impatience
to be at home. Transient clouds darkened my imagination, and in those
clouds I saw events from which I shrunk; but a sentence or two of the
Rambler's conversation gave me firmness, and I considered that I was upon an
expedition for which I had wished for years, and the recollection of which
would be a treasure to me for life.

Sunday, 29th August

Mr Keith breakfasted with us. Dr Johnson expatiated rather too strongly upon
the benefits derived to Scotland from the Union, and the bad state of our
people before it. I am entertained with his copious exaggeration upon that
subject; but I am uneasy when people are by, who do not know him as well
as I do, and may be apt to think him narrow-minded.* I therefore diverted the
subject.

The English chapel, to which we went this morning, was but mean. The
altar was a bare fir table, with a coarse stool for kneeling on, covered with
a piece of thick sail-cloth doubled, by way of cushion. The congregation was
small. Mr Tait, the clergyman, read prayers very well, though with much of
the Scotch accent. He preached on 'Love your Enemies'. It was remarkable
that, when talking of the connections amongst men, he said, that some
connected themselves with men of distinguished talents, and since they could
not equal them, tried to deck themselves with their merit, by being their
companions. The sentence was to this purpose. It had an odd coincidence
with what might be said of my connecting myself with Dr Johnson.

After church, we walked down to the Quay. We then went to Macbeth's
castle. I had a romantick satisfaction in seeing Dr Johnson actually in it.
It perfectly corresponds with Shakspeare's description, which Sir Joshua
Reynolds has so happily illustrated, in one of his notes on our immortal poet:

* It is remarkable that Dr Johnson read this gentle remonstrance, and took no notice of it to me.

> This castle hath a pleasant seat: the air
> Nimbly and sweetly recommends itself
> Unto our gentle sense, &c.

Just as we came out of it, a raven perched on one of the chimney-tops, and croaked. Then I repeated

> '. . . The raven himself is hoarse,
> That croaks the fatal enterance of Duncan
> Under my battlements.'

We dined at Mr Keith's. Mrs Keith was rather too attentive to Dr Johnson, asking him many questions about his drinking only water. He repressed that observation, by saying to me, 'You may remember that Lady Errol took no notice of this.'

Dr Johnson has the happy art (for which I have heard my father praise the old Earl of Aberdeen) of instructing himself, by making every man he meets tell him something of what he knows best. He led Keith to talk to him of the Excise in Scotland, and, in the course of conversation, mentioned that his friend Mr Thrale, the great brewer, paid twenty thousand pounds a year to the revenue; and that he had four casks, each of which holds sixteen hundred barrels – above a thousand hogsheads.

After this there was little conversation that deserves to be remembered. I shall therefore here again glean what I have omitted on former days. Dr Gerard, at Aberdeen, told us, that when he was in Wales, he was shewn a valley inhabited by Danes, who still retain their own language, and are quite a distinct people. Dr Johnson thought it could not be true, or all the kingdom must have heard of it. He said to me, as we travelled, 'these people, sir, that Gerard talks of, may have somewhat of a *peregrinity* in their dialect, which relation has augmented to a different language'. I asked him if *peregrinity* was an English word: he laughed, and said, 'No.' I told him this was the second time that I had heard him coin a word. When Foote broke his leg, I observed that it would make him fitter for taking off George Faulkner as Peter Paragragh, poor George having a wooden leg.[113] Dr Johnson at that time said, 'George will rejoice at the *depeditation* of Foote'; and when I challenged that word, laughed, and owned he had made it, and added that he had not made above three or four in his dictionary.*

---

* When upon the subject of this *peregrinity*, he told me some particulars concerning the compilation of his *Dictionary*, and concerning his throwing off Lord Chesterfield's patronage, of which very erroneous accounts have been circulated. These particulars, with others which he afterwards gave me – as also his celebrated letter to Lord Chesterfield, which he dictated to me – I reserve for his *Life*.

Having conducted Dr Johnson to our inn, I begged permission to leave him for a little, that I might run about and pay some short visits to several good people of Inverness. He said to me, 'You have all the old-fashioned principles, good and bad.' I acknowledge I have. That of attention to relations in the remotest degree, or to worthy persons, in every state whom I have once known, I inherit from my father. It gave me much satisfaction to hear every body at Inverness speak of him with uncommon regard. Mr Keith and Mr Grant, whom we had seen at Mr M'Aulay's, supped with us at the inn. We had roasted kid, which Dr Johnson had never tasted before. He relished it much.

Monday, 30th August

This day we were to begin our *equitation*, as I said; for *I* would needs make a word too.[114] It is remarkable, that my noble, and to me most constant friend, the Earl of Pembroke (who, if there is too much ease on my part, will please to pardon what his benevolent, gay, social intercourse, and lively correspondence, have insensibly produced) has since hit upon the very same word. The title of the first edition of his lordship's very useful book was, in simple terms, *A Method of Breaking Horses and Teaching Soldiers to Ride*. The title of the second edition is, *Military Equitation*.

We might have taken a chaise to Fort Augustus, but, had we not hired horses at Inverness, we should not have found them afterwards: so we resolved to begin here to ride. We had three horses, for Dr Johnson, myself, and Joseph, and one which carried our portmanteaus, and two Highlanders who walked along with us, John Hay and Lauchland Vass, whom Dr Johnson has remembered with credit in his *Journey*, though he has omitted their names. Dr Johnson rode very well.[115]

About three miles beyond Inverness, we saw, just by the road, a very complete specimen of what is called a Druid's temple. There was a double circle, one of very large, the other of smaller stones. Dr Johnson justly observed, that, 'to go and see one druidical temple is only to see that it is nothing, for there is neither art nor power in it; and seeing one is quite enough'.[116]

It was a delightful day. Lochness, and the road upon the side of it, shaded with birch trees, and the hills above it, pleased us much. The scene was as sequestered and agreeably wild as could be desired, and for a time engrossed all our attention.

To see Dr Johnson in any new situation is always an interesting object to me; and, as I saw him now for the first time on horseback, jaunting about at his ease in quest of pleasure and novelty, the very different occupations of his former laborious life, his admirable productions, his *London*, his *Rambler*, &c. &c. immediately presented themselves to my mind, and the contrast made a strong impression on my imagination.

When we had advanced a good way by the side of Lochness, I perceived a little hut, with an old looking woman at the door of it. I thought here might be a scene that would amuse Dr Johnson; so I mentioned it to him. 'Let's go in,' said he. We dismounted, and we and our guides entered the hut. It was a wretched little hovel of earth only, I think, and for a window had only a small hole, which was stopped with a piece of turf, that was taken out occasionally to let in light. In the middle of the room or space which we entered, was a fire of peat, the smoke going out at a hole in the roof. She had a pot upon it, with goat's flesh, boiling. There was at one end under the same roof, but divided by a kind of partition made of wattles, a pen or fold in which we saw a good many kids.

Dr Johnson was curious to know where she slept. I asked one of the guides, who questioned her in Erse. She answered with a tone of emotion, saying (as he told us) she was afraid we wanted to go to bed to her.[117] This *coquetry*, or whatever it may be called, of so wretched a being, was truly ludicrous. Dr Johnson and I afterwards were merry upon it. I said, it was he who alarmed the poor woman's virtue. 'No, sir,' said he, 'she'll say, "There came a wicked young fellow, a wild dog, who I believe would have ravished me, had there not been with him a grave old gentleman, who repressed him: but when he gets out of the sight of his tutor, I'll warrant you he'll spare no woman he meets, young or old."' 'No, sir,' I replied, 'she'll say, "There was a terrible ruffian who would have forced me, had it not been for a civil decent young man who, I take it, was an angel sent from heaven to protect me."'

Dr Johnson would not hurt her delicacy, by insisting on 'seeing her bed-chamber', like Archer in *The Beaux' Stratagem*. But my curiosity was more ardent; I lighted a piece of paper, and went into the place where the bed was. There was a little partition of wicker, rather more neatly done than that for the fold, and close by the wall was a kind of bedstead of wood with heath upon it by way of bed; at the foot of which I saw some sort of blankets or covering rolled up in a heap. The woman's name was Fraser; so was her husband's. He was a man of eighty. Mr Fraser of Balnain allows him to live in this hut, and keep sixty goats, for taking care of his woods, where he then was. They had five children, the eldest only thirteen. Two were gone to Inverness to buy meal; the rest were looking after the goats. This contented family had four stacks of barley, twenty-four sheaves in each. They had a few fowls. We were informed that they lived all the spring without meal, upon milk and curds and whey alone. What they get for their goats, kids, and fowls, maintains them during the rest of the year.

She asked us to sit down and take a dram. I saw one chair. She said she was as happy as any woman in Scotland. She could hardly speak any English except a few detached words. Dr Johnson was pleased at seeing, for the first time, such a state of human life. She asked for snuff. It is her luxury, and she uses a great deal. We had none; but gave her six pence a piece. She then brought out her whisky bottle. I tasted it; as did Joseph and our guides: so I gave her sixpence more. She sent us away with many prayers in Erse.

We dined at a publick house called the General's Hut, from General Wade, who was lodged there when he commanded in the North. Near it is the meanest parish kirk I ever saw.[118] It is a shame it should be on a high road. After dinner, we passed through a good deal of mountainous country. I had known Mr Trapaud, the deputy governour of Fort Augustus, twelve years ago, at a circuit at Inverness, where my father was judge. I sent forward one of our guides, and Joseph, with a card to him, that he might know Dr Johnson and I were coming up, leaving it to him to invite us or not. It was dark when we arrived. The inn was wretched. Government ought to build one, or give the resident governour an additional salary; as in the present state of things, he must necessarily be put to a great expence in entertaining travellers. Joseph announced to us, when we alighted, that the governour waited for us at the gate of the fort. We walked to it. He met us, and with much civility conducted us to his house. It was comfortable to find ourselves in a well built little square, and a neatly furnished house, in good company, and with a good supper before us; in short, with all the conveniencies of civilized life in the midst of rude mountains. Mrs Trapaud, and the governour's daughter, and her husband, Captain Newmarsh, were all most obliging and polite. The governour had excellent animal spirits, the conversation of a soldier, and somewhat of a Frenchman, to which his extraction entitles him.[119] He is brother to General Cyrus Trapaud.[120] We passed a very agreeable evening.

Tuesday, 31st August

The governour has a very good garden. We looked at it, and at the rest of the fort, which is but small, and may be commanded from a variety of hills around. We also looked at the galley or sloop belonging to the fort, which sails upon the Loch, and brings what is wanted for the garrison. Captains Urie and Darippe, of the 15th regiment of foot, breakfasted with us.[121] They had served in America, and entertained Dr Johnson much with an account of the

Indians. He said, he could make a very pretty book out of them, were he to stay there. Governour Trapaud was much struck with Dr Johnson. 'I like to hear him,' said he; 'it is so majestick. I should be glad to hear him speak in your court.' He pressed us to stay dinner; but I considered that we had a rude road before us, which we could more easily encounter in the morning, and that it was hard to say when we might get up, were we to sit down to good entertainment, in good company: I therefore begged the governour would excuse us. Here too, I had another very pleasing proof how much my father is regarded. The governour expressed the highest respect for him, and bade me tell him, that, if he would come that way on the northern circuit, he would do him all the honours of the garrison.

Between twelve and one we set out, and travelled eleven miles, through a wild country, till we came to a house in Glenmorison, called Anoch, kept by a M'Queen.* Our landlord was a sensible fellow: he had learnt his grammar, and Dr Johnson justly observed, that 'a man is the better for that as long as he lives.'[122] There were some books here: a *Treatise against Drunkenness*, translated from the French; a volume of the *Spectator*; a volume of Prideaux's *Connection*, and Cyrus's *Travels*. M'Queen said he had more volumes; and his pride seemed to be much piqued that we were surprised at his having books.

Near to this place we had passed a party of soldiers, under a serjeant's command, at work upon the road. We gave them two shillings to drink. They came to our inn, and made merry in the barn. We went and paid them a visit, Dr Johnson saying, 'Come, let's go and give 'em another shilling a-piece.' We did so; and he was saluted 'My Lord' by all of them. He is really generous, loves influence, and has the way of gaining it. He said, 'I am quite feudal, sir.' Here I agree with him. I said, I regretted I was not the head of a clan; however, though not possessed of such an hereditary advantage, I would always endeavour to make my tenants follow me. I could not be a *patriarchal* chief, but I would be a *feudal* chief.

The poor soldiers got too much liquor. Some of them fought, and left blood upon the spot, and cursed whisky next morning. The house here was built of thick turfs, and thatched with thinner turfs and heath. It had three rooms in length, and a little room which projected. Where we sat, the side-walls were *wainscotted*, as Dr Johnson said, with wicker, very neatly plaited. Our landlord had made the whole with his own hands.

* *A* M'Queen is a Highland mode of expression. An Englishman would say *one* M'Queen. But where there are clans or tribes of men, distinguished by patronymick surnames, the individuals of each are considered as if they were of different species, at least as much as nations are distinguished; so that a *M'Queen*, a *M'Donald*, a *M'Lean*, is said, as we say a Frenchman, an Italian, a Spaniard.

After dinner, M'Queen sat by us a while, and talked with us. He said, all the Laird of Glenmorison's people would bleed for him, if they were well used; but that seventy men had gone out of the Glen to America. That he himself intended to go next year; for that the rent of his farm, which twenty years ago was only five pounds, was now raised to twenty pounds. That he could pay ten pounds, and live; but no more. Dr Johnson said, he wished M'Queen Laird of Glenmorison, and the laird to go to America. M'Queen very generously answered, he should be sorry for it; for the laird could not shift for himself in America as he could do.

I talked of the officers whom we had left to day; how much service they had seen, and how little they got for it, even of fame. JOHNSON. 'Sir, a soldier gets as little as any man can get.' BOSWELL. 'Goldsmith has acquired more fame than all the officers last war, who were not Generals.' JOHNSON. 'Why, sir, you will find ten thousand fit to do what they did, before you find one who does what Goldsmith has done. You must consider, that a thing is valued according to its rarity. A pebble that paves the street is in itself more useful than the diamond upon a lady's finger.' I wish our friend Goldsmith had heard this.

I yesterday expressed my wonder that John Hay, one of our guides, who had been pressed aboard a man of war, did not choose to continue in it longer than nine months, after which time he got off. JOHNSON. 'Why, sir, no man will be a sailor, who has contrivance enough to get himself into a jail; for, being in a ship is being in a jail, with the chance of being drowned.'

We had tea in the afternoon, and our landlord's daughter, a modest civil girl, very neatly drest, made it for us. She told us, she had been a year at Inverness, and learnt reading and writing, sewing, knotting, working lace, and pastry. Dr Johnson made her a present of a book which he had bought at Inverness.*

The room had some deals laid across the joists, as a kind of ceiling. There

* This book has given rise to much inquiry, which has ended in ludicrous surprise. Several ladies, wishing to learn the kind of reading which the great and good Dr Johnson esteemed most fit for a young woman, desired to know what book he had selected for this Highland nymph. 'They never adverted,' said he, 'that I had no *choice* in the matter. I have said that I presented her with a book which I *happened* to have about me.' And what was this book? My readers, prepare your features for merriment. It was Cocker's *Arithmetick*! Wherever this was mentioned, there was a loud laugh, at which Dr Johnson, when present, used sometimes to be a little angry. One day, when we were dining at General Oglethorpe's, where we had many a valuable day, I ventured to interrogate him, 'But, sir, is it not somewhat singular that you should *happen* to have Cocker's *Arithmetick* about you on your journey? What made you buy such a book at Inverness?' He gave me a very sufficient answer. 'Why, sir, if you are to have but one book with you upon a journey, let it be a book of science. When you have read through a book of entertainment, you know it, and it can do no more for you; but a book of science is inexhaustible.'

were two beds in the room, and a woman's gown was hung on a rope to make a curtain of separation between them. Joseph had sheets, which my wife had sent with us, laid on them. We had much hesitation, whether to undress, or lie down with our clothes on. I said at last, 'I'll plunge in! There will be less harbour for vermin about me, when I am stripped!' Dr Johnson said, he was like one hesitating whether to go into the cold bath. At last he resolved too. I observed, he might serve a campaign. JOHNSON. 'I could do all that can be done by patience: whether I should have strength enough, I know not.' He was in excellent humour. To see the *Rambler* as I saw him to-night, was really an amusement. I yesterday told him, I was thinking of writing a poetical letter to him, *On his Return from Scotland*, in the stile of Swift's humorous epistle in the character of Mary Gulliver to her husband, Captain Lemuel Gulliver, on his return to England from the country of the *Houyhnhums*:

> At early morn I to the market haste,
> Studious in ev'ry thing to please thy taste.
> A curious *fowl* and *sparagrass* I chose;
> (For I remember you were fond of those:)
> Three shillings cost the first, the last sev'n groats;
> Sullen you turn from both, and call for OATS.[123]

He laughed, and asked in whose name I would write it. I said, in Mrs Thrale's. He was angry. 'Sir, if you have any sense of decency or delicacy, you won't do that!' BOSWELL. 'Then let it be in Cole's, the landlord of the Mitre tavern; where we have so often sat together.' JOHNSON. 'Ay, that may do.'

After we had offered up our private devotions, and had chatted a little from our beds, Dr Johnson said, 'God bless us both, for Jesus Christ's sake! Good night!' I pronounced '*Amen*.' He fell asleep immediately. I was not so fortunate for a long time. I fancied myself bit by innumerable vermin under the clothes; and that a spider was travelling from the wainscot towards my mouth. At last I fell into insensibility.

Wednesday, 1st September

I awaked very early. I began to imagine that the landlord, being about to emigrate, might murder us to get our money, and lay it upon the soldiers in the barn. Such groundless fears will arise in the mind, before it has resumed its vigour after sleep! Dr Johnson had had the same kind of ideas; for he told me afterwards, that he considered so many soldiers, having seen us, would be witnesses, should any harm be done, and that circumstance, I suppose, he considered as a security. When I got up, I found him sound asleep in his miserable stye, as I may call it, with a coloured handkerchief tied round his head. With difficulty could I awaken him. It reminded me of Henry the Fourth's fine soliloquy on sleep; for there was here as 'uneasy a pallet' as the poet's imagination could possibly conceive.

A red coat of the 15th regiment, whether officer, or only serjeant, I could not be sure, came to the house, in his way to the mountains to shoot deer, which it seems the Laird of Glenmorison does not hinder any body to do. Few, indeed, can do them harm. We had him to breakfast with us. We got away about eight. M'Queen walked some miles to give us a convoy. He had, in 1745, joined the Highland army at Fort Augustus, and continued in it till after the battle of Culloden. As he narrated the particulars of that ill-advised, but brave attempt, I could not refrain from tears. There is a certain association of ideas in my mind upon that subject, by which I am strongly affected. The very Highland names, or the sound of a bagpipe, will stir my blood, and fill me with a mixture of melancholy and respect for courage; with pity for an unfortunate and superstitious regard for antiquity, and thoughtless inclination for war; in short, with a crowd of sensations with which sober rationality has nothing to do.[124]

We passed through Glensheal, with prodigious mountains on each side. We saw where the battle was fought in the year 1719;[125] Dr Johnson owned he was now in a scene of as wild nature as he could see; but he corrected me sometimes in my inaccurate observations. 'There,' said I, 'is a mountain like a cone.' JOHNSON. 'No, sir. It would be called so in a book; and when a man comes to look at it, he sees it is not so. It is indeed pointed at the top; but one side of it is larger than the other.' Another mountain I called immense. JOHNSON. 'No; it is no more than a considerable protuberance.'

We came to a rich green valley, comparatively speaking, and stopped a while to let our horses rest and eat grass.* We soon afterwards came to

---

* Dr Johnson, in his *Journey*, thus beautifully describes his situation here: 'I sat down on a bank, such as a writer of romance might have delighted to feign. I had, indeed, no trees to whisper over my head; but a clear rivulet streamed at my feet. The day was calm, the air soft, and all was rudeness, silence, and solitude. Before me, and on either side, were high hills, which, by hindering the eye from ranging, forced the mind to find entertainment for itself. Whether I spent the hour well, I know not; for here I first conceived the thought of this narration.' The *Critical Reviewers*, with a spirit and expression worthy of the subject, say, 'We congratulate the publick on the event with which this quotation concludes, and are fully persuaded that the hour in which the entertaining traveller conceived this narrative will be considered, by every reader of taste, as a fortunate event in the annals of literature. Were it suitable to the talk in which we are at present engaged, to indulge ourselves in a poetical flight, we would invoke the winds of the Caledonian mountains to blow for ever, with their softest breezes, on the bank where our author reclined, and request of Flora, that it might be perpetually adorned with the gayest and most fragrant productions of the year.'

Auchnasheal, a kind of rural village, a number of cottages being built together, as we saw all along in the Highlands. We passed many miles this day without seeing a house, but only little summer-huts, called *shielings*. Evan Campbell, servant to Mr Murchison, factor to the Laird of Macleod in Glenelg, ran along with us to-day. He was a very obliging fellow. At Auchnasheal, we sat down on a green turf-seat at the end of a house; they brought us out two wooden dishes of milk, which we tasted. One of them was frothed like a syllabub. I saw a woman preparing it with such a stick as is used for chocolate, and in the same manner. We had a considerable circle about us, men, women and children, all M'Craas, Lord Seaforth's people. Not one of them could speak English. I observed to Dr Johnson, it was much the same as being with a tribe of Indians. JOHNSON. 'Yes, sir; but not so terrifying.' I gave all who chose it, snuff and tobacco. Governour Trapaud had made us buy a quantity at Fort Augustus, and put them up in small parcels. I also gave each person a bit of wheat bread, which they had never tasted before. I then gave a penny apiece to each child. I told Dr Johnson of this; upon which he called to Joseph and our guides, for change for a shilling, and declared that he would distribute among the children. Upon this being announced in Erse, there was a great stir; not only did some children come running down from neighbour-ing huts, but I observed one black-haired man, who had been with us all along, had gone off, and returned, bringing a very young child. My fellow traveller then ordered the children to be drawn up in a row; and he dealt about his copper, and made them and their parents all happy. The poor M'Craas, whatever may be their present state, were of considerable estimation in the year 1715, when there was a line in a song,

And aw the brave M'Craas are coming.*

There was great diversity in the faces of the circle around us: Some were

*The M'Craas, or Macraes, were since that time brought into the king's army, by the late Lord Seaforth. When they lay in Edinburgh castle in 1778, and were ordered to embark for Jersey, they with a number of other men in the regiment, for different reasons, but especially an apprehension that they were to be sold to the East-India Company, though enlisted not to be sent out of Great-Britain without their own consent, made a determined mutiny and encamped upon the lofty mountain, Arthur's Seat, where they remained three days and three nights; bidding defiance to all the force in Scotland. At last they came down, and embarked peaceably, having obtained formal articles of capitulation, signed by Sir Adolphus Oughton, commander in chief, General Skene, deputy commander, the Duke of Buccleugh, and the Earl of Dunmore, which quieted them. Since the secession of the Commons of Rome to the *Mons Sacer*, a more spirited exertion has not been made. I gave great attention to it from first to last, and have drawn up a particular account of it. Those brave fellows have since served their country effectually at Jersey, and also in the East Indies, to which, after being better informed, they voluntarily agreed to go.

237

as black and wild in their appearance as any American savages whatever. One woman was as comely almost as the figure of Sappho, as we see it painted. We asked the old woman, the mistress of the house where we had the milk, (which by the bye, Dr Johnson told me, for I did not observe it myself, was built not of turf, but of stone,) what we should pay. She said, what we pleased. One of our guides asked her, in Erse, if a shilling was enough. She said, 'Yes.' But some of the men bade her ask more. This vexed me; because it shewed a desire to impose upon strangers, as they knew that even a shilling was high payment. The woman, however, honestly persisted in her price; so I gave her half a crown. Thus we had one good scene of life uncommon to us. The people were very much pleased, gave us many blessings, and said they had not had such a day since the old Laird of Macleod's time.

Dr Johnson was much refreshed by this repast. He was pleased when I told him he would make a good chief. He said, 'Were I a chief, I would dress my servants better than myself, and knock a fellow down if he looked saucy to a Macdonald in rags: but I would not treat men as brutes. I would let them know why all of my clan were to have attention paid to them. I would tell my upper servants why, and make them tell the others.'

We rode on well, till we came to the high mountain called the Rattakin,[126] by which time both Dr Johnson and the horses were a good deal fatigued. It is a terrible steep climb, notwithstanding the road is formed slanting along it; however, we made it out. On the top of it we met Captain M'Leod of Balmenoch (a Dutch officer who had come from Sky) riding with his sword slung across him. He asked, 'Is this Mr Boswell?' which was a proof that we were expected. Going down the hill on the other side was no easy task. As Dr Johnson was a great weight, the two guides agreed that he should ride the horses alternately. Hay's were the two best, and the Doctor would not ride but upon one or other of them, a black or a brown. But, as Hay complained much after ascending the Rattakin, the Doctor was prevailed with to mount one of Vass's greys. As he rode upon it down hill, it did not go well; and he grumbled. I walked on a little before, but was excessively entertained with the method taken to keep him in good humour. Hay led the horse's head, talking to Dr Johnson as much as he could; and (having heard him, in the forenoon, express a pastoral pleasure on seeing the goats browzing) just when the Doctor was uttering his displeasure, the fellow cried, with a very Highland accent, 'See such pretty goats!' Then he whistled, *whu!* and made them jump. Little did he conceive what Doctor Johnson was. Here now was a common ignorant Highland clown imagining that he could divert, as one does a child, *Dr Samuel Johnson!* The ludicrousness, absurdity, and extraordinary contrast between what the fellow fancied, and the reality, was truly comick.

It grew dusky; and we had a very tedious ride for what was called five miles; but I am sure would measure ten. We had no conversation. I was riding forward to the inn at Glenelg, on the shore opposite to Sky, that I might take proper measures, before Dr Johnson, who was now advancing in dreary silence, Hay leading his horse, should arrive. Vass also walked by the side of his horse, and Joseph followed behind: as therefore he was thus attended, and seemed to be in deep meditation, I thought there could be no harm in leaving him for a little while. He called me back with a tremendous shout, and was really in a passion with me for leaving him. I told him my intentions, but he was not satisfied, and said, 'Do you know, I should as soon have thought of picking a pocket, as doing so.' BOSWELL. 'I am diverted with you, sir.' JOHNSON. 'Sir, I could never be diverted with incivility. Doing such a thing, makes one lose confidence in him who has done it, as one cannot tell what he may do next.' His extraordinary warmth confounded me so much, that I justified myself but lamely to him; yet my intentions were not improper. I wished to get on, to see how we were to be lodged, and how we were to get a boat; all which I thought I could best settle myself, without his having any trouble. To apply his great mind to minute particulars, is wrong: it is like taking an immense balance, such as is kept on quays for weighing cargoes of ships, to weigh a guinea. I knew I had neat little scales, which would do better; and that his attention to every thing which falls in his way, and his uncommon desire to be always in the right, would make him weigh, if he knew of the particulars: it was right therefore for me to weigh them, and let him have them only in effect. I however continued to ride by him, finding he wished I should do so.

As we passed the barracks at Bernéra,[127] I looked at them wishfully, as soldiers have always every thing in the best order: but there was only a serjeant and a few men there. We came on to the inn at Glenelg.[128] There was no provender for our horses: so they were sent to grass, with a man to watch them. A maid shewed us up stairs into a room damp and dirty, with bare walls, a variety of bad smells, a coarse black greasy fir table, and forms of the same kind; and out of a wretched bed started a fellow from his sleep, like Edgar in *King Lear*, 'Poor Tom's a-cold'.*

This inn was furnished with not a single article that we could either eat or drink; but Mr Murchison, factor to the Laird of Macleod in Glenelg, sent us a bottle of rum and some sugar, with a polite message, to acquaint us, that he was very sorry that he did not hear of us till we had passed his house, other-

---

* It is amusing to observe the different images which this being presented to Dr Johnson and me. The Doctor, in his *Journey*, compares him to a *Cyclops*.

wise he should have insisted on our sleeping there that night; and that, if he were not obliged to set out for Inverness early next morning, he would have waited upon us. Such extraordinary attention from this gentleman, to entire strangers, deserves the most honourable commemoration.

Our bad accommodation here made me uneasy, and almost fretful. Dr Johnson was calm. I said, he was so from vanity. JOHNSON. 'No, sir, it is from philosophy.' It pleased me to see that the *Rambler* could practise so well his own lessons.

I resumed the subject of my leaving him on the road, and endeavoured to defend it better. He was still violent upon that head, and said, 'Sir, had you gone on, I was thinking that I should have returned with you to Edinburgh, and then have parted from you, and never spoken to you more.'

I sent for fresh hay, with which we made beds for ourselves, each in a room equally miserable. Like Wolfe, we had a 'choice of difficulties'.[129] Dr Johnson made things easier by comparison. At M'Queen's, last night, he observed, that few were so well lodged in a ship. To-night he said, we were better than if we had been upon the hill. He lay down buttoned up in his great coat. I had my sheets spread on the hay, and my clothes and great coat laid over me, by way of blankets.

Thursday, 2d September

I had slept ill. Dr Johnson's anger had affected me much. I considered that, without any bad intention, I might suddenly forfeit his friendship; and was impatient to see him this morning. I told him how uneasy he had made me, by what he had said, and reminded him of his own remark at Aberdeen, upon old friendships being hastily broken off. He owned, he had spoken to me in passion; that he would not have done what he threatened; and that, if he had, he should have been ten times worse than I; that forming intimacies, would indeed be 'limning the water',[130] were they liable to such sudden dissolution; and he added, 'Let's think no more on't.' BOSWELL. 'Well then, sir, I shall be easy. Remember, I am to have fair warning in case of any quarrel. You are never to spring a mine upon me. It was absurd in me to believe you.' JOHNSON. 'You deserved about as much, as to believe me from night to morning.'

After breakfast, we got into a boat for Sky. It rained much when we set off, but cleared up as we advanced. One of the boatmen, who spoke English, said, that a mile at land was two miles at sea. I then observed, that from Glenelg to Armidale in Sky, which was our present course, and is called twelve, was only six miles: but this he could not understand. 'Well,' said Dr Johnson, 'never talk to me of the native good sense of the Highlanders. Here is a fellow who calls one mile two, and yet cannot comprehend that twelve such imaginary miles make in truth but six.'

We reached the shore of Armidale before one o'clock. Sir Alexander M'Donald came down to receive us. He and his lady (formerly Miss Bosville of Yorkshire) were then in a house built by a tenant at this place,[131] which is in the district of Slate, the family mansion here having been burned in Sir Donald Macdonald's time.

The most ancient seat of the chief of the Macdonalds in the Isle of Sky was at Duntulm, where there are the remains of a stately castle. The principal residence of the family is now at Mugstot, at which there is a considerable building.[132] Sir Alexander and Lady Macdonald had come to Armidale in their way to Edinburgh, where it was necessary for them to be soon after this time.

Armidale is situated on a pretty bay of the narrow sea, which flows between the main land of Scotland and the Isle of Sky. In front there is a grand prospect of the rude mountains of Moidart and Knoidart. Behind are hills gently rising and covered with a finer verdure than I expected to see in this climate, and the scene is enlivened by a number of little clear brooks.

Sir Alexander Macdonald having been an Eton scholar, and being a gentleman of talents, Dr Johnson had been very well pleased with him in London. But my fellow traveller and I were now full of the old Highland spirit, and were dissatisfied at hearing of racked rents and emigration; and finding a chief not surrounded by his clan. Dr Johnson said, 'Sir, the Highland chiefs should not be allowed to go farther south than Aberdeen. A strong-minded man, like Sir James Macdonald, may be improved by an English education; but in general, they will be tamed into insignificance.'

We found here Mr Janes[133] of Aberdeenshire, a naturalist. Janes said he had been at Dr Johnson's in London, with Ferguson the astronomer. JOHNSON. 'It is strange that, in such distant places, I should meet with any one who knows me. I should have thought I might hide myself in Sky.'

Friday, 3d September

This day proving wet, we should have passed our time very uncomfortably, had we not found in the house two chests of books, which we eagerly ransacked. After dinner, when I alone was left at table with the few Highland gentlemen who were of the company, having talked with very high respect of Sir James Macdonald, they were all so much affected as to shed tears. One of them was Mr Donald Macdonald, who had been lieutenant of grenadiers in the Highland regiment, raised by Colonel Montgomery, now Earl of Eglintoune, in the war before last; one of those regiments which the late Lord Chatham prided himself in having brought from 'the mountains of the north': by doing which he contributed to extinguish in the Highlands the remains of disaffection to the present Royal Family. From this gentleman's conversation, I first learnt how very popular his Colonel was among the highlanders; of which I had such continued proofs, during the whole course of my tour, that on my return I could not help telling the noble Earl himself, that I did not before know how great a man he was.

We were advised by some persons here to visit Rasay,[134] in our way to Dunvegan, the seat of the Laird of Macleod.[135] Being informed that the Rev. Mr Donald M'Queen was the most intelligent man in Sky, and having been favoured with a letter of introduction to him, by the learned Sir James Foulis,[136] I sent it to him by an express, and requested he would meet us at Rasay; and at the same time enclosed a letter to the Laird of Macleod, informing him that we intended in a few days to have the honour of waiting on him at Dunvegan.

Dr Johnson this day endeavoured to obtain some knowledge of the state of the country; but complained that he could get no distinct information about any thing, from those with whom he conversed.

Saturday, 4th September

My endeavours to rouse the English-bred chieftain, in whose house we were, to the feudal and patriarchal feelings, proving ineffectual, Dr Johnson this morning tried to bring him to our way of thinking. JOHNSON. 'Were I in your place, sir, in seven years I would make this an independant island. I would roast oxen whole, and hang out a flag as a signal to the Macdonalds to come and get beef and whisky.' Sir Alexander was still starting difficulties. JOHNSON. 'Nay, sir; if you are born to object, I have done with you. Sir, I would have a magazine of arms.' SIR ALEXANDER. 'They would rust.' JOHNSON. 'Let there be men to keep them clean. Your ancestors did not use to let their arms rust.'

We attempted in vain to communicate to him a portion of our enthusiasm. He bore with so polite a good-nature our warm, and what some might call Gothick, expostulations, on this subject, that I should not forgive myself, were I to record all that Dr Johnson's ardour led him to say.[137] This day was little better than a blank.

Sunday, 5th September

I walked to the parish church of Slate, which is a very poor one. There are no church bells in the island. I was told there were once some; what has become of them, I could not learn. The minister not being at home, there was no service. I went into the church and saw the monument of Sir James Macdonald,[138] which was elegantly executed at Rome, and has the following inscription, written by his friend, George Lord Lyttelton:[139]

To the memory
Of SIR JAMES MACDONALD, BART.
Who in the flower of youth,
Had attained to so eminent a degree of knowledge
in Mathematics, Philosophy, Languages,
And in every other branch of useful and polite learning,
As few have acquired in a long life
Wholly devoted to study:
Yet to this erudition he joined
What can rarely be found with it,
Great talents for business,
Great propriety of behaviour,
Great politeness of manners!
His eloquence was sweet, correct, and flowing;
His memory vast and exact;
His judgement strong and acute;
All which endowments, united
With the most amiable temper
And every private virtue,
Procured him, not only in his own country,
But also from foreign nations,
The highest marks of esteem.
In the year of our Lord
1766,
The 25th of his life,
After a long and extremely painful illness,
Which he supported with admirable patience and fortitude,
He died at Rome,
Where, notwithstanding the difference of religion,
Such extraordinary honours were paid to his memory,
As had never graced that of any other British subject,
Since the death of Sir Philip Sydney.
The fame he left behind him is the best consolation
To his afflicted family,

243

And to his countrymen in this isle,
For whose benefit he had planned
Many useful improvements,
Which his fruitful genius suggested,
And his active spirit promoted,
Under the sober direction
Of a clear and enlightened understanding.
Reader, bewail our loss,
And that of all Britain.
In testimony of her love,
And as the best return she can make
To her departed son,
For the constant tenderness and affection
Which, even to his last moments,
He shewed for her,
His much afflicted mother,
The LADY MARGARET MACDONALD,
Daughter to the EARL of EGLINTOUNE,
Erected this Monument,
A.D. 1768.*

---

* This extraordinary young man, whom I had the pleasure of knowing intimately, having been deeply regretted by his country, the most minute particulars concerning him must be interesting to many. I shall therefore insert his two last letters to his mother, Lady Margaret Macdonald, which her ladyship has been pleased to communicate to me.

MY DEAR MOTHER,   *Rome, July* 9th, 1766.

Yesterday's post brought me your answer to the first letter in which I acquainted you of my illness. Your tenderness and concern upon that account are the same I have always experienced, and to which I have often owed my life. Indeed it never was in so great danger as it has been lately; and though it would have been a very great comfort to me to have had you near me, yet perhaps I ought to rejoice, on your account, that you had not the pain of such a spectacle. I have been now a week in Rome, and wish I could continue to give you the same good accounts of my recovery as I did in my last: but I must own that, for three days past, I have been in a very weak and miserable state, which however seems to give no uneasiness to my physician. My stomach has been greatly out of order, without any visible cause; and the palpitation does not decrease. I am told that my stomach will soon recover its tone, and that the palpitation must cease in time. So I am willing to believe; and with this hope support the little remains of spirits which I can be supposed to have, on the forty-seventh day of such an illness. Do not imagine I have relapsed – I only recover slower than I expected. If my letter is shorter than usual, the cause of it is a dose of physick, which has weakened me so much to-day, that I am not able to write a long letter. I will make up for it next post, and remain always

Your most sincerely affectionate son,
J. MACDONALD.

He grew gradually worse; and on the night before his death he wrote as follows from Frescati:

Dr Johnson said, the inscription should have been in Latin, as every thing intended to be universal and permanent, should be.

This being a beautiful day, my spirits were cheered by the mere effect of climate. I had felt a return of spleen during my stay at Armidale, and had it not been that I had Dr Johnson to contemplate, I should have sunk into dejection; but his firmness supported me. I looked at him, as a man whose head is turning giddy at sea looks at a rock, or any fixed object. I wondered at his tranquillity. He said, 'Sir, when a man retires into an island, he is to turn his thoughts intirely to another world. He has done with this.' BOSWELL. 'It appears to me, sir, to be very difficult to unite a due attention to this world, and that which is to come; for, if we engage eagerly in the affairs of life, we are apt to be totally forgetful of a future state; and, on the other hand, a steady contemplation of the awful concerns of eternity renders all objects here so insignificant, as to make us indifferent and negligent about them.' JOHNSON. 'Sir, Dr Cheyne has laid down a rule to himself on this subject, which should be imprinted on every mind: "To neglect nothing to secure my eternal peace, more than if I had been certified I should die within the day: nor to mind any thing that my secular obligations and duties demanded of me, less than if I had been ensured to live fifty years more." '[140]

I must here observe, that though Dr Johnson appeared now to be philosophically calm, yet his genius did not shine forth as in companies, where I have listened to him with admiration. The vigour of his mind was, however, sufficiently manifested, by his discovering no symptoms of feeble relaxation in the dull, 'weary, flat and unprofitable' state in which we now were placed.

I am inclined to think that it was on this day he composed the following *Ode upon the Isle of Sky*, which a few days afterwards he shewed me at Raysay:[141]

MY DEAR MOTHER,

Though I did not mean to deceive you in my last letter from Rome, yet certainly you would have very little reason to conclude of the very great and constant danger I have gone through ever since that time. My life, which is still almost entirely desperate, did not at that time appear to me so, otherwise I should have represented, in its true colours, a fact which acquires very little horror by that means, and comes with redoubled force by deception. There is no circumstance of danger and pain of which I have not had the experience, for a continued series of above a fortnight; during which time I have settled my affairs, after my death, with as much distinctness as the hurry and the nature of the thing could admit of. In case of the worst, the Abbé Grant will be my executor in this part of the world, and Mr Mackenzie in Scotland, where my object has been to make you and my younger brother as independent of the eldest as possible.

ODA

Ponti profundis clausa recessibus,
Strepens procellis, rupibus obsita,
Quam grata defesso virentem
Skia sinum nebulosa pandis.

His cura, credo, sedibus exulat;
His blanda certe pax habitat locis:
Non ira, non mœror quietis
Insidias meditatur horis.

At non cavata rupe latescere,
Menti nec ægræ montibus aviis
Prodest vagari, nec frementes
E scopulo numerare fluctus.

Humana virtus non sibi sufficit,
Datur nec æquum cuique animum sibi
Parare posse, ut Stoicorum
Secta crepet nimis alta fallax.

Exœstuantis pectoris impetum,
Rex summe, solus tu regis arbiter,
Mentisque, te tollente, surgunt,
*Te recidunt moderante fluctus.**

After supper, Dr Johnson told us, that Isaac Hawkins Browne drank freely for thirty years, and that he wrote his poem, *De Animi Immortalitate*, in some of the last of these years.[142] I listened to this with the eagerness of one, who, conscious of being himself fond of wine, is glad to hear that a man of so much genius and good thinking as Browne had the same propensity.

Monday, 6th September

We set out, accompanied by Mr Donald M'Leod (late of Canna) as our guide. We rode for some time along the district of Slate, near the shore. The houses

---

*VARIOUS READINGS. Line 2. In the manuscript, Dr Johnson, instead of *rupibus obsita*, had written *imbribus uvida*, and *uvida nubibus*, but struck them both out. Lines 15 & 16. Instead of these two lines, he had written, but afterwards struck out, the following:

Parare posse, utcunque jactet
Grandiloquus nimis alta Zeno.

in general are made of turf, covered with grass. The country seemed well peopled. We came into the district of Strath, and passed along a wild moorish tract of land till we arrived at the shore. There we found good verdure, and some curious whin-rocks, or collections of stones like the ruins of the foundations of old buildings. We saw also three cairns of considerable size.

About a mile beyond Broadfoot, is Corrichatachin, a farm of Sir Alexander Macdonald's, possessed by Mr M'Kinnon,* who received us with a hearty welcome, as did his wife, who was what we call in Scotland a *lady-like* woman. Mr Pennant, in the course of his tour to the Hebrides, passed two nights at this gentleman's house. On its being mentioned, that a present had here been made to him of a curious specimen of Highland antiquity, Dr Johnson said, 'Sir, it was more than he deserved: the dog is a Whig.'

We here enjoyed the comfort of a table plentifully furnished, the satisfaction of which was heightened by a numerous and cheerful company; and we for the first time had a specimen of the joyous social manners of the inhabitants of the Highlands. They talked in their own ancient language, with fluent vivacity, and sung many Erse songs with such spirit, that, though Dr Johnson was treated with the greatest respect and attention, there were moments in which he seemed to be forgotten. For myself, though but a lowlander, having picked up a few words of the language, I presumed to mingle in their mirth, and joined in the choruses with as much glee as any of the company. Dr Johnson being fatigued with his journey, retired early to his chamber, where he composed the following Ode, addressed to Mrs Thrale:[143]

ODA

Permeo terras, ubi nuda rupes
Saxeas miscet nebulis ruinas,
Torva ubi rident steriles coloni
   Rura labores.

---

*That my readers may have my narrative in the style of the country through which I am travelling, it is proper to inform them, that the chief of a clan is denominated by his *surname* alone, as M'Leod, M'Kinnon, M'Intosh. To prefix *Mr* to it would be a degradation from *the* M'Leod, &c. My old friend, the Laird of M'Farlane, the great antiquary, took it highly amiss, when General Wade called him Mr M'Farlane. Dr Johnson said, he could not bring himself to use this mode of address; it seemed to him to be too familiar, as it is the way in which, in all other places, intimates or inferiors are addressed. When the chiefs have *titles*, they are denominated by them, as *Sir James Grant, Sir Allan M'Lean.* The other Highland gentlemen, of landed property, are denominated by their *estates*, as *Rasay, Boisdale*; and the wives of all of them have the title of *ladies*. The *tacksmen*, or principal tenants, are named by their farms, as *Kingsburgh, Corrichatachin*; and their wives are called the *mistress* of Kingsburgh, the *mistress* of Corrichatachin. Having given this explanation, I am at liberty to use that mode of speech which generally prevails in the Highlands and the Hebrides.

Pervagor gentes, hominum ferorum
Vita ubi nullo decorata cultu
Squallet informis, tugurique fumis
                    Fœda latescit.

Inter erroris salebrosa longi,
Inter ignotæ strepitus loquelæ,
Quot modis mecum, quid agat, requiro,
                    Thralia dulcis?

Seu viri curas pia nupta mulcet,
Seu fovet mater sobolem benigna,
Sive cum libris novitate pascet
                    Sedula mentem;

Sit memor nostri, fideique merces,
Stet fides constans, meritoque blandum
Thraliæ discant resonare nomen
                    Littora Skiæ.

Scriptum in Skia, Sept. 6, 1773.

Tuesday, 7th September

Dr Johnson was much pleased with his entertainment here. There were many good books in the house: Hector Boethius in Latin; Cave's *Lives of the Fathers*; Baker's *Chronicle*; Jeremy Collier's *Church History*; Dr Johnson's small *Dictionary*; Craufurd's *Officers of State*, and several more: a mezzotinto of Mrs Brooks the actress (by some strange chance in Sky); and also a print of Macdonald of Clanranald, with a Latin inscription about the cruelties after the battle of Culloden, which will never be forgotten.

It was a very wet stormy day; we were therefore obliged to remain here, it being impossible to cross the sea to Rasay.

I employed a part of the forenoon in writing this *Journal*. The rest of it was somewhat dreary, from the gloominess of the weather, and the uncertain state which we were in, as we could not tell but it might clear up every hour. Nothing is more painful to the mind than a state of suspence, especially when it depends upon the weather, concerning which there can be so little calculation. As Dr Johnson said of our weariness on the Monday at Aberdeen, 'Sensation is sensation.' Corrichatachin, which was last night a hospitable house, was, in my mind, changed to-day into a prison. After dinner I read some of Dr Macpherson's *Dissertations on the Ancient Caledonians*. I was disgusted by the unsatisfactory conjectures as to antiquity, before the days of record. I was happy when tea came. Such, I take it, is the state of those who live in the country. Meals are wished for from the cravings of vacuity of mind, as well as from the desire of eating. I was hurt to find even such a temporary feebleness, and that I was so far from being that robust wise man who is sufficient for his own happiness. I felt a kind of lethargy of indolence. I did not exert myself to get Dr Johnson to talk, that I might not have the labour of writing down his conversation. He inquired here, if there were any remains of the second sight. Mr M'Pherson, Minister of Slate, said, he was *resolved* not to believe it, because it was founded on no principle. JOHNSON. 'There are many things then, which we are sure are true, that you will not believe. What principle is there, why a loadstone attracts iron? Why an egg produces a chicken by heat? Why a tree grows upwards, when the natural tendency of all things is downwards? Sir, it depends upon the degree of evidence that you have.' Young Mr M'Kinnon mentioned one M'Kenzie, who is still alive, who had often fainted in his presence, and when he recovered, mentioned visions which had been presented to him. He told Mr M'Kinnon, that at such a place he should meet a funeral, and that such and such people would be the bearers, naming four; and three weeks afterwards he saw what M'Kenzie had predicted. The naming the very spot in a country where a funeral comes a long way, and the very people as bearers, when there are so many out of whom a choice may be made, seems extraordinary. We should have sent for M'Kenzie, had we not been informed that he could speak no English. Besides, the facts were not related with sufficient accuracy.

Mrs M'Kinnon, who is a daughter of old Kingsburgh, told us that her father was one day riding in Sky, and some women, who were at work in a field on the side of the road, said to him, they had heard two *taiscks* (that is, two voices of persons about to die), and what was remarkable, one of them was an *English taisck*, which they never heard before. When he returned, he at that very place met two funerals, and one of them was that of a woman who had come from the main land, and could speak only English. This, she remarked, made a great impression upon her father.

How all the people here were lodged, I know not.[144] It was partly done by separating man and wife, and putting a number of men in one room, and of women in another.

Wednesday, 8th September

When I waked, the rain was much heavier than yesterday; but the wind had abated. By breakfast, the day was better, and in a little while it was calm and clear. I felt my spirits much elated. The propriety of the expression, *'the sun-shine of the breast'*, now struck me with peculiar force; for the brilliant rays penetrated into my very soul. We were all in better humour than before. Mrs M'Kinnon, with unaffected hospitality and politeness, expressed her happiness in having such company in her house, and appeared to understand and relish Dr Johnson's conversation, as indeed all the company seemed to do. When I knew she was old Kingsburgh's daughter, I did not wonder at the good appearance which she made.

She talked as if her husband and family would emigrate, rather than be oppressed by their landlord; and said, 'how agreeable would it be, if these gentlemen should come in upon us when we are in America'. Somebody observed that Sir Alexander Macdonald was always frightened at sea. JOHNSON. *'He* is frightened at sea; and his tenants are frightened when he comes to land.'

We resolved to set out directly after breakfast. We had about two miles to ride to the sea-side, and there we expected to get one of the boats belonging to the fleet of bounty herring-busses[145] then on the coast, or at least a good country fishing-boat. But while we were preparing to set out, there arrived a man with the following card from the Reverend Mr Donald M'Queen:

Mr M'Queen's compliments to Mr Boswell, and begs leave to acquaint him that, fearing the want of a proper boat, as much as the rain of yesterday, might have caused a stop, he is now at Skianwden with Macgillichallum's* carriage, to convey him and Dr Johnson to Rasay, where they will meet with a most hearty welcome, and where Macleod, being on a visit, now attends their motions.

Wednesday afternoon.

This card was most agreeable; it was a prologue to that hospitable and truly polite reception which we found at Rasay. In a little while arrived Mr Donald M'Queen himself; a decent minister, an elderly man with his own black hair, courteous, and rather slow of speech, but candid, sensible and well informed, nay learned. Along with him came, as our pilot, a gentleman whom I had a great desire to see, Mr Malcolm Macleod, one of the Rasay family, celebrated in the year 1745-6.[146] He was now sixty-two years of age, hale, and well proportioned, with a manly countenance, tanned by the weather, yet having a ruddiness in his cheeks, over a great part of which his rough beard extended. His eye was quick and lively, yet his look was not fierce, but he appeared at once firm and good-humoured. He wore a pair of brogues, tartan hose which came up only near to his knees, and left them bare, a purple camblet

---

* The Highland expression for Laird of Rasay.

kilt, a black waistcoat, a short green cloth coat bound with gold cord, a yellowish bushy wig, a large blue bonnet with a gold thread button. I never saw a figure that gave a more perfect representation of a Highland Gentleman. I wished much to have a picture of him just as he was. I found him frank and *polite*, in the true sense of the word.[147]

The good family at Corrichatachin said, they hoped to see us on our return. We rode down to the shore; but Malcolm walked with graceful agility.

We got into Rasay's *carriage*, which was a good strong open boat made in Norway. The wind had now risen pretty high, and was against us; but we had four stout rowers, particularly a Macleod, a robust, black-haired fellow, half naked, and bear-headed, something between a wild Indian and an English tar. Dr Johnson sat high on the stern, like a magnificent Triton. Malcolm sung an Erse song, the chorus of which was *'Hatyin foam foam eri'*, with words of his own.[148] The tune resembled *'Owr the muir amang the heather'*,[149] the boatmen and Mr M'Queen chorused, and all went well. At length Malcolm himself took an oar, and rowed vigorously. We sailed along the coast of Scalpa, a rugged island, about four miles in length. Dr Johnson proposed that he and I should buy it, and found a good school, and an episcopal church (Malcolm said, he would come to it), and have a printing-press, where he would print all the Erse that could be found.

Here I was strongly struck with our long projected scheme of visiting the Hebrides being realized. I called to him, 'We are contending with seas;' which I think were the words of one of his letters to me. 'Not much,' said he; and though the wind made the sea lash considerably upon us, he was not discomposed. After we were out of the shelter of Scalpa, and in the sound between it and Rasay, which extended about a league, the wind made the sea very rough. I did not like it. JOHNSON. 'This now is the Atlantick. If I should tell at a tea table in London, that I have crossed the Atlantick in an open boat, how they'd shudder, and what a fool they'd think me to expose myself to such danger.' He then repeated Horace's ode,[150]

> *Otium Divos rogat in patenti*
> *Prensus Ægæo . . .*

In the confusion and hurry of this boisterous sail, Dr Johnson's spurs, of which Joseph had charge, were carried over-board into the sea, and lost. This was the first misfortune that had befallen us. Dr Johnson was a little angry at first, observing that 'there was something wild in letting a pair of spurs be carried into the sea out of a boat'; but then he remarked, that, as Janes the naturalist had said upon losing his pocket book, it was rather an inconvenience than a loss. He told us, he now recollected that he dreamt the night before, that he put his staff into a river, and chanced to let it go, and it was carried down the stream and lost. 'So now you see,' said he, 'that I have lost my spurs; and this story is better than many of those which we have concerning second sight and dreams.' Mr M'Queen said he did not believe in second sight; that he never met with any well attested instances; and if he should, he should impute them to chance; because all who pretend to that quality often fail in their predictions, though they take a great scope, and sometimes interpret literally, sometimes figuratively, so as to suit the events. He told us, that, since he came to be minister of the parish where he now is, the belief of witchcraft, or charms, was very common, insomuch that he had many prosecutions before his session (the parochial ecclesiastical court) against women, for having by these means carried off the milk from people's cows. He disregarded them; and there is not now the least vestige of that superstition. He preached against it; and in order to give a strong proof to the people that there was nothing in it, he said from the pulpit, that every woman in the parish was welcome to take the milk from his cows, provided she did not touch them.

Dr Johnson asked him as to *Fingal*. He said he could repeat some passages in the original, that he heard his grandfather had a copy of it; but that he could not affirm that Ossian composed all that poem as it is now published. This came pretty much to what Dr Johnson had maintained; though he goes farther, and contends that it is no better than such an epick poem as he could make from the song of Robin Hood; that is to say, that, except a few passages, there is nothing truly ancient but the names and some vague traditions.[151] Mr M'Queen alledged that Homer was made up of detached fragments. Dr Johnson denied this; observing, that it had been one work originally, and that you could not put a book of the Iliad out of its place; and he believed the same might be said of the Odyssey.

The approach to Rasay was very pleasing. We saw before us a beautiful bay, well defended by a rocky coast; a good family mansion; a fine verdure about it, with a considerable number of trees; and beyond it hills and mountains in gradation of wildness. Our boatmen sung with great spirit. Dr Johnson observed, that naval musick was very ancient. As we came near the shore, the singing of our rowers was succeeded by that of reapers, who were busy at work, and who seemed to shout as much as to sing, while they worked with a bounding activity. Just as we landed, I observed a cross, or rather the ruins of one, upon a rock, which had to me a pleasing vestige of religion. I perceived a large company coming out from the house. We met them as we walked up. There were Rasay himself; his brother Dr Macleod; his nephew the Laird of M'Kinnon; the Laird of Macleod; Colonel Macleod of

Talisker, an officer in the Dutch service, a very genteel man, and a faithful branch of the family; Mr Macleod of Muiravenside, best known by the name of Sandie Macleod, who was long in exile on account of the part which he took in 1745; and several other persons. We were welcomed upon the green, and conducted into the house, where we were introduced to Lady Rasay, who was surrounded by a numerous family, consisting of three sons and ten daughters. The Laird of Rasay is a sensible, polite, and most hospitable gentleman. I was told that his island of Rasay, and that of Rona (from which the eldest son of the family has his title), and a considerable extent of land which he has in Sky, do not altogether yield him a very large revenue: and yet he lives in great splendour; and so far is he from distressing his people, that, in the present rage for emigration, not a man has left his estate.

It was past six o'clock when we arrived. Some excellent brandy was served round immediately, according to the custom of the Highlands, where a dram is generally taken every day. They call it a *scatch*.[152] On a side-board was placed for us, who had come off the sea, a substantial dinner, and a variety of wines. Then we had coffee and tea. I observed in the room several elegantly bound books and other marks of improved life. Soon afterwards a fiddler appeared, and a little ball began. Rasay himself danced with as much spirit as any man, and Malcolm bounded like a roe. Sandie Macleod, who has at times an excessive flow of spirits, and had it now, was, in his days of absconding, known by the name of *M'Cruslick*,[153] which it seems was the designation of a kind of wild man in the Highlands, something between Proteus and Don Quixotte; and so he was called here. He made much jovial noise. Dr Johnson was so delighted with this scene, that he said, 'I know not how we shall get away.' It entertained me to observe him sitting by, while we danced, sometimes in deep meditation, sometimes smiling complacently, sometimes looking upon Hooke's *Roman History*, and sometimes talking a little amidst the noise of the ball, to Mr Donald M'Queen, who anxiously gathered knowledge from him. He was pleased with M'Queen and said to me, 'This is a critical man, sir.[154] There must be great vigour of mind to make him cultivate learning so much in the isle of Sky, where he might do without it. It is wonderful how many of the new publications he has. There must be a snatch of every opportunity.' Mr M'Queen told me that his brother (who is the fourth generation of the family following each other as ministers of the parish of Snizort) and he joined together, and bought from time to time such books as had reputation. Soon after we came in, a black cock and grey hen, which had been shot, were shewn, with their feathers on, to Dr Johnson, who had never seen that species of bird before. We had a company of thirty at supper; and all was good humour and gaiety, without intemperance.

Thursday, 9th September

At breakfast this morning, among a profusion of other things, there were oat-cakes, made of what is called *graddaned* meal, that is, meal made of grain separated from the husks, and toasted by fire, instead of being threshed and kiln dried. This seems to be bad management, as so much fodder is consumed by it. Mr M'Queen however defended it, by saying, that it is doing the thing much quicker, as one operation effects what is otherwise done by two. His chief reason however was, that the servants of Sky are, according to him, a faithless pack, and steal what they can; so that much is saved by the corn passing but once through their hands, as at each time they pilfer some. It appears to me, that the graddaning is a strong proof of the laziness of the highlanders, who will rather make fire act for them, at the expence of fodder, than labour themselves. There was also, what I cannot help disliking at breakfast, cheese: it is the custom over all the Highlands to have it; and it often smells very strong, and poisons to a certain degree the elegance of an Indian repast. The day was showery; however, Rasay and I took a walk, and had some cordial conversation. I conceived a more than ordinary regard for this worthy gentleman. His family has possessed this island above four hundred years. It is the remains of the estate of Macleod of Lewis, whom he represents. When we returned, Dr Johnson walked with us to see the old chapel. He was in fine spirits. He said, 'This is truely the patriarchal life: this is what we came to find.'

After dinner, M'Cruslick, Malcolm, and I, went out with guns, to try if we could find any black-cock; but we had no sport, owing to a heavy rain. I saw here what is called a Danish fort.[155] Our evening was passed as last night was. One of our company,[156] I was told, had hurt himself by too much study, particularly of infidel metaphysicians, of which he gave a proof, on second sight being mentioned. He immediately retailed some of the fallacious arguments of Voltaire and Hume against miracles in general. Infidelity in a Highland gentleman appeared to me peculiarly offensive. I was sorry for him, as he had otherwise a good character. I told Dr Johnson that he had studied himself into infidelity. JOHNSON. 'Then he must study himself out of it again. That is the way. Drinking largely will sober him again.'

Friday, 10th September

Having resolved to explore the island of Rasay, which could be done only on foot, I last night obtained my fellow-traveller's permission to leave him for a day, he being unable to take so hardy a walk. Old Mr Malcolm M'Cleod, who had obligingly promised to accompany me, was at my bedside between five and six. I sprang up immediately, and he and I, attended by two other gentlemen, traversed the country during the whole of this day. Though we had passed over not less than four-and-twenty miles of very rugged ground, and had a Highland dance on the top of Dun Can, the highest mountain in the island, we returned in the evening not at all fatigued, and piqued ourselves at not being outdone at the nightly ball by our less active friends, who had remained at home.

My survey of Rasay did not furnish much which can interest my readers; I shall therefore put into as short a compass as I can, the observations upon it, which I find registered in my journal. It is about fifteen English miles long, and four broad. On the south side is the laird's family seat, situated on a pleasing low spot.[157] The old tower of three stories, mentioned by Martin, was taken down soon after 1746, and a modern house supplies its place. There are very good grass-fields and corn-lands about it, well dressed. I observed, however, hardly any inclosures, except a good garden plentifully stocked with vegetables, and strawberries, raspberries, currants, &c.

On one of the rocks just where we landed, which are not high, there is rudely carved a square, with a crucifix in the middle. Here, it is said, the lairds of Rasay, in old times, used to offer up their devotions. I could not approach the spot, without a grateful recollection of the event commemorated by this symbol.

A little from the shore, westward, is a kind of subterraneous house. There has been a natural fissure, or separation of the rock, running towards the sea, which has been roofed over with long stones, and above them turf has been laid. In that place the inhabitants used to keep their oars. There are a number of trees near the house, which grow well; some of them of a pretty good size. They are mostly plane and ash. A little to the west of the house is an old ruinous chapel, unroofed, which never has been very curious. We here saw some human bones of an uncommon size. There was a heel-bone, in particular, which Dr Macleod said was such, that if the foot was in proportion, it must have been twenty-seven inches long. Dr Johnson would not look at the bones. He started back from them with a striking appearance of horrour. Mr M'Queen told us, it was formerly much the custom, in these isles, to have human bones lying above ground, especially in the windows of churches. On the south of the chapel is the family burying place. Above the door, on the east end of it, is a small bust or image of the Virgin Mary, carved upon a stone which makes part of the wall. There is no church upon the island. It is annexed to one of the parishes of Sky; and the minister comes and preaches either in Rasay's house, or some other house, on certain

Sundays. I could not but value the family seat more, for having even the ruins of a chapel close to it. There was something comfortable in the thought of being so near a piece of consecrated ground. Dr Johnson said, 'I look with reverence upon every place that has been set apart for religion'; and he kept off his hat while he was within the walls of the chapel.

The eight crosses, which Martin mentions as pyramids for deceased ladies, stood in a semicircular line, which contained within it the chapel. They marked out the boundaries of the sacred territory within which an asylum was to be had. One of them, which we observed upon our landing, made the first point of the semicircle. There are few of them now remaining. A good way farther north, there is a row of buildings about four feet high: they run from the shore on the east along the top of a pretty high eminence, and so down to the shore on the west, in much the same direction with the crosses. Rasay took them to be the marks for the asylum; but Malcolm thought them to be false sentinels, a common deception, of which instances occur in Martin, to make invaders imagine an island better guarded. Mr Donald M'Queen, justly in my opinion, supposed the crosses which form the inner circle to be the church's land-marks.

The south end of the island is much covered with large stones or rocky strata. The laird has enclosed and planted part of it with firs, and he shewed me a considerable space marked out for additional plantations.

Dun Can is a mountain three computed miles from the laird's house. The ascent to it is by consecutive risings, if that expression may be used when vallies intervene, so that there is but a short rise at once; but it is certainly very high above the sea. The palm of altitude is disputed for by the people of Rasay and those of Sky; the former contending for Dun Can, the latter for the mountains in Sky, over against it. We went up the east side of Dun Can pretty easily. It is mostly rocks all around, the points of which hem the summit of it. Sailors, to whom it is a good object as they pass along, call it Rasay's cap. Before we reached this mountain, we passed by two lakes. Of the first, Malcolm told me a strange fabulous tradition. He said, there was a wild beast in it, a sea-horse, which came and devoured a man's daughter; upon which the man lighted a great fire, and had a sow roasted at it, the smell of which attracted the monster. In the fire was put a spit. The man lay concealed behind a low wall of loose stones, and he had an avenue formed for the monster, with two rows of large flat stones, which extended from the fire over the summit of the hill, till it reached the side of the loch. The monster came, and the man with the red-hot spit destroyed it. Malcolm shewed me the little hiding-place, and the rows of stones. He did not laugh when he told this story. I recollect having seen in the *Scots Magazine*, several years ago, a poem upon a similar tale, perhaps the same, translated from the Erse, or Irish, called *Albin and the Daughter of Mey*.[158]

There is a large tract of land, possessed as a common, in Rasay. They have no regulations as to the number of cattle. Every man puts upon it as many as he chooses. From Dun Can northward, till you reach the other end of the island, there is much good natural pasture unincumbered by stones. We passed over a spot, which is appropriated for the exercising ground. In 1745, a hundred fighting men were reviewed here, as Malcolm told me, who was one of the officers that led them to the field. They returned home all but about fourteen. What a princely thing is it to be able to furnish such a band! Rasay has the true spirit of a chief. He is, without exaggeration, a father to his people.

There is plenty of lime-stone in the island, a great quarry of free-stone,[159] and some natural woods, but none of any age, as they cut the trees for common country uses. The lakes, of which there are many, are well stocked with trout. Malcolm catched one of four-and-twenty pounds weight in the loch next to Dun Can, which, by the way, is certainly a Danish name, as most names of places in these islands are.

The old castle, in which the family of Rasay formerly resided, is situated upon a rock very near the sea: the rock is not one mass of stone, but a concretion of pebbles and earth, so firm that it does not appear to have mouldered. In this remnant of antiquity I found nothing worthy of being noticed, except a certain accommodation rarely to be found at the modern houses of Scotland, and which Dr Johnson and I fought for in vain at the Laird of Rasay's new-built mansion, where nothing else was wanting.[160] I took the liberty to tell the laird it was a shame there should be such a deficiency in civilized times. He acknowledged the justice of the remark. But perhaps some generations may pass before the want is supplied. Dr Johnson observed to me, how quietly people will endure an evil, which they might at any time very easily remedy; and mentioned as an instance, that the present family of Rasay had possessed the island for more than four-hundred years, and never made a commodious landing place, though a few men with pickaxes might have cut an ascent of stairs out of any part of the rock in a week's time.

The north end of Rasay is as rocky as the south end. From it I saw the little Isle of Fladda, belonging to Rasay, all fine green ground; and Rona, which is of so rocky a soil that it appears to be a pavement. I was told however that it has a great deal of grass, in the interstices. The laird has it all in his own hands. At this end of the island of Rasay is a cave in a striking situation. It is in a recess of a great cleft, a good way up from the sea. Before it the ocean roars, being dashed against monstrous broken rocks; grand and aweful *propugnacula*.[161] On the right hand of it is a longitudinal cave, very low at the entrance, but higher as you advance. The sea having scooped it out, it seems strange and unaccountable that the interior part, where the water must have operated with less force, should be loftier than that which is more immediately exposed to its violence. The roof of it is all covered with a kind of petrifications formed by drops, which perpetually distil from it. The first cave has been a place of much safety. I find a great difficulty in describing visible objects. I must own too that the old castle and cave, like many other things, of which one hears much, did not answer my expectations. People are every where apt to magnify the curiosities of their country.

This island has abundance of black cattle, sheep, and goats; a good many horses, which are used for ploughing, carrying out dung, and other works of husbandry. I believe the people never ride. There are indeed no roads through the island, unless a few detached beaten tracks deserve that name. Most of the houses are upon the shore; so that all the people have little boats, and catch fish. There is great plenty of potatoes here. There are black-cock in extraordinary abundance, moor-fowl, plover and wild pigeons, which seemed to me to be the same as we have in pigeon-houses, in their state of nature. Rasay has no pigeon-house. There are no hares nor rabbits in the island, nor was there ever known to be a fox, till last year, when one was landed on it by some malicious person, without whose aid he could not have got thither, as that animal is known to be a very bad swimmer. He has done much mischief. There is a great deal of fish caught in the sea round Rasay; it is a place where one may live in plenty, and even in luxury. There are no deer; but Rasay told us he would get some.

They reckon it rains nine months in the year in this island, owing to its being directly opposite to the western coast of Sky, where the watery clouds are broken by high mountains. The hills here, and indeed all the healthy grounds in general, abound with the sweet-smelling plant which the high-landers call *gaul*,[162] and (I think) with dwarf juniper in many places. There is enough of turf, which is their fuel, and it is thought there is a mine of coal. Such are the observations which I made upon the island of Rasay, upon comparing it with the description given by Martin, whose book we had with us.

There has been an ancient league between the families of Macdonald and Rasay. Whenever the head of either family dies, his sword is given to the head of the other. The present Rasay has the late Sir James Macdonald's sword. Old Rasay joined the Highland army in 1745, but prudently guarded against a forfeiture, by previously conveying his estate to the present gentleman, his eldest son. On that occasion, Sir Alexander, father of the late Sir James Macdonald, was very friendly to his neighbour. 'Don't be afraid, Rasay,' said he; 'I'll use all my interest to keep you safe; and if your estate should be taken, I'll buy it for the family.' And he would have done it.

Let me now gather some gold dust – some more fragments of Dr Johnson's conversation, without regard to order of time. He said, he thought very highly of Bentley;[163] that no man now went so far in the kinds of learning that he cultivated; that the many attacks on him were owing to envy, and to a desire of being known, by being in competition with such a man; that it was safe to attack him, because he never answered his opponents, but let them die away. It was attacking a man who would not beat them, because his beating them would make them live the longer. And he was right not to answer; for, in his hazardous method of writing, he could not but be often enough wrong; so it was better to leave things to their general appearance, than own himself to have erred in particulars. He said, Mallet was the prettiest drest puppet about town, and always kept good company.[164] That, from his way of talking, he saw, and always said, that he had not written any part of the *Life of the Duke of Marlborough*, though perhaps he intended to do it at some time, in which case he was not culpable in taking the pension. That he imagined the duchess furnished the materials for her *Apology*, which Hooke wrote, and Hooke furnished the words and the order, and all that in which the art of writing consists. That the duchess had not superior parts, but was a bold frontless woman, who knew how to make the most of her opportunities in life. That Hooke got a *large* sum of money for writing her *Apology*. That he wondered Hooke should have been weak enough to insert so profligate a maxim, as that to tell another's secret to one's friend, is no breach of confidence; though perhaps Hooke, who was a virtuous man, as his *History* shews, and did not wish her well, though he wrote her *Apology*, might see its ill tendency, and yet insert it at her desire. He was acting only ministerially. I apprehend, however, that Hooke was bound to give his best advice. I speak as a lawyer. Though I have had clients whose causes I could not, as a private man, approve; yet, if I undertook them, I would not do any thing that might be prejudicial to them, even at their desire, without warning them of their danger.

Saturday, 11th September

It was a storm of wind and rain; so we could not set out. I wrote some of this *Journal*, and talked awhile with Dr Johnson in his room, and passed the day, I cannot well say how, but very pleasantly. I was here amused to find Mr Cumberland's comedy of the *Fashionable Lover*, in which he has very well drawn a Highland character, Colin M'Cleod, of the same name with the family under whose roof we now were. Dr Johnson was much pleased with the Laird of Macleod, who is indeed a most promising youth, and with a noble spirit struggles with difficulties, and endeavours to preserve his people. He has been left with an incumbrance of forty thousand pounds debt,[165] and annuities to the amount of thirteen hundred pounds a year. Dr Johnson said, 'If he gets the better of all this, he'll be a hero; and I hope he will. I have not met with a young man who had more desire to learn, or who has learnt more. I have seen nobody that I wish more to do a kindness to than Macleod.' Such was the honourable elogium, on this young chieftain, pronounced by an accurate observer, whose praise was never lightly bestowed.

There is neither justice of peace, nor constable in Rasay. Sky has Mr M'Cleod of Ulinish, who is the sheriff substitute, and no other justice of peace. The want of the execution of justice is much felt among the islanders. Macleod very sensibly observed, that taking away the heritable jurisdictions had not been of such service in the islands, as was imagined. They had not authority enough in lieu of them. What could formerly have been settled at once, must now either take much time and trouble, or be neglected. Dr Johnson said, 'A country is in a bad state, which is governed only by laws; because a thousand things occur for which laws cannot provide, and where authority ought to interpose. Now destroying the authority of the chiefs set the people loose. It did not pretend to bring any positive good, but only to cure some evil; and I am not well enough acquainted with the country to know what degree of evil the heritable jurisdictions occasioned.' I maintained hardly any; because the chiefs generally acted right, for their own sakes.

Dr Johnson was now wishing to move. There was not enough of intellectual entertainment for him, after he had satisfyed his curiosity, which he did, by asking questions, till he had exhausted the island; and where there was so numerous a company, mostly young people, there was such a flow of familiar talk, so much noise, and so much singing and dancing, that little opportunity was left for his energetick conversation. He seemed sensible of this; for when I told him how happy they were at having him there, he said, 'Yet we have not been able to entertain them much.' I was fretted, from irritability of nerves, by M'Cruslick's too obstreperous mirth. I complained of it to my friend, observing we should be better if he was gone. 'No, sir,' said he. 'He puts something into our society, and takes nothing out of it.' Dr Johnson, however, had several opportunities of instructing the company; but I am sorry to say, that I did not pay sufficient attention to what passed, as his discourse now turned chiefly on mechanicks, agriculture and such subjects, rather than on science and wit. Last night Lady Rasay shewed him the operation of *wawking* cloth, that is, thickening it in the same manner as is done by a mill. Here it is performed by women, who kneel upon the ground, and rub it with both their hands, singing an Erse song all the time. He was asking questions while they were performing this operation, and, amidst their loud and wild howl, his voice was heard even in the room above.

They dance here every night. The queen of our ball was the eldest Miss Macleod, of Rasay, an elegant well-bred woman, and celebrated for her beauty over all those regions, by the name of Miss Flora Rasay.* There seemed to be no jealousy, no discontent among them; and the gaiety of the scene was such, that I for a moment doubted whether unhappiness had any place in Rasay. But my delusion was soon dispelled, by recollecting the following lines of my fellow-traveller:

> Yet hope not life from grief or danger free,
> Nor think the doom of man revers'd for thee![166]

Sunday, 12th September

It was a beautiful day, and although we did not approve of travelling on Sunday, we resolved to set out, as we were in an island from whence one must take occasion as it serves. Macleod and Talisker sailed in a boat of Rasay's for Sconser, to take the shortest way to Dunvegan. M'Cruslick went with them to Sconser, from whence he was to go to Slate, and so to the main land. We were resolved to pay a visit at Kingsburgh, and see the celebrated Miss Flora Macdonald, who is married to the present Mr Macdonald of Kingsburgh; so took that road, though not so near. All the family, but Lady Rasay, walked down to the shore to see us depart. Rasay himself went with us in a large boat, with eight oars, built in his island; as did Mr Malcolm M'Cleod, Mr Donald M'Queen, Dr Macleod, and some others. We had a most pleasant sail between Rasay and Sky; and passed by a cave, where Martin says fowls were caught by lighting fire in the mouth of it. Malcolm remembers this. But it is not now practised, as few fowls come into it.

We spoke of death. Dr Johnson on this subject observed, that the boastings

---

* She had been some time at Edinburgh, to which she again went, and was married to my worthy neighbour, Colonel Mure Campbell, now Earl of Loudoun; but she died soon afterwards, leaving one daughter.

of some men, as to dying easily, were idle talk, proceeding from partial views. I mentioned Hawthornden's *Cypress Grove*,[167] where it is said that the world is a mere show; and that it is unreasonable for a man to wish to continue in the show-room, after he has seen it. Let him go cheerfully out, and give place to other spectators. JOHNSON. 'Yes, sir, if he is sure he is to be well, after he goes out of it. But if he is to grow blind after he goes out of the show-room, and never to see any thing again; or if he does not know whither he is to go next, a man will not go cheerfully out of a show-room. No wise man will be contented to die, if he thinks he is to go into a state of punishment. Nay, no wise man will be contented to die, if he thinks he is to fall into annihilation: for however unhappy any man's existence may be, he yet would rather have it, than not exist at all. No; there is no rational principle by which a man can die contented, but a trust in the mercy of God, through the merits of Jesus Christ.' This short sermon, delivered with an earnest tone, in a boat upon the sea, which was perfectly calm, on a day appropriated to religious worship, while every one listened with an air of satisfaction, had a most pleasing effect upon my mind.

Pursuing the same train of serious reflection, he added, that it seemed certain that happiness could not be found in this life, because so many had tried to find it, in such a variety of ways, and had not found it.

We reached the harbour of Portree, in Sky, which is a large and good one. There was lying in it a vessel to carry off the emigrants, called the *Nestor*. It made a short settlement of the differences between a chief and his clan:

> ... *Nestor componere lites*
> *Inter Peleiden festinat & inter Atriden.*[168]

We approached her, and she hoisted her colours. Dr Johnson and Mr M'Queen remained in the boat: Rasay and I, and the rest went on board of her. She was a very pretty vessel, and, as we were told, the largest in Clyde. Mr Harrison, the captain shewed her to us. The cabin was commodious, and even elegant. There was a little library, finely bound. Portree has its name from King James the Fifth having landed there in his tour through the Western Isles, *Ree* in Erse being King, as *Re* is in Italian; so it is *Port-Royal*. There was here a tolerable inn. On our landing, I had the pleasure of finding a letter from home; and there were also letters to Dr Johnson and me, from Lord Elibank,[169] which had been sent after us from Edinburgh. His lordship's letter to me was as follows:

Dear Boswell,

I flew to Edinburgh the moment I heard of Mr Johnson's arrival; but so defective was my intelligence, that I came too late.

It is but justice to believe, that I could never forgive myself, nor deserve to be forgiven by others, if I was to fail in any mark of respect to that very great genius. — I hold him in the highest veneration; for that very reason I was resolved to take no share in the merit, perhaps guilt, of inticing him to honour this country with a visit.—I could not persuade myself there was any thing in Scotland worthy to have a Summer of Samuel Johnson bestowed on it; but since he has done us that compliment, for heaven's sake inform me of your motions. I will attend them most religiously; and though I should regret to let Mr Johnson go a mile out of his way on my account, old as I am, I shall be glad to go five hundred miles to enjoy a day of his company. Have the charity to send a council-post* with intelligence; the post does not suit us in the country. At any rate write to me. I will attend you in the north, when I shall know where to find you.

> I am,
> My dear Boswell,
> Your sincerely
> Obedient humble servant,
> ELIBANK.

August 21st, 1773.

The letter to Dr Johnson was in these words:

Dear Sir,

I was to have kissed your hands at Edinburgh, the moment I heard of you; but you were gone.

I hope my friend Boswell will inform me of your motions. It will be cruel to deprive me an instant of the honour of attending you. As I value you more than any King in Christendom, I will perform that duty with infinitely greater alacrity than any courtier. I can contribute but little to your entertainment; but, my sincere esteem for you gives me some title to the opportunity of expressing it.

I dare say you are by this time sensible that things are pretty much the same, as when Buchanan complained of being born *solo et seculo inerudito*.[170] Let me hear of you, and be persuaded that none of your admirers is more sincerely devoted to you, than,

> Dear Sir,
> Your most obedient,
> And most humble servant,
> ELIBANK.

Dr Johnson, on the following Tuesday, answered for both of us, thus:

MY LORD,

On the rugged shore of Skie, I had the honour of your lordship's letter, and can with great truth declare, that no place is so gloomy but that it would be cheered by such a testimony of regard, from a mind so well qualified to estimate characters,

---

* A term in Scotland for a special messenger, such as was formerly sent with dispatches by the lords of the council.

and to deal out approbation in its due proportions. If I have more than my share, it is your lordship's fault; for I have always reverenced your judgment too much, to exalt myself in your presence by any false pretensions.

Mr Boswell and I are at present at the disposal of the winds, and therefore cannot fix the time at which we shall have the honour of seeing your lordship. But we should either of us think ourselves injured by the supposition that we would miss your lordship's conversation, when we could enjoy it; for I have often declared that I never met you without going away a wiser man.

I am, my Lord,

Your lordship's most obedient

And most humble servant,

SAM. JOHNSON.

At Portree, Mr Donald M'Queen went to church and officiated in Erse, and then came to dinner. Dr Johnson and I resolved that we should treat the company, so I played the landlord, or master of the feast, having previously ordered Joseph to pay the bill.

Sir James Macdonald intended to have built a village here, which would have done great good. A village is like a heart to a country. It produces a perpetual circulation, and gives the people an opportunity to make profit of many little articles, which would otherwise be in a good measure lost. We had here a dinner, *et præterea nihil*.[171] Dr Johnson did not talk. When we were about to depart, we found that Rasay had been before-hand with us, and that all was paid: I would fain have contested this matter with him, but seeing him resolved, I declined it. We parted with cordial embraces from him and worthy Malcolm. In the evening Dr Johnson and I remounted our horses, accompanied by Mr M'Queen and Dr Macleod. It rained very hard. We rode what they call six miles, upon Rasay's lands in Sky, to Dr Macleod's house. On the road Dr Johnson appeared to be somewhat out of spirits. When I talked of our meeting Lord Elibank, he said, 'I cannot be with him much. I long to be again in civilized life; but can stay but for a short while' (he meant at Edinburgh). He said, 'Let us go to Dunvegan to-morrow.' 'Yes,' said I, 'if it is not a deluge.' 'At any rate,' he replied. This shewed a kind of fretful impatience; nor was it to be wondered at, considering our disagreeable ride. I feared he would give up Mull and Icolmkill, for he said something of his apprehensions of being detained by bad weather in going to Mull and Iona. However I hoped well. We had a dish of tea at Dr Macleod's, who had a pretty good house, where was his brother, a half-pay officer. His lady was a polite, agreeable woman. Dr Johnson said, he was glad to see that he was so well married, for he had an esteem for physicians. The doctor accompanied us to Kingsburgh, which is called a mile farther; but the computation of Sky has no connection whatever with real distance.[172]

I was highly pleased to see Dr Johnson safely arrived at Kingsburgh,[173] and received by the hospitable Mr Macdonald, who, with a most respectful attention, supported him into the house. Kingsburgh was completely the figure of a gallant highlander, exhibiting 'the graceful mien and manly looks', which our popular Scotch song has justly attributed to that character. He had his tartan plaid thrown about him, a large blue bonnet with a knot of black ribband like a cockade, a brown short coat of a kind of duffil, a tartan waistcoat with gold buttons and gold button-holes, a bluish philibeg, and tartan hose. He had jet black hair tied behind, and was a large stately man, with a steady sensible countenance.

There was a comfortable parlour with a good fire, and a dram went round. By and by supper was served, at which there appeared the lady of the house, the celebrated Miss Flora Macdonald. She is a little woman, of a genteel appearance, and uncommonly mild and well bred. To see Dr Samuel Johnson, the great champion of the English Tories, salute Miss Flora Macdonald in the isle of Sky, was a striking sight; for though somewhat congenial in their notions, it was very improbable they should meet here.

Miss Flora Macdonald (for so I shall call her) told me, she heard upon the main land, as she was returning home about a fortnight before, that Mr Boswell was coming to Sky, and one Mr Johnson, a young English buck, with him. He was highly entertained with this fancy. Giving an account of the afternoon which we passed at Anock, he said, 'I, being a *buck*, had miss in to make tea.' He was rather quiescent tonight, and went early to bed. I was in a cordial humour, and promoted a cheerful glass. The punch was excellent. Honest Mr M'Queen observed that I was in high glee, 'my *governour*[174] being gone to bed'. Yet in reality my heart was grieved, when I recollected that Kingsburgh was embarrassed in his affairs, and intended to go to America.[175] However, nothing but what was good was present, and I pleased myself in thinking that so spirited a man should be well every where. I slept in the same room with Dr Johnson. Each had a neat bed, with tartan curtains, in an upper chamber.

Monday, 13th September

The room where we lay was a celebrated one. Dr Johnson's bed was the very bed in which the grandson of the unfortunate King James the Second*

---

*I do not call him *the Prince of Wales*, or *the Prince*, because I am quite satisfied that the right which the House of Stuart had to the throne is extinguished. I do not call him the *Pretender*, because it appears to me as an insult to one who is still alive, and, I suppose, thinks very differently. It may be a parliamentary expression; but it is not a gentlemanly expression. I *know*, and I exult in having it in my power to tell, that *the only person* in the world who is intitled to be offended lay, on one of the nights after the failure of his rash attempt in 1745–6, while he was eluding the pursuit of the emissaries of government, which had offered thirty thousand pounds as a reward for apprehending him. To see Dr Samuel Johnson lying in that bed, in the isle of Sky, in the house of Miss Flora Macdonald, struck me with such a group of ideas as it is not easy for words to describe, as they passed through the mind. He smiled and said, 'I have had no ambitious thoughts in it.'* The room was decorated with a great variety of maps and prints. Among others, was Hogarth's print of Wilkes grinning, with the cap of liberty on a pole by him. That too was a curious circumstance in the scene this morning; such a contrast was Wilkes to the above group. It reminded me of Sir William Chambers's *Account of Oriental Gardening*, in which we are told all odd, strange, ugly, and even terrible objects, are introduced, for the sake of variety; a wild extravagance of taste which is so well ridiculed in the celebrated *Epistle* to him.[176] The following lines of that poem immediately occurred to me;

> Here too, O king of vengeance! in thy fane,
> Tremendous Wilkes shall rattle his gold chain.

Upon the table in our room I found in the morning a slip of paper, on which Dr Johnson had written with his pencil these words:

Quantum cedat virtutibus aurum.†

What he meant by writing them I could not tell.‡ He had caught cold a day or two ago, and the rain yesterday having made it worse, he was become very deaf. At breakfast he said, he would have given a good deal rather than not

---

at this delicacy, thinks and feels as I do; and has liberality of mind and generosity of sentiment enough to approve of my tenderness for what even *has been* Blood Royal. That he is *a prince* by *courtesy*, cannot be denied; because his mother was the daughter of Sobiesky, king of Poland. I shall, therefore, *on that account alone*, distinguish him by the name of *Prince Charles Edward*.

* This perhaps, was said in allusion to some lines ascribed to *Pope*, on his lying, at John Duke of Argyle's, at Adderbury, in the same bed in which Wilmot, Earl of Rochester, had slept.

> With no poetick ardour fir'd,
> I press the bed where Wilmot lay;
> That here he liv'd; or here expir'd,
> Begets no numbers, grave or gay.

† With virtue weigh'd, what worthless trash is gold!

‡ Since the first edition of this book, an ingenious friend has observed to me, that Dr Johnson had probably been thinking on the reward which was offered by government for the apprehension of the grandson of King James II and that he meant by these words to express his admiration of the highlanders, whose fidelity and attachment had resisted the golden temptation that had been held out to them.

have lain in that bed. I owned he was the lucky man; and observed, that without doubt it had been contrived between Mrs Macdonald and him. She seemed to acquiesce; adding, 'You know young *bucks* are always favourites of the ladies.' He spoke of Prince Charles being here, and asked Mrs Macdonald, '*Who* was with him? We were told, madam, in England, there was one Miss Flora Macdonald with him.' She said, 'they were very right'; and perceiving Dr Johnson's curiosity, though he had delicacy enough not to question her, very obligingly entertained him with a recital of the particulars which she herself knew of that escape, which does so much honour to the humanity, fidelity, and generosity, of the highlanders. Dr Johnson listened to her with placid attention, and said, 'All this should be written down.'

From what she told us, and from what I was told by others personally concerned, and from a paper of information which Rasay was so good as to send me, at my desire, I have compiled the following abstract, which, as it contains some curious anecdotes, will, I imagine not be uninteresting to my readers, and even, perhaps, be of some use to future historians.

Prince Charles Edward, after the battle of Culloden, was conveyed to what is called the Long Island, where he lay for some time concealed. But intelligence having been obtained where he was, and a number of troops having come in quest of him, it became absolutely necessary for him to quit that country without delay. Miss Flora Macdonald, then a young lady, animated by what she thought the sacred principle of loyalty, offered, with the magnanimity of a heroine, to accompany him in an open boat to Sky, though the coast they were to quit was guarded by ships. He dressed himself in women's clothes, and passed as her supposed maid, by the name of Betty Bourke, an Irish girl. They got off undiscovered, though several shots were fired to bring them to, and landed at Mugstot, the seat of Sir Alexander Macdonald. Sir Alexander was then at Fort Augustus, with the Duke of Cumberland; but his lady was at home. Prince Charles took his post upon a hill near the house. Flora Macdonald waited on Lady Margaret, and acquainted her of the enterprise in which she was engaged. Her ladyship, whose active benevolence was ever seconded by superior talents, shewed a perfect presence of mind, and readiness of invention, and at once settled that Prince Charles should be conducted to old Rasay, who was himself concealed with some select friends. The plan was instantly communicated to Kingsburgh, who was dispatched to the hill to inform the Wanderer, and carry him refreshments. When Kingsburgh approached, he started up, and advanced, holding a large knotted stick, and in appearance ready to knock him down, till he said, 'I am Macdonald of Kingsburgh, come to serve your highness.' The Wanderer answered, 'It is well,' and was satisfied with the plan.

Flora Macdonald dined with Lady Margaret, at whose table there sat an officer of the army, stationed here with a party of soldiers, to watch for Prince Charles in case of his flying to the isle of Sky. She afterwards often laughed in good humour with this gentleman, on her having so well deceived him.

After dinner, Flora Macdonald on horseback, and her supposed maid, and Kingsburgh, with a servant carrying some linen, all on foot, proceeded towards that gentleman's house. Upon the road was a small rivulet which they were obliged to cross. The Wanderer, forgetting his assumed sex, that his clothes might not be wet, held them up a great deal too high. Kingsburgh mentioned this to him, observing, it might make a discovery. He said he would be more careful for the future. He was as good as his word; for the next brook they crossed, he did not hold up his clothes at all, but let them float upon the water. He was very awkward in his female dress. His size was so large, and his strides so great, that some women whom they met reported that they had seen a very big woman, who looked like a man in woman's clothes, and that perhaps it was (as they expressed themselves) the *Prince*, after whom so much search was making.

At Kingsburgh he met with a most cordial reception; seemed gay at supper, and after it indulged himself in a cheerful glass with his worthy host. As he had not had his clothes off for a long time, the comfort of a good bed was highly relished by him, and he slept soundly till next day at one o'clock.

The mistress of Corrichatachin told me, that in the forenoon she went into her father's room, who was also in bed, and suggested to him her apprehensions that a party of the military might come up, and that his guest had better not remain here too long. Her father said, 'Let the poor man repose himself after his fatigues; and as for me, I care not, though they take off this old grey head ten or eleven years sooner than I should die in the course of nature.' He then wrapped himself in the bed-clothes, and again fell fast asleep.

On the afternoon of that day, the Wanderer, still in the same dress, set out for Portree, with Flora Macdonald and a man servant. His shoes being very bad, Kingsburgh provided him with a new pair, and taking up the old ones, said, 'I will faithfully keep them till you are safely settled at St James's. I will then introduce myself by shaking them at you, to put you in mind of your night's entertainment and protection under my roof.' He smiled, and said, 'Be as good as your word!' Kingsburgh kept the shoes as long as he lived. After his death, a zealous Jacobite gentleman gave twenty guineas for them.

Old Mrs Macdonald, after her guest had left the house, took the sheets in which he had lain, folded them carefully, and charged her daughter that they should be kept unwashed, and that, when she died, her body should be wrapped in them as a winding sheet. Her will was religiously observed.

Upon the road to Portree, Prince Charles changed his dress, and put on man's clothes again; a tartan short coat and a waistcoat, with philibeg and short hose, a plaid, and a wig and bonnet.

Mr Donald M'Donald, called Donald Roy, had been sent express to the present Rasay, then the young laird, who was at that time at his sister's house, about three miles from Portree, attending his brother, Dr Macleod, who was recovering of a wound he had received at the battle of Culloden. Mr M'Donald communicated to young Rasay the plan of conveying the Wanderer to where old Rasay was; but was told that old Rasay had fled to Knoidart, a part of Glengary's estate. There was then a dilemma what should be done. Donald Roy proposed that he should conduct the Wanderer to the main land; but young Rasay thought it too dangerous at that time, and said it would be better to conceal him in the island of Rasay, till old Rasay could be informed where he was, and give his advice what was best. But the difficulty was, how to get him to Rasay. They could not trust a Portree crew, and all the Rasay boats had been destroyed, or carried off by the military except two belonging to Malcolm M'Leod, which he had concealed somewhere.

Dr Macleod being informed of this difficulty, said he would risk his life once more for Prince Charles; and it having occurred, that there was a little boat upon a fresh water lake in the neighbourhood, young Rasay and Dr Macleod, with the help of some women, brought it to the sea, by extraordinary exertion, across a Highland mile of land, one half of which was bog, and the other a steep precipice.

These gallant brothers, with the assistance of one little boy, rowed the small boat to Rasay, where they were to endeavour to find Captain M'Leod, as Malcolm was then called, and get one of his good boats, with which they might return to Portree, and receive the Wanderer; or, in case of not finding him, they were to make the small boat serve, though the danger was considerable.

Fortunately, on their first landing, they found their cousin Malcolm, who, with the utmost alacrity, got ready one of his boats, with two strong men, John M'Kenzie, and Donald M'Friar. Malcolm, being the oldest man, and most cautious, said, that as young Rasay had not hitherto appeared in the unfortunate business, he ought not to run any risk; but that Dr Macleod and himself, who were already publickly engaged, should go on this expedition. Young Rasay answered, with an oath, that he would go, at the risk of his life and fortune. 'In God's name then,' said Malcolm, 'let us proceed.' The two boatmen, however, now stopped short, till they should be informed of their destination; and M'Kenzie declared he would not move an oar till he knew where they were going. Upon which they were both sworn to secrecy; and the business being imparted to them, they were eager to put off to sea without loss of time. The boat soon landed about half a mile from the inn at Portree.

All this was negotiated before the Wanderer got forward to Portree. Malcolm M'Leod, and M'Friar, were dispatched to look for him. In a short time he appeared, and went into the publick house. Here Donald Roy, whom he had seen at Mugstot, received him, and informed him of what had been concerted. He wanted silver for a guinea, but the landlord had only thirteen shillings. He was going to accept of this for his guinea; but Donald Roy very judiciously observed, that it would discover him to be some great man; so he desisted. He slipped out of the house, leaving his fair protectress, whom he never again saw; and Malcolm Macleod was presented to him by Donald Roy, as a captain in his army. Young Rasay and Dr Macleod had waited, in impatient anxiety, in the boat. When he came, their names were announced to him. He would not permit the usual ceremonies of respect, but saluted them as his equals.

Donald Roy staid in Sky, to be in readiness to get intelligence, and give an alarm in case the troops should discover the retreat to Rasay; and Prince Charles was then conveyed in a boat to that island in the night. He slept a little upon the passage, and they landed about day-break. There was some difficulty in accommodating him with a lodging, as almost all the houses in the island had been burnt by soldiery. They repaired to a little hut, which some shepherds had lately built, and having prepared it as well as they could, and made a bed of heath for the stranger, they kindled a fire, and partook of some provisions which had been sent with him from Kingsburgh. It was observed, that he would not taste wheat-bread, or brandy, while oat-bread and whisky lasted; 'for these,' said he, 'are my own country's bread and drink'. This was very engaging to the highlanders.

Young Rasay being the only person of the company that durst appear with safety, he went in quest of something fresh for them to eat; but though he was amidst his own cows, sheep, and goats, he could not venture to take any of them for fear of a discovery, but was obliged to supply himself by stealth. He therefore caught a kid, and brought it to the hut in his plaid, and it was killed and drest, and furnished them a meal which they relished much. The distressed Wanderer, whose health was now a good deal impaired by hunger, fatigue, and watching, slept a long time, but seemed to be frequently disturbed. Malcolm told me he would start from broken slumbers, and speak to himself in different languages, French, Italian, and English. I must however acknowledge, that it is highly probable that my worthy friend Malcolm did not know precisely the difference between French and Italian. One of his expressions in English was, 'O God! Poor Scotland!'

While they were in the hut, M'Kenzie and M'Friar, the two boatmen, were placed as sentinels upon different eminences; and one day an incident happened, which must not be omitted. There was a man wandering about the island, selling tobacco. Nobody knew him, and he was suspected to be a spy. M'Kenzie came running to the hut, and told that this suspected person was approaching. Upon which the three gentlemen, young Rasay, Dr Macleod, and Malcom, held a council of war upon him, and were unanimously of opinion that he should instantly be put to death. Prince Charles, at once assuming a grave and even severe countenance, said, 'God forbid that we should take away a man's life, who may be innocent, while we can preserve our own.' The gentlemen however persisted in their resolution, while he as strenuously continued to take the merciful side. John M'Kenzie, who sat watching at the door of the hut, and overheard the debate, said in Erse, 'Well, well; he must be shot. You are the king, but we are the parliament, and will do what we choose.' Prince Charles, seeing the gentlemen smile, asked what the man had said, and being told it in English, he observed that he was a clever fellow, and, notwithstanding the perilous situation in which he was, laughed loud and heartily. Luckily the unknown person did not perceive that there were people in the hut, at least did not come to it, but walked on past it, unknowing of his risk. It was afterwards found out that he was one of the Highland army, who was himself in danger. Had he come to them, they were resolved to dispatch him; for, as Malcolm said to me, 'We could not keep him with us, and we durst not let him go. In such a situation, I would have shot my brother, if I had not been sure of him.' John M'Kenzie was at Rasay's house, when we were there.* About eighteen years before, he hurt one of his legs when dancing, and being obliged to have it cut off, he now was going about with a wooden leg. The story of his being a *Member of Parliament* is not yet forgotten. I took him out a little way from the house, gave him a shilling to drink Rasay's health, and led him into a detail of the particulars which I have just related. With less foundation, some writers have traced the idea of a parliament, and of the British constitution, in rude and early times. I was curious to know if he had really heard, or understood, any thing of that subject, which, had he

* This old Scottish *Member of Parliament*, I am informed, is still living (1785).

been a greater man, would probably have been eagerly maintained. 'Why, John,' said I, 'did you think the king should be controuled by a parliament?' He answered, 'I thought, sir, there were many voices against one.'

The conversation then turning on the times, the Wanderer said, that to be sure, the life he had led of late was a very hard one; but he would rather live in the way he now did, for ten years, than fall into the hands of his enemies. The gentlemen asked him, what he thought his enemies would do with him, should he have the misfortune to fall into their hands. He said, he did not believe they would dare to take his life publickly, but he dreaded being privately destroyed by poison or assassination. He was very particular in his inquiries about the wound which Dr Macleod had received at the battle of Culloden, from a ball which entered at one shoulder, and went cross to the other. The doctor happened still to have on the coat which he wore on that occasion. He mentioned, that he himself had his horse shot under him at Culloden; that the ball hit the horse about two inches from his knee, and made him so unruly that he was obliged to change him for another. He threw out some reflections on the conduct of the disastrous affair at Culloden, saying, however, that perhaps it was rash in him to do so. I am now convinced that his suspicions were groundless; for I have had a good deal of conversation upon the subject with my very worthy and ingenious friend, Mr Andrew Lumisden, who was under secretary to Prince Charles, and afterwards principal secretary to his father at Rome, who, he assured me, was perfectly satisfied both of the abilities and honour of the generals who commanded the highland army on that occasion. Mr Lumisden has written an account of the three battles in 1745–6, at once accurate and classical. Talking of the different Highland corps, the gentlemen who were present wished to have his opinion which were the best soldiers. He said, he did not like comparisons among those corps: they were all best.

He told his conductors, he did not think it advisable to remain long in any one place; and that he expected a French ship to come for him to Lochbroom, among the Mackenzies. It then was proposed to carry him in one of Malcolm's boats to Lochbroom, though the distance was fifteen leagues coastwise. But he thought this would be too dangerous, and desired that at any rate, they might first endeavour to obtain intelligence. Upon which young Rasay wrote to his friend, Mr M'Kenzie of Applecross, but received an answer, that there was no appearance of any French ship.

It was therefore resolved that they should return to Sky, which they did, and landed in Strath, where they reposed in a cow-house belonging to Mr Niccolson of Scorbreck. The sea was very rough, and the boat took in a good deal of water. The Wanderer asked if there was danger, as he was not used to such a vessel. Upon being told there was not, he sung an Erse song with much vivacity. He had by this time acquired a good deal of the Erse language.

Young Rasay was now dispatched to where Donald Roy was, that they might get all the intelligence they could; and the Wanderer, with much earnestness, charged Dr Macleod to have a boat ready, at a certain place about seven miles off, as he said he intended it should carry him upon a matter of great consequence; and gave the doctor a case, containing a silver spoon, knife, and fork, saying, 'keep you that till I see you', which the doctor understood to be two days from that time. But all these orders were only blinds; for he had another plan in his head, but wisely thought it safest to trust his secrets to no more persons than was absolutely necessary. Having then desired Malcolm to walk with him a little way from the house, he soon opened his mind, saying, 'I deliver myself to you. Conduct me to the Laird of M'Kinnon's country.' Malcolm objected that it was very dangerous, as so many parties of soldiers were in motion. He answered. 'There is nothing now to be done without danger.' He then said, that Malcolm must be the master, and he the servant; so he took the bag, in which his linen was put up, and carried it on his shoulder; and observing that his waistcoat, which was of scarlet tartan, with a gold twist button, was finer than Malcolm's, which was of a plain ordinary tartan, he put on Malcolm's waistcoat, and gave him his; remarking at the same time, that it did not look well that the servant should be better dressed than the master.

Malcolm, though an excellent walker, found himself excelled by Prince Charles, who told him, he should not much mind the parties that were looking for him, were he once but a musquet shot from them; but that he was somewhat afraid of the highlanders who were against him. He was well used to walking in Italy, in pursuit of game; and he was even now so keen a sportsman, that, having observed some partridges, he was going to take a shot; but Malcolm cautioned him against it, observing that the firing might be heard by the tenders who were hovering upon the coast.

As they proceeded through the mountains, taking many a circuit to avoid any houses, Malcolm, to try his resolution, asked him what they should do, should they fall in with a party of soldiers: he answered. 'Fight to be sure!' Having asked Malcolm if he should be known in his present dress, and Malcolm having replied he would, he said, 'Then I'll blacken my face with powder.' 'That,' said Malcolm, 'would discover you at once.'

'Then,' said he, 'I must be put in the greatest dishabille possible.' So he pulled off his wig, tied a handkerchief round his head, and put his night-cap over it, tore the ruffles from his shirt, took the buckles out of his shoes, and made Malcolm fasten them with strings; but still Malcolm thought he would be known. 'I have so odd a face,' said he, 'that no man ever saw me but he would know me again.'

He seemed unwilling to give credit to the horrid narrative of men being massacred in cold blood, after victory had declared for the army commanded by the Duke of Cumberland. He could not allow himself to think that a general could be so barbarous.

When they came within two miles of M'Kinnon's house, Malcolm asked if he chose to see the laird. 'No,' said he, 'by no means. I know M'Kinnon to be as good and as honest a man as any in the world, but he is not fit for my purpose at present. You must conduct me to some other house; but let it be a gentleman's house.' Malcolm then determined that they should go to the house of his brother-in-law, Mr John M'Kinnon, and from thence be conveyed to the main land of Scotland, and claim the assistance of Macdonald of Scothouse. The Wanderer at first objected to this, because Scothouse was cousin to a person of whom he had suspicions. But he acquiesced in Malcolm's opinion.

When they were near Mr John M'Kinnon's house, they met a man of the name of Ross, who had been a private soldier in the Highland army. He fixed his eyes steadily on the Wanderer in his disguise, and having at once recognized him, he clapped his hands, and exclaimed, 'Alas! is this the case?' Finding that there was now a discovery, Malcolm asked, 'What's to be done?' 'Swear him to secrecy,' answered Prince Charles. Upon which Malcolm drew his dirk, and on the naked blade, made him take a solemn oath, that he would say nothing of his having seen the Wanderer, till his escape should be made publick.

Malcolm's sister, whose house they reached pretty early in the morning, asked him who the person was that was along with him. He said it was one Lewis Caw, from Crieff, who being a fugitive like himself, for the same reason, he had engaged him as his servant, but that he had fallen sick. 'Poor man!' said she, 'I pity him. At the same time my heart warms to a man of his appearance.' Her husband was gone a little way from home; but was expected every minute to return. She set down to her brother a plentiful Highland breakfast. Prince Charles acted the servant very well, sitting at a respectful distance, with his bonnet off. Malcolm then said to him, 'Mr Caw, you have as much need of this as I have; there is enough for us both: you had better draw nearer and share with me.' Upon which he rose, made a profound bow, sat down at table with his supposed master, and eat very heartily. After this there came in an old woman, who, after the mode of ancient hospitality, brought warm water, and washed Malcolm's feet. He desired her to wash the feet of the poor man who attended him. She at first seemed averse to this, from pride, as thinking him beneath her, and in the periphrastick language of the highlanders and the Irish, said warmly, 'Though I wash your father's son's feet, why should I wash his father's son's feet?' She was however persuaded to do it.

They then went to bed, and slept for some time; and when Malcolm awaked, he was told that Mr John M'Kinnon, his brother-in-law, was in sight. He sprang out to talk to him before he shoulld see Prince Charles. After saluting him, Malcolm, pointing to the sea, said, 'What, John, if the prince should be prisoner on board one of those tenders?' 'God forbid!' replied John. 'What if we had him here?' said Malcolm. 'I wish we had,' answered John; 'we should take care of him.' 'Well, John,' said Malcolm, 'he is in your house.' John, in a transport of joy, wanted to run directly in, and pay his obeisance; but Malcolm stopped him, saying, 'Now is your time to behave well, and do nothing that can discover him.' John composed himself, and having sent away all his servants upon different errands, he was introduced into the presence of his guest, and was then desired to go and get ready a boat lying near his house, which, though but a small leaky one, they resolved to take, rather than go to the Laird of M'Kinnon. John M'Kinnon, however, thought otherwise; and upon his return told them, that his chief and Lady M'Kinnon were coming in the laird's boat. Prince Charles said to his trusty Malcolm. 'I am sorry for this, but must make the best of it.' M'Kinnon then walked up from the shore, and did homage to the Wanderer. His lady waited in a cave, to which they all repaired, and were entertained with cold meat and wine. Mr Malcolm M'Leod being now superseded by the Laird of M'Kinnon, desired leave to return, which was granted him, and Prince Charles wrote a short note, which he subscribed 'James Thompson', informing his friends that he had got away from Sky, and thanking them for their kindness; and he desired this might be speedily conveyed to young Rasay and Dr Macleod, that they might not wait longer in expectation of seeing him again. He bade a cordial adieu to Malcolm, and insisted on his accepting of a silver stock-buckle, and ten guineas from his purse, though, as Malcolm told me, it did not appear to contain above forty. Malcolm at first begged to be excused, saying, that he had a few guineas at his service; but Prince Charles answered, 'You will have need of money. I shall get enough when I come upon the main land.'

The Laird of M'Kinnon then conveyed him to the opposite coast of Knoidart. Old Rasay, to whom intelligence had been sent, was crossing at the same time to Sky; but as they did not know of each other, and each had apprehensions, the two boats kept aloof.

*

These are the particulars which I have collected concerning the extraordinary concealment and escapes of Prince Charles, in the Hebrides. He was often in imminent danger. The troops traced him from the Long Island, across Sky, to Portree, but there lost him.

Here I stop, having received no farther authentick information of his fatigues and perils before he escaped to France. Kings and subjects may both take a lesson of moderation from the melancholy fate of the House of Stuart; that kings may not suffer degradation and exile, and subjects may not be harrassed by the evils of a disputed succession.

Let me close the scene on that unfortunate House with the elegant and pathetick reflections of Voltaire, in his *Histoire Generale*. '*Que les hommes privés,*' says that brilliant writer, speaking of Prince Charles, '*qui se croyent malheureux, jettent les yeux sur ce prince et ses ancêtres.*'[177]

In another place he thus sums up the sad story of the family in general:

Il n'y a aucun exemple dans l'histoire d'une maison si longtems infortunée. Le premier des Rois d'Écosse, qui eut le nom de Jacques, apres avoir été dix-huit ans prisonnier en Angleterre, mourut assassiné, avec sa femme, par la main de ses sujets. Jacques II, son fils, fut tué à vingt-neuf ans en combattant contre les Anglois. Jacques III, mis en prison par son peuple, fut tué ensuite par les revoltés, dans une battaille. Jacques IV perit dans un combat qu'il perdit. Marie Stuart, sa petite fille, chassée, de son trone, fugitive en Angleterre, ayant langui dix-huit ans en prison, se vit condamnée à mort par des juges Anglais, et eut la tête tranchée. Charles I, petit fils de Marie, Roi d'Écosse et d'Angleterre, vendu par les Écossois, et jugé à mort par les Anglais, mourut sur un échauffaut dans la place publique. Jacques, son fils, septième du nom, et deuxieme en Angleterre, fut chassé de ses trois royaumes; et pour comble de malheur on contesta à son fils sa naissance; le fils ne tenta de remonter sur le trone de ces peres, que pour faire périr ses amis par des bourreaux; et nous avons vu le Prince Charles Edouard, reunuissant en vain les vertus de ses peres, et le courage du Roy Jean Sobieski, son ayeul maternel, executer les exploits et essuyer les malheurs les plus incroyables. Si quelque chose justifie ceux qui croyent une fatalité à laquelle rien ne peut se soustraire, c'est cette suite continuelle de malheurs qui a persecuté la maison de Stuart, pendant plus de trois-cent années.

The gallant Malcolm was apprehended[178] in about ten days after they separated, put aboard a ship and carried prisoner to London. He said, the prisoners in general were very ill treated in their passage; but there were soldiers on board who lived well, and sometimes invited him to share with them: that he had the good fortune not to be thrown into jail, but was confined in the house of a messenger, of the name of Dick. To his astonishment, only one witness could be found against him, though he had been so openly engaged; and therefore, for want of sufficient evidence, he was set at liberty. He added, that he thought himself in such danger, that he would gladly have compounded for banishment.[179] Yet, he said, he should never be so ready for death as he then was. There is philosophical truth in this. A man will meet death much more firmly at one time than another. The enthusiasm even of a mistaken principle warms the mind, and sets it above the fear of death; which in our cooler moments, if we really think of it, cannot but be terrible, or at least very awful.

Miss Flora Macdonald being then also in London, under the protection of Lady Primrose,[180] that lady provided a post-chaise to convey her to Scotland, and desired she might choose any friend she pleased to accompany her. She chose Malcolm. 'So,' said he, with a triumphant air, 'I went to London to be hanged, and returned in a post-chaise with Miss Flora Macdonald.'

Mr Macleod of Muiravènside, whom we saw at Rasay, assured us that Prince Charles was in London in 1759,[181] and that there was then a plan in agitation for restoring his family. Dr Johnson could scarcely credit this story, and said, there could be no probable plan at that time. Such an attempt could not have succeeded, unless the King of Prussia had stopped the army in Germany; for both the army and the fleet would, even without orders, have fought for the King, to whom they had engaged themselves.

Having related so many particulars concerning the grandson of the unfortunate King James the Second; having given due praise to fidelity and generous attachment, which, however erroneous the judgement may be, are honourable for the heart; I must do the highlanders the justice to attest, that I found every where amongst them a high opinion of the virtues of the King now upon the throne, and an honest disposition to be faithful subjects to his majesty, whose family had possessed the sovereignty of this country so long, that a change, even for the abdicated family, would now hurt the best feelings of all his subjects.

The *abstract* point of *right* would involve us in a discussion of remote and perplexed questions; and after all, we should have no clear principle of decision. That establishment, which, from political necessity, took place in 1688, by a breach in the succession of our kings, and which, whatever benefits may have accrued from it, certainly gave a shock to our monarchy, the able and constitutional Blackstone, wisely rests on the solid footing of authority: 'Our ancestors having most indisputably a competent jurisdiction to decide this great and important question, and having, in fact, decided it, it is now become our duty, at this distance of time, to acquiesce in their determination.'*

* *Commentaries on the Laws of England*, Book I, chap. 3.

Mr Paley, the present Archdeacon of Carlisle, in his *Principles of Moral and Political Philosophy*, having, with much clearness of argument, shewn the duty of submission to civil government to be founded neither on an indefeasible *jus divinum*, nor on *compact*,[182] but on *expediency*, lays down this rational position:

Irregularity in the first foundation of a state, or subsequent violence, fraud, or injustice, in getting possession of the supreme power, are not sufficient reasons for resistance, after the government is once peaceably settled. No subject of the British Empire conceives himself engaged to vindicate the justice of the Norman claim or conquest, or apprehends that his duty in any manner depends upon that controversy. So likewise, if the house of Lancaster, or even the posterity of Cromwell, had been at this day seated upon the throne of England, we should have been as little concerned to enquire how the founder of the family came there.*

In conformity with this doctrine, I myself, though fully persuaded that the House of Stuart had originally no right to the crown of Scotland; for that Baliol, and not Bruce, was the lawful heir; should yet have thought it very culpable to have rebelled, on that account, against Charles the First, or even a prince of that house much nearer the time, in order to assert the claim of the posterity of Baliol.

---

* Book VI, chap. 3. Since I have quoted Mr Archdeacon Paley upon one subject, I cannot but transcribe, from his excellent work, a distinguished passage in support of the Christian Revelation. After shewing, in decent but strong terms, the unfairness of the *indirect* attempts of modern infidels to unsettle and perplex religious principles, and particularly the irony, banter, and sneer, of one whom he politely calls 'an eloquent historian', the archdeacon thus expresses himself:

'Seriousness is not constraint of thought; nor levity, freedom. Every mind which wishes the advancement of truth and knowledge, in the most important of all human researches, must abhor this licentiousness, as violating no less the laws of reasoning than the rights of decency. There is but one description of men to whose principles it ought to be tolerable. I mean that class of reasoners who can see *little* in Christianity even supposing it to be true. To such adversaries we address this reflection. Had Jesus Christ delivered no other declaration than the following, "The hour is coming in the which all that are in the graves shall hear his voice, and shall come forth, – they that have done well unto the resurrection of life, and they that have done evil unto the resurrection of damnation," he had pronounced a message of inestimable importance, and well worthy of that splendid apparatus of prophecy and miracles with which his mission was introduced and attested – a message in which the wisest of mankind would rejoice to find an answer to their doubts, and rest to their inquiries. It is idle to say that a future state had been discovered already. It had been discovered as the Copernican System was; it was one guess amongst many. He alone discovers who *proves*; and no man can prove this point but the teacher who testifies by miracles that his doctrine comes from God' (Book V, chap. 9).

If infidelity be disingenuously dispersed in every shape that is likely to allure, surprise, or beguile the imagination – in a fable, a tale, a novel, a poem, in books of travels, of philosophy, of natural history, as Mr Paley has well observed – I hope it is fair in me thus to meet such poison with an unexpected antidote, which I cannot doubt will be found powerful.

However convinced I am of the justice of that principle, which holds allegiance and protection to be reciprocal, I do however acknowledge, that I am not satisfied with the cold sentiment which would confine the exertions of the subject within the strict line of duty. I would have every breast animated with the *fervour* of loyalty; with that generous attachment which delights in doing somewhat more than is required, and makes 'service perfect freedom'. And, therefore, as our most gracious Sovereign, on his accession to the throne, gloried in being born a Briton; so, in my more private sphere, *Ego me nunc denique natum gratulor.*[183] I am happy that a disputed succession no longer distracts our minds; and that a monarchy, established by law, is now so sanctioned by time, that we can fully indulge those feelings of loyalty which I am ambitious to excite. They are feelings which have ever actuated the inhabitants of the Highlands and the Hebrides. The plant of loyalty is there in full vigour, and the Brunswick graft now flourishes like a native shoot. To that spirited race of people I may with propriety apply the elegant lines of a modern poet, on the 'facile temper of the beauteous sex':

> Like birds new-caught, who flutter for a time,
> And struggle with captivity in vain;
> But by-and-by they rest, they smooth their plumes,
> And to *new masters* sing their former notes.*

Surely such notes are much better than the querulous growlings of suspicious Whigs and discontented Republicans.

Kingsburgh conducted us in his boat, across one of the lochs, as they call them, or arms of the sea, which flow in upon all the coasts of Sky, to a mile beyond a place called Grishinish.[184] Our horses had been sent round by land to meet us. By this sail we saved eight miles of bad riding.[185] Dr Johnson said, 'When we take into the computation what we have saved, and what we have gained, by this agreeable sail, it is a great deal.' He observed, 'it is very disagreeable riding in Sky. The way is so narrow, one only at a time can travel, so it is quite unsocial; and you cannot indulge in meditation by yourself, because you must be always attending to the steps which your horse takes.' This was a just and clear description of its inconveniencies.

The topick of emigration being again introduced, Dr Johnson said, that 'a rapacious chief would make a wilderness of his estate'. Mr Donald M'Queen told us, that the oppression, which then made so much noise, was owing

---

* *Agis*, a tragedy, by John Home.

279

to landlords listening to bad advice in the letting of their lands; that interested and designed people flattered them with golden dreams of much higher rents than could reasonably be paid; and that some of the gentlemen tacksmen, or upper tenants, were themselves in part the occasion of the mischief, by over-rating the farms of others. That many of the tacksmen, rather than comply with exorbitant demands, had gone off to America, and impoverished the country, by draining it of its wealth; and that their places were filled by a number of poor people, who had lived under them, properly speaking, as servants, paid by a certain proportion of the produce of the lands, though called sub-tenants. I observed, that if the men of substance were once banished from a Highland estate, it might probably be greatly reduced in its value; for one bad year might ruin a set of poor tenants, and men of any property would not settle in such a country, unless from the temptation of getting land extremely cheap; for an inhabitant of any good county in Britain, had better go to America than to the Highlands or the Hebrides. Here, therefore was a consideration that ought to induce a chief to act a more liberal part, from a mere motive of interest, independent of the lofty and honourable principle of keeping a clan together, to be in readiness to serve his king. I added, that I could not help thinking a little arbitrary power in the sovereign, to control the bad policy and greediness of the chiefs, might sometimes be of service. In France a chief would not be permitted to force a number of the king's subjects out of the country. Dr Johnson concurred with me, observing, that 'were an oppressive chieftain a subject of the French king, he would probably be admonished by a *letter*'.

During our sail, Dr Johnson asked about the use of the dirk, with which he imagined the highlanders cut their meat. He was told, they had a knife and fork besides, to eat with. He asked, how did the women do? and was answered, some of them had a knife and fork too; but in general the men, when they had cut their meat, handed their knives and forks to the women, and they themselves eat with their fingers. The old tutor of Macdonald always eat fish with his fingers, alledging that a knife and fork gave it a bad taste. I took the liberty to observe to Dr Johnson, that he did so. 'Yes,' said he; 'but it is because I am short-sighted, and afraid of bones, for which reason I am not fond of eating many kinds of fish, because I must use my fingers.'

Dr M'Pherson's *Dissertations on Scottish Antiquities*, which he had looked at when at Corrichatachin, being mentioned, he remarked, that 'you might read half an hour, and ask yourself what you had been reading: there were so many words to so little matter, that there was no getting through the book'.

As soon as we reached the shore, we took leave of Kingsburgh, and mounted our horses. We passed through a wild moor, in many places so soft that we were obliged to walk, which was very fatiguing to Dr Johnson. Once he had advanced on horseback to a very bad step. There was a steep declivity on his left, to which he was so near, that there was not room for him to dismount in the usual way. He tried to alight on the other side, as if he had been a 'young buck' indeed, but in the attempt he fell at his length upon the ground; from which, however, he got up immediately without being hurt. During this dreary ride, we were sometimes relieved by a view of branches of the sea, that universal medium of connection amongst mankind. A guide, who had been sent with us from Kingsburgh, explored the way (much in the same manner as, I suppose, is pursued in the wilds of America) by observing certain marks known only to the inhabitants. We arrived at Dunvegan late in the afternoon.[186] The great size of the castle, which is partly old and partly new, and is built upon a rock close to the sea, while the land around it presents nothing but wild, moorish, hilly, and craggy appearances, gave a rude magnificence to the scene. Having dismounted, we ascended a flight of steps, which was made by the late Macleod, for the accomodation of persons coming to him by land, there formerly being, for security, no other access to the castle but from the sea; so that visitors who came by the land were under the necessity of getting into a boat, and sailed round to the only place where it could be approached. We were introduced into a stately dining-room, and received by Lady Macleod, mother of the laird, who, with his friend Talisker, having been detained on the road, did not arrive till some time after us.

We found the lady of the house a very polite and sensible woman, who had lived for some time in London, and had there been in Dr Johnson's company. After we had dined, we repaired to the drawing-room, where some of the young ladies of the family, with their mother, were at tea. This room had formerly been the bed-chamber of Sir Roderick Macleod, one of the old lairds; and he chose it, because, behind it, there was a considerable cascade, the sound of which disposed him to sleep. Above his bed was this inscription: SIR RORIE M'LEOD OF DUNVEGAN, KNIGHT. GOD SEND GOOD REST! Rorie is the contraction of Roderick. He was called Rorie *More*, that is, great Rorie, not from his size, but from his spirit. Our entertainment here was in so elegant a style, and reminded my fellow-traveller so much of England, that he became quite joyous. He laughed, and said, 'Boswell, we came in at the wrong end of this island.' 'Sir,' said I, 'it was best to keep this for the last.' He answered, 'I would have it both first and last.'

Tuesday, 14th September

Dr Johnson said in the morning, 'Is not this a fine lady?' There was not a word now of his 'impatience to be in civilized life'; though indeed I should beg pardon – he found it here. We had slept well, and lain long. After breakfast we surveyed the castle, and the garden. Mr Bethune,[187] the parish minister, Magnus M'Leod, of Claggan, brother to Talisker, and M'Leod, of Bay, two substantial gentlemen of the clan, dined with us. We had admirable venison, generous wine; in a word, all that a good table has. This was really the hall of a chief. Lady M'Leod had been much obliged to my father, who had settled by arbitration, a variety of perplexed claims between her and her relation, the Laird of Brodie, which she now repaid by particular attention to me. M'Leod started the subject of making women do penance in the church for fornication. JOHNSON. 'It is right, sir. Infamy is attached to the crime, by universal opinion, as soon as it is known. I would not be the man who would discover it, if I alone knew it, for a woman may reform; nor would I commend a parson who divulges a woman's first offence; but being once divulged, it ought to be infamous. Consider, of what importance to society the chastity of women is. Upon that all the property in the world depends. We hang a thief for stealing a sheep; but the unchastity of a woman transfers sheep, and farm and all, from the right owner. I have much more reverence for a common prostitute than for a woman who conceals her guilt. The prostitute is known. She cannot deceive: she cannot bring a strumpet into the arms of an honest man, without his knowledge.' BOSWELL. 'There is, however, a great difference between the licentiousness of a single woman, and that of a married woman.' JOHNSON. 'Yes, sir; there is a great difference between stealing a shilling, and stealing a thousand pounds; between simply taking a man's purse, and murdering him first, and then taking it. But when one begins to be vicious, it is easy to go on. Where single women are licentious, you rarely find faithful married women.' BOSWELL. 'And yet we are told that in some nations in India, the distinction is strictly observed.' JOHNSON. 'Nay, don't give us India. That puts me in mind of Montesquieu, who is really a fellow of genius too in many respects; whenever he wants to support a strange opinion, he quotes you the practice of Japan or of some other distant country, of which he knows nothing. To support polygamy, he tells you of the island of Formosa, where there are ten women born for one man. He had but to suppose another island, where there are ten men born for one woman, and so make a marriage between them.'*

* What my friend treated as so wild a supposition, has actually happened in the western islands of Scotland, if we may believe Martin, who tells it of the islands of Col and Tyr-yi, and says that it is proved by the parish registers.

At supper, Lady Macleod mentioned Dr Cadogan's book on the gout.[188] JOHNSON. 'It is a good book in general, but a foolish one in particulars. It is good in general, as recommending temperance and exercise, and cheerfulness. In that respect it is only Dr Cheyne's book told in a new way; and there should come out such a book every thirty years, dressed in the mode of the times. It is foolish, in maintaining that the gout is not hereditary, and that one fit of it, when gone, is like a fever when gone.' Lady Macleod objected that the author does not practice what he teaches.* JOHNSON. 'I cannot help that, madam. That does not make his book the worse. People are influenced more by what a man says, if his practice is suitable to it, because they are blockheads. The more intellectual people are, the readier will they attend to what a man tells them. If it is just, they will follow it, be his practice what it will. No man practises so well as he writes. I have, all my life long, been lying till noon; yet I tell all young men, and tell them with great sincerity, that nobody who does not rise early will ever do any good. Only consider! You read a book; you are convinced by it; you do not know the authour. Suppose you afterwards know him, and find that he does not practice what he teaches; are you to give up your former conviction? At this rate you would be kept in a state of equilibrium, when reading every book, till you knew how the authour practised.' 'But,' said Lady M'Leod, 'you would think better of Dr Cadogan, if he acted according to his principles.' JOHNSON. 'Why, madam, to be sure, a man who acts in the face of light, is worse than a man who does not know so much; yet I think no man should be the worse thought of for publishing good principles. There is something noble in publishing truth, though it condemns one's self.' I expressed some surprize at Cadogan's recommending good humour, as if it were quite in our power to attain it. JOHNSON. 'Why, sir, a man grows better humoured as he grows older. He improves by experience. When young, he thinks himself of great consequence, and every thing of importance. As he advances in life, he learns to think himself of no consequence, and little things of little importance; and so he becomes more patient, and better pleased. All good humour and complaisance are acquired. Naturally a child seizes directly what it sees, and thinks of pleasing itself only. By degrees, it is taught to please others, and to prefer others; and that this will ultimately produce the greatest happiness. If a man is not convinced of that, he never will practice it. Common language speaks the truth as to this: we say, a person is well *bred*.

*This was a general reflection against Dr Cadogan, when his very popular book was first published. It was said, that whatever precepts he might give to others, he himself indulged freely in the bottle. But I have since had the pleasure of becoming acquainted with him, and, if his own testimony may be believed (and I have never heard it impeached), his course of life has been conformable to his doctrine.

As it is said, that all material motion is primarily in a right line, and is never *per circuitum*,[189] never in another form, unless by some particular cause; so it may be said intellectual motion is.' Lady M'Leod asked, if no man was naturally good. JOHNSON. 'No, madam, no more than a wolf.' BOSWELL. 'Nor no woman, sir?' JOHNSON. 'No, sir.' Lady M'Leod started at this, saying, in a low voice, 'This is worse than Swift.'

M'Leod of Ulinish had come in the afternoon. We were a jovial company at supper. The laird, surrounded by so many of his clan, was to me a pleasing sight. They listened with wonder and pleasure, while Dr Johnson harangued. I am vexed that I cannot take down his full train of eloquence.

Wednesday, 15th September

The gentlemen of the clan went away early in the morning to the harbour of Lochbradale,[190] to take leave of some of their friends who were going to America. It was a very wet day. We looked at Rorie More's horn, which is a large cow's horn, with the mouth of it ornamented with silver curiously carved. It holds rather more than a bottle and a half. Every laird of M'Leod, it is said, must, as a proof of his manhood, drink it off full of claret, without laying it down. From Rorie More many of the branches of the family are descended; in particular, the Talisker branch; so that his name is much talked of. We also saw his bow, which hardly any man now can bend, and his *glaymore*, which was wielded with both hands, and is of a prodigious size. We saw here some old pieces of iron armour, immensely heavy. The broadsword now used, though called the *glaymore* (i.e. the *great sword*), is much smaller than that used in Rorie More's time.[191] There is hardly a target now to be found in the Highlands. After the disarming act, they made them serve as covers to their butter-milk barrels; a kind of change, like beating spears into pruning-hooks.

Sir George Mackenzie's *Works* (the folio edition) happened to lie in a window in the dining room. I asked Dr Johnson to look at the *Characteres Advocatorum*. He allowed him power of mind, and that he understood very well what he tells; but said, that there was too much declamation, and that the Latin was not correct. He found fault with *approprinquabant*, in the character of Gilmour.[192] I tried him with the opposition between *gloria* and *palma*, in the comparison between Gilmour and Nisbet, which Lord Hailes, in his *Catalogue of the Lords of Session*, thinks difficult to be understood. The words are, *penes illum gloria, penes hunc palma*. In a short *Account of the Kirk of Scotland*, which I published some years ago, I applied these words to the two contending parties, and explained them thus: 'The popular party has most eloquence; Dr Robertson's party most influence.' I was very desirous to hear Dr Johnson's explication. JOHNSON. 'I see no difficulty. Gilmour was admired for his parts; Nisbet carried his cause by the skill in law. *Palma* is victory.'[193] I observed, that the character of Nicholson, in this book resembled that of Burke: for it is said, in one place, *in omnes lusos & jocos se sæpe resolvebat;** and, in another, *sed accipitris more e conspectu aliquando astantium sublimi se protrahens volatu, in prædam miro impetu descendebat.*† JOHNSON. 'No, sir; I never heard Burke make a good joke in my life.' BOSWELL. 'But, sir, you will allow he is a hawk.' Dr Johnson, thinking that I meant this of his joking, said, 'No, sir, he is not the hawk there. He is the beetle in the mire.' I still adhered to my metaphor. 'But he *soars* as the hawk.' JOHNSON. 'Yes, sir; but he catches nothing.' M'Leod asked, what is the particular excellence of Burke's eloquence? JOHNSON. 'Copiousness and fertility of allusion; a power of diversifying his matter, by placing it in various relations. Burke has great information, and great command of language; though, in my opinion, it has not in every respect the highest elegance.' BOSWELL. 'Do you think, sir, that Burke has read Cicero much?' JOHNSON. 'I don't believe it, sir. Burke has great knowledge, great fluency of words, and great promptness of ideas, so that he can speak with great illustration on any subject that comes before him. He is neither like Cicero, nor like Demosthenes, nor like any one else, but speaks as well as he can.'

In the 65th page of the first volume of Sir George Mackenzie, Dr Johnson pointed out a paragraph beginning with 'Aristotle', and told me there was an error in the text, which he bade me try to discover. I was lucky enough to hit it at once. As the passage is printed, it is said that the devil answers *even* in *engines*. I corrected it to – *ever* in *ænigmas*. 'Sir,' said he, 'you are a good critick. This would have been a great thing to do in the text of an ancient authour.'

Thursday, 16th September

Last night much care was taken of Dr Johnson, who was still distressed by his cold. He had hitherto most strangely slept without a night-cap. Miss M'Leod made him a large flannel one, and he was prevailed with to drink a little brandy when he was going to bed. He has great virtue, in not drink-

*He often indulged himself in every species of pleasantry and wit.

† But like the hawk, having soared with a lofty flight to a height which the eye could not reach, he was want to swoop upon his quarry with wonderful rapidity.

ing wine or any fermented liquor, because, as he acknowledged to us, he could not do it in moderation. Lady M'Leod would hardly believe him, and said, 'I am sure, sir, you would not carry it too far.' JOHNSON. 'Nay, madam, it carried me. I took the opportunity of a long illness to leave it off. It was then prescribed to me not to drink wine; and having broken off the habit, I have never returned to it.'

In the argument on Tuesday night, about natural goodness, Dr Johnson denied that any child was better than another, but by difference of instruction; though, in consequence of greater attention being paid to instruction by one child than another, and of a variety of imperceptible causes, such as instruction being counteracted by servants, a notion was conceived, that of two children, equally well educated, one was naturally much worse than another. He owned, this morning, that one might have a greater aptitude to learn than another, and that we inherit dispositions from our parents. 'I inherited,' said he, 'a vile melancholy from my father, which has made me mad all my life, at least not sober.' Lady M'Leod wondered he should tell this. 'Madam,' said I, 'he knows that with that madness he is superior to other men.'

I have often been astonished with what exactness and perspicuity he will explain the process of any art. He this morning explained to us all the operation of coining, and, at night, all the operation of brewing, so very clearly, that Mr M'Queen said, when he heard the first, he thought he had been bred in the Mint; when he heard the second, that he had been bred a brewer.

I was elated by the thought of having been able to entice such a man to this remote part of the world. A ludicrous, yet just image presented itself to my mind, which I expressed to the company. I compared myself to a dog who has got hold of a large piece of meat, and runs away with it to a corner, where he may devour it in peace, without any fear of others taking it from him. 'In London, Reynolds, Beauclerk, and all of them, are contending who shall enjoy Dr Johnson's conversation. We are feasting upon it, undisturbed, at Dunvegan.'

It was still a storm of wind and rain. Dr Johnson however walked out with M'Leod, and saw Rorie More's cascade in full perfection. Colonel M'Leod, instead of being all life and gaiety, as I have seen him, was at present grave, and somewhat depressed by his anxious concern about M'Leod's affairs, and by finding some gentlemen of the clan by no means disposed to act a generous or affectionate part to their chief in his distress, but bargaining with him as with a stranger. However, he was agreeable and polite, and Dr Johnson said, he was a very pleasing man. My fellow-traveller and I talked of going to Sweden; and, while we were settling our plan, I expressed a pleasure in the prospect of seeing the king. JOHNSON. 'I doubt, sir, if he would speak to us.' Colonel M'Leod said, 'I am sure Mr Boswell would speak to *him*.' But, seeing me a little disconcerted by his remark, he politely added, 'and with great propriety'. Here let me offer a short defence of that propensity in my disposition, to which this gentleman alluded. It has procured me much happiness. I hope it does not deserve so hard a name as either forwardness or impudence. If I know myself, it is nothing more than an eagerness to share the society of men distinguished either by their rank or their talents, and a diligence to attain what I desire. If a man is praised for seeking knowledge, though mountains and seas are in his way, may he not be pardoned, whose ardour, in the pursuit of the same object, leads him to encounter difficulties as great, though of a different kind?

After the ladies were gone from table, we talked of the highlanders not having sheets; and this led us to consider the advantage of wearing linen. JOHNSON. 'All animal substances are less cleanly than vegetables. Wool, of which flannel is made, is an animal substance; flannel therefore is not so cleanly as linen. I remember I used to think tar dirty; but when I knew it to be only a preparation of the juice of the pine, I thought so no longer. It is not disagreeable to have the gum that oozes from a plumb-tree upon your fingers, because it is vegetable, but if you have any candle-grease, any tallow upon your fingers, you are uneasy till you rub it off. I have often thought, that, if I kept a seraglio, the ladies should all wear linen gowns, or cotton – I mean stuffs made of vegetable substances. I would have no silk; you cannot tell when it is clean: it will be very nasty before it is perceived to be so. Linen detects its own dirtiness.'

To hear the grave Dr Samuel Johnson, 'that majestick teacher of moral and religious wisdom', while sitting solemn in an arm-chair in the Isle of Sky, talk, *ex cathedra*, of his keeping a seraglio, and acknowledge that the supposition had *often* been in his thoughts, struck me so forcibly with ludicrous contrast, that I could not but laugh immoderately. He was too proud to submit, even for a moment, to be the object of ridicule, and instantly retaliated with such keen sarcastick wit, and such a variety of degrading images, of every one of which I was the object, that, though I can bear such attacks as well as most men, I yet found myself so much the sport of all the company, that I would gladly expunge from my mind every trace of this severe retort.

Talking of our friend Langton's house in Lincolnshire, he said, 'the old house of the family was burnt. A temporary building was erected in its room; and to this day they have been always adding as the family increased. It is like a shirt made for a man when he was a child, and enlarged always as he grows older.'

We talked to-night of Luther's allowing the Landgrave of Hesse two wives, and that it was with the consent of the wife to whom he was first married. JOHNSON. 'There was no harm in this, so far as she was only concerned, because *volenti non fit injuria*.[194] But it was an offence against the general order of society, and against the law of the Gospel, by which one man and one woman are to be united. No man can have two wives, but by preventing somebody else from having one.'

Friday, 17th September

After dinner yesterday, we had a conversation upon cunning. M'Leod said that he was not afraid of cunning people; but would let them play their tricks about him like monkeys. 'But,' said I, 'they scratch'; and Mr M'Queen added, 'they'll invent new tricks, as soon as you find out what they do.' JOHNSON. 'Cunning has effect from the credulity of others, rather than from the abilities of those who are cunning. It requires no extraordinary talents to lie and deceive.' This led us to consider whether it did not require great abilities to be very wicked. JOHNSON. 'It requires great abilities to have the *power* of being very wicked; but not to *be* very wicked. A man who has the power, which great abilities procure him, may use it well or ill; and it requires more abilities to use it well, than to use it ill. Wickedness is always easier than virtue; for it takes the short cut to every thing. It is much easier to steal a hundred pounds, than to get it by labour, or any other way. Consider only what act of wickedness requires great abilities to commit it, when once the person who is to do it has the power; for *there* is the distinction. It requires great abilities to conquer an army, but none to massacre it after it is conquered.'

The weather this day was rather better than any that we had since we came to Dunvegan. Mr M'Queen had often mentioned a curious piece of antiquity near this which he called a temple of the goddess Anaitis.[195] Having often talked of going to see it, he and I set out after breakfast, attended by his servant, a fellow quite like a savage. I must observe here, that in Sky there seems to be much idleness; for men and boys follow you, as colts follow passengers upon a road. The usual figure of a Sky boy, is a *lown*[196] with bare legs and feet, a dirty kilt, ragged coat and waistcoat, a bare head, and a stick in his hand, which, I suppose, is partly to help the lazy rogue to walk, partly to serve as a kind of a defensive weapon. We walked what is called two miles, but is probably four, from the castle, till we came to the sacred place. The country around is a black dreary moor on all sides, except to the sea-coast, towards which there is a view through a valley, and the farm of Bay shews some good land. The place itself is green ground, being well drained, by means of a deep glen on each side, in both of which there runs a rivulet with a good quantity of water, forming several cascades, which make a considerable appearance and sound. The first thing we came to was an earthen mound, or dyke, extending from the one precipice to the other. A little farther on, was a strong stone-wall, not high, but very thick, extending in the same manner. On the outside of it were the ruins of two houses, one on each side of the entry or gate to it. The wall is built all along of uncemented stones, but of so large a size as to make a very firm and durable rampart. It has been built all about the consecrated ground, except where the precipice is deep enough to form an enclosure of itself. The sacred spot contains more than two acres.[197] There are within it the ruins of many houses, none of them large, a *cairn*, and many graves marked by clusters of stones. Mr M'Queen insisted that the ruin of a small building, standing east and west, was actually the temple of the goddess Anaitis, where her statue was kept, and from whence processions were made to wash it in one of the brooks. There is, it must be owned, a hollow road visible for a good way from the entrance; but Mr M'Queen, with the keen eye of an antiquary, traced it much farther than I could perceive it. There is not above a foot and a half in height of the walls now remaining; and the whole extent of the building was never, I imagine, greater than an ordinary Highland house. Mr M'Queen has collected a great deal of learning on the subject of the temple of Anaitis; and I had endeavoured, in my journal, to state such particulars as might give some idea of it, and of the surrounding scenery; but from the great difficulty of describing visible objects, I found my account so unsatisfactory, that my readers would probably have exclaimed

And write about it, *Goddess*, and about it;[198]

and therefore I have omitted it.

When we got home, and were again at table with Dr Johnson, we first talked of portraits. He agreed in thinking them valuable in families. I wished to know which he preferred, fine portraits, or those of which the merit was resemblance. JOHNSON. 'Sir, their chief excellence is being like.' BOSWELL. 'Are you of that opinion as to the portraits of ancestors, whom one has never seen?' JOHNSON. 'It then becomes of more consequence that they should be like; and I would have them in the dress of the times, which makes a piece of history. One should like to see how Rorie More looked.

Truth, sir, is of the greatest value in these things.' Mr M'Queen observed, that if you think it of no consequence whether portraits are like, if they are but well painted, you may be indifferent whether a piece of history is true or not, if well told.

Dr Johnson said at breakfast to day, 'that it was but of late that historians bestowed pains and attention in consulting records, to attain to accuracy. Bacon, in writing his *History of Henry VII*, does not seem to have consulted any, but to have just taken what he found in other histories, and blended it with what he learnt by tradition.' He agreed with me that there should be a chronicle kept in every considerable family, to preserve the characters and transactions of successive generations.

After dinner I started the subject of the temple of Anaitis. Mr M'Queen had laid stress on the name given to the place by the country people, Ainnit; and added, 'I knew not what to make of this piece of antiquity, till I met with the *Anaitidis delubrum* in Lydia, mentioned by Pausanias and the elder Pliny.' Dr Johnson, with his usual acuteness, examined Mr M'Queen as to the meaning of the word Ainnit, in Erse; and it proved to be a *water-place*, or a place near water, 'which,' said Mr M'Queen, 'agrees with all the descriptions of the temples of that goddess, which were situated near rivers, that there might be water to wash the statue'. JOHNSON. 'Nay, sir, the argument from the name is gone. The name is exhausted by what we see. We have no occasion to go to a distance for what we can pick up under our feet. Had it been an accidental name, the similarity between it and Anaitis might have had something in it; but it turns out to be a mere physiological name.' Macleod said, Mr M'Queen's knowledge of etymology had destroyed his conjecture. JOHNSON. 'You have one possibility for you, and all possibilities against you. It is possible it may be the temple of Anaitis. But it is also possible that it may be a fortification; or it may be a place of Christian worship, as the first Christians often chose remote and wild places, to make an impression on the mind; or, if it was a heathen temple, it may have been built near a river, for the purpose of lustration; and there is such a multitude of divinities, to whom it may have been dedicated, that the chance of its being a temple of Anaitis is hardly any thing. It is like throwing a grain of sand upon the sea-shore to-day, and thinking you may find it to-morrow. No, sir, this temple, like many an ill-built edifice, tumbles down before it is roofed in.' In his triumph over the reverend antiquarian, he indulged himself in a conceit; for, some vestige of the *altar* of the goddess being much insisted on in support of the hypothesis, he said, 'Mr M'Queen is fighting *pro* aris *et focis*.'[199]

It was wonderful how well time passed in a remote castle, and in dreary weather. After supper, we talked of Pennant. It was objected that he was superficial. Dr Johnson defended him warmly. He said, 'Pennant has greater variety of inquiry than almost any man, and has told us more than perhaps one in ten thousand could have done, in the time that he took. He has not said what he was to tell; so you cannot find fault with him, for what he has not told. If a man comes to look for fishes, you cannot blame him if he does not attend to fowls.' 'But,' said Colonel M'Leod, 'he mentions the unreasonable rise of rents in the Highlands, and says, "the gentlemen are for emptying the bag, without filling it"; for that is the phrase he uses. Why does he not tell how to fill it?' JOHNSON. 'Sir, there is no end of negative criticism. He tells what he observes, and as much as he chooses. If he tells what is not true, you may find fault with him; but, though he tells that the land is not well cultivated, he is not obliged to tell how it may be well cultivated. If I tell that many of the highlanders go bare-footed, I am not obliged to tell how they may get shoes. Pennant tells a fact. He need go no farther, except he pleases. He exhausts nothing; and no subject whatever has yet been exhausted. But Pennant has surely told a great deal. Here is a man six feet high, and you are angry because he is not seven.' Notwithstanding this eloquent *Oratio pro Pennantio*, which they who have read this gentleman's *Tours*, and recollect the Savage and the Shopkeeper at Monboddo will probably impute to the spirit of contradiction,[200] I still think that he had better have given more attention to fewer things, than have thrown together such a number of imperfect accounts.

Saturday, 18th September

Before breakfast, Dr Johnson came up to my room, to forbid me to mention that this was his birth-day;[201] but I told him I had done it already; at which he was displeased; I suppose from wishing to have nothing particular done on his account. Lady M'Leod and I got into a warm dispute. She wanted to build a house upon a farm which she has taken, about five miles from the castle, and to make gardens and other ornaments there; all of which I approved of; but insisted that the seat of the family should always be upon the rock of Dunvegan. JOHNSON. 'Ay, in time we'll build all round this rock. You may make a very good house at the farm; but it must not be such as to tempt the Laird of M'Leod to go thither to reside. Most of the great families of England have a secondary residence, which is called a join-ture-house:[202] let the new house be of that kind.' The lady insisted that the rock was very inconvenient; that there was no place near it where a good garden could be made; that it must always be the rude place; that it was a Herculean labour to make a dinner here. I was vexed to find the alloy of modern refinement in a lady who had so much old family spirit. 'Madam,' said I, 'if once you quit this rock, there is no knowing where you may settle. You move five miles first, then to St Andrews, as the late laird did; then to Edinburgh; and so on till you end at Hampstead, or in France. No, no; keep to the rock: it is the very jewel of the estate. It looks as if it had been let down from heaven by the four corners,[203] to be the residence of a chief. Have all the comforts and conveniencies of life upon it, but never leave Rorie More's cascade.' 'But,' said she, 'is it not enough if we keep it? Must we never have more convenience than Rorie More had? He had his beef brought to dinner in one basket, and his bread in another. Why not as well be Rorie More all over, as live upon his rock? And should not we tire, in looking perpetually on this rock? It is very well for you, who have a fine place, and every thing easy, to talk thus, and think of chaining honest folks to a rock. You would not live upon it yourself.' 'Yes, madam,' said I, 'I would live upon it, were I Laird of M'Leod, and should be unhappy if I were not upon it.' JOHNSON (with a strong voice, and most determined manner). 'Madam, rather than quit the old rock, Boswell would live in the pit; he would make his bed in the dungeon.' I felt a degree of elation, at finding my resolute feudal enthusiasm thus confirmed by such a sanction. The lady was puzzled a little. She still returned to her pretty farm – rich ground, fine garden. 'Madam,' said Dr Johnson, 'were they in Asia, I would not leave the rock.' My opinion on this subject is still the same. An ancient family residence ought to be a primary object; and though the situation of Dunvegan be such that little can be done here in gardening, or pleasure-ground, yet, in addition to the veneration acquired by the lapse of time, it has many circumstances of natural grandeur, suited to the seat of a Highland chief: it has the sea, islands, rocks, hills, a noble cascade; and when the family is again in opulence, something may be done by art.

Mr Donald M'Queen went away to-day, in order to preach at Bracadale next day. We were so comfortably situated at Dunvegan, that Dr Johnson could hardly be moved from it. I proposed to him that we should leave it on Monday. 'No, sir,' said he, 'I will not go before Wednesday. I will have some more of this good.' However, as the weather was at this season so bad, and so very uncertain, and we had a great deal to do yet, Mr M'Queen and I prevail'd with him to agree to set out on Monday, if the day should be good. Mr M'Queen though it was inconvenient for him to be absent from his harvest, engaged to wait on Monday at Ulinish for us. When he was going away, Dr Johnson said, 'I shall ever retain a great regard for you'; then asked him if he had the *Rambler*. Mr M'Queen said,

'No; but my brother has it.' JOHNSON. 'Have you the *Idler?*' M'QUEEN. 'No, sir.' JOHNSON. 'Then I will order one for you at Edinburgh, which you will keep in remembrance of me.' Mr M'Queen was much pleased with this. He expressed to me, in the strongest terms, his admiration of Dr Johnson's wonderful knowledge, and every other quality for which he is distinguished. I asked Mr M'Queen, if he was satisfied with being a minister in Sky. He said he was; but he owned that his forefathers having been so long there, and his having been born there, made a chief ingredient in forming his contentment. I should have mentioned, that on our left hand, between Portree and Dr Macleod's house, Mr M'Queen told me there had been a college of the Knights Templars; that tradition said so; and that there was a ruin remaining of their church, which had been burnt: but I confess Dr Johnson has weakened my belief in remote tradition. In the dispute about Anaitis, Mr M'Queen said, Asia Minor was peopled by Scythians, and, as they were the ancestors of the Celts, the same religion might be in Asia Minor and Sky. JOHNSON. 'Alas! sir, what can a nation that has not letters tell of its original? I have always difficulty to be patient when I hear authors gravely quoted, as giving accounts of savage nations, which accounts they had from the savages themselves. What can the M'Craas tell about themselves a thousand years ago? There is no tracing the connection of ancient nations, but by language; and therefore I am always sorry when any language is lost, because languages are the pedigree of nations. If you find the same language in distant countries, you may be sure that the inhabitants of each have been the same people; that is to say, if you find the languages a good deal the same; for a word here and there being the same, will not do. Thus Butler, in his *Hudibras*, remembering that *Penguin*, in the Straits of Magellan, signifies a bird with a white head, and that the same word has, in Wales, the signification of a white-headed wench (*pen* head, and *guin* white), by way of ridicule, concludes that the people of those Straits are Welch.'[204]

A young gentleman of the name of M'Lean, nephew to the Laird of the Isle of Muck, came this morning; and, just as we sat down to dinner, came the Laird of the Isle of Muck himself, his lady, sister to Talisker, two other ladies their relations, and a daughter of the late M'Leod of Hamer, who wrote a treatise on the second sight, under the designation of *Theophilus Insulanus*. It was somewhat droll to hear this laird called by his title. *Muck* would have founded ill; so he was called *Isle of Muck*, which went off with great readiness. The name, as now written, is unseemly, but is not so bad in the original Erse, which is *Mouach*, signifying the Sows' Island. Buchanan calls it *Insula Porcorum*. It is so called from its form. Some call it Isle of *Monk*. The laird insists that this is the proper name. It was formerly church-land belonging to Icolmkill, and a hermit lived in it. It is two miles long, and about three quarters of a mile broad. The laird said, he had seven score of souls upon it. Last year he had eighty persons inoculated, mostly children, but some of them eighteen years of age. He agreed with the surgeon to come and do it, at half a crown a head. It is very fertile in corn, of which they export some; and its coasts abound in fish. A taylor comes there six times in a year. They get a good blacksmith from the Isle of Egg.

Sunday, 19th September

It was rather worse weather than any that we had yet. At breakfast Dr Johnson said, 'Some cunning men choose fools for their wives, thinking to manage them, but they always fail. There is a spaniel fool and a mule fool. The spaniel fool may be made to do by beating. The mule fool will neither do by words or blows; and the spaniel fool often turns mule at last: and suppose a fool to be made do pretty well, you must have the continual trouble of making her do. Depend upon it, no woman is the worse for sense and knowledge.' Whether afterwards he meant merely to say a polite thing, or to give his opinion, I could not be sure; but he added, 'Men know that women are an over-match for them, and therefore they choose the weakest or most ignorant. If they did not think so, they never could be afraid of women knowing as much as themselves.' In justice to the sex, I think it but candid to acknowledge, that, in a subsequent conversation, he told me that he was serious in what he had said.

He came to my room this morning before breakfast, to read my *Journal*, which he has done all along. He often before said, 'I take great delight in reading it.' To-day he said, 'You improve: it grows better and better.' I observed, there was a danger of my getting a habit of writing in a slovenly manner. 'Sir,' said he, 'it is not written in a slovenly manner. It might be printed, were the subject fit for printing.'* While Mr Beaton[205] preached to us in the dining-room, Dr Johnson sat in his own room, where I saw lying before him a volume of Lord Bacon's works, the *Decay of Christian Piety*, Monboddo's *Origin of Language*, and Sterne's *Sermons*. He asked me to-day, how it happened that we were so little together: I told him, my *Journal* took up much time. Yet, on reflection, it appeared strange to me, that although I will run from one end of London to another, to pass an

---

* As I have faithfully recorded so many minute particulars, I hope I shall be pardoned for inserting so flattering an encomium on what is now offered to the publick.

hour with him, I should omit to seize any spare time to be in his company, when I am settled in the same house with him. But my *Journal* is really a task of much time and labour, and he forbids me to contract it.

I omitted to mention, in its place, that Dr Johnson told Mr M'Queen that he had found the belief of the second sight universal in Sky, except among the clergy, who seemed determined against it. I took the liberty to observe to Mr M'Queen, that the clergy were actuated by a kind of vanity. 'The world,' say they, 'takes us to be credulous men in a remote corner. We'll shew them that we are more enlightened than they think.' The worthy man said, that his disbelief of it was from his not finding sufficient evidence; but I could perceive that he was prejudiced against it.

After dinner to-day, we talked of the extraordinary fact of Lady Grange's being sent to St Kilda, and confined there for several years, without any means of relief.* Dr Johnson said, if M'Leod would let it be known that he had such a place for naughty ladies, he might make it a very profitable island. We had, in the course of our tour, heard of St Kilda poetry. Dr Johnson observed, 'it must be very poor, because they have very few images.' BOSWELL. 'There may be a poetical genius shewn in combining these, and in making poetry of them.' JOHNSON. 'Sir, a man cannot make fire but in proportion as he has fuel. He cannot coin guineas but in

---

* The true story of this lady, which happened in this century, is as frightfully romantick as if it had been the fiction of a gloomy fancy. She was the wife of one of the Lords of Session in Scotland, a man of the very first blood of his country. For some mysterious reasons, which have never been discovered,[206] she was seized and carried off in the dark, she knew not by whom, and by nightly journies was conveyed to the Highland shores, from whence she was transported by sea to the remote rock of St Kilda, where she remained, amongst its few wild inhabitants, a forlorn prisoner, but had a constant supply of provisions, and a woman to wait on her. No inquiry was made after her, till she at last found means to convey a letter to a confidential friend, by the daughter of a Catechist, who concealed it in a clue of yarn. Information being thus obtained at Edinburgh, a ship was sent to bring her off; but intelligence of this being received, she was conveyed to M'Leod's island of Herries, where she died.

In Carstares's *State Papers*, we find an authentick narrative of Connor, a Catholick priest, who turned Protestant, being seized by some of Lord Seaforth's people, and detained prisoner in the island of Herries several years; he was fed with bread and water, and lodged in a house where he was exposed to the rains and cold. Sir James Ogilvy writes (June 18, 1667) that the Lord Chancellor, the Lord Advocate, and himself, were to meet next day, to take effectual methods to have this redressed. Connor was then still detained (p. 310). This shews what private oppression might in the last century be practised in the Hebrides.

In the same collection, the Earl of Argyle gives a picturesque account of an embassy from 'the great M'Neil of Barra', as that insular chief used to be denominated. 'I received a letter yesterday from M'Neil of Barra, who lives very far off, sent by a gentleman in all formality, offering his service, which had made you laugh to see his entry. His style of his letter runs as if he were of another kingdom' (p. 643).

proportion as he has gold.' At tea he talked of his intending to go to Italy in 1775. M'Leod said, he would like Paris better. JOHNSON. 'No, sir; there are none of the French literati now alive, to visit whom I would cross a sea. I can find in Buffon's book all that he can say.'*[207]

After supper he said, 'I am sorry that prize-fighting is gone out; every art should be preserved, and the art of defence is surely important.[208] It is absurd that our soldiers should have swords, and not be taught the use of them. Prize-fighting made people accustomed not to be alarmed at seeing their own blood, or feeling a little pain from a wound. I think the heavy *glaymore* was an ill-contrived weapon. A man could only strike once with it. It employed both his hands, and he must of course be soon fatigued with wielding it; so that if his antagonist could only keep playing a while, he was sure of him. I would fight with a dirk against Rorie More's sword. I could ward off a blow with a dirk, and then run in upon my enemy. When within that heavy sword, I have him; he is quite helpless, and I could stab him at my leisure, like a calf. It is thought by sensible military men, that the English do not enough avail themselves of their superior strength of body against the French; for that must always have a great advantage in pushing with bayonets. I have heard an officer say, that if women could be made to stand, they would do as well as men in a mere interchange of bullets from a distance: but, if a body of men should come close up to them, then to be sure they must be overcome; now (said he), in the same manner the weaker-bodied French must be overcome by our strong soldiers.'

The subject of duelling was introduced. JOHNSON. 'There is no case in England where one or other of the combatants *must* die: if you have overcome your adversary by disarming him, that is sufficient, though you should not kill him; your honour, or the honour of your family, is restored, as much as it can be by a duel. It is cowardly to force your antagonist to renew the combat, when you know that you have the advantage of him by superior skill. You might just as well go and cut his throat while he is asleep in his bed. When a duel begins, it is supposed there may be an equality; because it is not always skill that prevails. It depends much on presence of mind; nay on accidents. The wind may be in a man's face. He may fall. Many such things may decide the superiority. A man is sufficiently punished, by being called out, and subjected to the risk that is in a duel.' But on my suggesting that the injured person is equally subjected to risk, he fairly owned he could not explain the rationality of duelling.

*I doubt the justice of my fellow-traveller's remark concerning the French literati, many of whom, I am told, have considerable merit in conversation, as well as in their writings. That of Monsieur de Buffon, in particular, I am well assured is highly instructive and entertaining.

Monday, 20th September

When I awaked, the storm was higher still. It abated about nine, and the sun shone; but it rained again very soon, and it was not a day for travelling. At breakfast, Dr Johnson told us, 'there was once a pretty good tavern in Catharine Street in the Strand, where very good company met in an evening, and each man called for his own half pint of wine, or gill, if he pleased; they were frugal men, and nobody paid but for what he himself drank. The house furnished no supper; but a woman attended with muttonpies, which any body might purchase. I was introduced to this company by Cumming the Quaker, and used to go there sometimes when I drank wine. In the last age, when my mother lived in London, there were two sets of people, those who gave the wall, and those who took it; the peaceable and the quarrelsome. When I returned to Lichfield, after having been in London, my mother asked me, whether I was one of those who gave the wall, or those who took it. Now, it is fixed that every man keeps to the right; or, if one is taking the wall, another yields it, and it is never a dispute.' He was very severe on a lady, whose name was mentioned.[209] He said, he would have sent her to St Kilda. That she was as bad as negative badness could be, and stood in the way of what was good: that insipid beauty would not go a great way; and that such a woman might be cut out of a cabbage, if there was a skilful artificer.

M'Leod was too late in coming to breakfast. Dr Johnson said, laziness was worse than the toothache. BOSWELL. 'I cannot agree with you, sir; a bason of cold water, or a horse whip, will cure laziness.' JOHNSON. 'No, sir; it will only put off the fit; it will not cure the disease. I have been trying to cure my laziness all my life, and could not do it.' BOSWELL. 'But if a man does in a shorter time what might be the labour of a life, there is nothing to be said against him.' JOHNSON (perceiving at once that I alluded to him and his *Dictionary*). 'Suppose that flattery to be true, the consequence would be, that the world would have no right to censure a man; but that will not justify him to himself.'

After breakfast, he said to me, 'A Highland chief should now endeavour to do every thing to raise his rents, by means of the industry of his people. Formerly, it was right for him to have his house full of idle fellows; they were his defenders, his servants, his dependants, his friends. Now they may be better employed. The system of things is now so much altered, that the family cannot have influence but by riches, because it has no longer the power of ancient feudal times. An individual of a family may have it; but it cannot now belong to a family, unless you could have a perpetuity of men with the same views. M'Leod has four times the land that the Duke of Bedford has. I think, with his spirit, he may in time make himself the greatest man in the king's dominions; for land may always be improved to a certain degree. I would never have any man sell land, to throw money into the funds, as is often done, or to try any other species of trade. Depend upon it, this rage of trade will destroy itself. You and I shall not see it; but the time will come when there will be an end of it. Trade is like gaming. If a whole company are gamesters, play must cease; for there is nothing to be won. When all nations are traders, there is nothing to be gained by trade, and it will stop first where it is brought to the greatest perfection. Then the proprietors of land only will be the great men.' I observed, it was hard that M'Leod should find ingratitude in so many of his people. JOHNSON. 'Sir, gratitude is a fruit of great cultivation; you do not find it among gross people.' I doubt of this. Nature seems to have implanted gratitude in all living creatures. The lion, mentioned by Aulus Gellius, had it.* It appears to me that culture, which brings luxury and selfishness with it, has a tendency rather to weaken than promote this affection.

Dr Johnson said this morning, when talking of our setting out, that he was in the state in which Lord Bacon represents kings. He desired the end, but did not like the means. He wished much to get home, but was unwilling to travel in Sky. 'You are like kings too in this, sir,' said I, 'that you must act under the direction of others.'

Tuesday, 21st September

The uncertainty of our present situation having prevented me from receiving any letters from home for some time, I could not help being uneasy. Dr Johnson had an advantage over me, in this respect, he having no wife or child to occasion anxious apprehensions in his mind. It was a good morning; so we resolved to set out. But, before quitting this castle, where we have been so well entertained, let me give a short description of it.

Along the edge of the rock, there are the remains of a wall, which is now covered with ivy. A square court is formed by buildings of different ages, particularly some towers, said to be of great antiquity; and at one place there is a row of false cannon of stone. There is a very large unfinished pile, four stories high, which we were told was here when Leod, the first of this family, came from the Isle of Man, married the heiress of the M'Crails, the ancient possessors of Dunvegan, and afterwards acquired

* Aul. Gellius, Lib. v. c. xiv.

by conquest as much land as he had got by marriage. He surpassed the house of Austria; for he was *felix* both *bella genere* et *nubere.*[210] John Breck M'Leod, the grandfather of the late laird, began to repair the castle, or rather to complete it: but he did not live to finish his undertaking. Not doubting, however, that he should do it, he, like those who have had their epitaphs written before they died, ordered the following inscription, composed by the minister of the parish, to be cut upon a broad stone above one of the lower windows, where it still remains to celebrate what was not done, and to serve as a memento of the uncertainty of life, and the presumption of man:

Joannes Macleod Beganoduni Dominus gentis suæ Philarchus, Durinesiæ Haraiæ Vaternesiæ, &c: Baro D. Floræ Macdonald matrimoniali vinculo conjugatus turrem hanc Beganodunensem proavorum habitaculum longe vetustissimum diu penitus labefectatam Anno æræ vulgaris MDCLXXXVI instauravit.

Quem stabilire juvat proavorum tecta vetusta,
Omne scelus fugiat, justitiamque colat.
Vertit in aerias turres magalia virtus,
Inque casas humiles tecta superba nefas.[211]

M'Leod and Talisker accompanied us. We passed by the parish church of Durinish. The church-yard is not enclosed, but a pretty murmuring brook runs along one side of it. In it is a pyramid erected to the memory of Thomas Lord Lovat, by his son Lord Simon, who suffered on Towerhill. It is of freestone, and, I suppose, about thirty feet high.[212] There is an inscription on a piece of white marble inserted in it, which I suspect to have been the composition of Lord Lovat himself, being much in his pompous style:

This pyramid was erected by SIMON LORD FRASER of LOVAT, in honour of Lord THOMAS his Father, a Peer of Scotland, and Chief of the great and ancient clan of the FRASERS. Being attacked for his birthright by the family of ATHOLL, then in power and favour with KING WILLIAM, yet, by the valour and fidelity of his clan, and the assistance of the CAMPBELLS, the old friends and allies of his family, he defended his birthright with such greatness and fermety of soul, and such valour and activity, that he was an honour to his name, and a good pattern to all brave Chiefs of clans. He died in the month of May, 1699, in the 63d year of his age, in Dunvegan, the house of the LAIRD of MAC LEOD, whose sister he had married: by whom he had the above SIMON LORD FRASER, and several other children. And, for the great love he bore to the family of MAC LEOD, he desired to be buried near his wife's relations, in the place where two of her uncles lay. And his son LORD SIMON, to shew to posterity his great affection for his mother's kindred, the brave MAC LEODS, chooses rather to leave his father's bones with them, than carry them to his own burial-place, near Lovat.

I have preserved this inscription, though of no great value, thinking it characteristical of a man who has made some noise in the world. Dr Johnson said, it was poor stuff, such as Lord Lovat's butler might have written.

I observed, in this church-yard, a parcel of people assembled at a funeral, before the grave was dug. The coffin, with the corpse in it, was placed on the ground, while the people alternately assisted in making a grave. One man, at a little distance, was busy cutting a long turf for it, with the crooked spade which is used in Sky; a very aukward instrument. The iron part of it is like a plough-coulter. It has a rude tree for a handle, in which a wooden pin is placed for the foot to press upon. A traveller might, without further inquiry, have set this down as the mode of burying in Sky. I was told, however, that the usual way is to have a grave previously dug.

I observed to-day, that the common way of carrying home their grain here is in loads on horse-back. They have also a few sleds, or *cars*, as we call them in Ayrshire, clumsily made, and rarely used.

We got to Ulinish about six o'clock, and found a very good farm-house, of two stories. Mr M'Leod of Ulinish, the sheriff-substitute of the island, was a plain honest gentleman, a good deal like an English justice of peace; not much given to talk, but sufficiently sagacious, and somewhat droll. His daughter, though she was never out of Sky, was a very well-bred woman. Our reverend friend, Mr Donald M'Queen, kept his appointment, and met us here.

Talking of Phipps's voyage to the North Pole,[213] Dr Johnson observed, that it 'was conjectured that our former navigators have kept too near land, and so have found the sea frozen far north, because the land hinders the free motion of the tide; but, in the wide ocean, where the waves tumble at their full convenience, it is imagined that the frost does not take effect'.

Wednesday, 22d September

In the morning I walked out, and saw a ship, the *Margaret* of Clyde, pass by with a number of emigrants on board. It was a melancholy sight. After breakfast, we went to see what was called a subterraneous house, about a mile off. It was upon the side of a rising-ground. It was discovered by a fox's having taken up his abode in it, and in chasing him, they dug into it. It was very narrow and low, and seemed about forty feet in length. Near it, we found the foundations of several small huts, built of stone. Mr M'Queen, who is always for making every thing as ancient as possible, boasted that it was the dwelling of some of the first inhabitants of the island, and observed, what a curiosity it was to find here a specimen of the houses of the Aborigines, which he believed could be found no where else; and it was plain that they lived without fire. Dr Johnson remarked, that they who made this were not in the rudest state; for that it was more difficult to make *it* than to build a house; therefore certainly those who made it were in possession of houses, and had this only as a hiding-place. It appeared to me, that the vestiges of houses, just by it, confirmed Dr Johnson's opinion.

From an old tower, near this place, is an extensive view of Loch Braccadil, and, at a distance, of the isles of Barra and South Uist; and on the landside, the Cuillin, a prodigious range of mountains, capped with rocky pinnacles in a strange variety of shapes. They resemble the mountains near Corté in Corsica, of which there is a very good print. They make part of a great range for deer, which, though entirely devoid of trees, is in these countries called a forest.²¹⁴

In the afternoon, Ulinish carried us in his boat to an island possessed by him, where we saw an immense cave, much more deserving the title of *antrum immane* than that of the Sybil described by Virgil, which I likewise have visited.²¹⁵ It is one hundred and eighty feet long, about thirty feet broad, and at least thirty feet high. This cave, we were told, had a remarkable echo; but we found none. They said it was owing to the great rains having made it damp. Such are the excuses by which the exaggeration of Highland narratives is palliated. There is a plentiful garden at Ulinish (a great rarity in Sky), and several trees; and near the house is a hill, which has an Erse name, signifying 'the hill of strife', where, Mr M'Queen informed us, justice was of old administered. It is like the *mons placiti* of Scone, or those hills which are called *laws*, such as Kelly *law*, North Berwick *law*, and several others. It is singular that this spot should happen now to be the sheriff's residence.

We had a very cheerful evening, and Dr Johnson talked a good deal on the subject of literature. Speaking of the noble family of Boyle, he said, that all the Lord Orrerys, till the present, had been writers. The first wrote several plays; the second was Bentley's antagonist; the third wrote the *Life of Swift*, and several other things; his son Hamilton wrote some papers in the *Adventurer* and *World*. He told us, he was well acquainted with Swift's Lord Orrery. He said, he was a feeble-minded man; that, on the publication of Dr Delany's *Remarks* on his book, he was so much alarmed that he was afraid to read them. Dr Johnson comforted him, by telling him they were both in the right; that Delany had seen most of the good side of Swift, Lord Orrery most of the bad. M'Leod asked, if it was not wrong in Orrery to expose the defects of a man with whom he lived in intimacy. JOHNSON. 'Why no, sir, after the man is dead; for then it is done historically.' He added, 'If Lord Orrery had been rich, he would have been a very liberal patron. His conversation was like his writings, neat and elegant, but without strength. He grasped at more than his abilities could reach; tried to pass for a better talker, a better writer, and a better thinker than he was. There was a quarrel between him and his father, in which his father was to blame; because it arose from the son's not allowing his wife to keep company with his father's mistress. The old lord shewed his resentment in his will – leaving his library from his son, and assigning, as his reason, that he could not make use of it.'

I mentioned the affectation of Orrery, in ending all his letters on the *Life of Swift* in studied varieties of phrase, and never in the common mode of 'I am', &c. an observation which I remember to have been made several years ago by old Mr Sheridan. This species of affectation in writing, as a foreign lady of distinguished talents once remarked to me, is almost peculiar to the English. I took up a volume of Dryden, containing the *Conquest of Granada*, and several other plays, of which all the dedications had such studied conclusions. Dr Johnson said, such conclusions were more elegant, and, in addressing persons of high rank (as when Dryden dedicated to the Duke of York), they were likewise more respectful. I agreed that *there* it was much better: it was making his escape from the royal presence with a genteel sudden timidity, in place of having the resolution to stand still, and make a formal bow.

Lord Orrery's unkind treatment of his son in his will, led us to talk of the dispositions a man should have when dying. I said, I did not see why a man should act differently with respect to those of whom he thought ill when in health, merely because he was dying. JOHNSON. 'I should not scruple to speak against a party, when dying; but should not do it against an individual. It is told of Sixtus Quintus,[216] that on his death-bed, in the intervals of his last pangs, he signed death-warrants.' Mr M'Queen said, he should not do so; he would have more tenderness of heart. JOHNSON. 'I believe I should not either; but Mr M'Queen and I are cowards. It would not be from tenderness of heart; for the heart is as tender when a man is in health as when he is sick, though his resolution may be stronger. Sixtus Quintus was a sovereign as well as a priest; and, if the criminals deserved death, he was doing his duty to the last. You would not think a judge died ill, who should be carried off by an apoplectick fit while pronouncing sentence of death. Consider a class of men whose business it is to distribute death: soldiers, who die scattering bullets. Nobody thinks they die ill on that account.'

Talking of biography, he said, he did not think that the life of any literary man in England had been well written. Beside the common incidents of life, it should tell us his studies, his mode of living, the means by which he attained to excellence, and his opinion of his own works.[217] He told us, he had sent Derrick to Dryden's relations, to gather materials for his *Life*; and he believed Derrick had got all that he himself should have got; but it was nothing. He added, he had a kindness for Derrick, and was sorry he was dead.

His notion as to the poems published by Mr M'Pherson, as the works of Ossian, was not shaken here. Mr M'Queen always evaded the point of authenticity, saying only that Mr M'Pherson's pieces fell far short of those he knew in Erse, which were said to be Ossian's. JOHNSON. 'I hope they do. I am not disputing that you may have poetry of great merit; but that M'Pherson's is not a translation from ancient poetry. You do not believe it. I say before you, you do not believe it, though you are very willing that the world should believe it.' Mr M'Queen made no answer to this. Dr Johnson proceeded, 'I look upon M'Pherson's *Fingal* to be as gross an imposition as ever the world was troubled with. Had it been really an ancient work, a true specimen how men thought at that time, it would have been a curiosity of the first rate. As a modern production, it is nothing.' He said, he could never get the meaning of an Erse song explained to him. They told him, the chorus was generally unmeaning. 'I take it,' said he, 'Erse songs are like a song which I remember: it was composed in Queen Elizabeth's time, on the Earl of Essex; and the burthen was

"Radaratoo, radarate, radara tadara tandore."'

'But surely,' said Mr M'Queen, 'there were words to it, which had meaning.' JOHNSON. 'Why, yes, sir; I recollect a stanza, and you shall have it:

"O! then bespoke the prentices all,
Living in London, both proper and tall,
For Essex's sake they would fight all.
    Radaratoo, radarate, radara, tadara, tandore."'*

---

*This droll quotation, I have since found, was from a song in honour of the Earl of Essex, called 'Queen Elizabeth's Champion', which is preserved in a collection of *Old Ballads*, in three volumes, published in London in different years, between 1720 and 1730. The full verse is as follows:

Oh! then bespoke the prentices all,
Living in London, both proper and tall,
In a kind letter sent straight to the Queen,
For Essex's sake they would fight all.
        Raderer too, tandaro te,
        Raderer, tandorer, tan do re.

When Mr M'Queen began again to expatiate on the beauty of Ossian's poetry, Dr Johnson entered into no further controversy, but, with a pleasant smile, only cried, 'Ay, ay; *Radaratoo, radarate.*'

Thursday, 23d September

I took *Fingal* down to the parlour in the morning, and tried a test proposed by Mr Roderick M'Leod, son to Ulinish. Mr M'Queen had said he had some of the poem in the original. I desired him to mention any passage in the printed book, of which he could repeat the original. He pointed out one in page 50 of the quarto edition, and read the Erse, while Mr Roderick M'Leod and I looked on the English; and Mr M'Leod said, that it was pretty like what Mr M'Queen had recited. But when Mr M'Queen read a description of Cuchullin's sword in Erse, together with a translation of it in English verse, by Sir James Foulis, Mr M'Leod said, that was much more like than Mr M'Pherson's translation of the former passage. Mr M'Queen then repeated in Erse a description of one of the horses in Cuchillin's car. Mr M'Leod said, Mr M'Pherson's English was nothing like it.

When Dr Johnson came down, I told him that I had now obtained some evidence concerning *Fingal*; for that Mr M'Queen had repeated a passage in the original Erse, which Mr M'Pherson's translation was pretty like; and reminded him that he himself had once said, he did not require Mr M'Pherson's Ossian to be more like the original than Pope's Homer. JOHNSON. 'Well, sir, this is just what I always maintained. He has found names, and stories, and phrases, nay passages in old songs, and with them has blended his own compositions, and so made what he gives to the world as the translation of an ancient poem.' If this was the case, I observed, it was wrong to publish it as a poem in six books. JOHNSON. 'Yes, sir; and to ascribe it to a time too when the Highlanders knew nothing of *books*, and nothing of *six*; or perhaps were got the length of counting six. We have been told, by Condamine, of a nation[218] that could count no more than four. This should be told to Monboddo; it would help him.[219] There is as much charity in helping a man down-hill, as in helping him up-hill.' BOSWELL. 'I don't think there is as much charity.' JOHNSON. 'Yes, sir, if his *tendency* be downwards. Till he is at the bottom, he flounders; get him once there, and he is quiet. Swift tells, that Stella had a trick, which she learned from Addison, of encouraging a man in absurdity, instead of endeavouring to extricate him.'

Mr M'Queen's answers to the inquiries concerning Ossian were so unsatisfactory, that I could not help observing, that, were he examined in a court of justice, he would find himself under a necessity of being more explicit. JOHNSON. 'Sir, he has told Blair a little too much, which is published; and he sticks to it. He is so much at the head of things here, that he has never been accustomed to be closely examined; and so he goes on quite smoothly.' BOSWELL. 'He has never had any body to work him.' JOHNSON. 'No, sir; and a man is seldom disposed to work himself; though he ought to work himself, to be sure.' Mr M'Queen made no reply.*

Having talked of the strictness with which witnesses are examined in courts of justice, Dr Johnson told us, that Garrick, though accustomed to face multitudes, when produced as a witness in Westminster Hall, was so disconcerted by a new mode of publick appearance, that he could not understand what was asked. It was a cause where an actor claimed a *free benefit*; that is to say, a benefit without paying the expence of the house; but the meaning of the term was disputed. Garrick was asked, 'Sir, have you a free benefit?' 'Yes.' 'Upon what terms have you it?' 'Upon ... the terms ... of ... a free benefit.' He was dismissed as one from whom no information could be obtained. Dr Johnson is often too hard on our friend Mr Garrick. When I asked him, why he did not mention him in the Preface to his Shakspeare, he said, 'Garrick has been liberally paid for any thing he has done for Shakspeare. If I should praise him, I should much more praise the nation who paid him. He has not made Shakspeare better known;† he cannot illustrate Shakspeare: So I have reasons enough against mentioning him, were reasons necessary. There should be reasons *for* it.' I spoke of Mrs Montague's very high praises of Garrick.[220] JOHNSON. 'Sir, it is fit she should say so much, and I should say nothing. Reynolds is fond of her book, and

---

*I think it but justice to say, that I believe Dr Johnson meant to ascribe Mr M'Queen's conduct to inaccuracy and enthusiasm, and did not mean any severe imputation against him.

† It has been triumphantly asked, 'Had not the plays of Shakspeare lain dormant for many years before the appearance of Mr Garrick? Did he not exhibit the most excellent of them frequently for thirty years together, and render them extremely popular by his own inimitable performance?' He undoubtedly did. But Dr Johnson's assertion has been misunderstood. Knowing as well as the objectors what has been just stated, he must necessarily have meant, that 'Mr Garrick did not as *a critick* make Shakspeare better known; he did not *illustrate* any one *passage* in any of his plays by acuteness of disquisition, sagacity of conjecture:' and what had been done with any degree of excellence in *that* way was the proper and immediate subject of his preface. I may add in support of this explanation the following anecdote, related to me by one of the ablest commentators on Shakspeare, who knew much of Dr Johnson: 'Now I have quitted the theatre,' cries Garrick, 'I will sit down and read Shakspeare.' ' 'Tis time you should,' exclaimed Johnson, 'for I much doubt if you ever examined one of his plays from the first scene to the last.'

I wonder at it; for neither I, nor Beauclerk, nor Mrs Thrale, could get through it.'*

Last night Dr Johnson gave us an account of the whole process of tanning, and of the nature of milk, and the various operations upon it, as making

*No man has less inclination to controversy than I have, particularly with a lady. But as I have claimed, and am conscious of being entitled to, credit, for the strictest fidelity, my respect for the publick obliges me to take notice of an insinuation which tends to impeach it.

Mrs Piozzi (late Mrs Thrale), to her *Anecdotes of Dr Johnson*, added the following postscript:

Naples, Feb. 10, 1786.

Since the foregoing went to the press, having seen a passage from Mr Boswell's *Tour to the Hebrides*, in which it is said, that I could not get through Mrs Montague's *Essay on Shakspeare*, I do not delay a moment to declare, that, on the contrary, I have always commended it myself, and heard it commended by every one else; and few things would give me more concern than to be thought incapable of tasting, or unwilling to testify my opinion of its excellence.

It is remarkable that this postscript is so expressed, as not to point out the person who said that Mrs Thrale could not get through Mrs Montague's book; and therefore I think it necessary to remind Mrs Piozzi, that the assertion concerning her was Dr Johnson's, and not mine. The second observation that I shall make on this postscript is, that it does not deny the fact asserted, though I must acknowledge from the praise it bestows on Mrs Montague's book, it may have been designed to convey that meaning.

What Mrs Thrale's opinion is or was, or what she may or may not have said to Dr Johnson concerning Mrs Montague's book, it is not necessary for me to inquire. It is only incumbent on me to ascertain what Dr Johnson said to me. I shall therefore confine myself to a very short state of the fact.

The unfavourable opinion of Mrs Montague's book, which Dr Johnson is here reported to have given, is known to have been that which is uniformly expressed, as many of his friends well remember. So much for the authenticity of the paragraph, as far as it relates to his own sentiments. The words containing the assertion, to which Mrs Piozzi objects, are printed from my manuscript *Journal*, and were taken down at the time. The *Journal* was read by Dr Johnson, who pointed out some inaccuracies, which I corrected, but did not mention any inaccuracy in the paragraph in question: and what is still more material, and very flattering to me, a considerable part of my *Journal*, containing this paragraph, *was read several years ago by Mrs Thrale herself*, who had it for some time in her possession, and returned it to me, without intimating that Dr Johnson had mistaken her sentiments.

When the first edition of my *Journal* was passing through the press, it occurred to me, that a peculiar delicacy was necessary to be observed in reporting the opinion of one literary lady concerning the performance of another; and I had such scruples on that head, that in the proof sheet I struck out the name of Mrs Thrale from the above paragraph, and two or three hundred copies of my book were actually printed and published without it; of these Sir Joshua Reynolds's copy happened to be one. But while the sheet was working off, a friend, for whose opinion I have great respect, suggested that I had no right to deprive Mrs Thrale of the high honour which Dr Johnson had done her, by stating her opinion along with that of Mr Beauclerk, as coinciding with, and, as it were, sanctioning his own. The observation appeared to me so weighty and conclusive, that I hastened to the printing house, and, as a piece of justice, restored Mrs Thrale to that place from which a too scrupulous delicacy had excluded her.

On this simple state of facts I shall make no observation whatever.

whey, &c. His variety of information is surprizing; and it gives one much satisfaction to find such a man bestowing his attention on the useful arts of life. Ulinish was much struck with his knowledge; and said, 'He is a great orator, sir; it is musick to hear this man speak.' A strange thought struck me, to try if he knew any thing of an art, or whatever it should be called, which is no doubt very useful in life, but which lies far out of the way of a philosopher and poet; I mean the trade of a butcher. I enticed him into the subject, by connecting it with the various researches into the manners and customs of uncivilized nations, that have been made by our late navigators into the South Seas. I began with observing, that Mr (now Sir Joseph) Banks tells us, that the art of slaughtering animals was not known in Otaheite, for, instead of bleeding to death their dogs (a common food with them), they strangle them. This he told me himself; and I supposed that their hogs were killed in the same way. Dr Johnson said, 'This must be owing to their not having knives, though they have sharp stones with which they can cut a carcase in pieces tolerably.' By degrees, he shewed that he knew something even of butchery. 'Different animals,' said he, 'are killed differently. An ox is knocked down, and a calf stunned; but a sheep has its throat cut, without any thing being done to stupify it. The butchers have no view to the ease of the animals, but only to make them quiet, for their own safety and convenience. A sheep can give them little trouble. Hales is of opinion, that every animal should be blooded, without having any blow given to it, because it bleeds better.' BOSWELL. 'That would be cruel.' JOHNSON. 'No, sir; there is not much pain, if the jugular vein be properly cut.' Pursuing the subject, he said, the kennels[221] of Southwark ran with blood two or three days in the week; that he was afraid there were slaughter-houses in more streets in London than one supposes (speaking with a kind of horrour of butchering), and yet, he added, 'any of us would kill a cow, rather than not have beef'. I said we *could* not. 'Yes,' said he, 'any one may. The business of a butcher is a trade indeed, that is to say, there is an apprenticeship served to it; but it may be learnt in a month.'

I mentioned a club in London, at the Boar's Head in Eastcheap, the very tavern where Falstaff and his joyous companions met; the members of which all assume Shakspeare's characters. One is Falstaff, another Prince Henry, another Bardolph, and so on. JOHNSON. 'Don't be of it, sir. Now that you have a name, you must be careful to avoid many things, not bad in themselves, but which will lessen your character.* This every man who has a

---

* I do not see why I might not have been of this club without lessening my character. But Dr Johnson's caution against supposing one's self concealed in London, may be very useful to prevent some people from doing many things, not only foolish, but criminal.

name must observe. A man who is not publickly known may live in London as he pleases, without any notice being taken of him; but it is wonderful how a person of any consequence is watched. There was a Member of Parliament, who wanted to prepare himself to speak on a question that was to come in the House; and he and I were to talk it over together. He did not wish it should be known that he talked with me; so he would not let me come to his house, but came to mine. Some time after he had made his speech in the house, Mrs Cholmondeley, a very airy lady, told me, "Well, you could make nothing of him!" naming the gentleman, which was a proof that he was watched. I had once some business to do for government, and I went to Lord North's. Precaution was taken that it should not be known. It was dark before I went; yet a few days after I was told, "Well, you have been with Lord North." That the door of the Prime Minister should be watched, is not strange; but that a Member of Parliament should be watched, or that my door should be watched, is wonderful.'

We set out this morning on our way to Talisker, in Ulinish's boat, having taken leave of him and his family. Mr Donald M'Queen still favoured us with his company, for which we were much obliged to him. As we sailed along Dr Johnson got into one of his fits of railing at the Scots. He owned that they had been a very learned nation for a hundred years, from about 1550 to about 1650; but that they afforded the only instance of a people among whom the arts of civil life did not advance in proportion with learning; that they had hardly any trade, any money, or any elegance, before the Union; that it was strange that, with all the advantages possessed by other nations, they had not any of those conveniencies and embellishments which are the fruit of industry, till they came in contact with a civilized people. 'We have taught you,' said he, 'and we'll do the same in time to all barbarous nations, to the Cherokees, and at last to the Ouran-Outangs'; laughing with as much glee as if Monboddo had been present. BOSWELL. 'We had wine before the Union.' JOHNSON. 'No, sir; you had some weak stuff, the refuse of France, which would not make you drunk.' BOSWELL. 'I assure you, sir, there was a great deal of drunkenness.' JOHNSON. 'No, sir; there were people who died of dropsies, which they contracted in trying to get drunk.'[222]

I must here gleen some of his conversation at Ulinish, which I have omitted. He repeated his remark, that a man in a ship was worse than a man in a jail. 'The man in a jail,' said he, 'has more room, better food, and commonly better company, and is in safety.' 'Ay; but,' said Mr M'Queen, 'the man in the ship has the pleasing hope of getting to shore.' JOHNSON. 'Sir, I am not talking of a man's getting to shore; but a man while he is in a ship: and then, I say, he is worse than a man while he is in a jail. A man in a jail *may* have the "pleasing hope" of getting out. A man confined for only a limited time, actually *has* it.' M'Leod mentioned his schemes for carrying on fisheries with spirit, and that he would wish to understand the construction of boats. I suggested that he might go to a dock-yard and work, as Peter the Great did. JOHNSON. 'Nay, sir, he need not work. Peter the Great had not the sense to see that the mere mechanical work may be done by any body, and that there is the same art in constructing a vessel, whether the boards are well or ill wrought. Sir Christopher Wren might as well have served his time to a bricklayer, and first, indeed, to a brick-maker.'

There is a beautiful little island in the Loch of Dunvegan, called Isa. M'Leod said, he would give it to Dr Johnson, on condition of his residing on it three months in the year; nay one month. Dr Johnson was highly amused with the fancy. I have seen him please himself with little things, even with mere ideas like the present. He talked a great deal of this island – how he would build a house there, how he would fortify it, how he would have cannon, how he would plant, how he would sally out, and *take* the isle of Muck; and then he laughed with uncommon glee, and could hardly leave off. I have seen him do so at a small matter that struck him, and was a sport to no one else. Mr Langton told me, that one night he did so while the company were all grave about him: only Garrick, in his significant smart manner, darting his eyes around, exclaimed, '*Very* jocose, to be sure!' M'Leod encouraged the fancy of Dr Johnson's becoming owner of an island; told him, that it was the practice in this country to name every man by his lands; and begged leave to drink to him in that mode: '*Island Isa*, your health!' Ulinish, Talisker, Mr M'Queen, and I, all joined in our different manners, while Dr Johnson bowed to each, with much good humour.

We had good weather, and a fine sail this day. The shore was varied with hills, and rocks, and corn-fields, and bushes, which are here dignified with the name of natural wood. We landed near the house of Ferneley, a farm possessed by another gentleman of the name of M'Leod, who, expecting our arrival, was waiting on the shore, with a horse for Dr Johnson. The rest of us walked. At dinner, I expressed to M'Leod the joy which I had in seeing him on such cordial terms with his clan. 'Government,' said he, 'has deprived us of our ancient power; but it cannot deprive us of our domestick satisfactions. I would rather drink punch in one of their houses' (meaning the houses of his people) 'than be enabled by their hardships, to have claret in my own.' This should be the sentiment of every chieftain.

All that he can get by raising his rents, is more luxury in his own house. Is it not better to share the profits of his estate, to a certain degree, with his kinsmen, and thus have both social intercourse and patriarchal influence?

We had a very good ride, for about three miles, to Talisker, where Colonel M'Leod introduced us to his lady. We found here Mr Donald M'Lean, the young Laird of Col (nephew to Talisker), to whom I delivered the letter with which I had been favoured by his uncle, Professor M'Leod, at Aberdeen. He was a little lively young man. We found he had been a good deal in England, studying farming, and was resolved to improve the value of his father's lands, without oppressing his tenants, or losing the ancient Highland fashions.

Talisker is a better place than one commonly finds in Sky. It is situated in a rich bottom. Before it is a wide expanse of sea, on each hand of which are immense rocks; and, at some distance in the sea, there are three columnal rocks rising to sharp points. The billows break with prodigious force and noise on the coast of Talisker. There are here a good many well-grown trees. Talisker is an extensive farm. The possessor of it has, for several generations, been the next heir to M'Leod, as there has been but one son always in that family. The court before the house is most injudiciously paved with the round blueish-grey pebbles which are found upon the sea-shore; so that you walk as if upon cannon-balls driven into the ground.

After supper, I talked of the assiduity of the Scottish clergy, in visiting and privately instructing their parishioners, and observed how much in this they excelled the English clergy. Dr Johnson would not let this pass. He tried to turn it off, by saying, 'There are different ways of instructing. Our clergy pray and preach.' M'Leod and I pressed the subject, upon which he grew warm, and broke forth: 'I do not believe your people are better instructed. If they are, it is the blind leading the blind; for your clergy are not instructed themselves.' Thinking he had gone a little too far, he checked himself, and added, 'When I talk of the ignorance of your clergy, I talk of them as a body: I do not mean that there are not individuals who are learned' (looking at Mr M'Queen). 'I suppose there are such among the clergy in Muscovy. The clergy of England have produced the most valuable books in support of religion, both in theory and practice. What have your clergy done, since you sunk into presbyterianism? Can you name one book of any value, on a religious subject, written by them?' We were silent. 'I'll help you. Forbes wrote very well; but I believe he wrote before episcopacy was quite extinguished.'[223] And then pausing a little, he said, 'Yes, you have Wishart against Repentance.'* BOSWELL. 'But, sir, we are not contending for the superior learning of our clergy, but for their superior assiduity.' He bore us down again, with thundering against their ignorance, and said to me, 'I see you have not been well taught; for you have not charity.' He had been in some measure forced into this warmth, by the exulting air which I assumed; for, when he began, he said, 'Since you *will* drive the nail!' He again thought of good Mr M'Queen, and, taking him by the hand, said, 'Sir, I did not mean any disrespect to you.'

Here I must observe, that he conquered by deserting his ground, and not meeting the argument as I had put it. The assiduity of the Scottish clergy is certainly greater than that of the English. His taking up the topick of their not having so much learning, was, though ingenious, yet a fallacy in logick. It was as if there should be a dispute whether a man's hair is well dressed, and Dr Johnson should say, 'Sir, his hair cannot be well dressed; for he has a dirty shirt. No man who has not clean linen has his hair well dressed.' When some days afterwards he read this passage, he said, 'No, sir; I did not say that a man's hair could not be well dressed because he has not clean linen, but because he is bald.'

He used one argument against the Scottish clergy being learned, which I doubt was not good. 'As we believe a man dead till we know that he is alive; so we believe men ignorant till we know that they are learned.' Now our maxim in law is, to presume a man alive, till we know he is dead. However, indeed, it may be answered, that we must first know he has lived; and that we have never known the learning of the Scottish clergy. Mr M'Queen, though he was of opinion that Dr Johnson had deserted the point really in dispute, was much pleased with what he said, and owned to me, he thought it very just; and Mrs M'Leod was so much captivated by his eloquence, that she told me 'I was a good advocate for a bad cause.'

Friday, 24th September

This was a good day. Dr Johnson told us, at breakfast, that he rode harder at a fox chase than any body. 'The English,' said he, 'are the only nation who ride hard a-hunting. A Frenchman goes out upon a managed horse, and capers in the field, and no more thinks of leaping a hedge than of mounting a breach. Lord Powerscourt laid a wager, in France, that he would ride

* This was a dexterous mode of description, for the purpose of his argument; for what he alluded to was, a sermon published by the learned Dr William Wishart, formerly principal of the college at Edinburgh, to warn men *against* confiding in a death-bed *repentance*, of the inefficacy of which he entertained notions very different from those of Dr Johnson.[224]

a great many miles in a certain short time. The French academicians set to work, and calculated that, from the resistance of the air, it was impossible. His lordship however performed it.'

Our money being nearly exhausted, we sent a bill for thirty pounds, drawn on Sir William Forbes and Co. to Lochbraccadale, but our messenger found it very difficult to procure cash for it;[225] at length, however, he got us value from the master of a vessel which was to carry away some emigrants. There is a great scarcity of specie in Sky. Mr M'Queen said he had the utmost difficulty to pay his servants' wages, or to pay for any little thing which he has to buy. The rents are paid in bills, which the drovers give. The people consume a vast deal of snuff and tobacco, for which they must pay ready money; and pedlers, who come about selling goods, as there is not a shop in the island, carry away the cash. If there were encouragement given to fisheries and manufacturers, there might be a circulation of money introduced. I got one-and-twenty shillings in silver at Portree, which was thought a wonderful store.

Talisker, Mr M'Queen, and I, walked out, and looked at no less than fifteen different waterfalls near the house, in the space of about a quarter of a mile. We also saw Cuchullin's well, said to have been the favourite spring of that ancient hero. I drank of it. The water is admirable. On the shore are many stones full of crystallizations in the heart.

Though our obliging friend, Mr M'Lean, was but the young laird, he had the title of Col constantly given him. After dinner he and I walked to the top of Prieshwell, a very high rocky hill, from whence there is a view of Barra, the Long Island, Bernera, the Loch of Dunvegan, part of Rum, part of Rasay, and a vast deal of the isle of Sky. Col, though he had come into Sky with an intention to be at Dunvegan, and pass a considerable time in the island, most politely resolved first to conduct us to Mull, and then to return to Sky. This was a very fortunate circumstance; for he planned an expedition for us of more variety than merely going to Mull. He proposed we should flee the islands of Egg, Muck, Col, and Tyr-yi.[226] In all these islands he could shew us every thing worth seeing; and in Mull he said he should be as if at home, his father having lands there, and he a farm.

Dr Johnson did not talk much to-day, but seemed intent in listening to the schemes of future excursion, planned by Col. Dr Birch, however, being mentioned, he said, he had more anecdotes than any man. I said, Percy had a great many; that he flowed with them like one of the brooks here. JOHNSON. 'If Percy is like one of the brooks here, Birch was like the river Thames. Birch excelled Percy in that, as much as Percy excels Goldsmith.' I mentioned Lord Hailes as a man of anecdote. He was not pleased with him, for publishing only such memorials and letters as were unfavourable for the Stuart family. 'If,' said he, 'a man fairly warns you, "I am to give all the ill; do you find the good", he may: but if the object which he professes be to give a view of a reign, let him tell all the truth. I would tell truth of the two Georges, or of that scoundrel, King William. Granger's *Biographical History* is full of curious anecdote, but might have been better done. The dog is a Whig. I do not like much to see a Whig in any dress; but I hate to see a Whig in a parson's gown.'

Saturday, 25th September

It was resolved that we should set out, in order to return to Slate, to be in readiness to take boat whenever there should be a fair wind. Dr Johnson remained in his chamber writing a letter, and it was long before we could get him into motion. He did not come to breakfast, but had it sent to him. When he had finished his letter, it was twelve o'clock, and we should have set out at ten. When I went up to him, he said to me, 'Do you remember a song which begins,[227]

> "Every island is a prison
>   Strongly guarded by the sea;
> Kings and princes, for that reason,
>   Prisoners are, as well as we." '

I suppose he had been thinking of our confined situation. He would fain have gone in a boat from hence, instead of riding back to Slate. A scheme for it was proposed. He said, 'We'll not be driven tamely from it': but it proved impracticable.

We took leave of M'Leod and Talisker, from whom we parted with regret. Talisker, having been bred to physick, had a tincture of scholarship in his conversation, which pleased Dr Johnson, and he had some very good books; and being a colonel in the Dutch service, he and his lady, in consequence of having lived abroad, had introduced the ease and politeness of the continent into this rude region.

Young Col was now our leader. Mr M'Queen was to accompany us half a day more. We stopped at a little hut, where we saw an old woman grinding with the *quern*, the ancient Highland instrument, which it is said was used by the Romans, but which, being very slow in its operation, is almost entirely gone into disuse.[228]

The walls of the cottages in Sky, instead of being one compacted mass of stones, are often formed by two exterior surfaces of stone, filled up with earth in the middle, which makes them very warm. The roof is generally bad. They are thatched, sometimes with straw, sometimes with heath, sometimes with fern. The thatch is secured by ropes of straw, or of heath; and, to fix the ropes, there is a stone tied to the end of each. These stones hang round the bottom of the roof, and make it look like a lady's hair in papers; but I should think that, when there is wind, they would come down, and knock people on the head.[229]

We dined at the inn at Sconser,[230] where I had the pleasure to find a letter from my wife. Here we parted from our learned companion, Mr Donald M'Queen. Dr Johnson took leave of him very affectionately, saying, 'Dear sir, do not forget me!' We settled, that he should write an account of the Isle of Sky, which Dr Johnson promised to revise. He said, Mr M'Queen should tell all that he could; distinguishing what he himself knew, what was traditional, and what conjectural.

We sent our horses round a point of land, that we might shun some very bad road; and resolved to go forward by sea. It was seven o'clock when we got into our boat. We had many showers, and it soon grew pretty dark. Dr Johnson sat silent and patient. Once he said, as he looked on the black coast of Sky – black, as being composed of rocks seen in the dusk – 'This is very solemn.' Our boatmen were rude singers, and seemed so like wild Indians, that a very little imagination was necessary to give one an impression of being upon an American river. We landed at Strolimus, from whence we got a guide to walk before us, for two miles, to Corrichatachin. Not being able to procure a horse for our baggage, I took one portmanteau before me, and Joseph another. We had but a single star to light us on our way. It was about eleven when we arrived. We were most hospitably received by the master and mistress, who were just going to bed, but, with unaffected ready kindness, made a good fire, and at twelve o'clock at night had supper on the table.

James Macdonald, of Knockow, Kingsburgh's brother, whom we had seen at Kingsburgh, was there. He shewed me a bond granted by the late Sir James Macdonald, to old Kingsburgh, the preamble of which does so much honour to the feelings of that much-lamented gentleman, that I thought it worth transcribing. It was as follows:

I, Sir James Macdonald, of Macdonald, Baronet, now, after arriving at my perfect age, from the friendship I bear to Alexander Macdonald of Kingsburgh, and in return for the long and faithful services done and performed by him to my deceased father, and to myself during my minority, when he was one of my Tutors and Curators; being resolved, now that the said Alexander Macdonald is advanced in years, to contribute my endeavours for making his old age placid and comfortable, therefore he grants him an annuity of fifty pounds sterling.

Dr Johnson went to bed soon. When one bowl of punch was finished, I rose, and was near the door, in my way up stairs to bed; but Corrichatachin said, it was the first time Col had been in his house, and he should have his bowl; and would not I join in drinking it? The heartiness of my honest landlord, and the desire of doing social honour to our very obliging conductor, induced me to sit down again. Col's bowl was finished; and by that time we were well warmed. A third bowl was soon made, and that too was finished. We were cordial, and merry to a high degree; but of what passed I have no recollection, with any accuracy. I remember calling Corrichatachin by the familiar appellation of Corri, which his friends do. A fourth bowl was made, by which time Col, and young M'Kinnon, Corrichatachin's son, slipped away to bed. I continued a little with Corri and Knockow; but at last I left them. It was near five in the morning when I got to bed.

Sunday, 26th September

I awaked at noon, with a severe head-ach. I was much vexed that I should have been guilty of such a riot, and afraid of a reproof from Dr Johnson. I thought it very inconsistent with that conduct which I ought to maintain, while the companion of the *Rambler*. About one he came into my room, and accosted me, 'What, drunk yet?' His tone of voice was not that of severe upbraiding; so I was relieved a little. 'Sir,' said I, 'they kept me up.' He answered, 'No, you kept them up, you drunken dog.' This he said with good-humoured *English* pleasantry. Soon afterwards, Corrichatachin, Col, and other friends assembled round my bed. Corri had a brandy-bottle and glass with him, and insisted I should take a dram. 'Ay,' said Dr Johnson, 'fill him drunk again. Do it in the morning, that we may laugh at him all day. It is a poor thing for a fellow to get drunk at night, and sculk to bed, and let his friends have no sport.' Finding him thus jocular, I became quite easy; and when I offered to get up, he very good-naturedly said, 'You need be in no such hurry now.'* I took my host's advice, and drank some

---

* My ingenuously relating this occasional instance of intemperance has I find been made the subject both of serious criticism and ludicrous banter. With the banterers I shall not trouble myself, but I wonder that those who pretend to the appellation of serious criticks should not have had sagacity enough to perceive that here, as in every other part of the present work, my principal object was to delineate Dr Johnson's manners and character. In justice to him I would not omit an anecdote, which, though in some degree to my own disadvantage, exhibits in so strong a light the indulgence and good humour with which he could treat those excesses in his friends, of which he highly disapproved.

brandy, which I found an effectual cure for my head-ach. When I rose, I went into Dr Johnson's room, and taking up Mrs M'Kinnon's prayer-book, I opened it at the twentieth Sunday after Trinity, in the epistle for which I read, 'And be not drunk with wine, wherein there is excess.' Some would have taken this as a divine interposition.

Mrs M'Kinnon told us at dinner, that old Kingsburgh, her father, was examined at Mugstot, by General Campbell,[231] as to the particulars of the dress of the person who had come to his house in woman's clothes, along with Miss Flora M'Donald; as the General had received intelligence of that disguise. The particulars were taken down in writing, that it might be seen how far they agreed with the dress of the 'Irish girl' who went with Miss Flora from the Long Island. Kingsburgh, she said, had but one song, which he always sung when he was merry over a glass. She dictated the words to me, which are foolish enough:

> Green sleeves and pudding pies,
> Tell me where my mistress lies,
> And I'll be with her before the rise,
> Fiddle and aw' together.
>
> May our affairs abroad succeed,
> And may our king come home with speed,
> And all pretenders shake for dread,
> And let *his* health go round.
>
> To all our injured friends in need,
> This side and beyond the Tweed!
> Let all pretenders shake for dread,
> And let *his* health go round.
> Green sleeves, &c.

While the examination was going on, the present Talisker, who was there as one of M'Leod's militia, could not resist the pleasantry of asking Kingsburgh, in allusion to his only song, 'Had she *green sleeves?*' Kingsburgh gave him no answer. Lady Margaret M'Donald was very angry at Talisker for joking on such a serious occasion, as Kingsburgh was really in danger of his life.[232] Mrs M'Kinnon added that Lady Margaret was quite adored in

---

In some other instances, the criticks have been equally wrong as to the true motive of my recording particulars, the objections to which I saw as clearly as they. But it would be an endless talk for an authour to point out upon every occasion the precise object he has in view. Contenting himself with the approbation of readers of discernment and taste, he ought not to complain that some are found who cannot or will not understand him.

Sky. That when she travelled through the island, the people ran in crowds before her, and took the stones off the road, lest her horse should stumble and she be hurt. Her husband, Sir Alexander, is also remembered with great regard. We were told that every week a hogshead of claret was drunk at his table.

This was another day of wind and rain; but good cheer and good society helped to beguile the time. I felt myself comfortable enough in the afternoon. I then thought that my last night's riot was no more than such a social excess as may happen without much moral blame; and recollected that some physicians maintained, that a fever produced by it was, upon the whole, good for health: so different are our reflections on the same subject, at different periods; and such the excuses with which we palliate what we know to be wrong.

Monday, 27th September

Mr Donald M'Leod, our original guide, who had parted from us at Dunvegan, joined us again to-day. The weather was still so bad that we could not travel. I found a closet here, with a good many books, beside those that were lying about. Dr Johnson told me, he found a library in his room at Talisker; and observed, that it was one of the remarkable things of Sky, that there were so many books in it.

Though we had here great abundance of provisions, it is remarkable that Corrichatachin has literally no garden: not even a turnip, a carrot or a cabbage. After dinner, we talked of the crooked spade used in Sky, already described, and they maintained that it was better than the usual garden-spade, and that there was an art in tossing it, by which those who were accustomed to it could work very easily with it. 'Nay,' said Dr Johnson, 'it may be useful in land where there are many stones to raise; but it certainly is not a good instrument for digging good land. A man may toss it, to be sure; but he will toss a light spade much better: its weight makes it an incumbrance. A man *may* dig any land with it; but he has no occasion for such a weight in digging good land. You may take a field-piece to shoot sparrows; but all the sparrows you can bring home will not be worth the charge.' He was quite social and easy amongst them; and, though he drank no fermented liquor, toasted Highland beauties with great readiness. His conviviality engaged them so much, that they seemed eager to shew their attention to him, and vied with each other in crying out, with a strong Celtick pronunciation, 'Toctor Shonson, Toctor Shonson, your health!'

This evening one of our married ladies, a lively pretty little woman, good-humouredly sat down upon Dr Johnson's knee, and, being encouraged by some of the company, put her hands round his neck, and kissed him. 'Do it again,' said he, 'and let us see who will tire first.' He kept her on his knee some time, while he and she drank tea. He was now like a *buck* indeed. All the company were much entertained to find him so easy and pleasant. To me it was highly comick, to see the grave philosopher – the *Rambler* – toying with a Highland beauty! But what could he do? He must have been surly, and weak too, had he not behaved as he did. He would have been laughed at, and not more respected, though less loved.

He read to-night, to himself, as he sat in company, a great deal of my *Journal*, and said to me, 'The more I read of this, I think the more highly of you.' The gentlemen sat a long time at their punch, after he and I had retired to our chambers. The manner in which they were attended struck me as singular: the bell being broken, a smart lad lay on a table in the corner of the room, ready to spring up and bring the kettle, whenever it was wanted. They continued drinking, and singing Erse songs, till near five in the morning, when they all came into my room, where some of them had beds. Unluckily for me, they found a bottle of punch in a corner, which they drank; and Corrichatachin went for another, which they also drank. They made many apologies for disturbing me. I told them, that, having been kept awake by their mirth, I had once thoughts of getting up, and joining them again. Honest Corrichatachin said, 'To have had you done so, I would have given a cow.'

Tuesday, 28th September

The weather was worse than yesterday. I felt as if imprisoned. Dr Johnson said, it was irksome to be detained thus: yet he seemed to have less uneasiness, or more patience, than I had. What made our situation worse here was, that we had no rooms that we could command; for the good people had no notion that a man could have any occasion but for a mere sleeping-place; so, during the day, the bed-chambers were common to all the house. Servants eat in Dr Johnson's; and mine was a kind of general rendezvous of all under the roof, children and dogs not excepted. As the gentlemen occupied the parlour, the ladies had no place to sit in, during the day, but Dr Johnson's room. I had always some quiet time for writing in it, before he was up; and, by degrees, I accustomed the ladies to let me sit in it after breakfast, at my *Journal*, without minding me.

Dr Johnson was this morning for going to see as many islands as we could; not recollecting the uncertainty of the season, which might detain us in one place for many weeks. He said to me, 'I have more the spirit of adventure than you.' For my part, I was anxious to get to Mull, from whence we might almost any day reach the main land.

Dr Johnson mentioned, that the few ancient Irish gentlemen yet remaining have the highest pride of family; that Mr Sandford, a friend of his, whose mother was Irish, told him, that O'Hara (who was true Irish, both by father and mother) and he, and Mr Ponsonby, son to the Earl of Besborough, the greatest man of the three, but of an English family, went to see one of those ancient Irish,²³³ and that he distinguished them thus: 'O'Hara, you are welcome! Mr Sandford, your mother's son, is welcome! Mr Ponsonby, you may sit down.'

He talked both of threshing and thatching. He said, it was very difficult to determine how to agree with a thresher. 'If you pay him by the day's wages, he will thresh no more than he pleases; though, to be sure, the negligence of a thresher is more easily detected than that of most labourers, because he must always make a sound while he works. If you pay him by the piece, by the quantity of grain which he produces, he will thresh only while the grain comes freely, and, though he leaves a good deal in the ear, it is not worth while to thresh the straw over again; nor can you fix him to do it sufficiently, because it is so difficult to prove how much less a man threshes than he ought to do. Here then is a dilemma: but, for my part, I would engage him by the day; I would rather trust his idleness than his fraud.' He said, a roof thatched with Lincolnshire reeds would last seventy years, as he was informed when in that county; and that he told this in London to a great thatcher, who said, he believed it might be true. Such are the pains that Dr Johnson takes to get the best information on every subject.

He proceeded: 'It is difficult for a farmer in England to find day-labourers, because the lowest manufacturers can always get more than a day-labourer. It is of no consequence how high the wages of manufacturers are; but it would be of very bad consequence to raise the wages of those who procure the immediate necessaries of life, for that would raise the price of provisions. Here then is a problem for politicians. It is not reasonable that the most useful body of men should be the worst paid; yet it does not appear how it can be ordered otherwise. It were to be wished, that a mode for its being otherwise were found out. In the mean time, it is better to give temporary assistance by charitable contributions to poor labourers, at times when provisions are high, than to raise their wages; because, if wages are once raised, they will never get down again.'

Happily the weather cleared up between one and two o'clock, and we got ready to depart; but our kind host and hostess would not let us go without taking a 'snatch', as they called it; which was in truth a very good dinner. While the punch went round, Dr Johnson kept a close whispering conference with Mrs M'Kinnon, which, however, was loud enough to let us hear that the subject of it was the particulars of Prince Charles's escape. The company were entertained and pleased to observe it. Upon that subject, there was something congenial between the soul of Dr Samuel Johnson, and that of an isle of Sky farmer's wife. It is curious to see people, how far soever removed from each other in the general system of their lives, come close together on a particular point which is common to each. We were merry with Corrichatachin, on Dr Johnson's whispering with his wife. She, perceiving this, humorously cried, 'I am in love with him. What is it to live and not to love?' Upon her saying something, which I did not hear, or cannot recollect, he seized her hand eagerly, and kissed it.

As we were going, the Scottish phrase of 'honest man!' which is an expression of kindness and regard,[234] was again and again applied by the company to Dr Johnson. I was also treated with much civility; and I must take some merit from my assiduous attention to him, and from my contriving that he shall be easy wherever he goes, that he shall not be asked twice to eat or drink any thing (which always disgusts him), that he shall be provided with water at his meals, and many such little things, which, if not attended to would fret him. I also may be allowed to claim some merit in leading the conversation: I do not mean leading, as in an orchestra, by playing the first fiddle; but leading as one does in examining a witness – starting topics, and making him pursue them. He appears to me like a great mill, into which a subject is thrown to be ground. It requires, indeed, fertile minds to furnish materials for this mill. I regret whenever I see it unemployed; but sometimes I feel myself quite barren, and having nothing to throw in. I know not if this mill be a good figure; though Pope makes his mind a mill for turning verses.

We set out about four. Young Corrichatachin went with us. We had a fine evening, and arrived in good time at Ostig, the residence of Mr Martin M'Pherson, minister of Slate. It is a pretty good house, built by his father, upon a farm near the church. We were received here with much kindness by Mr and Mrs M'Pherson, and his sister, Miss M'Pherson, who pleased Dr Johnson much, by singing Erse songs, and playing on the guittar. He afterwards sent her a present of his *Rasselas*. In his bed-chamber was a press stored with books, Greek, Latin, French, and English, most of which had belonged to the father of our host, the learned Dr M'Pherson; who, though his *Dissertations* have been mentioned in a former page as un-satisfactory, was a man of distinguished talents. Dr Johnson looked at a Latin paraphrase of the song of Moses, written by him, and published in the *Scots Magazine* for 1747, and said, 'It does him honour; he has a great deal of Latin, and good Latin.' Dr M'Pherson published also in the same magazine, June 1739, an original Latin ode, which he wrote from the Isle of Barra, where he was minister for some years. It is very poetical, and exhibits a striking proof how much all things depend upon comparison: for Barra, it seems, appeared to him so much worse than Sky, his *natale solum*, that he languished for its 'blessed mountains', and thought himself buried alive amongst barbarians where he was. My readers will probably not be displeased to have a specimen of this ode:[235]

> *Hei mihi! quantos patior dolores,*
> *Dum procul specto juga ter beata;*
> *Dum feræ Barræ steriles arenas*
> > *Solus oberro.*

> *Ingemo, indignor, crucior, quod inter*
> *Barbaros Thulen lateam colentes;*
> *Torpeo languens, morior sepultus,*
> > *Carcere cœco.*

After wishing for wings to fly over to his dear country, which was in his view, from what he calls 'Thule', as being the most western isle of Scotland, except St Kilda; after describing the pleasures of society, and the miseries of solitude, he at last, with becoming propriety, has recourse to the only sure relief of thinking men – *Sursum corda*, the hope of a better world – and disposes his mind to resignation:

> *Interim fiat, tua, rex, voluntas:*
> *Erigor sursum quoties subit spes*
> *Certa migrandi Solymam supernam,*
> > *Numinis aulam.*

He concludes in a noble strain of orthodox piety:

> *Vita tum demum vocitanda vita est.*
> *Tum licet gratos socios habere,*
> *Seraphim et sanctos Triadem verendam*
> > *Concelebrantes.*

Wednesday, 29th September

After a very good sleep, I rose more refreshed than I had been for some nights. We were now at but a little distance from the shore, and saw the sea from our windows, which made our voyage seem nearer. Mr M'Pherson's manners and address pleased us much. He appeared to be a man of such intelligence and taste as to be sensible of the extraordinary powers of his illustrious guest. He said to me, 'Dr Johnson is an honour to mankind; and, if the expression may be used, is an honour to religion.'

Col, who had gone yesterday to pay a visit at Camuscross, joined us this morning at breakfast. Some other gentlemen also came to enjoy the entertainment of Dr Johnson's conversation. The day was windy and rainy, so that we had just seized a happy interval for our journey last night. We had good entertainment here, better accommodation than at Corrichatachin, and time enough to ourselves. The hours slipped along imperceptibly. We talked of Shenstone. Dr Johnson said, he was a good layer-out of land, but would not allow him to approach excellence as a poet. He said, he believed he had tried to read all his *Love Pastorals*, but did not get through them. I repeated the stanza,

> ' "She gazed as I slowly withdrew;
> My path I could hardly discern;
> So sweetly she bade me adieu,
> I thought that she bade me return." '

He said, 'That seems to be pretty.' I observed that Shenstone, from his short maxims in prose, appeared to have some power of thinking; but Dr Johnson would not allow him that merit. He agreed, however, with Shenstone, that it was wrong in the brother of one of his correspondents to burn his letters; 'for,' said he, 'Shenstone was a man whose correspondence was an honour.' He was this afternoon full of critical severity, and dealt about his censures on all sides. He said, Hammond's *Love Elegies* were poor things.[236] He spoke contemptuously of our lively and elegant, though too licentious, lyrick bard, Hanbury Williams, and said, 'he had no fame, but from boys who drank with him'.[237]

While he was in this mood, I was unfortunate enough, simply perhaps, but, I could not help thinking, undeservedly, to come within 'the whiff and wind of his fell sword'. I asked him, if he had ever been accustomed to wear a night-cap. He said 'No.' I asked, if it was best not to wear one. JOHNSON. 'Sir, I had this custom by chance, and perhaps no man shall ever know whether it is best to sleep with or without a night-cap.' Soon afterwards he was laughing at some deficiency in the Highlands, and said, 'One might as well go without shoes and stockings.' Thinking to have a little hit at his own deficiency, I ventured to add, 'or without a night-cap, sir'. But I had better have been silent; for he retorted directly, 'I do not see the connection there' (laughing). 'Nobody before was ever foolish enough to ask whether it was best to wear a night-cap or not. This comes of being a little wrong-headed.' He carried the company along with him: and yet the truth is, that if he had always worn a night-cap, as is the common practice, and found the highlanders did not wear one, he would have wondered at their barbarity; so that my hit was fair enough.

Thursday, 30th September

There was as great a storm of wind and rain as I have almost ever seen, which necessarily confined us to the house; but we were fully compensated by Dr Johnson's conversation. He said, he did not grudge Burke's being the first man in the House of Commons, for he was the first man every where; but he grudged that a fellow who makes no figure in company, and has a mind as narrow as the neck of a vinegar cruet, should make a figure in the House of Commons, merely by having the knowledge of a few forms, and being furnished with a little occasional information.* He told us, the first time he saw Dr Young was at the house of Mr Richardson, the author of *Clarissa*. He was sent for, that the doctor might read to him his *Conjectures on Original Composition*, which he did, and Dr Johnson made his remarks; and he was surprised to find Young receive as novelties, what he thought very common maxims. He said, he believed Young was not a great scholar, nor had studied regularly the art of writing; that there were very fine things in his *Night Thoughts*, though you could not find twenty lines together without some extravagance. He repeated two passages from his *Love of Fame* – the characters of Brunetta and Stella, which he praised highly. He said Young pressed him much to come to Wellwyn. He always intended it, but never went. He was sorry when Young died. The cause of quarrel between Young and his son, he told us, was, that his son insisted Young should turn away a clergyman's widow, who lived with him, and who, having acquired great influence over the father, was saucy to the son. Dr Johnson said, she could not conceal her resentment at him, for saying to Young, that 'an old man should not

---

* He did not mention the name of any particular person; but those who are conversant with the political world will probably recollect more persons than one to whom this observation may be applied.

resign himself to the management of any body.' I asked him, if there was any improper connection between them. 'No, sir, no more than between two statues. He was past fourscore, and she a very coarse woman. She read to him, and, I suppose, made his coffee, and frothed his chocolate, and did such things as an old man wishes to have done for him.'

Dr Dodridge being mentioned, he observed that 'he was author of one of the finest epigrams in the English language. It is in Orton's *Life* of him. The subject is his family-motto, *Dum vivimus, vivamus*; which, in its primary signification, is, to be sure, not very suitable to a Christian divine; but he paraphrased it thus:

> "Live, while you live, the *epicure* would say,
> And seize the pleasures of the present day.
> Live, while you live, the sacred *preacher* cries,
> And give to God each moment as it flies.
> Lord, in my views let both united be;
> I live in *pleasure*, when I live to *thee*." '

I asked if it was not strange that government should permit so many infidel writings to pass without censure. JOHNSON. 'Sir, it is mighty foolish. It is for want of knowing their own power. The present family on the throne came to the crown against the will of nine tenths of the people. Whether those nine tenths were right or wrong, it is not our business now to inquire. But such being the situation of the royal family, they were glad to encourage all who would be their friends. Now you know every bad man is a Whig; every man who has loose notions. The Church was all against this family. They were, as I say, glad to encourage any friends; and therefore, since their accession, there is no instance of any man being kept back on account of his bad principles; and hence this inundation of impiety.' I observed that Mr Hume, some of whose writings were very unfavourable to religion, was, however, a Tory. JOHNSON. 'Sir, Hume is a Tory by chance, as being a Scotchman; but not upon a principle of duty; for he has no principle. If he is any thing, he is a Hobbist.'

There was something not quite serene in his humour to night, after supper; for he spoke of hastening away to London, without stopping much at Edinburgh. I reminded him, that he had General Oughton and many others to see. JOHNSON. 'Nay, I shall neither go in jest, nor stay in jest. I shall do what is fit.' BOSWELL. 'Ay, sir, but all I desire is, that you will let me tell you when it is fit.' JOHNSON. 'Sir, I shall not consult you.' BOSWELL. 'If you are to run away from us, as soon as you get loose, we will keep you confined in an island.' He was, however, on the whole, very good company. Mr Donald M'Leod expressed very well the gradual impression made by Dr Johnson on those who are so fortunate as to obtain his acquaintance. 'When you see him first, you are struck with awful reverence; then you admire him; and then you love him cordially.'

I read this evening some part of Voltaire's *History of the War in 1741*, and of Lord Kames against *Hereditary Indefeasible Right*. This is a very slight circumstance, with which I should not trouble my reader, but for the sake of observing, that every man should keep minutes of whatever he reads. Every circumstance of his studies should be recorded; what books he has consulted; how much of them he has read; at what times; how often the same authors; and what opinions he formed of them, at different periods of his life. Such an account would much illustrate the history of his mind.

Friday, 1st October

I shewed to Dr Johnson verses in a magazine, on his *Dictionary*, composed of uncommon words taken from it:

Little of *Anthropopathy* has he, &c.[238]

He read a few of them, and said, 'I am not answerable for all the words in my *Dictionary*.' I told him, that Garrick kept a book of all who had either praised or abused him. On the subject of his own reputation, he said, 'Now that I see it has been so current a topick, I wish I had done so too; but it could not well be done now, as so many things are scattered in newspapers.' He said he was angry at a boy of Oxford, who wrote in his defence against Kenrick;[239] because it was doing him hurt to answer Kenrick. He was told afterwards, the boy was to come to him to ask a favour. He first thought to treat him rudely, on account of his meddling in that business; but then he considered, he had meant to do him all the service in his power, and he took another resolution; he told him he would do what he could for him, and did so, and the boy was satisfied. He said, he did not know how his pamphlet was done, as he had read very little of it. The boy made a good figure at Oxford, but died. He remarked, that attacks on authors did them much service. 'A man who tells me my play is very bad, is less my enemy than he who lets it die in silence. A man, whose business it is to be talked of, is much helped at being attacked.' Garrick, I observed, had been often so helped. JOHNSON. 'Yes, sir; though Garrick had more opportunities than almost any man, to keep the publick in mind of him, by exhibiting himself to such numbers, he would not have had so much

325

reputation, had he not been so much attacked. Every attack produces a defence; and so attention is engaged. There is no sport in mere praise, when people are all of a mind.' BOSWELL. 'Then Hume is not the worse for Beattie's attack?'[240] JOHNSON. 'He is, because Beattie has confuted him. I do not say, but that there may be some attacks which will hurt an author. Though Hume suffered from Beattie, he was the better for other attacks.' (He certainly could not include in that number those of Dr Adams, and Mr Tytler.) BOSWELL. 'Goldsmith is the better for attacks.' JOHNSON. 'Yes, sir; but he does not think so yet. When Goldsmith and I published, each of us something, at the same time, we were given to understand that we might review each other. Goldsmith was for accepting the offer. I said, No; set reviewers at defiance. It was said to old Bentley, upon the attacks against him, "Why, they'll write you down." "No, sir," he replied; "depend upon it, no man was ever written down but by himself." ' He observed to me afterwards, that the advantages authours derived from attacks, were chiefly in subjects of taste, where you cannot confute, as so much may be said on either side. He told me he did not know who was the authour of the *Adventures of a Guinea*,[241] but that the bookseller had sent the first volume to him in manuscript, to have his opinion if it should be printed; and he thought it should.

The weather being now somewhat better, Mr James M'Donald, factor to Sir Alexander M'Donald in Slate, insisted that all the company at Ostig should go to the house at Armidale, which Sir Alexander had left, having gone with his lady to Edinburgh, and be his guests, till we had an opportunity of sailing to Mull. We accordingly got there to dinner; and passed our day very cheerfully, being no less than fourteen in number.

Saturday, 2d October

Dr Johnson said, that 'a chief and his lady should make their house like a court. They should have a certain number of the gentlemen's daughters to receive their education in the family, to learn pastry and such things from the housekeeper, and manners from my lady. That was the way in the great families in Wales; at Lady Salisbury's, Mrs Thrale's grandmother, and at Lady Philips's.[242] I distinguish the families by the ladies, as I speak of what was properly their province. There were always six young ladies at Sir John Philips's: when one was married, her place was filled up. There was a large school-room, where they learnt needlework and other things.' I observed, that, at some courts in Germany, there were academies for the pages, who are the sons of gentlemen, and receive their education without any expence to their parents. Dr Johnson said, that manners were best learnt at those courts. 'You are admitted with great facility to the prince's company, and yet must treat him with much respect. At a great court, you are at such a distance that you get no good.' I said, 'Very true: a man sees the court of Versailles, as if he saw it on a theatre.' He said, 'The best book that ever was written upon good breeding, *Il Corteggiano*, by Castiglione,[243] grew up at the little court of Urbino, and you should read it.' I am glad always to have his opinion of books. At Mr M'Pherson's, he commended Whitby's *Commentary*,[244] and said, he had heard him called rather lax; but he did not perceive it. He had looked at a novel, called *The Man of the World*, at Rasay, but thought there was nothing in it. He said to-day, while reading my *Journal*, 'This will be a great treasure to us some years hence.'

Talking of a very penurious gentleman[245] of our acquaintance, he observed, that he exceeded *L'Avare* in the play. I concurred with him, and remarked that he would do well, if introduced in one of Foote's farces; that the best way to get it done, would be to bring Foote to be entertained at his house for a week, and then it would be *facit indignatio*.[246] JOHNSON. 'Sir, I wish he had him. I, who have eaten his bread, will not give him to him, but I should be glad he came honestly by him.'

He said, he was angry at Thrale, for sitting at General Oglethorpe's without speaking. He censured a man for degrading himself to a non-entity. I observed, that Goldsmith was on the other extreme; for he spoke at all ventures. JOHNSON. 'Yes, sir; Goldsmith, rather than not speak, will talk of what he knows himself to be ignorant, which can only end in exposing him.' 'I wonder,' said I, 'if he feels that he exposes himself. If he was with two taylors ...' 'Or with two founders,' said Dr Johnson, interrupting me, 'he would fall a talking on the method of making cannon, though both of them would soon see that he did not know what metal a cannon is made of.' We were very social and merry in his room this forenoon. In the evening the company danced as usual. We performed, with much activity, a dance which, I suppose, the emigration from Sky has occasioned. They call it 'America'. Each of the couples, after the common involutions and evolutions, successively whirls round in a circle, till all are in motion; and the dance seems intended to shew how emigration catches, till a whole neighbourhood is set afloat. Mrs M'Kinnon told me, that last year when a ship sailed from Portree for America, the people on shore were almost distracted when they saw their relations go off; they lay down on the ground, tumbled, and tore the grass with their teeth. This year there was not a tear shed. The people on shore seemed to think that they would soon follow. This indifference is a mortal sign for the country.

We danced to night to the musick of the bagpipe, which made us beat the ground with prodigious force. I thought it better to endeavour to conciliate the kindness of the people of Sky, by joining heartily in their amusements, than to play the abstract scholar. I looked on this tour to the Hebrides as a copartnership between Dr Johnson and me. Each was to do all he could to promote its success; and I have some reason to flatter myself, that my gayer exertions were of service to us. Dr Johnson's immense fund of knowledge and wit was a wonderful source of admiration and delight to them; but they had it only at times; and they required to have the intervals agreeably filled up, and even little elucidations of his learned text. I was also fortunate enough frequently to draw him forth to talk, when he would otherwise have been silent. The fountain was at times locked up, till I opened the spring. It was curious to hear the Hebridians, when any dispute happened while he was out of the room, saying, 'Stay till Dr Johnson comes: say that to *him!*'

Yesterday Dr Johnson said, 'I cannot but laugh, to think of myself roving among the Hebrides at sixty. I wonder where I shall rove at fourscore!' This evening he disputed the truth of what is said, as to the people of St Kilda catching cold whenever strangers come. 'How can there,' said he, 'be a physical effect without a physical cause?' He added, laughing, 'the arrival of a ship full of strangers would kill them; for, if one stranger gives them one cold, two strangers must give them two colds; and so in proportion.' I wondered to hear him ridicule this, as he had praised M'Aulay[247] for putting it in his book: saying, that it was manly in him to tell a fact, however strange, if he himself believed it. He said, the evidence was not adequate to the improbability of the thing; that if a physician, rather disposed to be incredulous, should go to St Kilda, and report the fact, then he would begin to look about him. They said, it was annually proved by M'Leod's steward, on whose arrival all the inhabitants caught cold. He jocularly remarked, 'the steward always comes to demand something from them; and so they fall a coughing. I suppose the people in Sky all take a cold, when —' (naming a certain person) 'comes.'[248] They said, he came only in summer. JOHNSON. 'That is out of tenderness to you. Bad weather and he, at the same time, would be too much.'

Sunday, 3d October

Joseph reported that the wind was still against us. Dr Johnson said, 'A wind, or not a wind? that is the question'; for he can amuse himself at times with a little play of words, or rather sentences. I remember when he turned his cup at Aberbrothick, where we drank tea, he muttered, *Claudite jam rivos, pueri.*[249] I must again and again apologize to fastidious readers, for recording such minute particulars. They prove the scrupulous fidelity of my *Journal*. Dr Johnson said it was a very exact picture of a portion of his life.

While we were chatting in the indolent stile of men who were to stay here all this day at least, we were suddenly roused at being told that the wind was fair, that a little fleet of herring-busses was passing by for Mull, and that Mr Simpson's vessel was about to sail. Hugh M'Donald, the skipper, came to us, and was impatient that we should get ready, which we soon did. Dr Johnson, with composure and solemnity, repeated the observation of Epictetus, that, 'as man has the voyage of death before him, whatever may be his employment, he should be ready at the master's call; and an old man should never be far from the shore, lest he should not be able to get himself ready'. He rode, and I and the other gentlemen walked, about an English mile to the shore, where the vessel lay. Dr Johnson said, he should never forget Sky, and returned thanks for all civilities. We were carried to the vessel in a small boat which she had, and we set sail very briskly about one o'clock. I was much pleased with the motion for many hours. Dr Johnson grew sick, and retired under cover, as it rained a good deal. I kept above, that I might have fresh air, and finding myself not affected by the motion of the vessel, I exulted in being a stout seaman, while Dr Johnson was quite in a state of annihilation. But I was soon humbled; for after imagining that I could go with ease to America or the East Indies, I became very sick, but kept above board, though it rained hard.

As we had been detained so long in Sky by bad weather, we gave up the scheme that Col had planned for us of visiting several islands, and contented ourselves with the prospect of seeing Mull, and Icolmkill and Inchkenneth, which lie near to it.

Mr Simpson was sanguine in his hopes for a-while, the wind being fair for us. He said, he would land us at Icolmkill that night. But when the wind failed, it was resolved we should make for the sound of Mull, and land in the harbour of Tobermorie. We kept near the five herring vessels for some time; but afterwards four of them got before us, and one little wherry fell behind us. When we got in full view of the point of Ardnamurchan, the wind changed, and was directly against our getting into the sound. We were then obliged to tack, and get forward in that tedious manner. As we advanced, the storm grew greater, and the sea very rough. Col then began to talk of making for Egg, or Canna, or his own island. Our skipper said, he would get us into the Sound. Having struggled for this a good while in vain, he said, he would push forward till we were near the land of Mull, where we might cast anchor, and lie till the morning; for although, before this, there had been a good moon, and I had pretty distinctly seen not only the land of Mull, but up the Sound, and the country of Morven as at one end of it, the night was now grown very dark.[250] Our crew consisted of one M'Donald, our skipper, and two sailors, one of whom had but one eye; Mr Simpson himself, Col, and Hugh M'Donald his servant, all helped. Simpson said, he would willingly go for Col, if young Col or his servant would undertake to pilot us to a harbour; but, as the island is low land, it was dangerous to run upon it in the dark. Col and his servant appeared a little dubious. The scheme of running for Canna seemed then to be embraced; but Canna was ten leagues off, all out of our way; and they were afraid to attempt the harbour of Egg. All these different plans were sucessively in agitation. The old skipper still tried to make for the land of Mull, but then it was considered that there was no place there where we could anchor in safety. Much time was lost in striving against the storm. At last it became so rough, and threatened to be so much worse, that Col and his servant took more courage, and said they would undertake to hit one of the harbours in Col.[251] 'Then let us run for it in God's name,' said the skipper; and instantly we turned towards it. The little wherry which had fallen behind us, had hard work. The master begged that, if we made for Col, we should put out a light to him. Accordingly one of the sailors waved a glowing peat for some time. The various difficulties that were started, gave me a good deal of apprehension, from which I was relieved, when I found we were to run for a harbour before the wind. But my relief was but of short duration; for I soon heard that our sails were very bad, and were in danger of being torn in pieces, in which case we should be driven upon the rocky shore of Col. It was very dark, and there was a heavy and incessant rain. The sparks of the burning peat flew so much about, that I dreaded the vessel might take fire. Then, as Col was a sportman, and had powder on board, I figured that we might be blown up. Simpson and he appeared a little frightened, which made me more so; and the perpetual talking, or rather shouting, which was carried on in Erse, alarmed me still more. A man is always suspicious of what is saying in an unknown tongue; and, if fear be his passion at the time, he grows more afraid. Our vessel often lay so much on one side, that I trembled lest she should be overset, and indeed they told me afterwards, that they had run her sometimes to within an inch of the water, so anxious were they to make what haste they could before the night should be worse. I now saw what I never saw before, a prodigious sea, with immense billows coming upon a vessel, so as that it seemed hardly possible to escape. There was something grandly horrible in the sight. I am glad I have seen it once. Amidst all these terrifying circumstances, I endeavoured to compose my mind. It was not easy to do it; for all the stories that I had heard of the dangerous sailing among the Hebrides, which is proverbial, came full upon my recollection. When I thought of those who were dearest to me, and would suffer severely, should I be lost, I upbraided myself, as not having a sufficient cause for putting myself in such danger. Piety afforded me comfort; yet I was disturbed by the objections that have been made against a particular providence, and by the arguments of those who maintain that it is in vain to hope that the petitions of an individual, or even of congregations, can have any influence with the Deity; objections which have been often made, and which Dr Hawkesworth has lately revived, in his preface to the *Voyages to the South Seas*; but Dr Ogden's excellent doctrine on the efficacy of intercession prevailed.

It was half an hour after eleven before we set ourselves in the course for Col. As I saw them all busy doing something, I asked Col, with much earnestness, what I could do. He, with a happy readiness, put into my hand a rope, which was fixed to the top of one of the masts, and told me to hold it till he bade me pull. If I had considered the matter, I might have seen that this could not be of the least service; but his object was to keep me out of the way of those who were busy working the vessel, and at the same time to divert my fear, by employing me, and making me think that I was of use. Thus did I stand firm to my post, while the wind and rain beat upon me, always expecting a call to pull my rope.

The man with one eye steered; old M'Donald, and Col and his servant, lay upon the fore-castle, looking sharp out for the harbour. It was necessary to carry much 'cloth', as they termed it, that is to say, much sail, in order to keep the vessel off the shore of Col. This made violent plunging in a rough sea. At last they spied the harbour of Lochiern, and Col cried, 'Thank God, we are safe!' We ran up till we were opposite to it, and soon afterwards we got into it, and cast anchor.

Dr Johnson had all this time been quiet and unconcerned. He had lain down on one of the beds, and having got free from sickness, was satisfied. The truth is, he knew nothing of the danger we were in: but, fearless and unconcerned, might have said, in the words which he has chosen for the motto to his *Rambler*.

Quo me cunque rapit tempestas, deferor hospes.*

Once, during the doubtful consultations, he asked whither we were going; and upon being told that it was not certain whether to Mull or Col, he cried, 'Col for my money!' I now went down, with Col and Mr Simpson, to visit him. He was lying in philosophick tranquillity with a greyhound of Col's at his back, keeping him warm. Col is quite the *Juvenis qui gaudet canibus*.[252] He had, when we left Talisker, two greyhounds, two terriers, a pointer, and a large Newfoundland water-dog. He lost one of his terriers by the road, but had still five dogs with him. I was very ill, and very desirous to get to shore. When I was told that we could not land that night, as the storm had now increased, I looked so miserably, as Col afterwards informed me, that what Shakspeare has made the Frenchman say of the English soldiers, when scantily dieted, 'Piteous they will look, like drowned mice!'[253] might, I believe, have been well applied to me. There was in the harbour, before us, a Campbelltown vessel, the *Betty*, Kenneth Morison master, taking in kelp, and bound for Ireland. We sent our boat to beg beds for two gentlemen, and that the master would send his boat, which was larger than ours. He accordingly did so, and Col and I were accommodated in his vessel till the morning.

Monday, 4th October

About eight o'clock we went in the boat to Mr Simpson's vessel, and took in Dr Johnson. He was quite well, though he had tasted nothing but a dish of tea since Saturday night. On our expressing some surprise at this, he said, that, 'when he lodged in the Temple, and had no regular system of life, he had fasted for two days at a time, during which he had gone about visiting, though not at the hours of dinner or supper; that he had drunk tea, but eaten no bread; that this was no intentional fasting, but happened just in the course of a literary life'.

There was a little miserable publick-house close upon the shore, to which we should have gone, had we landed last night: but this morning Col resolved to take us directly to the house of Captain Lauchlan M'Lean, a descendant of his family, who had acquired a fortune in the East Indies, and taken

*For as the tempest drives, I shape my way. FRANCIS.

a farm in Col. We had about an English mile to go to it. Col and Joseph, and some others, ran to some little horses, called here 'Shelties', that were running wild on a heath, and catched one of them. We had a saddle with us, which was clapped upon it, and a straw-halter was put on its head. Dr Johnson was then mounted, and Joseph very slowly and gravely led the horse. I said to Dr Johnson, 'I wish, sir, *the club* saw you in this attitude.'*

It was a very heavy rain, and I was wet to the skin. Captain M'Lean had but a poor temporary house, or rather hut; however, it was a very good haven to us. There was a blazing peat-fire, and Mrs M'Lean, daughter of the minister of the parish, got us tea. I felt still the motion of the sea. Dr Johnson said, it was not in imagination, but a continuation of motion on the fluids, like that of the sea itself after the storm is over.

There were some books on the board which served as a chimney-piece. Dr Johnson took up Burnet's *History of his own Times*. He said, 'The first part of it is one of the most entertaining books in the English language; it is quite dramatick: while he went about every where, saw every where, and heard every where. By the first part, I mean so far as it appears that Burnet himself was actually engaged in what he has told; and this may be easily distinguished.' Captain M'Lean censured Burnet, for his high praise of Lauderdale in a dedication, when he shews him in his history to have been so bad a man. JOHNSON. 'I do not myself think that a man should say in a dedication what he could not say in a history. However, allowance should be made; for there is a great difference. The known style of a dedication is flattery: it professes to flatter. There is the same difference between what a man says in a dedication, and what he says in a history, as between a lawyer's pleading a cause, and reporting it.'

The day passed away pleasantly enough. The wind became fair for Mull in the evening, and Mr Simpson resolved to sail next morning: but having been thrown into the island of Col, we were unwilling to leave it unexamined, especially as we considered that the Campbell-town vessel would sail for Mull in a day or two, and therefore we determined to stay.

---

* This curious exhibition may perhaps remind some of my readers of the ludicrous lines, made, during Sir Robert Walpole's administration, on Mr George (afterwards Lord) Littelton, though the figures of the two personages must be allowed to be very different:

> But who is this astride the pony;
> So long, so lean, so lank, so bony?
> Dat be de great orator, Littletony.

Tuesday, 5th October

I rose, and wrote my *Journal* till about nine; and then went to Dr Johnson, who sat up in bed and talked and laughed. I said, it was curious to look back ten years, to the time when we first thought of visiting the Hebrides. How distant and improbable the scheme then appeared! Yet here we were actually among them. 'Sir,' said he, 'people may come to do any thing almost, by talking of it. I really believe, I could talk myself into building a house upon island Isa, though I should probably never come back again to see it. I could easily persuade Reynolds to do it; and there would be no great sin in persuading him to do it. Sir, he would reason thus: "What will it cost me to be there once in two or three summers? Why, perhaps, five hundred pounds; and what is that, in comparison of having a fine retreat, to which a man can go, or to which he can send a friend?" He would never find out that he may have this within twenty miles of London. Then I would tell him, that he may marry one of the Miss M'Leods, a lady of great family. Sir, it is surprising how people will go to a distance for what they may have at home. I knew a lady who came up from Lincolnshire to Knightsbridge with one of her daughters and gave five guineas a week for a lodging and a warm bath; that is, mere warm water. *That*, you know, could not be had in *Lincolnshire!* She said, it was made either too hot or too cold there.'[254]

After breakfast, Dr Johnson and I, and Joseph, mounted horses, and Col and the captain walked with us about a short mile across the island. We paid a visit to the Reverend Mr Hector M'Lean. His parish consists of the islands of Col and Tyr-yi. He was about seventy-seven years of age, a decent ecclesiastick, dressed in a full suit of black clothes, and a black wig. He appeared like a Dutch pastor, or one of the assembly of divines at Westminster. Dr Johnson observed to me afterwards, 'that he was a fine old man, and was as well-dressed, and had as much dignity in his appearance as the dean of a cathedral'. We were told, that he had a valuable library, though but poor accomodation for it, being obliged to keep his books in large chests. It was curious to see him and Dr Johnson together. Neither of them heard very distinctly; so each of them talked in his own way, and at the same time. Mr M'Lean said, he had a confutation of Bayle, by Leibnitz. JOHNSON. 'A confutation of Bayle, sir! What part of Bayle do you mean? The greatest part of his writings is not confutable: it is historical and critical.' Mr M'Lean said, 'the irreligious part'; and proceeded to talk of Leibnitz's controversy with Clarke, calling Leibnitz a great man. JOHNSON. 'Why, sir, Leibnitz persisted in affirming that Newton called space *sensorium numinis*[255], notwithstanding he was corrected, and desired to observe that Newton's words were *quasisensorium numinis*. No, sir; Leibnitz was as paltry a fellow as I know. Out of respect to Queen Caroline, who patronized him, Clarke treated him too well.'

During the time that Dr Johnson was thus going on, the old minister was standing with his back to the fire, cresting up erect, pulling down the front of his periwig, and talking what a great man Leibnitz was. To give an idea of the scene, would require a page with two columns; but it ought rather to be represented by two good players. The old gentleman said, Clarke was very wicked, for going so much into the Arian system. 'I will not say he was wicked,' said Dr Johnson; 'he might be mistaken.' M'LEAN. 'He was wicked, to shut his eyes against the Scriptures; and worthy men in England have since confuted him to all intents and purposes.' JOHNSON. 'I know not *who* has confuted him to *all intents and purposes*.' Here again there was a double talking, each continuing to maintain his own argument, without hearing exactly what the other said.

I regretted that Dr Johnson did not practice the art of accommodating himself to different sorts of people. Had he been softer with this venerable old man, we might have had more conversation; but his forcible spirit, and impetuosity of manner, may be said to spare neither sex nor age. I have seen even Mrs Thrale stunned; but I have often maintained, that it is better he should retain his own manner. Pliability of address I conceive to be inconsistent with that majestick power of mind which he possesses, and which produces such noble effects. A lofty oak will not bend like a supple willow.

He told me afterwards, he liked firmness in an old man, and was pleased to see Mr M'Lean so orthodox. 'At his age, it is too late for a man to be asking himself questions as to his belief.'

We rode to the northern part of the island, where we saw the ruins of a church or chapel. We then proceeded to a place called Grissipol, or the Rough Pool.

At Grissipol we found a good farm house, belonging to the Laird of Col, and possessed by Mr M'Sweyn. On the beach here there is a singular variety of curious stones. I picked up one very like a small cucumber. By the by, Dr Johnson told me, that Gay's line in the *Beggar's Opera*, 'As men should serve a cucumber,' &c. has no waggish meaning, with reference to men flinging away cucumbers as too *cooling*, which some have thought; for it has been a common saying of physicians in England, that a cucumber should be well sliced, and dressed with pepper and vinegar, and then thrown out, as good for nothing. Mr M'Sweyn's predecessors had been in Sky from a very remote period, upon the estate belonging to M'Leod; probably before

M'Leod had it. The name is certainly Norwegian, from Sueno, King of Norway. The present Mr M'Sweyn left Sky upon the late M'Leod's raising his rents. He then got this farm from Col.

He appeared to be near fourscore; but looked as fresh, and was as strong as a man of fifty. His son Hugh looked older; and, as Dr Johnson observed, had more the manners of an old man than he. I had often heard of such instances, but never saw one before. Mrs M'Sweyn was a decent old gentlewoman. She was dressed in tartan, and could speak nothing but Erse. She said, she taught Sir James M'Donald Erse, and would teach me soon. I could now sing a verse of the song *Hatyin foam'eri*, made in honour of Allan, the famous Captain of Clanranald, who fell at Sherrif-muir; whose servant, who lay on the field watching his master's dead body, being asked next day who that was, answered, 'He was a man yesterday.'

We were entertained here with a primitive heartiness.[256] Whisky was served round in a shell, according to the ancient Highland custom. Dr Johnson would not partake of it; but, being desirous to do honour to the modes 'of other times', drank some water out of the shell.

In the forenoon Dr Johnson said, 'it would require great resignation to live in one of these islands.' BOSWELL. 'I don't know, sir; I have felt myself at times in a state of almost mere physical existence, satisfied to eat, drink, and sleep, and walk about, and enjoy my own thoughts; and I can figure a continuation of this.' JOHNSON. 'Ay, sir; but if you were shut up here, your own thoughts would torment you: you would think of Edinburgh or London, and that you could not be there.'

We set out after dinner for Breacacha, the family seat of the Laird of Col, accompanied by the young laird, who had now got a horse, and by the younger Mr M'Sweyn, whose wife had gone thither before us, to prepare every thing for our reception, the laird and his family being absent at Aberdeen. It is called Breacacha, or the Spotted Field, because in summer it is enamelled with clover and daisies, as young Col told me. We passed by a place where there is a very large stone, I may call it a *rock* – 'a vast weight for Ajax'. The tradition is, that a giant threw such another stone at his mistress, up to the top of a hill, at a small distance; and that she in return, threw this mass down to him. It was all in sport.

Malo me petit lasciva puella.[257]

As we advanced, we came to a large extent of plain ground. I had not seen such a place for a long time. Col and I took a gallop upon it by way of race. It was very refreshing to me, after having been so long taking short steps in hilly countries. It was like stretching a man's legs after being cramped in a short bed. We also passed close by a large extent of sand-hills, near two miles square. Dr Johnson said, 'he never had the image before. It was horrible, if barrenness and danger could be so.' I heard him, after we were in the house of Breacacha, repeating to himself, as he walked about the room,

' "And smother'd in the dusty whirlwind, dies." '[258]

Probably he had been thinking of the whole of the simile in *Cato*, of which that is the concluding line; the sandy desert had struck him so strongly. The sand has of late been blown over a good deal of meadow; and the people of the island say, that their fathers remembered much of the space which is now covered with sand, to have been under tillage. Col's house is situated on a bay called Breacacha Bay. We found here a neat new-built gentleman's house, better than any we had been in since we were at Lord Errol's.[259] Dr Johnson relished it much at first, but soon remarked to me, that 'there was nothing becoming a chief about it: it was a mere trades-man's box.' He seemed quite at home, and no longer found any difficulty in using the Highland address; for as soon as we arrived, he said, with a spirited familiarity, 'Now, *Col*, if you could get us a dish of tea.' Dr Johnson and I had each an excellent bed-chamber. We had a dispute which of us had the best curtains. His were rather the best, being of linen; but I insisted that my bed had the best posts, which was undeniable. 'Well,' said he, 'if you *have* the best *posts*, we will have you tied to them and whipped.' I mention this slight circumstance, only to shew how ready he is, even in mere trifles, to get the better of his antagonist, by placing him in a ludicrous view. I have known him sometimes use the same art, when hard pressed in serious disputation. Goldsmith, I remember, to retaliate for many a severe defeat which he has suffered from him, applied to him a lively saying in one of Cibber's comedies, which puts this part of his character in a strong light. 'There is no arguing with Johnson; for, *if his pistol misses fire, he knocks you down with the but-end of it.*'

Wednesday, 6th October

After a sufficiency of sleep, we assembled at breakfast. We were just as if in barracks. Every body was master. We went and viewed the old castle of Col, which is not far from the present house, near the shore, and founded on a rock. It has never been a large feudal residence, and has nothing about it that requires a particular description. Like other old inconvenient buildings of the same age, it exemplified Gray's picturesque lines,

Huge windows that exclude the light,
And passages that lead to nothing.

It may however be worth mentioning, that on the second story we saw a vault, which was, and still is, the family prison. There was a woman put into it by the laird, for theft, within these ten years; and any offender would be confined there yet; for, from the necessity of the thing, as the island is remote from any power established by law, the laird must exercise his jurisdiction to a certain degree.

We were shewn, in a corner of this vault, a hole, into which Col said greater criminals used to be put. It was now filled up with rubbish of different kinds. He said, it was of a great depth. 'Ay,' said Dr Johnson, smiling, 'all such places, that *are filled up*, were of a great depth.' He is very quick in shewing that he does not give credit to careless or exaggerated accounts of things. After seeing the castle, we looked at a small hut near it. It is called *Teigh Franchich*, i.e. the Frenchman's House. Col could not tell us the history of it. A poor man with a wife and children now lived in it. We went into it, and Dr Johnson gave them some charity. There was but one bed for all the family, and the hut was very smoky. When he came out, he said to me, '*Et hoc secundum sententiam philosophorum est esse beatus.*'[260] BOSWELL. 'The philosophers, when they placed happiness in a cottage, supposed cleanliness and no smoke.' JOHNSON. 'Sir, they did not think about either.'

We walked a little in the laird's garden, in which endeavours have been used to rear some trees; but, as soon as they got above the surrounding wall, they died. Dr Johnson recommended sowing the seeds of hardy trees, instead of planting.

Col and I rode out this morning, and viewed a part of the island. In the course of our ride, we saw a turnip-field, which he had hoed with his own hands. He first introduced this kind of husbandry into the Western islands. We also looked at an appearance of lead, which seemed very promising. It has been long known; for I found letters to the late laird, from Sir John Areskine and Sir Alexander Murray, respecting it.

After dinner came Mr M'Lean, of Corneck, brother to Isle of Muck, who is a cadet of the family of Col. He possesses the two ends of Col, which belong to the Duke of Argyll. Corneck had lately taken a lease of them at a very advanced rent, rather than let the Campbells get a footing in the island, one of whom had offered nearly as much as he. Dr Johnson well observed, that, 'landlords err much when they calculate merely what their land *may* yield. The rent must be in a proportionate ratio of what the land may yield, and of the power of the tenant to make it yield. A tenant cannot make by his land, but according to the corn and cattle which he has. Suppose you should give him twice as much land as he has, it does him no good, unless he gets also more stock. It is clear then, that the Highland landlords, who let their substantial tenants leave them, are infatuated; for the poor small tenants cannot give them good rents, from the very nature of things. They have not the means of raising more from their farms.' Corneck, Dr Johnson said, was the most distinct man that he had met with in these isles; he did not shut his eyes, or put his fingers in his ears, which he seemed to think was a good deal the mode with most of the people whom we have seen of late.

Thursday, 7th October

Captain M'Lean joined us this morning at breakfast. There came on a dreadful storm of wind and rain, which continued all day, and rather increased at night. The wind was directly against our getting to Mull. We were in a strange state of abstraction from the world: we could neither hear from our friends, nor write to them. Col had brought Daille *On the Fathers*, Lucas *On Happiness*, and More's *Dialogues*, from the Reverend Mr M'Lean's, and Burnet's *History of his own Times*, from Captain M'Lean's; and he had of his own some books of farming, and Gregory's *Geometry*. Dr Johnson read a good deal of Burnet, and of Gregory, and I observed he made some geometrical notes in the end of his pocket-book. I read a little of Young's *Six Weeks Tour through the Southern Counties*; and Ovid's *Epistles*, which I had bought at Inverness, and which helped to solace many a weary hour.

We were to have gone with Dr Johnson this morning to see the mine; but were prevented by the storm. While it was raging, he said, 'We may be glad we are not *damnati ad metalla*.'[261]

Friday, 8th October

Dr Johnson appeared to day very weary of our present confined situation. He said, 'I want to be on the main land, and go on with existence. This is a waste of life.'

I shall here insert, without regard to chronology, some of his conversation at different times.

'There was a man some time ago, who was well received for two years, among the gentlemen of Northamptonshire, by calling himself my brother. At last he grew so impudent as by his influence to get tenants turned out of their farms. Allen the printer, who is of that county, came to me, asking, with much appearance of doubtfulness, if I had a brother; and upon being assured I had none alive, he told me of the imposition, and immediately wrote to the country, and the fellow was dismissed. It pleased me to hear that so much was got by using my name. It is not every name that can carry double; do both for a man's self and his brother' (laughing). 'I should be glad to see the fellow. However, I could have done nothing against him. A man can have no redress for his name being used, or ridiculous stories being told of him in the news-papers, except he can shew that he has suffered damage. Some years ago a foolish piece was published, said to be written "by S. Johnson". Some of my friends wanted me to be very angry about this. I said, it would be in vain; for the answer would be, S. Johnson may be Simon Johnson, or Simeon Johnson, or Solomon Johnson; and even if the full name, Samuel Johnson, had been used, it might be said; "it is not you; it is a much cleverer fellow."

'Beauclerk and I, and Langton, and Lady Sydney Beauclerk, mother to our friend, were one day driving in a coach by Cuper's Gardens,[262] which were then unoccupied. I, in sport, proposed that Beauclerk and Langton, and myself should take them; and we amused ourselves with scheming how we should all do our parts. Lady Sydney grew angry, and said, "an old man should not put such things in young people's heads". She had no notion of a joke, sir; had come late into life, and had a mighty unpliable understanding.

'Carte's *Life of the Duke of Ormond*[263] is considered as a book of authority; but it is ill-written. The matter is diffused in too many words; there is no animation, no compression, no vigour. Two good volumes in duodecimo might be made out of the two in folio.'

Talking of our confinement here, I observed, that our discontent and impatience could not be considered as very unreasonable; for that we were just in the state of which Seneca complains so grievously, while in exile in Corsica. 'Yes,' said Dr Johnson, 'and he was not farther from home than we are.' The truth is, he was much nearer.

There was a good deal of rain to-day, and the wind was still contrary. Corneck attended me, while I amused myself in examining a collection of papers belonging to the family of Col. The first laird was a younger son of the chieftain M'Lean, and got the middle part of Col for his patrimony. Dr Johnson having given a very particular account of the connection between this family and a branch of the family of Camerons, called M'Lonich, I shall only insert the following document (which I found in Col's cabinet), as a proof of its continuance, even to a late period:

To the Laird of Col.

Dear Sir,

The long-standing tract of firm affectionate friendship 'twixt your worthy predecessors and ours affords us such assurance, as that we may have full relyance on your favour and undoubted friendship, in recommending the bearer, Ewen Cameron, our cousin, son to the deceast Dugall M'Connill of Innermaillie, sometime in Glenpean, to your favour and conduct, who is a man of undoubted honesty and discretion, only that he has the misfortune of being alledged to have been accessory to the killing of one of M'Martin's family about fourteen years ago, upon which alledgeance the M'Martins are now so sanguine on revenging, that they are fully resolved for the deprivation of his life; to the preventing of which you are relyed on by us, as the only fit instrument and a most capable person. Therefore your favour and protection is expected and intreated, during his good behaviour; and failing of which behaviour, you'll please to use him as a most insignificant person deserves.

Sir, he had, upon the alledgeance foresaid, been transported, at Lochiel's desire, to France, to gratify the M'Martins, and upon his return home, about five years ago, married: But now he is so much theatened by the M'Martins, that he is not secure enough to stay where he is, being Ardmurchan, which occasions this trouble to you. Wishing prosperity and happiness to attend still yourself, worthy Lady, and good family, we are, in the most affectionate manner,

> Dear sir,
> Your most obliged, affectionate,
> and most humble servants,
> DUGALL CAMERON, *of Strone.*
> DUGALL CAMERON, *of Barr.*
> DUGALL CAMERON, *of Inveriskvouilline.*
> DUGALL CAMERON, *of Invinvalie.*

Strone, 11th March, 1737.

Ewen Cameron was protected, and his son has now a farm from the Laird of Col, in Mull.

The family of Col was very loyal in the time of the great Montrose, from whom I found two letters in his own hand-writing. The first is as follows.

For my very loving friend the Laird of Coall.

Sir,

I must heartily thank you for all your willingness and good affection to his Majesty's service, and particularly the sending alongs of your son, to who I will heave ane particular respect, hopeing also that you will still continue ane goode instrument for the advanceing ther of the King's service, for which, and all your former loyal carriages, be confident you shall find the effects of his Mas favour, as they can be witnessed you by

> Your very faithful friende,

Strethearne, 20 Jan. 1646 MONTROSE.

The other is,

For the Laird of Col.

Sir,

Having occasion to write to your fields, I cannot be forgetful of your willingness and good affection to his Majesty's service. I acknowledge to you, and thank you heartily for it, assuring, that in what lies in my power, you shall find the good. Mean while, I shall expect that you will continue your loyal endeavours, in wishing those slack people that are about you, to appear more obedient than they do, and loyal in their prince's service; whereby I assure you, you shall find me ever

Your faithful friend,

Petty, 17 April, 1646.   MONTROSE.*

I found some uncouth lines on the death of the present laird's father, intituled 'Nature's Elegy upon the Death of Donald Maclean of Col'. They are not worth insertion. I shall only give what is called his Epitaph, which Dr Johnson said, 'was not so very bad'.

> Nature's minion, Virtue's wonder,
> Art's corrective here lyes under.

I asked, what 'Art's corrective' meant. 'Why, sir,' said he, 'that the laird was so exquisite, that he set Art right, when she was wrong.'

I found several letters to the late Col, from my father's old companion at Paris, Sir Hector M'Lean, one of which was written at the time of settling the colony in Georgia. It dissuades Col from letting people go there, and assures him there will soon be an opportunity of employing them better at home. Hence it appears that emigration from the Highlands, though not in such numbers at a time as of late, has always been practised. Dr Johnson observed, that, 'the lairds, instead of improving their country, diminished their people'.

There are several districts of sandy desart in Col. There are forty-eight lochs of fresh water; but many of them are very small – meer pools. About one half of them, however, have trout and eel. There is a great number of horses in the island, mostly of a small size. Being over-stocked, they sell some in Tir-yi, and on the main land. Their black cattle, which are chiefly rough-haired, are reckoned remarkably good. The climate being very mild in winter, they never put their beasts in any house. The lakes are never frozen so as to bear a man; and snow never lies above a few hours.[264] They have a good many sheep, which they eat mostly themselves, and sell but

---

* It is observeable that men of the first rank spelt very ill in the last century. In the first of these letters I have preserved the original spelling.

a few. They have goats in several places. There are no foxes; no serpents, toads, or frogs, nor any venomous creature. They have otters and mice here; but had no rats till lately that an American vessel brought them. There is a rabbit-warren on the north-east of the island, belonging to the Duke of Argyle. Young Col intends to get some hares, of which there are none at present. There are no black-cock, muir-fowl, nor partridges; but there are snipe, wild-duck, wild-geese, and swans, in winter; wild-pidgeons, plover, and great number of starlings; of which I shot some, and found them pretty good eating. Woodcocks come hither, though there is not a tree upon the island. There are no rivers in Col; but only some brooks, in which there is a great variety of fish. In the whole isle there are but three hills, and none of them considerable, for a Highland country. The people are very industrious. Every man can tan. They get oak, and birch-bark, and lime, from the main land. Some have pits; but they commonly use tubs. I saw brogues very well tanned; and every man can make them. They all make candles of the tallow of their beasts, both moulded and dipped; and they all make oil of the livers of fish. The little fish called cuddies[265] produce a great deal. They sell some oil out of the island, and they use it much for light in their houses, in little iron lamps, most of which they have from England; but of late their own blacksmith makes them. He is a good work-man; but he has no employment in shoeing horses, for they all go unshod here, except some of a better kind belonging to young Col, which were now in Mull. There are two carpenters in Col; but most of the inhabitants can do something as boat-carpenters. They can all dye. Heath is used for yellow; and for red, a moss which grows on stones. They make broad-cloth, and tartan, and linen, of their own wool and flax, sufficient for their own use; as also stockings. Their bonnets come from the main land. Hard-ware and several small articles are brought annually from Greenock, and sold in the only shop in the island, which is kept near the house, or rather hut, used for publick worship, there being no church in the island. The inhabitants of Col have increased considerably within these thirty years, as appears from the parish registers. There are but three considerable tacksmen on Col's part of the island: the rest is let to small tenants, some of whom pay so low a rent as four, three, or even two guineas. The highest is seven pounds, paid by a farmer, whose son goes yearly on foot to Aberdeen for education, and in summer returns, and acts as a school-master in Col. Dr Johnson said, 'There is something noble in a young man's walking two hundred miles and back again, every year, for the sake of learning.'

This day a number of people came to Col, with complaints of each others' trespasses. Corneck, to prevent their being troublesome, told them, that the lawyer from Edinburgh was here, and if they did not agree, he would take them to task. They were alarmed at this; said, they had never been used to go to law, and hoped Col would settle matters himself. In the evening Corneck left us.

Saturday, 9th October

As, in our present confinement, any thing that had even the name of curious was an object of attention, I proposed that Col should show me the great stone, mentioned in a former page, as having been thrown by a giant to the top of a mountain. Dr Johnson, who did not like to be left alone, said he would accompany us as far as riding was practicable. We ascended a part of the hill on horseback, and Col and I scrambled up the rest. A servant held our horses, and Dr Johnson placed himself on the ground, with his back against a large fragment of rock. The wind being high, he let down the cocks of his hat, and tied it with his handkerchief under his chin. While we were employed in examining the stone, which did not repay our trouble in getting to it, he amused himself with reading Gataker *On Lots and on the Christian Watch*, a very learned book, of the last age,[266] which had been found in the garret of Col's house, and which he said was a treasure here. When we descried him from above, he had a most eremitical appearance; and on our return told us, he had been so much engaged by Gataker, that he had never missed us. His avidity for variety of books, while we were in Col, was frequently expressed; and he often complained that so few were within his reach. Upon which I observed to him, that it was strange he should complain of want of books, when he could at any time make such good ones.

We next proceeded to the lead mine. In our way we came to a strand of some extent, where we were glad to take a gallop, in which my learned friend joined with great alacrity. Dr Johnson, mounted on a large bay mare without shoes, and followed by a foal, which had some difficulty in keeping up with him, was a singular spectacle.

After examining the mine, we returned through a very uncouth district, full of sand hills; down which, though apparent precipices, our horses carried us with safety, the sand always gently sliding away from their feet. Vestiges of houses were pointed out to us, which Col, and two others who had joined us, asserted had been overwhelmed with sand blown over them. But, on going close to one of them, Dr Johnson shewed the absurdity of the notion, by remarking, that 'it was evidently only a house abandoned, the stones of which had been taken away for other purposes; for the large stones, which

344

form the lower part of the walls, were still standing higher than the sand. If *they* were not blown over, it was clear nothing higher than they could be blown over.' This was quite convincing to me; but it made not the least impression on Col and the others, who were not to be argued out of a Highland tradition.

We did not sit down to dinner till between six and seven. We lived plentifully here, and had a true welcome. In such a season, good firing was of no small importance. The peats were excellent, and burned cheerfully. Those at Dunvegan, which were damp, Dr Johnson called 'a sullen fuel'. Here a Scottish phrase was singularly applied to him. One of the company having remarked that he had gone out on a stormy evening, and brought in a supply of peats from the stack, old Mr M'Sweyn said, 'that was *main honest!'*

Blenheim being occasionally mentioned, he told me he had never seen it: he had not gone formerly; and he would not go now, just as a common spectator, for his money: he would not put it in the power of some man about the Duke of Marlborough to say, 'Johnson was here; I knew him, but I took no notice of him.' He said, he should be very glad to see it, if properly invited, which in all probability would never be the case, as it was not worth his while to seek for it. I observed, that he might be easily introduced there by a common friend of ours, nearly related to the duke. He answered, with an uncommon attention to delicacy of feeling, 'I doubt whether our friend be on such a footing with the duke as to carry any body there; and I would not give him the uneasiness of seeing that I knew he was not, or even of being himself reminded of it.'

Sunday, 10th October

There was this day the most terrible storm of wind and rain that I ever remember. It made such an awful impression on us all, as to produce, for some time, a kind of dismal quietness in the house. The day was passed without much conversation: only, upon my observing that there must be something bad in a man's mind, who does not like to give leases to his tenants, but wishes to keep them in a perpetual wretched dependence on his will, Dr Johnson said, 'You are right: it is a man's duty to extend comfort and security among as many people as he can. He should not wish to have his tenants mere *Ephemeræ* – mere beings of an hour.' BOSWELL. 'But, sir, if they have leases, is there not some danger that they may grow insolent? I remember you yourself once told me, an English tenant was so independent, that, if provoked, he would *throw* his rent at his landlord.'

JOHNSON. 'Depend upon it, sir, it is the landlord's own fault, if it is thrown at him. A man may always keep his tenants in dependence enough, though they have leases. He must be a good tenant indeed, who will not fall behind in his rent, if his landlord will let him; and if he does fall behind, his landlord has him at his mercy. Indeed, the poor man is always much at the mercy of the rich; no matter whether landlord or tenant. If the tenant lets his landlord have a little rent before-hand, or has lent him money, then the landlord is in his power. There cannot be a greater man than a tenant who has lent money to his landlord; for he has under subjection the very man to whom he should be subjected.'

Monday, 11th October

We had some days ago engaged the Campbell-town vessel to carry us to Mull, from the harbour where she lay. The morning was fine, and the wind fair and moderate; so we hoped at length to get away.

Mrs M'Sweyn, who officiated as our landlady here, had never been on the main land. On hearing this, Dr Johnson said to me, before her, 'That is rather being behind-hand with life. I would at least go and see Glenelg.' BOSWELL. 'You yourself, sir, have never seen, till now, any thing but your native island.' JOHNSON. 'But, sir, by seeing London, I have seen as much of life as the world can shew.' BOSWELL. 'You have not seen Pekin.' JOHNSON. 'What is Pekin? Ten thousand Londoners would *drive* all the people of Pekin: they would drive them like deer.'

We set out about eleven for the harbour; but, before we reached it, so violent a storm came on, that we were obliged again to take shelter in the house of Captain M'Lean, where we dined, and passed the night.

Tuesday, 12th October

After breakfast, we made a second attempt to get to the harbour; but another storm soon convinced us that it would be in vain. Captain M'Lean's house being in some confusion, on account of Mrs M'Lean being expected to lie-in, we resolved to go to Mr M'Sweyn's, where we arrived very wet, fatigued, and hungry. In this situation, we were somewhat disconcerted by being told that we should have no dinner till late in the evening; but should have tea in the mean time. Dr Johnson opposed this arrangement; but they persisted, and he took the tea very readily. He said to me afterwards, 'You must consider, sir, a dinner here is a matter of great consequence. It is a thing to be first planned, and then executed. I suppose the mutton was brought some miles off, from some place where they knew there was a sheep killed.'

Talking of the good people with whom we were, he said, 'Life has not got at all forward by a generation in M'Sweyn's family; for the son is exactly formed upon the father. What the father says, the son says; and what the father looks, the son looks.'

There being little conversation to-night, I must endeavour to recollect what I may have omitted on former occasions. When I boasted, at Rasay, of my independency of spirit, and that I could not be bribed, he said, 'Yes, you may be bribed by flattery.' At the Reverend Mr M'Lean's, Dr Johnson asked him, if the people of Col had any superstitions. He said, 'No.' The cutting peats at the increase of the moon was mentioned as one; but he would not allow it, saying, it was not a superstition, but a whim. Dr Johnson would not admit the distinction. There were many superstitions, he maintained, not connected with religion; and this was one of them. On Monday we had a dispute at the Captain's, whether sand-hills could be fixed down by art. Dr Johnson said, 'How *the devil* can you do it?' but instantly corrected himself, 'How can you do it?' I never before heard him use a phrase of that nature.

He has particularities which it is impossible to explain. He never wears a night-cap, as I have already mentioned; but he puts a handkerchief on his head in the night. The day that we left Talisker, he bade us ride on. He then turned the head of his horse back towards Talisker, stopped for some time; then wheeled round to the same direction with ours, and then came briskly after us. He sets open a window in the coldest day or night, and stands before it. It may do with his constitution; but most people, amongst whom I am one, would say, with the frogs in the fable, 'This may be sport to you; but it is death to us.' It is in vain to try to find a meaning in every one of his particularities, which, I suppose, are mere habits, contracted by chance; of which every man has some that are more or less remarkable. His speaking to himself, or rather repeating, is a common habit with studious men accustomed to deep thinking; and, in consequence of their being thus rapt, they will even laugh by themselves, if the subject which they are musing on is a merry one. Dr Johnson is often uttering pious ejaculations, when he appears to be talking to himself; for sometimes his voice grows stronger, and parts of the Lord's Prayer are heard. I have sat beside him with more than ordinary reverence on such occasions.*

* It is remarkable, that Dr Johnson should have read this account of some of his own peculiar habits, without saying any thing on the subject, which I hoped he would have done.

In our tour, I observed that he was disgusted whenever he met with coarse manners. He said to me, 'I know not how it is, but I cannot bear low life: and I find others, who have as good a right as I to be fastidious, bear it better, by having mixed more with different sorts of men. You would think that I have mixed pretty well too.'

He read this day a good deal of my *Journal*, written in a small book with which he had supplied me, and was pleased, for he said, 'I wish thy books were twice as big.' He helped me to fill up blanks which I had left in first writing it, when I was not quite sure of what he had said, and he corrected any mistakes that I had made. 'They call me a scholar,' said he, 'and yet how very little literature is there in my conversation.' BOSWELL. 'That, sir, must be according to your company. You would not give literature to those who cannot taste it. Stay till we meet Lord Elibank.'

We had at last a good dinner, or rather supper, and were very well satisfied with our entertainment.

Wednesday, 13th October

Col called me up, with intelligence that it was a good day for a passage to Mull; and just as we rose, a sailor from the vessel arrived for us. We got all ready with dispatch. Dr Johnson was displeased at my bustling, and walking quickly up and down. He said, 'It does not hasten us a bit. It is getting on horseback in a ship. All boys do it; and you are longer a boy than others.' He himself has no alertness, or whatever it may be called; so he may dislike it, as *Oderunt hilarem tristes*.[267]

Before we reached the harbour, the wind grew high again. However, the small boat was waiting, and took us on board. We remained for some time in uncertainty what to do: at last it was determined, that, as a good part of the day was over, and it was dangerous to be at sea at night, in such a vessel, and such weather, we should not sail till the morning tide, when the wind would probably be more gentle. We resolved not to go ashore again, but lie here in readiness. Dr Johnson and I had each a bed in the cabbin. Col sat at the fire in the forecastle, with the captain, and Joseph, and the rest. I eat some dry oatmeal, of which I found a barrel in the cabbin. I had not done this since I was a boy. Dr Johnson owned that he too was fond of it when a boy; a circumstance which I was highly pleased to hear from him, as it gave me an opportunity of observing that, notwithstanding his joke on the article of oats, he was himself a proof that this kind of food was not peculiar to the people of Scotland.

Thursday, 14th October

When Dr Johnson awaked this morning, he called, 'Lanky!' having, I suppose, been thinking of Langton; but corrected himself instantly, and cried, 'Bozzy!' He has a way of contracting the names of his friends. Goldsmith feels himself so important now, as to be displeased at it. I remember one day, when Tom Davies was telling that Dr Johnson said, 'We are all in labour for a name to Goldy's play,' Goldsmith cried, 'I have often desired him not to call me Goldy.'

Between six and seven we hauled our anchor, and set sail with a fair breeze; and, after a pleasant voyage, we got safely and agreeably into the harbour of Tobermorie, before the wind rose, which it always has done, for some days, about noon.

Tobermorie is an excellent harbour.[268] An island lies before it, and it is surrounded by a hilly theatre. The island is too low, otherwise this would be quite a secure port; but, the island not being a sufficient protection, some storms blow very hard here. Not long ago, fifteen vessels were blown from their moorings. There are sometimes sixty or seventy sail here: to-day there were twelve or fourteen vessels. To see such a fleet was the next thing to seeing a town. The vessels were from different places; Clyde, Campbelltown, Newcastle, &c. One was returning to Lancaster from Hamburgh. After having been shut up so long in Col, the sight of such an assemblage of moving habitations, containing such a variety of people, engaged in different pursuits, gave me much gaiety of spirit. When we had landed, Dr Johnson said, 'Boswell is now all alive. He is like Antæus; he gets new vigour whenever he touches the ground.' I went to the top of a hill fronting the harbour, from whence I had a good view of it. We had here a tolerable inn. Dr Johnson had owned to me this morning, that he was out of humour. Indeed, he shewed it a good deal in the ship; for when I was expressing my joy on the prospect of our landing in Mull, he said, he had no joy, when he recollected that it would be five days before he should get to the main land. I was afraid he would now take a sudden resolution to give up seeing Icolmkill. A dish of tea, and some good bread and butter, did him service, and his bad humour went off. I told him, that I was diverted to hear all the people whom we had visited in our tour, say, 'Honest man! he's pleased with every thing; he's always content!' 'Little do they know,' said I. He laughed, and said, 'You rogue!'

We sent to hire horses to carry us across the island of Mull to the shore opposite to Inchkenneth, the residence of Sir Allan M'Lean, uncle to young Col, and chief of the M'Leans, to whose house we intended to go the next day. Our friend Col went to visit his aunt, the wife of Dr Alexander M'Lean, a physician, who lives about a mile from Tobermorie.

Dr Johnson and I sat by ourselves at the inn, and talked a good deal. I told him, that I had found, in Leandro Alberti's *Description of Italy*,[269] much of what Addison has given us in his *Remarks*. He said, 'The collection of passages from the Classicks[270] has been made by another Italian: it is, however, impossible to detect a man as a plagiary in such a case, because all who set about making such a collection must find the same passages; but, if you find the same applications in another book, then Addison's learning in his *Remarks* tumbles down. It is a tedious book; and, if it were not attached to Addison's previous reputation, one would not think much of it. Had he written nothing else, his name would not have lived. Addison does not seem to have gone deep in Italian literature: he shews nothing of it in his subsequent writings. He shews a great deal of French learning. There is, perhaps, more knowledge circulated in the French language than in any other. There is more original knowledge in English.' 'But the French,' said I, 'have the art of accommodating literature.' JOHNSON. 'Yes, sir; we have no such book as Moreri's *Dictionary*.'[271] BOSWELL. 'Their *Ana*[272] are good.' JOHNSON. 'A few of them are good; but we have one book of that kind better than any of them; Selden's *Table-talk*. As to original literature, the French have a couple of tragick poets who go round the world, Racine and Corneille, and one comick poet, Molière.' – BOSWELL. 'They have Fenelon.' JOHNSON. 'Why, sir, *Telemachus* is pretty well.' BOSWELL. 'And Voltaire, sir.' JOHNSON. 'He has not stood his trial yet. And what makes Voltaire chiefly circulate is collection; such as his *Universal History*.' BOSWELL. 'What do you say to the Bishop of Meaux?' JOHNSON. 'Sir, nobody reads him.'* He would not allow Massillon and Bourdaloue to go round the world. In general, however, he gave the French much praise for their industry.

He asked me whether he had mentioned, in any of the papers of the *Rambler*, the description in Virgil of the entrance into Hell, with an application to the press; 'for,' said he, 'I do not much remember them'. I told him, 'No.' Upon which he repeated it:

> *Vestibulum ante ipsum, primisque in faucibus orci,*
> *Luctus et ultrices posuere cubilia Curæ;*
> *Pallentesque habitant Morbi, tristisque Senectus,*

---

*I take leave to enter my strongest protest against this judgement. Bossuet I hold to be one of the first luminaries of religion and literature. If there are who do not read him, it is full time they should begin.

Et Metus, et malesuada Fames, et turpis Egestas,
Terribiles visu formæ; Lethumque, Laborque. *

'Now,' said he, 'almost all these apply exactly to an authour; all these are the concomitants of a printing-house.' I proposed to him to dictate an essay on it, and offered to write it. He said, he would not do it then, but perhaps would write one at some future period.

The Sunday evening that we sat by ourselves at Aberdeen, I asked him several particulars of his early years, which he readily told me; and I wrote them down before him. This day I proceeded in my inquiries, also writing them in his presence. I have them on detached sheets. I shall collect authentick materials for *The Life of Samuel Johnson, LL. D.*; and, if I survive him, I shall be one who will most faithfully do honour to his memory. I have now a vast treasure of his conversation, at different times, since the year 1762, when I first obtained his acquaintance; and, by assiduous inquiry, I can make up for not knowing him sooner.†

A Newcastle ship-master, who happened to be in the house, intruded himself upon us. He was much in liquor, and talked nonsense about his being a man for 'Wilkes and Liberty', and against the ministry. Dr Johnson was angry, that 'a fellow should come into *our* company, who was fit for *no* company'. He left us soon.

Col returned from his aunt, and told us, she insisted that we should come to her house that night. He introduced to us Mr Campbell, the Duke of Argyle's factor in Tyr-yi. He was a genteel, agreeable man. He was going to Inveraray, and promised to put letters into the post-office for us. I now found that Dr Johnson's desire to get on the main land, arose from his anxiety to have an opportunity of conveying letters to his friends.[273]

After dinner, we proceeded to Dr M'Lean's, which was about a mile from our inn. He was not at home, but we were received by his lady and daughter, who entertained us so well, that Dr Johnson seemed quite happy. When we had supped, he asked me to give him some paper to write letters. I begged

---

* Just in the gate, and in the jaws of hell,
  Revengeful cares, and sullen sorrows dwell;
  And pale diseases, and repining age;
  Want, fear, and famine's unresisted rage;
  Here toils and death, and death's half-brother, sleep,
  Forms terrible to view, their sentry keep.
  DRYDEN.

† It is no small satisfaction to me to reflect, that Dr Johnson read this, and, after being apprised of my intention, communicated to me, at subsequent periods, many particulars of his life, which probably could not otherwise have been preserved.

he would write short ones, and not *expatiate*, as we ought to set off early. He was irritated by this, and said, 'What must be done, must be done: the thing is past a joke.' 'Nay, sir,' said I, 'write as much as you please; but do not blame me, if we are kept six days before we get to the main land. You were very impatient in the morning: but no sooner do you find yourself in good quarters, than you forget that you are to move.' I got him paper enough, and we parted in good humour.

Let me now recollect whatever particulars I have omitted. In the morning I said to him, before we landed at Tobermorie, 'We shall see Dr M'Lean, who has written the *History of the M'Leans*.' JOHNSON. 'I have no great patience to stay to hear the history of the M'Leans. I would rather hear the history of the Thrales.' When on Mull, I said, 'Well, sir, this is the fourth of the Hebrides that we have been upon.' JOHNSON. 'Nay, we cannot boast of the number we have seen. We thought we should see many more. We thought of sailing about easily from island to island; and so we should, had we come at a better season; but we, being wise men, thought it would be summer all the year where *we* were. However, sir, we have seen enough to give us a pretty good notion of the system in insular life.'

Let me not forget, that he sometimes amused himself with very slight reading; from which, however, his conversation shewed that he contrived to extract some benefit. At Captain M'Lean's he read a good deal in *The Charmer*, a collection of songs.

Friday, 15th October

We this morning found that we could not proceed, there being a violent storm of wind and rain, and the rivers being impassable. When I expressed my discontent at our confinement, Dr Johnson said, 'Now that I have had an opportunity of writing to the main land, I am in no such haste.' I was amused with his being so easily satisfied; for the truth was, that the gentleman who was to convey our letters, as I was now informed, was not to set out for Inveraray for some time; so that it was probable we should be there as soon as he: however, I did not undeceive my friend, but suffered him to enjoy his fancy.

Dr Johnson asked, in the evening, to see Dr M'Lean's books. He took down Willis *De Anima Brutorum*,[274] and pored over it a good deal.

Miss M'Lean produced some Erse poems by John M'Lean, who was a famous bard in Mull, and had died only a few years ago. He could neither read nor write. She read and translated two of them; one, a kind of elegy on Sir John M'Lean's being obliged to fly his country in 1715; another, a dialogue between two Roman Catholick young ladies, sisters, whether it was better to be a nun or to marry. I could not perceive much poetical imagery in the translation. Yet all of our company who understood Erse, seemed charmed with the original. There may, perhaps, be some choice of expression, and some excellence of arrangement, that cannot be shewn in translation.

After we had exhausted the Erse poems, of which Dr Johnson said nothing, Miss M'Lean gave us several tunes on a spinnet, which, though made so long ago, as in 1667, was still very well toned. She sung along with it. Dr Johnson seemed pleased with the musick, though he owns he neither likes it, nor has hardly any perception of it. At Mr M'Pherson's, in Slate, he told us, that 'he knew a drum from a trumpet, and a bagpipe from a guitar, which was about the extent of his knowledge of musick'. To-night he said, that, 'if he had learnt musick, he should have been afraid he would have done nothing else but play. It was a method of employing the mind, without the labour of thinking at all, and with some applause from a man's self.'

We had the musick of the bagpipe every day, at Armidale, Dunvegan, and Col. Dr Johnson appeared fond of it, and used often to stand for some time with his ear close to the great drone.

The penurious gentleman of our acquaintance, formerly alluded to, afforded us a topick of conversation to-night. Dr Johnson said, I ought to write down a collection of the instances of his narrowness, as they almost exceeded belief. Col told us, that O'Kane, the famous Irish harper, was once at that gentleman's house. He could not find in his heart to give him any money, but gave him a key for a harp, which was finely ornamented with gold and silver, and with a precious stone, and was worth eighty or a hundred guineas. He did not know the value of it; and when he came to know it, he would fain have had it back; but O'Kane took care that he should not. JOHNSON. 'They exaggerate the value; every body is so desirous that he should be fleeced. I am very willing it should be worth eighty or a hundred guineas; but I do not believe it.' BOSWELL. 'I do not think O'Kane was obliged to give it back.' JOHNSON. 'No, sir. If a man with his eyes open, and without any means used to deceive him, gives me a thing, I am not to let him have it again when he grows wiser. I like to see how avarice defeats itself; how, when avoiding to part with money, the miser gives something more valuable.' Col said, the gentleman's relations were angry at his giving away the harp-key, for it had been long in the family. JOHNSON. 'Sir, he values a new guinea more than an old friend.'

Col also told us, that the same person having come up with a serjeant and twenty men, working on the high road, he entered into discourse with the serjeant, and then gave him sixpence for the men to drink. The serjeant asked, 'Who is this fellow?' Upon being informed, he said, 'If I had known who he was, I should have thrown it in his face.' JOHNSON. 'There is much want of sense in all this. He had no business to speak with the serjeant. He might have been in haste, and trotted on. He had not learnt to be a miser: I believe we must take him apprentice.' BOSWELL. 'He would grudge giving half a guinea to be taught.' JOHNSON. 'Nay, sir, you must teach him *gratis*. You must give him an opportunity to practice your precepts.'

Let me now go back, and glean *Johnsoniana*. The Saturday before we sailed from Slate, I sat awhile in the afternoon with Dr Johnson in his room, in a quiet serious frame. I observed, that hardly any man was accurately prepared for dying; but almost every one left something undone, something in confusion; that my father, indeed, told me he knew one man (Carlisle of Limekilns), after whose death all his papers were found in exact order; and nothing was omitted in his will. JOHNSON. 'Sir, I had an uncle who died so; but such attention requires great leisure, and great firmness of mind. If one was to think constantly of death, the business of life would stand still. I am no friend to making religion appear too hard. Many good people have done harm, by giving severe notions of it. In the same way, as to learning: I never frighten young people with difficulties; on the contrary, I tell them that they may very easily get as much as will do very well. I do not indeed tell them that they will be *Bentleys*.'

The night we rode to Col's house, I said, 'Lord Elibank is probably wondering what is become of us.' JOHNSON. 'No, no; he is not thinking of us.' BOSWELL. 'But recollect the warmth with which he wrote. Are we not to believe a man, when he says he has a great desire to see another? Don't you believe that I was very impatient for your coming to Scotland?' JOHNSON. 'Yes, sir; I believe you were; and I was impatient to come to you. A young man feels so, but seldom an old man.' I however convinced him that Lord Elibank, who has much of the spirit of a young man, might feel so. He asked me if our jaunt had answered expectation. I said it had much exceeded it. I expected much difficulty with him, and had not found it. 'And,' he added, 'wherever we have come, we have been received like princes in their progress.'

He said, he would not wish not to be disgusted in the Highlands; for that would be to lose the power of distinguishing, and a man might then lie down in the middle of them. He wished only to conceal his disgust.

At Captain M'Lean's, I mentioned Pope's friend, Spence. JOHNSON. 'He was a weak conceited man.'* BOSWELL. 'A good scholar, sir?' JOHNSON. 'Why, no, sir.' BOSWELL. 'He was a pretty scholar.' JOHNSON. 'You have about reached him.'

Last night at the inn, when the factor in Tyr-yi spoke of his having heard that a roof was put on some part of the buildings at Icolmkill, I unluckily said, 'It will be fortunate if we find a cathedral with a roof on it.' I said this from a foolish anxiety to engage Dr Johnson's curiosity more. He took me short at once. 'What, sir? How can you talk so? If we shall *find* a cathedral roofed! As if we were going to a *terra incognita;* when every thing that is at Icolmkill is so well known. You are like some New England men who came to the mouth of the Thames. "Come," said they, "let us go up and see what sort of inhabitants there are here." They talked, sir, as if they had been to go up the Susquehannah, or any other American river.'

Saturday, 16th October

This day there was a new moon, and the weather changed for the better. Dr Johnson said of Miss M'Lean, 'She is the most accomplished lady that I have found in the Highlands. She knows French, musick, and drawing, sews neatly, makes shell-work, and can milk cows; in short, she can do every thing. She talks sensibly, and is the first person whom I have found, that can translate Erse poetry literally.' We set out, mounted on little Mull horses. Mull corresponded exactly with the idea which I had always had of it; a hilly country, diversified with heath and grass, and many rivulets. Dr Johnson was not in very good humour. He said, it was a dreary country, much worse than Sky. I differed from him, 'O, sir,' said he, 'a most dolorous country!'

We had a very hard journey to-day. I had no bridle for my sheltie, but only a halter; and Joseph rode without a saddle. At one place, a loch having swelled over the road, we were obliged to plunge through pretty deep water. Dr Johnson observed, how helpless a man would be, were he travelling here alone, and should meet with any accident; and said, 'he longed to get to a country of saddles and bridles'. He was more out of humour to-day, than he has been in the course of our tour, being fretted to find that his

* Mr Langton thinks this must have been the hasty expression of a splenetick moment, as he has heard Dr Johnson speak of Mr Spence's judgement in criticism with so high a degree of respect, as to shew that this was not his settled opinion of him. Let me add that, in the preface to the *Preceptor*, he recommends Spence's *Essay on Pope's Odyssey*, and that his admirable *Lives of the English Poets* are much enriched by Spence's *Anecdotes of Pope*.

little horse could scarcely support his weight; and having suffered a loss, which, though small in itself, was of some consequence to him, while travelling the rugged steeps of Mull, where he was at times obliged to walk. The loss that I allude to was that of the large oak-stick, which, as I formerly mentioned, he had brought with him from London. It was of great use to him in our wild peregrination; for, ever since his last illness in 1766, he has had a weakness in his knees, and has not been able to walk easily. It had too the properties of a measure; for one nail was driven into it at the length of a foot; another at that of a yard. In return for the services it had done him, he said, this morning he would make a present of it to some museum; but he little thought he was so soon to lose it. As he preferred riding with a switch, it was intrusted to a fellow to be delivered to our baggage-man, who followed us at some distance; but we never saw it more. I could not persuade him out of a suspicion that it had been stolen. 'No, no, my friend,' said he, 'it is not to be expected that any man in Mull, who has got it, will part with it. Consider, sir, the value of such a *piece of timber* here!'

As we travelled this forenoon, we met Dr M'Lean, who expressed much regret at his having been so unfortunate as to be absent while we were at his house.

We were in hopes to get to Sir Allan Maclean's at Inchkenneth,[275] to-night; but the eight miles, of which our road was said to consist, were so very long, that we did not reach the opposite coast of Mull till seven at night, though we had set out about eleven in the forenoon; and when we did arrive there, we found the wind strong against us. Col determined that we should pass the night at M'Quarrie's, in the island of Ulva, which lies between Mull and Inchkenneth; and a servant was sent forward to the ferry, to secure the boat for us: but the boat was gone to the Ulva side, and the wind was so high that the people could not hear him call; and the night so dark that they could not see a signal. We should have been in a very bad situation, had there not fortunately been lying in the little sound of Ulva an Irish vessel, the *Bonnetta*, of Londonderry, Captain M'Lure, master. He himself was at M'Quarrie's; but his men obligingly came with their long-boat, and ferried us over.

M'Quarrie's house was mean; but we were agreeably surprised with the appearance of the master, whom we found to be intelligent, polite, and much a man of the world. Though his clan is not numerous, he is a very ancient chief, and has a burial place at Icolmkill. He told us, his family had possessed Ulva for nine hundred years; but I was distressed to hear that it was soon to be sold for the payment of his debts.[276]

Captain M'Lure, whom we found here, was of Scotch extraction, and properly a M'Leod, being descended of some of the M'Leods who went with Sir Normand of Bernera to the battle of Worcester, and after the defeat of the royalists, fled to Ireland, and, to conceal themselves, took a different name. He told me, there was a great number of them about Londonderry; some of good property. I said, they should now resume their real name. The Laird of M'Leod should go over, and assemble them, and make them all drink the large horn full, and from that time they should be M'Leods. The captain informed us, he had named his ship the *Bonnetta*, out of gratitude to Providence; for once, when he was sailing to America with a good number of passengers, the ship in which he then sailed was becalmed for five weeks, and during all that time, numbers of the fish bonnetta swam close to her, and were caught for food; he resolved therefore, that the ship he should next get, should be called the *Bonnetta*.

M'Quarrie told us a strong instance of the second sight. He had gone to Edinburgh, and taken a man-servant along with him. An old woman, who was in the house, said one day, 'M'Quarrie will be at home to-morrow, and will bring two gentlemen with him'; and she said, she saw his servant return in red and green. He did come home next day. He had two gentlemen with him; and his servant had a new red and green livery, which M'Quarrie had bought for him at Edinburgh, upon a sudden thought, not having the least intention when he left home to put his servant in livery, so that the old woman could not have heard any previous mention of it. This, he assured us, was a true story.

M'Quarrie insisted that the *mercheta mulierum*, mentioned in our old charters, did really mean the privilege which a lord of a manor, or a baron, had, to have the first night of all his vassals' wives. Dr Johnson said, the belief of such a custom having existed was also held in England, where there is a tenure called Borough-English, by which the eldest child does not inherit, from a doubt of his being the son of the tenant.*[277] M'Quarrie told us, that still, on the marriage of each of his tenants, a sheep is due to him; for which the composition is fixed at five shillings. I suppose, Ulva is the only place where this custom remains.

Talking of the sale of an estate of an ancient family, which was said to have been purchased much under its value by the confidential lawyer of that family, and it being mentioned that the sale would probably be set aside by a suit in equity, Dr Johnson said, 'I am very willing that this sale

* Sir William Blackstone says in his Commentaries, that 'he cannot find that ever this custom prevailed in England'; and therefore he is of opinion that it could not have given rise to Borough-English.

should be set aside, but I doubt much whether the suit will be successful; for the argument for avoiding the sale is founded on vague and indeterminate principles, as that the price was too low, and that there was a great degree of confidence placed by the seller in the person who became the purchaser. Now, how low should a price be? or what degree of confidence should there be to make a bargain be set aside? a bargain, which is a wager of skill between man and man. If, indeed, any fraud can be proved, that will do.'

When Dr Johnson and I were by ourselves at night, I observed of our host, *'aspectum generosum habet.'* *'Et generosum animum,'*[278] he added. For fear of being overheard in the small Highland houses, I often talked to him in such Latin as I could speak, and with as much of the English accent as I could assume, so as not to be understood, in case our conversation should be too loud for the space.

We had each an elegant bed in the same room; and here it was that a circumstance occurred, as to which he has been strangely misunderstood. From his description of his chamber, it has erroneously been supposed, that his bed being too short for him, his feet, during the night, were in the mire; whereas he has only said, that when he undressed, he felt his feet in the mire: that is, the clay-floor of the room, on which he stood before he went into bed, was wet, in consequence of the windows being broken, which let in the rain.

Sunday, 17th October

Being informed that there was nothing worthy of observation in Ulva, we took boat, and proceeded to Inchkenneth, where we were introduced by our friend Col to Sir Allan M'Lean, the chief of his clan, and to two young ladies, his daughters. Inchkenneth is a pretty little island, a mile long, and about half a mile broad, all good land.

As we walked up from the shore, Dr Johnson's heart was cheered by the sight of a road marked with cart-wheels, as on the main land; a thing which we had not seen for a long time. It gave us a pleasure similar to that which a traveller feels, when, whilst wandering on what he fears is a desert island, he perceives the print of human feet.

Military men acquire excellent habits of having all conveniencies about them. Sir Allan M'Lean, who had been long in the army, and had now a lease of the island, had formed a commodious habitation, though it consisted but of a few small buildings, only one story high. He had, in his little apartments, more things than I could enumerate in a page or two.[279]

Among other agreeable circumstances, it was not the least, to find here a parcel of the *Caledonian Mercury*, published since we left Edinburgh; which I read with that pleasure which every man feels who has been for some time secluded from the animated scenes of the busy world.

Dr Johnson found books here. He bade me buy Bishop Gastrell's *Christian Institutes*,[280] which was lying in the room. He said, 'I do not like to read any thing on a Sunday, but what is theological; not that I would scrupulously refuse to look at any thing which a friend should shew me in a newspaper; but in general, I would read only what is theological. I read just now some of Drummond's *Travels*, before I perceived what books were here. I then took up Derham's *Physico-Theology*.'[281]

Every particular concerning this island having been so well described by Dr Johnson, it would be superfluous in me to present the publick with the observations that I made upon it, in my *Journal*.

I was quite easy with Sir Allan almost instantaneously. He knew the great intimacy that had been between my father and his predecessor, Sir Hector, and was himself of a very frank disposition. After dinner, Sir Allan said he had got Dr Campbell about a hundred subscribers to his *Britannia Elucidata* (a work since published under the title of *A Political Survey of Great Britain*), of whom he believed twenty were dead, the publication having been so long delayed.[282] JOHNSON. 'Sir, I imagine the delay of publication is owing to this; that, after publication, there will be no more subscribers, and few will send the additional guinea to get their books: in which they will be wrong; for there will be a great deal of instruction in the work. I think highly of Campbell. In the first place, he has very good parts. In the second place, he has very extensive reading; not, perhaps, what is properly called learning, but history, politicks, and, in short, that popular knowledge which makes a man very useful. In the third place, he has learned much by what is called the *vox viva*. He talks with a great many people.'

Speaking of this gentleman, at Rasay, he told us, that he one day called on him, and they talked of Tull's *Husbandry*.[283] Dr Campbell said something. Dr Johnson began to dispute it. 'Come,' said Dr Campbell, 'we do not want to get the better of one another: we want to encrease each other's ideas.' Dr Johnson took it in good part, and the conversation then went on coolly and instructively. His candour in relating this anecdote does him much credit, and his conduct on that occasion proves how easily he could be persuaded to talk from a better motive than 'for victory'.

Dr Johnson here shewed so much of the spirit of a highlander, that he won Sir Allan's heart: indeed, he has shewn it during the whole of our tour. One night, in Col, he strutted about the room with a broad-sword and target, and made a formidable appearance; and, another night, I took the liberty to put a large blue bonnet on his head. His age, his size, and his bushy grey wig, with this covering on it, presented the image of a venerable *senachi*:[284] and, however unfavourable to the Lowland Scots, he seemed much pleased to assume the appearance of an ancient Caledonian. We only regretted that he could not be prevailed with to partake of the social glass. One of his arguments against drinking, appears to me not convincing. He urged, that, 'in proportion as drinking makes a man different from what he is before he has drunk, it is bad; because it has so far affected his reason'. But may it not be answered, that a man may be altered by it *for the better*; that his spirits may be exhilarated, without his reason being affected? On the general subject of drinking, however, I do not mean positively to take the other side. I am *dubius, non improbus*.[285]

In the evening, Sir Allan informed us that it was the custom of his house to have prayers every Sunday; and Miss M'Lean read the evening service, in which we all joined. I then read Ogden's second and ninth sermons on prayer, which, with their other distinguished excellence, have the merit of being short. Dr Johnson said, that it was the most agreeable Sunday he had ever passed; and it made such an impression on his mind, that he afterwards wrote the following Latin verses upon Inchkenneth:[286]

INSULA SANCTI KENNETHI

Parva quidem regio, sed relligione priorum
  Nota, Caledonias panditur inter aquas;
Voce ubi Cennethus populos domuisse feroces
  Dicitur, et vanos dedocuisse deos.
Huc ego delatus placido per cœrula cursu
  Scire locum volui quid daret ille novi.
Illic Leniades humili regnabat in aula,
  Leniades magnis nobilitatus avis:
Una duas habuit casa cum genitore puellas,
  Quas Amor undarum fingeret esse deas:
Non tamen inculti gelidis latuere sub antris,
  Accola Danubii qualia sævus habet;
Mollia non deerant vacuæ solatia vitæ,
  Sive libros poscant otia, sive lyram.
Luxerat illa dies, legis gens docta supernæ
  Spes hominum ac curas cum procul esse jubet,
Ponti inter strepitus sacri non munera cultus
  Cessarunt; pietas hic quoque cura fuit:
Quid quod sacrifici versavit femina libros,

Legitimas faciunt pectora pura preces.
Quo vagor ulterius? quod ubique requiritur hic est;
Hic secura quies, hic et honestus amor.[287]

Monday, 18th October

We agreed to pass this day with Sir Allan, and he engaged to have every thing in order for our voyage to-morrow.

Being now soon to be separated from our amiable friend young Col, his merits were all remembered. At Ulva he had appeared in a new character, having given us a good prescription for a cold. On my mentioning him with warmth, Dr Johnson said, 'Col does every thing for us: we will erect a statue to Col.' 'Yes,' said I, 'and we will have him with his various attributes and characters, like Mercury, or any other of the heathen gods. We will have him as a pilot; we will have him as a fisherman, as a hunter, as a husbandman, as a physician.'

I this morning took a spade, and dug a little grave in the floor of a ruined chapel, near Sir Allan M'Lean's house, in which I buried some human bones I found there. Dr Johnson praised me for what I had done, though he owned, he could not have done it. He shewed in the chapel at Rasay his horrour at dead men's bones. He shewed it again at Col's house. In the charter-room there was a remarkable large shin-bone; which was said to have been a bone of John Garve, one of the lairds. Dr Johnson would not look at it; but started away.

At breakfast, I asked, 'What is the reason that we are angry at a trader's having opulence?' JOHNSON. 'Why, sir, the reason is (though I don't undertake to prove that there is a reason), we see no qualities in trade that should entitle a man to superiority. We are not angry at a soldier's getting riches, because we see that he possesses qualities which we have not. If a man returns from a battle, having lost one hand, and with the other full of gold, we feel that he deserves the gold; but we cannot think that a fellow, by sitting all day at a desk, is entitled to get above us.' BOSWELL. 'But, sir, may we not suppose a merchant to be a man of an enlarged mind, such as Addison in the *Spectator* describes Sir Andrew Freeport to have been?' JOHNSON. 'Why, sir, we may suppose any fictitious character. We may suppose a philosophical day-labourer, who is happy in reflecting that, by his labour, he contributes to the fertility of the earth, and to the support of his fellow-creatures; but we find no such philosophical day-labourer. A merchant may, perhaps, be a man of an enlarged mind; but there is nothing in trade connected with an enlarged mind.'

I mentioned that I heard Dr Solander say he was a Swedish Laplander.[288] JOHNSON. 'Sir, I don't believe he is a Laplander. The Laplanders are not much above four feet high. He is as tall as you; and he has not the copper colour of a Laplander.' BOSWELL. 'But what motive could he have to make himself a Laplander?' JOHNSON. 'Why, sir, he must either mean the word Laplander in a very extensive sense, or may mean a voluntary degradation of himself. "For all my being the great man that you see me now, I was originally a barbarian"; as if Burke should say, "I came over a wild Irishman," which he might say in his present state of exaltation.'

Having expressed a desire to have an island like Inchkenneth, Dr Johnson set himself to think what would be necessary for a man in such a situation. 'Sir, I should build me a fortification, if I came to live here; for, if you have it not, what should hinder a parcel of ruffians to land in the night, and carry off every thing you have in the house, which, in a remote country, would be more valuable than cows and sheep? Add to all this the danger of having your throat cut.' BOSWELL. 'I would have a large dog.' JOHNSON. 'So you may, sir; but a large dog is of no use but to alarm.' He, however, I apprehend, thinks too lightly of the power of that animal. I have heard him say, that he is afraid of no dog. 'He would take him up by the hinder legs, which would render him quite helpless, and then knock his head against a stone, and beat out his brains.' Topham Beauclerk told me, that at his house in the country, two large ferocious dogs were fighting. Dr Johnson looked steadily at them for a little while; and then, as one would separate two little boys, who are foolishly hurting each other, he ran up to them, and cuffed their heads till he drove them asunder. But few men have his intrepidity, Herculean strength, or presence of mind. Most thieves or robbers would be afraid to encounter a mastiff.

I observed, that, when young Col talked of the lands belonging to his family, he always said, '*my* lands'. For this he had a plausible pretence; for he told me, there has been a custom in this family, that the laird resigns the estate to the eldest son when he comes of age, reserving to himself only a certain life-rent. He said, it was a voluntary custom; but I think I found an instance in the charter-room, that there was such an obligation in a contract of marriage. If the custom was voluntary, it was only curious; but if founded on obligation, it might be dangerous; for I have been told, that in Otaheité, whenever a child is born (a son, I think), the father loses his right to the estate and honours, and that this unnatural, or rather absurd custom, occasions the murder of many children.

Young Col told us he could run down a greyhound; 'for,' said he, 'the dog runs himself out of breath, by going too quick, and then I get up with him.' I accounted for his advantage over the dog, by remarking that Col had the faculty of reason, and knew how to moderate his pace, which the dog had not sense enough to do. Dr Johnson said, 'He is a noble animal. He is as complete an islander as the mind can figure. He is a farmer, a sailor, a hunter, a fisher: he will run you down a dog: if any man has a *tail*, it is Col. He is hospitable; and he has an intrepidity of talk, whether he understands the subject or not. I regret that he is not more intellectual.'

Dr Johnson observed, that there was nothing of which he would not undertake to persuade a Frenchman in a foreign country. 'I'll carry a Frenchman to St Paul's Church-yard, and I'll tell him, "by our law you may walk half round the church; but, if you walk round the whole, you will be punished capitally", and he will believe me at once. Now, no Englishman would readily swallow such a thing: he would go and inquire of somebody else.' The Frenchman's credulity, I observed, must be owing to his being accustomed to implicit submission; whereas every Englishman reasons upon the laws of his country, and instructs his representatives, who compose the legislature.

This day was passed in looking at a small island adjoining Inchkenneth, which afforded nothing worthy of observation; and in such social and gay entertainments as our little society could furnish.

Tuesday, 19th October

After breakfast we took leave of the young ladies, and of our excellent companion Col, to whom we had been so much obliged. He had now put us under the care of his chief; and was to hasten back to Sky. We parted from him with very strong feelings of kindness and gratitude; and we hoped to have had some future opportunity of proving to him the sincerity of what we felt; but in the following year he was unfortunately lost in the Sound between Ulva and Mull; and this imperfect memorial, joined to the high honour of being tenderly and respectfully mentioned by Dr Johnson, is the only return which the uncertainty of human events has permitted us to make to this deserving young man.

Sir Allan, who obligingly undertook to accompany us to Icolmkill had a strong good boat, with four stout rowers. We coasted along Mull till we reached Gribon, where is what is called Mackinnon's cave, compared with which that at Ulinish is inconsiderable. It is in a rock of a great height, close to the sea. Upon the left of its entrance there is a cascade, almost perpendicular from the top to the bottom of the rock. There is a tradition that it was conducted thither artificially, to supply the inhabitants of the cave with water. Dr Johnson gave no credit to this tradition. As, on the one hand, his faith in the Christian religion is firmly founded upon good grounds; so, on the other, he is incredulous when there is no sufficient reason for belief; being in this respect just the reverse of modern infidels, who, however nice and scrupulous in weighing the evidences of religion, are yet often so ready to believe the most absurd and improbable tales of another nature, that Lord Hailes well observed, a good essay might be written *Sur la credulité des Incredules.*

The height of this cave I cannot tell with any tolerable exactness: but it seemed to be very lofty, and to be a pretty regular arch. We penetrated, by candlelight, a great way; by our measurement, no less than four hundred and eighty-five feet. Tradition says, that a piper and twelve men once advanced into this cave, nobody can tell how far; and never returned. At the distance to which we proceeded the air was quite pure; for the candle burned freely, without the least appearance of the flame growing globular; but as we had only one, we thought it dangerous to venture farther, lest, should it have been extinguished, we should have had no means of ascertaining whether we could remain without danger. Dr Johnson said, this was the greatest natural curiosity he had ever seen.

We saw the island of Staffa, at no very great distance, but could not land upon it, the surge was so high on its rocky coast.

Sir Allan, anxious for the honour of Mull, was still talking of its *woods*, and pointing them out to Dr Johnson, as appearing at a distance on the skirts of that island, as we sailed along. JOHNSON. 'Sir, I saw at Tobermorie what they called a wood, which I unluckily took for *heath*. If you shew me what I shall take for *furze*, it will be something.'

In the afternoon we went ashore on the coast of Mull, and partook of a cold repast, which we carried with us. We hoped to have procured some rum or brandy for our boatmen and servants, from a publick-house near where we landed; but unfortunately a funeral a few days before had exhausted all their store. Mr Campbell however, one of the Duke of Argyle's tacksmen, who lived in the neighbourhood, on receiving a message from Sir Allan, sent us a liberal supply.

We continued to coast along Mull, and passed by Nuns' Island, which, it is said, belonged to the nuns of Icolmkill, and from which, we were told, the stone for the buildings there was taken. As we sailed along by moonlight, in a sea somewhat rough, and often between black and gloomy rocks, Dr Johnson said, 'If this be not *roving among the Hebrides*, nothing is.' The repetition of words which he had so often previously used, made a strong impression on my imagination; and, by a natural course of thinking, led me to consider how our present adventures would appear to me at a future period.

I have often experienced, that scenes through which a man has passed, improve by lying in the memory: they grow mellow. *Acti labores sunt jucundi.*[289] This may be owing to comparing them with present listless ease. Even harsh scenes acquire a softness by length of time:* and some are like very loud sounds, which do not please, or at least do not please so much, till you are removed to a certain distance. They may be compared to strong coarse pictures, which will not bear to be viewed near. Even pleasing scenes improve by time, and seem more exquisite in recollection, than when they were present; if they have not faded to dimness in the memory. Perhaps, there is so much evil in every human enjoyment, when present – so much dross mixed with it – that it requires to be refined by time; and yet I do not see why time should not melt away the good and the evil in equal proportions; why the shade should decay, and the light remain in preservation.

After a tedious sail, which, by our following various turnings of the coast of Mull, was extended to about forty miles, it gave us no small pleasure to perceive a light in the village of Icolmkill, in which almost all the inhabitants of the island live, close to where the ancient building stood. As we approached the shore, the tower of the cathedral, just discernable in the air, was a picturesque object.

When we had landed upon the sacred place, which, as long as I can remember, I had thought on with veneration, Dr Johnson and I cordially embraced. We had long talked of visiting Icolmkill; and, from the lateness of the season, were at times very doubtful whether we should be able to effect our purpose. To have seen it, even alone, would have given me great satisfaction; but the venerable scene was rendered much more pleasing by the company of my great and pious friend, who was no less affected by it than I was; and who has described the impressions it should make on the mind, with such strength of thought, and energy of language, that I shall quote his words, as conveying my own sensations much more forcibly than I am capable of doing:

We are now treading that illustrious island, which was once the luminary of the Caledonian regions, whence savage clans and roving barbarians derived the benefits of knowledge, and the blessings of religion. To abstract the mind from all local emotion would be impossible, if it were endeavoured, and would be foolish if it were

---

*I have lately observed that this thought has been elegantly expressed by Cowley:
> Things which offend when present, and affright,
> In memory, well painted, move delight.

possible. Whatever withdraws us from the power of our senses, whatever makes the past, the distant, or the future, predominate over the present, advances us in the dignity of thinking beings. Far from me, and from my friends, be such frigid philosophy as may conduct us indifferent and unmoved over any ground which has been dignified by wisdom, bravery or virtue. That man is little to be envied, whose patriotism would not gain force upon the plain of Marathon, or whose piety would not grow warmer among the ruins of Iona!*

Upon hearing that Sir Allan M'Lean was arrived, the inhabitants, who still consider themselves as the people of M'Lean, to whom the island formerly belonged, though the Duke of Argyle has at present possession of it, ran eagerly to him.

We were accommodated this night in a large barn, the island affording no lodging that we should have liked so well. Some good hay was strewed at one end of it, to form a bed for us, upon which we lay with our clothes on; and we were furnished with blankets from the village. Each of us had a portmanteau for a pillow. When I awaked in the morning, and looked round me, I could not help smiling at the idea of the Chief of the M'Leans, the great English moralist, and myself, lying thus extended in such a situation.

Wednesday, 20th October

Early in the morning we surveyed the remains of antiquity at this place, accompanied by an illiterate fellow, as cicerone, who called himself a descendant of a cousin of Saint Columba, the founder of the religious establishment here. As I knew that many persons had already examined them, and as I saw Dr Johnson inspecting and measuring several of the ruins of which he has since given so full an account, my mind was quiescent; and I resolved to stroll among them at my ease, to take no trouble to investigate minutely, and only receive the general impression of solemn antiquity, and the particular ideas of such objects as should of themselves strike my attention.

We walked from the monastery of nuns to the great church or cathedral, as they call it, along an old broken causeway. They told us, that this had been a street; and that there were good houses built on each side. Dr Johnson doubted if it was any thing more than a paved road for the nuns. The convent of monks, the great church, Oran's chapel, and four other chapels,

*Had our tour produced nothing else but this sublime passage, the world must have acknowledged that it was not made in vain. The present respectable President of the Royal Society was so much struck on reading it, that he clasped his hands together, and remained for some time in an attitude of silent admiration.[290]

are still to be discerned. But I must own that Icolmkill did not answer my expectations; for they were high, from what I had read of it, and still more from what I had heard and thought of it, from my earliest years. Dr Johnson said, it came up to his expectations, because he had taken his impression from an account of it subjoined to Sacheverel's *History of the Isle of Man*, where it is said, there is not much to be seen here. We were both disappointed, when we were shewn what are called the monuments of the kings of Scotland, Ireland, and Denmark, and of a king of France. There are only some grave-stones flat on the earth, and we could see no inscriptions. How far short was this of marble monuments, like those in Westminster Abbey, which I had imagined here! The grave-stones of Sir Allan M'Lean's family, and of that of M'Quarrie, had as good an appearance as the royal grave-stones; if they were royal, we doubted.

My easiness to give credit to what I heard in the course of our tour was too great. Dr Johnson's peculiar accuracy of investigation detected much traditional fiction, and many gross mistakes. It is not to be wondered at, that he was provoked by people carelessly telling him, with the utmost readiness and confidence, what he found, on questioning them a little more, was erroneous. Of this there were innumerable instances.

I left him and Sir Allan to breakfast in our barn, and stole back again to the cathedral, to indulge in solitude and devout meditation.[291] While contemplating the venerable ruins, I reflected with much satisfaction, that the solemn scenes of piety never lose their sanctity and influence, though the cares and follies of life may prevent us from visiting them, or may even make us fancy that their effects are only 'as yesterday, when it is past', and never again to be perceived. I hoped, that, ever after having been in this holy place, I should maintain an exemplary conduct. One has a strange propensity to fix upon some point of time from whence a better course of life may begin.

Being desirous to visit the opposite shore of the island, where Saint Columba is said to have landed, I procured a horse from one M'Ginnis, who ran along as my guide. The M'Ginnises are said to be a branch of the clan of M'Lean. Sir Allan had been told that this man had refused to send him some rum, at which the knight was in great indignation. 'You rascal!' said he. 'Don't you know that I can hang you, if I please?' Not averting to the chieftain's power over his clan, I imagined that Sir Allan had known of some capital crime that the fellow had committed, which he could discover, and so get him condemned; and said, 'How so?' 'Why,' said Sir Allan, 'are they not all my people?' Sensible in my inadvertency, and most willing to contribute what I could towards the continuation of feudal authority, 'Very true,' said I. Sir Allan went on: 'Refuse to send rum to me, you rascal! Don't you know that, if I order you to go and cut a man's throat, you are to do it?' 'Yes, an't please your honour! and my own too, and hang myself too.' The poor fellow denied that he had refused to send the rum. His making these professions was not merely a pretence in presence of his chief; for after he and I were out of Sir Allan's hearing, he told me, 'Had he sent his dog for the rum, I would have given it: I would cut my bones for him.' It was very remarkable to find such an attachment to a chief, though he had then no connection with the island, and had not been there for fourteen years. Sir Allan, by way of upbraiding the fellow, said, 'I believe you are a *Campbell*.'

The place which I went to see is about two miles from the village. They call it Portawherry, from the wherry in which Columba came; though, when they shew the length of his vessel, as marked on the beach by two heaps of stones, they say, 'Here is the length of the *currach*,' using the Erse word.

Icolmkill is a fertile island. The inhabitants export some cattle and grain; and I was told, they import nothing but iron and salt. They are industrious, and make their own woollen and linen cloth; and they brew a good deal of beer, which we did not find in any of the other islands.

We set sail again about mid-day, and in the evening landed on Mull, near the house of the Reverend Mr Neal M'Leod, who having been informed of our coming, by a message from Sir Allan, came out to meet us. We were this night very agreeably entertained at his house. Dr Johnson observed to me, that he was the cleanest-headed man that he had met in the Western islands. He seemed to be well acquainted with Dr Johnson's writings, and courteously said, 'I have been often obliged to you, though I never had the pleasure of seeing you before.'

He told us, he had lived for some time in St Kilda, under the tuition of the minister or catechist there, and had there first read Horace and Virgil. The scenes which they describe must have been a strong contrast to the dreary waste around him.

Thursday, 21st October

This morning the subject of politicks was introduced. JOHNSON. 'Pulteney was as paltry a fellow as could be. He was a Whig, who pretended to be honest; and you know it is ridiculous for a Whig to pretend to be honest. He cannot hold it out.' He called Mr Pitt a meteor; Sir Robert Walpole a fixed star. He said, 'It is wonderful to think that all the force of government was required to prevent Wilkes from being chosen the chief magistrate of London, though the liverymen knew he would rob their shops, knew he would debauch their daughters.'*

BOSWELL. 'The history of England is so strange, that, if it were not so well vouched as it is, it would hardly be credible.' JOHNSON. 'Sir, if it were told as shortly, and with as little preparation for introducing the different events, as the history of the Jewish kings, it would be equally liable to objections of improbability.' Mr M'Leod was much pleased with the justice and novelty of the thought. Dr Johnson illustrated what he had said, as follows: 'Take, as an instance, Charles the First's concessions to his parliament, which were greater and greater, in proportion as the parliament grew more insolent, and less deserving of trust. Had these concessions been related nakedly, without any detail of the circumstances which generally led to them, they would not have been believed.'

Sir Allan M'Lean bragged, that Scotland had the advantage of England, by its having more water. JOHNSON, 'Sir, we would not have your water, to take the vile bogs which produced it. You have too much! A man who is drowned has more water than either of us'; and then he laughed. (But this was surely robust sophistry: for the people of taste in England, who have seen Scotland, own that its variety of rivers and lakes makes it naturally more beautiful than England, in that respect.) Pursuing his victory over Sir Allan, he proceeded: 'Your country consists of two things, stone and water. There is, indeed, a little earth above the stone in some places, but a very little; and the stone is always appearing. It is like a man in rags; the naked skin is still peeping out.'

He took leave of Mr M'Leod, saying, 'Sir, I thank you for your entertainment, and your conversation.'

Mr Campbell, who had been so polite yesterday, came this morning on

*I think it incumbent on me to make some observation on this strong satirical sally on my classical companion, Mr Wilkes. Reporting it lately from memory, in his presence, I expressed it thus: 'They knew he would rob their shops, *if he durst*; they knew he would debauch their daughters, *if he could*', which, according to the French phrase, may be said *renchérir* on Dr Johnson; but on looking into my *Journal*, I found it as above, and would by no means make any addition. Mr Wilkes received both readings with a good humour that I cannot enough admire. Indeed both he and I (as, with respect to myself, the reader has more than once had occasion to observe in the course of this *Journal*) are too fond of a *bon mot*, not to relish it, though we should be ourselves the object of it.

Let me add, in justice to the gentleman here mentioned, that at a subsequent period, he *was* elected chief magistrate of London, and discharged the duties of that high office with great honour to himself, and advantage to the city. Some years before Dr Johnson died, I was fortunate enough to bring him and Mr Wilkes together; the consequence of which was, that they were ever afterwards on easy and not unfriendly terms. The particulars I shall have great pleasure in relating at large in my *Life of Dr Johnson*.

purpose to breakfast with us, and very obligingly furnished us with horses to proceed on our journey to Mr M'Lean's of Lochbuy, where we were to pass the night. We dined at the house of Dr Alexander M'Lean, another physician in Mull, who was so much struck with the uncommon conversation of Dr Johnson, that he observed to me, 'This man is just a *hogshead* of sense.'

Dr Johnson said of the *Turkish Spy*,[292] which lay in the room, that it told nothing but what every body might have known at that time; and that what was good in it, did not pay you for the trouble of reading to find it.

After a very tedious ride, through what appeared to me the most gloomy and desolate country I had ever beheld, we arrived, between seven and eight o'clock, at Moy, the seat of the Laird of Lochbuy. Buy, in Erse, signifies yellow, and I at first imagined that the loch or branch of the sea here, was thus denominated, in the same manner as the Red Sea; but I afterwards learned that it derived its name from a hill above it, which being of a yellowish hue, has the epithet of *Buy*.

We had heard much of Lochbuy's being a great roaring braggadocio, a kind of Sir John Falstaff, both in size and manners; but we found that they had swelled him up to a fictitious size, and clothed him with imaginary qualities. Col's idea of him was equally extravagant, though very different: he told us, he was quite a Don Quixote; and said, he would give a great deal to see him and Dr Johnson together. The truth is, that Lochbuy proved to be only a bluff, comely, noisy old gentleman, proud of his hereditary consequence, and a very hearty and hospitable landlord. Lady Lochbuy was sister to Sir Allan M'Lean, but much older. He said to me, 'They are quite *Antediluvians*.' Being told that Dr Johnson did not hear well, Lochbuy bawled out to him, 'Are you of the Johnstons of Glencro, or of Ardnamurchan?' Dr Johnson gave him a significant look, but made no answer; and I told Lochbuy that he was not John*ston*, but John*son*, and that he was an Englishman.

Lochbuy some years ago tried to prove himself a weak man, liable to imposition, or, as we term it in Scotland, a *facile* man, in order to set aside a lease which he had granted; but failed in the attempt. On my mentioning this circumstance to Dr Johnson, he seemed much surprized that such a suit was admitted by the Scottish law, and observed, that 'in England no man is allowed to *stultify* himself.'*

---

* This maxim, however, has been controverted. See Blackstone's *Commentaries*, Vol. II, p. 292; and the authorities there quoted.

Sir Allan, Lochbuy, and I, had the conversation chiefly to ourselves to-night: Dr Johnson, being extremely weary, went to bed soon after supper.

Friday, 22d October

Before Dr Johnson came to breakfast, Lady Lochbuy said, 'he was a *dungeon* of wit'; a very common phrase in Scotland to express a profound-ness of intellect, though he afterwards told me, that he never had heard it. She proposed that he should have some cold sheep's head for breakfast. Sir Allan seemed displeased at his sister's vulgarity, and wondered how such a thought should come into her head. From a mischievous love of sport, I took the lady's part; and very gravely said, 'I think it is but fair to give him an offer of it. If he does not choose it, he may let it alone.' 'I think so,' said the lady, looking at her brother with an air of victory. Sir Allan, finding the matter desperate, strutted about the room, and took snuff. When Dr Johnson came in, she called to him, 'Do you choose any cold sheep's-head, sir?' 'No, Madam,' said he, with a tone of surprise and anger. 'It is here, sir,' said she, supposing he had refused it to save the trouble of bring-ing it in. They thus went on at cross purposes, till he confirmed his refusal in a manner not to be misunderstood; while I sat quietly by, and enjoyed my success.

After breakfast, we surveyed the old castle, in the pit or dungeon of which Lochbuy had some years before taken upon him to imprison several persons; and though he had been fined a considerable sum by the Court of Justiciary, he was so little affected by it, that while we were examining the dungeon, he said to me, with a smile, 'Your father knows something of this' (alluding to my father's having sat as one of the judges on his trial). Sir Allan whispered me, that the laird could not be persuaded, that he had lost his heritable jurisdiction.

We then set out for the ferry, by which we were to cross to the main land of Argyleshire. Lochbuy and Sir Allan accompanied us. We were told much of a war-saddle, on which this reputed Don Quixote used to be moun-ted; but we did not see it, for the young laird had applied it to a less noble purpose, having taken it to Falkirk fair *with a drove of black cattle*.

We bade adieu to Lochbuy, and to our very kind conductor, Sir Allan M'Lean, on the shore of Mull, and then got into the ferry-boat, the bottom of which was strewed with branches of trees or bushes, upon which we sat. We had a good day and a fine passage, and in the evening landed at Oban, where we found a tolerable inn.[293] After having been so long con-fined at different times in islands, from which it was always uncertain when we could get away, it was comfortable to be now on the main land, and to know that, if in health, we might get to any place in Scotland or England in a certain number of days.

Here we discovered from the conjectures which were formed, that the people on the main land were intirely ignorant of our motions; for in a Glasgow news-paper we found a paragraph, which, as it contains a just and well-turned compliment to my illustrious friend, I shall here insert:

> We are well assured that Dr Johnson is confined by tempestuous weather to the isle of Sky; it being unsafe to venture, in a small boat upon such a stormy surge as is very common there at this time of the year. Such a philosopher, detained on an almost barren island, resembles a whale left upon the strand. The latter will be welcome to every body, on account of his oil, his bone, &c. and the other will charm his companions, and the rude inhabitants, with his superior knowledge and wisdom, calm resignation, and unbounded benevolence.

Saturday, 23d October

After a good night's rest, we breakfasted at our leisure. We talked of Goldsmith's *Traveller*, of which Dr Johnson spoke highly; and, while I was helping him on with his great coat, he repeated from it the character of the British nation, which he did with such energy, that the tear started into his eye:

> ' "Stern o'er each bosom reason holds her state.
> With daring aims irregularly great,
> Pride in their port, defiance in their eye,
> I see the lords of humankind pass by,
> Intent on high designs, a thoughtful band,
> By forms unfashion'd; fresh from nature's hand;
> Fierce in their native hardiness of soul,
> True to imagin'd right, above control,
> While ev'n the peasant boasts these rights to scan,
> And learns to venerate himself as man." '

We could get but one bridle here, which, according to the maxim *detur digniori*,[294] was appropriated to Dr Johnson's sheltie. I and Joseph rode with halters. We crossed in a ferry-boat a pretty wide lake, and on the farther side of it, close by the shore, found a hut for our inn.[295] We were much wet. I changed my clothes in part, and was at pains to get myself well dried. Dr Johnson resolutely kept on all his clothes, wet as they were, letting them steam before the smoky turf fire. I thought him in the wrong; but his firmness was, perhaps, a species of heroism.

I remember but little of our conversation. I mentioned Shenstone's saying of Pope, that he had the art of condensing sense more than any body. Dr Johnson said, 'It is not true, sir. There is more sense in a line of Cowley than in a page' (or a sentence of ten lines – I am not quite certain of the very phrase) 'of Pope.' He maintained that Archibald, Duke of Argyle, was a narrow man. I wondered at this; and observed, that his building so great a house at Inveraray was not like a narrow man. 'Sir,' said he, 'when a narrow man has resolved to build a house, he builds it like another man. But Archibald, Duke of Argyle, was narrow in his ordinary expences, in his quotidian expences.'

The distinction is very just. It is in the ordinary expences of life that a man's liberality or narrowness is to be discovered. I never heard the word *quotidian* in this sense, and I imagined it to be a word of Dr Johnson's own fabrication; but I have since found it in Young's *Night Thoughts* (Night fifth):

Death's a destroyer of quotidian prey.

and in my friend's *Dictionary*, supported by the authorities of Charles I and Dr Donne.

It rained very hard as we journied on after dinner. The roar of torrents from the mountains, as we passed along in the dusk, and the other circumstances attending our ride this evening, have been mentioned with so much animation by Dr Johnson, that I shall not attempt to say any thing on the subject.

We got at night to Inveraray, where we found an excellent inn.[296] Even here, Dr Johnson would not change his wet clothes.

The prospect of good accommodation cheered us much. We supped well; and after supper, Dr Johnson, whom I had not seen taste any fermented liquor during all our travels, called for a gill of whisky. 'Come,' said he, 'let me know what it is that makes a Scotchman happy!' He drank it all but a drop, which I begged leave to pour into my glass, that I might say we had drunk whisky together. I proposed Mrs Thrale should be our toast. He would not have *her* drunk in whisky, but rather 'some insular lady', so we drank one of the ladies whom we had lately left. He owned tonight, that he got as good a room and bed as at an English inn.

I had here the pleasure of finding a letter from home, which relieved me from the anxiety I had suffered, in consequence of not having received any account of my family for many weeks. I also found a letter from Mr Garrick, which was a regale as agreeable as a pineapple would be in a desert.

He had favoured me with his correspondence for many years; and when Dr Johnson and I were at Inverness, I had written to him as follows:

Inverness,

My dear Sir, Sunday, 29 August, 1773

Here I am, and Mr Samuel Johnson actually with me. We were a night at Fores, in coming to which, in the dusk of the evening, we passed over a bleak and blasted heath where Macbeth met the witches. Your old preceptor repeated, with much solemnity, the speech

> How far is't called to Fores? What are these,
> So wither'd and so wild in their attire, &c.

This day we visited the ruins of Macbeth's castle at Inverness. I have had great romantick satisfaction in seeing Johnson upon the classical scenes of Shakspeare in Scotland; which I really looked upon as almost as improbable as that 'Birnam wood should come to Dunsinane'. Indeed, as I have always been accustomed to view him as a permanent London object, it would not be much more wonderful to me to see St Paul's church moving along where we now are. As yet we have travelled in postchaises; but to-morrow we are to mount on horseback, and ascend into the mountains by Fort Augustus, and so on to the ferry, where we are to cross to Sky. We shall see that island fully, and then visit some more of the Hebrides; after which we are to land in Argyleshire, proceed by Glasgow to Auchinleck, repose there a competent time, and then return to Edinburgh, from whence the Rambler will depart for old England again, as soon as he finds it convenient. Hitherto we have had a very prosperous expedition. I flatter myself *servetur ad imum, qualis ab incepto processerit*.[297] He is in excellent spirits, and I have a rich journal of his conversation. Look back, Davy,* to Litchfield; run up through the time that has elapsed since you first knew Mr Johnson, and enjoy with me his present extraordinary tour. I could not resist the impulse of writing to you from this place. The situation of the old castle corresponds exactly to Shakspeare's description. While we were there to-day, it happened oddly, that a raven perched upon one of the chimney-tops, and croaked. Then I in my turn repeated

> 'The raven himself is hoarse,
> That croaks the fatal entrance of Duncan,
> Under my battlements.'

I wish you had been with us. Think what enthusiastick happiness I shall have to see Mr Samuel Johnson walking among the romantick rocks and woods of my ancestors at Auchinleck! Write to me at Edinburgh. You owe me his verses on great George and tuneful Cibber,[298] and the bad verses which led him to make his fine

---

*I took the liberty of giving this familiar appellation to my celebrated friend, to bring in a more lively manner to his remembrance the period when he was Dr Johnson's pupil.

ones on Philips the musician. Keep your promise, and let me have them. I offer my very best compliments to Mrs Garrick, and ever am

Your warm admirer and friend,

To David Garrick, Esq;   JAMES BOSWELL,
London.

His answer was as follows,

Hampton,

Dear Sir,   September 14, 1773,

You stole away from London, and left us all in the lurch; for we expected you one night at the club, and knew nothing of your departure. Had I payed you what I owed you, for the book you bought for me, I should only have grieved for the loss of your company, and slept with a quiet conscience; but, wounded as it is, it must remain so till I see you again, though I am sure our good friend Mr Johnson will discharge the debt for me, if you will let him. Your account of your journey to *Fores*, the *raven, old castle*, &c. &c. made me half mad. Are you not rather too late in the year for fine weather, which is the life and soul of seeing places? I hope your pleasure will continue *qualis ab incepto*, &c.

Your friend ——*[299] threatens me much. I only wish that he would put his threats in execution, and, if he prints his play, I will forgive him. I remember he complained to you, that his bookseller called for the money for some copies of his —— , which I subscribed for, and that I desired him to call again. The truth is, that my wife was not at home, and that for weeks together I have not ten shillings in my pocket. However, had it been otherwise, it was not so great a crime to draw his poetical vengeance upon me. I despise all that he can do, and am glad that I can so easily get rid of him and his ingratitude. I am hardened both to abuse and ingratitude.

You, I am sure, will no more recommend your poetasters to my civility and good offices.

Shall I recommend to you a play of Eschylus (the Prometheus), published and translated by poor old Morell, who is a good scholar, and an acquaintance of mine? It will be but half a guinea, and your name shall be put in the list I am making for him. You will be in very good company.

Now for the Epitaphs!

[These, together with the verses on George the Second, and Colley Cibber, as his Poet Laureat, of which imperfect copies are gone about, will appear in my Life of Dr Johnson.*]*

* I have suppressed my friend's name from an apprehension of wounding his sensibility; but I would not withhold from my readers a passage which shews Mr Garrick's mode of writing as the Manager of a Theatre, and contains a pleasing trait of his domestick life. His judgment of dramatick pieces, so far as concerns their exhibition on the stage, must be allowed to have considerable weight. But from the effect which a perusal of the tragedy here condemned had upon myself, and from the opinions of some eminent criticks, I venture to pronounce that it has much poetical merit; and its author has distinguished himself by several performances which shew that the epithet *poetaster* was, in the present instance, much misapplied.

I have no more paper, or I should have said more to you. My love and respects to Mr Johnson.

Yours ever,
D. GARRICK.

I can't write. I have the gout in my hand.
To James Boswell, Esq., Edinburgh.

Sunday, 24th October

We passed the forenoon calmly and placidly. I prevailed on Dr Johnson to read aloud Ogden's sixth sermon on prayer, which he did with a distinct expression, and pleasing solemnity. He praised my favourite preacher, his elegant language, and remarkable acuteness; and said, he fought infidels with their own weapons.

As a specimen of Ogden's manner, I insert the following passage from the sermon which Dr Johnson now read. The preacher, after arguing against that vain philosophy which maintains, in conformity with the hard principle of eternal necessity, or unchangeable predetermination, that the only effect of prayer for others, although we are exhorted to pray for them, is to produce good dispositions in ourselves towards them; thus expresses himself:

A plain man may be apt to ask, But if this then, though enjoined in the holy Scriptures, is to be my real aim and intention, when I am taught to pray for other persons, why is it that I do not plainly so express it? Why is not the form of the petition brought nearer to the meaning? Give them, say I to our heavenly father, what is good. But this, I am to understand, will be as it will be, and is not for me to alter. What is it then that I am doing? I am desiring to become charitable myself; and why may I not plainly say so? Is there shame in it, or impiety? The wish is laudable: why should I form designs to hide it?

Or is it, perhaps, better to be brought about by indirect means, and in this artful manner? Alas! who is it that I would impose on? From whom can it be, in this commerce, that I desire to hide any thing? When, as my Saviour commands me, I have 'entered into my closet, and shut my door', there are but two parties privy to my devotions, God and my own heart; which of the two am I deceiving?

He wished to have more books, and, upon inquiring if there were any in the house, was told that a waiter had some, which were brought to him; but I recollect none of them, except Hervey's *Meditations*.[300] He thought slightingly of this admired book. He treated it with ridicule, and would not allow even the scene of the dying husband and father to be pathetick. I am not an impartial judge; for Hervey's *Meditations* engaged my affections in my early years. He read a passage concerning the moon, ludicrously, and shewed how easily he could, in the same style, make reflections on that planet, the very reverse of Hervey's, representing her as treacherous to mankind. He did this with much humour; but I have not preserved the particulars. He then indulged a playful fancy, in making a *Meditation on a Pudding*, of which I hastily wrote down, in his presence, the following note; which, though imperfect, may serve to give my readers some idea of it.

MEDITATION ON A PUDDING

Let us seriously reflect of what a pudding is composed. It is composed of flour that once waved in the golden grain, and drank the dews of the morning; of milk pressed from the swelling udder by the gentle hand of the beauteous milk-maid, whose beauty and innocence might have recommended a worse draught; who, while she stroked the udder, indulged no ambitious thoughts of wandering in palaces, formed no plans for the destruction of her fellow-creatures: milk, which is drawn from the cow, that useful animal, that eats the grass of the field, and supplies us with that which made the greatest part of the food of mankind in the age which the poets have agreed to call golden. It is made with an egg, that miracle of nature, which the theoretical Burnet has compared to creation. An egg contains water within its beautiful smooth surface; and an unformed mass, by the incubation of the parent, becomes a regular animal, furnished with bones and sinews, and covered with feathers. Let us consider; can there be more wanting to complete the Meditation on a Pudding? If more is wanting, more may be found. It contains salt, which keeps the sea from putrefaction: salt, which is made the image of intellectual excellence, contributes to the formation of a pudding.

In a magazine I found a saying of Dr Johnson's, something to this purpose; that the happiest part of a man's life is what he passes lying awake in bed in the morning. I read it to him. He said, 'I may, perhaps, have said this; for nobody, at times, talks more laxly than I do.' I ventured to suggest to him, that this was dangerous from one of his authority.

I spoke of living in the country, and upon what footing one should be with neighbours. I observed that some people were afraid of being on too easy a footing with them, from an apprehension that their time would not be their own. He made the obvious remark, that it depended much on what kind of neighbours one has, whether it was desirable to be on an easy footing with them, or not. I mentioned a certain baronet,[301] who told me, he never was happy in the country, till he was not on speaking terms with his neighbours, which he contrived in different ways to bring about. 'Lord — ,[302] said he, 'stuck along; but at last the fellow pounded my pigs, and then I got rid of him.' JOHNSON. 'Nay, sir, My Lord got rid of Sir John, and shewed how little he valued him, by putting his pigs in the pound.'

I told Dr Johnson I was in some difficulty how to act at Inveraray. I had reason to think that the Duchess of Argyle disliked me, on account of my zeal in the Douglas cause;[303] but the Duke of Argyle had always been pleased to treat me with great civility. They were now at the castle, which is a very short walk from our inn; and the question was, whether I should go and pay my respects there. Dr Johnson, to whom I had stated the case, was clear that I ought; but, in his usual way, he was very shy of discovering a desire to be invited there himself. Though from a conviction of the benefit of subordination to society, he has always shewn great respect to persons of high rank, when he happened to be in their company, yet his pride of character has ever made him guard against any appearance of courting the great. Besides, he was impatient to go to Glasgow, where he expected letters. At the same time he was, I believe, secretly not unwilling to have attention paid him by so great a chieftain, and so exalted a nobleman. He insisted that I should not go to the castle this day before dinner, as it would look like seeking an invitation. 'But,' said I, 'if the duke invites us to dine with him to-morrow, shall we accept?' 'Yes, sir,' I think he said, 'to be sure.' But, he added, 'He won't ask us!' I mentioned, that I was afraid my company might be disagreeable to the duchess. He treated this objection with a manly disdain: '*That*, sir, he must settle with his wife.' We dined well. I went to the castle just about the time when I supposed the ladies would be retired from dinner. I sent in my name; and, being shewn in, found the amiable duke sitting at the head of his table with several gentlemen. I was most politely received, and gave his grace some particulars of the curious journey which I had been making with Dr Johnson. When we rose from table, the duke said to me, 'I hope you and Dr Johnson will dine with us to-morrow.' I thanked his grace; but told him, my friend was in a great hurry to get back to London. The duke, with a kind complacency, said, 'He will stay one day; and I will take care he shall see this place to advantage.' I said, I should be sure to let him know his grace's invitation. As I was going away, the duke said, 'Mr Boswell, won't you have some tea?' I thought it best to get over the meeting with the duchess this night; so respectfully agreed. I was conducted to the drawing-room by the duke, who announced my name; but the duchess, who was sitting with her daughter, Lady Betty Hamilton, and some other ladies, took not the least notice of me. I should have been mortified at being thus coldly received by a lady of whom I, with the rest of the world, have always entertained a very high admiration, had I not been consoled by the obliging attention of the duke.

When I returned to the inn, I informed Dr Johnson of the Duke of Argyle's invitation, with which he was much pleased, and readily accepted of it.

We talked of a violent contest which was then carrying on, with a view to the next general election for Ayrshire; where one of the candidates, in order to undermine the old and established interest, had artfully held himself out as a champion for the independency of the county against aristocratick influence, and had persuaded several gentlemen into a resolution to oppose every candidate who was supported by peers. 'Foolish fellows!' said Dr Johnson. 'Didn't they see that they are as much dependent upon the peers one way as the other. The peers have but to *oppose* a candidate, to ensure him success. It is said, the only way to make a pig go forward, is to pull him back by the tail. These people must be treated like pigs.'

Monday, 25th October

My acquaintance, the Reverend Mr John M'Aulay, one of the ministers of Inveraray,[304] and brother to our good friend at Calder, came to us this morning, and accompanied us to the castle, where I presented Dr Johnson to the Duke of Argyle. We were shewn through the house; and I never shall forget the impression made upon my fancy by some of the ladies' maids tripping about in neat morning dresses. After seeing for a long time little but rusticity, their lively manner, and gay inviting appearance, pleased me so much, that I thought, for the moment, I could have been a knight-errant for them.*

We then got into a low one-horse chair, ordered for us by the duke, in which we drove about the place. Dr Johnson was much struck by the grandeur and elegance of this princely seat. He thought, however, the castle too low, and wished it had been a story higher. He said, 'What I admire here, is the total defiance of expence.' I had a particular pride in shewing him a great number of fine old trees, to compensate for the nakedness which had made such an impression on him on the eastern coast of Scotland.

When we came in, before dinner, we found the duke and some gentlemen in the hall. Dr Johnson took much notice of the large collection of arms, which are excellently disposed there. I told what he had said to Sir Alexander McDonald, of his ancestors not suffering their arms to rust. 'Well,' said the doctor, 'but let us be glad we live in times when arms *may* rust. We can sit to-day at his grace's table, without any risk of being attacked, and perhaps sitting down again wounded or maimed.' The duke placed Dr Johnson next himself at table. I was in fine spirits; and though sensible that I had the misfortune of not being in favour with the duchess, I was

---

*On reflection, at the distance of several years, I wonder that my venerable fellow-traveller should have read this passage without censuring my levity.

not in the least disconcerted, and offered her grace some of the dish that was before me. It must be owned that I was in the right to be quite unconcerned, if I could. I was the Duke of Argyle's guest; and I had no reason to suppose that he adopted the prejudices and resentments of the Duchess of Hamilton.

I knew it was the rule of modern high life not to drink to any body; but, that I might have the satisfaction for once to look the duchess in the face, with a glass in my hand, I with a respectful air addressed her, 'My Lady Duchess, I have the honour to drink your grace's good health.' I repeated the words audibly, and with a steady countenance. This was, perhaps, rather too much; but some allowance must be made for human feelings.

The duchess was very attentive to Dr Johnson. I know not how a middle state came to be mentioned. Her grace wished to hear him on that point. 'Madam,' said he, 'your own relation, Mr Archibald Campbell, can tell you better about it than I can. He was a bishop of the nonjuring communion, and wrote a book upon the subject.'* He engaged to get it for her grace. He afterwards gave a full history of Mr Archibald Campbell, which I am sorry I do not recollect particularly. He said, Mr Campbell had been bred a violent Whig, but afterwards 'kept *better company*, and became a Tory'. He said this with a smile, in pleasant allusion, as I thought, to the opposition between his own political principles and those of the duke's clan. He added that Mr Campbell, after the Revolution, was thrown in gaol on account of his tenets; but, on application by letter to the old Lord Townshend, was released: that he always spoke of his Lordship with great gratitude, saying, 'though a *Whig*, he had humanity'.

Dr Johnson and I passed some time together, in June 1784, at Pembroke College, Oxford, with the Reverend Dr Adams, the master; and I having expressed a regret that my note relative to Mr Archibald Campbell was imperfect, he was then so good as to write with his own hand, on the blank page of my *Journal*, opposite to that which contains what I have now men-

---

* As this book is now become very scarce, I shall subjoin the title, which is curious:

'The Doctrines of a Middle State between Death and the Resurrection: Of Prayers for the Dead: And the Necessity of Purification; plainly proved from the holy Scriptures, and the Writings of the Fathers of the Primitive Church: And acknowledged by several learned Fathers and great Divines of the Church of England and others since the Reformation. To which is added, an Appendix concerning the Descent of the Soul of Christ into Hell, while his Body lay in the Grave. Together with the Judgment of the Reverend Dr Hickes concerning this Book, so far as relates to a Middle State, particular Judgment, and Prayers for the Dead as it appeared in the first Edition. And a Manuscript of the Right Reverend Bishop Overall upon the Subject of a Middle State, and never before printed. Also, a Preservative against several of the Errors of the Roman Church, in six small Treatises. By the Honourable Archibald Campbell.' Folio, 1721.

tioned, the following paragraph; which, however, is not quite so full as the narrative he gave at Inveraray:

The Honourable Archibald Campbell was, I believe, the nephew of the Marquis of Argyle. He began life by engaging in Monmouth's rebellion, and, to escape the law, lived some time in Surinam. When he returned, he became zealous for episcopacy and monarchy; and at the Revolution adhered not only to the Nonjurors, but to those who refused to communicate with the Church of England, or to be present at any worship where the usurper was mentioned as king. He was, I believe, more than once apprehended in the reign of King William, and once at the accession of George. He was the familiar friend of Hicks and Nelson; a man of letters, but injudicious; and very curious and inquisitive, but credulous. He lived in 1743, or 44, about 75 years old.[305]

The subject of luxury having been introduced, Dr Johnson defended it. 'We have now,' said he, 'a splendid dinner before us. Which of all these dishes is unwholsome?' The duke asserted, that he had observed the grandees of Spain diminished in their size by luxury. Dr Johnson politely refrained from opposing directly an observation which the duke himself had made; but said, 'Man must be very different from other animals, if he is diminished by good living; for the size of all other animals is increased by it.' I made some remark that seemed to imply a belief in second sight. The duchess said, 'I fancy you will be a *Methodist*.' This was the only sentence her grace deigned to utter to me; and I take it for granted, she thought it a good hit on my *credulity* in the Douglas cause.

A gentleman in company, after dinner, was desired by the duke to go to another room, for a specimen of curious marble, which his grace wished to shew us. He brought a wrong piece, upon which the duke sent him back again. He could not refuse; but, to avoid any appearance of servility, he whistled as he walked out of the room, to show his independency. On my mentioning this afterwards to Dr Johnson, he said, it was a nice trait of character.

Dr Johnson talked a great deal, and was so entertaining, that Lady Betty Hamilton, after dinner, went and placed her chair close to his, leaned upon the back of it, and listened eagerly. It would have made a fine picture to have drawn the Sage and her at this time in their several attitudes. He did not know, all the while, how much he was honoured. I told him afterwards. I never saw him so gentle and complaisant as this day.

We went to tea. The duke and I walked up and down the drawing-room, conversing. The duchess still continued to shew the same marked coldness for me; for which, though I suffered from it, I made every allowance, considering the very warm part that I had taken for Douglas, in the cause in which she thought her son deeply interested. Had not her grace discovered some displeasure towards me, I should have suspected her of insensibility or dissimulation.

Her grace made Dr Johnson come and sit by her, and asked him why he made his journey so late in the year. 'Why, madam,' said he, 'you know Mr Boswell must attend the Court of Session, and it does not rise till the twelfth of August.' She said, with some sharpness, 'I *know nothing* of Mr Boswell.' Poor Lady Lucy Douglas, to whom I mentioned this, observed, 'She knew *too much* of Mr Boswell.' I shall make no remark on her grace's speech. I indeed felt it as rather too severe; but when I recollected that my punishment was inflicted by so dignified a beauty, I had that kind of consolation which a man would feel who is strangled by a *silken cord*. Dr Johnson was all attention to her grace. He used afterwards a droll expression, upon her enjoying the three titles of Hamilton, Brandon, and Argyle. Borrowing an image from the Turkish empire, he called her a 'Duchess with three tails'.

He was much pleased with our visit at the castle of Inveraray. The Duke of Argyle was exceedingly polite to him, and, upon his complaining of the shelties which he had hitherto ridden being too small for him, his grace told him he should be provided with a good horse to carry him next day.

Mr John M'Aulay passed the evening with us at our inn. When Dr Johnson spoke of people whose principles were good, but whose practice was faulty, Mr M'Aulay said, he had no notion of people being in earnest in their good professions, whose practice was not suitable to them. The Doctor grew warm, and said, 'Sir, you are so grossly ignorant of human nature, as not to know that a man may be very sincere in good principles, without having good practice?'

Dr Johnson was unquestionably in the right; and whoever examines himself candidly, will be satisfied of it, though the inconsistency between principles and practice is greater in some men than in others.

I recollect very little of this night's conversation. I am sorry that indolence came upon me towards the conclusion of our journey, so that I did not write down what passed with the same assiduity as during the greatest part of it.

Tuesday, 26th October

Mr M'Aulay breakfasted with us, nothing hurt or dismayed by his last night's correction. Being a man of good sense, he had a just admiration of Dr Johnson.

Either yesterday morning, or this, I communicated to Dr Johnson, from Mr M'Aulay's information, the news that Dr Beattie had got a pension of two hundred pounds a year. He sat up in his bed, clapped his hands, and cried, 'O brave we!' a peculiar exclamation of his when he rejoices.*

As we sat over our tea, Mr Home's *Tragedy of Douglas* was mentioned. I put Dr Johnson in mind, that once, in a coffee-house at Oxford, he called to old Mr Sheridan, 'How came you, sir, to give Home a gold medal for writing that foolish play?' and defied Mr Sheridan to shew ten good lines in it. He did not insist they should be together; but that there were not ten good lines in the whole play. He now persisted in this. I endeavoured to defend that pathetick and beautiful tragedy, and repeated the following passage:

> ' "... Sincerity,
> Thou first of virtues! let no mortal leave
> Thy onward path, although the earth should gape,
> And from the gulph of hell destruction cry,
> To take dissimulation's winding way." '

JOHNSON. 'That will not do, sir. Nothing is good but what is consistent with truth or probability, which this is not. Juvenal, indeed, gives us a noble picture of inflexible virtue:

> *Esto bonus miles, tutor bonus, arbiter idem*
> *Integer: ambiguæ si quando citabere testis,*
> *Incertæque rei, Phalaris licet imperet, ut sis*
> *Falsus, et admoto dictet perjuria tauro,*
> *Summum crede nefas animam præferre pudori,*
> *Et propter vitam vivendi perdere causas.†*

---

* Having mentioned, more than once, that my *Journal* was perused by Dr Johnson, I think it proper to inform my readers that this is the last paragraph which he read.

> † An honest guardian, arbitrator just,
> Be thou; thy station deem a sacred trust.
> With thy good sword maintain thy country's cause;
> In every action venerate its laws:
> The lie suborn'd if falsely urg'd to swear,
> Though torture wait thee, torture firmly bear;
> To forfeit honour, think the highest shame,
> And life too dearly bought by loss of fame;
> Nor, to preserve it, with thy virtue give
> That for which only man should wish to live.

For this and the other translations to which no signature is affixed, I am indebted to the friend whose observations are mentioned in notes.[306]

He repeated the lines with great force and dignity; then added, 'And, after this, comes Johnny Hoe, with his *earth gaping*, and his *destruction crying* – Pooh!'*

While we were lamenting the number of ruined religious buildings which we had lately seen, I spoke with peculiar feeling to the miserable neglect of the chapel belonging to the palace of Holyrood House, in which are deposited the remains of many of the kings of Scotland, and of many of our nobility. I said, it was a disgrace to the country that it was not repaired: and particularly complained that my friend Douglas, the representative of a great house, and proprietor of a vast estate, should suffer the sacred spot where his mother lies interred, to be unroofed, and exposed to all the inclemencies of the weather. Dr Johnson, who, I know not how, had formed an opinion on the Hamilton side, in the Douglas cause, slily answered, 'Sir, sir, don't be too severe upon the gentleman; don't accuse him of want of filial piety! Lady Jane Douglas was not *his* mother.'[307] He roused my zeal so much that I took the liberty to tell him he knew nothing of the cause; which I do most seriously believe was the case.

We were now 'in a country of bridles and saddles', and set out fully equipped. The Duke of Argyle was obliging enough to mount Dr Johnson on a stately steed from his grace's stable. My friend was highly pleased, and Joseph said, 'He now looks like a bishop.'

We dined at the inn at Tarbat,[308] and at night came to Rosedow, the beautiful seat of Sir James Colquhoun,[309] on the banks of Lochlomond, where I, and any friends whom I have introduced, have ever been received with kind and elegant hospitality.

Wednesday, 27th October

When I went into Dr Johnson's room this morning, I observed to him how wonderfully courteous he had been at Inveraray, and said, 'You were quite a fine gentleman, when with the duchess.' He answered, in good humour, 'Sir, I look upon myself as a very polite man': and he was right, in a proper manly sense of the word. As an immediate proof of it, let me observe, that he would not send back the Duke of Argyle's horse without a letter of thanks, which I copied.

---

*I am sorry that I was unlucky in my quotation. But notwithstanding the acuteness of Dr Johnson's criticism, and the power of his ridicule, the *Tragedy of Douglas* still continues to be generally and deservedly admired.

To his Grace the Duke of ARGYLE.

My Lord,

That kindness which disposed your grace to supply me with the horse, which I have now returned, will make you pleased to hear that he has carried me well.

By my diligence in the little commission with which I was honoured by the duchess, I will endeavour to shew how highly I value the favours which I have received, and how much I desire to be thought,

My lord,

Your grace's most obedient,

and most humble servant,

SAM. JOHNSON.

Rosedow, Oct. 29, 1773.

The duke was so attentive to his respectable guest, that on the same day, he wrote him an answer, which was received at Auchinleck:

To Dr JOHNSON, *Auchinleck, Ayrshire.*

Sir,

I am glad to hear your journey from this place was not unpleasant, in regard to your horse. I wish I could have supplied you with good weather, which I am afraid you felt the want of.

The Duchess of Argyle desires her compliments to you, and is much obliged to you for remembering her commission. I am, sir,

Your most obedient humble servant,

ARGYLE.

Inveraray, Oct. 29, 1773.

I am happy to insert every memorial of the honour done to my great friend. Indeed, I was at all times desirous to preserve the letters which he received from eminent persons, of which, as of all other papers, he was very negligent; and I once proposed to him, that they should be committed to my care, as his *Custos Rotulorum.*[310] I wish he had complied with my request, as by that means many valuable writings might have been preserved, that are now lost.*

After breakfast, Dr Johnson and I were furnished with a boat, and sailed about upon Lochlomond, and landed on some of the islands which are

---

* As a remarkable instance of his negligence, I remember some years ago to have found lying loose in his study, and without the cover, which contained the address, a letter to him from Lord Thurlow, to whom he had made an application as Chancellor, in behalf of a poor literary friend. It was expressed in such terms of respect for Dr Johnson, that, in my zeal for his reputation, I remonstrated warmly with him on his strange inattention, and obtained his permission to take a copy of it; by which probably it has been preserved, as the original I have reason to suppose is lost.

interspersed. He was much pleased with the scene, which is so well known by the accounts of various travellers, that it is unnecessary for me to attempt any description of it.

I recollect none of his conversation, except that, when talking of dress, he said, 'Sir, were I to have any thing fine, it should be very fine. Were I to wear a ring, it should not be a bauble, but a stone of great value. Were I to wear a laced or embroidered waistcoat, it should be very rich. I had once a very rich laced waistcoat, which I wore the first night of my tragedy.'

Lady Helen Colquhoun being a very pious woman, the conversation, after dinner, took a religious turn. Her ladyship defended the presbyterian mode of publick worship; upon which Dr Johnson delivered those excellent arguments for a form of prayer which he has introduced into his *Journey*. I am myself fully convinced that a form of prayer for publick worship is in general most decent and edifying. *Solennia verba*[311] have a kind of prescriptive sanctity, and make a deeper impression on the mind than extemporaneous effusions, in which, as we know not what they are to be, we cannot readily acquiesce. Yet I would allow also of a certain portion of extempore address, as occasion may require. This is the practice of the French Protestant churches. And although the office of forming supplications to the throne of Heaven is, in my mind, too great a trust to be indiscriminately committed to the discretion of every minister, I do not mean to deny that sincere devotion may be experienced when joining in prayer with those who use no Liturgy.

We were favoured with Sir James Colquhoun's coach to convey us in the evening to Cameron, the seat of Commissary Smollet[312]. Our satisfaction of finding ourselves again in a comfortable carriage was very great. We had a pleasing conviction of the commodiousness of civilization, and heartily laughed at the ravings of those absurd visionaries who have attempted to persuade us of the superior advantages of a state of nature.

Mr Smollet was a man of considerable learning, with abundance of animal spirits; so that he was a very good companion for Dr Johnson, who said to me, 'We have had more solid talk here than at any place where we have been.'

I remember Dr Johnson gave us this evening an able and eloquent discourse on the origin of evil, and on the consistency of moral evil with the power and goodness of God. He shewed us how it arose from our free agency, an extinction of which would be a still greater evil than any we experience. I know not that he said any thing absolutely new, but he said a great deal wonderfully well; and perceiving us to be delighted and satisfied, he concluded his harangue with an air of benevolent triumph over an objection which has distressed many worthy minds: 'This then is the answer to the question, πόθεν τὸ κακόν?'[313] Mrs Smollet whispered me, that it was the best sermon she had ever heard. Much do I upbraid myself for having neglected to preserve it.

Thursday, 28th October

Mr Smollet pleased Dr Johnson, by producing a collection of news-papers in the time of the Usurpation, from which it appeared that all sorts of crimes were very frequent during that horrible anarchy. By the side of the high road to Glasgow, at some distance from his house, he had erected a pillar to the memory of his ingenious kinsman, Dr Smollet; and he consulted Dr Johnson as to an inscription for it. Lord Kames, who, though he had a great store of knowledge, with much ingenuity, and uncommon activity of mind, was no profound scholar, had it seems recommended an English inscription. Dr Johnson treated this with great contempt, saying 'An English inscription would be a disgrace to Dr Smollet'; and, in answer to what Lord Kames had urged, as to the advantage of its being in English, because it would be generally understood, I observed, that all to whom Dr Smollet's merit could be an object of respect and imitation, would understand it as well in Latin; and that surely it was not meant for the Highland drovers, or other such people, who pass and repass that way.

We were then shewn a Latin inscription, proposed for this monument. Dr Johnson sat down with an ardent and liberal earnestness to revise it, and greatly improved it by several additions and variations. I unfortunately did not take a copy of it, as it originally stood; but I have happily preserved every fragment of what Dr Johnson wrote:[314]

> *Quisquis ades, viator,*
> *Vel mente felix, vel studiis cultus,*
> *Immorare paululum memoriæ*
> TOBIÆ SMOLLET M.D.
> *Viri iis virtutibus*
> *Quas in homine et cive*
> *Et laudes, et imiteris,*
>
> . . . . .
> *Postquam mira . . .*
> *Se . . . .*
>
> . . . .

387

Tali tantoque viro, suo patrueli,

. . . . . .

Hanc columnam,
Amoris eheu! inane monumentum,
In ipsis Leviniæ ripis,
Quas primis infans vagitibus personuit,
Versiculisque jam fere moriturus illustravit,
Ponendam curavit*

. . . .

* The epitaph which has been inscribed on the pillar erected on the banks of the Leven, in honour of Dr Smollet, is as follows. The part which was written by Dr Johnson, it appears, has been altered; whether for the better, the reader will judge. The alterations are distinguished by italicks.

Siste viator!
Si lepores ingeniique venam benignam,
Si morum callidissimum pictorem,
Unquam es miratus,
Immorare paululum memoriæ
TOBIÆ SMOLLET, M.D.
Viri virtutibus *hisce*
Quas in homine et cive
Et laudes et imiteris,
Haud mediocriter ornati:
Qui in literis variis versatus,
Postquam felicitate *sibi propria*
Sese posteris commendaverat,
Morte acerba raptus
Anno œtatis 51
Eheu! quam procul a patria!
Prope Liburni portum in Italia,
Jacet sepultus.
Tali tantoque viro, patrueli suo,
Cui in decursu lampada
Se potius tradidisse decuit,
Hanc Columnam,
Amoris, eheu! inane monumentum
In ipsis Leviniæ ripis,
Quas *versiculis sub exitu vitæ illustratas*
Primis infans vagitibus personuit,
Ponendam curavit
JACOBUS SMOLLET de Bonhill
Abi et reminscere,
Hoc quidem honore,
Non modo defuncti memoriæ,
Verum etiam exemplo, prospectum esse;
Aliis enim, si modo digni sint,
Idem erit virtutis præmium!

We had this morning a singular proof of Dr Johnson's quick and retentive memory. Hay's translation of Martial was lying in a window. I said, I thought it was pretty well done, and shewed him a particular epigram, I think, of ten, but am certain of eight, lines. He read it, and tossed away the book, saying 'No, it is *not* pretty well.' As I persisted in my opinion, he said, 'Why, sir, the original is thus' (and he repeated it); 'and this man's translation is thus,' and then he repeated that also, exactly, though he had never seen it before, and read it over only once, and that too, without any intention of getting it by heart.

Here a post-chaise, which I had ordered from Glasgow, came for us, and we drove on in high spirits. We stopped at Dunbarton, and though the approach to the castle there is very steep, Dr Johnson ascended it with alacrity, and surveyed all that was to be seen. During the whole of our tour he shewed uncommon spirit, could not bear to be treated like an old or infirm man, and was very unwilling to accept of any assistance, insomuch that, at our landing at Icolmkill, when Sir Allan McLean and I submitted to be carried on men's shoulders from the boat to the shore, as it could not be brought quite close to land, he sprang into the sea, and waded vigorously out.

On our arrival at the Saracen's Head Inn, at Glasgow, I was made happy by good accounts from home; and Dr Johnson, who had not received a single letter since we left Aberdeen, found here a great many, the perusal of which entertained him much. He enjoyed in imagination the comforts which we could now command, and seemed to be in high glee. I remember, he put a leg up on each side of the grate, and said, with a mock solemnity, by way of soliloquy, but loud enough for me to hear it, 'Here am I, an *English* man, sitting by a *coal* fire.'

Friday, 29th October

The professors of the university being informed of our arrival, Dr Stevenson, Dr Reid, and Mr Anderson, breakfasted with us. Mr Anderson accompanied us while Dr Johnson viewed this beautiful city. He had told me, that one day in London, when Dr Adam Smith was boasting of it, he turned to him and said, 'Pray, sir, have you ever seen Brentford?' This was surely a strong instance of his impatience, and spirit of contradiction. I put him in mind of it to-day, while he expressed his admiration of the elegant buildings, and whispered him, 'Don't you feel some remorse?'

We were received in the college by a number of the professors, who shewed all due respect to Dr Johnson; and then we paid a visit to the principal, Dr Leechman, at his own house, where Dr Johnson had the satisfaction of being told that his name had been gratefully celebrated in one of the parochial congregations in the Highlands, as the person to whose influence it was chiefly owing, that the New Testament was allowed to be translated into the Erse language. It seems some political members of the Society in Scotland for propagating Christian Knowledge, had opposed this pious under-taking, as tending to preserve the distinction between the Highlanders and Lowlanders. Dr Johnson wrote a long letter upon the subject to a friend, which being shewn to them, made them ashamed, and afraid of being pub-lickly exposed; so they were forced to a compliance. It is now in my posses-sion, and is, perhaps, one of the best productions of his masterly pen.[315]

Professors Reid and Anderson, and the two Messieurs Foulis, the Elzevirs of Glasgow,[316] dined and drank tea with us at our inn, after which the professors went away; and I, having a letter to write, left my fellow-traveller with Messieurs Foulis. Though good and ingenious men, they had that unsettled speculative mode of conversation which is offensive to a man regularly taught at an English school and university. I found that, instead of listening to the dictates of the Sage, they had teazed him with questions and doubtful disputations. He came in a flutter to me, and desired I might come back again, for he could not bear these men. 'O ho! sir,' said I, 'you are flying to me for refuge!' He never, in any situation, was at a loss for a ready repartee. He answered, with quick vivacity, 'It is of two evils choos-ing the least.' I was delighted with this flash bursting from the cloud which hung upon his mind, closed my letter directly, and joined the company.

We supped at Professor Anderson's. The general impression upon my memory is, that we had not much conversation at Glasgow where the professors, like their brethren at Aberdeen, did not venture to expose them-selves much to the battery of cannon which they knew might play upon them. Dr Johnson, who was fully conscious of his own superior powers, afterwards praised Principal Robertson for his caution in this respect. He said to me, 'Robertson, sir, was in the right. Robertson is a man of eminence, and the head of a college at Edinburgh. He had a character to maintain, and did well not to risk its being lessened.'

Saturday, 30th October

We set out towards Ayrshire. I sent Joseph on to Loudoun, with a message, that, if the earl[317] was at home, Dr Johnson and I would have the honour to dine with him. Joseph met us on the road, and reported that the earl 'jumped for joy', and said, 'I shall be very happy to see them.' We were received with a most pleasing courtesy by his lordship, and by the countess his mother, who, in her ninety-fifth year, had all her faculties quite un-impaired. This was a very cheering sight to Dr Johnson, who had an extra-ordinary desire for long life. Her ladyship was sensible and well-informed, and had seen a great deal of the world. Her lord had held several high offices, and she was sister to the great Earl of Stair.

I cannot here refrain from paying a just tribute to the character of John Earl of Loudoun, who did more service to the county of Ayr in general, as well as to individuals in it, than any man we have ever had. It is pain-ful to think that he met with much ingratitude from persons both in high and low rank: but such was his temper, such his knowledge of 'base man-kind,'[*] that, as if he had expected no other return, his mind was never soured, and he retained his good-humour and benevolence to the last. The tenderness of his heart was proved in 1745-6, when he had an important command in the Highlands, and behaved with a generous humanity to the unfortunate. I cannot figure a more honest politician; for, though his interest in our county was great, and generally successful, he not only did not deceive by fallacious promises, but was anxious that people should not deceive them-selves by too sanguine expectations. His kind and dutiful attention to his mother was unremitted. At his house was true hospitality; a plain but a plentiful table; and every guest, being left at perfect freedom, felt himself quite easy and happy. While I live, I shall honour the memory of this amiable man.

At night, we advanced a few miles farther, to the house of Mr Campbell of Treesbank, who was married to one of my wife's sisters, and were enter-tained very agreeably by a worthy couple.

Sunday, 31st October

We reposed here in tranquillity. Dr Johnson was pleased to find a numer-ous and excellent collection of books, which had mostly belonged to the Reverend Mr John Campbell, brother of our host. I was desirous to have procured for my fellow traveller, to-day, the company of Sir John Cuning-hame, of Caprington, whose castle was but two miles from us. He was a very distinguished scholar, long abroad, and during part of the time lived much with the learned Cuninghame, the opponent of Bentley as a critick upon Horace.[318] He wrote Latin with great elegance, and, what is very remarkable, read Homer and Ariosto through every year. I wrote to him to request he would come to us; but unfortunately he was prevented by in-disposition.

[*] The unwilling gratitude of base mankind. POPE.

Monday, 1st November

Though Dr Johnson was lazy, and averse to move, I insisted that he should go with me, and pay a visit to the Countess of Eglintoune, mother of the late and present earl.[319] I assured him, he would find himself amply recompensed for the trouble; and he yielded to my solicitations, though with some unwillingness. We were well mounted, and had not many miles to ride. He talked of the attention that is necessary in order to distribute our charity judiciously. 'If thoughtlessly done, we may neglect the most deserving objects; and, as every man has but a certain proportion to give, if it is lavished upon those who first present themselves, there may be nothing left for such as have a better claim. A man should first relieve those who are nearly connected with him, by whatever tie; and then, if he has any thing to spare, may extend his bounty to a wider circle.'

As we passed very near the castle of Dundonald, which was one of the many residencies of the kings of Scotland, and in which Robert the Second lived and died, Dr Johnson wished to survey it particularly. It stands on a beautiful rising ground, which is seen at a great distance on several quarters, and from whence there is an extensive prospect of the rich district of Cuninghame, the western sea, the isle of Arran, and a part of the northern coast of Ireland. It has long been unroofed; and, though of considerable size, we could not, by any power of imagination, figure it as having been a suitable habitation for majesty. Dr Johnson, to irritate my old Scottish enthusiasm, was very jocular on the homely accommodation of 'King Bob', and roared and laughed till the ruins echoed.

Lady Eglintoune, though she was now in her eighty-fifth year, and had lived in the retirement of the country for almost half a century, was still a very agreeable woman. She was of the noble house of Kennedy, and had all the elevation which the consciousness of such birth inspires. Her figure was majestick, her manners high-bred, her reading extensive, and her conversation elegant. She had been the admiration of the gay circles of life, and the patroness of poets. Dr Johnson was delighted with his reception here. Her principles in Church and state were congenial with his. She knew all his merit, and had heard much of him from her son, Earl Alexander, who loved to cultivate the acquaintance of men of talents, in every department.

All who knew his lordship, will allow that his understanding and accomplishments were of no ordinary rate. From the gay habits which he had early acquired, he spent too much of his time with men, and in pursuits far beneath such a mind as his. He afterwards became sensible of it, and turned his thoughts to objects of importance; but was cut off in the prime of his life. I cannot speak, but with emotions of the most affectionate regret, of one, in whose company many of my early days were passed, and to whose kindness I was much indebted.

Often must I have occasion to upbraid myself, that soon after our return to the main land, I allowed indolence to prevail over me so much, as to shrink from the labour of continuing my *Journal* with the same minuteness as before; sheltering myself in the thought, that we had done with the Hebrides; and not considering, that Dr Johnson's *Memorabilia* were likely to be more valuable when we were restored to a more polished society. Much has thus been irrecoverably lost.

In the course of our conversation this day, it came out, that Lady Eglintoune was married the year before Dr Johnson was born; upon which she graciously said to him, that she might have been his mother; and that she now adopted him; and when we were going away, she embraced him, saying, 'My dear son, farewell!' My friend was much pleased with this day's entertainment, and owned that I had done well to force him out.

Tuesday, 2d November

We were now in a country not only 'of saddles and bridles', but of post-chaises; and having ordered one from Kilmarnock, we got to Auchinleck before dinner.[320]

My father was not quite a year and a half older than Dr Johnson; but his conscientious discharge of his laborious duty as a judge in Scotland, where the law proceedings are almost all in writing, a severe complaint which ended in his death, and the loss of my mother, a woman of almost unexampled piety and goodness, had before this time in some degree affected his spirits, and rendered him less disposed to exert his faculties: for he had originally a very strong mind, and cheerful temper. He assured me, he never had felt one moment of what is called low spirits, or uneasiness, without a real cause. He had a great many good stories, which he told uncommonly well, and he was remarkable for 'humour, *incolumi gravitate*',[321] as Lord Monboddo used to characterize it. His age, his office, and his character, had long given him an acknowledged claim to great attention, in whatever company he was; and he could ill brook any diminution of it. He was as sanguine a Whig and Presbyterian, as Dr Johnson was a Tory and Church of England man: and as he had not much leisure to be informed of Dr Johnson's great merits by reading his works, he had a partial and unfavourable notion of him, founded on his supposed political tenets; which were so discordant to his own, that, instead of speaking of him with that respect to which he was entitled, he used to call him 'a *Jacobite fellow*'. Knowing all this, I should not have ventured to bring them together, had not my father, out of kindness to me, desired me to invite Dr Johnson to his house.

I was very anxious that all should be well; and begged of my friend to avoid three topicks, as to which they differed very widely; Whiggism, Presbyterianism, and – Sir John Pringle.[322] He said courteously, 'I shall certainly not talk on subjects which I am told are disagreeable to a gentleman under whose roof I am; especially, I shall not do so to *your father*.'

Our first day went off very smoothly. It rained, and we could not get out; but my father shewed Dr Johnson his library, which, in curious editions of the Greek and Roman classicks, is, I suppose, not excelled by any private collection in Great Britain. My father had studied at Leyden, and been very intimate with the Gronovii, and other learned men there. He was a sound scholar, and, in particular, had collated manuscripts and different editions of Anacreon, and others of the Greek lyric poets, with great care; so that my friend and he had much matter for conversation, without touching on the fatal topicks of difference.

Dr Johnson found here Baxter's *Anacreon*, which he told me he had long inquired for in vain, and began to suspect there was no such book. Baxter was the keen antagonist of Barnes.[323] His life is in the *Biographia Britannica*. My father has written many notes on this book, and Dr Johnson and I talked of having it reprinted.

Wednesday, 3d November

It rained all day, and gave Dr Johnson an impression of that incommodiousness of climate in the west, of which he has taken notice in his *Journey*; but, being well accommodated, and furnished with variety of books, he was not dissatisfied.

Some gentlemen of the neighbourhood came to visit my father; but there was little conversation. One of them asked Dr Johnson how he liked the Highlands. The question seemed to irritate him, for he answered, 'How, sir, can you ask me what obliges me to speak unfavourably of a country where I have been hospitably entertained? Who *can* like the Highlands? – I like the inhabitants very well.' The gentleman asked no more questions.

Let me now make up for the present neglect, by again gleaning from the past. At Lord Monboddo's, after the conversation upon the decrease of learning in England, his Lordship mentioned *Hermes* by Mr Harris of Salisbury, as the work of a living authour, for whom he had a great respect. Dr Johnson said nothing at the time; but when we were in our post-chaise, told me, he thought Harris 'a coxcomb'. This he said of him, not as a man, but as an authour; and I give his opinions of men and books, faithfully, whether they agree with my own, or not. I do admit, that there always appeared to me something of affectation in Mr Harris's manner of writing; something of a habit of clothing plain thoughts in analytick and categorical formality. But all his writings are imbued with learning; and all breathe that philanthropy and amiable disposition, which distinguished him as a man.*

At another time, during our tour, he drew the character of a rapacious Highland chief with the strength of Theophrastus or la Bruyère; concluding with these words: 'Sir, he has no more the soul of a chief, than an attorney who has twenty houses in a street, and considers how much he can make by them.'

He this day, when we were by ourselves, observed, how common it was for people to talk from books; to retail the sentiments of others, and not their own; in short, to converse without any originality of thinking. He was pleased to say, 'You and I do not talk from books.'

Thursday, 4th November

I was glad to have at length a very fine day, on which I could shew Dr Johnson the place of my family, which he has honoured with so much attention in his *Journey*. He is, however, mistaken in thinking that the Celtick name, *Auchinleck*, has no relation to the natural appearance of it. I believe every Celtick name of a place will be found very descriptive. *Auchinleck* does not signify a 'stony field', as he has said, but a 'field of flag stones'; and this place has a number of rocks, which abound in strata of that kind. The 'sullen dignity of the old castle', as he has forcibly expressed it, delighted him exceedingly. On one side of the rock on which its ruins

---

* This gentleman, though devoted to the study of grammar and dialecticks, was not so absorbed in it as to be without a sense of pleasantry, or to be offended at his favourite topicks being treated lightly. I one day met him in the street, as I was hastening to the House of Lords, and told him, I was sorry I could not stop, being rather too late to attend an appeal of the Duke of Hamilton against Douglas. 'I thought,' said he, 'their contest had been over long ago.' I answered, 'The contest concerning Douglas's filiation was over long ago; but the contest now is, who shall have the estate.' Then, assuming the air of 'an antient sage philosopher', I proceeded thus: 'Were I to *predicate* concerning him, I should say, the contest formerly was, What *is* he? The contest now is, What *has* he?' 'Right,' replied Mr Harris, smiling, 'you have done with *quality*, and have got into *quantity*.'

stand, runs the river Lugar, which is here of considerable breadth, and is bordered by other high rocks, shaded with wood. On the other side runs a brook, skirted in the same manner, but on a smaller scale. I cannot figure a more romantick scene.

I felt myself elated here, and expatiated to my illustrious mentor on the antiquity and honourable alliances of my family, and on the merits of its founder, Thomas Boswell, who was highly favoured by his sovereign, James IV of Scotland, and fell with him at the battle of Flodden field; and in the glow of what, I am sensible, will, in a commercial age, be considered as genealogical enthusiasm, did not omit to mention what I was sure my friend would not think lightly of, my relation to the Royal Personage, whose liberality, on his accession to the throne, had given him comfort and independence. I have, in a former page, acknowledged my pride of ancient blood, in which I was encouraged by Dr Johnson: my readers therefore will not be surprised at my having indulged it on this occasion.

Not far from the old castle is a spot of consecrated earth, on which may be traced the foundations of an ancient chapel, dedicated to St Vincent, and where in old times 'was the place of graves' for the family. It grieves me to think that the remains of sanctity here, which were considerable, were dragged away, and employed in building a part of the house of Auchinleck, of the middle age; which was the family residence, till my father erected that 'elegant modern mansion', of which Dr Johnson speaks so handsomely. Perhaps this chapel may one day be restored.

Dr Johnson was pleased, when I shewed him some venerable old trees, under the shade of which my ancestors had walked. He exhorted me to plant assiduously, as my father had done to a great extent.

As I wandered with my reverend friend in the groves of Auchinleck, I told him, that, if I survived him, it was my intention to erect a monument to him here, among scenes which, in my mind, were all classical; for in my youth I had appropriated to them many of the descriptions of the Roman poets. He could not bear to have death presented to him in any shape; for his constitutional melancholy made the king of terrours more frightful. He turned off the subject, saying, 'Sir, I hope to see your grand-children!'

This forenoon he observed some cattle without horns, of which he has taken notice in his *Journey*, and seems undecided whether they be of a particular race. His doubts appear to have had no foundation; for my respectable neighbour, Mr Fairlie, who, with all his attention to agriculture, finds time both for the Classicks and his friends, assures me they are a distinct species, and that, when any of their calves have horns, a mixture of breed can be traced. In confirmation of his opinion, he pointed out to me the following passage in Tacitus, *Ne armentis quidem suus honor, aut gloria frontis* (De mor. Germ. § 5)[324] which he wondered had escaped Dr Johnson.

On the front of the house of Auchinleck is this inscription:

> ... *Quod petis, hic est;*
> *Est Ulubris, animus si te non deficit æquus.*[325]

It is characteristick of the founder; but the *animus æquus* is, alas! not inheritable, nor the subject of devise. He always talked to me as if it were in a man's own power to attain it; but Dr Johnson told me that he owned to him, when they were alone, his persuasion that it was in a great measure constitutional, or the effect of causes which do not depend on ourselves, and that Horace boasts too much, when he says, *æquum mi animum ipse parabo.*[326]

Friday, 5th November

The Reverend Mr Dun, our parish minister, who had dined with us yesterday, with some other company, insisted that Dr Johnson and I should dine with him to-day. This gave me an opportunity to shew my friend the road to the church, made by my father at a great expence, for above three miles, on his own estate, through a range of well enclosed farms, with a row of trees on each side of it. He called it the *Via sacra,*[327] and was very fond of it. Dr Johnson, though he held notions far distant from those of the Presbyterian clergy, yet could associate on good terms with them. He indeed occasionally attacked them. One of them discovered a narrowness of information concerning the dignitaries of the Church of England, among whom may be found men of the greatest learning, virtue, and piety, and of a truly apostolic character. He talked before Dr Johnson, of fat bishops and drowsy deans; and, in short, seemed to believe the illiberal and profane scoffings of professed satyrists, or vulgar railers. Dr Johnson was so highly offended, that he said to him, 'Sir, you know no more of our church than a Hottentot.' I was sorry that he brought this upon himself.

Saturday, 6th November

I cannot be certain, whether it was on this day, or a former, that Dr Johnson and my father came in collision. If I recollect right, the contest began while my father was shewing him his collection of medals; and Oliver Cromwell's coin unfortunately introduced Charles the First, and Toryism. They became exceedingly warm, and violent, and I was very much distressed by being present at such an altercation between the two men, both of whom I reverenced; yet I durst not interfere. It would certainly be very unbecoming in me to exhibit my honoured father, and my respected friend, as intellectual gladiators, for the entertainment of the publick; and therefore I suppress what would, I dare say, make an interesting scene in this dramatick sketch, this account of the transit of Johnson over the Caledonian hemisphere.

Yet I think I may, without impropriety, mention one circumstance, as an instance of my father's address. Dr Johnson challenged him, as he did us all at Talisker, to point out any theological works of merit written by Presbyterian ministers in Scotland. My father, whose studies did not lie much in that way, owned to me afterwards, that he was somewhat at a loss how to answer, but that luckily he recollected having read in catalogues the title of Durham *On the Galatians*; upon which he boldly said, 'Pray, sir, have you read Mr Durham's excellent commentary on the Galatians?' 'No, sir,' said Dr Johnson.[328] By this lucky thought my father kept him at bay, and for some time enjoyed his triumph; but his antagonist soon made a retort, which I forbear to mention.

In the course of their altercation, Whiggism and Presbyterianism, Toryism and Episcopacy, were terribly buffeted. My worthy hereditary friend, Sir John Pringle, never having been mentioned, happily escaped without a bruise.

My father's opinion of Dr Johnson may be conjectured from the name he afterwards gave him, which was *Ursa Major*.[329] But it is not true, as has been reported, that it was in consequence of my saying that he was a *constellation* of genius and literature. It was a sly abrupt expression to one of his brethren on the bench of the Court of Session, in which Dr Johnson was then standing; but it was not said in his hearing.

Sunday, 7th November

My father and I went to publick worship in our parish-church, in which I regretted that Dr Johnson would not join us; for, though we have there no form of prayer, nor magnificent solemnity, yet, as God is worshipped in spirit and in truth, and the same doctrines preached as in the Church of England, my friend would certainly have shewn more liberality, had he attended. I doubt not, however, but he employed his time in private to very good purpose. His uniform and fervent piety was manifested on many occasions during our tour, which I have not mentioned. His reason for not joining in Presbyterian worship has been recorded in a former page.

Monday, 8th November

Notwithstanding the altercation that had passed, my father who had the dignified courtesy of an old Baron, was very civil to Dr Johnson, and politely attended him to the post-chaise, which was to convey us to Edinburgh.

Thus they parted. They are now in another, and a higher, state of existence: and as they were both worthy Christian men, I trust they have met in happiness. But I must observe, in justice to my friend's political principles, and my own, that they have met in a place where there is no room for *Whiggism*.

We came at night to a good inn at Hamilton.[330] I recollect no more.

Tuesday, 9th November

I wished to have shewn Dr Johnson the Duke of Hamilton's house, commonly called the *Palace* of Hamilton, which is close by the town.[331] It is an object which, having been pointed out to me as a splendid edifice, from my earliest years, in travelling between Auchinleck and Edinburgh, has still great grandeur in my imagination. My friend consented to stop, and view the outside of it, but could not be persuaded to go into it.

We arrived this night at Edinburgh, after an absence of eighty-three days. For five weeks together, of the tempestuous season, there had been no account received of us. I cannot express how happy I was on finding myself again at home.

Wednesday, 10th November

Old Mr Drummond, the bookseller, came to breakfast. Dr Johnson and he had not met for ten years. There was respect on his side, and kindness on Dr Johnson's. Soon afterwards Lord Elibank came in, and was much pleased at seeing Dr Johnson in Scotland.[332] His lordship said, 'hardly any thing seemed to him more improbable'. Dr Johnson had a very high opinion of him. Speaking of him to me, he characterized him thus: 'Lord Elibank has read a great deal. It is true, I can find in books all that he has read; but he has a great deal of what is in books, proved by the test of real life.' Indeed, there have been few men whose conversation discovered more knowledge enlivened by fancy. He published several small pieces of distinguished merit; and has left some in manuscript, in particular an account of the expedition against Carthagena, in which he served as an officer in the army. His writings deserve to be collected. He was the early patron of Dr Robertson, the historian, and Mr Home, the tragick poet; who, when they were ministers of country parishes, lived near his seat. He told me, 'I saw these lads had talents, and they were much with me.' I hope they will pay a grateful tribute to his memory.

The morning was chiefly taken up by Dr Johnson's giving him an account of our tour. The subject of difference in political principles was introduced. JOHNSON. 'It is much increased by opposition. There was a violent Whig, with whom I used to contend with great eagerness. After his death I felt my Toryism much abated.' I suppose he meant Mr Walmsley of Lichfield, whose character he has drawn so well in his life of Edmund Smith.

Mr Nairne came in, and he and I accompanied Dr Johnson to Edinburgh castle, which he owned was 'a great place'. But I must mention, as a striking instance of that spirit of contradiction to which he had a strong propensity, when Lord Elibank was some days after talking of it with the natural elation of a Scotchman, or of any man who is proud of a stately fortress in his own country, Dr Johnson affected to despise it, observing that, 'it would make a good *prison* in *England*'.[333]

Lest it should be supposed that I have suppressed one of his sallies against my country, it may not be improper here to correct a mistaken account that has been circulated, as to his conversation this day. It has been said, that being desired to attend to the noble prospect from the Castle Hill, he replied, 'Sir, the noblest prospect that a Scotchman ever sees, is the high road that leads him to London.' This lively sarcasm was thrown out at a tavern in London, in my presence, many years before.

We had with us to day at dinner, at my house, the Lady Dowager Colvill, and Lady Anne Erskine, sisters of the Earl of Kelly; the Honourable Archibald Erskine, who has now succeeded to that title; Lord Elibank; the Reverend Dr Blair; Mr Tytler, the acute vindicator of Mary Queen of Scots, and some other friends.

Fingal being talked of, Dr Johnson, who used to boast that he had, from the first, resisted both Ossian and the giants of Patagonia, averred his positive disbelief of its authenticity.[334] Lord Elibank said, 'I am sure it is not McPherson's. Mr Johnson, I keep company a great deal with you; it is known I do. I may borrow from you better things than I can say myself, and give them as my own; but, if I should, every body will know whose they are.' The Doctor was not softened by this compliment. He denied merit to *Fingal*, supposing it to be the production of a man who has had the advantages that the present age affords; and said, 'nothing is more easy than to write enough in that style if once you begin'.* One gentleman in company expressing his opinion 'that *Fingal* was certainly genuine, for that he had heard a great part of it repeated in the original', Dr Johnson indignantly asked him, whether he understood the original; to which an answer being given in the negative, 'Why then,' said Dr Johnson, 'we see to what *this* testimony comes: thus it is.'

I mentioned this as a remarkable proof how liable the mind of man is to credulity, when not guarded by such strict examination as that which Dr Johnson habitually practised. The talents and integrity of the gentleman who made the remark, are unquestionable; yet, had not Dr Johnson made him advert to the consideration, that he who does not understand a language, cannot know that something which is recited to him is in that language, he might have believed, and reported to this hour, that he had 'heard a great part of *Fingal* repeated in the original'.

For the satisfaction of those on the north of the Tweed, who may think Dr Johnson's account of Caledonian credulity and inaccuracy too strong, it is but fair to add, that he admitted the same kind of ready belief might be found in his own country. 'He would undertake,' he said, 'to write an epick poem on the story of Robin Hood, and half England, to whom the names and places he should mention in it are familiar, would believe and declare they had heard it from their earliest years.'

One of his objections to the authenticity of *Fingal*, during the conversation at Ulinish, is omitted in my *Journal*, but I perfectly recollect it. 'Why is not the original deposited in some publick library, instead of exhibiting attestations of its existence? Suppose there were a question in a court of justice, whether a man be dead or alive. You aver he is alive, and you bring fifty witnesses to swear it: I answer, "Why do you not produce the man?"' This is an argument founded on one of the first principles of the *law of evidence*, which Gilbert[335] would have held to be irrefragable.

I do not think it incumbent on me to give any precise decided opinion upon this question, as to which I believe more than some, and less than others. The subject appears to have now become very uninteresting to the publick. That *Fingal* is not from beginning to end a translation from the Gallick, but that *some* passages have been supplied by the editor to connect the whole, I have heard admitted by very warm advocates for its authenticity. If this be the case, why are not these distinctly ascertained? Antiquaries, and admirers of the work, may complain, that they are in a situation similar

---

*I desire not to be understood as agreeing *entirely* with the opinions of Dr Johnson, which I relate without any remark. The many imitations, however, of *Fingal*, that have been published, confirm this observation in a considerable degree.

to that of the unhappy gentleman whose wife informed him, on her death-bed, that one of their reputed children was not his; and, when he eagerly begged her to declare which of them it was, she answered, 'That you shall never know', and expired, leaving him in irremediable doubt as to them all.

I beg leave to say something upon second sight, of which I have related two instances, as they impressed my mind at the time. I own, I returned from the Hebrides with a considerable degree of faith in the many stories of that kind which I heard with a too easy acquiescence, without any close examination of the evidence: but, since that time, my belief in those stories has been much weakened, by reflecting on the careless inaccuracy of narrative in common matters, from which we may certainly conclude that there may be the same in what is more extraordinary. It is but just, however, to add, that the belief in second sight is not peculiar to the Highlands and Isles.

Some years after our tour, a cause was tried in the Court of Session, where the principal fact to be ascertained was, whether a ship-master, who used to frequent the Western Highlands and Isles, was drowned in one particular year, or in the year after. A great number of witnesses from those parts were examined on each side, and swore directly contrary to each other, upon this simple question. One of them, a very respectable chieftain, who told me a story of second sight, which I have not mentioned, but which I too implicitly believed, had in this case, previous to this publick examination, not only said, but attested under his hand, that he had seen the ship-master in the year subsequent to that in which the court was finally satisfied he was drowned. When interrogated with the strictness of judicial inquiry, and under the awe of an oath, he recollected himself better, and retracted what he had formerly asserted, apologizing for his inaccuracy, by telling the judges, 'A man will *say* what he will not *swear*.' By many he was much censured, and it was maintained that every gentleman would be as attentive to truth without the sanction of an oath, as with it. Dr Johnson, though he himself was distinguished at all times by a scrupulous adherence to truth, controverted this proposition; and, as a proof that this was not, though it ought to be, the case, urged the very different decisions of elections under Mr Grenville's Act, from those formerly made. 'Gentlemen will not pronounce upon oath, what they would have said, and voted in the House without that sanction.'

However difficult it may be for men who believe in preternatural communications, in modern times, to falsify those who are of a different opinion, they may easily refute the doctrine of their opponents, who impute a belief in second sight to superstition. To entertain a visionary notion that one

sees a distant or future event, may be called superstition; but the correspondence of the fact or event with such an impression on the fancy, though
certainly very wonderful, *if proved*, has no more connection with superstition,
than magnetism or electricity.

After dinner, various topicks were discussed; but I recollect only one particular. Dr Johnson compared the different talents of Garrick and Foote, as
companions, and gave Garrick greatly the preference for elegance, though
he allowed Foote extraordinary powers of entertainment. He said, 'Garrick
is restrained by some principle; but Foote has the advantage of an unlimited
range. Garrick has some delicacy of feeling; it is possible to put him out;
you may get the better of him; but Foote is the most incompressible fellow
that I ever knew: when you have driven him into a corner, and think you
are sure of him, he runs through between your legs, or jumps over your
head, and makes his escape.'

Dr Erskine and Mr Robert Walker, two very respectable ministers of Edinburgh, supped with us, as did the Reverend Dr Webster. The conversation
turned on the Moravian missions, and on the Methodists. Dr Johnson observed in general, that missionaries were too sanguine in their accounts
of their success among savages, and that much of what they tell is not
to be believed. He owned that the Methodists had done good; had spread
religious impressions among the vulgar part of mankind: but, he said, they
had great bitterness against other Christians, and that he never could get
a Methodist to explain in what he excelled others; that it always ended
in the indispensible necessity of hearing one of their preachers.

Thursday, 11th November

Principal Robertson came to us as we sat at breakfast; he advanced to Dr
Johnson, repeating a line of Virgil, which I forget. I suppose, either

Post varios casus, per tot discrimina rerum, *

or

... multum ille et terris jactatus, et alto. †

Every body had accosted us with some studied compliment on our return.
Dr Johnson said, 'I am really ashamed of the congratulations which we
receive. We are addressed as if we had made a voyage to Nova Zembla,
and suffered five persecutions in Japan.' And he afterwards remarked, that,

* Through various hazards and events we move.
† Long labours both by sea and land he bore. DRYDEN.

'to see a man come up with a formal air, and a Latin line, when we had no fatigue and no danger, was provoking.' I told him, he was not sensible of the danger, having lain under cover in the boat during the storm: he was like the chicken, that hides its head under its wing, and then thinks itself safe.[336]

Lord Elibank came to us, as did Sir William Forbes. The rash attempt in 1745 being mentioned, I observed, that it would make a fine piece of history. Dr Johnson said it would. Lord Elibank doubted whether any man of this age could give it impartially. JOHNSON. 'A man, by talking with those of different sides, who were actors in it, and putting down all that he hears, may in time collect the materials of a good narrative. You are to consider, all history was at first oral. I suppose Voltaire was fifty years in collecting his *Louis XIV* which he did in the way that I am proposing.' ROBERTSON. 'He did so. He lived much with all the great people who were concerned in that reign, and heard them talk of every thing; and then either took Mr Boswell's way, of writing down what he heard, or, which is as good, preserved it in his memory; for he has a wonderful memory.' With the leave, however, of this elegant historian, no man's memory can preserve facts or sayings with such fidelity as may be done by writing them down when they are recent. Dr Robertson said, 'it was now full time to make such a collection as Dr Johnson suggested; for many of the people who were then in arms, were dropping off; and both Whigs and Jacobites were now come to talk with moderation.' Lord Elibank said to him, 'Mr Robertson, the first thing that gave me a high opinion of you, was your saying in the Select Society,* while parties ran high, soon after the year 1745, that you did not think worse of a man's moral character for his having been in rebellion. This was venturing to utter a liberal sentiment, while both sides had a detestation of each other.'

Dr Johnson observed, that being in rebellion from a notion of another's right, was not connected with depravity; and that we had this proof of it, that all mankind applauded the pardoning of rebels; which they would not do in the case of robbers and murderers. He said, with a smile, that 'he wondered that the phrase of *unnatural* rebellion should be so much used, for that all rebellion was natural to man'.

As I kept no journal of any thing that passed after this morning, I shall, from memory, group together this and the other days, till that on which Dr Johnson departed for London. They were in all nine days; on which he dined at Lady Colvill's, Lord Hailes's, Sir Adolphus Oughton's, Sir Alex-

* A society for debate in Edinburgh, consisting of the most eminent men.

ander Dick's, Principal Robertson's, Mr McLaurin's, and thrice at Lord Elibank's seat in the country, where we also passed two nights. He supped at the Honourable Alexander Gordon's, now one of our judges, by the title of Lord Rockville; at Mr Nairne's, now also one of our judges, by the title of Lord Dunsinan; at Dr Blair's, and Mr Tytler's; and at my house thrice, one evening with a numerous company, chiefly gentlemen of the law; another with Mr Menzies of Culdares, and Lord Monboddo, who disengaged himself on purpose to meet him; and the evening on which we returned from Lord Elibank's, he supped with my wife and me by ourselves.

He breakfasted at Dr Webster's, at old Mr Drummond's, and at Dr Blacklock's; and spent one forenoon at my uncle Dr Boswell's, who shewed him his curious museum; and, as he was an elegant scholar, and a physician bred in the school of Boerhaave, Dr Johnson was pleased with his company.

On the mornings when he breakfasted at my house, he had, from ten o'clock till one or two, a constant levee of various persons, of very different characters and descriptions. I could not attend him, being obliged to be in the Court of Session; but my wife was so good as to devote the greater part of the morning to the endless task of pouring out tea for my friend and his visitors.

Such was the disposition of his time at Edinburgh. He said one evening to me, in a fit of langour, 'Sir, we have been harrassed by invitations.' I acquiesced. 'Ay, sir,' he replied; 'but how much worse would it have been, if we had been neglected?'

From what has been recorded in this *Journal*, it may well be supposed that a variety of admirable conversation has been lost, by my neglect to preserve it. I shall endeavour to recollect some of it, as well as I can.

At Lady Colvill's, to whom I am proud to introduce any stranger of eminence, that he may see what dignity and grace is to be found in Scotland, an officer observed, that he had heard Lord Mansfield was not a great English lawyer. JOHNSON. 'Why, sir, supposing Lord Mansfield not to have the splendid talents which he possesses, he must be a great English lawyer, from having been so long at the bar, and having passed through so many of the great offices of the law. Sir, you may as well maintain that a carrier, who has driven a packhorse between Edinburgh and Berwick for thirty years, does not know the road, as that Lord Mansfield does not know the law of England.'

At Mr Nairne's, he drew the character of Richardson, the author of *Clarissa*, with a strong yet delicate pencil. I lament much that I have not preserved it: I only remember that he expressed a high opinion of his talents and virtues; but observed, that 'his perpetual study was to ward off petty inconveniencies, and procure petty pleasures; that his love of continual superiority was such, that he took care to be always surrounded by women, who listened to him implicitly, and did not venture to controvert his opinions; and that his desire of distinction was so great, that he used to give large vails[337] to the Speaker Onslow's servants, that they might treat him with respect'.

On the same evening, he would not allow that the private life of a judge, in England, was required to be so strictly decorous as I supposed. 'Why then, sir,' said I, 'according to your account, an English judge may just live like a gentleman.' JOHNSON. 'Yes, sir – if he *can*.'

At Mr Tytler's, I happened to tell that one evening, a great many years ago, when Dr Hugh Blair and I were sitting together in the pit of Drury-lane play-house, in a wild freak of youthful extravagance, I entertained the audience *prodigiously*, by imitating the lowing of a cow. A little while after I had told this story, I differed from Dr Johnson, I suppose too confidently, upon some point, which I now forget. He did not spare me. 'Nay, sir,' said he, 'if you cannot talk better as a man, I'd have you bellow like a cow.'*

At Dr Webster's, he said, that he believed hardly any man died without affectation. This remark appears to me to be well founded, and will account for many of the celebrated death-bed sayings which are recorded.

On one of the evenings at my house, when he told that Lord Lovat boasted to an English nobleman, that though he had not his wealth, he had two thousand men whom he could at any time call into the field, the Honourable Alexander Gordon observed, that those two thousand men brought him to the block. 'True, sir,' said Dr Johnson: 'but you may just as well argue, concerning a man who has fallen over a precipice to which he has walked too near, "His two legs brought him to that" – is he not the better for having two legs?'

At Dr Blair's I left him, in order to attend a consultation, during which he and his amiable host were by themselves. I returned to supper, at which were Principal Robertson, Mr Nairne, and some other gentlemen. Dr Robertson and Dr Blair, I remember, talked well upon subordination and government; and, as my friend and I were walking home, he said to me, 'Sir, these two doctors are good men, and wise men.' I begged of Dr Blair to recollect what he could of the long conversation that passed between

---

* As I have been scrupulously exact in relating anecdotes concerning other persons, I shall not withhold any part of this story, however ludicrous. – I was so successful in this boyish frolick, that the universal cry of the galleries was, '*Encore* the cow! *Encore* the cow!' In the pride of my heart, I attempted imitations of some other animals, but with very inferior effect. My reverend friend, anxious for my fame, with an air of the utmost gravity and earnestness, addressed me thus: 'My dear sir, I would *confine* myself to the *cow*!'

Dr Johnson and him alone, this evening, and he obligingly wrote to me as follows:

Dear Sir,   *March 3, 1785.*

... As so many years have intervened, since I chanced to have that conversation with Dr Johnson in my house, to which you refer, I have forgotten most of what then passed, but remember that I was both instructed and entertained by it. Among other subjects, the discourse happening to turn on modern Latin poets, the Dr expressed a very favourable opinion of Buchanan, and instantly repeated, from beginning to end, an ode of his, intituled *Calendæ Maiæ* (the eleventh in his *Miscellaneorum Liber*), beginning with these words, *Salvete sacris deliciis sacræ*,[338] with which I had formerly been unacquainted; but upon perusing it, the praise which he bestowed upon it, as one of the happiest of Buchanan's poetical compositions, appeared to me very just. He also repeated to me a Latin ode he had composed in one of the western islands, from which he had lately returned. We had much discourse concerning his excursion to those islands, with which he expressed himself as having been highly pleased; talked in a favourable manner of the hospitality of the inhabitants; and particularly spoke much of his happiness in having you for his companion; and said, that the longer he knew you, he loved and esteemed you the more. This conversation passed in the interval between tea and supper, when we were by ourselves. You, and the rest of the company who were with us at supper, have often taken notice that he was uncommonly bland and gay that evening, and gave much pleasure to all who were present. This is all that I can recollect distinctly of that long conversation.

Yours sincerely,

HUGH BLAIR.

At Lord Hailes's, we spent a most agreeable day; but again I must lament that I was so indolent as to let almost all that passed evaporate into oblivion. Dr Johnson observed there, that 'it is wonderful how ignorant many officers of the army are, considering how much leisure they have for study, and the acquisition of knowledge.' I hope he was mistaken; for he maintained that many of them were ignorant of things belonging immediately to their own profession; 'for instance, many cannot tell how far a musket will carry a bullet;' in proof of which, I suppose, he mentioned some particular person, for Lord Hailes, from whom I solicited what he could recollect of that day, writes to me as follows:

As to Dr Johnson's observation about the ignorance of officers, in the length that a musket will carry, my brother, Colonel Dalrymple, was present, and he thought that the doctor was either mistaken, by putting the question wrong, or that he had conversed on the subject with some person out of service.

Was it upon that occasion that he expressed no curiosity to see the room at Dumfermline, where Charles I was born? 'I know that he was born,' said he; 'no matter where.' Did he envy us the birth-place of the king?

Near the end of his *Journey*, Dr Johnson has given liberal praise to Mr Braidwood's academy for the deaf and dumb. When he visited it, a circumstance occurred which was truly characteristical of our great lexicographer. 'Pray,' said he, 'can they pronounce any *long* words?' Mr Braidwood informed him they could. Upon which Dr Johnson wrote one of his *sequipedalia verba*,[339] which was pronounced by the scholars, and he was satisfied. My readers may perhaps wish to know what the word was; but I cannot gratify their curiosity. Mr Braidwood told me, it remained long in his school, but had been lost before I made my inquiry.*

Dr Johnson one day visited the Court of Session. He thought the mode of pleading there too vehement, and too much addressed to the passions of the judges. 'This,' said he, 'is not the Areopagus.'

At old Mr Drummond's, Sir John Dalrymple quaintly said, the two noblest animals in the world were, a Scotch highlander and an English sailor. 'Why, sir,' said Dr Johnson, 'I shall say nothing as to the Scotch highlander; but as to the English sailor, I cannot agree with you.' Sir John said, he was generous in giving away his money. JOHNSON. 'Sir, he throws away his money, without thought, and without merit. I do not call a tree generous, that sheds its fruit at every breeze.' Sir John having affected to complain of the attacks made upon his *Memoirs*, Dr Johnson said, 'Nay, sir, do not complain. It is advantageous to an authour, that his book should be attacked as well as praised. Fame is a shuttlecock. If it be struck only at one end of the room, it will soon fall to the ground. To keep it up, it must be struck at both ends.' Often have I reflected on this since; and, instead of being angry at many of those who have written against me, have smiled to think that they were unintentionally subservient to my fame, by using a battle-door to make me *virum volitare per ora*.[340]

At Sir Alexander Dick's, from that absence of mind to which every man is at times subject, I told, in a blundering manner, Lady Eglingtoune's complimentary adoption of Dr Johnson as her son; for I unfortunately stated that her ladyship adopted him as her son, in consequence of her having been married the year *after* he was born. Dr Johnson instantly corrected me. 'Sir, don't you perceive that you are defaming the countess? For, sup-

* One of the best criticks of our age 'does not wish to prevent the admirers of the incorrect and nerveless style which generally prevailed for a century before Dr Johnson's energetick writings were known, from enjoying the laugh that this story may produce, in which he is very ready to join them'. He, however, requests me to observe, that 'my friend very properly chose a *long* word on this occasion, not, it is believed, from any predilection for polysyllables (though he certainly had a due respect for them), but in order to put Mr Braidwood's skill to the strictest test, and to try the efficacy of his instruction by the most difficult exertion of the organs of his pupils'.

posing me to be her son, and that she was not married till the year after my birth, I must have been her *natural* son.' A young lady of quality, who was present, very handsomely said, 'Might not the son have justified the faults?' My friend was much flattered by this compliment, which he never forgot. When in more than ordinary spirits, and talking of his journey in Scotland, he has called to me, 'Boswell, what was it that the young lady of quality said of me at Sir Alexander Dick's?' Nobody will doubt that I was happy in repeating it.

My illustrious friend, being now desirous to be again in the great theatre of life and animated exertion, took a place in the coach, which was to set out for London on Monday the 22d of November. Sir John Dalrymple pressed him to come on the Saturday before, to his house at Cranston, which being twelve miles from Edinburgh, upon the middle road to Newcastle (Dr Johnson had come to Edinburgh by Berwick, and along the naked coast), it would make his journey easier, as the coach would take him up at a more reasonable hour than that at which it sets out. Sir John, I perceived, was ambitious of having such a guest; but, as I was well assured, that at this very time he had joined with some of his prejudiced countrymen in railing at Dr Johnson, and had said, he wondered how any gentleman of Scotland could keep company with him, I thought he did not deserve the honour: yet, as it might be a convenience to Dr Johnson, I contrived that he should accept the invitation, and engaged to conduct him. I resolved that, on our way to Sir John's, we should make a little circuit by Roslin Castle, and Hawthornden,³⁴¹ and wished to set out soon after breakfast; but young Mr Tytler came to shew Dr Johnson some essays which he had written; and my great friend, who was exceedingly obliging when thus consulted, was detained so long that it was, I believe, one o'clock before we got into our post-chaise. I found that we should be too late for dinner at Sir John Dalrymple's, to which we were engaged: but I would by no means lose the pleasure of seeing my friend at Hawthornden, of seeing *Sam Johnson* at the very spot where *Ben Johnson* visited the learned and poetical Drummond.

We surveyed Roslin Castle, the romantick scene around it, and the beautiful Gothick chapel, and dined and drank tea at the inn; after which we proceeded to Hawthornden, and viewed the caves; and I all the while had *Rare Ben* in my mind, and was pleased to think that this place was now visited by another celebrated wit of England.

By this time 'the waning night was growing old', and we were yet several miles from Sir John Dalrymple's. Dr Johnson did not seem much troubled at our having treated the baronet with so little attention to politeness; but when I talked of the grievous disappointment it must have been to him that we did not come to the *feast* that he had prepared for us (for he told us he had killed a seven-year-old sheep on purpose), my friend got into a merry mood, and jocularly said, 'I dare say, sir, he has been very sadly distressed. Nay, we do not know but the consequence may have been fatal. Let me try to describe his situation in his own historical style. I have as good a right to make him think and talk, as he has to tell us how people thought and talked a hundred years ago, of which he has no evidence. All history, so far as it is not supported by contemporary evidence, is romance ... Stay now ... Let us consider!' He then (heartily laughing all the while) proceeded in his imitation, I am sure to the following effect, though now, at the distance of almost twelve years, I cannot pretend to recollect all the precise words:

'Dinner being ready, he wondered that his guests were not yet come. His wonder was soon succeeded by impatience. He walked about the room in anxious agitation; sometimes he looked at his watch, sometimes he looked out at the window with an eager gaze of expectation, and revolved in his mind the various accidents of human life. His family beheld him with mute concern. "Surely," said he, with a sigh, "they will not fail me." The mind of man can bear a certain pressure; but there is a point when it can bear no more. A rope was in his view, and he died a Roman death.'*

It was very late before we reached the seat of Sir John Dalrymple, who, certainly with some reason was not in very good humour. Our conversation was not brilliant. We supped, and went to bed in ancient rooms, which would have better suited the climate of Italy in summer, than that of Scotland in the month of November.

I recollect no conversation of the next day, worth preserving, except one saying of Dr Johnson, which will be a valuable text for many decent old dowagers, and other good company, in various circles to descant upon. He said, 'I am sorry I have not learnt to play at cards. It is very useful in life: it generates kindness, and consolidates society.' He certainly could not mean deep play.

My friend and I thought we should be more comfortable at the inn at

---

* 'Essex was at that time confined to the same chamber of the Tower from which his father Lord Capel had been led to death, and in which his wife's grandfather had inflicted a voluntary death upon himself. When he saw his friend carried to what he reckoned certain fate, their common enemies enjoying the spectacle, and reflected that it was he who had forced Lord Howard upon the confidence of Russel, he retired, and, by a *Roman death*, put an end to his misery.'

Dalrymple's *Memoirs of Great Britain and Ireland*,
Vol. I, p. 36.

Blackfields,[342] two miles farther on. We therefore went thither in the evening, and he was very entertaining; but I have preserved nothing but the pleasing remembrance, and his verses on George the Second and Cibber, and his epitaph on Parnell, which he was then so good as to dictate to me. We breakfasted together next morning, and then the coach came, and took him up. He had, as one of his companions in it, as far as Newcastle, the worthy and ingenious Dr Hope, botanical professor at Edinburgh. Both Dr Johnson and he used to speak of their good fortune in thus accidentally meeting; for they had much instructive conversation, which is always a most valuable enjoyment, and, when found where it is not expected, is peculiarly relished.

I have now completed my account of our tour to the Hebrides. I have brought Dr Johnson down to Scotland, and seen him into the coach which in a few hours carried him back into England. He said to me often, that the time he spent in this tour was the pleasantest part of his life, and asked me if I would lose the recollection of it for five hundred pounds. I answered I would not; and he applauded my setting such a value on an accession of new images in my mind.

Had it not been for me, I am persuaded Dr Johnson never would have undertaken such a journey; and I must be allowed to assume some merit from having been the cause that our language has been enriched with such a book as that which he published on his return; a book which I never read but with the utmost admiration, as I had such opportunities of knowing from what very meagre materials it was composed.

NOTES

Johnson: A Journey to the Western Islands of Scotland

1. William Nairne, later Lord Dunsinane.
2. Fifeshire.
3. Sixteenth-century poet and controversialist, 1506–82. His Latin verse is nearly as good as Johnson thought it.
4. Robert Arbuthnot.
5. Robert Watson, Professor of Logic, Rhetoric, etc.
6. They are still standing and still beautiful.
7. His body was slung from a window where he had witnessed the burning to death of the Protestant George Wishart.
8. St Salvator's and St Leonard's were united in 1734. St Mary's survived.
9. The first edition has 'decent' which the second thoughts of Oxford and the eternal thoughts of Yale accept. I prefer 'recent', proposed in 1924.
10. St Mary's.
11. James Murison, Principal of St Mary's.
12. Thomas Hay, Earl of Kinnoul.
13. Can it have been the thorn tree planted by Mary Queen of Scots, Johnson's heroine?
14. Sir John Davies, 1569–1626, *Discoverie of the True Causes Why Ireland Was Never Entirely Subdued until the Beginning of his Majesties Happy Reign* (1612). Often quoted in Johnson's *Dictionary*.
15. Arbroath, at the mouth of the Brothock Water.
16. It flourished down to 1606 and was never deliberately destroyed.
17. Episcopalian. It can also mean a chapel with the liturgy in English, not Gaelic. At Inveraray the Duke of Argyll built a Gaelic and an English chapel back to back under one roof. The army pulled its spire down in 1941.
18. An early evolutionist of pleasing eccentricity, 1714–99.
19. This is a slip of memory, as Boswell points out.
20. Boece died in 1536. He wrote a Latin history and description of Scotland used by Holinshed and known to Shakespeare, but unreliable.
21. 1587–1641. Johnson tried in vain to buy his poems in Aberdeen, and was still after a copy of his own in February 1777.
22. In 1444.
23. In the sixteenth century.
24. By a slip of the pen Johnson wrote 'eight'.
25. The old Episcopalian Church imposed by Charles I refused the new loyalty oath of 1693. It was a persecuted sect, forbidden to assemble for worship, and its ministers were poor and vagrant, particularly after 1745. But certain chapels were allowed to have ministers of Irish or English (never Scottish) Episcopal ordination,

with the English liturgy (never the less Protestant liturgy of the old Episcopalians, who carried it with them in exile to America).

26. Lady Diana Middleton.

27. Now crumbling into ruin.

28. He is thinking about some famous lines of Lucretius. The present Lady Erroll has built a residence in Swedish style under the walls of the old castle and decorated her headland with Armada cannon.

29. Erroll's younger brother.

30. The name Coot was often given to the Guillemot. The name Cooter is unknown to Murray's Oxford Dictionary, and was perhaps misheard.

31. This water is Buchan Ness.

32. Boswell wrongly questions this usage.

33. The second thoughts of R. W. Chapman in 1930 suggested 'rovers'. Wrongly, I think.

34. He seems to mean Memsie, north of Strichen, but that is not a circle of standing stones, at least not now.

35. The Earl of Buchan in 1390.

36. 1567, when Moray was Regent.

37. Johnson had originally added here savage sentences about his native Lichfield. He deleted them during publication out of old affection for the Dean and they survive in very few copies. 'There is now, as I have heard, a body not less decent or virtuous than the Scottish Council longing to melt the lead of an English Cathedral. What they shall melt it were just they should swallow.'

38. In 1764, discussed in the Introduction to this edition. I thought it a fine book until I read Martin on the same subject.

39. Valentine White, the Factor.

40. George Ferne, Master of the Stores. For Fort George, see Introduction.

41. Mentioned in the Introduction to this edition.

42. See Defoe's *Tour through the Whole Island of Great Britain* (1762). Over ninety years, oral tradition is often reliable.

43. In a letter he reports that a professor told him, 'they taught us to raise cabbage and make shoes', and so they may have done, when they settled. Cromwellian soldiers went native in more places than one.

44. Arthur Johnston's Latin *Flower of Great Contemporary Scottish Poets* (Amsterdam, 1637). May's *Supplement* was a continuation of Lucan. I am unable to comprehend Johnson's admiration of him. How can so awful a poet in English be any good in Latin?

45. Noted in the 1762 edition of Defoe's *Tour*.

46. Built after the 1745 war. Boswell puts it along the south side of Loch Ness, crossing to the north of the Great Glen only at Fort Augustus, between the lochs.

47. Boswell's servant, Joseph Ritter.

48. By a slip of the pen Johnson wrote 'thirteenth'.

49. 700 feet (over 116 fathoms), so far as I can discover.

50. Yes. It has never been recorded to freeze.

51. In Plutarch's *Life of Alexander*. But the theme was common in Hellenistic philosophizing.

52. Said to be a dialect word from the midland counties, though I would have thought it more widespread.

53. A Hanoverian road-building military man, a Field Marshal.

54. This is treated in the Introduction to the present edition.

55. Lachlan Macqueen.

56. Prideaux was born in 1648; the *Connection* (between the Old and New Testaments), a most popular work in its day, was published in 1716–18.

57. Cocker's *Arithmetic* (1678).

58. Boswell says it was much discussed while Johnson was at Edinburgh.

59. Scholars have identified the exact spot, not always in the same place.

60. Herodotus, 4.2.

61. This road is still thought alarming by those unused to mountain roads.

62. Murchison, says Boswell.

63. Mrs Boswell.

64. Misprinted, perhaps, as 'twentieth' in the first edition.

65. Of Sleat, later a peer. He was a close ally of the Macleods. He was educated at Eton, where, Johnson privately remarked, 'he was tamed into insignificance'.

66. John Jeans.

67. John Campbell's *A Political Survey of Britain*. Published in 1774, after Johnson's expedition. The account of the trees was at second hand.

68. In 1746. Many highlanders were too poor to change at once. The inn by the bridge that joins Seil to the mainland used to hire out trousers to islanders as they left the islands.

69. He died in 1764.

70. They are just beginning to return to the west of Scotland after coming close to extermination.

71. A Roman epicure to whom Latin writings on cookery, composed much later, were ascribed.

72. Misprinted as 'free' in the first edition.

73. Learned authors complain that this is properly spelt *sgailc*.

74. Burnt taste or smell. Did any reader understand both *empyreumatick* and *sgailc*?

75. He bought some and had them sent to London. You still can, if you must.

76. Raasay lies close to Skye, opposite Portree. Raasay is some fifteen miles by one mile.

77. Kilmuir.

78. Macleod of Raasay was furious that this should be said, and Johnson apologized. Dunvegan was the principal fortress on Skye, where the Macleods in the early eighteenth century employed their own Gaelic bard, quartet of musicians, jester, barber, etc.

79. This is still true here and there in western Scotland.

80. Tea plantations in India and Ceylon were devised to shorten the journey from China; the plant itself was Chinese.

81. Martin mentions these enormous sea-otters. I have seen a very big otter killed by hounds in Devonshire, but these sound like a separate species. Martin gives them a white spot on the breast.

82. Calling to action.

83. Johnson's friend, the natural scientist, later Sir Joseph Banks (1743–1820). His expedition was from 1768 to 1771. His greatest contribution was to botany.

84. 1745.

85. Martin Martin, discussed in the Introduction.

86. He is thinking of Martin's reports of local holy days and processions, and what they commemorated. Extreme Protestants disapproved of them.

87. The first edition has 'art' but the Oxford suggestion 'act' must be right.

88. Where Ulysses is kindly entertained in the *Odyssey*. If not in fairyland, Phaeacia is Corfu.

89. He said the same of Sconser, as Boswell pointed out to him.

90. The famous Jacobite heroine who saved the life of Prince Charles. Later she emigrated to America but, disapproving of the disloyalty of those colonies, she returned to Scotland. The house survives in great beauty.

91. Editors puzzle over this.

92. The chief was her son. Johnson's 'bread and butter' letter is preserved at Dunvegan.

93. Johnson later discovered he had told this story twice. He cut it out from the second place in his book (page 125).

94. The horn is extant. It holds two bottles of claret.

95. At Mallaig twenty-five years ago, there being hardly more than two surnames in the town, people were known by their houses' names. The piper was Ron Seaview.

96. He was Substitute Sheriff of Skye, of which Ulinish was a western promontory, north of Loch Harport.

97. Coal-fish or Pollock, a cousin of the queenly Cod.

98. An island some way south of Skye and its smaller neighbours.

99. Peter the Great.

100. An offshore island of Mull, famous for its monastery of the early Dark Ages whose monks brought Christianity to Scotland.

101. Another offshore island. Unity Mitford's father Lord Redesdale bought it before the war in his daughter Jessica's name: he hoped to live out the war there. Jessica married a Californian; they sold the island, but it is still private property.

102. Martin, son of John the co-author or ghost-writer of Macaulay's *St Kilda*.

103. The English thought the lost weight of Scottish cattle that had walked to London was due to mountain rearing. Welsh cattle were called 'Welsh runts'.

104. When St Kilda was deserted, the enormous and extremely ancient field-mice exterminated their more recent domestic rivals.

105. Lady Louchaun and Lady Eglintoune.

106. Lauchlan MacQuarrie of Ulva.

107. Sir Ambrose Crowley, the Stourbridge ironmaster satirized by Addison.

108. In the *Gentleman's Magazine*, October 1749.

109. The Highland veterans settled in America formed a highly effective kilted regiment in Canada in the War of Independence a few years later.

110. Gaulish tribal migrations devastated the ancient world more than once. The Galatians are an example; they still spoke Gaulish in the fourth century AD.

111. The Black Watch; the 'Old Highland Regiment'; the forty-second.

112. Provençal, Romansh, Spanish.

113. Charred to charcoal.

114. Most of what is now said about Macrimmon traditions was faked in the nineteenth century. The colleges of pipers were like those colleges of bardic poetry that survived into the eighteenth century in Ireland.

115. He was called Donald Maclean.

116. He refers to the plight of the Episcopalians. William III had established Presbyterianism in Scotland.

117. A set form; a written liturgy.

118. Johnson is mistaken about this. Catholics were more numerous.

119. The *Gruagach* mentioned by Macaulay on St Kilda.

120. Johnson's credulity over second sight was ridiculed at the Literary Club in London. Boswell said Johnson was only 'willing to believe: I am full of belief'. 'Then cork it up,' said George Colman.

121. *Taibhse.*

122. Martin Macpherson of Sleat, born on Barra. Johnson may also be thinking of Martin Martin.

123. Misprinted as 'Bayle', not a notably cold reasoner. The reading 'Boyle', often suspected, was established in *Notes and Queries*, 1952.

124. *Seanachaidh.* Campion in his *History of Ireland* says: 'One office in the house of great men is a tale-teller, who bringeth his Lord on sleep, with tales vain and frivolous,' which is what *seanachaidh* (teller of tales) must mean.

125. Sir James Foulis of Colinton.

126. These social roles overlapped.

127. Not true in Ireland in Campion's day (1573) or at Dunvegan in the eighteenth century, where an Irish-trained bard was retained.

128. The grollocking of a stag, the wrapping of various tasty entrails in the tongue, a word unrecorded by Murray which I spell by guesswork, is still in use and still implies that the gillie has his choice pieces.

129. At Dunvegan he had seen a vast claymore (great sword, broadsword) which Boswell drew not badly in his notes, and which still survives there.

130. This story was engraved in stone.

131. This is untrue.

132. This was published only in 1694. A new version was approved in 1751 and published in 1753.

133. Sir John Pryce in 1573. The quarrel over antiquity of civilized language goes back to a Bodleian manuscript (Dunstan's) in which runes are interpreted as Welsh by Nennius (or his dog) and prove Welsh to be older than English.

134. The poems of John Maclean of Mull were written down by Dr Hector Maclean.

135. James Macpherson in the sixties, an impostor in whose 'Ossian' Napoleon and all Europe believed. There was a real Osheen (or Ossian) credited, rather as Homer was, with Irish epic verse then unknown to scholars.

136. William Bedell, Bishop of Kilmore (died 1642), whose Bible was published in the 1680s.

137. Donald Macqueen. It is said that he denied he would not answer.

138. He still means the impostor Macpherson. 'Publisher' means person responsible.

139. Monsters supposed to dwell in Patagonia, near the straits Magellan first tried to navigate.

140. Here Johnson, wilfully or ignorantly, underestimates a dangerous adventure. Coll is well south of Rhum and Skye, just west of Mull.

141. Captain Lauchlan Maclean, who had served in Bengal.

142. Donald Maclean, 'young Col'.

143. This sounds like a Shetland pony. At the age of sixteen I could bestride one with both feet on the ground.

144. Dr Samuel Clarke, it seems: an early-eighteenth-century Whig Protestant divine (died 1729). Dr Johnson admired (with reservations) his sermons.

145. One of these, like a small pickaxe, is to be seen in the West Highland Museum at Fort William.

146. Breacacha, where the castle ruins still stand.

147. Coll is twelve miles by four, on average.

148. The lochs are full of brown trout. What is he talking about?

149. The winds around Tyree and Coll are indeed remarkable.

150. Ben Hogh.

151. Stonehenge was 'brought by Gyants from Affrique' to the plains of Kildare, thence to Britain.

152. Who could fight.

153. 26,400 acres, with several mountains approaching 3,000 feet. The greatest remaining refuge outside Russia of the Manx Shearwater.

154. 325 persons in 1772, reduced to one family by 1828.

155. George III, on reading this book, declared his suspicion that Johnson was a Papist and a Jacobite.

156. As Martin had already hinted, Johnson had at first repeated a story here, and put in this last paragraph to cover the mistake. See note 93.

157. Neil Maclean.

158. Donald Maclean. Johnson sent him his *Dictionary*, which stayed in his family until 1929. Now it is at Trinity College, Cambridge.

159. Substituting.

160. Imposed by Parliament in 1697, and superseded by a beer-tax in 1880.

161. Duart, finely sketched by Paul Sandby (Boswell corrects the spelling incorrectly).

162. The old kings of Ulster sat naked in a cauldron with a white cow they killed and then boiled. They ate without implements, sitting in the broth and sharing with their people.

163. It existed in Ireland also.

164. *Macaladh.*

165. *Dalta.*

166. Modern Tobermory.

167. Virgil and such writers on farming.

168. Lauchlan MacQuarrie. The Irish boat was *Bonnetta* of Londonderry; the Master was Captain McLure.

169. Quoted in Pennant's *Tour.*

170. Johnson seems to refer to Robert Plot's *History of Staffordshire*, 1686.

171. See note 101.

172. The Macleans had seen their lands eroded by the Campbells (Argylls), and lost land in 1715 and 1745.

173. We know from Boswell that there was no prayer for the Hanoverian Royal Family.

174. Iona.

175. On 12 November.

176. On 25 September 1774.

177. J. Spon, *Voyage du Levant* (1678). G. Wheler (the more usual spelling), *Journey into Greece* (1682). They travelled together mostly, but their books, each of which names them both, differ in many details.

178. Iona virtually conjoins Mull. It is a question whether Johnson's description of Iona, the most ancient Christian holy place in Scotland, does not owe some colouring to St Patrick's Purgatory in the account of Ireland by Sir John Davies.

179. Boswell, who swore an oath there, claimed it was one stone.

180. Kings of Scotland, Lords of the Isles, and many chiefs of Scotland, Ireland, Norway, and it is said France, lie on Iona.

181. Originally misprinted or misremembered as Maclean.

182. Survives as stables, Lochbuies 1750–90. The older Moy Castle exists as a ruin.

183. Given particular routes both in Wales and in Scotland, this would be an acceptable exaggeration.

184. Boswell says from the colour of a hill.

185. A sixteenth-century Bishop of Ross talking about the Orkneys.

186. On the main droving route from the Western Isles.

187. The house, a magnificent Gothick toy, was newly built, and the town was rising. Johnson stayed at the inn, which is still in service.

188. In Scotland.

189. Misprinted as Mr.

190. His letters suggest he is thinking of the Duchess of Douglas.

191. Fellows of the Royal Society.

192. Defoe's son-in-law, a journalist.

193. Gilbert Burnet (1643–1715). He made his observations at Geneva.

NOTES

Boswell: The Journal of a Tour to the Hebrides

1. Boswell's *Account of Corsica*, 1768.

2. Boswell often stayed with Paoli in London.

3. Edmond Malone (1741–1812) met Johnson in 1765 but Boswell only in 1781. He was an Irish barrister, writer and scholar who settled in London in 1777, issued a *Supplement* to Johnson's *Shakespeare* in 1780, and announced his own edition (1790) in 1783. It was Malone who arranged for Johnson's memorial in the Abbey.

4. Sir Walter James, who published as 'Verax'.

5. Johnson had written that Shakespeare 'may now begin to assume the dignity of an ancient'.

6. Boswell found this quotation, which refers to James I of England, at Corrichatachin on 27 September 1773.

7. A French border village near Geneva.

8. *Macbeth*, I, iii.

9. Lord Elibank (1703–78) was a retired colonel and a pamphleteer, Robertson a historian and Beattie a poet, all famous learned men.

10. Allusion to Ovid, *Heroides* 1.2: 'Don't write back to me, come in person.'

11. Gray met Beattie at Glamis Castle in 1765.

12. Brother of Lord Eldon. He became Lord Stowell.

13. Edinburgh. A bad inn, now demolished, where breakfast never appeared before nine.

14. Before the New Town was built this was a grand address like Albany in Piccadilly, where gentlemen could live a civilized life.

15. One of Boswell's executors. Wrote a *Life* of Dr Beattie. Forbes is a disyllable.

16. 'It is nothing if the other fellow doesn't know it.'

17. The chapel was demolished in 1822.

18. No. 8, Queen Street. He resigned in 1775 and died in 1778.

19. An inheritance case in which Boswell appeared. The Lords reversed the Scottish verdict.

20. Dr John Arbuthnot (1667–1735), FRS, friend of Swift and Pope.

21. Beattie (1735–1803), being established as a poet, became a sage. In 1770 he attacked Hume in an *Essay on Truth*.

22. Allusion to a line of Pope. Johnson wondered whether being a blockhead made Hume a rogue, or vice versa.

23. Charles Hay, later Lord Newton, a fellow-student of Boswell.

24. This last passage is by Malone.

25. Pembroke College, Oxford; but their times there did not overlap.

26. Burke.

27. Thomas Cooke (1703–56), *Hesiod* (1728); one volume only of Plautus (1746). The subscribers included Garrick, Handel, Chesterfield, etc. He was in the Dunciad.

28. Samuel Foote (1720–77), actor and dramatist. His uncle, a naval commander, was hanged for fratricide. The quarrel was over money. As a result, Foote inherited a fortune.

29. She believed she was in constant private communication with God.

30. Restored in 1883.

31. 'These are our miseries'.

32. His notes on the collation of Hebrew manuscripts had appeared in 1770, and his work was extremely controversial. He never finished it, but he was a great and formidable scholar.

33. On Folly Bridge.

34. A Dublin bookseller.

35. 'Unequal to himself'.

36. An early evolutionist.

37. 'At supper we had such a conflux of company that I could scarcely support the tumult,' Johnson wrote in a letter.

38. Sir Matthew Hale has been suggested.

39. Thomas Blacklock (1721–91), a poet blind from infancy, who almost became Professor of Greek at Aberdeen.

40. By Baron d'Holbach (1770). Voltaire hated this book as much as Boswell did.

41. Anne Vane, the Prince of Wales's mistress, and Catherine Sedley, James the II's.

42. One of Boswell's closest friends: he became a judge.

43. Both versions adapt Virgil (*Aeneid* II. 368) into prose.

44. 'Believe a mind capable of so great things survived its dying body'.

45. Minister of the Tolbooth, a convivial kinsman of Boswell's.

46. Rochester, imitating Horace (*Satires* I. 10).

47. Later Lord Dunsinnan and a judge.

48. In a *Discourse on Duels*. He was a French courtier of Mary Queen of Scots.

49. The island is still defended. It lies close to the rail bridge.

50. Ferries crossed from Leith to near Kinghorn, not far from the modern bridges.

51. We are moving up the east coast of Scotland.

52. *Poems and Addresses from his Scottish Progress in 1617* (Edinburgh, 1618).

53. Sixteenth-century Scottish Latin poet.

54. Pitcairne's reputation nowadays has sunk out of sight and Prior's is sinking.

55. At ten, as we learn from Boswell's *Diaries.*

56. It is not known who the cartographer was.

57. Croatian soldiers, thought to be brutish. Did they grease shirts to make them waterproof?

58. George Martine. He wrote the account in 1683 and it was published in 1797.

59. This pamphlet was published in 1728.

60. He means the upper room of the University Library, a decent, plain, classical room.

61. Which portrayed his murder in 1679.

62. The Reverend David Lindsay, the properly constituted Episcopalian Minister of St Andrew's. Johnson said, 'Sir, I honour him.' Johnson would have wished it said that Boswell's levity in this passage is inappropriate and excessively provincial.

63. Of his sermons written for the Reverend H. H. Aston, one survives.

64. One of Horace's most famous Odes (II. 14).

65. 1680–1740. Seven volumes, 1740–51.

66. Then principal of Glasgow University.

67. Not far from Kinghorn. In 1822 Boswell's eldest son was carried dying from a duel at Kinghorn to his kinsman's house at Balmuto.

68. A Pembroke man who inherited Vauxhall Gardens. Wealthy, amusing and pleasant; Johnson loved him.

69. To judge from his Welsh journey, it was for constipation.

70. In the Midlands, stone walls may properly be called stone hedges to this day.

71. It was never built.

72. 'Fertile happy crops'. Returning late one night, Monboddo went out again with candles to inspect his turnips.

73. 'Something royal'.

74. Bishop of Gloucester.

75. Someone has written in the margin of the Bodleian copy: 'Also Ld Mansfield, who patronized him for his attachment to Pope'.

76. Bishop of London. His father was an even more learned theologian, and his grandfather a bookseller whose premises were burnt out in the Fire of London.

77. Frank Barber was Johnson's beloved servant and friend, and the beneficiary of his will.

78. The father and grandfather of this boy, both Edmund Waller, sat in the same parliament (1747). The boy was really a great-great-grandson of the poet.

79. Under Milton's picture.

80. Published in 1747.

81. Baxter wrote in 1658, Grotius in 1617.

82. Langton.

83. Ascribed to Bacon in 1629.

84. Latin poet and former Principal of Marischal College.

85. Fashionable Scottish physician in London (appointed to the King in 1774).

86. George Graham, an Eton master.

87. Cumming wrote (1742) before Leechman preached (1743). Controversy was very heated.

88. Horace, Odes I. 2.

89. Two or three thousand books, now in the Mitchell Library at Glasgow.

90. 'Generalizations conceal tricks'.

91. 'Nabob' at this time meant any rich nobody, like those who returned rich from the East.

92. Enthusiasm for these was so great that at Taymouth Castle in the 1750s Lord Glenorchy built himself one. Pennant was keen on them.

93. Surely a tomb.

94. Published in French in 1755, in English in 1768. Monboddo met the girl in Paris in 1765.

95. Sir James Lowther died in 1755, the richest English commoner.

96. The second Duke of Gordon, a Catholic, was a friend of the Duke of Tuscany. At the time of Boswell's writing, his grandson was the duke; his daughter married a Duke of Richmond and the Gordon title passed into that family.

97. A vast column of rock supposed to commemorate the retreat of the Danes, called Swene's Stone.

98. By Richard Glover. These are fashionable poets.

99. By Richard Gifford of Balliol, quoted under 'Wheel' in Johnson's *Dictionary* but misquoted here.

100. Such tokens are to be seen in the West Highland Museum at Oban.

101. Discussed in the Introduction. Macaulay's brother was Argyll's minister at Inverary.

102. This is now certain (from letters).

103. John Campbell of Cawdor, who died in Pembrokeshire.

104. The antiquarian observations are inexpert.

105. Intellectual arguments apart, the ungovernable extremism and independence of Protestantism in Scotland and the ineradicable survival there of the Roman Church must surely both have something to do with the refusal to be manipulated by foreigners.

106. Up the east coast, across the Great Glen, a hop to Skye, then island-hopping south to Mull and Iona. Not far, really.

107. A famous Jacobite who lived on Benbecula.

108. Baretti, whom Boswell disliked. The story is untrue.

109. Aulay Macaulay served a year at seventeen or so as a Lieutenant of Marines, then lived on half pay; he died in 1842 aged eighty.

110. Eyre Coote was broken by an unjust court-martial after an act of gallantry in the 1745 rebellion, and transferred to the Indian army where he did very well and soon returned as Commander-in-Chief.

111. He was Commander-in-Chief in North Britain from 1768 until his death at Bath in 1780 (he was born in 1720). His father was ADC to Marlborough and Colonel of the Coldstream Guards. Adolphus was a successful fighting soldier in his youth. Johnson had met him at Edinburgh.

112. The name of MacGregor was forbidden and abolished by a Scottish law of 1603.

113. In Foote's comedy *The Orators*.

114. Of course this daft claim is unjustified. The word is recorded in 1562 and in Boswell's circle Gibbon had already used it.

115. He was proud of his dashing reputation in the hunting field.

116. Still called Druids' Temple, a Neolithic burial site.

117. Well may she have feared. Moray Maclaren has pointed out that in this same hut an English officer had committed rape and murder not long before.

118. Boleskine is the church (or was). A 1776 survey marks it as ruins and it is not easy to pinpoint now. It stood near Foyers.

119. He was sixty.

120. He saved George II by stopping his bolting horse at Dettingen.

121. Ourry and D'Aripé.

122. This gentleman–innkeeper lived to be ninety; he read poetry in Latin and wrote it in Gaelic. He was an unrepentant Jacobite, a veteran of 1745.

123. By Pope, not Swift.

124. They were passing places full of heroic memories of the 1745 campaign.

125. It ended an abortive Jacobite rising in that year.

126. Rattachan, on the border of Ross and Cromarty with Inverness-shire.

127. Built in 1719 to hold two hundred men. Its ruins survive.

128. Gone and untraceable.

129. Wolfe, in a despatch shortly before his last battle.

130. Quoted previously by Dr Johnson at Aberdeen.

131. The site of Armadale Castle.

132. Monkstadt, built in 1740.

133. John Jeans, mineralogist.

134. Raasay is another island.

135. On Skye.

136. A good Gaelic scholar and an antiquary respected in his time.

137. He did record it, but censored it from his journal before publication.

138. The church was abandoned in 1876 and the monument shifted to a new one.

139. Poet, man of letters and patron; also an amiable, mildly corrupt and absent-minded politician. I doubt whether Boswell or even Johnson knew that a speech by Lyttelton was chiefly responsible for abolishing hereditary jurisdiction in Scotland.

140. Cheyne's *English Malady* (1733).

141. The import of this splendid poem, which recalls Gray as well as Horace, is 'Skye, refuge in a stormy sea, island without anxiety! No use for the sick mind to seek such refuges: one is not master of a level mind. Thou, God, alone rulest the storms in the heart.'

142. At forty-eight in 1754; he died in 1760.

143. A pleasant, very able Horatian lyric. Its purport is that these are grim regions; in whatever charming occupation she may be, let Mrs Thrale remember him, and let Skye resound with her honour.

144. Thirteen in five rooms, all but the foreigners sharing beds.

145. A bounty, that is a subsidy, of thirty shillings a ton. 'Buss' is a very old word in several European languages, but its origin is unknown. 'Busse' in old French meant a cask or barrel. In English 'busses' were fishing ships of two or three masts, often Dutch: 'bus' in old Dutch meant 'box'.

146. These cousins escorted Prince Charles Edward in his flight from the Hanoverians.

147. In return, the old boy liked Boswell, and wrote him a jolly letter on the birth of his son.

148. 'He was a man yesterday'. Song in honour of the Clanranald, who died in battle in 1715.

149. Or 'Comin' thro' the craigs o' Kyle', a folksong recorded by Burns.

150. *Odes* II. 16.

151. Johnson is right about Macpherson's Ossian, but that mysterious bard did figure in Irish Gaelic poetry, and so did Fingal. About the nature of epic poetry he is wrong, because he does not understand oral traditional poetry at all. He thinks Newton could have written an epic. Robin Hood is not as flimsy as Johnson believes, either.

152. Or he may have written *scalck*. The Gaelic spelling is *sgailc*. If that is a help to any reader, God bless him.

153. A McCruslick is a kind of mountain Puck or hobgoblin.

154. Boswell thought him obstinately opinionated.

155. Untraced. Could he mean Brochel, ancient stronghold of the Macleods?

156. The Laird of MacKinnon, who died by suicide in 1796.

157. Now a hotel.

158. Not much in common, scholars say.

159. More tractable stone to be carved like butter; he may mean sandstone, but there are tractable limestones also.

160. He means a lavatory, a loo, a jakes, an indoor toilet. The one in the castle vented outside the walls. To my knowledge such arrangements persisted here and there in Europe until the late 1950s.

161. 'Outer defences'.

162. Bog myrtle. The Isle of Eriska in its outer skirts is ˜till deliciously scented with this plant. Having known it only on mountain tops, I was amazed its smell could be so intense.

163. The great classical scholar.

164. Atheistic Scottish man of letters whom Johnson utterly despised and frequently mentioned with scorn. He had died about ten years before the journey.

165. He died in 1801 in debt not for forty, as at first, but for seventy thousand pounds, and had sold land on Harris.

166. Johnson's *Vanity of Human Wishes*. Boswell misquoted this. We have restored it as he would have wished.

167. William Drummond of Hawthornden.

168. Horace, *Epistles* I. 2. 11. Like many of Boswell's allusions, this adds nothing to the purpose.

169. Seventy-year-old lawyer, soldier and man of letters, of great prestige in Scotland.

170. 'On an unlearned soil in an unlearned age'.

171. 'And that was all'.

172. The same is true in much of western Scotland to this day, as it often is in south-west England.

173. A very beautiful house still standing.

174. Tutor.

175. They went the next year, but Flora detested the disloyalty of the colonies and returned in 1779. Her husband followed in 1784.

176. By Gray's and Walpole's friend, poet and country parson, just out in 1773.

177. *Siècle de Louis XV*, slightly misquoted.

178. By John Macleod of Talisker, a colonel.

179. Transportation as a slave to America.

180. Was she the widow of Hugh, third Viscount Primrose, a lieutenant-colonel who died in 1741? The family were officially Whigs.

181. He means 1750, when George II was in Germany and Prussia threatened Hanover.

182. That is, we are bound neither by the eternal law of God nor by contract between government and governed.

183. 'I am pleased to be born now' (Ovid).

184. Grishornish.

185. Seventeen, actually.

186. This castle survives and the Macleods still live in it.

187. Pronounced and sometimes spelt Beaton, minister of Duirinish, son of the minister of Kilmuir.

188. Published in 1771.

189. In a roundabout course.

190. Modern Lochbracadale.

191. These relics are still to be seen.

192. He was right to do so.

193. He was again right to see no difficulty.

194. 'If you wish the injury you are not injured'.

195. Goddess of the Oxus, worshipped by the Greeks as Artemis Anaitis.

196. Loon, peasant.

197. An early monastic site recently discussed by C. Thomas, *Early Christian Archaeology of North Britain* (Glasgow/Oxford, 1971), pp. 45–6.

198. Pope's *Dunciad*, 4.252.

199. 'For altar and hearth', a tag from Cicero.

200. In dispute with Monboddo, Johnson admitted he might have taken the side of savages if someone else had supported shopkeepers.

201. He was sixty-four.

202. Dower house.

203. Like the New Jerusalem.

204. Penguin was the original name for Great Auks. Drake's chaplain in 1578 apparently recorded it as a Welsh name for birds, and in 1582 British sailors knew it as a Welsh word. Some auks do have white heads as penguins have. The French claim that *pingouin* (1598) is a Dutch word. Could it be Breton, like the St Malo Islands, Îles Malouines, Malvinas, our Falkland Islands?

205. Beaton or Bethune (see note 188).

206. She knew of her husband's Jacobite intrigues and threatened him. Lovat kidnapped her. Her husband was the Earl of Mar's brother.

207. Famous encyclopedic naturalist (1707–88), with whom Pennant corresponded; see Introduction.

208. Mrs Thrale recorded that Johnson knew a lot about it. His father's brother was unbeaten at Smithfield for a year in boxing and wrestling.

209. Lady Macdonald.

210. 'Both in war *and* marriage'.

211. This inscription is not worth translating.

212. Twenty-five.

213. That very summer. He was looking for a northern route to India. Nelson was one of his midshipmen.

214. Common Anglo-Norman usage.

215. Thought to be by the Alban lake.

216. A spirited Renaissance pope.

217. The *Lives of the Poets* were to come.

218. In South America; not a likely tale.

219. Monboddo thought it merely chance that ourang-outangs lacked language. He believed men were animals and savage life threw light on civilization. As a Scottish Judge of Appeal he was often a minority of one.

220. In her *Essay on Shakespeare*. Shakespeare's plays were widely read and some of them sometimes played earlier in the century; Garrick revived him in the London theatre.

221. Canals, channels, gutters. Coleridge could still use the word: 'Mark the faint light-beam on the Kennell'd Mud'.

222. Johnson thought one would drown in claret before getting drunk on it.

223. Published 1702, but lived 1592–1648.

224. Published in his *Discourses* in 1753.

225. Donald Macleod got drunk and gave some of the money away.

226. It is a pity Johnson missed the living tradition of Gaelic poetry on Tyree. But the winds make it often hard to approach under sail.

227. The printed version (1749) begins:

> Welcome, welcome, brother debtor
> To this poor but merry place.

228. By no means confined to the Highlands or the Romans.

229. They do not. They are still in use in Scotland.

230. Later the Sconser Lodge Hotel.

231. Alexander Macdonald of Kingsburgh, father-in-law to Flora Macdonald and factor to Sir Alexander Macdonald of Sleat. Campbell was Commander in western Scotland and cousin and heir to the Duke of Argyll.

232. He was imprisoned in Edinburgh and released by amnesty in 1747.

233. Macdermot of Coolavin, Sligo.

234. In common seventeenth-century English it meant a decent, loyal royalist.

235. Lame and thumping verses. Their purport is how awful it feels to be stuck on Barra, but one can always hope for heaven.

236. 'He that courts his mistress with Roman imagery deserves to lose her,' was said of Hammond.

237. Sir Charles Hanbury Williams (1708–59), a diplomat with an itch to write. His works were only published in 1822. He died by suicide after a Russian winter and a redundant mission.

238. Verses by John Maclaurin, whose *Works* appeared in 1798. Johnson had met him in Edinburgh. Boswell and Maclaurin cooperated at times.

239. The boy was James Barclay. Kenrick attacked Johnson's *Shakespeare*. Barclay's pamphlet is wild, juvenile and amusing. There is a copy in Birmingham Public Library.

240. In an *Essay on Truth*.

241. *Chrysal, Or the Adventures of a Guinea* (1760–65), by Charles Johnstone (1760–65).

242. At Picton Castle.

243. Published in 1528.

244. *On the New Testament* (1703).

245. Sir A. Macdonald.

246. 'Indignation makes me write' (Juvenal).

247. On St Kilda.

248. Sir A. Macdonald.

249. 'Shut up the streams, my boys' (Virgil).

250. The danger was very great indeed, as anyone who has sailed in this area will confirm.

251. Extremely hazardous.

252. 'The lad who likes dogs' (Horace, *Ars Poetica*, 161).

253. *2 Henry VI*, I, ii.

254. Mrs Langton, Johnson's friend's mother.

255. 'The extent of God's consciousness' (infinity).

256. Boswell censors from his own record the remark 'We had here the best goose that I ever eat.'

257. 'The wanton girl aims at me with an apple' (Virgil).

258. From Addison's *Cato*.

259. It survives, lived in by a retired Scottish brigadier.

260. 'And this is what the philosophers call happy'.

261. 'Condemned to the mines'.

262. Pleasure-gardens on the Thames opposite Somerset House, shut down by an act of George II, then reopened from 1753 to 1759.

263. Published in 1736.

264. It seldom snows at or near sea-level in western Scotland, though streaks of snow on the mountains can outlast the summer.

265. A lesser cousin of the noble Cod.

266. Published in 1619.

267. 'The melancholy hate the gay'.

268. Described by Sacheverell (1688) in his *Isle of Man* (see Introduction); a good natural harbour later to be built up and inhabited.

269. Published in 1550 with many later editions.

270. With a heavy reliance on Claudian.

271. *Le Grand Dictionnaire Historique* (1673; ten volume edition, 1759).

272. Books of *obiter dicta*, like Wottoniana.

273. To Mrs Thrale in particular, to whom his splendid letters survive.

274. Published in 1672. Willis was a doctor.

275. Small island with an ancient cross. Contains a hideous modern house built by the Mitford family who later sold the island.

276. Lauchlan MacQuarrie sold out in 1777, impoverished by profuse hospitality. He joined the army, served in America, and retired on half pay to live on Mull. His house on Ulva survives as cottages.

277. Borough English is Anglo-Norman *tenure en Burgh Engloys*, recorded from the fourteenth century onwards exactly as Johnson says.

278. 'He has a noble look.' 'And a noble mind.'

279. The old house survives as ruins.

280. Published in 1707.

281. Alexander Drummond, *Travels through Germany, Italy, Greece (etc.)* (1754): William Derham, *Physico-Theology* (1713).

282. First announced in 1755.

283. Jethro Tull's *Horse-hoing Husbandry.*

284. Literary retainer, tale-teller.

285. 'Doubtful, not wicked'.

286. Light and pleasant travel verses, whose purport is some compliments to the island, its people and the Sabbath. 'Why go further? Here is secure quiet and honest love.' He likes the girls there.

287. Johnson sent these verses to Boswell only in 1775. It was on this Sunday night in 1773 that Boswell went to pray at the lonely cross and was frightened by the thought of ghosts.

288. A Swede from Norrland, the next best thing.

289. A tag from Cicero.

290. Banks was the President. The admired passage from Johnson echoes *Rasselas*, chapter 11.

291. He read a sermon aloud in the cathedral and swore an oath of loyalty at the Swearing Stone.

292. They discussed this anonymous work again on 10 April 1783. It was by an Italian called Marana who died in 1693, and other writers later added bits to it for the London booksellers.

293. Oban, on the mainland, was a tiny place then; now it is a bustling harbour town, but it scarcely contains a tolerable inn.

294. 'Give it to the worthier'.

295. Loch Awe. The hut was at Port Sonachan, where the hotel now is.

296. The Duke built an ornamental Gothick castle of some beauty in a park, and a little town at his gates, including the Argyll Arms, a fine, solid inn.

297. 'He will be to the end what he was from the beginning' (Horace, *Ars Pœtica*, 126).

298. He got these out of Johnson later on the Scottish journey.

299. Mickle, whose *Chateaubriant, Or The Siege of Marseilles* Boswell had recommended.

300. Published in 1746 and 1748.

301. Sir John Dalrymple.

302. Lord Adam Gordon.

303. Lord Douglas versus the Duke of Hamilton, a famous disputed inheritance case. Lady Argyll was a Hamilton.

304. Lord Macaulay the historian's grandfather.

305. He died in June 1744. His grandfather, the Marquis, was beheaded by Charles II in 1661 and his uncle the Earl by James II in 1685. He was the last Archbishop of St Andrews.

306. Juvenal, *Satire* VIII. Translation by Malone.

307. The reader will not be surprised that Douglas was furious with Boswell over this story.

308. Now the Tarbet Hotel, landmark on a grim motor-route.

309. Who built Helensburgh and named it after his wife.

310. 'Keeper of the Rolls or Records'.

311. 'Solemn words'.

312. Cousin of the famous writer. The family own the house now.

313. 'Whence comes evil?'

314. The manuscript annotated by Johnson has been preserved at Cameron House, but the matter is not worth lengthy annotation here. Coleridge criticized the Latin that was engraved (at Renton) and Johnson's is better, but the style is too out of fashion now to be easily assessed.

315. Treated in Boswell's *Life of Johnson*.

316. Printers.

317. Lord Loudoun, once Governor of Virginia, but unsuccessful in public affairs.

318. Published an edition of Horace, not often consulted today, at The Hague in 1721 and died there in 1730, a bitter-mouthed man. Bentley, on the other hand, is constantly quoted and consulted.

319. She lived to be ninety-two; her hobby was taming rats.

320. Some ten miles from the main road from Glasgow to the south. Still a fine house in easy, rolling country.

321. Deadpan humour.

322. Boswell and his father loved and revered Pringle; Johnson had a low opinion of him and thought him slightly mad. This appears often in Boswell's *Life of Johnson*.

323. William Baxter (1650–1723) arrived at Harrow School, aged eighteen, knowing no language but Welsh. London schoolmaster and classical editor of some learning and perversity. His foe Joshua Barnes was a considerable scholar.

324. 'Not even cattle have their proper praise, the glory of their brows'.

325. 'What you seek is here; it is even at Ulubrae if a level mind is not wanting to you' (Horace, *Epistles* I. 11. 29).

326. 'I will supply myself a level mind'.

327. 'The Sacred Road', as at Rome.

328. Durham never wrote on the Galatians; he did write on Revelation.

329. 'The Great Bear'.

330. The Hamilton Arms, still operating.

331. Demolished in the 1920s. The town owns the grounds and some remains.

332. Johnson greatly admired his knowledge and experience. He was a soldier, a lawyer and a close observer of economics.

333. Maybe best seen from the north, not from Princes Street. It undeniably has the look of a prison. The great attractions of Edinburgh were built in the eighteenth and early nineteenth centuries.

334. Captain Byron had recently claimed to have seen giants in Patagonia.

335. *Law of Evidence* (1761).

336. Boswell was in a funk and Johnson was not, and that is that.

337. Tips.

338. I had several times attempted but never enjoyed Buchanan's Latin verse at all, until I noticed this recommendation of Johnson's. Johnson is right about it. He is a brilliant critic of neo-Latin. Both as poet and as critic he is at home in Latin as in English of all ages.

339. Six-syllable words.

340. Battledore and shuttlecock, the game of badminton. The Latin tag means 'to fly about through the mouths of men'.

341. Drummond's Hawthornden, a tower of bewitching beauty, was sold in the late 1970s. Roslin is famous for a late Gothic chapel elaborately carved in stone by Scandinavian woodworkers.

342. Some sixteen miles from Edinburgh on the Coldstream and Newcastle road, now a farm.